AMERICAN MUSEUM of NATURAL HISTORY

BIRDS
OF NORTH AMERICA

Editor-in-Chief
François Vuilleumier

EASTERN REGION

Content previously published in
Birds of North America

DORLING KINDERSLEY

DK

LONDON, NEW YORK, MUNICH, MELBOURNE, AND DELHI

DORLING KINDERSLEY

Senior Art Editors
Caroline Hill, Ina Stradins

Senior Editor
Angeles Gavira Guerrero

US Senior Editors
Shannon Beatty, Jill Hamilton

Project Editor
Nathan Joyce

Designers
Sonia Barbate, Helen McTeer

Editors
Jamie Ambrose, Lori Baird,
Tamlyn Calitz, Marcus Hardy,
Lizzie Munsey, Patrick
Newman, Siobhan O'Connor,
David Summers, Cressida
Tuson, Miezan van Zyl,
Rebecca Warren

Design Assistant
Becky Tennant

Editorial Assistant
Jaime Tenreiro

Creative Technical Support
Adam Brackenbury,
John Goldsmid

Production Editors
Joanna Byrne, Maria Elia

Production Controllers
Erika Pepe, Rita Sinha

Jacket Designer
Mark Cavanagh

Illustrators
John Cox, Andrew Mackay

Picture Editor
Neil Fletcher

Picture Researchers
Laura Barwick, Will Jones

Managing Art Editor
Michelle Baxter

Managing Editor
Sarah Larter

Publishing Manager
Liz Wheeler

Art Directors
Phil Ormerod, Bryn Walls

Publisher
Jonathan Metcalf

DK INDIA

Editorial Manager
Glenda Fernandes

Project Designer
Mahua Mandal

Senior Designer
Mini Dhawan

Editors
Megha Gupta, Rukmini
Kumar, Garima Sharma,
Dipali Singh

Picture Researcher
Sakshi Saluja

DTP Manager
Balwant Singh

Senior DTP Designer
Harish Aggarwal

DTP Designers
Shanker Prasad, Arjinder
Singh, Jaypal Singh, Bimlesh
Tiwary, Anita Yadav, Tanveer
Abbas Zaidi

**AMERICAN MUSEUM
OF NATURAL HISTORY**

Editor-in-chief
François Vuilleumier, Ph.D.

Project Coordinators
Alex Navissi, Caitlin Roxby,
Molly Leff

DEDICATION

F.V. dedicates this book to
the memory of John Bull,
John Farrand, and Stuart
Keith, top birders, field
guide authors, AMNH
colleagues, first-rate
ornithologists, and friends.

Material first published in
Birds of North America 2009. This edition
first published in the United States in 2011 by
DK Publishing
375 Hudson Street
New York, NY 10014

11 12 13   10 9 8 7 6 5 4 3 2 1

001—ND114—Feb/2011

Copyright © 2009, 2010, 2011 Dorling Kindersley
Limited
All rights reserved

A catalog record for this book is available from the
Library of Congress.

ISBN 978-0-7566-5867-0

DK books are available at special discounts when
purchased in bulk for sales promotions, premiums,
fund-raising, or educational use. For details, contact:
DK Publishing Special Markets, 375 Hudson Street,
New York, New York 10014 or SpecialSales@dk.com.

Printed and bound in China by L.Rex Printing
Co. Ltd.

Discover more at
www.dk.com

CONTRIBUTORS

David Bird, Ph.D.
Nicholas L. Block
Peter Capainolo
Matthew Cormons
Malcolm Coulter, Ph.D.
Joseph DiCostanzo
Shawneen Finnegan
Neil Fletcher
Ted Floyd
Jeff Groth, Ph.D.

Paul Hess
Brian Hiller
Rob Hume
Thomas Brodie Johnson
Kevin T. Karlson
Stephen Kress, Ph.D.
William Moskoff, Ph.D.
Bill Pranty
Michael L. P. Retter
Noah Strycker

Paul Sweet
Rodger Titman, Ph.D.
Elissa Wolfson

Map Editor
Paul Lehman

Project Coordinator
Joseph DiCostanzo

CONTENTS

PREFACE

THRUSHES
Back in the early 1900s, the great wildlife artist Louis Agassiz Fuertes already painted birds in the style of modern field guides, as shown in this plate from Chapman's *Handbook of the Birds of Eastern North America*.

With its eastern and western volumes, *Birds of North America* attempts to fill a gap in the North American bird book market. No other work offers, for every North American bird species, the same combination of stunning iconography, including beautiful photographs and precise distribution maps; scientifically accurate and readable accounts of salient characteristics; data on identification, behavior, habitat, voice, social structure, nest construction, breeding season, food, and conservation status; diagrams of flight patterns; statistics of size, wingspan, weight, clutch size, number of broods per year, and lifespan; and geographic information about breeding, wintering, and migration. Furthermore, no other bird book introduces, in such an up-to-date and lavishly illustrated manner, general material about birds: their evolution, classification, anatomy, flight, migration, navigation, courtship, mating, nests, and eggs. Scientific jargon has been avoided, but a glossary identifies concepts that benefit from an explanation. With its user-friendly format, these eastern and western guides to *Birds of North America* should permit readers either to enjoy studying one species account at a time, or browse to make cross comparisons.

Many field guides exist, as well as treatises on groups like gulls, hummingbirds, or sparrows; other books are dictionary-like, or focus on species of conservation concern. However, no bird book today can be called a "handbook," a concise reference work that can be conveniently carried around. I hope that these books will be useful in this role to all persons interested in birds, whether young or older, enthusiastic birder or beginner.

Historically, *Birds of North America* can be viewed as a successor to Frank M. Chapman's epochal *Handbook of the Birds of Eastern North America*, published in 1895. During his 54 years at the American Museum of Natural History in New York City, Chapman, dean of American ornithologists, blazed a trail that contributed substantially to what American ornithology, bird conservation, and birding have become. The facts that the new book has the imprint of the American Museum of Natural History, and that I, as its Editor-in-Chief, have worked there for 31 years as Curator of Ornithology and as Chairman of its Department of Ornithology, are not coincidental.

In his Handbook, Chapman treated all birds found in Eastern North America. The description of each species was followed by data on distribution, nest, and eggs, and a readable, often even brilliant text about habitat, behavior, and voice. The illustrations included plates by two pioneer American wildlife artists, Louis Agassiz Fuertes and Francis Lee Jaques, whose style inspired all those who followed them. Some of these

EASTERN AND WESTERN REGIONS

In a pioneering essay from 1908, Frank Chapman realized, on the basis of his own fieldwork, that the 100th Meridian corresponded to a rather clear-cut division of North American bird faunas into an Eastern and a Western region.
Of course there are exceptions and the 100th Meridian line is not something that the birds themselves recognize. The invisible barrier is located in a transitional zone between habitats that represent, respectively, Eastern versus Western landscape types or biomes. Some, but not all, modern field guides use the 100th Meridian as a division between East and West.

Arctic Circle

Western Region

Eastern Region

Tropic of Cancer

100° W

plates were, already then, executed in field guide fashion. Anybody who examines Chapman's *Handbook* today is struck by how modern it is. "Museum man" and "birder," Chapman was also a gifted educator and a good writer: a rare combination. Museum research gave him the taxonomic background, and fieldwork throughout North America sharpened his birding skills. As Editor-in-Chief of *Birds of North America*, working in the department Chapman created, enjoying the same extraordinary collection and library resources, and traveling as widely as he did, I have endeavored to make this new book a work of which he would have been proud. Don't leave home without it—and bring along binoculars and a pencil to jot down notes.

François Vuilleumier

François Vuilleumier
American Museum of Natural History,
New York City
February 2011

CATCHING THE LIGHT
The only hummingbird species breeding in the Eastern region is the Ruby-throated Hummingbird. With the right lighting, this male displays his brilliantly colored throat patch.

HOW THIS BOOK WORKS

This guide covers about 550 Eastern North American bird species. The species are arranged into three sections: the first profiles common species, each being given full-page treatment; the second covers rarer birds in quarter-page entries; the third section consists of a list of rare visitors.

▽ INTRODUCTION

The species are organized conventionally by order, family, and genus. Related birds appear together, preceded by a group introduction. The book follows the most up-to-date avian classification system, based on the latest scientific research.

MAPS

In this book, North America is defined as the area from the southern tip of Florida and the US–Mexico border northward to the Canadian High Arctic. Each species profile includes a map showing its range, with different colors reflecting seasonal movements.

KEY

	Resident all year
	Breeding distribution
	Nonbreeding distribution
	During migration

GROUP NAME
The common name of the group the species belong to is at the top of each page.

COMMON NAME

IN FLIGHT
Illustrations show the bird in flight, from above and/or below—differences of season, age, or sex are not always visible.

DESCRIPTION
Conveys the main features and essential character of the species including:

VOICE
A description of the species' calls and songs, given phonetically where possible.

NESTING
The type of nest and its usual location; the number of eggs in a clutch; the number of broods in a year; the breeding season.

FEEDING
How, where, and what the species feeds on.

SIMILAR SPECIES
Similar-looking species are identified and key differences pointed out.

LENGTH, WINGSPAN, AND WEIGHT
Length is tip of tail to tip of bill; measurements and weights are averages or ranges.

SOCIAL
The social unit the species is usually found in.

LIFESPAN
The length of life, in years, obtained from either zoo birds or from banding and recovery records of wild birds. The actual average or maximum life expectancy of many bird species is still unknown.

STATUS
The conservation status of the species; (p) means the data available is only provisional.

▽ COMMON SPECIES

The main section of the book features the 393 most commonly seen bird species in Eastern North America. Each entry is clear and detailed, following the same format.

ORIOLES AND BLACKBIRDS

Order Passeriformes	Family Icteridae

Baltimore Oriole

The Baltimore Oriole's brilliant colors are familiar to persons in the East because this bird is tolerant of hu presence. This species originally favored the American El nesting, but Dutch Elm disease decimated these trees. The since adapted to using sycamores, cottonwoods, and other for its nesting sites. Its ability to use suburban gardens and helped expand its range to areas densely occupied by hum Baltimore Oriole is Maryland's State Bird, somewhat iron

VOICE Loud, clear, melodious song comprising one ou several short notes in series, often of varying lengths.

NESTING Round-bottomed basket usually woven of g toward the end of branches; 4–5 eggs; 1 brood; May–Ju

FEEDING Hops or flits among leaves and branches pick and spiders; fond of caterpillars; also eats fruits and sips n

SIMILAR SPECIES

Length 8–10in (20–26cm)	Wingspan 10–12in (2
Social Solitary/Pairs	Lifespan Up to 11 yea

DATE SEEN	WHERE

394

MAPS
See panel, left. The occurrence caption describes the bird's preferred habitats and range within North America.

SYMBOLS

♂ Male	☘ Spring
♀ Female	☼ Summer
◑ Juvenile	🍂 Autumn
◕ Immature	❄ Winter

CLASSIFICATION

The top band of each entry provides the scientific names of order, family, and species (see glossary, pp. 473-474, for full definitions of these terms).

◁ RARE SPECIES

Over 100 less common birds are presented on pp. 443-470. Arranged in the same group order used in the main section, these entries consist of one photograph of the species accompanied by a description of the bird. Information on geographical distribution, occurrence, and voice is also given.

Species **Icterus galbula**

black head

black
upper
back

straight
blue-
gray bill

black
upper
breast

orange
underparts

MALE

FLIGHT: strong with rapid wing beats; full downstrokes during flight provide great power.

PERFECT FOR FORAGING
The Baltimore Oriole forages alone in dense foliage of trees and bushes or on the ground.

OCCURRENCE
Forest edges and tall, open mixed hardwoods, especially close to rivers; regularly uses forested parks, suburban and urban areas with abundant tall trees. Small numbers winter in southeastern US and Florida, but most birds move to Mexico, Colombia, and Venezuela.

Weight	1⅛–1¼oz (30–35g)
Status	**Secure**

NOTES

HABITAT/ BEHAVIOR
Photographs reveal the species in its habitat or show interesting behavior.

COLOR BAND
The information bands at the top and bottom of each entry are color-coded for each family.

PHOTOGRAPHS
These illustrate the species in different views and plumage variations. Significant differences relating to age, sex, and season (breeding/nonbreeding) are shown and the images labeled accordingly; if there is no variation, the images have no label. Unless stated otherwise, the bird shown is an adult.

FLIGHT PATTERNS
This feature illustrates and briefly describes the way the species flies. See panel below.

VAGRANTS ▷
Very rare and accidental visitors are listed at the back of the book with a brief indication of the species' status.

FLIGHT PATTERNS

Simple line diagrams are used to illustrate eight basic flight patterns.

wing beats

Woodpecker-like: bursts of wing beats between deeply undulating glides.

Finch-like: light, bouncy action with flurries of wing beats between deep, undulating glides.

Grouse-like: bursts of wing beats between short, straight glides.

Accipiter-like: straight, with several quick, deep beats between short glides.

Gull-like: continually flapping, with slow, steady wing beats; also glides.

Duck-like: continually flapping, with fast wing beats.

Buteo-like: deep, slow wing beats between soaring glides.

Swallow-like: swooping, with bursts of wing beats between glides.

9

EVOLUTION

O RNITHOLOGISTS AGREE THAT BIRDS evolved
from dinosaurs about 150 million years ago,
but there is still debate about the dinosaur group
from which they descended. Around 10,000 species
of birds exist today, living in many different kinds of
habitats across the world, from desert to Arctic tundra.
To reconstruct how avian evolution occurred, from
Archaeopteryx on up to the present, scientists use many
clues, especially fossil birds, and now DNA.

MISSING LINK?
Archaeopteryx, shown here, is
a 145-million-year-old fossil. It
had dinosaur-like teeth, but
bird-like feathers.

SPECIATION

What are species and how do they evolve? Species
are biological entities. When two species of a genus
overlap they rarely interbreed and produce hybrids. The
Northern Flicker has an eastern (yellow-shafted)
and a western (red-shafted) form; after the discovery
that these two forms interbreed in the Great Plains, the
flickers, which were formerly "split" into two species, are
now considered one. In other cases, a previously single
species, such as the Sage Grouse, has been divided. Such
examples illustrate how species evolve, first by geographic
separation, followed in time by overlap. This process can
take from tens of thousands to millions of years.

BIRD GENEALOGY

The diagram below is called a phylogeny, and shows how
selected groups of birds are related to each other. The timescale
at the top of the diagram is derived from both fossil and DNA

evidence, which allows ornithologists to estimate when
different lineages of birds diverged. The names of groups
shown in bold are those living in North America.

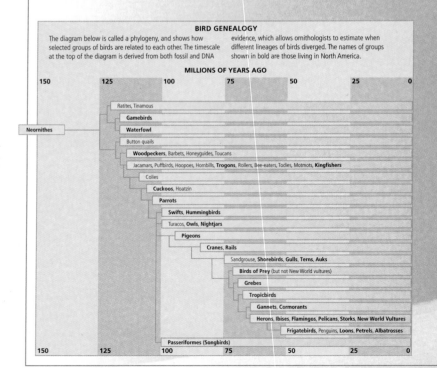

BLENDING IN

This magnificent species is diurnal, unlike most other owls, which are nocturnal. The Snowy Owl breeds in the Arctic tundra and if the ground is covered with snow, it blends in perfectly.

CONVERGENCE

The evolutionary process during which birds of two distantly related groups develop similarities is called convergence. Carrion-eating birds of prey are one example. Old World vultures belong to the hawk family (Accipitridae), while New World vultures are more closely related to storks. However, both groups are characterized by hooked bills, bare heads, and weak talons. Convergence can involve anatomy and behavior, as in the vultures, or other traits, including habitat preference.

PARALLEL EVOLUTION

The African longclaws (family Motacillidae) and North American meadowlarks (family Icteridae) show convergence in plumage color and pattern. Both groups live in grassland.

CAPE LONGCLAW

EASTERN MEADOWLARK

EXTINCTION

During the last 150 years, North America has lost the Passenger Pigeon, the Great Auk, the Carolina Parakeet, the Labrador Duck, and the Eskimo Curlew. Relentless hunting and habitat destruction are the main factors that have led to extinction. Some species that seemed doomed have had a reprieve. Thanks to a breeding and release program, the majestic California Condor soars once again over the Grand Canyon.

OVERHUNTING

The Passenger Pigeon was eradicated as a result of over hunting.

CLASSIFYING BIRDS

All past and present animal life is named and categorized into groups. Classifications reflect the genealogical relationships among groups, based on traits such as color, bones, or DNA. Birds make up the class "Aves," which includes "orders"; each "order" is made up of one or more "families." "Genus" is a subdivision of "family," and contains one or more "species." A species is a unique group of similar organisms that interbreed and produce fertile offspring. Some species have distinct populations, which are known as subspecies.

Aves (Birds)	Class
Passeriformes (Songbirds)	Order
Parulidae (Wood-warblers)	Family
Dendroica	Genus
Dendroica castanea Dendroica palmarum Dendroica tigrina	Species
D. p. palmarum	Subspecies

ANATOMY AND FLIGHT

IN SPITE OF THEIR EXTERNAL DIVERSITY, birds are remarkably similar internally. To allow flight, birds have a skeleton that is both rigid and light. Rigidity is achieved by the fusion of some bones, especially the lower vertebrae, while lightness is maintained by having hollow limb bones. These are connected to air sacs, which, in turn, are connected to the bird's lungs.

SKELETON
Avian skeletal features include the furcula (wishbone), the keeled sternum (breastbone), and the fused tail vertebrae.

"hand"

"forearm"

neck vertebrae

bill

furcula

fused tail vertebrae

keeled sternum

secondaries

FLIGHT ADAPTATIONS

For birds to be able to fly, they need light and rigid bones, a lightweight skull, and hollow wing and leg bones. In addition, pouch-like air sacs are connected to hollow bones, which reduce a bird's weight. The air sacs also function as a cooling system, which birds need because they have a high metabolic rate. The breast muscles, which are crucial for flight, attach to the keeled sternum (breastbone). Wing and tail feathers help support birds when airborne. Feathers wear out, and are regularly replaced during molt.

tail feathers

uppertail coverts

rump

BIRD BONE STRUCTURE
Most bird bones, except those of penguins and other flightless birds, are hollow, which reduces their weight. A honeycomb of internal struts makes the bones remarkably strong.

tertials

scapulars

LEGS, FEET, AND TOES

When you look at a bird's leg, you do not see its thigh, which is inside the body cavity, but the leg from the knee down. When we talk about a bird's feet we really mean its toes. The shin is a fused tibia and fibula. This fused bone plus the heel are known as the "tarso-metatarsus." The four examples below illustrate some toe arrangements.

UNDERPARTS
Underwing coverts have a regular pattern of overlapping rows. Short feathers cover the head, breast, belly, and flanks. In most birds, the toes are unfeathered.

primaries

axillaries

breast

bill

enables grip on ground

WALKING
Ground-foraging birds usually have a long hind claw.

enables strong grip on branches

CLIMBING
Most climbers have two toes forward and two backward.

webbing provides thrust in water

SWIMMING
Waterbirds have webbing between their toes.

used to grasp prey

HUNTING
Birds of prey have powerful toes and strong, sharp claws.

undertail coverts

belly

toes

FEATHERS

All birds, by definition, have feathers. These remarkable structures, which are modified scales, serve two main functions: insulation and flight. Special muscles allow birds to raise their feathers or to flatten them against the body. In cold weather, fluffed-out feathers keep an insulating layer of air between the skin and the outside. This insulating capacity is why humans often find wearing "down" jackets so effective against the cold. The first feathers that chicks have after hatching are down feathers. The rigidity of the flight feathers helps create a supporting surface that birds use to generate thrust and lift.

TYPES OF FEATHERS
Birds have three main kinds of feathers: down, contour, and flight feathers. The rigid axis of all feathers is called the "rachis."

DOWN FEATHER   CONTOUR FEATHER   FLIGHT FEATHER

primary coverts

secondary coverts

coverts

neck

nape

crown

chin

throat

mantle

alula (bastard wing)

UPPERPARTS
The wing feathers from the "hand" of the bird are the primaries, and those on the "forearm" are the secondaries. Each set has its accompanying row of coverts. The tertials are adjacent to the secondaries.

WING FUNCTIONS

Flapping, soaring, gliding, and hovering are among the ways birds use their wings. They also exhibit colors or patterns as part of territorial and courtship displays. Several birds, such as herons, open their wings like an umbrella when foraging in water for fish. An important aspect of wings is their relationship to a bird's weight. The ratio of a bird's wing area to weight is called wing loading, which may be affected also by wing shape. An eagle has a large wing area to weight ratio, which means it has lower wing loading, whereas a swallow has a small wing area to weight ratio, and therefore high wing loading. This means that the slow, soaring eagle is capable of much more energy-efficient flight than the fast, agile swallow.

LONG AND BROAD
The broad, long, rectangular wings of an eagle allow it to soar. The outstretched alulae (bastard wings) give it extra lift.

POINTED
Broad at their base and tapering toward a point, and bent at the wrist, a swallow's wings enable fast flight and sharp turns.

SHORT AND ROUND
Short, broad, and round wings permit warblers to move easily in dense vegetation.

WING AERODYNAMICS

The supporting surface of a bird's wing enables it to take off and stay aloft. Propulsion and lift are linked in birds—which use their wings for both—unlike in airplanes in which these two functions are separate. Large and heavy birds, like swans, flap their wings energetically to create propulsion, and need a long, watery runway before they can fly off. The California Condor can take off from a cliff with little or no wing flapping, but the Black and Turkey Vultures hop up from carrion then flap vigorously and finally use air flowing across their wings to soar. This diagram shows how airflow affects lift.

faster airflow   low air pressure

slower airflow   high air pressure   cross section of bird's wing

MIGRATION

Until recently, the mechanics, or the "how" of migration, was poorly understood. Today, however, ornithologists know that birds use a variety of cues including visual and magnetic, whether they migrate by day or by night. Birds do not leave northern breeding areas because of the winter cold, but because day-length is getting shorter and food scarcer.

NIGHT MIGRANTS
During migration, ornithologists can point a telescope on the moon and count the birds that cross its surface.

INSTINCTIVE MOVE

Even though many birds use visual cues and landmarks during their migration, for example, birds of prey flying along the Appalachians, "instinctive" behavior must control much of how and where they move. Instinct is a loose term that is hard to define, but ornithologists generally understand it as a genetically programmed activity. They assume that natural selection has molded a behavior as complex as migration by acting on birds' DNA; this hypothesis is reasonable, but hard to prove. Nevertheless, it would seem to be the only explanation why many juvenile shorebirds leave their breeding grounds after their parents, and yet find their way to their final destination.

REFUELING
Red Knots stop on their journey from Tierra del Fuego to the Arctic to eat horseshoe crab eggs.

NAVIGATION

One of the most puzzling aspects of migration is understanding how birds make their way from their summer breeding grounds to their winter destination. Ornithologists have devised experiments to determine the different components. Some of these components are innate, others learned. For example, if visual landmarks are hidden by fog, a faint sun can give birds a directional clue; if heavy clouds hide the sun, then the birds' magnetic compass may be used to ascertain their direction.

FINDING THE WAY
Birds coordinate information their brains receive from the sun, moon, stars, landmarks, and magnetite, or iron oxide, and use it as a compass.

OVERLAND FLIERS
Sandhill Cranes migrate over hills and mountains, from their Arctic tundra breeding grounds to the marshes of the Platte River in the midwestern US.

GLOBETROTTERS

Some bird species in North America are year-round residents, although a few individuals of these species move away from where they hatched at some time in the year. However, a large number of North American species are migratory. A few species breed in Alaska, but winter on remote southwest Pacific islands. Others breed in the Canadian Arctic Archipelago, fly over land and the Pacific Ocean, and spend the winter at sea off the coast of Peru. Many songbirds fly from the Gulf Coast to northern South America. The most amazing globetrotters, such as the Red Knot, fly all the way to Tierra del Fuego, making only a few stops along the way after their short breeding season in the Arctic tundra. The return journeys of some of these travelers are not over the same route—instead, their entire trip is elliptical in shape.

EPIC JOURNEY
The Arctic Tern is a notorious long-distance migrant, breeding in Arctic and Subartic regions, and wintering in the pack ice of Antarctica before returning north, a round-trip distance of at least 25,000 miles (40,000km).

KEY
→ Trans-Pacific route
→ Coastal Pacific route
→ Arctic to Pacific route
→ Trans-Gulf route
→ Atlantic to Caribbean route
→ Argentina to Arctic route
→ Arctic-Atlantic Neotropical route

NEOTROPICAL MIGRANT
Many wood-warblers, such as this Blackpoll Warbler, breed in boreal forests, before migrating to their wintering grounds in the Caribbean, or Central or South America.

MIGRATION ROUTES
The map above shows the range of migration routes that some North American species take to and from their breeding grounds.

V-FORMATION
Geese and other large waterbirds fly in a V-formation. The leader falls back and is replaced by another individual, saving energy for all the birds.

PARTIAL MIGRANT

The American Robin is a good example of a partial migrant, a species in which the birds of some populations are resident, whereas others migrate out of their breeding range. Most Canadian populations of the American Robin fly south, US populations are largely resident, and quite a few birds from either population spend the winter in the Southwest, Florida, or Mexico.

KEY ▓ Breeding distribution
▓ Resident all year
▓ Nonbreeding distribution

COURTSHIP AND MATING

WHETHER MONOGAMOUS OR NOT, males and females need to mate for their species to perpetuate itself. With most species, the male plays the dominant role of advertising a territory to potential mates using vocal or visual displays. Females then select a male, and if the two respond positively to each other, a period of courtship follows ending in mating. The next steps are nest building, egg laying, and rearing the young.

DANCING CRANES
During courtship, Sandhill Cranes perform spectacular dances, the two birds of a pair leaping into the air with wings opened and legs splayed.

DISPLAYS

Mutual attraction between the sexes starts with some sort of display, usually performed by the male. These displays can take a number of forms, from flashing dazzling breeding plumage, conducting elaborate dancing rituals, performing complex songs, offering food or nesting material, or actually building a nest. Some birds, such as grebes, have fascinatingly intricate ceremonies, in which both male and female simultaneously perform the same water-dance. Because they are usually very ritualized, displays help ornithologists understand relationships among birds.

WELCOME HOME
Northern Gannets greet their mates throughout the breeding season by rubbing bills together and opening their wings.

LADIES' CHOICE
On a lek (communal display area), male Sage-Grouse inflate chest pouches while females flock around them and select a mate. Sage-Grouse are found in the West.

COURTSHIP FEEDING

In some species, males offer food to their mate to maintain the pair-bond. For example, male terns routinely bring small fish to their mates in a nesting colony, spreading their wings and tail until the females accept the fish.

MAINTAINING RELATIONS
A male Northern Cardinal offers food to the female, which is a way of reinforcing their pair bond.

BREEDING

After mating, a nest is made, often by the female, where she lays from one to a dozen eggs. Not all birds make nests, however. Nightjars, for example, lay their eggs directly on the ground. In many species, incubation doesn't start until the female has laid all the eggs. Incubation, usually done by the female, varies from about 12 days to about 45 days. Songbirds breeding from the temperate zone northward to the Arctic show a range in clutch size, with more eggs produced in the North than in the South. The breeding process can fail at any stage, for example, a predator can eat the eggs or the chicks. Some birds will nest again after such a failure but others give up breeding for the season.

MATING TERNS
Mating is usually brief, and typically takes place on a perch or on the ground, but some species, like swifts, mate in the air. This male Black Tern balances himself by opening his wings.

MUTUAL PREENING
Many species of albatrosses, like these Black-footed Albatrosses from the Pacific, preen each other, with one bird softly nibbling the feathers on the other's head.

POLYGAMY
This Winter Wren collects nesting material for one of the several nests he will build.

MONOGAMOUS BONDS
Some birds, such as Snow Geese, remain paired for life after establishing a bond.

SINGLE FATHER

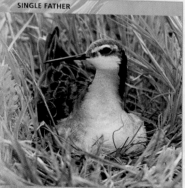

A male Red-necked Phalarope incubates eggs in the Arctic tundra. Phalaropes are well known for their reversal of breeding roles. The female, who is the larger and more colorful of the two sexes, aggressively competes for males, and after mating with several of them, plays no role in nest building, incubation, or caring for chicks, but tends to her territory instead. Although the chicks can feed by themselves immediately after hatching, they remain with a male before growing feathers and living on their own.

NESTS AND EGGS

M OST BIRD SPECIES BUILD THEIR OWN NEST, which is a necessary container for their eggs. Exceptions include some species of cuckoos and cowbirds, that lay their eggs in other species' nests. Nest-building is often done by the female alone, but in some species the male may help or even build it himself. Eggs are incubated either by females only, or by males and females, depending on the species. Eggs, consisting of 60 percent water, contain a fatty yolk for nourishment of the embryo as well as sugars and proteins. Eggshells are hard enough to sustain the weight of incubating parents, yet soft enough for a chick to break its way out. Hatching is an energy-draining process, and can last for several hours.

NEST TYPES

In addition to the four types shown below, nests range from a simple scrape in the ground with a few added pebbles to an elaborate woven basket-like structure. Plant matter forms basic nest material. This includes twigs, grass stems, bark, lichens, mosses, plant down, and rootlets. Some birds add mud to their nest for strength. Others incorporate animal hair or feathers to improve its softness and insulation. Female eider ducks line their nest with down feathers plucked from their belly. Some birds include bits of plastic or threads in their nests. Several species of flycatchers add shed snakeskins to their nests. Many birds make their nest or lay their eggs deep inside the empty burrows of other animals. Burrowing Owls nest in prairie dog burrows, where they coexist with the rodents.

UNTIDY NEST
Huge stick nests, built on top of dead trees, are the hallmark of Ospreys. They also readily use custom-made nesting platforms erected by humans specifically for them.

EGG CUP
A clutch of three blue robin's eggs rest in a cup lined with grass stems and strengthened with mud. Robins build their nests either in shrubs or trees.

NATURAL CAVITY
This Northern Saw-whet Owl is nesting at the bottom of a cavity, in a tree that has probably been excavated by a woodpecker.

NEST BOX
Cavity-nesting bluebirds have been affected by habitat loss, and compete with other birds for nest sites, which may include human-made structures.

COMPLEX WEAVE
New World orioles weave intricate nests from dried grass stems and other plant material, and hang them from the tip of branches, often high up in trees.

EGG SHAPES

There are six basic egg shapes among birds, as illustrated to the right. The most common egg shapes are longitudinal or elliptical. Murres lay pear-shaped eggs, an adaptation for nesting on the narrow ledges of sea cliffs; if an egg rolls, it does so in a tight circle and remains on the ledge. Spherical eggs with irregular red blotches are characteristic of birds of prey. Pigeons and doves lay white oval eggs, usually two per clutch. The eggs of many songbirds, including sparrows and buntings, are conical and have a variety of dark markings on a pale background.

COLOR AND SHAPE
Birds' eggs vary widely in terms of shape, colors, and markings. The American Robin's egg on the left is a beautiful blue.

PEAR SHAPED   **LONGITUDINAL**   **ELLIPTICAL**

OVAL   **CONICAL**   **SPHERICAL**

NEAT ARRANGEMENT
Many shorebirds, such as plovers and sandpipers, lay four conical eggs with the narrow ends pointed in toward each other.

HATCHING CONDITION

After a period of incubation, which varies from species to species, chicks break the eggshell, some of them using an egg tooth, a special bill feature that falls off after hatching. After a long and exhausting struggle, the chick eventually tumbles out of the shell fragments. The transition from the watery medium inside the egg to the air outside is a tremendous physiological switch. Once free of their shell, the hatchlings recover from the exertion and either beg food from their parents or feed on their own.

FOOD DELIVERY
Tern chicks, although able to move around, cannot catch the fish they need to survive, and must rely on their parents to provide food until they can fly.

FAST FEEDER
Coots, gallinules, and rails hatch with a complete covering of down, and can feed by themselves immediately after birth.

PARENTAL GUIDANCE
Birds of prey, such as these Snowy Owl owlets, need their parents to care for them longer than some other bird species, and do not leave the nest until their feathers are sufficiently developed for their first flight.

BROOD PARASITISM

Neither cowbirds in the New World nor cuckoos in the Old World make a nest. Female cowbirds deposit up to 20 eggs in the nests of several other species. If the foster parents accept the foreign egg, they will feed the chick of the parasite until it fledges. In the picture below, a tiny wood-warbler feeds its adopted chick, a huge cowbird hatchling that has overgrown the nest. Whereas some host species readily incubate the foreign egg, others reject it or abandon the nest.

IDENTIFICATION

Some species are easy to identify, but in many other cases, species identification is tricky. In North America, a notoriously difficult group in terms of identification is the wood-warblers, especially in the fall, when most species have similar greenish or yellowish plumage.

BLUEBIRD VARIATIONS
Species of the genus *Sialia*, such as the Mountain Bluebird above, and the Eastern Bluebird below, are easy to identify.

GEOGRAPHIC RANGE

Each bird species in North America lives in a particular area that is called its geographic range. Some species have a restricted range; for example, Kirtland's Warbler occurs only in Michigan. Other species, such as the Red-tailed Hawk, range from coast to coast and from northern Canada to Mexico. Species with a broad range usually breed in a variety of vegetation types, while species with narrow ranges often have a specialized habitat; Kirtland's Warblers' is jack pine woodland.

bright blue wings
white belly
chestnut flanks

SIZE AND WEIGHT

From hummingbird to Tundra Swan and from extra-light (¹⁄₁₆oz) to heavy (15lb), such is the range of sizes and weights found among the bird species of North America. Size can be measured in several ways, for example the length of a bird from bill-tip to tail-tip, or its wingspan. Size can also be estimated for a given bird in relationship with another that is familiar. For example, the less familiar Bicknell's Thrush can be compared with the well-known American Robin.

SIZE MATTERS
Smaller shorebirds, with shorter legs and bills, forage in shallow water, but larger ones have longer legs and bills and can feed in deeper water.

SEMIPALMATED PLOVER   **LESSER YELLOWLEGS**   **HUDSONIAN GODWIT**   **LONG-BILLED CURLEW**

GENERAL SHAPE

Just as birds come in all sizes, their body shapes vary, but size and shape are not necessarily correlated. In the dense reed beds in which it lives, the American Bittern's long and thin body blends in with stems. The round-bodied Sedge Wren hops in shrubby vegetation or near the ground where slimness is not an advantage. In dense forest canopy, the slender and long-tailed Yellow-billed Cuckoo can maneuver easily. Mourning Doves inhabit rather open habitats and their plumpness is irrelevant when it comes to their living space. The relative shape and length of the wings and tail are often, but not always, an important component on how a particular bird species behaves.

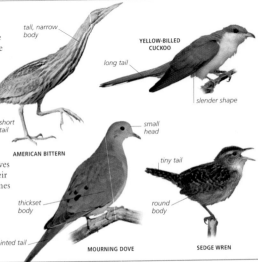

tall, narrow body
long tail
YELLOW-BILLED CUCKOO
slender shape
short tail
AMERICAN BITTERN
small head
tiny tail
thickset body
round body
long, pointed tail
MOURNING DOVE   **SEDGE WREN**

BILL SHAPE

These images show a range of bill shapes and sizes relative to the bird's head size. In general, bill form, including length or thickness, corresponds to the kinds of food a birds consumes. With its pointed bill, the Mountain Chickadee picks tiny insects from crevices in tree bark. At another extreme, dowitchers probe mud with their long thin bills, feeling for worms. The avocet swishes its bill back and forth in briny water, in search of shrimp.

worms and fruit

AMERICAN ROBIN

seeds and caterpillars

HOUSE FINCH

tiny insects, seeds

MOUNTAIN CHICKADEE

worms from deep mud

AMERICAN AVOCET

small shrimps in water

GREAT BLUE HERON fish

LONG-BILLED DOWITCHER

marine mollusks

SURF SCOTER

mammals and birds

GOLDEN EAGLE

WING SHAPE

Birds' wing shapes are correlated with their flight style. The long, round-tipped wings of the Red-tailed Hawk are perfect for soaring, while the tiny wings of hummingbirds are exactly what is needed to hover in front of flowers and then to back away after a meal of nectar. When flushed, quails flutter with their round wings and quickly drop down.

BROAD-TAILED HUMMINGBIRD

just a blur in flight

MOUNTAIN QUAIL

short and round

RED-TAILED HAWK

long, rounded

GREATER YELLOWLEGS

angled, pointed

AMERICAN WOODCOCK

broad and blunt

TAIL SHAPE

It is not clear why some songbirds, like the American Goldfinch, have a notched tail while other similar sized birds do not. Tail shapes vary as much as wing shapes, but are not so easily linked to a function or to the habitat in which a given species lives. Irrespective of shape, tails are needed for balance. In some birds, tail shape, color, and pattern are used in courtship displays or in defensive displays when threatened.

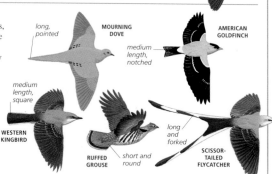

long, pointed

MOURNING DOVE

AMERICAN GOLDFINCH

medium length, notched

medium length, square

WESTERN KINGBIRD

RUFFED GROUSE

short and round

long and forked

SCISSOR-TAILED FLYCATCHER

COLORS AND MARKINGS

Melanin and carotenoid pigments determine color. Gray and brown-plumaged birds have melanin (under hormonal influence), yellow and red ones, carotenoid (derived from food). Flamingos are pink because they eat carotenoid-rich crustaceans. Diversity in color and markings also results from scattering of white light by feathers (producing blue colors) and optical interference (iridescence) due to the structural properties of some feathers (as in hummingbirds). Bare patches of skin are often used in displays.

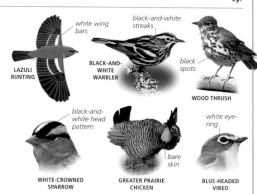

white wing bars

black-and-white streaks

LAZULI BUNTING

BLACK-AND-WHITE WARBLER

black spots

WOOD THRUSH

black-and-white head pattern

WHITE-CROWNED SPARROW

bare skin

GREATER PRAIRIE CHICKEN

white eye-ring

BLUE-HEADED VIREO

SPECIES GUIDE

GAMEBIRDS

THIS DIVERSE AND ADAPTABLE GROUP of birds thrives in habitats ranging from hot desert to frozen tundra. Gamebirds spend most of their time on the ground, springing loudly into the air when alarmed.

QUAILS

Among the most terrestrial of all gamebirds, quails are renowned for their great sociability, often forming large family groups, or "coveys," of up to 100 birds. The Northern Bobwhite is the only quail species found in the east, and ranges over a variety of habitats. Each of the five species found in western North America lives in a specific habitat or at a particular elevation.

DRESSED TO THRILL
With its striking plumage, Gambel's Quail is one of the best-known desert birds in southwestern North America.

GROUSE

The most numerous and widespread of gamebirds, the 12 different species of grouse can be divided into three groups based on their preferred habitats. Forest grouse include the Ruffed Grouse in the East, the Spruce Grouse in the North, and the Sooty Grouse and Dusky Grouse in the West.

Prairie grouse, including the Sharp-tailed Grouse, are found throughout the middle of the continent. All three tundra and mountaintop grouse or ptarmigans are found in the extreme North and the Rockies. Grouse often possess patterns that match their surroundings, providing camouflage from both animal and human predators.

GRASSLAND GROUSE
The aptly named Sharp-tailed Grouse is locally common in western prairies. It searches for grasshoppers in the summer.

PHEASANTS & PARTRIDGES

These Eurasian gamebirds were introduced into North America in the 19th and 20th centuries to provide additional targets for recreational hunters. While some introductions failed, species such as the colorful Ring-necked Pheasant adapted well and now thrive in established populations.

SNOW BIRD
The Rock Ptarmigan's white winter plumage camouflages it against the snow, helping hide it from predators.

| Order **Galliformes** | Family **Odontophoridae** | Species **Colinus virginianus** |

Northern Bobwhite

round wings

black-and-white face

short tail **MALE**

IN FLIGHT

tan throat

FEMALE

brown, beige, and black head pattern

thick, decurved bill

complex markings on upperparts

short wings

fine streaking on breast

MALE

FLIGHT: rapid and startling flight, followed by brief glide; seldom flies far before landing.

The Northern Bobwhite, a small, plump, chicken-like bird, is second only to the Ruffed Grouse among North American gamebirds in distribution across the eastern US states. Loved by hunters, when flushed it erupts in "coveys" of 10 to 20 individuals, bursting from groundcover and dispersing in many directions. Large numbers are raised in captivity and released to supplement wild populations for hunting.

VOICE Characteristic *bob-WHITE* or *bob-bob-WHITE* whistled by males in breeding season; call to reunite flock includes *hoi-lee* and *hoi* following dispersal.

NESTING Shallow depression lined with plant matter, located on ground within sight of an opening; 10–15 eggs; sometimes multiple broods per season; January–March.

FEEDING Forages for wide variety of plant matter (seeds, buds, leaves), and insects, snails, and spiders, depending on the season.

COVEY LIFE
Male, female, and immature Northern Bobwhites live together in tight flocks called coveys.

SIMILAR SPECIES

MONTEZUMA QUAIL

larger black-and-white facial pattern

dark sides with white spots

GRAY PARTRIDGE
see p.32

mostly gray

reddish cheeks

striped belly

OCCURRENCE
Widely distributed but only locally common in much of the eastern US, and in Mexico, southward to Guatemala. Most often associated with agricultural fields, it thrives in a patchwork of mixed young forests, fields, and brushy hedges. A permanent resident.

| Length **8–10in (20–25cm)** | Wingspan **11–14in (28–35cm)** | Weight **6oz (175g)** |
| Social **Small flocks** | Lifespan **Up to 6 years** | Status **Declining** |

DATE SEEN	WHERE	NOTES

| Order **Galliformes** | Family **Phasianidae** | Species *Meleagris gallopavo* |

Wild Turkey

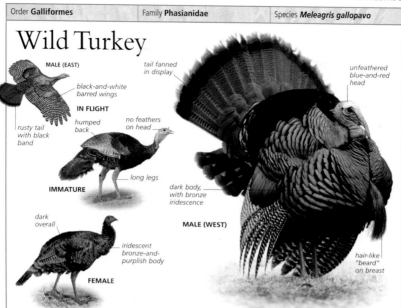

MALE (EAST)

tail fanned in display

black-and-white barred wings

IN FLIGHT

rusty tail with black band

humped back

no feathers on head

IMMATURE

long legs

dark overall

iridescent bronze-and-purplish body

FEMALE

unfeathered blue-and-red head

dark body, with bronze iridescence

MALE (WEST)

hair-like "beard" on breast

Once proposed by Benjamin Franklin as the national emblem of the US, the Wild Turkey—the largest gamebird in North America—was eliminated from most of its original range by the early 1900s due to over-hunting and habitat destruction. Since then, habitat restoration and the subsequent reintroduction of Wild Turkeys has been very successful.

VOICE Well-known gobble, given by males especially during courtship; female makes various yelps, clucks, and purrs, based on mood and threat level.

NESTING Scrape on ground lined with grass; placed against or under protective cover; 10–15 eggs; 1 brood; March–June.

FEEDING Omnivorous, it scratches in leaf litter on forest floor for acorns and other food, mostly vegetation; also takes plants and insects from agricultural fields.

FLIGHT: after running, leaps into the air with loud, rapid wing beats, then glides.

COLLECTIVE DISPLAY
Once the population expands into new areas, numerous males will be seen displaying together.

SIMILAR SPECIES

GREATER SAGE GROUSE

dark head

pointed tail

TURKEY VULTURE
see p.116

small red head

white breast

dark overall

OCCURRENCE
Found in mixed mature woodlands, fields with agricultural crops; also in various grasslands, close to swamps, but adaptable and increasingly common in suburban and urban habitats. Quite widespread, but patchily distributed across North America.

Length **2¾–4ft (0.9–1.2m)**	Wingspan **4–5ft (1.2–1.5m)**	Weight **10–24lb (4.5–11kg)**
Social **Flocks**	Lifespan **Up to 9 years**	Status **Secure**

DATE SEEN	WHERE	NOTES

Order **Galliformes**	Family **Phasianidae**	Species *Bonasa umbellus*

Ruffed Grouse

ADULT (RUFOUS FORM)

IN FLIGHT

brown-barred underparts

rusty tail with black band

spotted gray upperparts

heavy white spotting on brown upperparts

dark patch on neck

raised crest

feathered legs

gray-barred underparts

ADULT (GRAY FORM)

ADULT (RUFOUS FORM)

The Ruffed Grouse is perhaps the most widespread gamebird in North America. There are two color forms, rufous and gray, both allowing the birds to remain camouflaged and undetected on the forest floor, until they eventually burst into the air in an explosion of whirring wings. The male is well known for his extraordinary wing beating or "drumming" display, which he performs year-round, but most frequently in the spring.

VOICE Hissing notes, and soft *purrt, purrt, purrt* when alarmed, by both sexes; males "drumming" display when heard from distance resembles small engine starting, *thump…thump…thump...thump... thump…thuthuthuth.*

NESTING Shallow, leaf-lined bowl set against a tree trunk, rock or fallen log in forest; 6–14 eggs; 1 brood; March–June.

FEEDING Forages on ground for leaves, buds, and fruit; occasionally insects.

FLIGHT: an explosive take-off, usually at close range, glides for a short distance before landing.

SIMILAR SPECIES

SPRUCE GROUSE ♀
smaller overall;
see p.27

rusty orange tip

shorter tail

DUSKY GROUSE

larger and darker overall

heavier barring on chest

less barring

WARM RED
The rufous form of the Ruffed Grouse is more common in wetter parts of the continent.

OCCURRENCE
Found in young, mixed forests throughout the northern US and much of Canada except tundra. Southern edge of range extends along higher elevations of the Appalachians and middle levels of the Rocky Mountains, if suitable habitat is available.

Length **17–20in (43–51cm)**	Wingspan **20–23in (51–58cm)**	Weight **20–22oz (575–625g)**
Social **Solitary/Small flocks**	Lifespan **Up to 10 years**	Status **Secure**

DATE SEEN	WHERE	NOTES

| Order **Galliformes** | Family **Phasianidae** | Species **Canachites canadensis** |

Spruce Grouse

MALE (FRANKLIN'S)

ADULT

IN FLIGHT

white spots on black tail

paler overall

FEMALE C. c. canadensis (TAIGA)

heavy barring on underparts

bright red comb above eye

black throat

black breast

triangular white spots on underparts

MALE C. c. canadensis (TAIGA)

gray upperparts

heavily barred underparts

FEMALE C. c. franklinii (FRANKLIN'S)

Perhaps because of the remoteness of their habitat and lack of human contact, Spruce Grouse are not afraid of humans. This lack of wariness when approached has earned them the name "fool hens." Their specialized diet of pine needles causes the intestinal tract to expand in order to accommodate a large volume of food to compensate for its low nutritional value. There are two subspecies of Spruce Grouse (*C. c. canadensis* and *C. c. franklinii*) both of which have red and gray forms; "taiga" is the eastern one.

VOICE Mostly silent; males clap their wings during courtship display; females often utter long cackle at dawn and dusk.
NESTING Lined with moss, leaves, feathers; often at base of tree; naturally low area in forest floor 4–6 eggs; 1 brood; May–July.
FEEDING Feeds mostly on pine but also spruce needles; will eat insects, leaves, fruits, and seeds when available.

FLIGHT: generally avoids flying; when disturbed, bursts into flight on whirring wings.

RUFOUS BAND
The male "taiga" subspecies displays the thin rufous band on the tip of his tail.

SIMILAR SPECIES		
RUFFED GROUSE see p.26 spotted gray upperparts gray-barred underparts	**DUSKY GROUSE** longer, charcoal-gray tail	much larger grayer overall

OCCURRENCE
Present year-round in forests dominated by conifers, including Jack, Lodgepole, Spruce, Red Spruce, Black Spruce, Balsam Fir, Subalpine Fir, Hemlock, and Cedar. Found from western Alaska to the Atlantic Coast.

| Length **14–17in (36–43cm)** | Wingspan **21–23in (53–58cm)** | Weight **16oz (450g)** |
| Social **Solitary** | Lifespan **Up to 10 years** | Status **Secure** |

DATE SEEN	WHERE	NOTES

GAMEBIRDS

| Order **Galliformes** | Family **Phasianidae** | Species *Tympanuchus phasianellus* |

Sharp-tailed Grouse

tan eyebrow

naked pink skin

ADULT · mottled wings

long central tail feather

heavily mottled brown, white, and black upperparts

IN FLIGHT

pale, wedge-shaped tail, with protruding central feathers

white undertail feathers

MALE

brown wings with white dots

white underside, with dark brown arrowheads along flanks

FLIGHT: flushes from hiding with rapid wing beats, then switches to glide-flap-glide.

The most widespread of the three species in its genus, the Sharp-tailed Grouse is able to adapt to the greatest variety of habitats. It is not migratory, but undertakes seasonal movements between grassland summer habitats and woodland winter habitats. These birds are popular with hunters and are legal quarry in most of their range. Elements of this grouse's spectacular courtship display have been incorporated into the culture and dance of Native American people, including foot stomping and tail feather rattling.
VOICE Male calls a variety of unusual clucks, cooing, barks, and gobbles during courtship; females cluck with different intonations.
NESTING Shallow depression lined with plant matter close at hand as well as some feathers from female, usually near overhead cover; 10–12 eggs; 1 brood; March–May.
FEEDING Forages primarily for seeds, leaves, buds, and fruit; also takes insects and flowers when available.

PRAIRIE DANCER
The courtship dance of the Sharp-tailed Grouse heralds the arrival of spring to the grasslands.

OCCURRENCE
Has a northern and western distribution in North America, from Alaska (isolated population) southward to northern prairie states. Prefers a mixture of fallow and active agricultural fields combined with brushy forest edges and woodlots along river beds.

SIMILAR SPECIES

GREATER PRAIRIE CHICKEN see p.29 · shorter, square tail · more heavily barred · naked orange skin

RING-NECKED PHEASANT ♀ see p.33 · light brown · longer tail · scalloped pattern on underparts

| Length **15–19in (38–48cm)** | Wingspan **23–26in (58–66cm)** | Weight **26–34oz (750–950g)** |
| Social **Flocks** | Lifespan **Up to 7 years** | Status **Declining (p)** |

DATE SEEN	WHERE	NOTES

28

Order **Galliformes**	Family **Phasianidae**	Species *Tympanuchus cupido*

Greater Prairie Chicken

rounded wings

MALE

IN FLIGHT

square tail

no display feathers

FEMALE

two sets of feathers raised during display

orange skin over eye

display feathers against neck

barred overall

MALE

FLIGHT: bursts from cover with loud, rapid wing beats when approached.

MALE (DISPLAYING)

beard-like feathers

bright orange skin of "air sac"

Once common in prairie and woodland across central and eastern North America, populations of the Greater Prairie Chicken have been greatly reduced as their habitats gave way to agriculture. The Atlantic coast population (Heath Hen) became extinct in 1932. During the breeding season, males defend communal territories called "leks" and perform spectacular displays, inflating the air sacks on their necks, and "booming."
VOICE During courtship, males emit "booming" sounds like a three-part low hoot; also cackling calls.
NESTING Depression in soil lined with vegetation and feathers, in thick grass or other cover; 10–12 eggs; 1 brood; April–July.
FEEDING Eats berries, leaves, seeds, and grain; also insects.

BOOMING MALES
At a "lek" in the early morning, a male sends out a booming call and displays to attract a female.

SIMILAR SPECIES

SHARP-TAILED GROUSE see p.28
pink skin
pointed tail
slightly larger
"v"-shaped markings on underparts

LESSER PRAIRIE CHICKEN
pronged feathers
smaller overall
reddish orange skin

OCCURRENCE
Separate populations occur in the Dakotas, Minnesota, Colorado, Nebraska, Kansas, Illinois, Oklahoma, Texas, and Missouri. Breeds in openings mixed with oak-forested river corridors, especially where these interact with areas of native tallgrass prairie; resident year-round.

Length **15½–17½in (40–45cm)**	Wingspan **26–29in (66–74cm)**	Weight **30–36oz (850–1,000g)**
Social **Flocks**	Lifespan **Up to 4 years**	Status **Vulnerable**

DATE SEEN	WHERE	NOTES

Order **Galliformes**	Family **Phasianidae**	Species *Lagopus muta*

Rock Ptarmigan

brown-and-black barring

black tail

MALE (WINTER)

mostly gray upperparts

white wings

all-white wings

small bill

FEMALE (SUMMER)

small, round head

red comb

mottled belly

gray wing patch

IN FLIGHT

MALE (SUMMER)

"salt-and-pepper" barring on gray upperparts

small, delicate bill

black line between eye and bill

white plumage

FEMALE (WINTER)

white belly

MALE (WINTER)

MALE (SUMMER)

feathered feet and toes

FLIGHT: bursts into flight with rapid wing beats, followed by gliding and shallow flapping.

The Rock Ptarmigan is the most northern of the three ptarmigan species found in North America. Although some birds make a short migration to more southern wintering grounds, many remain on their breeding grounds year-round. This species is well known for its distinctive seasonal variation in plumage, which helps to camouflage it against its surroundings. Ptarmigan are a common food of the Inuit, who inhabit the same Arctic habitat.
VOICE Quiet; male call a raspy *krrrh*, also growls and clucks.
NESTING Small scrape or natural depression, lined with plant matter, often away from cover; 8–10 eggs; 1 brood; April–June.
FEEDING Feeds on buds, seeds, flowers, and leaves, especially birch and willow; eats insects in summer.

IN BETWEEN PLUMAGE
Various transitional plumage patterns can be seen on the Rock Ptarmigan in spring and fall.

SIMILAR SPECIES

WHITE-TAILED PTARMIGAN ⚥
all-white tail in winter;

smaller overall

WILLOW PTARMIGAN ⚥
see p.31

larger overall

lighter brown upperparts

OCCURRENCE
Local in dry, rocky tundra and shrubby ridge tops; will use edges of open meadows and dense evergreen stands along fairly high-elevation rivers and streams during winter. Occurs throughout the Northern Hemisphere in Arctic tundra from Iceland to Kamchatka in the Russian Far East.

Length **12½–15½in (32–40cm)**	Wingspan **19½–23½in (50–60cm)**	Weight **16–23oz (450–650g)**
Social **Winter flocks**	Lifespan **Up to 8 years**	Status **Secure**

DATE SEEN	WHERE	NOTES

Order **Galliformes**	Family **Phasianidae**	Species ***Lagopus lagopus***

Willow Ptarmigan

white between eye and black bill

red comb

reddish brown body

black tail

ADULT (WINTER)

black bill

all-white body

black bill

rich reddish brown body

IN FLIGHT

MALE (SUMMER)

lacks red comb

ADULT (WINTER)

dark, scaly bars

white belly

yellow-brown body

FEMALE (SUMMER)

MALE (SUMMER)

feathered feet

FLIGHT: strong, rapid wing beats before gliding; prefers to walk.

The most common and widespread of the three ptarmigan species, the Willow Ptarmigan is the state bird of Alaska. The Willow Ptarmigan is an unusual gamebird species, as male and female remain bonded throughout the chick-rearing process, in which the male is an active participant. The "Red Grouse" of British moors is a subspecies (*L. l. scotica*) of the Willow Ptarmigan.

VOICE Variety of purrs, clucks, hissing, meowing noises; *Kow-Kow-Kow* call given before flushing, possibly alerting others.

NESTING Shallow bowl scraped in soil, lined with plant matter, protected by overhead cover; 8–10 eggs; 1 brood; March–May.

FEEDING Mostly eats buds, stems, and seeds, but also flowers, insects, and leaves when available.

PERFECT BLEND-IN
Its reddish brown upperparts camouflage this summer ptarmigan in the shrubby areas it inhabits.

SIMILAR SPECIES

WHITE-TAILED PTARMIGAN ☼

browner plumage

smaller overall

ROCK PTARMIGAN ☼ see p.30

grayer plumage

darker

OCCURRENCE
Prefers tundra, in Arctic, sub-Arctic and subalpine regions. Thrives in willow thickets along low, moist river corridors; also in the low woodlands of the sub-Arctic tundra.

Length **14–17½in (35–44cm)**	Wingspan **22–24in (56–61cm)**	Weight **15–28oz (425–800g)**
Social **Winter flocks**	Lifespan **Up to 9 years**	Status **Secure**

DATE SEEN	WHERE	NOTES

Order **Galliformes**	Family **Phasianidae**	Species ***Perdix perdix***

Gray Partridge

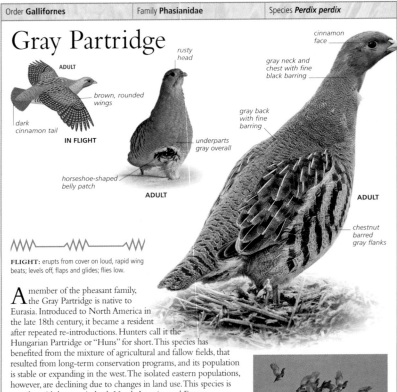

ADULT

rusty head

brown, rounded wings

dark cinnamon tail

IN FLIGHT

cinnamon face

gray neck and chest with fine black barring

gray back with fine barring

underparts gray overall

horseshoe-shaped belly patch

ADULT

ADULT

chestnut barred gray flanks

FLIGHT: erupts from cover on loud, rapid wing beats; levels off, flaps and glides; flies low.

A member of the pheasant family, the Gray Partridge is native to Eurasia. Introduced to North America in the late 18th century, it became a resident after repeated re-introductions. Hunters call it the Hungarian Partridge or "Huns" for short. This species has benefited from the mixture of agricultural and fallow fields, that resulted from long-term conservation programs, and its population is stable or expanding in the west. The isolated eastern populations, however, are declining due to changes in land use. This species is popular with hunters in both North America and Europe.

VOICE Short *kuk-kuk-kuk*, quickly and in a series when alarmed; *prruk-prruk* between adults and young when threatened.

NESTING Shallow depression in soil lined with vegetation, usually in hedgerows; 14–18 eggs; 1 brood; March–May.

FEEDING Eats mostly seeds and row crops such as corn and wheat; succulent green leaves in spring; insects when breeding.

NOISY TAKEOFF
When the Gray Partridge takes flight its wings make a loud, whirring sound.

SIMILAR SPECIES		

NORTHERN BOBWHITE ♀
see p.24
white streaks on rusty red body
buffy throat and face

CHUKAR
white face edged in black
red bill
black barring on white flanks

OCCURRENCE
Primarily agricultural fields of crops including corn, wheat, and oats, as well as associated hedgerows and fallow grasslands. Most birds are nonmigratory, but there is some movement by eastern birds after breeding.

Length **11–13in (28–33cm)**	Wingspan **17–20in (43–51cm)**	Weight **12–18oz (350–500g)**
Social **Family groups**	Lifespan **Up to 4 years**	Status **Secure**

DATE SEEN	WHERE	NOTES

Order **Galliformes**	Family **Phasianidae**	Species *Phasianus colchicus*

Ring-necked Pheasant

long tail

MALE

short, round wings

pale rump

pale brown body

bold black markings

green-black head

iridescent ear tufts

pointed tail

FEMALE

white neck ring

IN FLIGHT

orange-copper flanks

red face wattles

FEMALE

iridescent bronze sheen

MALE (DARK FORM)

long, pointed tail

FLIGHT: bursts vertically from cover on loud rapid wing beats; levels off, flaps, then glides.

barred underparts

MALE

A native of Asia, the variable-looking Ring-necked Pheasant was originally introduced in North America for recreational hunting purposes, and is now widely distributed across North America. Birds released after being bred in captivity are used to supplement natural reproduction for hunting purposes. In the wild, several females may lay eggs in the same nest—a phenomenon called "egg-dumping." There is a less common dark form, which can be distinguished principally because it lacks the distinctive white band around the neck.

VOICE Male emits a loud, raucous, explosive double note, *Karrk–KORK*, followed by loud wing-flapping; both sexes cackle when flushed.

NESTING Shallow bowl composed of grasses, usually on ground in tall grass or among low shrubs; 7–15 eggs; 1 brood; March–June.

FEEDING Feeds on corn and other grain, seeds, fruit, row crops, grass, leaves and shoots; eats insects when available.

SIMILAR SPECIES

GREATER SAGE GROUSE larger

SHARP-TAILED GROUSE slightly smaller; see p.28

shorter tail

long, dark tail

pale breast

dark belly

darker brown overall

FLUSHED OUT
The Ring-necked Pheasant is a powerful flier when alarmed or flushed out of its cover.

OCCURRENCE
Widespread across southern Canada and the US; prefers mixture of active agricultural crops (especially corn fields), fallow fields, and hedgerows; also cattail marshes and wooded river bottoms. The Ring-necked Pheasant is native to Asia from the Caucasus east to China.

Length **19½–28in (50–70cm)**	Wingspan **30–34in (76–86cm)**	Weight **1¼–6½lb (0.5–3kg)**
Social **Solitary/Flocks**	Lifespan **Up to 4 years**	Status **Secure**

DATE SEEN	WHERE	NOTES

WATERFOWL

Recent scientific studies indicate that waterfowl are closely related to gamebirds. Most species of waterfowl molt all their flight feathers at once after breeding, making them flightless for several weeks until they grow new ones.

GEESE

Ornithologists group geese and swans together into the subfamily Anserinae. Intermediate in body size and neck length between swans and ducks, geese are more terrestrial than either, and are often seen grazing on dry land. Like swans, geese pair for life. They are highly social, and most species are migratory, flying south for the winter in large flocks.

SWANS

Swans are essentially large, long-necked geese. Their heavier weight makes them ungainly on land, and they tend to be more aquatic than their smaller relatives. On water, however, they are extremely graceful. When feeding, a swan stretches its long neck to reach water plants at the bottom, submerging up to half its body as it does so. The Trumpeter Swan of the Northwest is North America's largest native waterfowl, growing up to 5ft (1.5m) long, and weighing up to 25lb (12kg).

DUCKS

Classified in their own subfamily, called the Anatinae, ducks are more varied than swans or geese, with many more species. They are loosely grouped by their feeding habits. Dabblers, or puddle ducks, such as the Mallard, teals, and wigeons, eat plants and animal matter, such as snails. They feed by upending on the surface of shallow water. By contrast diving ducks, a group that includes scaups, scoters, eiders, mergansers, and the Ruddy Duck, dive deep underwater for their food.

INSTANT TAKEOFF
Puddle ducks like the Mallard can shoot straight out of the water and into the air.

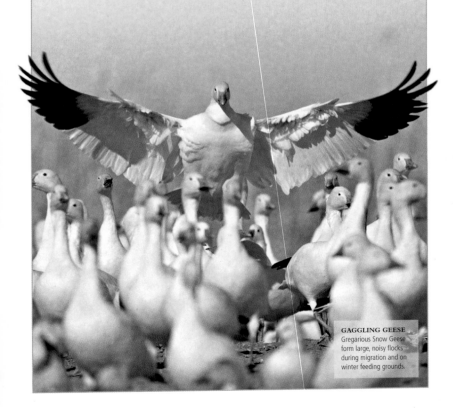

GAGGLING GEESE
Gregarious Snow Geese form large, noisy flocks during migration and on winter feeding grounds.

| Order **Anseriformes** | Family **Anatidae** | Species *Dendrocygna bicolor* |

Fulvous Whistling-Duck

ADULT

dark wings

white rump

tawny head and underparts

gray feet extend beyond tail

IN FLIGHT

tawny buff head and neck

faint crest

gray bill

ADULT

white flank plumes

barred back

tawny buff underparts

Although often thought of as dabbling ducks, whistling-ducks act more like swans, as they form long-term pairs, but without an elaborate courtship display, and the male helps to raise the brood. The Fulvous Whistling-Duck is a widespread species in tropical regions, but in the US it is closely associated with rice fields, where numbers of these noisy birds have steadily recovered from the use of pesticides in the 1960s.

VOICE High-pitched squeaky *pi-teeeew*; often calls in flight.

NESTING Simple bowl-shaped nest made of plant matter; among dense floating plants, or on ground; 6–20 eggs; 1 brood; April–September.

FEEDING Filter feeds on rice, seeds of water plants, insects, worms, snails, and clams by swimming, wading, or dabbling along or below the surface.

FLIGHT: fairly shallow wing beats; legs extend beyond tail.

BOTTOMS UP!
When feeding in water, the bird often up-ends to feed on snails and submerged rice seeds.

SHORT NECKED
The Fulvous Whistling-Duck is shorter-necked than its black-bellied relative, and can be confused with other ducks when its long legs are hidden.

SIMILAR SPECIES

BLACK-BELLIED WHISTLING-DUCK
see p.444

all-black tail

bold white wing stripe

longer neck

no white on flanks

NORTHERN PINTAIL ♀
see p.52

brown-and-black mottled plumage

OCCURRENCE
Permanent resident in southern Texas and Florida; range expands in summer to coastal Texas and Louisiana. In the US, often found in rice fields together with the Black-bellied Whistling-Duck. Casual vagrant as far north as British Columbia and Nova Scotia.

| Length **16½–20in (42–51cm)** | Wingspan **33–37in (85–93cm)** | Weight **19–34oz (550–975g)** |
| Social **Flocks** | Lifespan **Up to 7 years** | Status **Localized** |

DATE SEEN	WHERE	NOTES

Order **Anseriformes**	Family **Anatidae**	Species *Anser albifrons*

Greater White-fronted Goose

gray wing feathers

pink bill with white base

brownish gray head

ADULT

white rump band

IN FLIGHT

white flank streak

white tip to tail

darker chocolate-brown upperparts

dull yellowish orange bill

larger body

brown underparts with black bands

bright orange legs

MALE
A. a. frontalis (TUNDRA)

no belly barring

A. a. gambeli (TULE)

JUVENILE

The Greater White-fronted Goose is the most widespread goose in the Northern Hemisphere. It is easily distinguished by its black-barred belly and the patch of white at the base of its bill. There are five subspecies, two of which are commonly seen in North America. The "tundra" (*A. a. frontalis*), makes up the largest population, breeding in extreme northwestern Canada and Alaska. The "tule" (*A. a. gambeli*), while larger, occurs in smaller numbers, and breeds farther east in north-central Canada.

VOICE Laugh-like *klow-yo* or *klew-yo-yo;* very musical in a flock.
NESTING Bowl-shaped nest made of plant material, lined with down, constructed near water; 3–7 eggs; 1 brood; May–August.
FEEDING Eats sedges, grasses, berries, and plants on both land and water in summer; feeds on grasses, seeds, and grains in winter.

FLIGHT: strong, direct flight; flies alone, in multiple lines, or in a V-formation.

FLIGHT FORMATIONS
This heavy-bodied, powerful flier can often be seen in tightly packed flocks.

SIMILAR SPECIES

CANADA GOOSE
see p.39

black head, neck, and bill

white chin strap

HEAVY GRAZER
Grass is the major component of this goose's diet.

OCCURRENCE
Different habitats are utilized for breeding and wintering. Nesting areas include tundra ponds and lakes, dry rocky fields, and grassy slopes in Alaska and northern Canada. In winter, coastal marshes, inland wetlands, agricultural fields, and refuges are used in the southern US and eastern Mexico.

Length **25–32in (64–81cm)**	Wingspan **4¼–5¼ft (1.3–1.6m)**	Weight **4–6½lb (1.8–3kg)**
Social **Flocks**	Lifespan **Up to 22 years**	Status **Secure**

DATE SEEN	WHERE	NOTES

| Order **Anseriformes** | Family **Anatidae** | Species *Anser caerulescens* |

Snow Goose

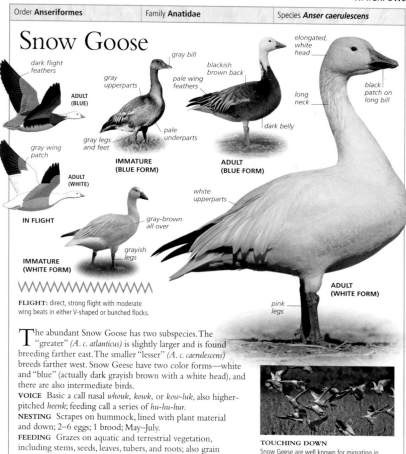

dark flight feathers

gray bill

ADULT (BLUE)

gray upperparts

blackish brown back

pale wing feathers

elongated, white head

long neck

black patch on long bill

IMMATURE (BLUE FORM)

gray legs and feet

pale underparts

dark belly

ADULT (BLUE FORM)

gray wing patch

ADULT (WHITE)

white upperparts

IN FLIGHT

gray-brown all over

grayish legs

IMMATURE (WHITE FORM)

ADULT (WHITE FORM)

FLIGHT: direct, strong flight with moderate wing beats in either V-shaped or bunched flocks.

pink legs

The abundant Snow Goose has two subspecies. The "greater" *(A. c. atlanticus)* is slightly larger and is found breeding farther east. The smaller "lesser" *(A. c. caerulescens)* breeds farther west. Snow Geese have two color forms—white and "blue" (actually dark grayish brown with a white head), and there are also intermediate birds.

VOICE Basic a call nasal *whouk*, *kowk*, or *kow-luk*, also higher-pitched *heenk*; feeding call a series of *hu-hu-hur*.

NESTING Scrapes on hummock, lined with plant material and down; 2–6 eggs; 1 brood; May–July.

FEEDING Grazes on aquatic and terrestrial vegetation, including stems, seeds, leaves, tubers, and roots; also grain and young leaves in agricultural fields in winter.

TOUCHING DOWN
Snow Geese are well known for migrating in flocks that number in the tens of thousands.

SIMILAR SPECIES

GREATER WHITE-FRONTED GOOSE
see p.36

dark head and neck

barred underparts

ROSS'S GOOSE
see p.38

white forehead

shorter bill

much smaller overall

OCCURRENCE
Breeding colonies in High Arctic from Wrangel Island in the West to Greenland in the East; a population of "lesser" Snow Geese breeds near Hudson Bay. Winters along interior valleys westward to coastal lowlands and central plateau of Mexico; Atlantic populations winter in coastal marshes.

Length **27–33in (69–83cm)**	Wingspan **4¼–5½ft (1.3–1.7m)**	Weight **3¾–6½lb (1.7–3kg)**
Social **Flocks**	Lifespan **Up to 27 years**	Status **Secure**

DATE SEEN	WHERE	NOTES

Order **Anseriformes**	Family **Anatidae**	Species *Anser rossii*

Ross's Goose

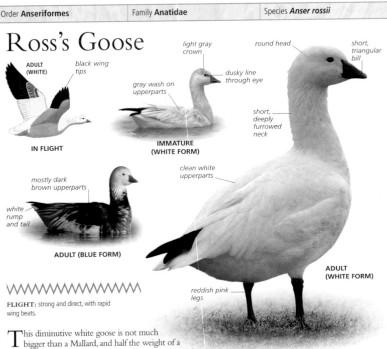

ADULT (WHITE)

black wing tips

IN FLIGHT

light gray crown

gray wash on upperparts

dusky line through eye

IMMATURE (WHITE FORM)

round head

short, triangular bill

short, deeply furrowed neck

clean white upperparts

mostly dark brown upperparts

white rump and tail

ADULT (BLUE FORM)

ADULT (WHITE FORM)

reddish pink legs

FLIGHT: strong and direct, with rapid wing beats.

This diminutive white goose is not much bigger than a Mallard, and half the weight of a Snow Goose; like its larger relative, it also has a "blue" form. About 95 percent of Ross's Geese nest at a single sanctuary in Arctic Canada, the rest breed along Hudson Bay and at several island locations. Hunting reduced the population to just 6,000 in the early 1950s, but the species has rebounded substantially, becoming more common along the East Coast as numbers increase.
VOICE Call a *keek keek keeek*, higher-pitched than Snow Goose; also a harsh, low *kork* or *kowk*; quiet when feeding.
NESTING Plant materials placed on ground, usually in colonies with Lesser Snow Geese; 3–5 eggs; 1 brood; June–August.
FEEDING Grazes on grasses, sedges, and small grains.

TRAVELING IN FAMILIES
Groups migrate thousands of miles together, for example from northern Canada to central California.

SIMILAR SPECIES

SNOW GOOSE white form; see p.37

larger bill

longer neck

pink legs

SNOW GOOSE blue form; see p.37

longer neck

black patch on bill

OCCURRENCE
Breeding grounds are amidst tundra in scattered, High Arctic locations. Main wintering areas in California. On the wintering grounds, it feeds in agricultural fields, and also grasslands. Roosts overnight in several types of wetlands.

Length **22½–25in (57–64cm)**	Wingspan **3¾ft (1.1m)**	Weight **1¾–4½lb (0.85–2kg)**
Social **Flocks**	Lifespan **Up to 21 years**	Status **Localized**

DATE SEEN	WHERE	NOTES

| Order **Anseriformes** | Family **Anatidae** | Species ***Branta canadensis*** |

Canada Goose

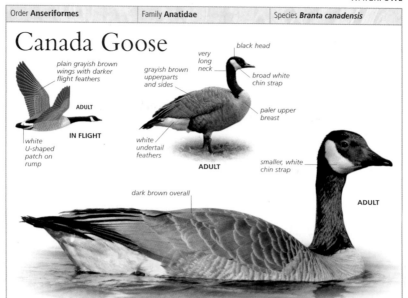

IN FLIGHT

plain grayish brown wings with darker flight feathers

ADULT

white U-shaped patch on rump

very long neck

black head

grayish brown upperparts and sides

broad white chin strap

paler upper breast

white undertail feathers

ADULT

smaller, white chin strap

dark brown overall

ADULT

ADULT

The Canada Goose is the most common, widespread, and familiar goose in North America. Given its vast range, it is not surprising that the Canada Goose should have much geographic variation. Twelve subspecies have been recognized. With the exception of the Cackling Goose, which has recently been separated, it is difficult to confuse it, with its distinctive white chin and neck, and grayish brown body, with any other species of goose. It is a monogamous species, and once pairs are formed, they stay together for life.

VOICE Male call a *honk* or *bark*; females have higher pitched *hrink*.

NESTING Scrape lined with available plant matter and down, near water; 1–2 broods; 2–12 eggs; May–August.

FEEDING Grazes on grasses, sedges, leaves, seeds, agricultural crops and berries; also insects.

FLIGHT: strong and direct with fairly slow, deep wing beats; often flies in V-formation.

TRICK OF THE LIGHT
A low sun can play tricks—these birds are actually pale grayish underneath.

SIMILAR SPECIES

GREATER WHITE-FRONTED GOOSE see p.36

white on base of pink bill

bright orange legs

CACKLING GOOSE see p.40

steep forehead

smaller overall

OCCURRENCE
Variety of inland breeding habitats near water, including grassy urban areas, marshes, prairie, parkland, coastal temperate forest, northern coniferous forest, and Arctic tundra. Winters in agricultural fields, mudflats, saltwater marshes, lakes, and rivers.

| Length **2¼–3½ft (0.7–1.1m)** | Wingspan **4¼–5½ft (1.3–1.7m)** | Weight **6½–9¾lb (3–4.4kg)** |
| Social **Flocks** | Lifespan **Up to 25 years** | Status **Secure** |

DATE SEEN	WHERE	NOTES

| Order **Anseriformes** | Family **Anatidae** | Species ***Branta hutchinsii*** |

Cackling Goose

plain grayish
brown wings

ADULT

small, black
head

white
U-shaped
patch on
rump

IN FLIGHT

broad, white
neck ring

black line
separates white
chin strap

darker breast

ADULT
B. h. leucopareia

dark
brown
breast

ADULT
B. h. minima

small
stubby
bill

white
chin
strap

no black
under
chin

pale
breast

black tail

ADULT
B. h. hutchinsii

The Cackling Goose has recently been split from the Canada Goose; it can be distinguished from the latter by its short stubby bill, steep forehead, and short neck. There are four subspecies of Cackling Goose, which vary in breast color, ranging from dark in *C. h. minima*, fairly dark in *C. h. leucopareia*, and pale in *C. h. hutchinsii*. The Cackling Goose is much smaller than all subspecies of Canada Goose, except the "lesser" Canada Goose, which has a longer neck and a less sloped forehead.
VOICE Male call a *honk* or *bark*; females have higher pitched *hrink*; also high-pitched yelps.
NESTING Scrape lined with available plant matter and down; 2–8 eggs; 1 brood; May–August.
FEEDING Consumes plants in summer; in winter, grazes on grass livestock and dairy pastures; also in agricultural fields.

FLIGHT: strong with rapid wing beats; flies in bunched V–formations.

LITTLE GEESE
Cackling Geese are tiny when seen together with the larger Canada Goose.

SIMILAR SPECIES

CANADA GOOSE
see p.39

more
sloped
forehead

larger overall
(except one
subspecies)

BRANT
see p.41

black
neck

barred
flanks

pale
belly

OCCURRENCE
At the northernmost fringe of the Canada Goose's range, in the tundra, it breeds on rocky tundra slopes from the Aleutians east to Baffin Island and Hudson Bay. Winters from British Columbia to California, also central US, Texas, and New Mexico in pastures and agricultural fields.

| Length 21½–30in (55–75cm) | Wingspan 4¼–5ft (1.3–1.5m) | Weight 2–6½lb (0.9–3kg) |
| Social **Flocks** | Lifespan **Unknown** | Status **Secure** |

DATE SEEN	WHERE	NOTES

| Order **Anseriformes** | Family **Anatidae** | Species *Branta bernicla* |

Brant

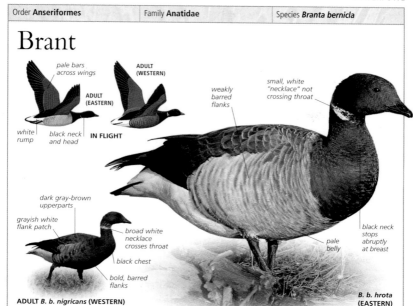

pale bars across wings

ADULT (EASTERN)

ADULT (WESTERN)

white rump *black neck and head* **IN FLIGHT**

weakly barred flanks

small, white "necklace" not crossing throat

dark gray-brown upperparts

grayish white flank patch

broad white necklace crosses throat

black chest

bold, barred flanks

ADULT *B. b. nigricans* (WESTERN)

black neck stops abruptly at breast

pale belly

***B. b. hrota* (EASTERN)**

A small-billed, dark, stocky sea goose, the Brant winters on both the east and west coasts of North America. There are two subspecies in the US (three overall)—the pale-bellied "Atlantic" Brant (*B. b. hrota*), found in the east, and the darker "black" Brant (*B. b. nigricans*), in the west. In addition, there is an intermediate gray-bellied form that winters in the Puget Sound region along the Washington State coast. Unlike other North American geese, the Brant feeds mainly on eelgrass in winter.

VOICE Nasal *cruk*, harsh-sounding in tone; rolling series of *cut cut cut cronk*, with an upward inflection at end.
NESTING Scrape lined with grass, plant matter, and down on islands or gravel spits; 3–5 eggs; 1 brood; May–July.
FEEDING Eats grass and sedges when nesting; eelgrass in winter; also green algae, salt marsh plants, and mollusks.

FLIGHT: rapid and strong; low, irregular flight formations.

GRASSY MEAL
In winter, Brants forage almost exclusively on eelgrass between the high and low tide marks.

SIMILAR SPECIES		
SNOW GOOSE (BLUE FORM) ♀ see p.37 *pale wing feathers*	**CANADA GOOSE** see p.39 *darker underparts*	*broad, white chin strap* *browner coloration*

OCCURRENCE
Breeds in colonies in northern Canada and Alaska, and winters along both Pacific and Atlantic coasts. The western breeding population of the Brant ("black") winters from the Aleutian Islands to northern Mexico, while the pale-bellied form ("Atlantic") is restricted in range to the East Coast.

Length **22–26in (56–66cm)**	Wingspan **3½–4ft (1.1–1.2m)**	Weight **2½–4lb (1–1.8kg)**
Social **Flocks**	Lifespan **Up to 25 years**	Status **Secure**

DATE SEEN	WHERE	NOTES

| Order **Anseriformes** | Family **Anatidae** | Species *Cygnus olor* |

Mute Swan

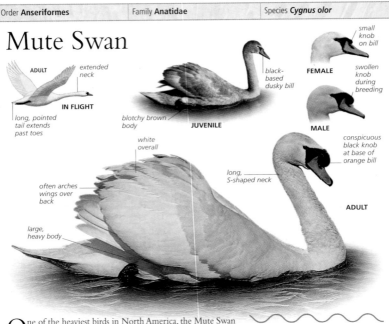

ADULT

extended neck

IN FLIGHT

long, pointed tail extends past toes

black-based dusky bill

blotchy brown body

JUVENILE

white overall

small knob on bill

FEMALE

swollen knob during breeding

MALE

conspicuous black knob at base of orange bill

often arches wings over back

long, S-shaped neck

large, heavy body

ADULT

One of the heaviest birds in North America, the Mute Swan was introduced from Europe because of its graceful appearance on water, if not on land, and easy domestication. However, this is an extremely territorial and aggressive bird. When threatened, it points its bill downwards, arches its wings, hisses, and then attacks. Displacement of native waterfowl species and overgrazing by this species have led to efforts to reduce its numbers in North America.

VOICE Not mute; hisses, grunts, snorts, and snores; during courtship, trumpets, although more quietly than other swans.
NESTING Platform nest of plant materials, built on ground near water; 4–8 eggs; 1–2 broods; March–October.
FEEDING Dabbles, dips, and upends, mainly for underwater plants, but occasionally for small creatures too.

FLIGHT: strong, steady wing beats; creating a distinctive whirring and throbbing sound.

FORMATION FLYING
Groups of Mute Swans will sometimes fly in a line, and at other times, as here, they will arrange themselves in a "V" formation.

SIMILAR SPECIES

TRUMPETER SWAN ⊙
see p.444

larger head

gray plumage

TUNDRA SWAN ⊙
much smaller; see p.43

pink at base of bill

straighter, black bill

straighter neck

OCCURRENCE
Bulk of population is found along the Atlantic Coast from Maine to North Carolina; smaller populations around the Great Lakes and southern British Columbia. Breeds and lives year-round on sluggish rivers, ponds, or lakes, preferring still water with emergent vegetation.

| Length **4–5ft (1.2–1.5m)** | Wingspan **6½–7½ft (2–2.3m)** | Weight **12–32lb (5.5–14.5kg)** |
| Social **Pairs/Family groups** | Lifespan **Up to 21 years** | Status **Localized** |

DATE SEEN	WHERE	NOTES

Order **Anseriformes**	Family **Anatidae**	Species **Cygnus columbianus**

Tundra Swan

eye stands out from face at close range

yellow facial skin next to eye

ADULT

small head and bill

dull grayish body

dirty pink bill

dark legs

IN FLIGHT

fairly thick neck

large yellow bill patch

JUVENILE

all-white plumage

BEWICK'S SWAN

ADULT

Nesting in the Arctic tundra, this well-named species is North America's most widespread and smallest swan. Two populations exist, with one wintering in the West, and the other along the East Coast. The Tundra Swan can be confused with the Trumpeter Swan, but their different calls immediately distinguish the two species. When they are silent, weight and bill structure are the best way to tell them apart. In Eurasia, this species is known as Bewick's Swan and possesses a larger yellow patch at the base of its bill.

VOICE Clear, high-pitched yodelling *whoo-hooo* calls mixed with garbles, yelping, and barking sounds.

NESTING Mound-shaped nest made of plant matter near water; 3–6 eggs; 1 brood; May–September.

FEEDING Eats aquatic vegetation, insects, mollusks; also grain.

FLIGHT: flight pattern like that of other swans but with slightly faster wing beats.

WINTER FLOCKS
Its size, white plumage, and flocking habits make the Tundra Swan a conspicuous species.

SIMILAR SPECIES

MUTE SWAN ♂see p.42

heavier bodied

pointed tail

TRUMPETER SWAN see p.444

all-black bill

more curved neck

straighter edge from eye to bill

OCCURRENCE
Nests around lakes and pools in northern tundra from the Aleutians to the Yukon, and east to northwest Québec. Winters in southern British Columbia, western US, and mid-Atlantic states, mostly New Jersey to south Carolina. Winter habitat includes shallow coastal bays, ponds, and lakes.

Length **4–5ft (1.2–1.5m)**	Wingspan **6¼–7¼ft (1.9–2.2m)**	Weight **12–18lb (5.5–8kg)**
Social **Flocks**	Lifespan **Up to 21 years**	Status **Secure**

DATE SEEN	WHERE	NOTES

| Order **Anseriformes** | Family **Anatidae** | Species *Aix sponsa* |

Wood Duck

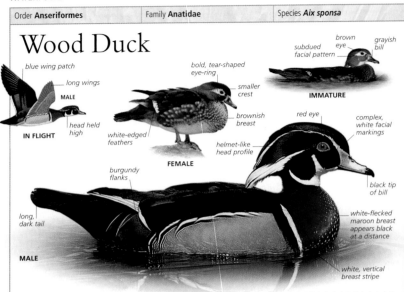

blue wing patch

long wings

MALE

head held high

IN FLIGHT

bold, tear-shaped eye-ring

smaller crest

white-edged feathers

brownish breast

helmet-like head profile

FEMALE

subdued facial pattern

brown eye

grayish bill

IMMATURE

red eye

complex, white facial markings

black tip of bill

white-flecked maroon breast appears black at a distance

burgundy flanks

long, dark tail

MALE

white, vertical breast stripe

The male Wood Duck is perhaps the most striking of all North American ducks. With its bright plumage, red eye and bill, and its long sleek crest that gives its head a helmet-shaped profile, the male is unmistakable. It is related to the Mandarin Duck of Asia. The Wood Duck is very dependent on mature swampy forestland. It is typically found on swamps, shallow lakes, ponds, and park settings that are surrounded by trees. Although it adapts to human activity, it is quite shy. When swimming, the Wood Duck can be seen jerking its head front to back. Of all waterfowl, this is the only species that regularly raises two broods each season.
VOICE Male gives a wheezy upslurred whistle *zweeet*; female's call a double-note, rising *oh-eek oh-eek*.
NESTING Nests in natural tree cavities or nest boxes in close proximity to water; 10–13 eggs; 2 broods; April–August.
FEEDING Forages for seeds, tree fruits, and small acorns; also spiders, insects, and crustaceans.

FLIGHT: rapid flight with deep wing beats; flies with head up; leaps straight off the water.

PLAIN BELLY
Wings raised, a male reveals one of the only plain areas of its plumage—its pale belly and underwing.

SIMILAR SPECIES

BUFFLEHEAD ♀
see p.66

white on cheek

shorter neck

shorter tail

HOODED MERGANSER ♀
narrower wings; see p.69

no eye-ring

long, tan crest

OCCURRENCE
Usually found throughout the year, along rivers, streams, and creeks, in swamps, and marshy areas. Has a preference for permanent bodies of water. If good aquatic feeding areas are unavailable, the Wood Duck feeds in open areas, including agricultural fields.

| Length **18½–21½in (47–54cm)** | Wingspan **26–29in (66–73cm)** | Weight **16–30oz (450–850g)** |
| Social **Small flocks** | Lifespan **Up to 18 years** | Status **Secure** |

DATE SEEN	WHERE	NOTES

Order **Anseriformes**	Family **Anatidae**	Species *Anas strepera*

Gadwall

conspicuous white patch

mostly white underwings

MALE (WINTER)

white belly **IN FLIGHT**

silvery gray area

rusty sides

MALE (ECLIPSE)

dark eyestripe

brown, scalloped back

white wing patch

FEMALE

brown, rounded head

dark grayish overall

black uppertail

black bill

MALE (WINTER)

orange-yellow legs

finely patterned gray flanks and breast

Although the Gadwall's appearance is somewhat somber, many birders consider this duck one of North America's most elegant species because of the subtlety of its plumage. Despite being common and widespread, Gadwalls are often overlooked because of their retiring behavior and relatively quiet vocalizations. This dabbling duck is slightly smaller and more delicate than the Mallard, yet female Gadwalls are often mistaken for female Mallards. Gadwalls associate with other species, especially in winter.

VOICE Low, raspy *meep* or *reb* given in quick succession; female *quack* similar to that of female Mallard, but higher-pitched and more nasal; high-pitched *peep*, or *pe-peep*; both sexes give *tickety-tickety-tickety* chatter while feeding.

NESTING Bowl nest made of plant material in a scrape; 8–12 eggs; 1 brood; April–August.

FEEDING Dabbles on the surface or below for seeds, aquatic vegetation, and invertebrates, including mollusks and insects.

FLIGHT: direct flight with fast wing beats; leaps straight off the water.

BROOD ON THE MOVE
Females lead their ducklings from their nest to a brood-rearing habitat that provides cover and ample food for the ducklings to forage.

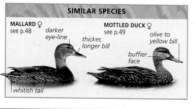

SIMILAR SPECIES

MALLARD ♀
see p.48

darker eye-line

thicker, longer bill

whitish tail

MOTTLED DUCK ♀
see p.49

olive to yellow bill

buffier face

OCCURRENCE
From the western prairie pothole country of Canada and the northern US, the Gadwall's range has expanded as it has adapted to man-made bodies of water, such as reservoirs and ponds. In winter, mostly found on lakes, marshes, and along rivers.

Length **18–22½in (46–57cm)**	Wingspan **33in (84cm)**	Weight **18–45oz (500–1,250g)**
Social **Winter flocks**	Lifespan **Up to 19 years**	Status **Secure**

DATE SEEN	WHERE	NOTES

Order **Anseriformes**	Family **Anatidae**	Species *Anas americana*

American Wigeon

MALE (BREEDING)

rufous-edged wing feathers

dark smudge around eye

gray head

white underwing patch

narrow, black line along bill

gray head contrasts with pinkish brown breast and flanks

warm brown breast and flanks

FEMALE

long, pointed tail

IN FLIGHT

cream forehead and crown

green band from eye to nape

black-tipped bill

MALE (BREEDING)

black rump

pinkish brown flanks

Often found in mixed flocks with other ducks, the American Wigeon is a common and widespread, medium-sized dabbling duck. This bird is an opportunist that loiters around other diving ducks and coots, feeding on the vegetation they dislodge. It is more social during migration and in the nonbreeding season than when breeding.

VOICE Slow and fast whistles; male's most common call a slow, high-pitched, wheezy, three-syllable *whew-whew-whew*, with middle note loudest; also, a faster *whee* whistle.

NESTING Depression lined with plant material and down, usually in tall grass away from water; 5–10 eggs; 1 brood; May–August.

FEEDING Grazes on grass, clover, algae, and, in agricultural fields; feeds on many seeds, insects, mollusks, and crustaceans during the breeding season.

FLIGHT: rapid, fairly deep wing beats; leaps almost vertically off the water.

COMING IN FOR LANDING
This male's cream-colored forehead is clearly visible, as is the sharp contrast between the white belly, and the pinkish breast and flanks.

FLAPPING WINGS
This bird has a white patch on its underwing, while the Eurasian Wigeon has a gray patch.

OCCURRENCE
The northernmost breeder of the dabbling ducks, occurs from Alaska to the Maritimes. Prefers pothole and grassland habitats; found almost anywhere near water in winter. Winters south to northern South America and the Caribbean, in freshwater and coastal bay habitats.

SIMILAR SPECIES

GADWALL ♀
see p.45

white patch

GREEN-WINGED TEAL ♂
see p.53

dark line through eye

black-and-orange bill

longer bill

green patch on wing

Length **17½–23in (45–58cm)**	Wingspan **33in (84cm)**	Weight **1⅛–3lb (0.5–1.3kg)**
Social **Flocks**	Lifespan **Up to 21 years**	Status **Secure**

DATE SEEN	WHERE	NOTES

Order **Anseriformes**	Family **Anatidae**	Species **Anas rubripes**

American Black Duck

rich violet patch

white underwing

MALE

dark tail **IN FLIGHT**

heavily streaked head and neck

olive bill

cinnamon-edged flank feathers

FEMALE

pale head

dark cap

narrow, dark eye-line

greenish yellow bill

dark body

MALE

The American Black Duck, a large dabbling duck, is closely related to the Mallard. In the past, the two species were separated by different habitat preferences—the American Black Duck preferring forested locations, and the Mallard favoring more open habitats. Over the years, these habitats became less distinct as the East was deforested and trees were planted in the Midwest. As a result, there are now many hybrids between the two species. It has also been argued that the introduction of Mallards to various areas in the East has further increased interbreeding. The American Black Duck breeds throughout a wide area in the northern part of its range. When breeding, males can be seen chasing away other males to maintain their territories.

VOICE Male's call a reedy *raeb*, given once or twice; female *quack* sounds very similar to Mallard.

NESTING Scrape lined with plant material and down, usually on ground or close to water; 4–10 eggs; 1 brood; March–September.

FEEDING An omnivore, the American Black Duck eats plant leaves and stems, roots, seeds, grains, fruit, aquatic plants, fish, and amphibians.

FLIGHT: fast, shallow, and regular; often flies in groups.

DARK PLUMAGE
This species is the darkest of all the Mallard-type ducks that occur in North America.

OCCURRENCE
Nests in eastern Canada and adjacent areas of the US in a variety of habitats including northerly and mixed hardwood forest, wooded uplands, bogs, salt- and freshwater marshes, and on islands. Resident in the central part of its range, but large numbers winter in saltwater marshes.

SIMILAR SPECIES

MALLARD ♀
see p.48

whitish tail

paler body

orange bill

MOTTLED DUCK ♀
see p.49

mottled brown upperparts

unstreaked face

Length **21½–23in (54–59cm)**	Wingspan **35–37in (88–95cm)**	Weight **1½–3½lb (0.7–1.6kg)**
Social **Flocks**	Lifespan **Up to 26 years**	Status **Secure**

DATE SEEN	WHERE	NOTES

Order **Anseriformes**	Family **Anatidae**	Species *Anas platyrhynchos*

Mallard

broad-based wings

short, round, pale tail

MALE (WINTER)

heavy body

FEMALE

olive-yellow bill

grayer head

MALE (SUMMER)

rusty underparts

orange bill with blackish patch

dark eye-line and cap

yellowish brown back

mottled brown belly

metallic green head

FEMALE

blue wing patch

warm gray body

bright yellow bill

narrow, white neck collar

brown underparts

IN FLIGHT

whitish outer tail feathers

short, black curls above white tail

MALE (WINTER)

chestnut-brown breast

The Mallard is perhaps the most familiar of all ducks, and occurs in the wild all across the Northern Hemisphere. It is the ancestor of most domestic ducks, and hybrids between the wild and domestic forms are frequently seen in city lakes and ponds, often with patches of white on the breast. Mating is generally a violent affair, but outside the breeding season the wild species is strongly migratory and gregarious, sometimes forming large flocks that may join with other species.

VOICE Male's call a quiet raspy *raab*; during courtship a high-pitched whistle; female call a *quack* or repeated in series.

NESTING Scrape lined with plant matter, usually near water, often on floating vegetation; 6–15 eggs; 1 brood; February–September.

FEEDING Feeds omnivorously on insects, crustaceans, mollusks, and earthworms when breeding; otherwise largely vegetarian; takes seeds, acorns, agricultural crops, aquatic vegetation, and bread.

FLIGHT: fast, shallow, and regular; often flies in groups.

STICKING TOGETHER
The mother leads her ducklings to water soon after they hatch. She looks after them until they can fend for themselves.

SIMILAR SPECIES	

GADWALL ♀
see p.45

slimmer body

steeper forehead

white wing patch

orange strip on bill

AMERICAN BLACK DUCK ♀
see p.47

dark tail

dark olive bill

darker brown overall

OCCURRENCE
Occurs throughout the region, choosing shallow water in natural wetlands, such as marshes, prairie potholes, ponds, and ditches; can also be found in man-made habitats such as city parks and reservoirs, preferring more open habitats in winter.

Length **19½–26in (50–65cm)**	Wingspan **32–37in (82–95cm)**	Weight **1⅞–3lb (0.9–1.4kg)**
Social **Flocks**	Lifespan **Up to 29 years**	Status **Secure**

DATE SEEN	WHERE	NOTES

| Order **Anseriformes** | Family **Anatidae** | Species *Anas fulvigula* |

Mottled Duck

iridescent blue-green wing patch

bright white underwing

MALE

IN FLIGHT

dark eye-line

dull green to orange-yellow bill

paler breast than male

duller orange legs than male

FEMALE

unstreaked face and throat

paler edges to dark body feathers

dark eye-line

dark body

pale buffy head and neck

no white on tail

olive-yellow bill

MALE

orange legs

A long with the American Black Duck, the Mottled Duck belongs to the so-called "Mallard complex," in which all three species are closely related and interbreed easily, especially with feral or semi-domesticated Mallards. There is concern that the fertile hybrid ducks produced may dilute the purity of the Mottled Duck population, and so eventually displace it. The Mottled Duck is a little smaller and darker than the similar female Mallard, and lacks a white edge to the blue wing patch.

VOICE Males give a variety of raspy *raab* calls; females *quack*.

NESTING Bowl-shaped depression constructed in dense grass; 8–12 eggs; 1 brood; January–September.

FEEDING Dabbles for aquatic vegetation, crustaceans, mollusks, insects, rice, seeds, and some small fish.

FLIGHT: direct with regular wing beats; flies at relatively low levels.

COLOR CONTRAST
The male Mottled Duck has a yellower bill than the smaller, orange-billed female.

STANDING MALE
This male has a cleaner, buffier face and brighter orange legs than the female Mottled Duck.

OCCURRENCE
Prefers shallow freshwater wetlands, breeding on coastal marshes. This nonmigratory species has distinct populations in the Gulf of Mexico between Alabama and Tamaulipas, and in central and southern Florida, though both populations may stray slightly outside this range in winter.

SIMILAR SPECIES

GADWALL ♀
white belly; see p.45

white wing patch

lighter upperparts

MALLARD ♀
bold white wing bars; see p.48

black on orange bill

larger, thicker neck

paler plumage

| Length **17½–24in (44–61cm)** | Wingspan **33–34in (83–87cm)** | Weight **21–46oz (0.6–1.4kg)** |
| Social **Flocks** | Lifespan **Up to 13 years** | Status **Declining** |

DATE SEEN	WHERE	NOTES

| Order **Anseriformes** | Family **Anatidae** | Species ***Anas discors*** |

Blue-winged Teal

powdery blue forewing
with green patch

**MALE
(BREEDING)**

white facial
crescent

white
underwing
stripe

IN FLIGHT

broken,
contrasting,
white eye-ring

grayish brown
overall

pale eyebrow,
dark cape,
and eye-line

FEMALE

pale spot
at base
of bill

white facial
crescent

black
bill

dark grayish
head

MALE (FALL)

black spots
on rich, buff-
brown breast
and flanks

white facial
crescent

long
blackish
bill

rich tan
flanks

warmer
brown overall

**MALE
(BREEDING)**

conspicuous
white patch

This small dabbling duck is a common and widespread North American breeding species. With a bold white crescent between bill and eye on its otherwise slate-gray head and neck, the male Blue-winged Teal is quite distinctive. The Blue-winged and Cinnamon Teals, together with the Northern Shoveler, constitute the three "blue-winged" ducks; this is a feature that is conspicuous when the birds are flying. The Cinnamon and the Blue-winged Teals are almost identical genetically and interbreed to form hybrids. The Blue-winged Teal winters mostly south of the US and migrates back north in spring.

VOICE Male a high-pitched, raspy *peew* or low-pitched *paay* during courtship; female a loud single *quack*.

NESTING Bowl-shaped depression lined with grasses, close to water's edge, in meadows; 6–14 eggs; 1 brood; April–September.

FEEDING Eats seeds of a variety of plants; feeds heavily on insect larvae, crustaceans, and snails, when breeding.

FLIGHT: fast, twisting flight; flies in compact, small groups.

OUTSTRETCHED WING
Wing stretch behavior shows the white feathers between the blue forewing and green speculum.

OCCURRENCE
Nests across North America, with highest numbers in the prairie and parkland regions of the midcontinent. Prefers shallow ponds or marshes during nesting; freshwater to brackish water and (less so) saltwater marshes during migration. In winter, prefers saline environments, including mangroves.

SIMILAR SPECIES

CINNAMON TEAL ♀
see p.471

plain face

warmer
brown

GREEN-WINGED TEAL ♀
see p.53

different
wing
pattern

streaked
rump

smaller, more
compact body

smaller
bill

| Length **14½–16in (37–41cm)** | Wingspan **23½–25in (60–64cm)** | Weight **11–18oz (300–500g)** |
| Social **Flocks** | Lifespan **Up to 17 years** | Status **Secure** |

DATE SEEN	WHERE	NOTES

| Order **Anseriformes** | Family **Anatidae** | Species *Anas clypeata* |

Northern Shoveler

dark, narrow eye-line

brown overall

dusky olive-gray to orange bill

FEMALE

grayish blue wing patch

pale blue wing patch

IN FLIGHT

whitish tail

long bill

FEMALE

heavy fronted

MALE

pale-edged, brown flank feathers

yellow eye

dark green head

large, dark spatula-shaped bill

MALE

white breast

black-and-white rump

chestnut belly and flanks

The Northern Shoveler is a common, medium-sized, dabbling duck found in North America and Eurasia. It is monogamous—pairs remain together longer than any other dabbler species. Its distinctive long bill is highly specialized; it is wider at the tip and contains thin, comb-like structures (called "lamellae") along the sides, used to filter food items from the water. Shovelers often form tight feeding groups, swimming close together as they sieve the water for prey.

VOICE Male call a nasal, muffled *thuk thuk…thuk thuk*; also a loud, nasal *paaaay*; female call a variety of *quacks*, singly or in a series of 4–5 descending notes.

NESTING Scrape lined with plant matter and down, in short plants, near water; 6–19 eggs; 1 brood; May–August.

FEEDING Forages for seeds; filters small crustaceans and mollusks out of the water.

FLIGHT: strong direct flight; male's wings make a rattling noise when taking off.

UPSIDE DOWN FEEDER
This male upends to feed below the water's surface, revealing his orange legs.

FILTER FEEDING
Their bills open, these ducks sieve small invertebrates from the water.

SIMILAR SPECIES

MALLARD ♀
larger; see p.48

slimmer bill

darker blue wing patch

CINNAMON TEAL ♀
see p.471

plainer plumage

plainer face

longer tail

OCCURRENCE
Widespread across North America, south of the tundra. Breeds in a variety of wetlands, in edges of shallow pools with nearby tall and short grasslands. Occurs in fresh- and salt marshes, ponds, and other shallow bodies of water in winter; does not feed on land.

| Length **17½–20in (44–51cm)** | Wingspan **27–33in (69–84cm)** | Weight **14–29oz (400–825g)** |
| Social **Flocks** | Lifespan **Up to 18 years** | Status **Secure** |

DATE SEEN	WHERE	NOTES

| Order **Anseriformes** | Family **Anatidae** | Species *Anas acuta* |

Northern Pintail

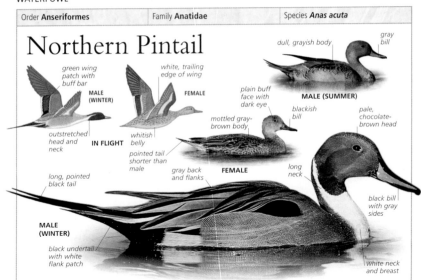

green wing patch with buff bar

MALE (WINTER)

outstretched head and neck

IN FLIGHT

white, trailing edge of wing

FEMALE

whitish belly

pointed tail shorter than male

plain buff face with dark eye

mottled gray-brown body

gray back and flanks

FEMALE

dull, grayish body

gray bill

MALE (SUMMER)

blackish bill

pale, chocolate-brown head

long neck

black bill with gray sides

long, pointed black tail

MALE (WINTER)

black undertail with white flank patch

white neck and breast

An elegant, long-necked dabbler, the Northern Pintail has extremely distinctive marking and a very long tail—in fact, the longest tail to be found on any freshwater duck. One of the earliest breeders in the year, these ducks begin nesting soon after the ice thaws. Northern Pintails were once one of the most abundant prairie breeding ducks. However, in recent decades, droughts, combined with the reduction of habitat on both their wintering and breeding grounds, have resulted in a significant decline in their population.

VOICE Male call a high-pitched rolling *prrreep prrreep;* lower-pitched wheezy *wheeeee*, which gets louder then drops off; female call a quiet, harsh *quack* or *kuk* singularly or as short series; also a loud *gaak*, often repeated.

NESTING Scrape lined with plant materials and down, usually in short grass, brush, or even in the open; 3–12 eggs; 1 brood; April–August.

FEEDING Feeds on grains, rice, seeds, aquatic weeds, insect larvae, crustaceans, and snails.

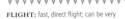

FLIGHT: fast, direct flight; can be very acrobatic in the air.

FEEDING TIME
Even when tipping up to feed, these pintails can be identified by their long, black, pointed tails.

SIMILAR SPECIES

GADWALL ♀
see p.45
shorter tail

orange-sided bill

white wing patch

AMERICAN WIGEON ♀
see p.46
shorter tail

darker gray head

chestnut breast and flanks

OCCURRENCE
Widely distributed in North America; breeding in open country in shallow wetlands or meadows in mountainous forest regions. Found in tidal wetlands and saltwater habitats in migration and winter; dry harvested and flooded agricultural fields in autumn and winter.

| Length **20–30in (51–76cm)** | Wingspan **35in (89cm)** | Weight **18–44oz (500–1,250g)** |
| Social **Flocks** | Lifespan **Up to 21 years** | Status **Declining** |

DATE SEEN	WHERE	NOTES

| Order **Anseriformes** | Family **Anatidae** | Species ***Anas crecca*** |

Green-winged Teal

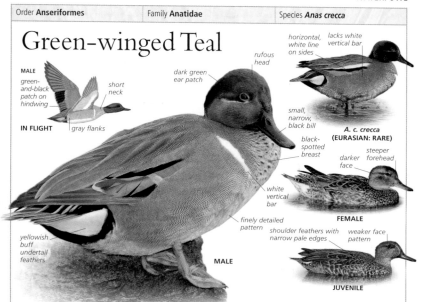

MALE
green-and-black patch on hindwing

short neck

IN FLIGHT   gray flanks

rufous head

dark green ear patch

horizontal, white line on sides   *lacks white vertical bar*

small, narrow, black bill

black-spotted breast

A. c. crecca (EURASIAN: RARE)

darker face   *steeper forehead*

FEMALE

white vertical bar

finely detailed pattern

shoulder feathers with narrow pale edges   *weaker face pattern*

yellowish buff undertail feathers

MALE

JUVENILE

The Green-winged Teal, the smallest North American dabbling duck, is slightly smaller than the Blue-winged and Cinnamon Teals, and lacks their blue wing patch. Its population is increasing, apparently because it breeds in more pristine habitats, and farther north, than the prairie ducks. The species has three subspecies, *A. c. crecca* (Eurasia), *A. c. carolinensis* (North America), and *A. c. nimia* (Aleutian Islands). *Carolinensis* males have a conspicuous vertical white bar, whereas Eurasian *crecca* males do not.

VOICE Male call a high-pitched, slightly rolling *crick crick*, similar to cricket; female a call quiet *quack*.

NESTING Shallow scrape on ground lined with nearby vegetation, often placed in dense vegetation near water; 6–9 eggs; 1 brood; April–September.

FEEDING Eats seeds, aquatic insects, crustaceans, and mollusks year-round; also feeds in grain fields in winter.

FLIGHT: fast flight; often flying in twisting, tight groups reminiscent of shorebird flocks.

SINGLE PARENT
The female duck is deserted by her partner during incubation, so she must provide all parental care.

SIMILAR SPECIES

BLUE-WINGED TEAL ♀
larger overall; see p.50
whitish spot at base of bill
different wing pattern

CINNAMON TEAL ♀
larger overall; see p.471
rich brown overall
longer bill
yellowish legs

OCCURRENCE
Breeds from the central US northward to Canada and Alaska; around ponds in forests and deciduous woodlands. Prefers shallow vegetated wetlands. In winter and migration, inland marshes, sloughs, agricultural fields, and coastal marshes. Winters south of the Caribbean and in southern Mexico.

| Length **12–15½in (31–39cm)** | Wingspan **20½–23in (52–59cm)** | Weight **7–16oz (200–450g)** |
| Social **Flocks** | Lifespan **Up to 20 years** | Status **Secure** |

DATE SEEN	WHERE	NOTES

| Order **Anseriformes** | Family **Anatidae** | Species *Aythya valisineria* |

Canvasback

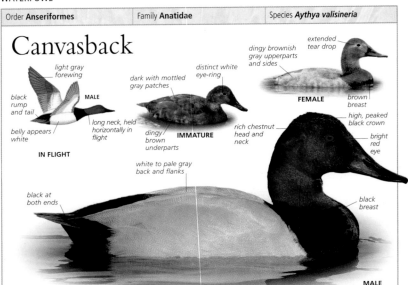

MALE

light gray forewing

black rump and tail

belly appears white

IN FLIGHT

long neck, held horizontally in flight

dark with mottled gray patches

distinct white eye-ring

dingy brown underparts

IMMATURE

dingy brownish gray upperparts and sides

extended tear drop

FEMALE

brown breast

rich chestnut head and neck

high, peaked black crown

bright red eye

white to pale gray back and flanks

black at both ends

black breast

MALE

A large, elegant, long-billed diving duck, the Canvasback is a bird of prairie pothole country. Its specialized diet of aquatic plants has resulted in a smaller population than other ducks. With legs set toward the rear, it is an accomplished swimmer and diver, and is rarely seen on land. Weather conditions and brood parasitism by Redheads determine how successful the Canvasback's nesting is from year to year.
VOICE Mostly silent except during courtship when males make soft *cooing* noises; females emit a grating *krrrrr krrrrrr krrrrr*; females give loud *quack* when taking off; during winter, both sexes make soft wheezing series of *rrrr rrrr rrrr* sounds.
NESTING Platform over water built of woven vegetation; occasionally on shore; 8–11 eggs; 1 brood; April–September.
FEEDING Mainly eats aquatic tubers, buds, root stalks, and shoots, particularly those of wild celery; also eats snails when preferred plants are unavailable.

FLIGHT: direct strong flight; one of the fastest ducks; forms V-shaped flocks.

DEEP WATER
Canvasbacks prefer deeper-bodied waters that support the aquatic vegetation they eat.

SIMILAR SPECIES

REDHEAD ♂
see p.55

shorter gray, black-tipped bill

yellow eye

LESSER SCAUP ♂
see p.58

darker gray on back

smaller overall

yellow eye

OCCURRENCE
Found in potholes, marshes, and ponds in prairie parkland, tundra; northerly forests preferred where their favorite foods grow. Winters in large numbers in large bays and lakes, and deltas, with smaller numbers scattered across North America and Mexico.

| Length **19–22in (48–56cm)** | Wingspan **31–35in (79–89cm)** | Weight **1¾–3½lb (0.8–1.6kg)** |
| Social **Flocks** | Lifespan **Up to 22 years** | Status **Secure** |

DATE SEEN	WHERE	NOTES

| Order **Anseriformes** | Family **Anatidae** | Species ***Aythya americana*** |

Redhead

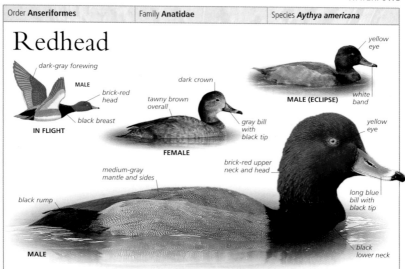

IN FLIGHT

dark-gray forewing

MALE

brick-red head

black breast

dark crown

tawny brown overall

gray bill with black tip

FEMALE

yellow eye

MALE (ECLIPSE)

white band

brick-red upper neck and head

yellow eye

long blue bill with black tip

medium-gray mantle and sides

black rump

MALE

black lower neck

The Redhead, a medium-sized diving duck belonging to the Pochard group, is native only to North America. Only when seen up close is it apparent that the male's seemingly gray upperparts and flanks are actually white, with dense, black, wavy markings. The Redhead often feeds at night and forages mostly around dusk and dawn, drifting during the day. It parasitizes other duck nests more than any other duck species, particularly those of the Canvasback and even other Redheads.

VOICE Male courtship call a wheezy rising then falling *whee ough*, also *meow*; female call a low, raspy *kurr kurr kurr*.

NESTING Weaves solid nest over water in dense vegetation such as cattails, lined with down; 7–14 eggs; 1 brood; May–September.

FEEDING Omniverous; feeds on aquatic plants, seeds, tubers, algae, insects, spiders, fish eggs, snails, and insect larvae; diet is variable depending on location.

FLIGHT: direct flight; runs on water prior to takeoff.

MALE DISPLAY
This male is performing a spectacular courtship display called a head throw, while remaining otherwise completely still on the water.

EASY IDENTIFICATION
The long blue bill with a whitish band and black tip is clearly visible in males.

SIMILAR SPECIES

CANVASBACK ♀
see p.54

wedge-shaped black bill

grayish back

RING-NECKED DUCK ♀
see p.56

peaked head shape

dark-brown back

OCCURRENCE
Breeds in shallow wetlands across the Great Basin and Prairie Pothole region, very densely in certain marsh habitats. The bulk of the population winters in coastal lagoons along the Atlantic Coast and the Gulf of Mexico.

Length **17–21in (43–53cm)**	Wingspan **30–31in (75–79cm)**	Weight **1⅜–3¼lbs (0.6–1.5kg)**
Social **Flocks**	Lifespan **Up to 21 years**	Status **Secure**

DATE SEEN	WHERE	NOTES

| Order **Anseriformes** | Family **Anatidae** | Species *Aythya collaris* |

Ring-necked Duck

dark forewing

MALE

bold white underwing

IN FLIGHT

dark brown back

bold white eye-ring

white band on bill

yellow eye

FEMALE

tall, peaked head

gray bill with white and black tip

thin chestnut ring (hard to see)

black neck and breast

rounded gray sides

MALE

A resident of freshwater ponds and lakes, the Ring-necked Duck is a fairly common medium-sized diving duck. A more descriptive and suitable name might have been Ring-billed Duck as the bold white band on the bill tip is easy to see whereas the thin chestnut ring around the neck can be very difficult to observe. The tall, pointed head is quite distinctive, peaking at the rear of the crown. When it sits on the water, this bird typically holds its head high.

VOICE Male normally silent; female makes low *kerp kerp* call.

NESTING Floating nest built in dense aquatic vegetation, often in marshes; 6–14 eggs; 1 brood; May–August.

FEEDING Feeds in water at all times, either by diving, tipping up, or dabbling for aquatic plant tubers and seeds; also eats aquatic invertebrates such as clams and snails.

FLIGHT: strong flier with deep, rapid wing beats; flight somewhat erratic.

UNIQUE BILL
A white outline around the base of the bill and the white band on the bill are unique markings.

FLAPPING WINGS
Bold white wing linings are apparent when the Ring-necked Duck flaps its wings.

OCCURRENCE
Breeds across Canada, south of the Arctic zone, in shallow freshwater marshes and bogs; sporadically in the western US. Winters in freshwater and brackish habitats such as swamps, lakes, estuaries, reservoirs, and flooded fields. Migrants are found in the Midwest near stands of wild rice.

SIMILAR SPECIES

LESSER SCAUP ♂
see p.58

wavy-patterned gray mantle

rounded head

TUFTED DUCK ♂
see p.471

crested tufts

white sides

| Length **15–18in (38–46cm)** | Wingspan **24–25in (62–63cm)** | Weight **1⅛–2lbs (500–900g)** |
| Social **Flocks** | Lifespan **Up to 20 years** | Status **Secure** |

DATE SEEN	WHERE	NOTES

| Order **Anseriformes** | Family **Anatidae** | Species *Aythya marila* |

Greater Scaup

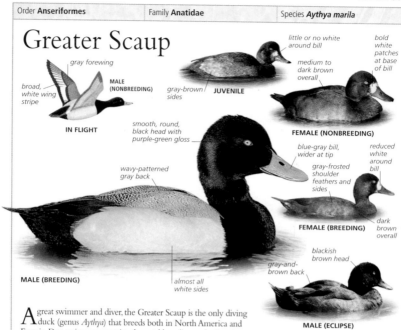

gray forewing

broad, white wing stripe

MALE (NONBREEDING)

gray-brown sides

JUVENILE

IN FLIGHT

little or no white around bill

bold white patches at base of bill

medium to dark brown overall

FEMALE (NONBREEDING)

smooth, round, black head with purple-green gloss

wavy-patterned gray back

blue-gray bill, wider at tip

gray-frosted shoulder feathers and sides

reduced white around bill

FEMALE (BREEDING)

dark brown overall

MALE (BREEDING)

almost all white sides

blackish brown head

gray-and-brown back

gray-and-brown back

MALE (ECLIPSE)

FLIGHT: strong, fast, and agile; flocks shift and twist during prolonged flight.

A great swimmer and diver, the Greater Scaup is the only diving duck (genus *Aythya*) that breeds both in North America and Eurasia. Due to its more restricted coastal breeding and wintering habitat preference, it is far less numerous in North America than its close relative, the Lesser Scaup. The Greater Scaup forms large, often sexually segregated flocks outside the breeding season. If both scaup species are present together, they will also segregate within the flocks according to species. Correct identification is difficult.

VOICE During courtship, male call a soft, fast, wheezy *week week wheew*; female gives a series of growled monotone *arrrr* notes.

NESTING Simple depression lined with grasses and down, nest sites need to have dense cover of vegetation from previous year; 6–10 eggs; 1 brood; May–September.

FEEDING Dives for aquatic plants, seeds, insects, crustaceans, snails, shrimp, and bivalves.

FOND OF FLOCKING
Greater Scaups flock together on the water. Males have distinct black-and-white markings.

SIMILAR SPECIES

CANVASBACK ♂
see p.54

chestnut brown head

black tail

LESSER SCAUP ♂
see p.58

slimmer head

grayer flanks

OCCURRENCE
Majority breed in western coastal Alaska on tundra wetlands; also in lower densities in northwest and eastern Canada. Almost all birds winter offshore, along the Atlantic and Pacific coasts, or on the Great Lakes due to increased food availability. Small groups found inland and midcontinent, on unfrozen water bodies.

| Length **15–22in (38–56cm)** | Wingspan **28–31in (72–79cm)** | Weight **1¼–3lb (0.6–1.4kg)** |
| Social **Flocks** | Lifespan **Up to 22 years** | Status **Declining** |

DATE SEEN	WHERE	NOTES

| Order **Anseriformes** | Family **Anatidae** | Species *Aythya affinis* |

Lesser Scaup

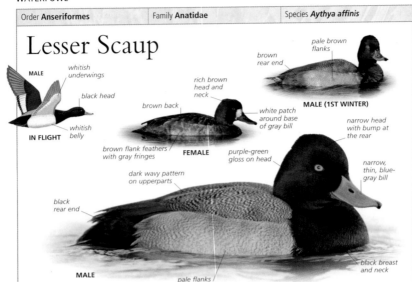

MALE
whitish underwings

black head

IN FLIGHT
whitish belly

pale brown flanks

brown rear end

MALE (1ST WINTER)

rich brown head and neck

brown back

white patch around base of gray bill

FEMALE
brown flank feathers with gray fringes

purple-green gloss on head

narrow head with bump at the rear

dark wavy pattern on upperparts

black rear end

narrow, thin, blue-gray bill

MALE
pale flanks

black breast and neck

The Lesser Scaup, far more numerous than its somewhat larger relative (their size and weight ranges overlap), is also the most abundant diving duck in North America. The two species are very similar in appearance and are best identified by shape. Identification must be done cautiously as head shape changes with position. For example, the crown feathers are flattened just before diving in both species; thus, scaups are best identified when they are not moving.

VOICE Males mostly silent except during courtship when they make a wheezy *wheeow wheeow wheeow* sound; females give repetitive series of grating *garrrf garrrf garrrf* notes.

NESTING Nest built in tall vegetation or under shrubs, sometimes far from water, also on islands and mats of floating vegetation; 8–11 eggs; 1 brood; May–September.

FEEDING Feeds mainly on leeches, crustaceans, mollusks, aquatic insects, and aquatic plants and seeds.

FLIGHT: rapid, direct flight; can jump off water more easily than other diving ducks.

PREENING SCAUP
Ducks are meticulous preeners, and the Lesser Scaup is no exception.

SIMILAR SPECIES

RING-NECKED DUCK ♀
see p.56
prominent white eye-ring
solid dark back

GREATER SCAUP ♀
see p.57
more tawny brown upperparts
more white around bill

OCCURRENCE
Breeds inland from Alaska to eastern Canada in open northern forests and forested tundra. Winters in the Caribbean, southern US, and south to northern South America. Majority winter along coasts; others winter inland on lakes and reservoirs.

Length **15½–17½in (39–45cm)**	Wingspan **27–31in (68–78cm)**	Weight **1–2¾lb (0.45–1.2kg)**
Social **Flocks**	Lifespan **Up to 18 years**	Status **Secure**

DATE SEEN	WHERE	NOTES

| Order **Anseriformes** | Family **Anatidae** | Species **Somateria spectabilis** |

King Eider

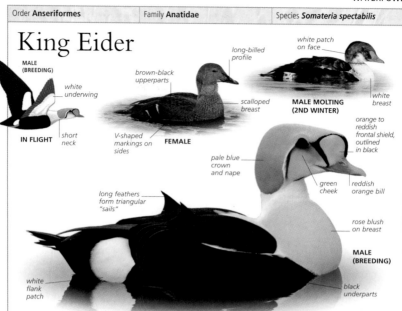

MALE (BREEDING)

white underwing

long-billed profile

brown-black upperparts

white patch on face

scalloped breast

MALE MOLTING (2ND WINTER)

white breast

IN FLIGHT short neck

V-shaped markings on sides **FEMALE**

pale blue crown and nape

orange to reddish frontal shield, outlined in black

green cheek reddish orange bill

long feathers form triangular "sails"

rose blush on breast

MALE (BREEDING)

white flank patch

black underparts

The scientific name of the King Eider, *spectabilis*, means "worth seeing," and its gaudy marking and coloring around the head and bill make it hard to mistake. Females resemble the somewhat larger and paler Common Eider. The female King Eider has a more rounded head, more compact body, and a longer bill than the male. King Eiders may dive down to 180ft (55m) when foraging.

VOICE Courting males give a repeated series of low, rolled dove-like *arrrrooooo* calls, each rising, then falling, followed by softer *cooos*; females give grunts and croaks.

NESTING Slight depression in tundra lined with nearby vegetation and down; 4–7 eggs; 1 brood; June–September.

FEEDING Dives for mollusks; other food items include crustaceans, starfish, and when breeding, insects and plants.

FLIGHT: direct and rapid flight; migrates in long lines, abreast in a broad front, or in clusters.

GROUP FLIGHT
Migratory King Eiders move in large groups to their northern breeding habitats.

SIMILAR SPECIES

| COMMON EIDER ♀ larger overall; see p.60 | longer, more wedge-shaped bill | BLACK SCOTER ♀ smaller overall; see p.64 | pale cheek and dark cap |
| flatter head | | longer, cocked tail | |

OCCURRENCE
Nests along coasts and farther inland than Spectacled or Steller's Eiders in the high Arctic, in a variety of habitats; around low marshes, lakes, and islands; prefers well-drained areas. During winter, found mostly along the southern edge of the ice pack, in coastal waters up to 66ft (20m) deep.

| Length **18½–25in (47–64cm)** | Wingspan **37in (94cm)** | Weight **2¾–4¾lb (1.2–2.1kg)** |
| Social **Flocks** | Lifespan **Up to 15 years** | Status **Secure** |

DATE SEEN	WHERE	NOTES

| Order **Anseriformes** | Family **Anatidae** | Species *Somateria mollissima* |

Common Eider

- black cap
- FEMALE
- brown overall
- olive-green wash on nape
- MALE (WINTER)
- IN FLIGHT
- whitish underwing
- black rump and tail
- dark brown overall
- **MALE (SUMMER)**
- greenish olive bill
- white flecking
- **MALE (2ND WINTER)**
- white breast, with rose tinge
- long, sloping forehead
- mottled, black-and-brown upperparts
- **FEMALE**
- **MALE (WINTER)**

The largest duck in North America, the Common Eider is also the most numerous, widespread, and variable of the eiders. Four of its seven subspecies occur in North America, and vary in the markings and color of their heads and bills. Male Common Eiders also have considerable seasonal plumage changes, and do not acquire their adult plumage until the third year.

VOICE Repeated hoarse, grating notes *korr-korr-korr*; male's owl-like *ah-WOO-ooo*; female's low, guttural notes *krrrr-krrrr-krrrr*.

NESTING Depression on ground lined with down and plant matter, often near water; 2–7 eggs; 1 brood; June–September.

FEEDING Forages in open water and areas of shallow water; dives in synchronized flocks for mollusks and crustaceans, but consumes its larger prey above the surface.

FLIGHT: strong flight with relatively slow wing beats; flies in undulating lines, low over the water.

BROODING FEMALE
Females line their nests with down and cover the eggs with it when leaving the nest.

SIMILAR SPECIES

KING EIDER ♀ smaller overall; see p.59
- flatter crown
- thicker neck
- shorter, more concave bill

SURF SCOTER ♀ see p.62
- shorter, wedge-shaped bill
- dark brown overall

OCCURRENCE
Arctic breeder, in both New and Old Worlds, on coastal islands, peninsulas, seldom along freshwater lakes and deltas. One population is sedentary in the Hudson and James Bays region; others winter in the Bering Sea, Hudson Bay, northern British Columbia, Gulf of St. Lawrence, and along the Atlantic Coast.

| Length **19½–28in (50–71cm)** | Wingspan **31–42in (80–108cm)** | Weight **2¾–5¾lb (1.2–2.6kg)** |
| Social **Flocks/Colonies** | Lifespan **Up to 21 years** | Status **Secure** |

DATE SEEN	WHERE	NOTES

| Order **Anseriformes** | Family **Anatidae** | Species *Histrionicus histrionicus* |

Harlequin Duck

MALE

dark wings above and below

short neck

pointed tail **IN FLIGHT**

dark sooty brown overall

broad face with whitish patches

scaly, pale brown lower breast and belly

FEMALE

slate-blue with bright rusty sides

two white bands perpendicular to breast and neck

two white facial spots

rust crown stripes

very round head

steep forehead

small dark bill

white bands down either side of back

white crescent

MALE

This small, hardy duck is a superbly skillful swimmer, diving to forage on the bottom of turbulent streams for its favorite insect prey. Despite the male's unmistakable plumage at close range, it looks very dark from a distance. With head and long tail held high, in winter it can be found among crashing waves, alongside larger and bigger-billed Surf and White-winged Scoters, who feed in the same habitat.

VOICE Male a high-pitched squeak earning it the nickname "sea mice"; female's call a raspy *ekekekekekek*.

NESTING Nests near water under vegetation or base of tree; also tree cavities; 3–9 eggs; 1 brood; April–September.

FEEDING Dives for insects and their larvae, and fish roe when breeding; in winter, eats mollusks, crustaceans, crabs, snails, fish roe, and barnacles.

FLIGHT: rapid and regular wing beats; usually flies low over water, in pairs or small groups.

MALE GROUPS
After the breeding season, many males may gather and forage together.

PAIR IN FLIGHT
Note the crisp white markings on the slate-blue male in flight.

OCCURRENCE
Breeds near rushing coastal and mountain streams. During winter, found in small groups or mixed in with other sea ducks close to the shore, particularly along shallow rocky shorelines, jetties, rocky beaches, and headlands. Eastern populations have a restricted range. Also breeds in Iceland.

SIMILAR SPECIES

SURF SCOTER ♀ see p.62

large, triangular bill

flatter head

elongated body

BUFFLEHEAD ♀ see p.66

larger head

oblong patch on cheek

| Length **13–21½in (33–54cm)** | Wingspan **22–26in (56–66cm)** | Weight **18–26oz (500–750g)** |
| Social **Small flocks** | Lifespan **Unknown** | Status **Secure** |

DATE SEEN	WHERE	NOTES

| Order **Anseriformes** | Family **Anatidae** | Species *Melanitta perspicillata* |

Surf Scoter

MALE
black wings overall

IN FLIGHT
compact body

whitish facial patches
dark brown overall
all-dark bill

FEMALE

black forehead
small white patch on nape

IMMATURE MALE (2ND WINTER)

white eye
white forehead
large, black spot on bill
swollen, orange bill with white base

white nape
velvety black feathers
long tail feathers

MALE

Surf Scoters, one of three species of scoters living in North America, migrate up and down both coasts, often with the other species. They take their name from the way they dive for mollusks on the sea floor, in shallow coastal waters, through heavy surf. Groups often dive and resurface in unison. Black and Surf Scoters can be difficult to tell apart as both have all-black wings. The underside of the Surf Scoter's wings are uniform black, wheras the Black Scoter has gray flight feathers, which contrast with the black underwing feathers.

VOICE Normally silent; courting male's variety of calls includes liquid gurgled *puk-puk*, bubbled whistles, and low croaks; female call a harsh *crahh*, reminiscent of a crow.

NESTING Ground nest lined with down and vegetation on brushy tundra, often under low branches of a conifer tree; 5–10 eggs; 1 brood; May–September.

FEEDING Dives for mollusks and other aquatic invertebrates.

FLIGHT: strong wing beats; flies in bunched up groups; male's wings hum or whistle in flight.

DISTINGUISHING FEATURES
The white forehead and bright orange bill, in addition to the red-orange legs and toes, identify male Surf Scoters.

OCCURRENCE
Nests on lake islands in forested regions of interior Alaska and northern Canada. Nonbreeders in summer and adults in winter are strictly coastal, with numbers decreasing from north to south along the Pacific coast. In the East, most overwinter in the mid-Atlantic coast region.

SIMILAR SPECIES

GREATER SCAUP ♀
see p.57
no white patches on cheek
thinner bill

WHITE-WINGED SCOTER ♀
see p.63
long, sloping forehead
longer bill

| Length **19–23½in (48–60cm)** | Wingspan **30in (77cm)** | Weight **1¾–2¾lb (0.8–1.2kg)** |
| Social **Flocks/Pairs** | Lifespan **Unknown** | Status **Secure** |

DATE SEEN	WHERE	NOTES

| Order **Anseriformes** | Family **Anatidae** | Species **Melanitta fusca** |

White-winged Scoter

long, sloping head

blackish bill

two distinct pale patches on face

IMMATURE FEMALE

white wing patch

ADULT

appears all-black in flight

IN FLIGHT

feathers extend onto the bill

dark brown overall

FEMALE

upturned white "comma" around white eye

all black with brownish sides

black knob at base of bill

pinkish red to yellow-orange bill

MALE

The White-winged Scoter is the largest of the three scoters. When visible, the white wing patch makes identification easy. Females are quite similar to immature male and female Surf Scoters and can be identified by head shape, extent of bill feathering, and shape of white areas on the face. When diving, this scoter leaps forward and up, arching its neck, and opens its wings when entering the water. Underwater, White-winged Scoters open their wings to propel and stabilize themselves.

VOICE Mostly silent; courting males emit a whistling note; female call a growly *karr*.

NESTING Depression lined with twigs and down in dense thickets, often far from water; 8–9 eggs; 1 brood; June–September.

FEEDING Dives for mollusks and crustaceans; sometimes eats fish and aquatic plants.

FLIGHT: direct with rapid wing beats; flies low over the water in small groups.

WHITE FLASH IN FLIGHT
Scoters often migrate or feed in mixed flocks. The white wing patches are striking in flight.

SIMILAR SPECIES

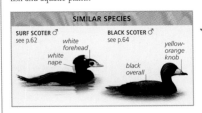

SURF SCOTER ♂
see p.62

white forehead

white nape

BLACK SCOTER ♂
see p.64

yellow-orange knob

black overall

OCCURRENCE
Majority breed in dense colonies in interior Alaska and western Canada on large freshwater or brackish lakes or ponds, sometimes on saltwater lakes. Winters along both coasts, large bays, inlets, and estuaries. Rarely winters inland, except on the Great Lakes.

| Length **19–23in (48–58cm)** | Wingspan **31in (80cm)** | Weight **2¾–4¾lb (0.9–1.9kg)** |
| Social **Flocks/Colonies** | Lifespan **Up to 18 years** | Status **Secure** |

DATE SEEN	WHERE	NOTES

Order **Anseriformes**	Family **Anatidae**	Species *Melanitta nigra*

Black Scoter

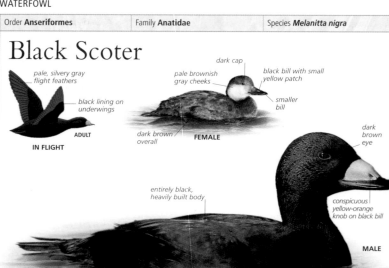

pale, silvery gray flight feathers

black lining on underwings

ADULT

IN FLIGHT

dark cap

pale brownish gray cheeks

black bill with small yellow patch

smaller bill

dark brown overall

FEMALE

dark brown eye

entirely black, heavily built body

conspicuous yellow-orange knob on black bill

MALE

Black Scoters, the most vocal of the scoters, are medium-sized sea ducks that winter along both coasts of North America. Riding high on the waves, they form dense flocks, often segregated by gender. While swimming, the Black Scoter sometimes flaps its wings and while doing so drops its neck low down, unlike the other two scoters. This scoter breeds in two widely separated sub-Arctic breeding areas and is one of the least studied ducks in North America. The Eurasian subspecies, known as the Common Scoter, has much less orange on its bill with a smaller knob at the base.

VOICE Male call a high-whistled *peeeur*, female a low raspy *kraaa*.

NESTING Depression lined with grass and down, often in tall grass on tundra; 5–10 eggs; 1 brood; May–September.

FEEDING Dives in saltwater for mollusks, crustaceans, and plant matter; feeds on aquatic insects and freshwater mussels.

FLIGHT: strong wing beats; male's wings make whistling sound during takeoff.

YELLOW BILL
Male Black Scoters are distinctive with their black plumage and yellow bill-knob.

SIMILAR SPECIES

SURF SCOTER ♀
see p.62

flatter crown

two whitish patches

WHITE-WINGED SCOTER ♀
see p.63

larger bill

more sloping head

longer bill

OCCURRENCE
Breeding habitat is somewhat varied, but is generally close to fairly shallow, small lakes. Winters along both coasts. Populations wintering farther north prefer water over cobbles, gravel, or offshore ledges, whereas in southern locations, sandier habitats are chosen.

Length **17–21in (43–53cm)**	Wingspan **31–35in (79–90cm)**	Weight **1¾–2¾lb (0.8–1.2kg)**
Social **Flocks**	Lifespan **Unknown**	Status **Declining**

DATE SEEN	WHERE	NOTES

| Order **Anseriformes** | Family **Anatidae** | Species *Clangula hyemalis* |

Long-tailed Duck

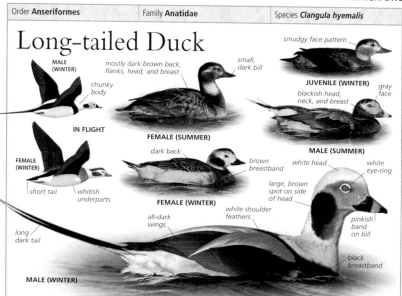

smudgy face pattern

MALE (WINTER)

mostly dark brown back, flanks, head, and breast

small, dark bill

chunky body

JUVENILE (WINTER)

gray face

blackish head, neck, and breast

IN FLIGHT

FEMALE (SUMMER)

MALE (SUMMER)

dark back

brown breastband

white head

white eye-ring

FEMALE (WINTER)

large, brown spot on side of head

short tail

whitish underparts

FEMALE (WINTER)

white shoulder feathers

pinkish band on bill

all-dark wings

long dark tail

black breastband

MALE (WINTER)

The Long-tailed Duck, which used to be called the Oldsquaw, is a small, compact sea duck. The male has two extremely long tail feathers, which are often held up in the air like a pennant. The male's loud calls are quite musical, and, when heard from a flock, have a chorus-like quality, hence the name *Clangula*, which is Latin for "loud." The Long-tailed Duck is capable of diving for a prolonged period of time, and can reach depths of 200ft (60m), making it one of the deepest diving ducks. Its three-part molt is more complex than that of other ducks.

VOICE Male call a *ang-ang-eeeooo* with yodelling quality; female barking *urk* or *uk* alarm call.

NESTING Shallow depression in ground lined with plant matter; 6–9 eggs; 1 brood; May–September.

FEEDING Dives to bottom of freshwater or saltwater habitats for mollusks, crustaceans, insects, fish, and roe.

FLIGHT: flies low over the water, somewhat erratically, with fast, fluttering wing beats.

UNMISTAKABLE MALE
In winter, dark wings, a white body with black breast-band, and a long tail make this male unmistakable.

SIMILAR SPECIES

BUFFLEHEAD ♀
see p.66

white wing patch

white cheek patch

BLACK GUILLEMOT ❋
see p.221

pale rump

white wing patches

OCCURRENCE
Breeds in Arctic and sub-Arctic, nesting in small groups on islands and peninsulas on lakes, less commonly on tundra and freshwater ponds on islands. Winters mostly along rocky coasts and headlands, protected bays, or on large freshwater lakes.

Length **14–23in (35–58cm)**	Wingspan **28in (72cm)**	Weight **18–39oz (500–1,100g)**
Social **Flocks**	Lifespan **Up to 22 years**	Status **Secure**

DATE SEEN	WHERE	NOTES

Order **Anseriformes**	Family **Anatidae**	Species *Bucephala albeola*

Bufflehead

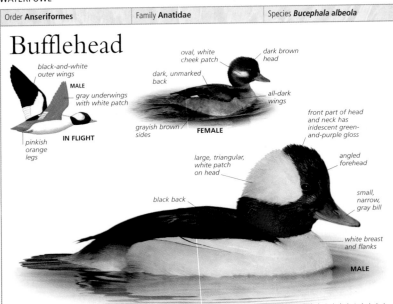

MALE

black-and-white outer wings

gray underwings with white patch

pinkish orange legs

IN FLIGHT

oval, white cheek patch

dark brown head

dark, unmarked back

all-dark wings

grayish brown sides

FEMALE

front part of head and neck has iridescent green-and-purple gloss

large, triangular, white patch on head

angled forehead

black back

small, narrow, gray bill

white breast and flanks

MALE

The smallest diving duck in North America, the Bufflehead is a close relative of the Common and Barrow's Goldeneyes. Males make a bold statement with their striking head pattern. In flight, males resemble the larger Common Goldeneye, yet the large white area on their head makes them easy to distinguish. The Common Goldeneye's wings create a whirring sound in flight whereas the Bufflehead's do not. The northern limit of the Bufflehead's breeding range corresponds to that of the Northern Flicker, as the ducks usually nest in abandoned Flicker cavities.

VOICE Male a low growl or squeal; chattering during breeding; female mostly silent except during courtship or calling to chicks.

NESTING Cavity nester, no nesting material added, near water; 7–9 eggs; 1 brood; April–September.

FEEDING Dives for aquatic invertebrates: usually insects in freshwater, mollusks and crustaceans in saltwater; also eats seeds.

FLIGHT: very rapid wing beats; no flight sound, unlike Goldeneyes.

IMMEDIATE TAKE OFF
Unlike other diving ducks, the small, compact Bufflehead can take off almost vertically.

OCCURRENCE
Breeds in forest from Alaska to eastern Canada, in woodlands near small lakes and permanent ponds, where young are raised. Winters largely along the Pacific and Atlantic Coasts with lower densities scattered across the continent, south to northern Mexico, and in Bermuda.

SIMILAR SPECIES

HOODED MERGANSER ♂
see p.69

smaller, with white cheek patch

RUDDY DUCK ♂ ❊
see p.72

dark cap

longer bill

larger size

Length **12½–15½in (32–39cm)**	Wingspan **21½–24in (54–61cm)**	Weight **10–18oz (275–500g)**
Social **Flocks**	Lifespan **Up to 15 years**	Status **Secure**

DATE SEEN	WHERE	NOTES

| Order **Anseriformes** | Family **Anatidae** | Species *Bucephala clangula* |

Common Goldeneye

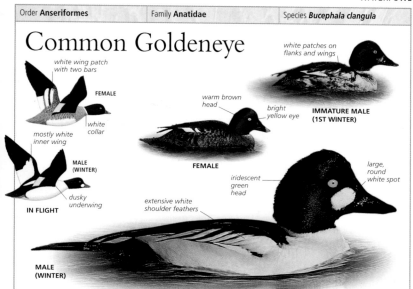

white wing patch with two bars

FEMALE

mostly white inner wing

white collar

MALE (WINTER)

IN FLIGHT

dusky underwing

white patches on flanks and wings

warm brown head

bright yellow eye

IMMATURE MALE (1ST WINTER)

FEMALE

iridescent green head

extensive white shoulder feathers

large, round white spot

MALE (WINTER)

Common Goldeneyes closely resemble Barrow's Goldeneyes. Found in North America and Eurasia, this is a medium-sized, compact diving duck. It is aggressive and very competitive with members of its own species, as well as other cavity-nesting ducks. It regularly lays eggs in the nests of other species—a behavior that is almost parasitic. Before diving, the Common Goldeneye flattens its feathers in preparation for underwater foraging. The female's head shape changes according to her posture.

VOICE Courting males make a faint *peent* call; females a harsh *gack* or repeated *cuk* calls.

NESTING Cavity nester in holes made by other birds, including Pileated Woodpeckers, in broken branches or hollow trees; also commonly uses nest boxes; 4–13 eggs; 1 brood; April–September.

FEEDING Dives during breeding season for insects; in winter, mollusks and crustaceans; sometimes eats fish and plant matter.

FLIGHT: rapid with fast wing beats; male's wings make a tinkling sound in flight.

MALE TAKING OFF
Quite a long takeoff, involving energetically running on the water, leaves a trail of spray.

OCCURRENCE
Breeds along wetlands, lakes, and rivers with clear water in northern forests, where large trees provide appropriate nest cavities. Winters across continent, with highest densities located from north New England to the mid-Atlantic on coastal bays and in the West from coastal southeast Alaska to British Columbia.

SIMILAR SPECIES		
BUFFLEHEAD ♀ see p.66	**BARROW'S GOLDENEYE** ♂ see p.68	

smaller overall

white oval patch behind eye

smaller bill

large crescent on face

Length **15½–20in (40–51cm)**	Wingspan **30–33in (77–83cm)**	Weight **19–44oz (550–1,300g)**
Social **Flocks**	Lifespan **Up to 15 years**	Status **Secure**

DATE SEEN	WHERE	NOTES

Order **Anseriformes**	Family **Anatidae**	Species ***Bucephala islandica***

Barrow's Goldeneye

darker brown head

steep forehead

small, yellow bill

black head with purple gloss

sloping crown

white wing patch

MALE

dark underwings

FEMALE (BREEDING)

narrow, white wing patch

IN FLIGHT

grayish brown wing feathers

IMMATURE MALE (1ST WINTER)

white neck

white "piano key" markings on sides

bold, white facial crescent

MALE

Barrow's Goldeneye is a slightly larger, darker version of the Common Goldeneye. Although the female can be identified by her different head structure, her bill color varies seasonally and geographically. Eastern Barrow's have blacker bills with less yellow, and western populations have entirely yellow bills, which darken in summer. During the breeding season, the majority of Barrow's Goldeneyes are found in mountainous regions of northwestern North America.

VOICE Males normally silent; courting males grunt *ka-KAA*; females *auc* call, slightly higher pitched than Common Goldeneye.

NESTING Tree cavity in holes formed by Pileated Woodpeckers, often broken limbs or hollow trees; also uses nest boxes; 6–12 eggs; 1 brood; April–September.

FEEDING Dives in summer for insects, some fish, and roe; in winter, mainly mollusks and crustaceans; some plant matter.

FLIGHT: rapid flight with fast, deep wing beats; flies near water surface on short flights.

COURTING DISPLAY
A male thrusts his head back and gives a guttural call. His feet then kick back, driving him forward.

SIMILAR SPECIES

GREATER SCAUP ♀
browner overall;
see p.57

longer neck

white patch

COMMON GOLDENEYE ♀
see p.67

more triangular head

warmer brown head

OCCURRENCE

Winters along the Pacific Coast between southeast Alaska and Washington, with small populations in eastern Canada. Smaller numbers found inland from the lower Colorado River to Yellowstone National Park. Eastern population is localized in winter with the highest count in St. Lawrence estuary.

Length **17–19in (43–48cm)**	Wingspan **28–30in (71–76cm)**	Weight **17–46oz (475–1,300g)**
Social **Flocks**	Lifespan **Up to 18 years**	Status **Secure**

DATE SEEN	WHERE	NOTES

| Order **Anseriformes** | Family **Anatidae** | Species *Lophodytes cucullatus* |

Hooded Merganser

triangular-shaped wings

black-and-white inner wing patch

MALE (BREEDING)

long tail **IN FLIGHT**

reddish-tinged crest (folded)

brownish gray flanks

brownish buff eye

yellow-based, thin, black bill

FEMALE

striking yellow eye

small, gray-brown crest (raised)

MALE (ECLIPSE)

longish tail, often raised

crested black-and-white head (crest not raised)

black back

yellow eye

thin, black, serrated bill

MALE (BREEDING)

white breast

warm brown flanks

bold vertical bars

This dapper, miniature fish-eater is the smallest of the three mergansers. Both male and female Hooded Mergansers have crests that they can raise or flatten. When the male raises his crest, the thin horizontal white stripe turns into a gorgeous white fan, surrounded by black. Although easily identified when swimming, the Hooded Merganser and the Wood Duck can be confused when seen in flight since they both are fairly small with bushy heads and long tails.

VOICE Normally silent; during courtship, males produce a low, growly, descending *pah-hwaaaaa*, reminiscent of a frog; females give a soft *rrrep*.

NESTING Cavity nester; nest lined with down feathers in a tree or box close to or over water; 6–15 eggs; 1 brood; February–June.

FEEDING Dives for fish, aquatic insects, and crayfish, preferably in clear and shallow fresh waters, but also in brackish waters.

FLIGHT: low, fast, and direct; shallow wing beats; quiet whirring noise produced by wings.

FANHEAD SPECTACULAR
The male's magnificent black-and-white fan of a crest is like a beacon in the late afternoon light.

SIMILAR SPECIES

WOOD DUCK ♀ see p.44

bold, white eye-ring

blue wing patch

RED-BREASTED MERGANSER ♀ see p.71

steel gray-and-white plumage

rustier head with ragged crest

OCCURRENCE
Prefers forested small ponds, marshes, or slow-moving streams during the breeding season. During winter, occurs in shallow water in both fresh- and saltwater bays, estuaries, rivers, streams, ponds, freshwater marshes, and flooded sloughs.

| Length **15½–19½in (40–49cm)** | Wingspan **23½–26in (60–66cm)** | Weight **16–31oz (450–875g)** |
| Social **Small flocks** | Lifespan **Unknown** | Status **Secure** |

DATE SEEN	WHERE	NOTES

Order **Anseriformes**	Family **Anatidae**	Species ***Mergus merganser***

Common Merganser

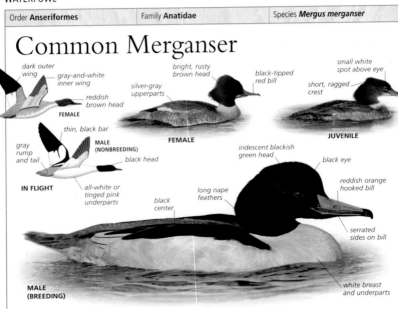

dark outer wing

gray-and-white inner wing

reddish brown head

FEMALE

bright, rusty brown head

black-tipped red bill

silver-gray upperparts

small white spot above eye

short, ragged crest

JUVENILE

gray rump and tail

thin, black bar

MALE (NONBREEDING)

black head

FEMALE

iridescent blackish green head

black eye

reddish orange hooked bill

IN FLIGHT

all-white or tinged pink underparts

long nape feathers

black center

serrated sides on bill

MALE (BREEDING)

white breast and underparts

The largest of the three merganser species in North America, the Common Merganser is called a Goosander in the UK. This large fish-eater is common and widespread, particularly in the northern portion of its range. It is often found in big flocks on lakes or smaller groups along rivers. It spends most of its time on the water, using its serrated bill to catch fish underwater.

VOICE Mostly silent, except when alarmed or during courtship; females give a low-pitched harsh *karr* or *gruk*, the latter also given in series; during courtship, males emit a high-pitched, bell-like note and other twangy notes; alarm call a hoarse *grrr* or *uak*.

NESTING Cavity nester sometimes high in trees; uses nest boxes, nests on ground; 6–17 eggs; 1 brood; April–September.

FEEDING Eats mostly fish (especially fond of trout and salmon, but also carp and catfish), aquatic invertebrates, frogs, small mammals, birds, and plants.

FLIGHT: fast with shallow wing beats; often flying low over the water.

FEEDING ON THE MOVE
This female Common Merganser is trying to swallow, head-first, a rather large fish.

SIMILAR SPECIES

COMMON GOLDENEYE ♂ see p.67

black-and-white pattern

white patch

RED-BREASTED MERGANSER ♀ see p.71

smaller, more lightly built

thinner bill

OCCURRENCE
Breeds in northern forests from Alaska to Newfoundland; winters south to north central Mexico. It winters farther north than most other waterfowl as long as water remains open. Prefers fresh-to saltwater locations.

Length **21½–28in (54–71cm)**	Wingspan **34in (86cm)**	Weight **1¾–4¾lb (0.8–2.1kg)**
Social **Flocks**	Lifespan **Up to 13 years**	Status **Secure**

DATE SEEN	WHERE	NOTES

| Order **Anseriformes** | Family **Anatidae** | Species **Mergus serrator** |

Red-breasted Merganser

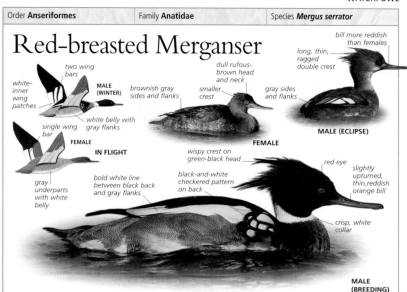

bill more reddish than females

long, thin, ragged double crest

MALE (ECLIPSE)

two wing bars

white-inner wing patches

MALE (WINTER)

brownish gray sides and flanks

dull rufous-brown head and neck

smaller crest

gray sides and flanks

single wing bar

white belly with gray flanks

FEMALE
IN FLIGHT

FEMALE

wispy crest on green-black head

red eye

slightly upturned, thin, reddish orange bill

gray underparts with white belly

bold white line between black back and gray flanks

black-and-white checkered pattern on back

crisp, white collar

MALE (BREEDING)

The Red-breasted Merganser, like the other saw-billed mergansers, is an elegant fish-eating duck. Both sexes are easily recognized by their long, sparse, somewhat ragged-looking double crest. Red-breasted Mergansers are smaller than Common Mergansers, but much larger than the Hooded. The Red-breasted Merganser, unlike the other two mergansers, nests on the ground, in loose colonies, often among gulls and terns, and is protected by its neighbors.

VOICE During courtship males make a raucous *yeow-yeow* call; females emit a raspy *krrr-krrr*.

NESTING Shallow depression on ground lined with down and plant material, near water; 5–11 eggs; 1 brood; May–July.

FEEDING Dives for small fish such as herring and minnows; also salmon eggs; at times flocks coordinate and drive fish together.

FLIGHT: fast flying duck with very rapid, regular, and shallow flapping.

KEEPING CLOSE
Red-breasted Mergansers are gregarious at all times of year, often feeding in loose flocks.

SIMILAR SPECIES

HOODED MERGANSER ♀
see p.69

fuller, cinnamon-tinged crest

darker back

smaller overall

COMMON MERGANSER ♀
see p.70

smaller bill

full crest

rusty-red head

larger and more robust

white breast and chin

OCCURRENCE
Most northern range of all the mergansers, nests across Arctic and sub-Arctic regions, tundra and northerly forests, along coasts, inland lakes, river banks, marsh edges, and coastal islands. Winters farther south than other mergansers, mostly in protected bays, estuaries, or on the Great Lakes.

| Length **20–25in (51–64cm)** | Wingspan **26–29in (66–74cm)** | Weight **1¾–2¾lb (0.8–1.3kg)** |
| Social **Flocks/Colonies** | Lifespan **Up to 9 years** | Status **Secure** |

DATE SEEN	WHERE		NOTES

| Order **Anseriformes** | Family **Anatidae** | Species *Oxyura jamaicensis* |

Ruddy Duck

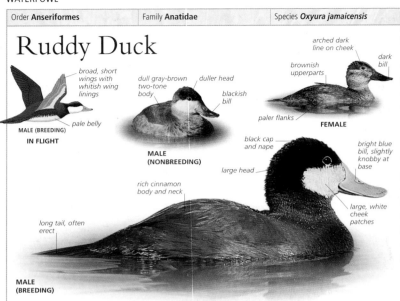

broad, short wings with whitish wing linings

dull gray-brown two-tone body

duller head

blackish bill

MALE (BREEDING) IN FLIGHT

pale belly

MALE (NONBREEDING)

arched dark line on cheek

brownish upperparts

dark bill

paler flanks

FEMALE

black cap and nape

large head

rich cinnamon body and neck

long tail, often erect

bright blue bill, slightly knobby at base

large, white cheek patches

MALE (BREEDING)

Small and stiff-tailed, the Ruddy Duck is comical in both its appearance and behavior. Both sexes often hold their tail in a cocked position, especially when sleeping. During courtship displays, the male points its long tail skyward while rapidly thumping its electric blue bill against its chest, ending the performance with an odd, bubbling sound. In another display, males make a popping sound by slapping their feet on the water's surface. Large feet, on legs set far back on its body, make the Ruddy Duck an excellent swimmer and diver; however, on land it is perhaps one of the most awkward of diving ducks. Females are known to push themselves along instead of walking.

VOICE Females give a nasal *raanh* and high pitched *eeek*; males vocally silent, but make popping noises with feet.

NESTING Platform, bowl-shaped nest built over water in thick emergent vegetation, rarely on land; 6–10 eggs; 1 brood; May–September.

FEEDING Dives for aquatic insects, larvae, crustaceans, and other invertebrates, particularly when breeding; during winter, also eats plants.

FLIGHT: rapid and direct, with fast wing beats; not very agile in flight, which seems labored.

HEAVY HEAD
A female "sitting" on the water streamlines her body before she dives, making her look large-headed.

SIMILAR SPECIES

MASKED DUCK ♂
see p.445

black tip to bill

black face

ruddy-colored back with black streaks

OCCURRENCE
Breeds in the prairie pothole region in wetland habitats; marshes, ponds, reservoirs, and other open shallow water with emergent vegetation and open areas. Majority winter on freshwater habitats from ponds to large lakes; smaller numbers found on brackish coastal marshes, bays, and estuaries.

| Length **14–17in (35–43cm)** | Wingspan **22–24in (56–62cm)** | Weight **11–30oz (300–850g)** |
| Social **Flocks** | Lifespan **Up to 13 years** | Status **Secure** |

DATE SEEN	WHERE	NOTES

LOONS

WORLDWIDE THERE ARE ONLY five species of loon, comprising a single genus (*Gavia*), a single family (the Gaviidae), and a single order (the Gaviiformes). The five species are limited to the Northern Hemisphere, where they are found in both northern North America and northern Eurasia. One feature of loons is that their legs are positioned so far to the rear of their body that they must shuffle on their bellies when they go from water to land. Not surprisingly, therefore, loons are almost entirely aquatic birds. In summer they are found on rivers, lakes, and ponds, where they nest close to the water's edge. After breeding, they occur along coasts, often after flying hundreds of miles away from their freshwater breeding grounds.

Excellent swimmers and divers, loons are unusual among birds in that their bones are less hollow than those of other groups. Consequently, loons can expel air from their lungs and compress their body feathers until they slowly sink beneath the surface.

LOON RANGER
The Common Loon has a wider range than any other in North America, as its name suggests.

They can remain submerged like this for several minutes. A loon's wings are relatively small in proportion to its body weight. This means that they have to run a long way across the surface of the water, flapping energetically, before they can become airborne. Once in the air they keep flapping and can fly at 60mph (95kmh).

FLIGHT SHAPE
The humped back and drooping neck of this Red-throated Loon are typical of loons in flight.

PROVIDING FOR THE FUTURE
A Red-throated Loon gives a fish to its chick to gulp down headfirst and whole.

| Order **Gaviiformes** | Family **Gaviidae** | Species *Gavia stellata* |

Red-throated Loon

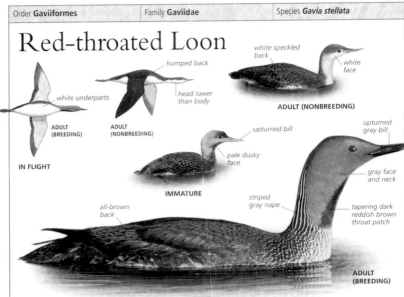

humped back

white underparts

white speckled back

white face

ADULT (NONBREEDING)

ADULT (BREEDING)

ADULT (NONBREEDING)

head lower than body

IN FLIGHT

upturned bill

pale dusky face

upturned gray bill

IMMATURE

gray face and neck

all-brown back

striped gray nape

tapering dark reddish brown throat patch

ADULT (BREEDING)

Even when seen from a distance, this elegant loon is almost unmistakable, with a pale, slim body, upward tilted head, and a thin, upturned bill. Unlike other Loons, the Red-throated Loon can leap straight into the air from both land and water, although most of the time it needs a "runway." The Red-throated Loon has an elaborate breeding ritual—side by side, a pair of birds races upright across the surface of water. Downy chicks climb onto the parents back only when very young.
VOICE High gull-like or even cat-like wail and low goose-like growl; vocal on breeding grounds, otherwise silent.
NESTING Scrape with mud and vegetation added during incubation, placed at water's edge in coastal and lake bays, shallow ponds, often at high altitudes; 2 eggs; 1 brood; April–July.
FEEDING Mainly eats fish; also spiders, crustaceans, and mollusks; flies long distances from shallow ponds when food is scarce.

FLIGHT: very direct; fast, with constant wing beats; head held lower than other loons.

TAKING OFF
While this bird is using the water's surface to take off, it can leap directly into flight from water and land.

SIMILAR SPECIES

YELLOW-BILLED LOON ❋ see p.471

RED-NECKED GREBE ❋ see p.86

massive, light-colored bill

larger overall

yellow in bill

darker back

smaller overall

OCCURRENCE
Lives in open areas within northern boreal forest, muskeg, and tundra; in Canadian Arctic Archipelago, sometimes in areas almost devoid of vegetation. Winters on the Great Lakes, and both coasts southwards to Florida and northern Mexico.

| Length **24–27in (61–69cm)** | Wingspan **3½ft (1.1m)** | Weight **3¼lb (1.5kg)** |
| Social **Solitary/Loose flocks** | Lifespan **Up to 23 years** | Status **Declining** |

DATE SEEN	WHERE	NOTES

| Order **Gaviiformes** | Family **Gaviidae** | Species *Gavia immer* |

Common Loon

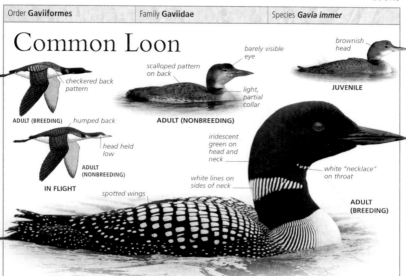

checkered back pattern

ADULT (BREEDING)   *humped back*

scalloped pattern on back

barely visible eye

light, partial collar

ADULT (NONBREEDING)

brownish head

JUVENILE

head held low

ADULT (NONBREEDING)

IN FLIGHT   spotted wings

iridescent green on head and neck

white lines on sides of neck

white "necklace" on throat

ADULT (BREEDING)

The Common Loon has the largest range of all loons in North America and is the only species to nest in a few of the northern states. It is slightly smaller than the Yellow-billed Loon but larger than the other three loons. It can remain underwater for well over 10 minutes, although it usually stays submerged for 40 seconds to 2 minutes while fishing, or a few more minutes if it is being pursued. Evidence shows that, occasionally, it interbreeds with its closest relative, the Yellow-billed Loon, in addition to the Arctic and Pacific Loons.

VOICE Most recognized call a 3–10 note falsetto yodel, rising, then fading; other calls similar in quality.

NESTING Simple scrape in large mound of vegetation, a few feet from open water; 2 eggs; 1 brood; April–June.

FEEDING Feeds primarily on fish underwater; also eats crustaceans, mollusks, amphibians, leeches, insects, and aquatic plants.

FLIGHT: fast, direct, with constant wing beats; head and neck held just above belly.

COZY RIDE
Downy Common Loon chicks climb up the backs of male and female adults for a safe ride.

BATHING RITUAL
Common Loons often shake their wings after bathing.

OCCURRENCE
Breeds across North America, Canada, and south to northern US. Winters on large ice-free lakes in Canada and the US, and along the Pacific and Atlantic Coasts, south to Baja California and Florida. In the Old World breeds only in Iceland.

| SIMILAR SPECIES | | |

YELLOW-BILLED LOON
see p.471

large, whitish or yellow bill

larger, checkered back pattern

RED-NECKED GREBE ❄
see p.86

much smaller overall

yellowish bill

brownish gray cheeks

| Length **26–36in (66–91cm)** | Wingspan **4¼–5ft (1.3–1.5m)** | Weight **4½–18lb (2–8kg)** |
| Social **Family groups** | Lifespan **Up to 30 years** | Status **Vulnerable** |

DATE SEEN	WHERE	NOTES

TUBENOSES

T HE NAME "TUBENOSES" IS GIVEN to several families of seabirds with tubular nostrils, which help get rid of excess salt and may enhance their sense of smell. Tubenoses are all members of the order Procellariiformes.

FLAP AND GLIDE
Shearwaters alternate stiff-winged flapping with gliding just over the ocean's surface or, in strong winds, glide in wide arcs, high above the waves.

ALBATROSSES
The long, narrow wings of albatrosses (family Diomedeidae) are perfectly suited for tackling the strong, constant winds that prevail on the southern oceans that form their main habitat. While they are expert gliders, albatrosses cannot take off from the ground without sufficient wing to give them lift.

SHEARWATERS
Shearwaters and gadfly petrels (family Procellariidae) are smaller than albatrosses. Like their larger relatives they are excellent gliders, but their lighter weight and proportionately shorter wings mean that they use more powered flight than albatrosses. They range over all the world's oceans. With its numerous islands, the Pacific Ocean is home to a greater variety of these seabirds than the Atlantic. During and after storms are the best times to look for shearwaters from the shore because this is when they drift away from the deep sea due to wind and waves.

STORM-PETRELS
The smallest tubenoses in North American waters, the storm-petrels (family Hydrobatidae) are also the most agile fliers. They often patter or "dance" as they fly just above the surface of the ocean in search of small fish, squid, and crustaceans. Storm-petrels spend most of their lives flying over the open sea, only visiting land in the breeding season, when they form colonies. The apparent fragility and small size of storm-petrels is belied by their ability to live as far away from land as their larger relatives, the shearwaters and albatrosses. Storm-petrels are nocturnal at their breeding colonies and nest under the ground, in burrows, or under rocks, two traits that reduce the effects of predation.

HOOKED BILL
All tubenoses have hooked bills in addition to their tubular nostrils.

STRONG PAIR BOND
After elaborate courtship displays, albatrosses generally pair for life. The rituals are simpler in later years.

| Order **Procellariiformes** | Family **Procellariidae** | Species *Fulmarus glacialis* |

Northern Fulmar

white patch on wing

ADULT (ATLANTIC FORM)

IN FLIGHT

paddle-like wings

dark gray overall

ADULT (DARK PACIFIC FORM)

gray back

small dark patch in front of eye

short, rounded, gray tail

ADULT (LIGHT PACIFIC FORM)

white head

thick, yellow bill

white underparts

ADULT (ATLANTIC FORM)

Possessing paddle-shaped wings and distinctive color patterns ranging from almost all-white to all-gray, the Northern Fulmar is among the most common seabirds in places like the Bering Sea. It breeds at high latitudes, then disperses south to offshore waters along both coasts of the continent. The Northern Fulmar can sometimes be seen in large mixed flocks containing albatrosses, shearwaters, and small petrels.

VOICE Mostly silent at sea; occasionally utters cackles and grunts.

NESTING Scrape in rock or soil on edge of cliff; 1 egg; 1 brood; May–October.

FEEDING Picks fish and offal from the surface of the ocean; also dives underwater to catch fish.

FLIGHT: snappy wing beats and long glides near the surface of the ocean.

FEEDING FRENZY
Large numbers of Northern Fulmars compete for the offal discarded by fishing trawlers.

SIMILAR SPECIES

SOOTY SHEARWATER see p.80

more slender wings

dark bill

dark overall

GREATER SHEARWATER see p.81

more slender wings

dark cap

white collar

OCCURRENCE
Breeds on remote, high, coastal cliffs in Alaska and Canada; winters at sea in offshore Pacific and Atlantic waters, generally farther north than most other seabirds. Breeds in Europe, northward to Greenland, Svalbard; also parts of Russia.

| Length 17½–19½in (45–50cm) | Wingspan 3¼–3½ft (1–1.1m) | Weight 16–35oz (0.45–1kg) |
| Social **Flocks** | Lifespan **Up to 50 years** | Status **Secure** |

| DATE SEEN | WHERE | NOTES |
| | | |

Order **Procellariiformes**	Family **Procellariidae**	Species ***Calonectris diomedea***

Cory's Shearwater

long, pointed wings

pale rump

ADULT

IN FLIGHT

dark wingtip and trailing edge

clean white underwing

all white belly

ADULT

scalloped pattern

grayish head and chin

yellow bill with dark tip

ADULT

white breast, with sooty-gray sides

Close observation of flocks of Cory's Shearwaters off the Atlantic coast has suggested the presence of two subspecies. The more common one, *C. d. borealis*, nests in the eastern Atlantic and is chunkier, with less white on the underwing. The other subspecies, *C. d. diomedea*, breeds in the Mediterranean, has a more slender build and a thinner bill, and more white on the underwing. Cory's Shearwater (either subspecies) has a relatively "languid" flight style that differs from that of other shearwaters in North Atlantic waters.

VOICE Mostly silent at sea; descending, lamb-like bleating.
NESTING Nests in burrow or rocky crevice; 1 egg; 1 brood; May–September.
FEEDING Dives into water or picks at surface for small schooling fish, and marine invertebrates such as squid.

FLIGHT: slow, deliberate wing beats interspersed with long glides; often arcs strongly on bent wings.

LAZY FLIERS
In calm weather Cory's Shearwaters look heavy and fly low, swooping higher in strong winds.

SIMILAR SPECIES

AUDUBON'S SHEARWATER see p.445
dark brown overall

GREATER SHEARWATER see p.81
dark head
brownish overall
white neck

OCCURRENCE
This species breeds in the Mediterranean and on islands of the eastern Atlantic, including the Azores, the Salvages, Madeira, and the Canaries. When nonbreeding, Cory's Shearwaters disperse widely over the Atlantic Ocean and the Gulf of Mexico.

Length **18in (46cm)**	Wingspan **3½ft (1.1m)**	Weight **28oz (800g)**
Social **Flocks**	Lifespan **Unknown**	Status **Secure**

DATE SEEN	WHERE	NOTES

| Order **Procellariiformes** | Family **Procellariidae** | Species ***Puffinus puffinus*** |

Manx Shearwater

long, pointed wings

black edge of wing

IN FLIGHT

white undertail feathers

snow white underparts

very dark brownish black upperparts

head is black above, white below

long, thin, hooked bill

crisp white underwings

dark upperwings

small head

dark, hooked bill

short tail

white throat

Most shearwaters are little known because of their nocturnal and oceanic habits, but the Manx is an exception. It is common in the British Isles, and ornithologists have been studying it there for decades. Long-term banding programs revealed that one bird flew over 3,000 miles (4,800km) from Massachusetts to its nesting burrow in Wales in just 12½ days, and that another was captured 56 years after it was first banded, making its accumulated migration-only mileage around 600,000 miles (1,000,000km).

VOICE Usually silent at sea, but at breeding sites, produces loud and raucous series of cries, *kah-kah-kah-kah-kah-HOWW*.

NESTING In burrow, in peaty soil, or rocky crevice; 1 egg; 1 brood; April–October.

FEEDING Dives into water, often with open wings and stays underwater, or picks at surface for small schooling fish and squid.

FLIGHT: rapid, stiff wing beats interspersed with glides; arcs high in strong winds.

PITTER-PATTER
Unlike gulls, shearwaters have to patter along the surface with their feet to achieve lift-off speed.

SIMILAR SPECIES	
BLACK-VENTED SHEARWATER *brownish upperparts* *paler head*	**AUDUBON'S SHEARWATER** see p.445 *longer tail* *slightly smaller overall*

OCCURRENCE
Breeds on many islands in eastern North Atlantic; restricted to islands off Newfoundland in North America. Regularly occurs off US east coast as far south as Florida. Rare in Gulf of Mexico and off the West Coast. Rarely seen from shore; cold-water shearwater.

| Length **13½in (34cm)** | Wingspan **33in (83cm)** | Weight **14–20oz (400–575g)** |
| Social **Migrant flocks** | Lifespan **Up to 55 years** | Status **Secure** |

DATE SEEN	WHERE	NOTES

Order **Procellariiformes**	Family **Procellariidae**	Species **Puffinus griseus**

Sooty Shearwater

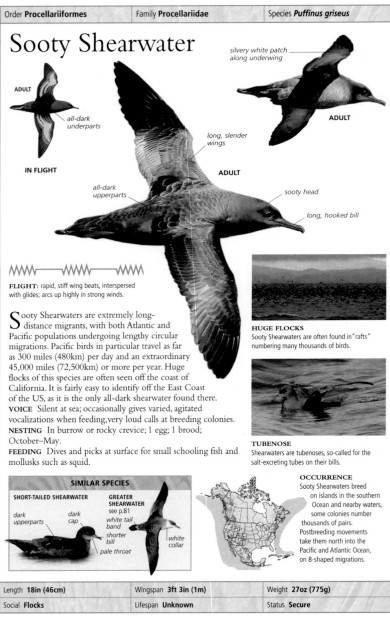

silvery white patch along underwing

ADULT

all-dark underparts

IN FLIGHT

long, slender wings

ADULT

ADULT

all-dark upperparts

sooty head

long, hooked bill

〜〜〜〜〜〜〜〜〜〜〜〜〜〜〜〜

FLIGHT: rapid, stiff wing beats, interspersed with glides; arcs up highly in strong winds.

Sooty Shearwaters are extremely long-distance migrants, with both Atlantic and Pacific populations undergoing lengthy circular migrations. Pacific birds in particular travel as far as 300 miles (480km) per day and an extraordinary 45,000 miles (72,500km) or more per year. Huge flocks of this species are often seen off the coast of California. It is fairly easy to identify off the East Coast of the US, as it is the only all-dark shearwater found there.

VOICE Silent at sea; occasionally gives varied, agitated vocalizations when feeding, very loud calls at breeding colonies.

NESTING In burrow or rocky crevice; 1 egg; 1 brood; October–May.

FEEDING Dives and picks at surface for small schooling fish and mollusks such as squid.

HUGE FLOCKS
Sooty Shearwaters are often found in "rafts" numbering many thousands of birds.

TUBENOSE
Shearwaters are tubenoses, so-called for the salt-excreting tubes on their bills.

SIMILAR SPECIES

SHORT-TAILED SHEARWATER

dark upperparts

dark cap

shorter bill

pale throat

GREATER SHEARWATER
see p.81

white tail band

white collar

OCCURRENCE
Sooty Shearwaters breed on islands in the southern Ocean and nearby waters, some colonies number thousands of pairs. Postbreeding movements take them north into the Pacific and Atlantic Ocean, on 8-shaped migrations.

Length **18in (46cm)**	Wingspan **3ft 3in (1m)**	Weight **27oz (775g)**
Social **Flocks**	Lifespan **Unknown**	Status **Secure**

DATE SEEN	WHERE	NOTES

| Order **Procellariiformes** | Family **Procellariidae** | Species **Puffinus gravis** |

Greater Shearwater

ADULT

dark, half "necklace" at sides of neck

dark smudge on center of belly

IN FLIGHT

darker outer wing feathers

brownish upperwings

white collar

dark cap

thin, black bill

thin, white band on rump

ADULT

A common species in North Atlantic waters, from northern Canada to Florida, the Greater Shearwater is similar in size to Cory's Shearwater and the birds scavenge together for scraps around fishing boats. However, their plumages and flight styles are quite different. While Cory's Shearwater has slow, labored wing beats, and glides high on broad, bowed, swept-back wings, Greater Shearwaters keep low, flapping hurriedly between glides on straight, narrow wings. The brown smudges on the belly (not always visible) and paler underwings of the Greater Shearwater also help distinguish the species.
VOICE Silent at sea; descending, lamb-like bleating at breeding sites.
NESTING Digs deep burrow in peaty or boggy soil; 1 egg; 1 brood; September–March.
FEEDING Feeds either from the surface, picking up items such as fish and squid, or makes shallow dives with open wings.

FLIGHT: fast, stiff wing beats interspersed with gliding; arcs high in windy conditions.

WHITE COLLAR
The Greater Shearwater's white collar is highly visible between its black cap and sooty back.

SIMILAR SPECIES

BLACK-CAPPED PETREL
see p.445

large, white rump

white forehead

MANX SHEARWATER
see p.79

darker plumage

smaller overall

OCCURRENCE
Nests on just a few islands in the middle of the South Atlantic. Total population probably well over 200 million. Postbreeding birds make a very long 8-shaped migration around the Atantic, spending late July–September in North Atlantic waters, usually offshore.

| Length **18in (46cm)** | Wingspan **3½ft (1.1m)** | Weight **30oz (850g)** |
| Social **Flocks** | Lifespan **At least 25 years** | Status **Secure** |

DATE SEEN	WHERE	NOTES

Order **Procellariiformes**	Family **Hydrobatidae**	Species *Oceanites oceanicus*

Wilson's Storm-Petrel

broad, pointed wings

white rump and lower flanks

pale bar on upperwing

ADULT

ADULT

IN FLIGHT

dark wings and body

small, black "tube nose"

"walking" on water

ADULT

short, square tail

yellow webbing between toes

Named after Alexander Wilson, often called the "father of North American ornithology," Wilson's Storm-Petrel is the quintessential small oceanic petrel. It is an extremely abundant species and breeds in the many millions on the Antarctic Peninsula and islands in Antarctica. After breeding, many move north to spend the summer off the Atlantic coast of North America. Here, they are a familiar sight to fishermen and birders at sea. By August they can be seen lingering, but by October they have flown south.
VOICE At sea, soft rasping notes; at breeding sites a variety of *coos*, *churrs*, and twitters during the night.
NESTING Mostly in rock crevices; also burrows where there is peaty soil; 1 egg; 1 brood; November–March.
FEEDING Patters on the water's surface, legs extended, picking up tiny crustaceans; also carrion, droplets of oil.

FLIGHT: flutters, low to ocean's surface, often "stalling" to drop to the surface and glean food.

FEEDING FLOCK
While flying, this bird "walks" on water, simultaneously picking food from the surface.

SIMILAR SPECIES		
BAND-RUMPED STORM-PETREL see p.445	**LEACH'S STORM-PETREL** see p.83	
square tail	smaller overall	white rump patch
		forked tail

OCCURRENCE
Breeds on the Antarctic Peninsula, many sub-Antarctic islands, and islands in the Cape Horn Archipelago. April –September or October, moves north, and is abundant off the coasts of New England, New York, and New Jersey July– September. With inshore winds, can often be seen from land.

Length **6¾in (17cm)**	Wingspan **16in (41cm)**	Weight **1¹⁄₁₆–1⁷⁄₁₆oz (30–40g)**
Social **Flocks**	Lifespan **Up to 10 years**	Status **Secure**

DATE SEEN	WHERE		NOTES

| Order **Procellariiformes** | Family **Hydrobatidae** | Species *Oceanodroma leucorhoa* |

Leach's Storm-Petrel

long, angled wings

white rump with thin, dark line down center

ADULT

IN FLIGHT

brown bar across blackish wings

ADULT

dark sooty black underwings

dark smudge beside eye

forked tail

FLIGHT: buoyant, deep wing beats low over ocean's surface, interrupted by twists and turns.

dark sooty brown underparts

ADULT

Leach's Storm-Petrel is widespread in both the Atlantic and Pacific Oceans, unlike most other storm-petrels. It breeds in colonies on islands off the coasts, coming to land at night and feeding offshore during the day, often many miles from the colony. This wide-ranging storm-petrel has both geographical and individual variation; most populations show a white rump, but others have a dark rump that is the same color as the rest of the body. Leach's Storm-Petrel can be distinguished from the similar Band-rumped Storm-Petrel by its notched tail and swooping flight.

VOICE At nesting sites, often from burrows, calls are long series of soft purring and chattering sounds.

NESTING Underground burrow on island free of predators such as rats; 1 egg; 1 brood; May–November.

FEEDING Gleans small crustaceans and small fish from the water's surface while in flight.

BALANCING ACT
Leach's Storm-Petrels will occasionally balance themselves with their toes while foraging.

SIMILAR SPECIES	
BAND-RUMPED STORM-PETREL see p.445	**BLACK STORM-PETREL**
white of rump extends toward belly	dark rump

OCCURRENCE
Breeds on islands in the Pacific Ocean from Alaska and the Aleutian Islands south to California; in the Atlantic Ocean, from Newfoundland to Maine. After breeding, it wanders widely on both oceans, keeping well out of sight of land.

Length **7–8½in (18–22cm)**	Wingspan **17½–19in (45–48cm)**	Weight **1⁹⁄₁₆–1¾oz (45–50g)**
Social **Colonies**	Lifespan **Up to 36 years**	Status **Secure**

DATE SEEN	WHERE	NOTES

GREBES

GREBES RESEMBLE LOONS and share many of their aquatic habits, but anatomical and molecular features show that they are actually unrelated. They are placed in a different order: the Podicipediformes. Grebes have streamlined bodies, which offer little resistance when diving and swimming. Underwater their primary means of propulsion is the sideways motion of their lobed toes. The legs are placed far back on a grebe's body, which greatly aids the bird when it swims above or below the surface. Grebes have short tails, and their trailing legs and toes serve as rudders when they fly. The position of the legs makes it impossible, however, for grebes to stand upright for long or easily walk on land. This means that grebes are tied to water even when breeding; and their nests are usually partially floating platforms, built on beds of water plants. Grebes' toes have broad lobes that splay when the bird thrusts forward through the water with its feet. They dive to catch fish with a short, forward arching spring. Unusual among birds, grebes swallow feathers, apparently to trap fish bones and protect their stomachs, then periodically disgorge them. Like loons, they can control their buoyancy by exhaling air and compressing their plumage so that they sink quietly below the surface. They are strong fliers and migratory.

PIED BILL
The black-and-white bill pattern clearly distinguishes this bird as the Pied-billed Grebe.

A FINE DISPLAY
This Horned Grebe reveals the colorful plumes on its head as part of its elaborate courtship display.

SIDE BY SIDE
This pair of Western Grebes is displaying their elaborate courtship behavior.

Order **Podicipediformes**	Family **Podicipedidae**	Species *Podilymbus podiceps*

Pied-billed Grebe

outstretched neck

ADULT (BREEDING)

lighter flight feathers

IN FLIGHT

yellowish bill

whitish throat

ADULT (NONBREEDING)

brown eye

whitish, hooked bill with a black ring

brownish gray body

ADULT (BREEDING)

reddish brown neck and breast

black throat patch

white undertail

The widest ranging of the North American grebes, the Pied-billed Grebe is tolerant of highly populated areas and is often seen breeding on lakes and ponds across North America. It is a powerful swimmer and can remain submerged for 16–30 seconds when it dives. In contrast to some of the elaborate displays from other grebe species, its courtship ritual is more vocal than visual and a pair usually duet-call in the mating season. Migration, conducted at night, is delayed until its breeding area ices up and food becomes scarce. The Pied-billed Grebe is capable of sustained flights of over 2,000 miles (3,200km).

VOICE Various grunts and wails; in spring, call a cuckoo-like repeated gobble *kup–kup–Kaow–Kaow–kaow*, gradually speeding up.

NESTING Floating nest of partially decayed plants and clipped leaves, attached to emergent vegetation in marshes and quiet waters; 4–7 eggs; 2 broods; April–October.

FEEDING Dives to catch a variety of crustaceans, fish, amphibians, insects, and other invertebrates; also picks prey from emergent vegetation, or catches them mid-air.

FLIGHT: strong, direct flight with rapid wing beats, but rarely seen.

BACK OFF
When alarmed, a Pied-billed Grebe may flap its wings in a defensive display.

SIMILAR SPECIES
LEAST GREBE ☼ see p.446

smaller bill

yellow eye

darker body

OCCURRENCE
Breeds on a variety of water bodies, including coastal brackish ponds, seasonal ponds, marshes, and even sewage ponds. Winters in the breeding area if food and open water are available, otherwise chooses still waters resembling its breeding habitat.

Length **12–15in (31–38cm)**	Wingspan **18–24in (46–62cm)**	Weight **13–17oz (375–475g)**
Social **Family groups**	Lifespan **At least 3 years**	Status **Vulnerable**

DATE SEEN	WHERE	NOTES
....	....	....
....	....	....
....	....	....
....	....	....
....	....	....

| Order **Podicipediformes** | Family **Podicipedidae** | Species **Podiceps grisegena** |

Red-necked Grebe

head and neck in line with body

white-edged inner wing

ADULT (BREEDING)

IN FLIGHT

brownish cap

pale, reddish brown crescent near ear

ADULT (NONBREEDING)

broad stripes on cheek and ear

mostly yellowish bill

JUVENILE

broad head with crest at rear

black cap

grayish white cheeks and throat

gray flanks

chestnut brown neck and chest

base of the bill yellow

ADULT (BREEDING)

The Red-necked Grebe is smaller than Western and Clark's Grebes, but larger than the other North American grebes. It migrates over short to medium distances and spends the winter along both coasts, where large flocks may be seen during the day. It runs along the water's surface to become airborne, although it rarely flies. This grebe doesn't come ashore often; it stands erect, but walks awkwardly, and prefers to sink to its breast and shuffle along.

VOICE Nasal, gull-like call on breeding grounds, evolves into bray, ends with whinny; also honks, rattles, hisses, purrs, and ticks.

NESTING Compact, buoyant mound of decayed and fresh vegetation in sheltered, shallow marshes and lakes, or artificial wetlands; 4–5 eggs; 1 brood; May–July.

FEEDING An opportunistic hunter, eats fish, crustaceans, aquatic insects, worms, mollusks, salamanders, and tadpoles.

FLIGHT: fast, direct, wing beats, with head and outstretched neck mostly level with line of body.

COURTSHIP DISPLAY
This courting pair face each other, with outstreched necks and raised neck feathers.

SIMILAR SPECIES

RED-THROATED LOON ❋
see p.74

no yellow on bill

white spots on back

white neck

HORNED GREBE ❋
see p.87

reddish eye
paler neck

OCCURRENCE
Breeds from northern prairies and forests, almost to the tree line in the northwest; limited to suitable interior bodies of water such as large marshes and small lakes. Winters primarily in estuaries, inlets, bays, and offshore shallows along Atlantic and Pacific Coasts; can also be found on the Great Lakes.

| Length **16½–22in (42–56cm)** | Wingspan **24–35in (61–88cm)** | Weight **1¾–3½lb (0.8–1.6kg)** |
| Social **Pairs/Loose flocks** | Lifespan **Up to 6 years** | Status **Vulnerable** |

DATE SEEN	WHERE	NOTES

| Order **Podicipediformes** | Family **Podicipedidae** | Species *Podiceps auritus* |

Horned Grebe

IN FLIGHT

ADULT (SUMMER) — neck and head in line with body

ADULT (WINTER) — white cheek, flattish top of head, white sides to neck

ADULT (SPRING MOLT) — gold streak from eye to nape

black crown, red eye, short, dark bill with whitish tip, black throat, rufous neck, white cheek

ADULT (SUMMER)

The timing of the Horned Grebe's migration depends largely on the weather—this species may not leave until its breeding grounds get iced over, nor does it arrive before the ice melts. Its breeding behavior is well documented since it is approachable on nesting grounds and has an elaborate breeding ritual. This grebe's so-called "horns" are in fact yellowish feather patches located behind its eyes, which it can raise at will.

VOICE At least 10 calls, but descending *aaanrrh* call most common in winter, ends in trill; muted conversational calls when birds are in groups.

NESTING Floating, soggy nest, hidden in vegetation, in small ponds and lake inlets; 3–9 eggs; 1 brood; May–July.

FEEDING Dives in open water or forages among plants, mainly for small crustaceans and insects, but also leeches, mollusks, amphibians, fish, and some vegetation.

FLIGHT: strong, rapid wing beats; runs on water to become airborne; rarely takes off from land.

HITCHING A RIDE
In common with other grebes, Horned Grebe chicks often ride on the back of a swimming parent.

SIMILAR SPECIES

RED-NECKED GREBE ✷ see p.86 — brownish cap, darker eye

EARED GREBE ✷ see p.88 — upturned bill, dark cheek

OCCURRENCE
Breeds in small freshwater, even slightly brackish, ponds and marshes, including man-made ponds. Prefers areas with open water and patches of sedges, cattails, and other wetland vegetation. Winters on saltwater close to shore; also on large bodies of freshwater. Also breeds in Eurasia.

| Length **12–15in (30–38cm)** | Wingspan **18–24in (46–62cm)** | Weight **11–20oz (300–575g)** |
| Social **Pairs/Loose flocks/Colonies** | Lifespan **Up to 5 years** | Status **Declining** |

DATE SEEN	WHERE	NOTES

| Order **Podicipediformes** | Family **Podicipedidae** | Species ***Podiceps nigricollis*** |

Eared Grebe

darker flanks

white patch on wing

browner plumage

ADULT (SUMMER)

outstretched neck

JUVENILE

dusky cheek

dusky white flanks

upturned bill

IN FLIGHT

grayish neck

large, wispy gold patch behind red eye

dark back

black neck

ADULT (WINTER)

black crest

red eye

thin, upturned bill

rufous breast and sides

ADULT (SUMMER)

The most abundant grebe in North America, the Eared Grebe is quite remarkable in terms of physiology. After breeding, it undergoes a complex and drastic reorganization of body-fat stores, along with changes in muscle, heart, and digestive organ mass to prepare it for fall migration. All of this increases the bird's energy reserves and body mass, but renders it flightless. It may have the longest periods of flightlessness of any flying bird—up to 10 months.

VOICE Various trills during courtship, including squeaky, rising *poo-eep*; sharp *chirp* when alarmed; usually silent at other times.

NESTING Sodden nest of decayed bottom plants anchored in thinly spaced reeds or submerged vegetation in shallow water of marshes, ponds, and lakes; 1 brood; 1–8 eggs; May–July.

FEEDING Forages underwater for small crustaceans and aquatic insects; also small fish and mollusks; consumes worms in winter.

FLIGHT: flies with neck outstretched, held at a low angle; rarely flies except during migration.

SALTY WATER
The Eared Grebe prefers salty water at all times except when breeding.

SIMILAR SPECIES

RED-NECKED GREBE ❋
see p.86

browner cap

thicker bill

HORNED GREBE ❋
see p.87

white tip on bill

more distinct white cheek

OCCURRENCE
Breeds in marshes, shallow lakes, and ponds. After breeding, many birds seek saline waters, such as Mono Lake, or lakes in Utah where their favorite foods thrive—brine shrimp and alkali flies. Winters in coastal bays of Pacific coast and is a vagrant on Atlantic coast. Also breeds in Eurasia.

| Length **12–14in (30–35cm)** | Wingspan **22½–24in (57–62cm)** | Weight **7–26oz (200–725g)** |
| Social **Flocks** | Lifespan **Up to 12 years** | Status **Secure** |

DATE SEEN	WHERE	NOTES
....	....	....
....	....	....
....	....	....
....	....	....
....	....	....

Families **Ciconiidae, Threskiornithidae, Ardeidae**

STORKS, IBISES, & HERONS

THESE ARE LARGE, WATER and wetland birds that have long legs and look rather similar, but have different habits. They eat fish and other aquatic prey as well as plants. Most breed in colonies.

IBISES

Birds of the marshlands or of dry land, ibises (Threskiornithidae) are characterized by rounded bodies; medium-length legs and strong feet that allow an easy, long-striding walk; short tails; rounded wings; and small, often bare, heads on curved necks, merging into long, curved bills. Gregarious birds, they fly in long lines or a "V" formation. Ibises feed mostly on insects, worms, small mollusks, and crustaceans, probing for them in the water and wet mud.

EYE-CATCHING IBIS
The White-faced Ibis has a distinctive white patch around its eye in the breeding season.

BITTERS, HERONS, AND EGRETS

These are mostly waterside birds (Ardeidae) with long, slender toes, broad, rounded wings, very short tails, forward-facing eyes, and dagger-shaped bills. Bitters and night-herons have smooth, dense feathers on their nape, while an egret's long, slender neck is tightly feathered, with an obvious "kink" that allows a lightning-fast stab for prey. Bitterns, herons, and egrets fly

EVER ALERT
The Green Heron stalks fish by watching and waiting patiently until prey is near.

with their legs trailing and their necks coiled back into their shoulders. Some make obvious bulky treetop nests and feed in the open, while others, especially bitterns, nest and feed secretively. In fact, often the only clue to a bittern's presence in a dense reedbed is the haunting, booming call it makes to keep in touch with its mate.

DANCING ON AIR
The Great Egret's courtship display often involves spreading its wings and leaping in a kind of aerial dance.

| Order **Ciconiiformes** | Family **Ciconiidae** | Species *Mycteria americana* |

Wood Stork

IN FLIGHT

ADULT

black-and-white wings

dark head

blackish, featherless head and upper neck

white body

long, decurved bill

ADULT

short, black tail

blackish gray legs

grayish, sparsely feathered head

pale yellow bill

JUVENILE

FLIGHT: flaps; using thermals, soars to great heights and glides, saving considerable energy.

The Wood Stork is the largest wading bird and the only stork that breeds in the US. It formerly bred mostly in south Florida, but as foraging conditions deteriorated, its population moved north and now mainly breeds north to North Carolina. During hot periods, the Wood Stork uses an extraordinary cooling method that involves defecation on its own legs.

VOICE Young give braying begging calls; adults usually silent; clatter bills during courting.

NESTING Large twig nest usually in swamps; colonial nesters, usually in trees over water for protection against predators; 2–4 eggs; 1 brood; December–August.

FEEDING Feeds on aquatic prey including fish, crabs, and insects; moves bill through water and detects prey movements.

FOOT STIRRING
Wood Storks often feed by stirring the bottom with their feet and feeling for prey with their bills.

SIMILAR SPECIES

GREAT EGRET see p.102

straight bill

black feet

SNOWY EGRET see p.106

smaller overall

yellow feet

much smaller overall

OCCURRENCE
Forested freshwater and coastal areas, swamps, and marshes; feeds in shallow wetlands. In the US, a southeastern species, breeding in Florida to North Carolina. Birds in Texas and Louisiana are postbreeders dispersing from Mexico. A few birds have been seen in southern California.

| Length **3ft 3in (100cm)** | Wingspan **5ft (1.5m)** | Weight **5½lb (2.5kg)** |
| Social **Flocks** | Lifespan **Up to 25 years** | Status **Endangered** |

DATE SEEN	WHERE	NOTES

| Order **Ciconiiformes** | Family **Threskiornithidae** | Species **Eudocimus albus** |

White Ibis

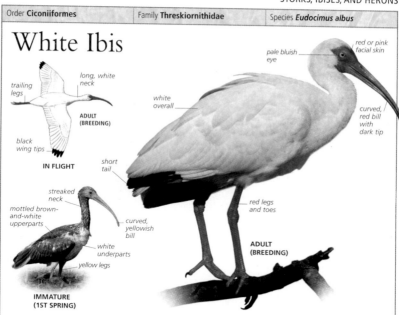

pale bluish eye

red or pink facial skin

curved, red bill with dark tip

ADULT (BREEDING)

long, white neck

trailing legs

white overall

black wing tips

IN FLIGHT

short tail

streaked neck

mottled brown-and-white upperparts

curved, yellowish bill

white underparts

yellow legs

IMMATURE (1ST SPRING)

red legs and toes

ADULT (BREEDING)

It is the shape that hints at the close relationship between the White Ibis and the darker Glossy and White-faced Ibises. Depending on the season, the White Ibis has a pink or flesh-colored face, bill, and legs set against its white plumage and black wing tips. When breeding, however, the legs, bill, and bare facial skin turn a vivid red. The 20,000–30,000 birds living in the southeastern US breed from Florida north to South Carolina, and along the Gulf Coast to Louisiana and Texas. The population moves around within this area, as do other large waders, depending on the water level.
VOICE Hoarse, croaking *kraah*; high-pitched calls during courtship.
NESTING Platform of sticks placed in trees or shrubs, often mangroves, over water; 2–4 eggs; 1 brood; March–October.
FEEDING Eats small crustaceans such as crayfish, small fish, and frogs; feeds in flocks in both estuarine and freshwater wetlands.

FLIGHT: rapid wing beats alternating with glides; soars on thermals to save energy.

HIGHLY GREGARIOUS
White Ibises are extremely social birds, flying, breeding, feeding, and roosting in large flocks.

SIMILAR SPECIES

GREAT EGRET see p.102

larger overall

black legs

SNOWY EGRET see p.106

shorter, straight bill

black bill

black legs

yellow feet

OCCURRENCE
Found in estuaries along the coast, also in freshwater marshes, swamps, and rice fields; breeds in colonies with other wading birds. Also occurs throughout Central America and northern South America from Venezuela to Colombia.

| Length **25in (64cm)** | Wingspan **3ft 2in (96cm)** | Weight **32oz (900g)** |
| Social **Flocks/Colonies** | Lifespan **Up to 16 years** | Status **Secure** |

DATE SEEN	WHERE	NOTES

| Order **Ciconiiformes** | Family **Threskiornithidae** | Species *Plegadis falcinellus* |

Glossy Ibis

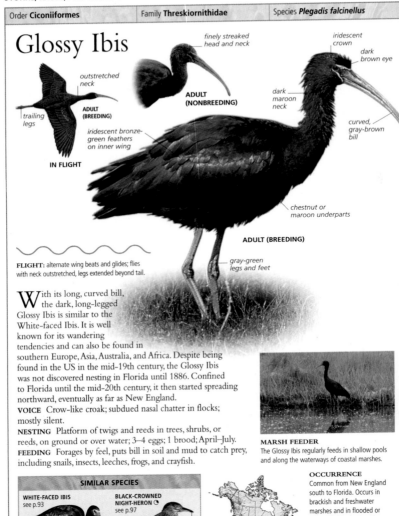

finely streaked head and neck

iridescent crown

dark brown eye

ADULT (NONBREEDING)

dark maroon neck

outstretched neck

ADULT (BREEDING)

trailing legs

iridescent bronze-green feathers on inner wing

IN FLIGHT

curved, gray-brown bill

chestnut or maroon underparts

ADULT (BREEDING)

FLIGHT: alternate wing beats and glides; flies with neck outstretched, legs extended beyond tail.

gray-green legs and feet

With its long, curved bill, the dark, long-legged Glossy Ibis is similar to the White-faced Ibis. It is well known for its wandering tendencies and can also be found in southern Europe, Asia, Australia, and Africa. Despite being found in the US in the mid-19th century, the Glossy Ibis was not discovered nesting in Florida until 1886. Confined to Florida until the mid-20th century, it then started spreading northward, eventually as far as New England.

VOICE Crow-like croak; subdued nasal chatter in flocks; mostly silent.

NESTING Platform of twigs and reeds in trees, shrubs, or reeds, on ground or over water; 3–4 eggs; 1 brood; April–July.

FEEDING Forages by feel, puts bill in soil and mud to catch prey, including snails, insects, leeches, frogs, and crayfish.

MARSH FEEDER
The Glossy Ibis regularly feeds in shallow pools and along the waterways of coastal marshes.

SIMILAR SPECIES

WHITE-FACED IBIS
see p.93

pink legs

white mask on pink face

BLACK-CROWNED NIGHT-HERON ⦵
see p.97

brown body

thick, straight bill

OCCURRENCE
Common from New England south to Florida. Occurs in brackish and freshwater marshes and in flooded or plowed fields; feeds with other waders in inland freshwater wetlands as well as coastal lagoons and estuaries.

| Length **23in (59cm)** | Wingspan **36in (92cm)** | Weight **13oz (375g)** |
| Social **Flocks/Colonies** | Lifespan **15–20 years** | Status **Secure (p)** |

DATE SEEN	WHERE	NOTES

| Order **Ciconiiformes** | Family **Threskiornithidae** | Species *Plegadis chihi* |

White-faced Ibis

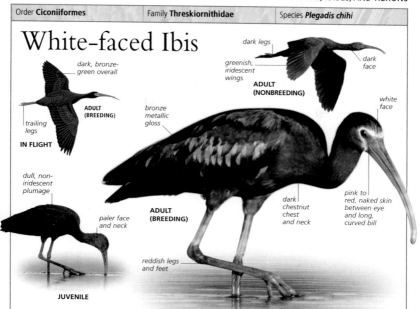

dark legs

greenish, iridescent wings

dark face

ADULT (NONBREEDING)

dark, bronze-green overall

ADULT (BREEDING)

white face

bronze metallic gloss

trailing legs

IN FLIGHT

dull, non-iridescent plumage

paler face and neck

ADULT (BREEDING)

dark chestnut chest and neck

pink to red, naked skin between eye and long, curved bill

reddish legs and feet

JUVENILE

The White-faced Ibis is not only the most widespread member of its family in North America but also the only ibis found commonly in its range. Very similar to the closely related Glossy Ibis, it is separable in winter only by its reddish eye and the absence of a thin blue line around the face, though the two are only likely to be seen together in the Louisiana area.

VOICE Generally silent; soft calls at the nest, including feeding calls, vocalizations after mating, and greeting calls to mates and chicks; outside breeding, a raucous *khah* or *krah*.

NESTING Flat or columnar nest lined with plant matter, such as cattail, or bulrush in low trees or shrubs over shallow water, or on ground on small islands; 2–5 eggs; 1 brood; May–July.

FEEDING Captures prey below soil by probing with bill; eats aquatic prey such as crayfish, small fish, and frogs.

FLIGHT: strong and direct, with rapid wing beats, alternating with glides; soars on thermals.

LARGE FLOCKS
The White-faced Ibis is social, feeding and traveling in flocks, which can be large.

SIMILAR SPECIES

GLOSSY IBIS
see p.92

darker legs

less white on face

BLACK-CROWNED NIGHT-HERON
see p.97

brown, streaked body

thick, straight bill

OCCURRENCE
Found in freshwater wetlands, especially in flooded fields, but also in marshes and lake edges with cattails and bulrushes. Although birds may disperse farther east after breeding, they are, for the most part, restricted to the western part of the United States, and in Central and South America.

| Length **23in (59cm)** | Wingspan **36in (92cm)** | Weight **22oz (625g)** |
| Social **Flocks/Colonies** | Lifespan **Up to 14 years** | Status **Secure** |

DATE SEEN	WHERE	NOTES
....	....	....
....	....	....
....	....	....
....	....	....
....	....	....

| Order **Ciconiiformes** | Family **Threskiornithidae** | Species *Ajaia ajaia* |

Roseate Spoonbill

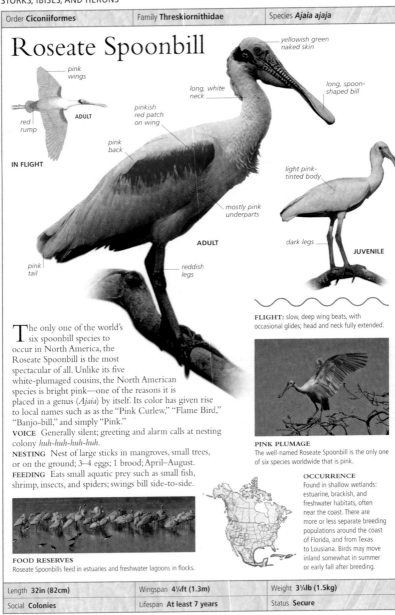

yellowish green naked skin

pink wings

long, white neck

pinkish red patch on wing

long, spoon-shaped bill

ADULT

red rump

pink back

IN FLIGHT

light pink-tinted body

mostly pink underparts

ADULT

dark legs

JUVENILE

pink tail

reddish legs

The only one of the world's six spoonbill species to occur in North America, the Roseate Spoonbill is the most spectacular of all. Unlike its five white-plumaged cousins, the North American species is bright pink—one of the reasons it is placed in a genus (*Ajaia*) by itself. Its color has given rise to local names such as as the "Pink Curlew," "Flame Bird," "Banjo-bill," and simply "Pink."

VOICE Generally silent; greeting and alarm calls at nesting colony *huh-huh-huh-huh*.

NESTING Nest of large sticks in mangroves, small trees, or on the ground; 3–4 eggs; 1 brood; April–August.

FEEDING Eats small aquatic prey such as small fish, shrimp, insects, and spiders; swings bill side-to-side.

FLIGHT: slow, deep wing beats, with occasional glides; head and neck fully extended.

PINK PLUMAGE
The well-named Roseate Spoonbill is the only one of six species worldwide that is pink.

OCCURRENCE
Found in shallow wetlands: estuarine, brackish, and freshwater habitats, often near the coast. There are more or less separate breeding populations around the coast of Florida, and from Texas to Lousiana. Birds may move inland somewhat in summer or early fall after breeding.

FOOD RESERVES
Roseate Spoonbills feed in estuaries and freshwater lagoons in flocks.

| Length **32in (82cm)** | Wingspan **4¼ft (1.3m)** | Weight **3¼lb (1.5kg)** |
| Social **Colonies** | Lifespan **At least 7 years** | Status **Secure** |

DATE SEEN	WHERE	NOTES

| Order **Ciconiiformes** | Family **Ardeidae** | Species ***Botaurus lentiginosus*** |

American Bittern

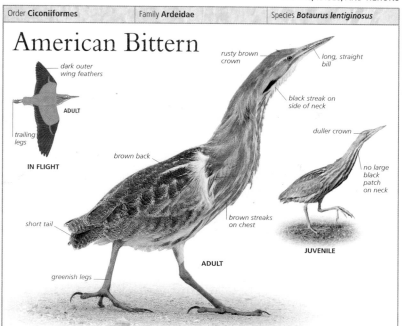

dark outer wing feathers

ADULT

trailing legs

IN FLIGHT

rusty brown crown

long, straight bill

black streak on side of neck

brown back

duller crown

no large black patch on neck

short tail

brown streaks on chest

greenish legs

JUVENILE

ADULT

The American Bittern's camouflaged plumage and secretive behavior help it to blend into the thick vegetation of its freshwater wetland habitat. It is heard much more often than it is seen; its call is unmistakable and has given rise to many evocative colloquial names, such as "thunder pumper."

VOICE Deep, resonant *pump-er-unk, pump-er-unk*; calls mainly at dawn, dusk, and nighttime, but also during the day in the early mating season.

NESTING Platform or mound constructed of available marsh vegetation, usually over shallow water; 2–7 eggs; 1 brood; April–August.

FEEDING Stands still or moves slowly, then strikes downward with bill to catch prey; eats fish, insects, crustaceans, snakes, amphibians, and small mammals.

FLIGHT: steady, deep, slightly stiff wing beats; usually flies relatively low and direct.

SIMILAR SPECIES

LEAST BITTERN
see p.96

black back

smaller overall

yellowish legs

BLACK-CROWNED NIGHT-HERON ◐
see p.97

white spots

thicker bill

LOOKING UP
Bitterns are secretive birds, but can occasionally be found walking slowly through reeds.

OCCURRENCE
Breeds in heavily vegetated freshwater wetlands across the northern US and southern Canada; also occasionally in estuarine wetlands; winters in southern and coastal wetlands where temperatures stay above freezing; can appear in any wetland habitat during migration.

| Length **23½–31in (60–80cm)** | Wingspan **3½–4¼ft (1.1–1.3m)** | Weight **13–20oz (375–575g)** |
| Social **Solitary** | Lifespan **At least 8 years** | Status **Declining** |

DATE SEEN	WHERE	NOTES

| Order **Ciconiiformes** | Family **Ardeidae** | Species *Ixobrychus exilis* |

Least Bittern

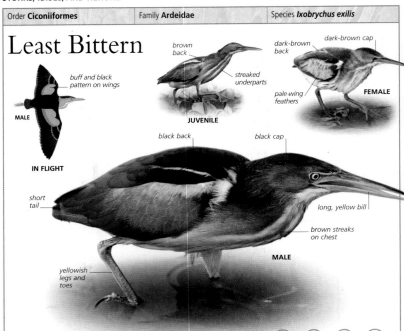

buff and black pattern on wings

MALE

IN FLIGHT

brown back

streaked underparts

JUVENILE

dark-brown back

dark-brown cap

pale-wing feathers

FEMALE

black back

black cap

short tail

long, yellow bill

brown streaks on chest

MALE

yellowish legs and toes

The smallest heron in North America, the Least Bittern is also one of the most colorful, but its secretive nature makes it easy to overlook in its densely vegetated marsh habitat. A dark color form, which was originally described in the 1800s as a separate species named Cory's Bittern, has rarely been reported in recent decades.

VOICE Soft *ku, ku, ku, ku, ku* display call; year-round, a loud *kak, kak, kak*.

NESTING Platform of marsh vegetation with sticks and stems added, usually within 30ft (9m) of open water; 2–7 eggs; 1 brood; April–August.

FEEDING Feeds on small fish, insects including dragonflies; also crustaceans; clings quietly to vegetation before striking prey, or stalks slowly.

FLIGHT: rapid wing beats; weak, direct flight; flies low, around top of vegetation.

OCCURRENCE
Breeds in summer in lowland freshwater marshes; less commonly in brackish and rarely in saltwater marshes; frequents similar habitat on migration; winters in brackish and saltwater marshes. Wide distribution in the Americas, south to Argentina.

SIMILAR SPECIES

AMERICAN BITTERN
see p.95

brown back

greenish legs

BLACK-CROWNED NIGHT-HERON ♂
see p.97

white spots

thicker bill

REED CREEPER
With its small, thin body, this species easily creeps through dense reeds in search of prey.

| Length **11–14in (28–36cm)** | Wingspan **15½–18in (40–46cm)** | Weight **2⅝–3³⁄₈oz (75–95g)** |
| Social **Solitary/Small flocks** | Lifespan **Unknown** | Status **Secure** |

DATE SEEN	WHERE	NOTES
....	....	....
....	....	....
....	....	....
....	....	....
....	....	....

| Order **Ciconiiformes** | Family **Ardeidae** | Species *Nycticorax nycticorax* |

Black-crowned Night-Heron

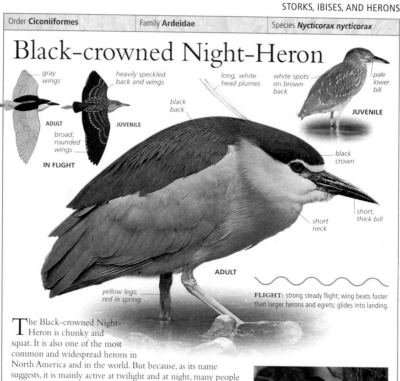

gray wings

heavily speckled back and wings

long, white head plumes

white spots on brown back

pale lower bill

JUVENILE

black back

ADULT

JUVENILE

broad, rounded wings

IN FLIGHT

black crown

short, thick bill

short neck

ADULT

yellow legs; red in spring

FLIGHT: strong steady flight; wing beats faster than larger herons and egrets; glides into landing.

The Black-crowned Night-Heron is chunky and squat. It is also one of the most common and widespread herons in North America and in the world. But because, as its name suggests, it is mainly active at twilight and at night, many people have never seen one. However, its distinctive barking call can be heard at night—even at the center of large cities.

VOICE Loud, distinctive *quark* or *wok*, often given in flight and around colonies.

NESTING Large stick nests built usually 20–40ft (6–12m) up in trees; 3–5 eggs; 1 brood; November–August.

FEEDING Feeds primarily on aquatic animals, such as fish, crustaceans, insects, and mollusks; also eggs and chicks of colonial birds, such as egrets, ibises, and terns.

LONG PLUMES
In breeding plumage, the plumes of the male of this species are longer than the female's.

SIMILAR SPECIES

YELLOW-CROWNED NIGHT-HERON see p.98 *gray neck*

GREEN HERON *rufous* smaller overall; *neck* see p.99

black-and-white head

thinner bill

OCCURRENCE
Widespread; can be found wherever there are waterbodies, such as lakes, ponds, streams; generally absent from higher elevations. Colonies often on islands or in marshes; colony sites may be used for decades. In winter, found in areas where water remains open.

| Length **23–26in (58–65cm)** | Wingspan **3½–4ft (1.1–1.2m)** | Weight **1½–2½lb (0.7–1kg)** |
| Social **Colonies** | Lifespan **Up to 21 years** | Status **Secure** |

DATE SEEN	WHERE	NOTES

| Order **Ciconiiformes** | Family **Ardeidae** | Species *Nyctanassa violacea* |

Yellow-crowned Night-Heron

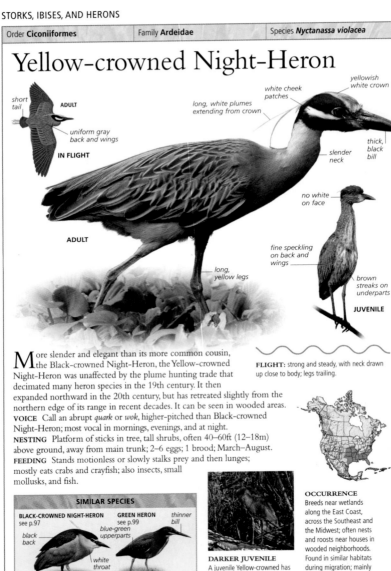

short tail

ADULT

uniform gray back and wings

IN FLIGHT

long, white plumes extending from crown

white cheek patches

yellowish white crown

thick, black bill

slender neck

ADULT

long, yellow legs

no white on face

fine speckling on back and wings

brown streaks on underparts

JUVENILE

More slender and elegant than its more common cousin, the Black-crowned Night-Heron, the Yellow-crowned Night-Heron was unaffected by the plume hunting trade that decimated many heron species in the 19th century. It then expanded northward in the 20th century, but has retreated slightly from the northern edge of its range in recent decades. It can be seen in wooded areas.

VOICE Call an abrupt *quark* or *wok*, higher-pitched than Black-crowned Night-Heron; most vocal in mornings, evenings, and at night.

NESTING Platform of sticks in tree, tall shrubs, often 40–60ft (12–18m) above ground, away from main trunk; 2–6 eggs; 1 brood; March–August.

FEEDING Stands motionless or slowly stalks prey and then lunges; mostly eats crabs and crayfish; also insects, small mollusks, and fish.

FLIGHT: strong and steady, with neck drawn up close to body; legs trailing.

SIMILAR SPECIES

BLACK-CROWNED NIGHT-HERON see p.97

black back

white throat

GREEN HERON see p.99

blue-green upperparts

thinner bill

DARKER JUVENILE
A juvenile Yellow-crowned has darker plumage than its Black-crowned counterpart.

OCCURRENCE
Breeds near wetlands along the East Coast, across the Southeast and the Midwest; often nests and roosts near houses in wooded neighborhoods. Found in similar habitats during migration; mainly coastal in winter.

| Length **19½–28in (50–70cm)** | Wingspan **3¼–3½ft (1–1.1m)** | Weight **23–28oz (650–800g)** |
| Social **Colonies** | Lifespan **At least 6 years** | Status **Secure (p)** |

DATE SEEN	WHERE	NOTES

| Order **Ciconiiformes** | Family **Ardeidae** | Species **Butorides virescens** |

Green Heron

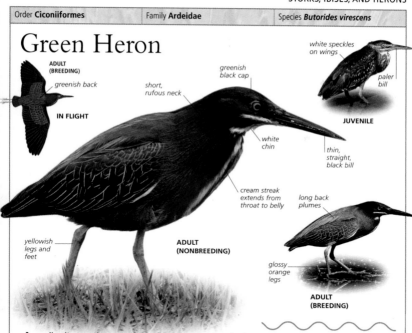

ADULT (BREEDING)

greenish back

IN FLIGHT

short, rufous neck

greenish black cap

white speckles on wings

paler bill

JUVENILE

white chin

thin, straight, black bill

cream streak extends from throat to belly

long back plumes

yellowish legs and feet

ADULT (NONBREEDING)

glossy orange legs

ADULT (BREEDING)

A small, solitary, and secretive bird of dense thicketed wetlands, the Green Heron can be difficult to observe. This dark, crested heron is most often seen flying away from a perceived threat, emitting a loud squawk. While the Green Heron of North and Central America has now been recognized as a separate species, it was earlier grouped with the Green-backed Heron (*B. striatus*), which is found in the tropics and subtropics throughout the world.

VOICE Squawking *keow* when flying from disturbance.
NESTING Nest of twigs often in bushes or trees, often over water but also on land; 1–2 broods; 3–5 eggs; March–July.
FEEDING Stands quietly on the shore or in shallow water and strikes quickly; mainly fish, but also frogs, insects, and spiders.

FLIGHT: direct, a bit plodding, and usually over short distances.

READY TO STRIKE
Green Herons usually catch their prey by lunging forward and downward with their whole body.

SIMILAR SPECIES

BLACK-CROWNED NIGHT-HERON ♂
see p.97

larger overall

YELLOW-CROWNED NIGHT-HERON ♂
see p.98

thicker bill

larger overall

OCCURRENCE
An inhabitant of swampy thickets, but occasionally dry land close to water across much of North America, but missing in the plains, the Rocky Mountains, and the western deserts that do not provide appropriate wetlands. Winters in coastal wetlands.

| Length **14½–15½in (37–39cm)** | Wingspan **25–27in (63–68cm)** | Weight **7–9oz (200–250g)** |
| Social **Solitary/Pairs/Small flocks** | Lifespan **Up to 10 years** | Status **Secure** |

DATE SEEN	WHERE	NOTES
....	....	....
....	....	....
....	....	....
....	....	....

| Order **Ciconiiformes** | Family **Ardeidae** | Species **Bubulcus ibis** |

Cattle Egret

rich buff on back

ADULT (BREEDING)

IN FLIGHT

all-white body

yellow bill

ADULT (NONBREEDING)

rich buff crown

yellow bill, reddish in spring

short neck

white body and wings

looks all-white in flight at long range

rich buff on breast in spring

dark legs and feet

ADULT (BREEDING)

ADULT (BREEDING)

yellow legs and feet

FLIGHT: flies with regular wing beats; neck crooked and legs extended.

Unlike most other herons, the Cattle Egret is a grassland species that rarely wades in water, and is most likely to be seen in association with livestock, feeding on the insects disturbed by their feet. It is thought to have originated in the shortgrass prairies of Africa and is now found worldwide. It was first seen in Florida in 1941, but expanded rapidly and has now bred in over 40 US states.

VOICE Generally silent; vocal at the nest: *rick-rack* common.
NESTING Nest of branches or plants placed in trees over ground; also in trees or shrubs over water; 2–5 eggs; 1 brood; March–October.
FEEDING Eats in groups, consumes insects, spiders as well as larger animals such as frogs; insects stirred up in grasslands by cattle.

VOCAL BREEDERS
This bird almost never calls away from a breeding colony, but is vocal near its nests.

SIMILAR SPECIES

GREAT EGRET see p.102

long bill

much larger

black legs and toes

SNOWY EGRET see p.106

black bill

yellow toes

OCCURRENCE
Since the 1940s, it has expanded to many habitats in much of North America, primarily in grasslands and prairies, but also wetland areas. In tropical regions, the Cattle Egrets flock around the cattle feeding in shallow wetlands.

| Length **20in (51cm)** | Wingspan **31in (78cm)** | Weight **13oz (375g)** |
| Social **Colonies** | Lifespan **Up to 17 years** | Status **Secure** |

DATE SEEN	WHERE	NOTES

Order **Ciconiiformes**	Family **Ardeidae**	Species ***Ardea herodias***

Great Blue Heron

dark wing tips

dark tail

brownish body

white face

dark bill

gray neck

ADULT

yellowish bill

crooked neck

JUVENILE

blue-gray body

IN FLIGHT

lighter-colored neck, almost beige

light bill

large, white bird

overall similar to Great Blue

shaggy plumes

light legs

WURDEMANN'S HERON (WHITE-HEADED FORM)

MALE

dark legs

GREAT WHITE HERON (WHITE FORM)

FLIGHT: deep-flapping, regular wing beats.

This is one of the three largest herons in the world—the Great Blue in North America, the Gray in Eurasia, and the Cocoi in South America—all of which are all interrelated, but classified separately. The Great Blue Heron is a common inhabitant of a variety of North American waterbodies, from marshes to swamps, as well as along sea coasts. Its majestic, deliberate flight is a highly wonderful sight to behold.
VOICE Mostly silent; gives a loud, barking squawk or *crank* in breeding colonies or when disturbed.
NESTING Nest of twigs and branches; usually in colonies, but also singly; in trees, often over water, but also over ground; 2–4 eggs; 1–2 broods; February–August.
FEEDING Catches prey with quick jab of bill; primarily fish.

LOFTY ABODE
Great Blue Herons nest in small colonies in trees, and often roost in them.

SIMILAR SPECIES

TRICOLORED HERON
see p.104
smaller overall

dark bill

white underparts

LITTLE BLUE HERON
smaller overall; see p.105

greenish legs

darker overall

OCCURRENCE
Across southern Canada and the US in wetlands, such as marshes, lake edges, and along rivers and swamps; also in marine habitats, especially tidal grass flats. The Great White Heron is common in mangroves in the Florida Keys; also West Indies and Yucatán.

Length **2¾–4¼ft (0.9–1.3m)**	Wingspan **5¼–6½ft (1.6–2m)**	Weight **4¾–5½lb (2.1–2.5kg)**
Social **Solitary/Flocks**	Lifespan **Up to 20 years**	Status **Secure**

DATE SEEN	WHERE	NOTES

Order **Ciconiiformes**	Family **Ardeidae**	Species **Ardea alba**

Great Egret

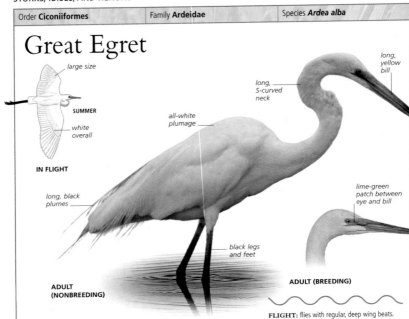

large size

SUMMER

white overall

IN FLIGHT

long, black plumes

long, yellow bill

long, S-curved neck

all-white plumage

lime-green patch between eye and bill

black legs and feet

ADULT (NONBREEDING)

ADULT (BREEDING)

FLIGHT: flies with regular, deep wing beats.

This large white heron is found on every continent except Antarctica. When feeding, the Great Egret would apparently rather forage alone than in flocks—it maintains space around itself, and will defend a territory of 10ft (3m) in diameter from other wading birds. This territory "moves" with the bird as it feeds. In years of scarce food supplies, a chick may kill a sibling, permitting the survival of at least one bird.

VOICE Largely vocal during courtship and breeding; otherwise, *kraak* or *cuk-cuk-cuk* when disturbed or in a combative encounter.
NESTING Nest of twigs in trees, over land or water; 2–4 eggs; 1 brood; March–July.
FEEDING Catches prey with quick thrust of bill; feeds on aquatic prey, primarily fish, also crustaceans.

TREE PERCHES
Great Egrets nest in trees and regularly perch in them when not feeding.

SIMILAR SPECIES

LITTLE BLUE HERON ♀
see p.105

smaller overall

two-toned bill

yellow-green legs

SNOWY EGRET
black bill;
see p.106

smaller overall

yellow feet

OCCURRENCE
Breeds in trees over water or on islands; forages in almost all types of freshwater and marine wetlands from marshes and ponds to rivers. Migratory over much of its North American range; more southerly populations resident. Distance migrated depends on severity of winter.

Length **3¼ft (1m)**	Wingspan **6ft (1.8m)**	Weight **1¾–3¼ft (0.8–1.5kg)**
Social **Solitary**	Lifespan **Up to 25 years**	Status **Secure**

DATE SEEN	WHERE	NOTES

| Order **Ciconiiformes** | Family **Ardeidae** | Species ***Egretta rufescens*** |

Reddish Egret

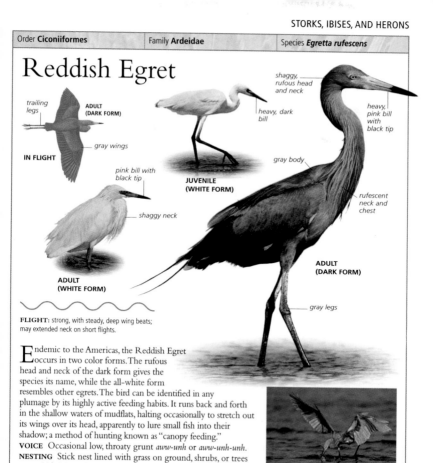

trailing legs

ADULT (DARK FORM)

IN FLIGHT

gray wings

shaggy, rufous head and neck

heavy, dark bill

heavy, pink bill with black tip

gray body

rufescent neck and chest

pink bill with black tip

JUVENILE (WHITE FORM)

shaggy neck

ADULT (DARK FORM)

ADULT (WHITE FORM)

gray legs

FLIGHT: strong, with steady, deep wing beats; may extended neck on short flights.

Endemic to the Americas, the Reddish Egret occurs in two color forms. The rufous head and neck of the dark form gives the species its name, while the all-white form resembles other egrets. The bird can be identified in any plumage by its highly active feeding habits. It runs back and forth in the shallow waters of mudflats, halting occasionally to stretch out its wings over its head, apparently to lure small fish into their shadow; a method of hunting known as "canopy feeding."

VOICE Occasional low, throaty grunt *aww-unh* or *aww-unh-unh*.

NESTING Stick nest lined with grass on ground, shrubs, or trees up to 30ft (10m) above ground, in colonies with other herons; 3–4 eggs; 1 brood; March–September.

FEEDING Almost exclusively eats small fish.

FISHING WITH OPEN WINGS
The Reddish Egret pounces on small fish with outspread wings when "canopy feeding."

SIMILAR SPECIES

TRICOLORED HERON see p.104

white line on throat

white belly

LITTLE BLUE HERON see p.105

bluish bill

greenish legs

OCCURRENCE
Found year-round in coastal lagoons, mudflats, and keys around Florida and the Gulf Coast; mostly nonmigratory; sometimes seen in southern California in winter; vagrants and post-breeders seen inland and north along the Atlantic coast. Breeds in Mexico, the West Indies, south to Belize.

| Length **26–32in (66–81cm)** | Wingspan **3½–4ft (1.1–1.2m)** | Weight **25–30oz (700–850g)** |
| Social **Colonies** | Lifespan **Up to 12 years** | Status **Localized** |

DATE SEEN	WHERE	NOTES
....	....	....
....	....	....
....	....	....
....	....	....

Order **Ciconiformes**	Family **Ardeidae**	Species *Egretta tricolor*

Tricolored Heron

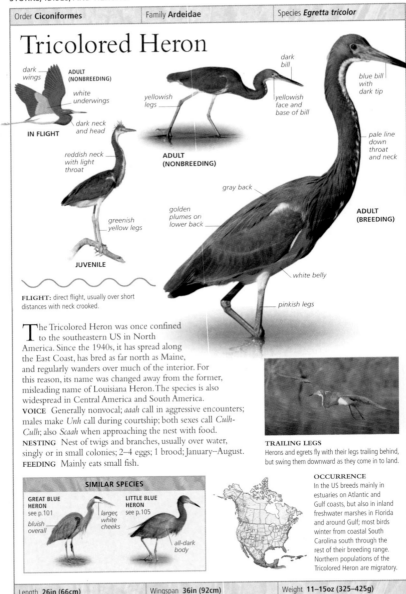

dark wings

ADULT (NONBREEDING)

white underwings

dark neck and head

IN FLIGHT

dark bill

yellowish legs

blue bill with dark tip

yellowish face and base of bill

ADULT (NONBREEDING)

reddish neck with light throat

pale line down throat and neck

gray back

golden plumes on lower back

greenish yellow legs

JUVENILE

ADULT (BREEDING)

white belly

FLIGHT: direct flight, usually over short distances with neck crooked.

pinkish legs

The Tricolored Heron was once confined to the southeastern US in North America. Since the 1940s, it has spread along the East Coast, has bred as far north as Maine, and regularly wanders over much of the interior. For this reason, its name was changed away from the former, misleading name of Louisiana Heron. The species is also widespread in Central America and South America.

VOICE Generally nonvocal; *aaah* call in aggressive encounters; males make *Unh* call during courtship; both sexes call *Culh-Culh*; also *Scaah* when approaching the nest with food.

NESTING Nest of twigs and branches, usually over water, singly or in small colonies; 2–4 eggs; 1 brood; January–August.

FEEDING Mainly eats small fish.

TRAILING LEGS

Herons and egrets fly with their legs trailing behind, but swing them downward as they come in to land.

SIMILAR SPECIES

GREAT BLUE HERON see p.101

bluish overall

larger, white cheeks

LITTLE BLUE HERON see p.105

all-dark body

OCCURRENCE

In the US breeds mainly in estuaries on Atlantic and Gulf coasts, but also in inland freshwater marshes in Florida and around Gulf; most birds winter from coastal South Carolina south through the rest of their breeding range. Northern populations of the Tricolored Heron are migratory.

Length **26in (66cm)**	Wingspan **36in (92cm)**	Weight **11–15oz (325–425g)**
Social **Solitary**	Lifespan **Up to 20 years**	Status **Secure**

DATE SEEN	WHERE	NOTES

| Order **Ciconiiformes** | Family **Ardeidae** | Species *Egretta caerulea* |

Little Blue Heron

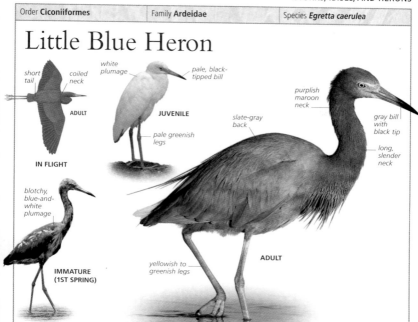

short tail

coiled neck

ADULT

white plumage

pale, black-tipped bill

JUVENILE

pale greenish legs

purplish maroon neck

slate-gray back

gray bill with black tip

long, slender neck

IN FLIGHT

blotchy, blue-and-white plumage

IMMATURE (1ST SPRING)

yellowish to greenish legs

ADULT

The shy and retreating Little Blue Heron is often overlooked because of its blue-gray color and secretive eating habits. First-year birds, which may be mistaken for Snowy Egrets, are white, and gradually acquire blue-gray, mottled feathers before eventually molting into their all-dark adult plumage. Immature birds are seen feeding together in open wetlands while adults feed alone in denser habitats, such as swamps and thick wetlands.

VOICE Vocal during courtship; generally silent.
NESTING Uses sticks and twigs, in trees or reeds, in wetlands or terrestrial habitats nearby; 2–4 eggs; 1 brood; April–September.
FEEDING Eats small fish, amphibians, crustaceans, and insects; stalks its prey, wading slowly in shallow waters or along the water's edge.

FLIGHT: deep and continuous wing beats; glides when descending and landing.

UNIQUE TRANSFORMATION
No other heron species undergoes such a complete change from an all-white juvenile to all-dark adult.

SIMILAR SPECIES

GREAT BLUE HERON see p.101

larger body

TRICOLORED HERON see p.104

white on face and crown

paler neck

white belly

OCCURRENCE
Breeds across much of southeast US in various wetlands, such as swamps, marshes, lakes, streams, rivers, and flooded fields, as well as estuarine and marine habitats, such as lagoons and tidal flats. Winters in similar habitat from southern California to Mexico and Central America.

| Length **24in (61cm)** | Wingspan **3ft 3in (100cm)** | Weight **11–13oz (325–375g)** |
| Social **Solitary** | Lifespan **10–20 years** | Status **Secure** |

DATE SEEN	WHERE	NOTES

Order **Ciconiiformes**	Family **Ardeidae**	Species *Egretta thula*

Snowy Egret

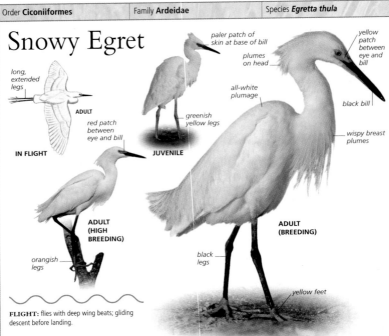

long, extended legs

ADULT

IN FLIGHT

red patch between eye and bill

paler patch of skin at base of bill

plumes on head

all-white plumage

greenish yellow legs

JUVENILE

yellow patch between eye and bill

black bill

wispy breast plumes

ADULT (HIGH BREEDING)

orangish legs

black legs

ADULT (BREEDING)

yellow feet

FLIGHT: flies with deep wing beats; gliding descent before landing.

A New World species, the Snowy Egret is similar to the Little Egret. It is very adaptable in estuarine and freshwater habitats. When foraging, it uses a wide variety of behaviors, including wing-flicking, foot-stirring, and foot-probing to get its prey moving, making it easier to capture.

VOICE High-pitched *Aargaarg* when flushed; low-pitched *Arg* and *Raah* aggressive calls; *Aarg* call during attacks and pursuits.

NESTING Small sticks, branches, and rushes over water or on land; also on ground, in shrubs, mangroves, and other trees; 3–5 eggs; 1 brood; March–August.

FEEDING Feeds on aquatic prey, from invertebrates, such as insects, shrimp, and prawns, to small fish, amphibians, and snakes.

WIDESPREAD SPECIES
Snowy Egrets feed in a wide variety of wetland habitats, using different foraging techniques.

SIMILAR SPECIES

GREAT EGRET see p.102

LITTLE BLUE HERON ♀ see p.105

yellow bill

black legs and feet

black legs and feet

OCCURRENCE
Found in a wide variety of wetlands throughout North America: from mangroves in Florida to marshlands in New England and the western US. Highly adaptable and widely found. Sites of breeding colonies may change from year to year within a set range.

Length **24in (62cm)**	Wingspan **3½ft (1.1m)**	Weight **12oz (350g)**
Social **Solitary**	Lifespan **Up to 22 years**	Status **Secure**

DATE SEEN	WHERE	NOTES

PELICANS & RELATIVES

PELICANS AND THEIR relatives belong to an order of large to huge fish-eating birds, Pelecaniformes, with four toes connected by leathery webs, and with fleshy, elastic pouches beneath their bills.

PELICANS

The pelican family includes seven large species, two of which—the American White Pelican and the Brown Pelican—breed in North America. All pelicans are buoyant swimmers and excellent fliers, capable of great lift on their long, broad wings with wing feathers spread. Flocks can be seen soaring to great heights on migration and when flying to feeding grounds. Pelicans feed by sweeping with open bills for fish, often cooperatively, or by plunging from a height to scoop up fish and water in their large, flexible bill pouches.

CORMORANTS

With 36 species worldwide, these are medium to large waterbirds, some marine, others freshwater, with broad, long wings, rounded tails, short, strong legs and hook-tipped bills often tilted upward when swimming. In flight, the

neck is extended and noticeably kinked. When hunting for fish, cormorants dive from the surface of the water, rolling smoothly

WING SPREADING
For this Neotropic Cormorant grooming includes spreading its wings to dry them in the sun. Neotropic Cormorants are rare in the East.

under or with a forward leap, and then swim underwater with closed wings, using their webbed toes for propulsion. Most are dark birds, apart from distinctive facial patterns on areas of bare skin which become more colorful in early spring. Most cormorants nest on cliff ledges, others use both cliffs and trees. There is one flightless and highly endangered cormorant species in the Galápagos Islands.

WATER BIRD
Webbed feet help Brown Pelicans negotiate water with ease, while strong wings allow easy takeoffs.

Order **Pelecaniformes**	Family **Fregatidae**	Species **Fregata magnificens**

Magnificent Frigatebird

long dark wings

JUVENILE

dark head

white on head

very powerful, long, hooked bill

variable white underparts

FEMALE

exceedingly long wings

red throat pouch

deeply forked tail

MALE

IN FLIGHT

glossy black plumage

MALE

FLIGHT: powerful but effortless soaring, alternating with fluid twists and turns.

One of North America's most skilled aerialists, the Magnificent Frigatebird is not seen perched except when nesting in mangroves or roosting on buoys. It is usually seen flying gracefully above bays, lagoons, or open ocean, but it never alights on the water's surface. Identifying the different species of frigatebirds is exceedingly difficult, but only the Magnificent Frigatebird occurs regularly in North American waters. This species is well known for its in-flight piracy and aggressive behavior. It will pursue birds of its own species and others, especially boobies in the tropics, stealing food from their bills.

VOICE Male call consists of whirring, rattling, and drumming sounds.

NESTING Flat or shallow depression in platform of twigs; 1 egg; 1 brood; November–May.

FEEDING Plucks small fish from water's surface, never wetting itself; regularly steals food from other birds.

long tail

INFLATED POUCH
Breeding males display their gaudy, flapping throat pouches by inflating them.

OCCURRENCE
Breeds mainly in coastal mangroves, but in North America, frigatebirds are usually seen away from nest sites, flying high in the sky over open water. Sometimes found well north of its usual Florida and Gulf Coast range, especially after hurricanes, and a few wander inland every year.

SIMILAR SPECIES

ANHINGA ♂
square-tipped, broader tail; see p.114

much longer neck

shorter wings

ANHINGA ♀
see p.114

silvery gray markings

pale front

Length **3ft 3in (100cm)**	Wingspan **7½ft (2.3m)**	Weight **39–60oz (1.1–1.7kg)**
Social **Colonies**	Lifespan **Up to 30 years**	Status **Secure**

DATE SEEN	WHERE	NOTES

Order **Pelecaniformes**	Family **Pelecanidae**	Species *Pelecanus erythrorhynchos*

American White Pelican

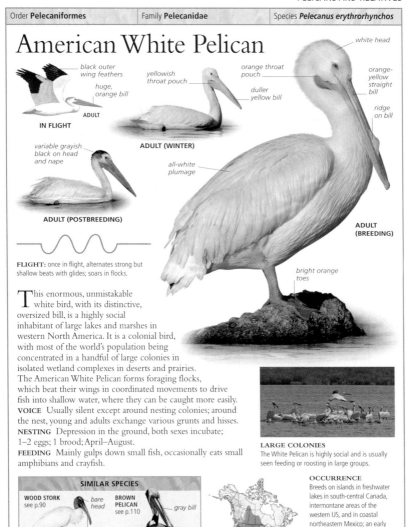

white head

orange-yellow straight bill

ridge on bill

orange throat pouch

black outer wing feathers

yellowish throat pouch

huge, orange bill

duller yellow bill

ADULT

IN FLIGHT

ADULT (WINTER)

variable grayish black on head and nape

all-white plumage

ADULT (POSTBREEDING)

ADULT (BREEDING)

bright orange toes

FLIGHT: once in flight, alternates strong but shallow beats with glides; soars in flocks.

This enormous, unmistakable white bird, with its distinctive, oversized bill, is a highly social inhabitant of large lakes and marshes in western North America. It is a colonial bird, with most of the world's population being concentrated in a handful of large colonies in isolated wetland complexes in deserts and prairies. The American White Pelican forms foraging flocks, which beat their wings in coordinated movements to drive fish into shallow water, where they can be caught more easily.
VOICE Usually silent except around nesting colonies; around the nest, young and adults exchange various grunts and hisses.
NESTING Depression in the ground, both sexes incubate; 1–2 eggs; 1 brood; April–August.
FEEDING Mainly gulps down small fish, occasionally eats small amphibians and crayfish.

LARGE COLONIES
The White Pelican is highly social and is usually seen feeding or roosting in large groups.

SIMILAR SPECIES

WOOD STORK see p.90
bare head
long thin legs

BROWN PELICAN see p.110
gray bill
curved bill
dark underparts

OCCURRENCE
Breeds on islands in freshwater lakes in south-central Canada, intermontane areas of the western US, and in coastal northeastern Mexico; an early spring migrant, often returning to breeding grounds in early March. Winters in coastal regions from California and Texas to Mexico and Central America.

Length **4¼–5½ft (1.3–1.7m)**	Wingspan **7¾–9½ft (2.4–2.9m)**	Weight **12–20lb (5.5–9kg)**
Social **Colonies**	Lifespan **Up to 26 years**	Status **Vulnerable**

DATE SEEN	WHERE	NOTES

| Order **Pelecaniformes** | Family **Pelecanidae** | Species ***Pelecanus occidentalis*** |

Brown Pelican

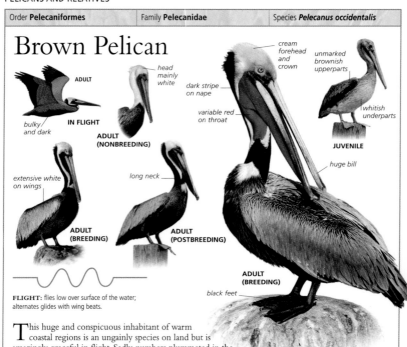

ADULT

bulky and dark — **IN FLIGHT**

head mainly white

ADULT (NONBREEDING)

cream forehead and crown

dark stripe on nape

variable red on throat

unmarked brownish upperparts

whitish underparts

JUVENILE

huge bill

extensive white on wings

ADULT (BREEDING)

long neck

ADULT (POSTBREEDING)

ADULT (BREEDING)

black feet

FLIGHT: flies low over surface of the water; alternates glides with wing beats.

This huge and conspicuous inhabitant of warm coastal regions is an ungainly species on land but is amazingly graceful in flight. Sadly, numbers plummeted in the 1960s when DDT was used widely as a pesticide, but it rapidly recovered in recent decades, and is now expanding its range northward along both coasts. The color of its throat varies according to geographic location and time of year.

VOICE Silent most of the time; vocal at nest colonies; adults and juveniles communicate with grunts and hisses; courting birds give a strange, deliberate *heart-hark*, repeated slowly.

NESTING Pile of debris, usually on ground; 2–3 eggs; 1 brood; February–August.

FEEDING Adults plunge headfirst into water to scoop up fish near the surface; does not herd fish, like the American White Pelican.

RESTING TOGETHER
Brown Pelicans are social most of the year, and can often be seen roosting in groups.

SIMILAR SPECIES

BLACK-FOOTED ALBATROSS
short bill
long, pointed wings

AMERICAN WHITE PELICAN
see p.109
orange bill
white plumage

OCCURRENCE
Found in and around warm coastal waters, flying above the water's surface over the cresting waves; small numbers breed in the interior US; individuals and small flocks can be found around docks and marinas.

| Length **4–4¼ft (1.2–1.3m)** | Wingspan **6½–7ft (2–2.1m)** | Weight **4–8¾lb (1.8–4kg)** |
| Social **Colonies** | Lifespan **Up to 10 years** | Status **Secure** |

DATE SEEN	WHERE	NOTES

| Order **Pelecaniformes** | Family **Sulidae** | Species *Morus bassanus* |

Northern Gannet

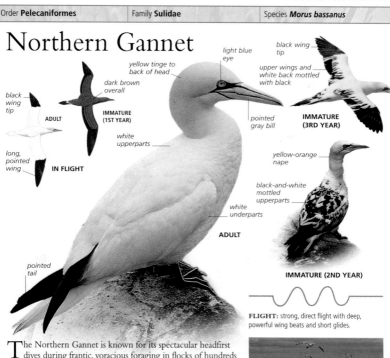

black wing tip

ADULT

yellow tinge to back of head

dark brown overall

IMMATURE (1ST YEAR)

white upperparts

long, pointed wing

IN FLIGHT

light blue eye

black wing tip

upper wings and white back mottled with black

IMMATURE (3RD YEAR)

pointed gray bill

yellow-orange nape

black-and-white mottled upperparts

white underparts

ADULT

pointed tail

white upperparts

IMMATURE (2ND YEAR)

FLIGHT: strong, direct flight with deep, powerful wing beats and short glides.

The Northern Gannet is known for its spectacular headfirst dives during frantic, voracious foraging in flocks of hundreds to thousands for surface-schooling fish. This bird nests in just six locations in northeastern Canada. The Northern Gannet was the first species to have its total world population estimated, at 83,000 birds in 1939. Numbers have since increased.

VOICE Loud landing call by both sexes *arrrr, arrah,* or *urrah rah rah*; hollow groan *oh-ah* uttered during take-off; *krok* call at sea.

NESTING Large pile of mud, seaweed, and rubbish, glued with guano, on bare rock or soil; 1 egg; 1 brood; April–November.

FEEDING Plunge-dives headfirst into water and often swims underwater to catch fish; eats mackerel, herring, capelin, and cod.

NESTING SITE
Northern Gannets prefer to nest in huge, noisy colonies on isolated rocky slopes or cliffs.

SIMILAR SPECIES		
LAYSAN ALBATROSS	**MASKED BOOBY** see p.471	black "mask"
more rounded tail	pinkish bill	yellow bill
white underwing with black patches	long, pointed wings	black inner wing feathers

OCCURRENCE
Breeds on isolated rock stacks, on small uninhabited islands in the eastern North Atlantic, or on steep, inaccessible cliffs in marine areas of northeastern North America; during migration and in winter, occurs in the waters of the continental shelf of the Gulf and Atlantic coast.

| Length 2¾–3½ft (0.8–1.1m) | Wingspan 5½ft (1.7m) | Weight 5–8lb (2.2–3.6kg) |
| Social **Flocks** | Lifespan **Up to 20 years** | Status **Localized** |

DATE SEEN	WHERE		NOTES

Order **Pelecaniformes**	Family **Phalacrocoracidae**	Species *Phalacrocorax auritus*

Double-crested Cormorant

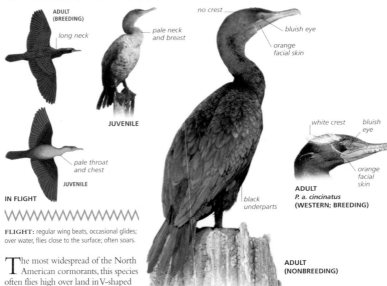

ADULT (BREEDING)

long neck

JUVENILE

pale neck and breast

no crest

bluish eye

orange facial skin

JUVENILE

pale throat and chest

IN FLIGHT

FLIGHT: regular wing beats, occasional glides; over water, flies close to the surface; often soars.

white crest

bluish eye

orange facial skin

ADULT
P. a. cincinatus
(WESTERN; BREEDING)

black underparts

ADULT (NONBREEDING)

The most widespread of the North American cormorants, this species often flies high over land in V-shaped flocks, but is mostly seen swimming with its head and neck visible, or resting on trees and rocks, sometimes with its wings spread. It dives from the surface of the water and chases fish underwater. using its webbed toes for propulsion.

VOICE Deep gruntlike calls while nesting, roosting, and fishing; *t-t-t-t* call before taking off and *urg-urg-urg* before landing; prolonged *arr-r-r-r-t-t* while mating, and *eh-hr* as threat.

NESTING Nests of twigs and sticks, seaweed, and trash, lined with grass; on ground, cliffs, or in trees; 3–5 eggs; 1 brood; April–August.

FEEDING Pursues slow-moving or schooling fish; feeds on insects, crustaceans, amphibians, and, rarely, on voles and snakes.

DRYING OFF
Like all cormorants, the Double-crested usually perches with wings spread, to dry its feathers.

SIMILAR SPECIES

BRANDT'S CORMORANT

throat pouch paler and less visible

NEOTROPIC CORMORANT
see p.447

shorter body

longer tail

OCCURRENCE
Breeds in a wide range of aquatic habitats, including ponds, artificial and natural lakes, slow-moving rivers, estuaries, lagoons, and seashores; winters on coastlines and sandbars in coastal inlets; roosts near catfish farms in some areas.

Length **28–35in (70–90cm)**	Wingspan **3½–4ft (1.1–1.2m)**	Weight **2¾–5½lb (1.2–2.5kg)**
Social **Flocks**	Lifespan **Up to 18 years**	Status **Secure**

DATE SEEN	WHERE	NOTES

| Order **Pelecaniformes** | Family **Phalacrocoracidae** | Species *Phalacrocorax carbo* |

Great Cormorant

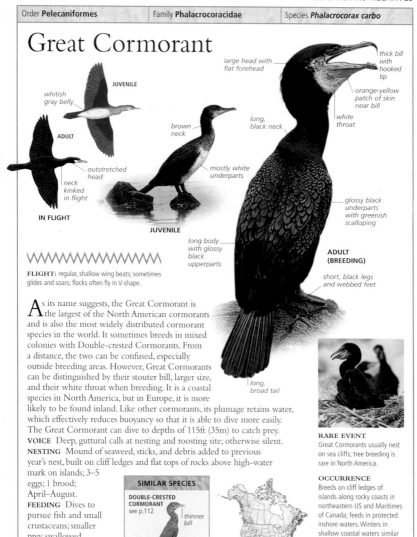

JUVENILE

whitish
gray belly

ADULT

large head with
flat forehead

thick bill
with
hooked
tip

orange-yellow
patch of skin
near bill

white
throat

brown
neck

long,
black neck

mostly white
underparts

outstretched
head

neck
kinked
in flight

IN FLIGHT

JUVENILE

long body
with glossy
black
upperparts

glossy black
underparts
with greenish
scalloping

**ADULT
(BREEDING)**

short, black legs
and webbed feet

long,
broad tail

FLIGHT: regular, shallow wing beats; sometimes
glides and soars; flocks often fly in V-shape.

As its name suggests, the Great Cormorant is
the largest of the North American cormorants
and is also the most widely distributed cormorant
species in the world. It sometimes breeds in mixed
colonies with Double-crested Cormorants. From
a distance, the two can be confused, especially
outside breeding areas. However, Great Cormorants
can be distinguished by their stouter bill, larger size,
and their white throat when breeding. It is a coastal
species in North America, but in Europe, it is more
likely to be found inland. Like other cormorants, its plumage retains water,
which effectively reduces buoyancy so that it is able to dive more easily.
The Great Cormorant can dive to depths of 115ft (35m) to catch prey.
VOICE Deep, guttural calls at nesting and roosting site; otherwise silent.
NESTING Mound of seaweed, sticks, and debris added to previous
year's nest, built on cliff ledges and flat tops of rocks above high-water
mark on islands; 3–5
eggs; 1 brood;
April–August.
FEEDING Dives to
pursue fish and small
crustaceans; smaller
prey swallowed
underwater, while
larger prey brought
to surface.

RARE EVENT
Great Cormorants usually nest
on sea cliffs; tree breeding is
rare in North America.

OCCURRENCE
Breeds on cliff ledges of
islands along rocky coasts in
northeastern US and Maritimes
of Canada; feeds in protected
inshore waters. Winters in
shallow coastal waters similar
to breeding habitat, but not
restricted to rocky shoreline;
winter habitat extends to
the Carolinas in the US.

SIMILAR SPECIES

**DOUBLE-CRESTED
CORMORANT**
see p.112

thinner
bill

see p.112

| Length **33–35in (84–90cm)** | Wingspan **4¼–5¼ft (1.3–1.6m)** | Weight **5¾–8¼lb (2.6–3.7kg)** |
| Social **Colonies** | Lifespan **Up to 14 years** | Status **Secure** |

DATE SEEN	WHERE	NOTES

Order **Pelecaniformes**	Family **Anhingidae**	Species *Anhinga anhinga*

Anhinga

FEMALE

dark brown overall

long neck

brown plumes on small, pointed head

dagger-like bill

JUVENILE

blotchy, silver-white markings on upperparts

pale tan neck and head

dark underwings

IN FLIGHT

long tail

MALE

black underparts

long tail with horizontal ridges

variable white upperparts

pale tan breast and neck

FEMALE

This resident of the Southeast coastal plain, locally called "Water Turkey," may be found swimming in murky swamps, roosting on tall trees, or soaring high overhead. The Anhinga is also known as the "snake bird"—a reference to its habit of swimming with its body immersed so deeply that only its long, thin, sinuous neck, pointed head, and sharp bill stick out above the water. Although they superficially resemble cormorants, the two species of Anhingas differ in many ways—particularly their long tails with unusual horizontal ridges.

VOICE Silent most of the time, but pairs may give various calls around nest; these vocalizations consist of soft rattles and trills, but are sometimes quite noisy, repeated *Krah-Krah*.

NESTING Loose platform of sticks in trees above water; 3–5 eggs; 1 brood; February–June.

FEEDING Jabs suddenly with its dagger-like bill, mostly for fish in calm freshwater habitats; also eats insects and shrimp.

FLIGHT: strong flier; neck and tail outstretched and wings held flat; often soars.

HANGING OUT TO DRY
Anhingas do not have waterproof plumage and so spend a lot of time drying off their wings.

SIMILAR SPECIES

DOUBLE-CRESTED CORMORANT
see p.112

hooked bill

shorter tail

DOUBLE-CRESTED CORMORANT ♂
see p.112

dark upperwings

shorter tail

OCCURRENCE
An inhabitant of southeastern wetlands south all the way to Argentina. Greatest concentrations in wooded wetlands, calm waters in swamps; often also seen in habitats far from open water. The second species occurs in the Old World tropics.

Length **35in (89cm)**	Wingspan **3½ft (1.1m)**	Weight **2¾lb (1.3kg)**
Social **Colonies**	Lifespan **Up to 10 years**	Status **Secure**

DATE SEEN	WHERE	NOTES

BIRDS OF PREY

THE DEFINING FEATURES of birds of prey, or raptors, are strong feet with sharp talons for catching and holding prey, and a powerful, hooked bill for tearing the catch to pieces. Vultures eat carrion not live prey.

VULTURES

Of the seven New World species of vulture, three occur in North America: the Black Vulture, the Turkey Vulture, which has an acute sense of smell that enables it to detect carrion hidden from sight

WEAK TOOL
In spite of its sharp beak, the Turkey Vulture cannot always break the skin of carcasses.

beneath the forest canopy, and the rare California Condor, the continent's largest soaring land bird. All three can stay in the air for hours on end, using the lift provided by updrafts to minimize the energy spent on wing flapping.

FALCONS

Ranging in size from the diminutive American Merlin, with northern breeding habitats, to the large, powerful Gyrfalcon, which nests in the Arctic, this group also includes the Kestrel, the Prairie Falcon, and perhaps the best-known raptor of all—the fast-diving Peregrine Falcon. Falcon prey ranges from insects to large mammals and birds.

EAGLES AND HAWKS

This group covers a wide range of raptors of varying sizes, from the the iconic Bald Eagle and the majestic Golden Eagle to smaller birds, such as the Northern Harrier, and various hawks and kites. These birds use a wide range of hunting methods. For example, forest-dwelling hawks rely on speed and stealth to pounce on small birds among the trees in a sudden, short dash. By contrast, the Osprey hovers over water until it sees a fish below, then dives steeply, pulling up at the last moment to pluck its prey clean out of the water with its talons.

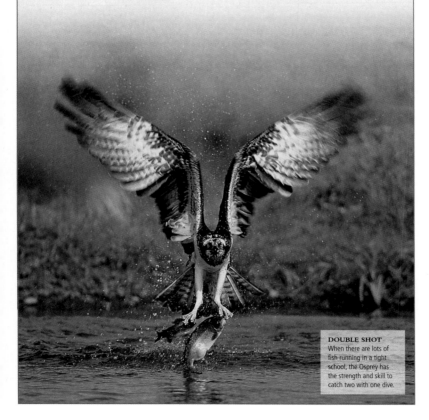

DOUBLE SHOT
When there are lots of fish running in a tight school, the Osprey has the strength and skill to catch two with one dive.

Order **Falconiformes**	Family **Cathartidae**	Species **Cathartes aura**

Turkey Vulture

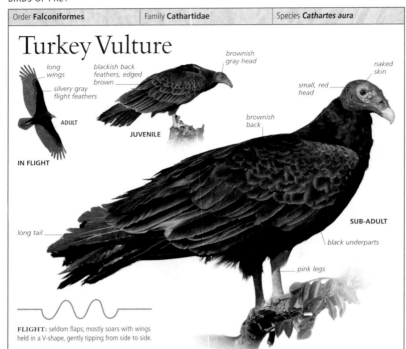

long wings

silvery gray flight feathers

ADULT

blackish back feathers, edged brown

JUVENILE

IN FLIGHT

long tail

brownish gray head

small, red head

naked skin

brownish back

SUB-ADULT

black underparts

pink legs

FLIGHT: seldom flaps; mostly soars with wings held in a V-shape, gently tipping from side to side.

The most widely distributed vulture in North America, the Turkey Vulture is found in most of the US and has expanded its range into southern Canada. It possesses a better sense of smell than the Black Vulture, which often follows it and displaces it from carcasses. The Turkey Vulture's habit of defecating down its legs, which it shares with the Wood Stork, may serve to cool it or to kill bacteria with its ammonia content.

VOICE Silent, but will hiss at intruders; also grunts.

NESTING Dark recesses, such as under large rocks or stumps, on rocky ledges in caves, and crevices, in mammal burrows and hollow logs, and abandoned buildings; 1–3 eggs; 1 brood; March–August.

FEEDING Feeds on a wide range of wild and domestic carrion, mostly mammals, also birds, reptiles, amphibians, and fish; occasionally takes live prey such as nestlings or trapped birds.

SOAKING UP THE SUN
Turkey Vultures often spread their wings to sun themselves and increase their body temperature.

SIMILAR SPECIES

BLACK VULTURE
see p.117

shorter tail

all-black body

OCCURRENCE
Generally forages and migrates over mixed farmland and forest; prefers to nest in forested or partly forested hillsides offering hidden ground protected from disturbance; roosts in large trees such as cottonwoods, on rocky outcrops, and on power line transmission towers; some winter in urban areas and near landfills.

Length **25–32in (64–81cm)**	Wingspan **5½–6ft (1.7–1.8m)**	Weight **4½lb (2kg)**
Social **Flocks**	Lifespan **At least 17 years**	Status **Secure**

DATE SEEN	WHERE	NOTES

| Order **Falconiformes** | Family **Cathartidae** | Species **Coragyps atratus** |

Black Vulture

naked, wrinkled, gray skin

silvery white patch on wing

ADULT

yellowish tip of bill

broad wings, spread at roost

IN FLIGHT

short, rounded tail

ADULT

black upperparts

black underparts

ADULT

long, grayish legs and feet

FLIGHT: rapid wing beats followed by glides on flat wings; soars using rising air currents.

Common in the southern and eastern states, the Black Vulture is often seen in large communal roosts in the evening. Communal roosts act as meeting places for adults and young, and possibly serve as information centers, where food locations are communicated. Maintaining long pair-bonds, Black Vultures remain together year-round. According to one study, parents will continue to feed their young for as long as eight months after fledging. When not feeding on roadkills along highways, Black Vultures spend time soaring above the landscape, in search of carrion.

VOICE Usually silent; hisses and barks occasionally.
NESTING No nest; lays eggs on ground in thickets or under stumps, in piles of rocks, seldom in old buildings; 2 eggs; 1 brood; January–August.
FEEDING Generally eats carrion (mostly large mammals) on the ground; also consumes live prey.

SIMILAR SPECIES

TURKEY VULTURE see p.116
red head
long tail

TURKEY VULTURE ♂ see p.116
brownish head
brownish body

DOMINANT SCAVENGER
The more aggressive Black Vultures often displace the Turkey Vultures at carcasses.

OCCURRENCE
Breeds in dense woodlands, caves, old buildings; forms roosts in stands of tall trees; forages in open habitats and near roads and highways; year-round resident throughout its range in southern and eastern states. Range expanding in the northeastern US.

| Length **24–27in (61–68cm)** | Wingspan **4½–5ft (1.4–1.5m)** | Weight **3½–5lb (1.6–2.2kg)** |
| Social **Loose colonies** | Lifespan **Up to 26 years** | Status **Secure** |

DATE SEEN	WHERE		NOTES

| Order **Falconiformes** | Family **Falconidae** | Species *Falco sparverius* |

American Kestrel

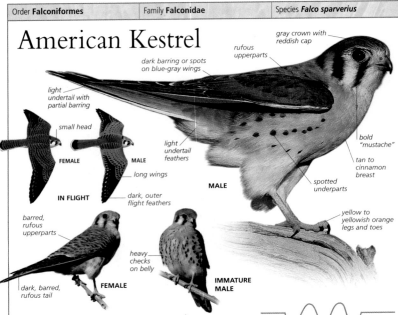

gray crown with reddish cap

rufous upperparts

dark barring or spots on blue-gray wings

light undertail with partial barring

small head

FEMALE   **MALE**

light undertail feathers

long wings

IN FLIGHT

dark, outer flight feathers

MALE

bold "mustache"

tan to cinnamon breast

spotted underparts

yellow to yellowish orange legs and toes

barred, rufous upperparts

heavy checks on belly

dark, barred, rufous tail   **FEMALE**

IMMATURE MALE

The smallest of the North American falcons, the American Kestrel features long pointed wings, a "tooth and notch" bill structure, and the dark brown eyes typical of falcons, though kestrels have shorter toes than other falcons. This may be due to the fact that kestrels often dive into long grass to capture insects and small mammals, which would be more difficult with long, thin toes. Male and female American Kestrels show differences in plumage, and also in size.

VOICE Common call a high-pitched *killy-killy-killy*.

NESTING Natural cavities, crevices, holes in dead trees, woodpeckers' holes, crevices in barns, man-made nest boxes if constructed and located properly; 4–5 eggs; 1 brood; April–June.

FEEDING Plunges for grasshoppers and crickets in spring and summer; small birds and mice in fall and winter; lizards and snakes.

FLIGHT: delicate and almost moth-like; may hover in one place for long, searching for prey.

HIGH FLIER
A male American Kestrel hovers over a field, its sharp eyes scanning the ground for insects and rodents.

SIMILAR SPECIES

MERLIN see p.119

no distinct stripes on head

SHARP-SHINNED HAWK see p.129

brownish upperparts

darker belly

longer toes

OCCURRENCE
From near the northern tree line in Alaska and Canada south, east, and west throughout most of North America. Occurs also in Central and South America. Habitat ranges from semi-open tree groves to grasslands, cultivated and fallow farmland, and open desert.

| Length **9in (23cm)** | Wingspan **22in (56cm)** | Weight **3½–4oz (100–125g)** |
| Social **Family groups** | Lifespan **10–15 years** | Status **Vulnerable** |

DATE SEEN	WHERE	NOTES

Order **Falconiformes**	Family **Falconidae**	Species *Falco columbarius*

Merlin

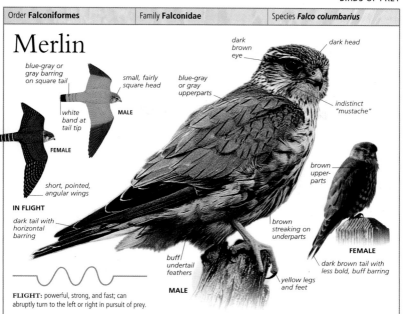

blue-gray or gray barring on square tail

small, fairly square head

blue-gray or gray upperparts

dark brown eye

dark head

MALE

white band at tail tip

indistinct "mustache"

FEMALE

brown upperparts

short, pointed, angular wings

IN FLIGHT

dark tail with horizontal barring

brown streaking on underparts

FEMALE

dark brown tail with less bold, buff barring

buff undertail feathers

yellow legs and feet

MALE

FLIGHT: powerful, strong, and fast; can abruptly turn to the left or right in pursuit of prey.

Merlins are small, fast-flying falcons that were formerly known as "pigeon hawks," because their shape and flight are similar to those strong fliers. Merlins can overtake and capture a wide variety of prey. They can turn on a dime, and use their long, thin toes, typical of falcons, to pluck birds from the air after launching a direct attack. Males are smaller than females, and different in color. Both males and females show geographical color variations.

VOICE Male call a high-pitched *ki-ki-ki-ki*; female call a low-pitched *kek-ek-ek-ek-ek*.

NESTING Small scrapes on ground in open country, or abandoned nests of other species, such as crows, in forested areas; 4–6 eggs; 1 brood; April–June.

FEEDING Catches small birds in midair, and occasionally birds as large as doves; also feeds on small mammals, including bats.

ABOUT TO ROUSE
An adult female Merlin sits on a moss-covered rock, about to "rouse," or fluff out and shake her feathers.

SIMILAR SPECIES

AMERICAN KESTREL see p.118

cinnamon flanks

tan breast

SHARP-SHINNED HAWK see p.129

rounder wings

barred underparts

longer tail

OCCURRENCE
Breeds from northern California east to Newfoundland, and south to Louisiana, Texas, and Mexico. Merlins can be seen hunting along coastlines, over marshlands and open fields, and in desert areas. Eastern birds migrate to southern areas.

Length **10in (25cm)**	Wingspan **24in (61cm)**	Weight **5–7oz (150–200g)**
Social **Pairs/Family groups**	Lifespan **10–15 years**	Status **Secure**

DATE SEEN	WHERE	NOTES

| Order **Falconiformes** | Family **Falconidae** | Species *Falco rusticolus* |

Gyrfalcon

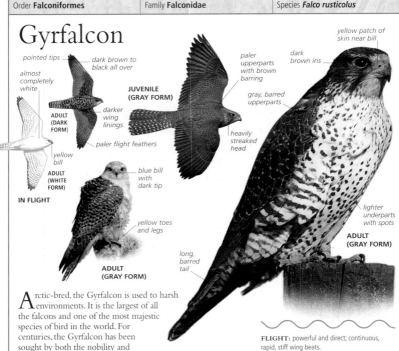

pointed tips

almost completely white

dark brown to black all over

JUVENILE (GRAY FORM)

darker wing linings

paler flight feathers

ADULT (DARK FORM)

yellow bill

ADULT (WHITE FORM)

IN FLIGHT

paler upperparts with brown barring

dark brown iris

yellow patch of skin near bill

gray, barred upperparts

heavily streaked head

lighter underparts with spots

blue bill with dark tip

yellow toes and legs

ADULT (GRAY FORM)

long, barred tail

ADULT (GRAY FORM)

Arctic-bred, the Gyrfalcon is used to harsh environments. It is the largest of all the falcons and one of the most majestic species of bird in the world. For centuries, the Gyrfalcon has been sought by both the nobility and falconers for its power, beauty, and gentle nature; today, it is also the mascot of the US Air Force Academy. It uses its speed to pursue prey in a "tail chase," sometimes striking its quarry on the ground, but also in flight. Three forms are known, ranging from almost pure white to gray and dark.

VOICE Loud, harsh *KYHa-KYHa-KYHa.*

NESTING Scrape on cliff, or old Common Ravens' nests; 2–7 eggs; 1 brood; April–July.

FEEDING Feeds mostly on large birds such as ptarmigan, pigeons, grouse; may also hunt mammals, such as lemmings.

FLIGHT: powerful and direct; continuous, rapid, stiff wing beats.

SNOWY PLUMAGE
A Gyrfalcon stands on an Arctic hillside. From a distance, it might be mistaken for a patch of snow.

| SIMILAR SPECIES | | |

PRAIRIE FALCON light, sandy brown upperparts; see p.121

light, brown-spotted underparts

PEREGRINE FALCON see p.122

dark "hood" on head

smaller overall

light, barred underparts

OCCURRENCE
Found in Arctic North America. Sometimes found in northern regions of the US. A truly Arctic species found in the most barren regions of the tundra, high mountains and foothills of the tundra, and Arctic and sub-Arctic evergreen forests and woodlands. Not common outside its breeding range.

| Length **22in (56cm)** | Wingspan **4ft (1.2m)** | Weight **2¾–4lb (1.2–1.8kg)** |
| Social **Solitary/Pairs** | Lifespan **15–30 years** | Status **Localized** |

DATE SEEN	WHERE	NOTES

Order **Falconiformes**	Family **Falconidae**	Species *Falco mexicanus*

Prairie Falcon

yellow eye-ring

yellow patch of skin near bill

light head and "mustache"

long, pointed wings

ADULT

light, sandy brown upperparts with incomplete barring

white cheek

longish tail

distinctive, triangle-shaped patch on wingpit feathers

light underparts with brown spots

IN FLIGHT

ADULT

yellow legs and toes

light undertail feathers

Prairie Falcons are light-colored, buoyant residents of the arid regions of North America. They blend in well with their surroundings (cliff faces and dry grass), where they are invisible to their prey. Prairie Falcons chase their prey close to the ground and do not often dive or "stoop" on prey from a great height. Ground squirrels are important prey items in some areas, and breeding is often linked with the squirrels' emergence. The sexes are very similar in coloration, though juveniles have a streaked rather than spotted breast. The underwing pattern with almost black feathers in the "wingpits" is distinctive; no other North American falcon shows this mark.

VOICE Repeated shrill *kik-kik-kik-kik-kik*.

NESTING Slight, shallow scrapes, almost always located on high cliff ledges or bluffs; 3–6 eggs; 1 brood; March–July.

FEEDING Feeds on small to medium-sized birds and small mammals, such as ground squirrels.

FLIGHT: fast flight; capable of soaring and diving; usually chases prey low above the ground.

STRIKING MUSTACHE
An inquisitive Prairie Falcon stares at the camera. The white cheek is obvious from this angle.

SIMILAR SPECIES		
MERLIN see p.119	**PEREGRINE FALCON ♂** see p.122	darker head
smaller overall		streaked underparts
heavily streaked underparts	yellow or bluish gray legs and toes	

OCCURRENCE
Interior North America, from central British Columbia east to western North Dakota and south to southern California, and Mexico, Arizona, northern Texas. Found in open plains, prairies, and grasslands, dotted with buttes or cliffs. A partial migrant, it moves east of its breeding range in winter.

Length **16in (41cm)**	Wingspan **3¼ (1m)**	Weight **22–30oz (625–850g)**
Social **Solitary/Pairs**	Lifespan **10–20 years**	Status **Localized**

DATE SEEN	WHERE	NOTES

| Order **Falconiformes** | Family **Falconidae** | Species *Falco peregrinus* |

Peregrine Falcon

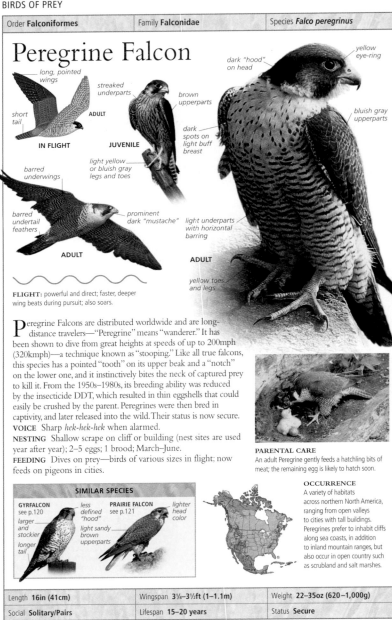

long, pointed wings

short tail

IN FLIGHT

streaked underparts

ADULT

brown upperparts

dark "hood" on head

yellow eye-ring

bluish gray upperparts

dark spots on light buff breast

JUVENILE

light yellow or bluish gray legs and toes

barred underwings

barred undertail feathers

prominent dark "mustache"

ADULT

light underparts with horizontal barring

ADULT

yellow toes and legs

FLIGHT: powerful and direct; faster, deeper wing beats during pursuit; also soars.

Peregrine Falcons are distributed worldwide and are long-distance travelers—"Peregrine" means "wanderer." It has been shown to dive from great heights at speeds of up to 200mph (320kmph)—a technique known as "stooping." Like all true falcons, this species has a pointed "tooth" on its upper beak and a "notch" on the lower one, and it instinctively bites the neck of captured prey to kill it. From the 1950s–1980s, its breeding ability was reduced by the insecticide DDT, which resulted in thin eggshells that could easily be crushed by the parent. Peregrines were then bred in captivity, and later released into the wild. Their status is now secure.

VOICE Sharp *hek-hek-hek* when alarmed.

NESTING Shallow scrape on cliff or building (nest sites are used year after year); 2–5 eggs; 1 brood; March–June.

FEEDING Dives on prey—birds of various sizes in flight; now feeds on pigeons in cities.

PARENTAL CARE
An adult Peregrine gently feeds a hatchling bits of meat; the remaining egg is likely to hatch soon.

SIMILAR SPECIES

GYRFALCON see p.120
less defined "hood"
larger and stockier
longer tail

PRAIRIE FALCON see p.121
lighter head color
light sandy brown upperparts

OCCURRENCE
A variety of habitats across northern North America, ranging from open valleys to cities with tall buildings. Peregrines prefer to inhabit cliffs along sea coasts, in addition to inland mountain ranges, but also occur in open country such as scrubland and salt marshes.

| Length **16in (41cm)** | Wingspan **3¼–3½ft (1–1.1m)** | Weight **22–35oz (620–1,000g)** |
| Social **Solitary/Pairs** | Lifespan **15–20 years** | Status **Secure** |

DATE SEEN	WHERE	NOTES

| Order **Falconiformes** | Family **Accipitridae** | Species *Pandion haliaetus* |

Osprey

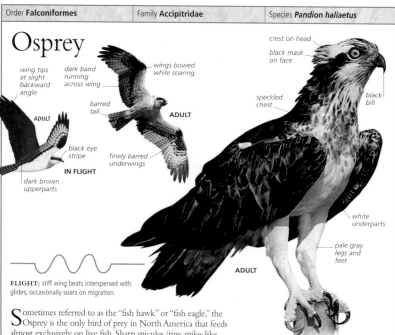

wing tips at slight backward angle

dark band running across wing

wings bowed while soaring

barred tail

ADULT

ADULT

crest on head

black mask on face

speckled chest

black bill

black eye stripe

finely barred underwings

IN FLIGHT

dark brown upperparts

white underparts

pale gray legs and feet

ADULT

FLIGHT: stiff wing beats interspersed with glides; occasionally soars on migration.

Sometimes referred to as the "fish hawk" or "fish eagle," the Osprey is the only bird of prey in North America that feeds almost exclusively on live fish. Sharp spicules (tiny, spike-like growths) on the pads of its feet, its reversible outer toes, and an ability to lock its talons in place enable it to hold onto slippery fish. Some populations declined between the 1950s and 1980s due to the use of dangerous pesticides. However, the ban on use of these chemicals, along with availability of artificial nest sites and a tolerance of nearby human activity has allowed the Osprey to return to its former numbers. The Osprey is Nova Scotia's official bird.

VOICE Slow, whistled notes, falling in pitch: *tiooop, tioooop, tiooop*; also screams by displaying male.

NESTING Twig nest on tree, cliff, rock pinnacles, boulders, ground; 1–4 eggs; 1 brood; March–August.

FEEDING Dives to catch fish up to top 3ft (90cm) of water.

IMPROVING AERODYNAMICS
Once caught, a fish is held with its head pointing forward reducing drag as the bird flies.

SIMILAR SPECIES

BALD EAGLE (2ND YEAR) see p.127

no crook in wings during flight

paler tail

GOLDEN EAGLE see p.137

dark brown head

brown, feathered legs

OCCURRENCE
Breeds in a wide variety of habitats: northern forests, near shallow reservoirs, along freshwater rivers and large lakes, estuaries and salt marshes, coastal deserts and desert saltflat lagoons. Migrates through and winters in similar habitats.

| Length **21–23in (53–58cm)** | Wingspan **5–6ft (1.5–1.8m)** | Weight **3–4½lb (1.4–2kg)** |
| Social **Solitary/Pairs** | Lifespan **Up to 25 years** | Status **Secure** |

DATE SEEN	WHERE	NOTES

Order **Falconiformes**	Family **Accipitridae**	Species **Elanoides forficatus**

Swallow-tailed Kite

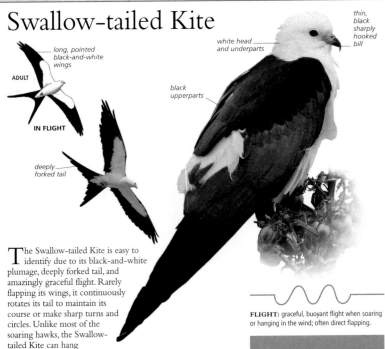

thin, black sharply hooked bill

white head and underparts

long, pointed black-and-white wings

ADULT

black uppparts

IN FLIGHT

deeply forked tail

The Swallow-tailed Kite is easy to identify due to its black-and-white plumage, deeply forked tail, and amazingly graceful flight. Rarely flapping its wings, it continuously rotates its tail to maintain its course or make sharp turns and circles. Unlike most of the soaring hawks, the Swallow-tailed Kite can hang motionless into the wind. This species lives in the southeastern US and migrates to South America. In their loose colonies of several pairs, nonbreeding birds associate with nesters.

VOICE Loud *klee-klee-klee* given by both sexes when excited or alarmed; a drawn-out *tew-whee* given during courtship.

NESTING Lined cup of small sticks, mostly in tall pine but also cypress and mangroves; 2 eggs; 1 brood; March–June.

FEEDING Feeds mainly on flying insects; also eats frogs, lizards, snakes, nestlings, and occasionally bats, fruit, and small fish.

FLIGHT: graceful, buoyant flight when soaring or hanging in the wind; often direct flapping.

AERIAL SNACK
Swallow-tailed Kites commonly eat smaller prey, such as insects, while on the wing.

OCCURRENCE
In swamps, lowland forests, freshwater and brackish marshes of Florida and the southeastern US; avoids arid areas. Needs tall trees for nesting, with open areas for foraging for small prey nearby. Tropical populations are found from Central America south to Argentina.

SIMILAR SPECIES

WHITE-TAILED KITE
see p.125

gray back

red eye

SWAINSON'S HAWK (LIGHT FORM)
see p.134

streaked head

square tail

Length **20–25in (51–64cm)**	Wingspan **4ft (1.2m)**	Weight **13–21oz (375–600g)**
Social **Colonies**	Lifespan **Unknown**	Status **Secure**

DATE SEEN	WHERE	NOTES

| Order **Falconiformes** | Family **Accipitridae** | Species *Elanus leucurus* |

White-tailed Kite

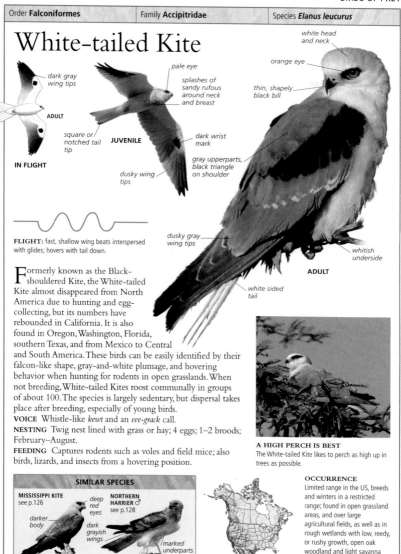

dark gray wing tips

ADULT

square or notched tail tip

IN FLIGHT

pale eye

splashes of sandy rufous around neck and breast

JUVENILE

dark wrist mark

dusky wing tips

white head and neck

orange eye

thin, shapely black bill

gray upperparts, black triangle on shoulder

dusky gray wing tips

whitish underside

ADULT

white sided tail

FLIGHT: fast, shallow wing beats interspersed with glides; hovers with tail down.

Formerly known as the Black-shouldered Kite, the White-tailed Kite almost disappeared from North America due to hunting and egg-collecting, but its numbers have rebounded in California. It is also found in Oregon, Washington, Florida, southern Texas, and from Mexico to Central and South America. These birds can be easily identified by their falcon-like shape, gray-and-white plumage, and hovering behavior when hunting for rodents in open grasslands. When not breeding, White-tailed Kites roost communally in groups of about 100. The species is largely sedentary, but dispersal takes place after breeding, especially of young birds.

VOICE Whistle-like *kewt* and an *eee-grack* call.
NESTING Twig nest lined with grass or hay; 4 eggs; 1–2 broods; February–August.
FEEDING Captures rodents such as voles and field mice; also birds, lizards, and insects from a hovering position.

A HIGH PERCH IS BEST
The White-tailed Kite likes to perch as high up in trees as possible.

SIMILAR SPECIES

MISSISSIPPI KITE see p.126

darker body

deep red eyes

NORTHERN HARRIER ♂ see p.128

dark grayish wings

marked underparts

OCCURRENCE
Limited range in the US, breeds and winters in a restricted range; found in open grassland areas, and over large agricultural fields, as well as in rough wetlands with low, reedy, or rushy growth, open oak woodland and light savanna woods. Especially fond of damp, riverside areas.

| Length **13–15in (33–38cm)** | Wingspan **3ft 3in–3½ft (1–1.1m)** | Weight **11–12oz (300–350g)** |
| Social **Colonies** | Lifespan **Up to 6 years** | Status **Secure** |

DATE SEEN	WHERE	NOTES

| Order **Falconiformes** | Family **Accipitridae** | Species *Ictinia mississippiensis* |

Mississippi Kite

white patch on inner wing feathers

ADULT

pale gray head with conspicuous dark eye patch

brick-red eye

unbarred, black tail

dark gray upperparts

flecked, brownish gray overall

JUVENILE

IN FLIGHT

long wings

brownish upperparts

JUVENILE

SUB-ADULT

FLIGHT: regular wing beats interspersed with glides; often soars with flight feathers extended.

The Mississippi Kite is locally abundant and nests in colonies in the central and southern Great Plains, but is less common and less colonial in the southeastern US. Foraging flocks of 25 or more individuals are common, and groups of ten or more roost near nests. In the West, the species nests in urban habitats, including city parks and golf courses. These urban birds can be aggressive, even attacking humans who venture too close to their nest. This graceful bird pursues its insect prey in flight. Mississippi Kites are long-distance migrants, wintering in South America.

VOICE High-pitched *phee-phew*; also multisyllabled *phee-ti-ti*.
NESTING Circular to oval nest of dead twigs, built in dead or well-foliaged tree; 1–3 eggs; 1 brood; March–July.
FEEDING Eats medium to large insects; also frogs, toads, lizards, box turtles, snakes, small birds, terrestrial mammals, and bats.

HIGH FLYING
Despite their falcon-like shape, these birds spend much of their time soaring, rather than perched.

SIMILAR SPECIES

PEREGRINE FALCON see p.122

larger overall

dark head

prominent black "mustache".

WHITE-TAILED KITE see p.125

dark shoulder patch

white underparts

OCCURRENCE
In the East, mostly mature bottomland forest or riverside woodland with open habitat nearby for foraging. Birds in the central and southern Great Plains prefer areas with numerous shelterbelts (windbreaks). Western birds use both rural woodland and suburban or urban habitat.

| Length **13–15in (33–38cm)** | Wingspan **35in (89cm)** | Weight **8–14oz (225–400g)** |
| Social **Colonies** | Lifespan **At least 8 years** | Status **Secure** |

DATE SEEN	WHERE	NOTES
....	....	....
....	....	....
....	....	....
....	....	....
....	....	....

| Order **Falconiformes** | Family **Accipitridae** | Species *Haliaeetus leucocephalus* |

Bald Eagle

JUVENILE dark head

ADULT white head — brown body — white tail

IN FLIGHT

dark eyestripe on whitish face

IMMATURE (3RD YEAR)

dark brown eyes

white belly and underwings mottled brown

dark brown overall

IMMATURE (2ND YEAR)

dark bill starting to turn yellow at base

IMMATURE (1ST YEAR)

dark chocolate-brown overall

pure white head with yellow eyes

yellow, hooked bill

long, wedge-shaped, white tail

yellow legs and toes

ADULT

FLIGHT: slow, powerful wing beats; soars and glides on broad, wide wings held at a right angle.

The Bald Eagle was selected by an act of Congress in 1782 as the national emblem of the US. With its white head and tail, this large bird of prey, although an opportunist, prefers to scavenge on carrion and steal prey from other birds, including Ospreys. It was nearing extinction because the use of DDT led to reproductive failure. Declared endangered in 1967, the bird's population has since rebounded.

VOICE Suprisingly high-pitched voice, 3–4 notes followed by a rapidly descending series.

NESTING Huge stick nest, usually in tallest tree; 1–3 eggs; 1 brood; March–September.

FEEDING Favors carrion, especially fish, also eats birds, mammals, reptiles; steals fish from Osprey.

SIMILAR SPECIES

FERRUGINOUS HAWK dark head; see p.449

GOLDEN EAGLE ♻ white in flight feathers; see p.137

whitish underparts

feathered legs

SUBSTANTIAL ABODE
Bald eagles make the largest stick nest of all raptors; it can weigh up to two tons.

OCCURRENCE
Widespread across Canada and much of the US. Breeds in forested areas near water; also shoreline areas ranging from undeveloped to relatively well-developed with marked human activity; winters along major river systems and in coastal areas and occasionally even in arid regions of southwest US.

| Length **28–38in (71–96cm)** | Wingspan **6½ft (2m)** | Weight **6½–14lb (3–6.5kg)** |
| Social **Solitary/Pairs** | Lifespan **Up to 28 years** | Status **Secure** |

DATE SEEN	WHERE	NOTES

| Order **Falconiformes** | Family **Accipitridae** | Species ***Circus cyaneus*** |

Northern Harrier

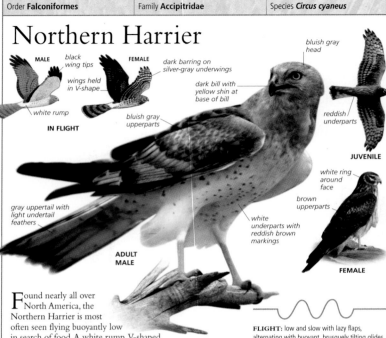

MALE — *black wing tips*

wings held in V-shape

white rump

IN FLIGHT

FEMALE — *dark barring on silver-gray underwings*

dark bill with yellow shin at base of bill

bluish gray upperparts

bluish gray head

reddish underparts

JUVENILE

gray uppertail with light undertail feathers

ADULT MALE

white underparts with reddish brown markings

white ring around face

brown upperparts

FEMALE

Found nearly all over North America, the Northern Harrier is most often seen flying buoyantly low in search of food. A white rump, V-shaped wings, and tilting flight make this species easily identifiable. The blue-gray males are quite different to the dark-brown females. The bird's most recognizable characteristic is its owl-like face, which contains stiff feathers to help channel in sounds from prey. Northern Harriers are highly migratory throughout their range.

VOICE Call given by both sexes in rapid succession at nest: *kek* becomes more high-pitched when intruders are spotted.

NESTING Platform of sticks on ground in open, wet field; 4–6 eggs; 1 brood; April–September.

FEEDING Mostly hunts rodents like mice and muskrats; also birds, frogs, reptiles; occasionally takes larger prey such as rabbits.

FLIGHT: low and slow with lazy flaps, alternating with buoyant, brusquely tilting glides.

WATERY DWELLING
To avoid predators, Northern Harriers prefer to raise their young on wet sites in tall, dense vegetation.

SIMILAR SPECIES

MISSISSIPPI KITE see p.126 — *whitish head*, *gray underparts*

ROUGH-LEGGED HAWK see p.136 — *dark eye patch*, *broader wings*, *shorter tail*

OCCURRENCE
Breeds in a variety of open wetlands: marshes, meadows, pastures, fallow fields across most of North America; winters in open habitats like deserts, coastal sand dunes, cropland, grasslands, marshy, and riverine areas.

| Length **18–20in (46–51cm)** | Wingspan **3½–4ft (1.1m–1.2m)** | Weight **11–26oz (300–750g)** |
| Social **Solitary/Pairs/Colonies** | Lifespan **Up to 16 years** | Status **Secure** |

DATE SEEN	WHERE	NOTES

| Order **Falconiformes** | Family **Accipitridae** | Species *Accipiter striatus* |

Sharp-shinned Hawk

grayish blue crown

reddish yellow eye

square-tipped tail

short, rounded wings

head appears small

grayish blue upperparts

slightly browner upperparts than male

JUVENILE

wide, dark, horizontal bars on gray tail

yellow legs and toes

IN FLIGHT

MALE

dark brown upperparts

light yellowish eye

wide, brown streaks on underparts

reddish brown bars on underparts

white, fluffy undertail feathers

ADULT

FEMALE

JUVENILE FEMALE

This small and swift hawk is quite adept at capturing birds, occasionally even taking species larger than itself. The Sharp-shinned Hawk's short, rounded wings and long tail allow it to make abrupt turns and lightning-fast dashes in thick woods and dense shrubby terrain. With needle-like talons, long, spindle-thin legs, and long toes, this hawk is well adapted to snatching birds in flight. The prey is plucked before being consumed or fed to the nestlings.

VOICE High-pitched, repeated *kiu kiu kiu* call; sometimes makes squealing sound when disturbed at nest.

NESTING Sturdy nest of sticks lined with twigs or pieces of bark; sometimes an old crow or squirrel nest; 3–4 eggs; 1 brood; March–June.

FEEDING Catches small birds, such as sparrows and wood-warblers, on the wing, or takes them unaware while perched.

FLIGHT: rapid, direct, and strong; nimble enough to maneuver in dense forest; soars during migration.

HUNTING BIRDS
A Sharp-shinned Hawk pauses on the ground with a freshly captured sparrow in its talons.

SIMILAR SPECIES

MERLIN
see p.119

light eye-stripe

long, pointed wings

COOPER'S HAWK
see p.130

larger overall

rounded tip of tail

OCCURRENCE
Deep coniferous forests and mixed hardwood–conifer woodlands across North America from the tree limit in northern Canada to the Gulf states. During fall migration sometimes seen in flocks of hundreds of individuals. Winters in Central America from Guatemala to Panama.

Length **11in (28cm)**	Wingspan **23in (58cm)**	Weight **3½–6oz (100–175g)**
Social **Solitary/Flocks**	Lifespan **At least 10 years**	Status **Secure**

DATE SEEN	WHERE	NOTES

| Order **Falconiformes** | Family **Accipitridae** | Species *Accipiter cooperii* |

Cooper's Hawk

broad, rounded wings

JUVENILE

long, barred tail with rounded tip

IN FLIGHT

dark crown

reddish eye

grayish blue upperparts

yellowish eyes

light underparts, with brown streaks

mottled dark brown upperparts

yellow legs and toes

brown tail

grayish blue overall

ADULT

JUVENILE

ADULT

gray tail with wide, dark bands

white band at tip of tail

FLIGHT: fast with rapid wing beats interspersed with glides; sometimes soars.

A secretive and inconspicuous bird, Cooper's Hawk was named by Charles Bonaparte, nephew of French Emperor Napoleon Bonaparte, for William C. Cooper, a noted New York naturalist. It is a typical woodland hawk, capable of quickly maneuvering through dense vegetation. Although it prefers to stay close to cover, it will venture out in search of food. Should a human approach the nest of a Cooper's Hawk, the brooding adult will quietly glide down and away from the nest tree rather than attack the intruder.

VOICE Most common call a staccato *ca-ca-ca-ca*; other vocalizations include as many as 40 different calls.

NESTING Medium-sized, stick nest, usually in a large deciduous tree; 4–5 eggs; 1 brood; April–May.

FEEDING Catches birds, such as robins and blackbirds; larger females can capture grouse; also eats chipmunks, small squirrels, and even bats.

DENSE BARRING
This hawk has characteristic fine, reddish brown, horizontal barring on its undersides.

OCCURRENCE
Breeds in woodlands across northern North America, southern Canada, and the northern US, south to Florida, Texas, and northwestern Mexico. Likes mature deciduous forests with leaf cover, and also roosts in conifers. Winters in southwestern US and Mexico.

SIMILAR SPECIES

NORTHERN HARRIER ♀
see p.128

larger overall

whitish underparts

square-tipped tail

SHARP-SHINNED HAWK
see p.129

much smaller head

| Length 15½–17½in (40–45cm) | Wingspan 28–34in (70–86cm) | Weight 13–19oz (375–525g) |
| Social **Solitary/Pairs** | Lifespan **At least 10 years** | Status **Secure** |

DATE SEEN	WHERE		NOTES

Order **Falconiformes**	Family **Accipitridae**	Species *Accipiter gentilis*

Northern Goshawk

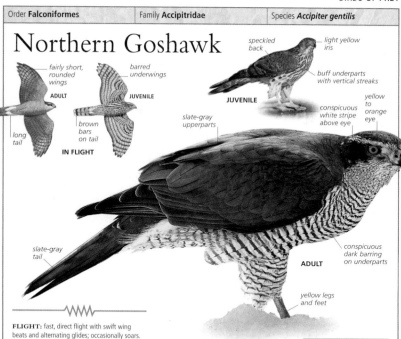

speckled back

light yellow iris

buff underparts with vertical streaks

JUVENILE

fairly short, rounded wings

barred underwings

ADULT

JUVENILE

yellow to orange eye

slate-gray upperparts

conspicuous white stripe above eye

brown bars on tail

long tail

IN FLIGHT

slate-gray tail

conspicuous dark barring on underparts

ADULT

yellow legs and feet

FLIGHT: fast, direct flight with swift wing beats and alternating glides; occasionally soars.

The powerful and agile Northern Goshawk is secretive by nature and not easily observed, even in regions where it is common. It has few natural enemies, but will defend its territories, nests, and young fiercely, by repeatedly diving and screaming at intruders that get too close. Spring hikers and turkey-hunters occasionally discover Northern Goshawks by wandering into their territory and being driven off by the angry occupants.

VOICE Loud, high-pitched *gek-gek-gek* when agitated.

NESTING Large stick structures lined with bark and plant matter in the mid- to lower region of tree; 1–3 eggs; 1 brood; May–June.

FEEDING Sits and waits on perch before diving rapidly; preys on birds as large as grouse and pheasants; also mammals, including hares and squirrels.

OCCASIONAL SOARER
A juvenile Northern Goshawk takes advantage of a thermal, soaring over its territory.

OCCURRENCE
Breeds in deep deciduous, coniferous, and mixed woodlands in northern North America, from the tundra–taiga border south to California, northern Mexico, and Pennsylvania in the eastern US, absent from east central US. The Northern Goshawk is widespread in northern Eurasia.

SIMILAR SPECIES

GYRFALCON (GRAY FORM) see p.120

longer, pointed wings

COOPER'S HAWK see p.130

brownish upperparts

no streaks on underparts

streaked underparts

Length **21in (53cm)**	Wingspan **3½ft (1.1m)**	Weight **2–3lb (0.9–1.4kg)**
Social **Solitary/Pairs**	Lifespan **Up to 20 years**	Status **Secure**

DATE SEEN	WHERE	NOTES

| Order **Falconiformes** | Family **Accipitridae** | Species *Buteo lineatus* |

Red-shouldered Hawk

ADULT
reddish leading edge on wings
translucent patch near wing tips
IN FLIGHT
brown, barred tail
JUVENILE
dark wing tips

brownish upperparts
mottled appearance
streaked breast
white spots on dark brown plumage
IMMATURE (1ST SPRING)

gray head with thin, dark streaks
red shoulder patch

rufous head
orangish breast
ADULT B. l. elegans (WESTERN)

black-and-white, barred tail
whitish undertail feathers

reddish and white barred breast
ADULT

yellow legs and feet

FLIGHT: occasional rapid flapping; soars in lazy circles over treetops with wings and tail spread.

The Red-shouldered Hawk has a remarkable distribution, with widespread populations in the East, Northeast, and Midwest then in the West, from Oregon to Baja California, despite a geographical gap of 1,000 miles (1,600km) between the two regions. Eastern birds are divided into four subspecies; western populations belong to the subspecies *B. l. elegans*. The red shoulder patches are not always evident, but the striped tail and translucent "windows" in the wings are easily identifiable.

VOICE Call a whistled *kee-aah*, accented on first syllable, descending on second.

NESTING Platform of sticks, dried leaves, bark, moss, and lichens in trees not far from water; 3–4 eggs; 1 brood; March–July.

FEEDING Catches mice, chipmunks, and voles; also snakes, toads, frogs, crayfish, and small birds.

SIMILAR SPECIES

BROAD-WINGED HAWK see p.133
chunkier body
shorter legs

RED-TAILED HAWK see p.135
no red on "shoulder"
no white tail bands
slightly larger overall

CHESTNUT WING
When seen from below, the reddish forewing of this adult hawk is clearly visible.

OCCURRENCE
Eastern populations breed in woodlands and forest, deciduous or mixed, whereas those in the West occur in oak woodlands and eucalyptus groves. In Florida, this species also lives in mangroves. Northeastern birds migrate to Mexico.

| Length **17–24in (43–61cm)** | Wingspan **3–3½ft (0.9–1.1m)** | Weight **17–27oz (475–775g)** |
| Social **Solitary/Flocks** | Lifespan **Up to 18 years** | Status **Declining (p)** |

DATE SEEN	WHERE	NOTES

| Order **Falconiformes** | Family **Accipitridae** | Species ***Buteo platypterus*** |

Broad-winged Hawk

indistinct "mustache"

dark border on edges of wings

one to two broad, white bands visible on tail

ADULT

upperparts brown with white flecking

ADULT

JUVENILE

pale tan wings with dark tips

IN FLIGHT

finely barred, all-brown tail

JUVENILE

pale outer wing feathers

pale underparts with conspicuous, tear-shaped, brown spots

short, yellow feet

IMMATURE

One of the most numerous of all North American birds of prey, the Broad-winged Hawk migrates in huge flocks or "kettles," with thousands of birds gliding on rising thermals. Some birds winter in Florida, but the majority average about 70 miles (110km) a day to log more than 4,000 miles (6,500km) before ending up in Brazil, Bolivia, and even some of the Caribbean islands. Compared to its two cousins, the Red-shouldered and Red-tailed Hawks, the Broad-winged Hawk is slightly smaller, but stockier. Adults are easily identified by a broad, white-and-black band on their tails. Broad-winged Hawks have two color forms, the light one being more common than the dark, sooty brown one.

VOICE High-pitched *peeoweee* call, first note shorter and higher-pitched.

NESTING Platform of fresh twigs or dead sticks, often on old squirrel, hawk, or crow nest in tree; 2–3 eggs; 1 brood; April–August.

FEEDING Eats small mammals, toads, frogs, snakes, grouse chicks, insects, and spiders; crabs in winter.

FLIGHT: circles above forest canopy with wings and tail spread; short flights from branch to branch.

WATCHING FOR PREY
From an elevated perch, this hawk scans for vertebrate prey such as rodents.

OCCURRENCE
Breeds across Canada (but not the Rockies) and in the eastern US (not west of the 100th meridian), in forested areas with deciduous, conifers, and mixed trees, with clearings and water nearby. Concentrations of migrants can be seen at bottlenecks such as the Isthmus of Tehuantepec and Panama.

SIMILAR SPECIES

RED-SHOULDERED HAWK
see p.132
larger overall

thin, white bands on tail

red patch on shoulder
more slender

RED-TAILED HAWK
see p.135
larger overall

dark band on belly

| Length **13–17in (33–43cm)** | Wingspan **32–39in (81–100cm)** | Weight **10–19oz (275–550g)** |
| Social **Flocks** | Lifespan **Up to 14 years** | Status **Secure** |

DATE SEEN	WHERE	NOTES

| Order **Falconiformes** | Family **Accipitridae** | Species ***Buteo swainsoni*** |

Swainson's Hawk

long pointed wings
dark wing tips

ADULT (LIGHT FORM)
JUVENILE (LIGHT FORM)

dark chest

IN FLIGHT

whitish head

spotted underparts

white face and chin

JUVENILE (LIGHT FORM)

reddish breast and belly
slender shape overall

ADULT (INTERMEDIATE FORM)

dark brown head and breast

spotted underparts

ADULT (DARK FORM)

longish tail

wing tips reach end of tail when perched

pale reddish upper chest

white underbelly

FLIGHT: soaring, buoyant flight with deep wing beats; will often hover and hang motionless.

ADULT (LIGHT FORM)

Swainson's Hawk is perhaps most famous for its spectacular 6,000-mile (9,650km) fall migration from the Canadian prairies to the lower regions of South America, when thousands can be observed soaring in the air at any one time. While migrating, this hawk averages 125 miles (200km) a day. There are three color forms: light, dark, and an intermediate form between the two.
VOICE Alarm call a shrill, plaintive scream *kreeeee* given by both sexes; high-pitched *keeeoooo* fading at the end.
NESTING Bulky, flimsy pile of sticks or various debris, in solitary tree or on utility poles; 1–4 eggs; 1 brood; April–July.
FEEDING Eats ground squirrels, pocket gophers, mice, voles, bats, rabbits; also snakes, lizards, songbirds.

ON THE LOOKOUT
This slim, elegant species will perch before diving for its prey.

OCCURRENCE
Breeds in scattered trees along streams; found in areas of open woodland, sparse shrubland, grasslands, and agricultural land; winters in native Argentinian grassland, and in harvested fields where grasshoppers are found abundantly.

SIMILAR SPECIES	
HARRIS'S HAWK see p.448	**RED-TAILED HAWK** see p.135

chestnut thighs and wing patches
long legs
white on tail

bulkier overall
shorter wings
red tail

Length **19–22in (48–56cm)**	Wingspan **4½ft (1.4m)**	Weight **1½–3lb (0.7–1.4kg)**
Social **Solitary/Pairs/Flocks**	Lifespan **Up to 19 years**	Status **Declining (p)**

DATE SEEN	WHERE	NOTES

Order **Falconiformes**	Family **Accipitridae**	Species ***Buteo jamaicensis***

Red-tailed Hawk

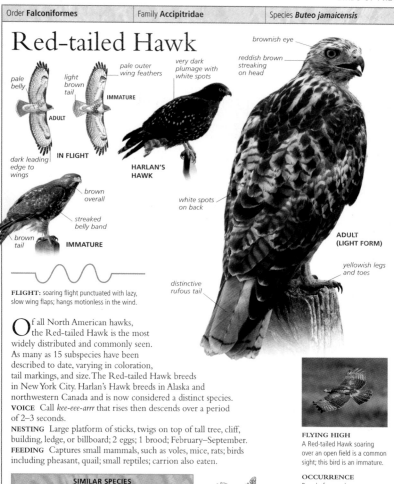

brownish eye

reddish brown streaking on head

pale outer wing feathers

very dark plumage with white spots

pale belly

light brown tail

IMMATURE

ADULT

dark leading edge to wings **IN FLIGHT**

HARLAN'S HAWK

brown overall

white spots on back

streaked belly band

brown tail **IMMATURE**

ADULT (LIGHT FORM)

yellowish legs and toes

distinctive rufous tail

FLIGHT: soaring flight punctuated with lazy, slow wing flaps; hangs motionless in the wind.

Of all North American hawks, the Red-tailed Hawk is the most widely distributed and commonly seen. As many as 15 subspecies have been described to date, varying in coloration, tail markings, and size. The Red-tailed Hawk breeds in New York City. Harlan's Hawk breeds in Alaska and northwestern Canada and is now considered a distinct species.

VOICE Call *kee-eee-arrr* that rises then descends over a period of 2–3 seconds.

NESTING Large platform of sticks, twigs on top of tall tree, cliff, building, ledge, or billboard; 2 eggs; 1 brood; February–September.

FEEDING Captures small mammals, such as voles, mice, rats; birds including pheasant, quail; small reptiles; carrion also eaten.

FLYING HIGH
A Red-tailed Hawk soaring over an open field is a common sight; this bird is an immature.

OCCURRENCE
Breeds, forages in open areas in wide range of habitats and altitudes: scrub desert, grasslands, agricultural fields and pastures, coniferous and deciduous woodland, and tropical rainforest. Prefers areas with tall perch sites; can be found in suburban woodlots.

SIMILAR SPECIES

FERRUGINOUS HAWK (LIGHT FORM) see p.449

larger bill

larger overall

mostly white underparts

ROUGH-LEGGED HAWK (DARK FORM) see p.136

dark band on white tail

Length **18–26in (46–65cm)**	Wingspan **3½–4¼ft (1.1–1.3m)**	Weight **1½–3¼lb (0.7–1.5kg)**
Social **Solitary/Pairs**	Lifespan **Up to 21 years**	Status **Secure**

DATE SEEN	WHERE	NOTES

| Order **Falconiformes** | Family **Accipitridae** | Species ***Buteo lagopus*** |

Rough-legged Hawk

FEMALE

black trailing edge

one line before tail tip

pale forehead

dark wing tips

ADULT

bold black patch

dark tail band

IN FLIGHT

short, broad head

MALE

JUVENILE

black belly

barred underparts

thin bands near tail tip

FLIGHT: strong wing beats; usually soars on thermals; frequently hovers in one spot.

white tail with faint black band at tip

plain gray brown or frosty feather edges

MALE

The Rough-legged Hawk is known for its extensive variation in plumage—some individuals are almost completely black, whereas others are much paler, very nearly cream or white. The year to year fluctuation in numbers of breeding pairs in a given region strongly suggest that this species is nomadic, moving about as a response to the availability of its rodent prey.

VOICE Wintering birds silent; breeding birds utter loud, cat-like mewing or thin whistles, slurred downward when alarmed.

NESTING Bulky mass of sticks, lined with grasses, sedges, feathers and fur from prey, constructed on cliff ledge; 2–6 eggs; 1 brood; April–August.

FEEDING Hovers in one spot over fields in search of prey; lemmings and voles in spring and summer; mice and shrews in winters; variety of birds, ground squirrels, and rabbits year-round.

ABUNDANT FOOD SUPPLY
When small mammals are abundant, these hawks produce large broods on cliff ledges in the tundra.

SIMILAR SPECIES

NORTHERN HARRIER ♀
see p.128

reddish underparts

longer wings

FERRUGINOUS HAWK
see p.449

reddish upperparts

white under-parts

OCCURRENCE
Breeds in rough, open country with low crags and cliffs, in high sub-Arctic and Arctic regions; found on the edge of extensive forest or forest clearings, and in treeless tundra, uplands, and alpine habitats. Winters in open areas with fields, marshes, and rough grasslands.

| Length **19–20in (48–51cm)** | Wingspan **4¼–4½ft (1.3–1.4m)** | Weight **1½–3lb (0.7–1.4kg)** |
| Social **Solitary** | Lifespan **Up to 18 years** | Status **Secure** |

DATE SEEN	WHERE	NOTES

| Order **Falconiformes** | Family **Accipitridae** | Species *Aquila chrysaetos* |

Golden Eagle

long, narrow white wing patches
IMMATURE
ADULT

holds wings in distinctive "V"

flat, broad head merges into heavy bill

golden feathers on long neck

brown overall

dark brown underparts

black tail band
IN FLIGHT

large, powerful bill

ADULT

heavy feathering on legs

pale head

dark plumage with variable white

white tail feathers

JUVENILE

FLIGHT: slow, steady wing beats; most often seen gliding or soaring.

Perhaps the most formidable of all North American birds of prey, the Golden Eagle is found mostly in the western part of the continent. It defends large territories ranging from 8–12 square miles (20–30 square kilometers), containing up to 14 nests. Although its appears sluggish, it is amazingly swift and agile, and employs a variety of hunting techniques to catch specific prey. Shot and poisoned by ranchers and trappers, it is unfortunately also faced with dwindling habitat and food sources due to human development.

VOICE Mostly silent, but breeding adults yelp and mew.

NESTING Large pile of sticks and vegetation on cliffs, in trees, and on man-made structures; 1–3 eggs; 1 brood; April–August.

FEEDING Eats mammals, such as hares, rabbits, ground squirrels, prairie dogs, marmots, foxes, and coyotes; also birds.

POWER AND STRENGTH
The Golden Eagle symbolizes all birds of prey, with its sharp talons, hooked bill, and large size.

SIMILAR SPECIES

BALD EAGLE ♂
see p.127
white head and neck

some pale wing feathers

FERRUGINOUS HAWK ♀
(DARK FORM)
see p.449

no golden tinge

smaller overall

OCCURRENCE
In North America occurs mostly in grasslands, wetlands, and rocky areas; breeds south to Mexico, in open and semi-open habitats from sea level to 12,000ft (3,500m) including tundra, shrublands, grasslands, coniferous forests, farmland, areas close to streams or rivers; winters in open habitat.

| Length **28–33in (70–84cm)** | Wingspan **6–7¼ft (1.8–2.2m)** | Weight **6½–13lb (3–6kg)** |
| Social **Solitary/Pairs** | Lifespan **Up to 39 years** | Status **Declining (p)** |

DATE SEEN	WHERE	NOTES

RAILS & RELATIVES

THE RALLIDAE, OR RAIL family, is a diverse group of small to medium-sized marsh birds. In the US and Canada, rallids, as they are known collectively, are represented by three rails, three crakes, two gallinules, and a coot. Rails and crakes inhabit dense marshland and are secretive, solitary, and inconspicuous, whereas coots and gallinules are seen on open water. Rallids are chicken-like birds with stubby tails and short, rounded wings. Rails have drab, camouflage coloring, and are long-legged, long-billed, and narrow-bodied. Crakes are smaller but similar, with shorter necks and stout, stubby bills. Both rails and crakes walk and run on the ground in marsh vegetation, but can swim well. Colorful gallinules include the Common Moorhen and the Purple Gallinule. Rallids look like weak flyers, but many migrate great distances at night. None has a specialized diet; their food includes insects, small crabs, slugs, snails, and plant matter. Rallids nest in pairs, the birds keep in close contact by calling loudly and clearly.

THIN AS A RAIL
This marsh-dwelling Clapper Rail has a narrow body that enables it to slip easily through reedbeds.

FLAT LANDING
Purple Gallinules can land safely on lily pads because their large toes spread their weight.

CRANES

CRANES ARE LARGE WADING BIRDS, superficially similar to storks and to the larger herons and egrets. However, several anatomical differences place them in a different family (Gruidae), within a different order (Gruiformes). The two North American crane species have much lighter bills than storks. Typically, too, long inner wing feathers form a "bustle" on a standing crane, giving it a different profile than a heron. Additionally, cranes fly with their necks straight out, rather than in the tight S-curve regularly seen in similar-sized herons. The Whooping Crane is the tallest bird in North America, standing nearly 5ft (1.5m) high.

CRANE RALLY
Large numbers of Sandhill Cranes gather on feeding grounds in winter, groups arriving in V-formation.

| Order **Gruiformes** | Family **Rallidae** | Species *Coturnicops noveboracensis* |

Yellow Rail

dark brown crown

stubby yellow to olive-gray bill

dark stripe runs from cheek to bill

buff or yellow breast

ADULT

dangling legs

ADULT

white patch on inner wing feathers

IN FLIGHT

long tan stripes on blackish background

short tail

FLIGHT: low, weak, short, and direct with stiff wing beats; dangling legs.

Although widespread, the diminutive, secretive, nocturnal Yellow Rail is extremely difficult to observe in its dense, damp, grassy habitat, and is detected mainly by its voice. The Yellow Rail, whose Latin name of *noveboracensis* means "New Yorker," has a small head, almost no neck, a stubby bill, a plump, almost tail-less body, and short legs. The bill of the male turns yellow in the breeding season; for the rest of the year, it is olive-gray like the female's. Although the Yellow Rail tends to dart for cover when disturbed, when it does fly, it reveals a distinctive white patch on its inner wing.

VOICE Two clicking calls followed by three more given by males, usually at night, reminiscent of two pebbles being struck together; also descending cackles, quiet croaking, and soft clucking.

NESTING Small cup of grasses and sedges, on the ground or in a plant tuft above water, concealed by overhanging vegetation; 8–10 eggs; 1 brood; May–June.

FEEDING Plucks seeds, aquatic insects, various small crustaceans, and mollusks (primarily small freshwater snails) from vegetation or ground; forages on the marsh surface or in shallow water, hidden by grass.

CURIOUS LISTENER
Imitating the "tick" calls of the Yellow Rail is often an effective way to lure it out into the open.

OCCURRENCE
Breeds in brackish and freshwater marshes and wet sedge meadows in Canada and the north central US; there is an isolated breeding population in Oregon. Winters predominantly in coastal marshes along the eastern seaboard.

SIMILAR SPECIES

SORA
see p.144

black streaks on brown upperparts

gray underparts

| Length **7¼in (18.5cm)** | Wingspan **11in (28cm)** | Weight **1¾oz (50g)** |
| Social **Pairs** | Lifespan **Unknown** | Status **Secure** |

DATE SEEN	WHERE	NOTES

| Order **Gruiformes** | Family **Rallidae** | Species *Laterallus jamaicensis* |

Black Rail

ADULT

white spotted back

reddish brown nape

IN FLIGHT

dark overall

slate-gray head

red eye

chestnut-brown nape and upper mantle

blackish upperparts, flecked with white

small, straight bill

dark gray breast and upper belly

darker gray underparts

ADULT (SUMMER)

greenish gray legs

FLIGHT: reluctant flier, short flights with dangling legs; longer flights; fast and direct.

This tiny, mouse-sized rail is so elusive that few people have ever seen it; consequently, much remains unknown about its life history and it is of great interest to birdwatchers. It is usually detected by its territorial call that is given during the breeding season from the cover of marsh grass. The best chance to see a Black Rail is when high tides force it to move to higher ground. Unfortunately, this is when it can fall prey to herons.

VOICE Distinctive, 3-note *kik-kee-do* given by male, mostly at night, during breeding season; makes low growl when agitated.

NESTING Small, deep cup of grasses and sedges placed on the ground, with an overhanging canopy of woven plants; 5–9 eggs; 2 broods; March–July.

FEEDING Forages on the wet marsh surface beneath the cover of grass for snails, insects, spiders, and seeds of marsh plants.

ELUSIVE BIRD
The highly secretive Black Rail is almost never seen by birdwatchers, and is a prize find.

OCCURRENCE
The Black Rail has a disjointed distribution across the US. It is found among reeds in freshwater, salt, and brackish marshes or wet meadows. It also occurs patchily in the West Indies (its scientific name is *jamaicensis*, after the island Jamaica), Central America, and South America.

SIMILAR SPECIES

VIRGINIA RAIL see p.143

larger overall

longer bill

SORA see p.144

downy back

yellow bill

Length **6in (15cm)**	Wingspan **9in (23cm)**	Weight **1¹⁄₁₆oz (30g)**
Social **Solitary**	Lifespan **Unknown**	Status **Secure**

DATE SEEN	WHERE	NOTES

| Order **Gruiformes** | Family **Rallidae** | Species ***Rallus longirostris*** |

Clapper Rail

ADULT
(GULF
COAST)

IN FLIGHT

gray
cheeks

drab gray
overall

long, down-
curved bill

brownish
cheeks

R. l. saturatus
(GULF COAST)

cinnamon
breast

long,
slender bill

pale underparts

long,
thick legs

R. l. obsoletus
(CALIFORNIA)

R. l. crepitans
(ATLANTIC)

Closely related to the King Rail, the Clapper Rail is a common and widespread species on the Atlantic and Gulf coasts. The Clapper Rail can be found in a variety of habitats but it is closely tied to brackish and saltwater marshes dominated by *Spartina* cord grass. However, in southern Florida, this rail is found close to mangrove swamps. The "Yuma" subspecies (*yumanensis*) occupies freshwater marshes in the interior. The Clapper Rail's distinctive, insistent calls are the best way to recognize its presence, as it is rarely seen.
VOICE Grunting calls; repeated loud *kek* notes.
NESTING Bulky cup of grasses and plant stems lined with finer material; bends growing plants to form a canopy; 4–14 eggs; 1 brood; March–August.
FEEDING Forages by crouching low and stalking through marsh, eating snails, insects, spiders, clams, fish, bird eggs, and seeds.

FLIGHT: low and weak; flies with outstretched neck and dangling legs.

LOUD AND CLEAR
The repeated, insistent *kek* call may be heard more than a mile away.

SIMILAR SPECIES

KING RAIL
see p.142

VIRGINIA RAIL
see p.143

smaller
overall

gray
face

black-
and-white
streaking
on flanks

black-and-
white barred
flanks

OCCURRENCE
Found mostly in saltwater and brackish marshes along the Atlantic Seaboard. Isolated populations are found in coastal California and inland in west and southwest North America, along the lower Colorado River. The Clapper Rail winters south of its breeding range.

| Length **14½in (37cm)** | Wingspan **19in (48cm)** | Weight **10oz (275g)** |
| Social **Solitary** | Lifespan **Up to 7 years** | Status **Localized** |

DATE SEEN	WHERE	NOTES

| Order **Gruiformes** | Family **Rallidae** | Species **Rallus elegans** |

King Rail

ADULT

rufous upperwing

heavy down-curved bill

IN FLIGHT

short tail

boldly barred, black-and-white flanks

reddish eye

brown stripe running down neck

boldly streaked upperparts

long, curved, yellow-orange bill

orangish breast

ADULT

This chicken-like marsh bird is the freshwater version of the Clapper Rail. These two species are known to interbreed where their ranges overlap. A scattered and localized breeder across eastern North America, the King Rail depends on extensive freshwater marsh habitats with tall, emergent reeds and cattails. Concealed by this vegetation, the King Rail is rarely seen and is most often detected by its distinctive calls.

VOICE Male call similar to Clapper Rail but lower; emits a loud *kik kik kik* during breeding season.

NESTING Cup of vegetation, often hidden by bent stems that form a canopy; 6–12 eggs; 2 broods; February–August.

FEEDING Forages in concealed locations for insects, snails, spiders, and crustaceans such as shrimps, crabs, and barnacles; also fish, frogs, and seeds.

FLIGHT: somewhat clumsy and labored; legs dangling; prefers to run.

LARGEST RAIL
Easily confused with the closely related Clapper Rail, this is the largest North American rail.

OCCURRENCE
Mostly breeds in freshwater marshes in the eastern US and in extreme southern Ontario. Also found throughout the year along the southern coast of the US, including Florida, and in central Mexico and Cuba.

SIMILAR SPECIES

CLAPPER RAIL
see p.141

flank barring diffused

grayer overall

VIRGINIA RAIL
see p.143

smaller overall

gray face

red bill

| Length **15in (38cm)** | Wingspan **20in (51cm)** | Weight **13oz (375g)** |
| Social **Pairs** | Lifespan **Unknown** | Status **Localized** |

DATE SEEN	WHERE	NOTES

Order **Gruiformes**	Family **Rallidae**	Species *Rallus limicola*

Virginia Rail

rufous upperwing

streaked black and brown upperparts

gray cheeks

ADULT (BREEDING)

dark outer wing feathers

IN FLIGHT

curved red bill

reddish brown breast

white undertail

black-and-white barring on flanks

diffused streaking

dark bill

reddish legs and toes

ADULT (BREEDING)

dark, blotchy breast

ADULT (NONBREEDING)

A smaller version of the King Rail, this freshwater marsh dweller is similar to its other relatives, more often heard than seen. Distributed in a wide range, the Virginia Rail spends most of its time in thick, reedy vegetation, which it pushes using its "rail thin" body and flexible vertebrae. Although it spends most of its time walking, it can swim and even dive to escape danger. The Virginia Rail is a partial migrant that leaves its northern breeding grounds in winter.

VOICE Series of pig-like grunting *oinks* that start loud and sharp, becoming steadily softer; also emits a series of double notes *ka-dik ka-dik*.

NESTING Substantial cup of plant material, concealed by bent-over stems; 5–12 eggs; 1–2 broods; April–July.

FEEDING Actively stalks prey or may wait and dive into water; primarily eats snails, insects, and spiders, but may also eat seeds.

FLIGHT: weak and struggling with outstretched neck and legs trailing behind.

HARD TO SPOT
The secretive Virginia Rail is difficult to spot in its reedy habitat.

SIMILAR SPECIES

CLAPPER RAIL see p.141

orange face

weak flank barring

KING RAIL see p.142

less gray face

larger overall

dark undertail

yellow-orange bill

OCCURRENCE
Breeds in freshwater habitats across North America, though is found throughout the year along the West Coast of the US. In winter, eastern populations move to saltwater and freshwater marshes in the southern US, including Florida, and in northern and central Mexico.

Length **9½in (24cm)**	Wingspan **13in (33cm)**	Weight **3oz (85g)**
Social **Pairs**	Lifespan **Unknown**	Status **Secure**

DATE SEEN	WHERE	NOTES

| Order **Gruiformes** | Family **Rallidae** | Species **Porzana carolina** |

Sora

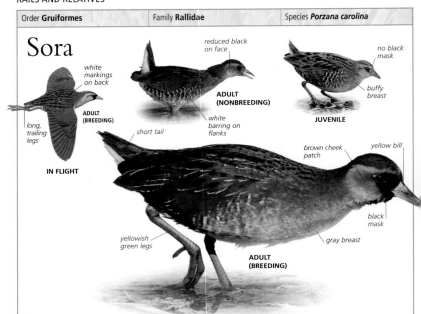

white markings on back

ADULT (BREEDING)

long, trailing legs

IN FLIGHT

reduced black on face

ADULT (NONBREEDING)

white barring on flanks

short tail

no black mask

buffy breast

JUVENILE

brown cheek patch

yellow bill

black mask

gray breast

yellowish green legs

ADULT (BREEDING)

Despite being the most widely distributed rail in North America, the Sora is rarely seen. It breeds in freshwater marshes and migrates hundreds of miles south in winter regardless of its weak and hesitant flight. It swims well, with a characteristic head-bobbing action. The Sora can be spotted walking at the edge of emergent vegetation—its yellow bill and black mask distinguish it from other rails.
VOICE Call a long, high, and loud, descending, horse-like whinny *ko-wee-hee-hee-hee-hee*; has an upslurred whistle.
NESTING Loosely woven basket of marsh vegetation suspended above water or positioned in clumps of vegetation on the water's surface; 8–11 eggs; 1 brood; May–June.
FEEDING Rakes vegetation with feet or pulls with bill in search of seeds of wetland plants, insects, spiders, and snails.

FLIGHT: appears weak, yet strenuous; wing beats hurried and constant.

CHICKEN-LIKE WALK
A rare sight, the Sora walks chicken-like through a marsh, its body in a low crouch.

SIMILAR SPECIES

YELLOW RAIL
see p.139

buffy streaks

VIRGINIA RAIL
see p.143

buffy breast

reddish legs

longer bill

OCCURRENCE
Breeds in freshwater marshes with emergent vegetation across most of temperate North America; rarely in salt marshes along the Atlantic Coast. Winters in freshwater, saltwater, and brackish marshes with spartina grass from the southern US to northern South America.

| Length **8½in (22cm)** | Wingspan **14in (36cm)** | Weight **2⅝oz (75g)** |
| Social **Solitary** | Lifespan **Unknown** | Status **Secure** |

DATE SEEN	WHERE	NOTES

| Order **Gruiformes** | Family **Rallidae** | Species ***Porphyrula martinica*** |

Purple Gallinule

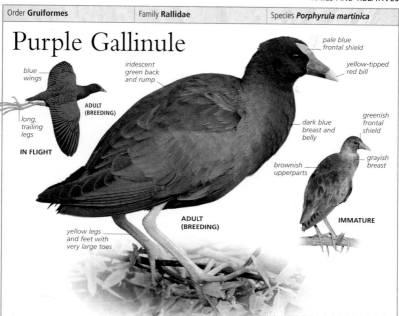

pale blue
frontal shield

yellow-tipped
red bill

blue
wings

iridescent
green back
and rump

**ADULT
(BREEDING)**

long,
trailing
legs

IN FLIGHT

dark blue
breast and
belly

greenish
frontal
shield

grayish
breast

brownish
upperparts

IMMATURE

**ADULT
(BREEDING)**

yellow legs
and feet with
very large toes

This vibrantly colored rail inhabits freshwater marshes in the southeastern US. The Purple Gallinule is extremely conspicuous due to its purple head and neck, bright red bill, and yellow legs. This species is well known for long distance vagrancy far outside its normal breeding range; it has been found as far away as Labrador, South Georgia, Switzerland, and South Africa.

VOICE Call a chicken-like clucking; also grunts and higher-pitched single notes.

NESTING Bulky cup of plant material built up slightly above the water's surface, usually placed in marsh vegetation; 5–10 eggs; 1 brood; April–August.

FEEDING Omnivorous diet; seeds, leaves, insects, spiders, and worms; will sometimes turn over lily pads to find aquatic insects.

FLIGHT: weak and slow with its heavy legs trailing behind.

EXTREMELY LONG TOES
The Purple Gallinule's long toes enable it to walk across floating vegetation.

OCCURRENCE
Breeds in lush wetlands containing emergent vegetation of the southeastern US; mostly freshwater marshes. Winter habitat similar to breeding; non-Florida populations withdraw southward in winter; Florida population nonmigratory.

SIMILAR SPECIES

COMMON MOORHEN
see p.146

red
frontal
shield

greenish
yellow
legs

AMERICAN COOT
see p.147

black
head

white
bill

black-
and-gray
plumage

| Length **13in (33cm)** | Wingspan **22in (56cm)** | Weight **8oz (225g)** |
| Social **Pairs** | Lifespan **Unknown** | Status **Localized** |

DATE SEEN	WHERE	NOTES

Order **Gruiformes**	Family **Rallidae**	Species **Gallinula chloropus**

Common Moorhen

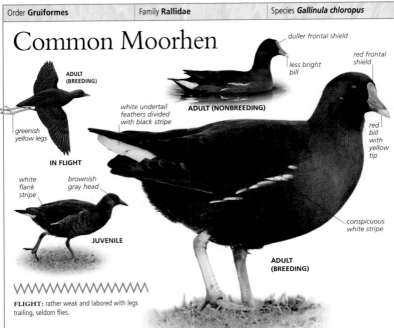

duller frontal shield

less bright bill

red frontal shield

ADULT (NONBREEDING)

ADULT (BREEDING)

white undertail feathers divided with black stripe

greenish yellow legs

red bill with yellow tip

IN FLIGHT

white flank stripe

brownish gray head

JUVENILE

conspicuous white stripe

ADULT (BREEDING)

FLIGHT: rather weak and labored with legs trailing, seldom flies.

The Common Moorhen is fairly widespread in the eastern US, although its distribution is more patchy in the western states. It has similarities in behavior and habitat to both the true rails and coots. Equally at home on land and water, its long toes allow it to walk easily over floating vegetation and soft mud. When walking or swimming, the Common Moorhen nervously jerks its short tail, revealing its white undertail feathers, and bobs its head.

VOICE A variety of hen-like clucks and cackles, including an explosive *krrooo*.

NESTING Bulky platform of aquatic vegetation with growing plants pulled over to conceal it, or close to water; 5–11 eggs, 1–3 broods; May–August, maybe year round in Florida.

FEEDING Forages mainly on aquatic and terrestrial plants and aquatic vegetation; also eats snails, spiders, and insects.

DUAL HABITAT
A walker and a swimmer, the Moorhen is equally at home on land and in water.

OCCURRENCE
Breeds in freshwater habitats in the eastern US and Canada; more localized in the West. Winters in warmer areas with open water, such as southern California and Mexico. Also found in Central and South America.

SIMILAR SPECIES

PURPLE GALLINULE see p.145 — blue frontal shield — bright yellow legs

AMERICAN COOT see p.147 — white bill — darker plumage

Length **14in (36cm)**	Wingspan **21in (53cm)**	Weight **11oz (325g)**
Social **Pairs**	Lifespan **Up to 10 years**	Status **Secure**

DATE SEEN	WHERE	NOTES

Order **Gruiformes**	Family **Rallidae**	Species *Fulica americana*

American Coot

black head
red eye

ADULT (BREEDING)

dark gray body

white bill

white-edged feathers

black ring on bill

IN FLIGHT

dull grayish plumage

JUVENILE

long, greenish yellow legs

lobed toes

ADULT (BREEDING)

This duck-like species is the most abundant and widely distributed of North American rails. Its lobed toes make it well adapted to swimming and diving, but are somewhat of an impediment on land. Its flight is clumsy; it becomes airborne with difficulty, running along the water surface before taking off. American Coots form large flocks on open water in winter, often associating with ducks—an unusual trait for a member of the rail family.

VOICE Various raucous clucks, grunts, and croaks and an explosive *keek*.

NESTING Bulky cup of plant material placed in aquatic vegetation on or near water; 5–15 eggs; 1–2 broods; April–July.

FEEDING Forages on or by diving under shallow water and on land; primarily herbivorous, but also eats snails, insects, spiders, tadpoles, fish, and even carrion.

FLIGHT: low and labored; runs for quite a long distance to take off.

SWIMMING AWAY
The red-headed, baldish looking American Coot chicks leave the nest a day after hatching.

SIMILAR SPECIES

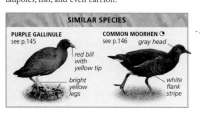

PURPLE GALLINULE
see p.145

red bill with yellow tip

bright yellow legs

COMMON MOORHEN ♀
see p.146   gray head

white flank stripe

OCCURRENCE
Breeds in open water habitats west of the Appalachians and in Florida. Moves from the northern parts of its range in winter to the southeastern US, where open water persists; also migrates to western and southern Mexico.

Length **15½in (40cm)**	Wingspan **24in (61cm)**	Weight **16oz (450g)**
Social **Flocks**	Lifespan **Up to 22 years**	Status **Secure**

DATE SEEN	WHERE	NOTES

Order **Gruiformes**	Family **Gruidae**	Species **Grus canadensis**

Sandhill Crane

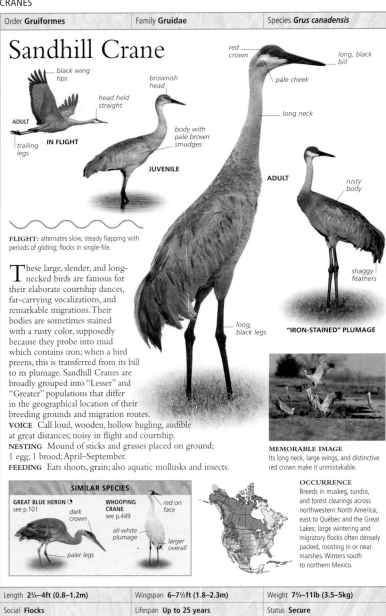

black wing tips

head held straight

ADULT

IN FLIGHT

trailing legs

brownish head

body with pale brown smudges

JUVENILE

red crown

long, black bill

pale cheek

long neck

ADULT

rusty body

shaggy feathers

"IRON-STAINED" PLUMAGE

long, black legs

FLIGHT: alternates slow, steady flapping with periods of gliding; flocks in single-file.

These large, slender, and long-necked birds are famous for their elaborate courtship dances, far-carrying vocalizations, and remarkable migrations. Their bodies are sometimes stained with a rusty color, supposedly because they probe into mud which contains iron; when a bird preens, this is transferred from its bill to its plumage. Sandhill Cranes are broadly grouped into "Lesser" and "Greater" populations that differ in the geographical location of their breeding grounds and migration routes.

VOICE Call loud, wooden, hollow bugling, audible at great distances; noisy in flight and courtship.

NESTING Mound of sticks and grasses placed on ground; 1 egg; 1 brood; April–September.

FEEDING Eats shoots, grain; also aquatic mollusks and insects.

MEMORABLE IMAGE
Its long neck, large wings, and distinctive red crown make it unmistakable.

SIMILAR SPECIES

GREAT BLUE HERON ◐
see p.101

dark crown

paler legs

WHOOPING CRANE
see p.449

red on face

all-white plumage

larger overall

OCCURRENCE
Breeds in muskeg, tundra, and forest clearings across northwestern North America, east to Québec and the Great Lakes; large wintering and migratory flocks often densely packed, roosting in or near marshes. Winters south to northern Mexico.

Length 2¾–4ft (0.8–1.2m)	Wingspan 6–7½ft (1.8–2.3m)	Weight 7¾–11lb (3.5–5kg)
Social **Flocks**	Lifespan **Up to 25 years**	Status **Secure**

DATE SEEN	WHERE	NOTES

Order **Gruiformes**	Family **Aramidae**	Species *Aramus guarauna*

Limpkin

dark wings

ADULT curved bill

IN FLIGHT

long, curvaceous neck

sparse white spotting on back

white speckles on neck

ADULT (SUMMER)

chocolate brown overall

⋀⋁⋀

FLIGHT: direct and heavy flight; legs are either drawn up into the body or left dangling behind.

long, gray legs

SNAILS FOR DINNER
Limpkins forage mainly for apple snails in quiet waterways in wooded southeastern swamps.

Similar to both herons and ibises, the Limpkin is actually related to the cranes, coots, and rails. It is at home in the swamps and marshes of southeastern North America, eating during the daylight, but remaining active at night. Individuals and small flocks tend to move slowly and deliberately, occasionally erupting into animated motions and wild wailing. This species's preferred food resource is threatened by habitat conversion and by competition from introduced species.
VOICE Call short whistles, abrupt barks, and medium length wails; often have an eerie quality.
NESTING Vegetation placed on ground or in tree; 5–6 eggs; 1–3 broods; February–July.
FEEDING Feeds in shallow water, on apple snails; also insects and spiders.

DEEP WADING
Although Limpkins often hide in vegetation, they sometimes wander into open water.

OCCURRENCE
Range limited to areas inhabited by apple snails. Breeds and forages in extensive marshes, wooded swamps, and swamp forests, but also ranges into disturbed habitats, including ditches, canals, and parks.

SIMILAR SPECIES

WOOD STORK ♂
lacks extensive white spotting; see p.90

gray facial skin

more sharply curved bill

WHITE-FACED IBIS ♂
see p.93

pale face

dull plumage

Length **26in (66cm)**	Wingspan **3ft 3in (100cm)**	Weight **2–2¾lbs (0.9–1.2kg)**
Social **Solitary**	Lifespan **Up to 12 years**	Status **Declining**

DATE SEEN	WHERE	NOTES

SHOREBIRDS, GULLS, & AUKS

THE DIVERSE SHOREBIRD, gull, and auk families together form the order Charadriiformes. They are small to medium-sized, mostly migratory birds, associated with aquatic habitats. Over 100 species are found in North America.

SHOREBIRDS

The various species popularly known as shorebirds belong to several different families. In North America there are the oystercatchers (Haematopodidae), the avocets and stilts (Recurvirostridae), the plovers (Charadriidae), the sandpipers (Scolopacidae); and the phalaropes (the subfamily Phalaropodinae, of Scolopacidae). They have long legs in proportion to their bodies, and a variety of bills, ranging from short to long, thin, thick, straight, down-curved and up-curved.

GULLS

The over 20 species of North American gulls in the family Laridae all share similar stout body shapes, sturdy bills, and webbed toes. Nearly all are scavengers. Closely associated with coastal areas, few gulls venture far out to sea. Some species are seen around fishing ports and harbors, or inland, especially in urban areas and garbage dumps.

TYPICAL GULL
Most large gulls, such as this Ring-billed Gull, have white heads and underparts with long dark wings and a bright sturdy bill.

TERNS

Terns are specialized long-billed predators that dive for fish. More slender and elegant than gulls, nearly all are immediately recognizable when breeding, due to their black caps and long, pointed bills. The related Black Skimmer also catches fish, but has a different bill.

AUKS, MURRES, & PUFFINS

Denizens of the northern oceans, these birds only come to land to breed. Most nest in colonies on sheer cliffs overlooking the ocean, but puffins excavate burrows in the ground, and some murrelets nest away from predators high up in treetops far inland.

COLOR-CHANGE BILL
The bright colors of a breeding Atlantic Puffin's bill fade to more muted tones in winter, after the breeding season.

ON THE MOVE
Dunlins and other sandpipers gather in large, highly coordinated flocks on migration.

| Order **Charadriiformes** | Family **Haematopodidae** | Species **Haematopus palliatus** |

American Oystercatcher

yellow eye

black head

orange-red eye-ring

white rump

prominent white wing bar

large, bulky body

dark brown upperparts

ADULT

long, orange-red bill

powerful wings

IN FLIGHT

white underparts

pale fringes on upperpart feathers

dull orange eye-ring

ADULT

dark eye

black tip to orange bill

thick, pinkish legs

JUVENILE

This large and noisy shorebird is conspicuous on beachfront habitats along the Atlantic and Gulf of Mexico coastlines. It is the heaviest of all North American shorebirds, and often runs on its thick, powerful legs to escape danger. This species is found in flocks of a few to several hundred birds in winter at its preferred feeding and roosting locations. Up to eight birds can be seen together in synchronized courtship flights, with their heads and necks bowed and wings arched upward.

VOICE Whistled, loud, clear descending *wheeu* call; alarm call sharp *wheep*; flight display call several sharp whistles accelerating into a series of descending piping notes.

NESTING Simple scrape with shell debris on coastal sandy beaches, dunes, and salt marshes; 2–3 eggs; 1 brood; April–May.

FEEDING Forages on slightly submerged shellfish beds; feeds by probing in subsoil; also by stabbing or hammering open bivalve shells with powerful bill.

FLIGHT: powerful, fast, direct flight with rapid shallow wing beats.

OPENING UP
This species uses its long, powerful bill to pry open or smash bivalve mollusks on rocks.

SIMILAR SPECIES

BLACK OYSTERCATCHER

all dark plumage

STRONG FLIER
Strong fliers, these birds use their long, powerful wings for swift, short-distance forays.

OCCURRENCE
Exclusive to saltwater coastal habitats; locally common from Massachusetts southward to Gulf Coast; also Caribbean south to Argentina, north from Chile to Baja California, Mexico. Occurs in southern California; recent nesting has been documented in Nova Scotia. Expanding northward on Atlantic Coast.

| Length **15½–17½in (40–44cm)** | Wingspan **29–32in (73–81cm)** | Weight **14–25oz (400–700g)** |
| Social **Flocks** | Lifespan **Up to 17 years** | Status **Secure** |

DATE SEEN	WHERE	NOTES

| Order **Charadriiformes** | Family **Recurvirostridae** | Species *Himantopus himantopus* |

Black-necked Stilt

long, angular, black wings

ADULT

no white spot above red eye

long, slender neck

IN FLIGHT

scaly appearance

black upperparts

slender, tapered body

MALE

long, bright pink legs

less contrasting head pattern than adult

shorter, stubbier bill

JUVENILE

white spot above red eye

black mask encircles eye

long, needle-like black bill

white underparts

brownish wash to back

duller legs than male

FEMALE

This tall, slender, elegant, and black-and-white shorebird is a familiar sight at ponds and lagoons in the western and southern US. Even among the shorebirds, it is remarkably long-legged, at times almost grotesquely so: in flight, it often crosses its trailing feet as if for extra control and support. Breeding takes place in small colonies, with several pairs sharing the same site. In winter, these tall birds are often seen in small flocks of about 25 individuals. These groups feed quietly in sheltered areas, but they aggressively drive visitors away with their raucous calls, dog-like yips, and noisy communal protests. The increased use of pesticides and loss of wetland habitat could cause a decline in its numbers in the future. US populations belong to subspecies *mexicanus*.

VOICE Flight and alarm call a loud, continuous poodle-like *yip-yip-yip*, given in a long series when alarmed.

NESTING Simple scrape lined with grass in soft soil; 4 eggs; 1 brood; April–May.

FEEDING Walks slowly in shallow water, picking food off surface; diet includes tadpoles, shrimp, snails, flies, worms, clams, small fish, and frogs.

FLIGHT: direct, but somewhat awkward due to long, trailing legs; deep wing beats.

FRIENDLY BUNCH
Black-necked Stilts are gregarious by nature, and often roost together in shallow water.

OCCURRENCE
Breeds around marshes, shallow grassy ponds, lake margins, and man-made waterbodies, such as reservoirs; uses similar habitats during migration and winter, as well as shallow lagoons, flooded fields, and mangrove swamps. Southern birds migrate locally only.

| Length **14–15½in (35–39cm)** | Wingspan **29–32in (73–81cm)** | Weight **4–8oz (125–225g)** |
| Social **Small flocks** | Lifespan **Up to 19 years** | Status **Secure** |

DATE SEEN	WHERE	NOTES

| Order **Charadriiformes** | Family **Recurvirostridae** | Species *Recurvirostra americana* |

American Avocet

striking black-and-white pattern

ADULT (BREEDING)

IN FLIGHT

white eye-ring

dark eye

cinnamon-colored head

long, thin, upturned bill

bold shoulder feathers

cinnamon-colored neck

white underparts

FEMALE

long, bluish legs

no cinnamon color on head and neck

white plumage

ADULT (NONBREEDING)

less upturned bill

MALE

FLIGHT: fast, direct, and graceful; very long legs extend beyond tail.

With its long, thin, and upturned bill, this graceful, long-legged shorebird is unmistakable when foraging. When it takes off, its striking plumage pattern is clearly visible. It is the only one of the four avocet species in the world that changes plumage when breeding. Breeding birds have a cinnamon head and neck, and bold, patterns on their black-and-white wings and upperparts. The American Avocet forms large flocks during migration and in winter.

VOICE Flight call a variable melodic *kleet*, loud and repetitive, given when alarmed and by foraging birds.

NESTING Simple scrape in shallow depression; 4 eggs; 1 brood; May–June.

FEEDING Uses specialized bill to probe, scythe, or jab a variety of aquatic invertebrates, small fish, and seeds; walks steadily in belly-deep water to chase its prey.

FORAGING FLOCK
These birds walk through shallow water in flocks searching mainly for insects and crustaceans.

OCCURRENCE
Breeds in temporary wetlands, in dry to arid regions. During migration and in winter, found in shallow water habitats, including ponds, reservoirs, fresh- and saltwater marshes, tidal mudflats, and lagoons. Each year, a flock of about 10,000 birds winters at Bolivar Flats, Texas. Regular East Coast visitor.

TRICKY BALANCE
During mating, the male supports himself with raised wings as the female extends her neck forward.

| Length **17–18½in (43–47cm)** | Wingspan **29–32in (74–81cm)** | Weight **10–12oz (275–350g)** |
| Social **Large flocks** | Lifespan **Up to 9 years** | Status **Secure** |

DATE SEEN	WHERE	NOTES

Order **Charadriiformes**	Family **Charadriidae**	Species *Pluvialis dominica*

American Golden Plover

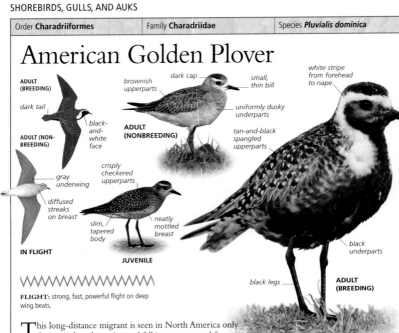

ADULT (BREEDING)
dark tail

black-and-white face

ADULT (NON-BREEDING)

gray underwing

diffused streaks on breast

IN FLIGHT

brownish upperparts

dark cap

small, thin bill

uniformly dusky underparts

tan-and-black spangled upperparts

ADULT (NONBREEDING)

crisply checkered upperparts

slim, tapered body

neatly mottled breast

JUVENILE

white stripe from forehead to nape

black underparts

black legs

ADULT (BREEDING)

FLIGHT: strong, fast, powerful flight on deep wing beats.

This long-distance migrant is seen in North America only during its lengthy spring and fall journeys to and from its high Arctic breeding grounds and wintering locations in southern South America. An elegant, slender, yet large plover, it prefers inland grassy habitats and plowed fields to coastal mudflats. The American Golden Plover's annual migration route includes a feeding stop at Labrador, then a 1,550–1,860 miles (2,500–3,000km) flight over the Atlantic Ocean to South America.
VOICE Flight call a whistled 2-note *queE-dle*, or *klee-u*, with second note shorter and lower pitched; male flight song a strong, melodious whistled *kid-eek*, or *kid-EEp*.
NESTING Shallow depression lined with lichens in dry, open tundra; 4 eggs; 1 brood; May–July.
FEEDING Forages in run, pause, and pluck sequence on insects, mollusks, crustaceans, and worms; also berries and seeds.

DISTRACTION TECHNIQUE
This breeding American Golden Plover is feigning an injury to its wing to draw predators away from its eggs or chicks in its nest.

SIMILAR SPECIES

PACIFIC GOLDEN PLOVER ✳
see p.471

longer legs

larger bill

PACIFIC GOLDEN PLOVER ♀
see p.471

checkered gold-and-black upperparts

pale golden wash

OCCURRENCE
Breeds in Arctic tundra habitats. In migration, it occurs in prairies, tilled farmlands, golf courses, pastures, airports; also mudflats, shorelines, and beaches. In spring, seen in Texas and Great Plains; in fall, uncommon in northeast Maritimes and New England; scarce along the Pacific Coast.

Length **9½–11in (24–28cm)**	Wingspan **23–28in (59–72cm)**	Weight **4–7oz (125–200g)**
Social **Solitary/Small flocks**	Lifespan **Unknown**	Status **Secure**

DATE SEEN	WHERE	NOTES
....	....	....
....	....	....
....	....	....
....	....	....
....	....	....

| Order **Charadriiformes** | Family **Charadriidae** | Species *Pluvialis squatarola* |

Black-bellied Plover

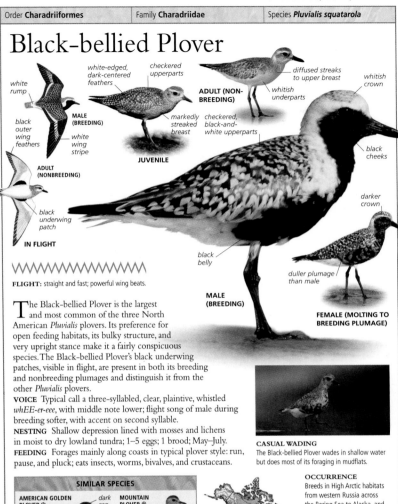

white rump

MALE (BREEDING)

black outer wing feathers

white wing stripe

white-edged, dark-centered feathers

checkered upperparts

ADULT (NONBREEDING)

JUVENILE

markedly streaked breast

checkered black-and-white upperparts

ADULT (NON-BREEDING)

diffused streaks to upper breast

whitish underparts

whitish crown

darker crown

black cheeks

MALE (BREEDING)

black belly

duller plumage than male

FEMALE (MOLTING TO BREEDING PLUMAGE)

IN FLIGHT

black underwing patch

FLIGHT: straight and fast; powerful wing beats.

The Black-bellied Plover is the largest and most common of the three North American *Pluvialis* plovers. Its preference for open feeding habitats, its bulky structure, and very upright stance make it a fairly conspicuous species. The Black-bellied Plover's black underwing patches, visible in flight, are present in both its breeding and nonbreeding plumages and distinguish it from the other *Pluvialis* plovers.

VOICE Typical call a three-syllabled, clear, plaintive, whistled *whEE-er-eee*, with middle note lower; flight song of male during breeding softer, with accent on second syllable.

NESTING Shallow depression lined with mosses and lichens in moist to dry lowland tundra; 1–5 eggs; 1 brood; May–July.

FEEDING Forages mainly along coasts in typical plover style: run, pause, and pluck; eats insects, worms, bivalves, and crustaceans.

CASUAL WADING
The Black-bellied Plover wades in shallow water but does most of its foraging in mudflats.

SIMILAR SPECIES

AMERICAN GOLDEN PLOVER ❊
see p.154

dingy, brownish upperparts

dark cap

MOUNTAIN PLOVER ❊
see p.449

sandy brown upperparts

white underparts

OCCURRENCE
Breeds in High Arctic habitats from western Russia across the Bering Sea to Alaska, and east to Baffin Island; winters primarily in coastal areas from southern Canada and US, south to southern South America. Found inland during migration. Migrates south all the way to South America.

| Length **10½–12in (27–30cm)** | Wingspan **29–32in (73–81cm)** | Weight **5–9oz (150–250g)** |
| Social **Flocks** | Lifespan **Up to 12 years** | Status **Secure** |

DATE SEEN	WHERE		NOTES
....	....		....
....	....		....
....	....		....
....	....		....
....	....		....

| Order **Charadriiformes** | Family **Charadriidae** | Species *Charadrius semipalmatus* |

Semipalmated Plover

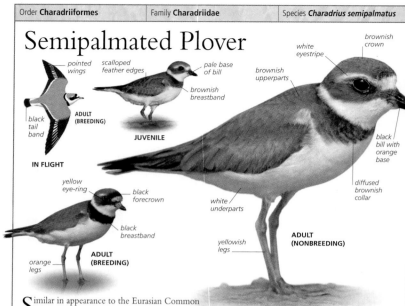

pointed wings

scalloped feather edges

black tail band

ADULT (BREEDING)

IN FLIGHT

pale base of bill

brownish breastband

JUVENILE

brownish crown

white eyestripe

brownish upperparts

black bill with orange base

diffused brownish collar

yellow eye-ring

black forecrown

black breastband

orange legs

ADULT (BREEDING)

white underparts

yellowish legs

ADULT (NONBREEDING)

Similar in appearance to the Eurasian Common Ringed Plover, the Semipalmated Plover is a small shorebird with a tapered shape. It is a familiar sight in a wide variety of habitats during migration and in winter, when these birds gather in loose flocks. A casual walk down a sandy beach between fall and spring might awaken up to 100 Semipalmated Plovers, sleeping in slight depressions in the sand, though flocks of up to 1,000 birds may also be encountered.

VOICE Flight call a whistled, abrupt double note, *chu-WEEp*, with soft emphasis on second syllable; courtship display song is a version of flight call followed by rough *r-r-r-r-r-r-r*, ending with a slurred, descending *yelp*.

NESTING Simple scrape on bare or slightly vegetated ground in Arctic tundra; 3–4 eggs; 1 brood; May–June.

FEEDING Forages in typical plover style: run, pause, and pluck; eats aquatic mollusks, crustaceans, flies, beetles, and spiders.

FLIGHT: straight, fast; with fluttering wing beats.

BY SIGHT AND FEEL
Semipalmated Plovers locate prey by sight or through the sensitive soles of their toes.

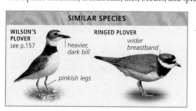

SIMILAR SPECIES

WILSON'S PLOVER see p.157

heavier, dark bill

pinkish legs

RINGED PLOVER

wider breastband

OCCURRENCE
Breeding habitat is Arctic or sub-Arctic tundra, well-drained gravel, shale, or other sparsely vegetated ground. During migration, mudflats, saltwater marshes, lake edges, tidal areas, and flooded fields. During winter, coastal or near coastal habitats.

| Length **6¾–7½in (17–19cm)** | Wingspan **17–20½in (43–52cm)** | Weight **1¹⁄₁₆–2½oz (30–70g)** |
| Social **Solitary/Flocks** | Lifespan **Up to 6 years** | Status **Secure** |

DATE SEEN	WHERE	NOTES

| Order **Charadriiformes** | Family **Charadriidae** | Species *Charadrius wilsonia* |

Wilson's Plover

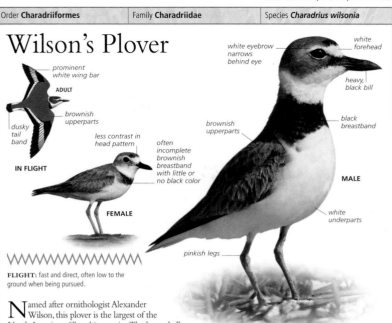

white eyebrow narrows behind eye

white forehead

heavy, black bill

ADULT

prominent white wing bar

brownish upperparts

dusky tail band

IN FLIGHT

brownish upperparts

black breastband

less contrast in head pattern

often incomplete brownish breastband with little or no black color

MALE

FEMALE

white underparts

pinkish legs

FLIGHT: fast and direct, often low to the ground when being pursued.

Named after ornithologist Alexander Wilson, this plover is the largest of the North American *Charadrius* species. The heavy belly of the Wilson's Plover gives it a very upright posture when it pauses, and its distinctive habit of running horizontally, low to the ground, is a familiar sight on beaches. The subspecies *C. w. beldingi* (Gulf of California and Mexico's Pacific coast) is smaller and darker, with a darker face. Wilson's Plover was listed as a species of "high concern" in 2000.

VOICE Flight call a short *pip*, or *pi-dit*; alarm calls include slurred whistle *tweet*, and short whistled *peet*; common distraction call a descending buzzy rattle, given in series.

NESTING Simple scrape in sand, dunes, and other coastal habitats; 3–4 eggs; 1 brood; April–June.

FEEDING Forages in typical plover style: run, pause, and pluck; mainly eats crustaceans, including fiddler crabs; also insects.

STRICTLY COASTAL
Wilson's Plover is strongly associated with coastal areas, where it forages at low tide.

SIMILAR SPECIES

SEMIPALMATED PLOVER ❋
see p.156

orange legs

smaller bill

smaller **PIPING PLOVER**
see p.159

orange bill

paler plumage

smaller overall

orange legs

black tip to bill

OCCURRENCE
Found primarily in coastal habitats, including open beaches, vegetated sand dunes, coastal lagoons, saltwater flats, and overwash areas. Located only in North American coastal regions of the southeast Atlantic and Gulf Coasts.

Length **6½–8in (16–20cm)**	Wingspan **15½–19½in (39–49cm)**	Weight **2–2½oz (55–70g)**
Social **Flocks**	Lifespan **Unknown**	Status **Declining**

DATE SEEN	WHERE	NOTES

Order **Charadriiformes**	Family **Charadriidae**	Species *Charadrius vociferus*

Killdeer

long wings

white wing bar

ADULT

reddish orange tail and rump

IN FLIGHT

long tail

rufous wash to back and wings

brownish upperparts

black collar encircling neck

red eye-ring

brownish crown

small, thin, black bill

MALE

second neck band crosses upper breast

white underparts

pinkish legs, sometimes with yellowish tinge

FLIGHT: fast, twisting flight with fluid wing beats.

This loud and vocal shorebird is the most widespread plover in North America, nesting in all southern Canadian provinces and across the US. The Killdeer's piercing call carries for long distances, sometimes causing other birds to fly away in fear of imminent danger. These birds often nest near human habitation, allowing a close observation of their vigilant parental nature with young chicks.
VOICE Flight call a rising, drawn out *deeee*; alarm call a loud, penetrating *dee-ee*, given repetitively; agitated birds also give series of *dee* notes, followed by rising trill.
NESTING Scrape on ground, sometimes in slight depression; 4 eggs; 1 brood (north), 2–3 broods (south); March–July.
FEEDING Forages in typical plover style: run, pause, and pick; eats a variety of invertebrates such as worms, snails, grasshoppers, and beetles; also small vertebrates and seeds.

CLEVER MANEUVER
The Killdeer lures intruders away from its nest with a "broken wing" display.

SIMILAR SPECIES

SEMIPALMATED PLOVER ❁
see p.156

single dark neckband

orange-yellow legs

smaller overall

WILSON'S PLOVER
see p.157

single, black collar

pinkish legs

short tail

OCCURRENCE
Widespread across Canada and the US, the Killdeer occurs in a wide variety of habitats. These include shorelines, mudflats, lake and river edges, sparsely grassy fields and pastures, golf courses, roadsides, parking lots, flat rooftops, driveways, and other terrestrial habitats.

Length **9–10in (23–26cm)**	Wingspan **23–25in (58–63cm)**	Weight **2¼–3⅛ oz (65–90g)**
Social **Small flocks**	Lifespan **Up to 10 years**	Status **Secure**

DATE SEEN	WHERE	NOTES
....	....	....
....	....	....
....	....	....
....	....	....
....	....	....

Order **Charadriiformes**	Family **Charadriidae**	Species **Charadrius melodus**

Piping Plover

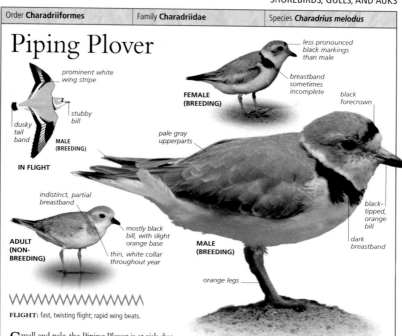

prominent white wing stripe

stubby bill

dusky tail band

MALE (BREEDING)

IN FLIGHT

less pronounced black markings than male

breastband sometimes incomplete

black forecrown

FEMALE (BREEDING)

pale gray upperparts

black-tipped, orange bill

dark breastband

MALE (BREEDING)

orange legs

indistinct, partial breastband

ADULT (NON-BREEDING)

mostly black bill, with slight orange base

thin, white collar throughout year

FLIGHT: fast, twisting flight; rapid wing beats.

Small and pale, the Piping Plover is at risk due to eroding coastlines, human disturbance, and predation by foxes, raccoons, and cats. With its pale gray back, it is well camouflaged along beaches or in dunes, but conservation measures, such as fencing off nesting beaches and control of predators, are necessary to restore populations. Two subspecies of the Piping Plover are recognized; one nests on the Atlantic Coast, and the other inland.
VOICE Clear, whistled *peep* call in flight; quiet *peep-lo* during courtship and contact; high-pitched *pipe-pipe-pipe* song.
NESTING Shallow scrape in sand, gravel, dunes, or salt flats; 4 eggs; 1 brood; April–May.
FEEDING Typical run, pause, and pluck plover feeding style; diet includes marine worms, insects, and mollusks.

VULNERABLE NESTS
The fragile nature of their preferred nesting sites has led to this species becoming endangered.

SIMILAR SPECIES

SEMIPALMATED PLOVER ✳
see p.156

dark, brown upperparts

SNOWY PLOVER ✳
see p.160

black bill

narrow, white collar

darker legs

OCCURRENCE
Found along beaches, in saline sandflats, and adjacent mudflats; during winter, found exclusively along the Atlantic and Gulf Coasts, sandflats, and mudflats. Inland subspecies nests on sand or gravel beaches adjacent to large lakes, rivers, and saline lakes.

Length **6½–7in (17–18cm)**	Wingspan **18–18½in (45–47cm)**	Weight **1⅝–2⅜ oz (45–65g)**
Social **Small flocks**	Lifespan **Up to 11 years**	Status **Vulnerable**

DATE SEEN	WHERE		NOTES

| Order **Charadriiformes** | Family **Charadriidae** | Species ***Charadrius alexandrinus*** |

Snowy Plover

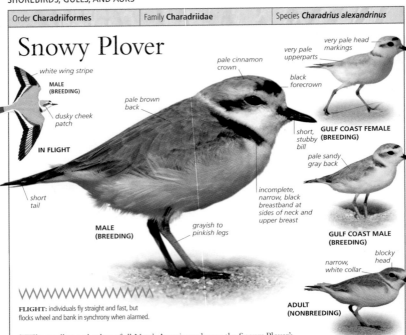

very pale head markings

very pale upperparts

GULF COAST FEMALE (BREEDING)

pale sandy gray back

GULF COAST MALE (BREEDING)

blocky head

narrow, white collar

ADULT (NONBREEDING)

white wing stripe

MALE (BREEDING)

dusky cheek patch

IN FLIGHT

short tail

pale cinnamon crown

black forecrown

pale brown back

short, stubby bill

incomplete, narrow, black breastband at sides of neck and upper breast

MALE (BREEDING)

grayish to pinkish legs

FLIGHT: individuals fly straight and fast, but flocks wheel and bank in synchrony when alarmed.

The smallest and palest of all North American plovers, the Snowy Plover's cryptic coloration blends in so well with its beach and dune habitat that it often remains unnoticed. This bird often runs faster and covers longer distances than other beach plovers, sprinting along the sand for extended spurts, like sanderlings. Nests are frequently destroyed by weather, disturbance, or predators, but the birds readily construct new nests, even up to six times in the face of regular losses. Nevertheless, habitat destruction has resulted in shrinking populations, and the species is designated as threatened along the Pacific Coast.

VOICE Repeated *tow-heet*; *purrt* and single *churr*; typically silent when not breeding, tinkling *ti* at roosts or before flight.

NESTING Shallow scrape in sand; 2–3 eggs; 2–3 broods; March–June.

FEEDING Feeds in run, pause, and pluck style on terrestrial and aquatic invertebrates, such as snails and clams.

TRULY SNOWY
The Snowy Plover breeds in sandy areas that are as pale as snow.

OCCURRENCE
Breeds on open beach and dune habitats on the Pacific and Gulf Coasts, and inland on brackish lakes in the Great Basin and southern Great Plains region. Coastal birds are only partially migratory, but most inland birds winter at the coast.

SIMILAR SPECIES

SEMIPALMATED PLOVER ♀
see p.156

brown breastband

plumper overall

PIPING PLOVER ♂
see p.159

orange legs

| Length **6–6½in (15–17cm)** | Wingspan **16–18in (41–46cm)** | Weight **1¼–2⅛oz (35–60g)** |
| Social **Large flocks** | Lifespan **Up to 4 years** | Status **Declining** |

DATE SEEN	WHERE	NOTES

| Order **Charadriiformes** | Family **Scolopacidae** | Species *Scolopax minor* |

American Woodcock

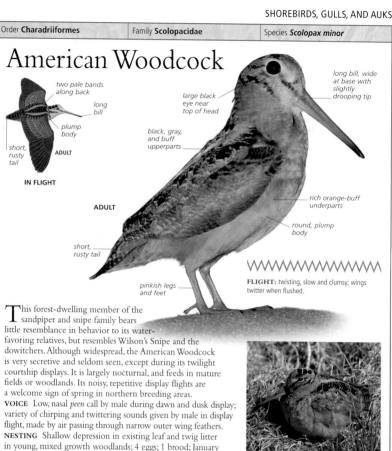

two pale bands
along back

long
bill

plump
body

short,
rusty
tail

ADULT

IN FLIGHT

large black
eye near
top of head

black, gray,
and buff
upperparts

long bill, wide
at base with
slightly
drooping tip

ADULT

rich orange-buff
underparts

round, plump
body

short,
rusty tail

pinkish legs
and feet

FLIGHT: twisting, slow and clumsy; wings
twitter when flushed.

This forest-dwelling member of the
sandpiper and snipe family bears
little resemblance in behavior to its water-
favoring relatives, but resembles Wilson's Snipe and the
dowitchers. Although widespread, the American Woodcock
is very secretive and seldom seen, except during its twilight
courtship displays. It is largely nocturnal, and feeds in mature
fields or woodlands. Its noisy, repetitive display flights are
a welcome sign of spring in northern breeding areas.
VOICE Low, nasal *peen* call by male during dawn and dusk display;
variety of chirping and twittering sounds given by male in display
flight, made by air passing through narrow outer wing feathers.
NESTING Shallow depression in existing leaf and twig litter
in young, mixed growth woodlands; 4 eggs; 1 brood; January
(southern populations) and April (northern populations).
FEEDING Probes deep in damp soil or mud; mostly for
earthworms, but also insects, snails, and some plants.

STAYING PUT
A foraging American Woodcock "caught" in an
open field will freeze before it flies off.

SIMILAR SPECIES		OCCURRENCE

WILSON'S SNIPE
see p.162
smaller
head

LONG-BILLED DOWITCHER
see p.164
smaller
head

more slender
shape

streaked
breast and
flanks

longer
legs

OCCURRENCE
Breeds from southern Canada
to southeastern US states, in
damp, second-growth forest,
overgrown fields and bogs. In
winter, found in similar habitat;
also found along marsh edges,
swamps, and damp, grassy
roadsides in Texas and Florida
in the southern US.

| Length **10–12in (25–31cm)** | Wingspan **16–20in (41–51cm)** | Weight **4–7oz (125–200g)** |
| Social **Solitary** | Lifespan **Up to 9 years** | Status **Secure** |

DATE SEEN	WHERE	NOTES

Order **Charadriiformes**	Family **Scolopacidae**	Species **Gallinago gallinago**

Wilson's Snipe

high-set large, dark eye

streaked face

long, pointed, angled wings

long bill

white, vertical streaks

long, tapered bill, slightly drooping at tip

ADULT

short tail

mostly brown upperparts

brown spots on breast and neck

IN FLIGHT

white underparts with barring on flanks

short russet tail

MALE

FLIGHT: extremely fast and zig-zagging, rapid wing beats; erratic-looking changes of direction.

Also known as the Common Snipe, this secretive and well camouflaged member of the sandpiper family has an unsettled taxonomic history. On its breeding grounds Wilson's Snipe produces rather eerie sounds during its aerial, mainly nocturnal, display flights. The birds fly up silently from the ground, then, from about 330ft (100m) up, they descend quickly, with their tail feathers spread, producing a unique, loud and vibrating sound through modified feathers. The North American populations belong to subspecies *delicata*.

VOICE Alarm and overhead flight call raspy *kraitsch*; perched and low flying breeding birds give repetitive, monotonous *kup-kup-kup-kup* in alarm or aggression; distinctive whistling sound during territorial displays.

NESTING Elaborate woven nest lined with fine grass on ground, sedge, or moss; 4 eggs; 1 brood; May–June.

FEEDING Forages in mud or shallow water; probes deep into subsoil; diet includes mostly insect larvae, but also crustaceans, earthworms, and mollusks.

RUSSET TAIL
Wilson's Snipe's russet-colored tail is usually hard to see, but it is evident on this preening bird.

OCCURRENCE
Widespread from Alaska to Québec and Labrador south of the tundra zone; breeds in a variety of wetlands, including marshes, bogs, and open areas with rich soil. Winters further south, where it prefers damp areas with vegetative cover, such as marshes, wet fields, and other bodies of water.

SIMILAR SPECIES

AMERICAN WOODCOCK see p.161	SHORT-BILLED DOWITCHER see p.163	LONG-BILLED DOWITCHER see p.164
plump body	smaller eye	no white streaks on back
buffy orange underparts	orange tint to breast	longer legs

Length **10–11in (25–28cm)**	Wingspan **17–19in (43–48cm)**	Weight **2⅞–5oz (80–150g)**
Social **Solitary**	Lifespan **Up to 10 years**	Status **Secure**

DATE SEEN	WHERE	NOTES

| Order **Charadriiformes** | Family **Scolopacidae** | Species *Limnodromus griseus* |

Short-billed Dowitcher

white slash from rump to mid-back

ADULT (BREEDING)

long, pointed wings

IN FLIGHT

orange-fringed feathers

flanks less heavily streaked

JUVENILE

dark-centered upperpart feathers

ADULT
L. g. griseus

greenish yellow legs

streaked flanks

orange wash to face, neck, breast, and underparts

long, stout bill

variable spotting on upper breast

slightly larger bill

ADULT
L. g. hendersoni

plain gray upperparts

white belly

ADULT (NONBREEDING)

WWWWWWWWWWWW

FLIGHT: swift, powerful with quick wing beats.

The Short-billed Dowitcher is a common visitor along the Atlantic, Gulf, and Pacific Coasts. Its remote and bug-infested breeding areas in northern bogs have hindered the study of its breeding behavior until recent years. There are three subspecies (*L. g. griseus*, *L. g. hendersoni*, and *L. g. caurinus*,) which differ in plumage, size, and respective breeding areas. Recent knowledge about shape and structure has helped ornithologists distinguish the Short-billed from the Long-billed Dowitcher.
VOICE Flight call low, plaintive *tu-tu-tu*, 3–4 notes; flight song *tu-tu, tu-tu, toodle-ee, tu-tu*, ending with low *anh-anh-anh*.
NESTING Simple depression, typically in sedge hummock; 4 eggs; 1 brood; May–June.
FEEDING Probes in "sewing machine" feeding style with water up to belly for aquatic mollusks, crustaceans, and insects.

ORANGE UNDERPARTS
In complete breeding plumage, the Short-billed Dowitcher is orange, even in late afternoon light.

SIMILAR SPECIES

WILSON'S SNIPE ♂
see p.162

shorter legs

LONG-BILLED DOWITCHER
see p.164

slightly thicker neck

slightly longer legs

OCCURRENCE
Breeds mostly in sedge meadows or bogs with interspersed spruce and tamaracks between sub-Arctic tundra and boreal forest. Migrates south to Central and South America, preferring coastal mudflats, salt marshes, or adjacent freshwater pools.

| Length **9–10in (23–25cm)** | Wingspan **18–20in (46–51cm)** | Weight **2½–5½oz (70–155g)** |
| Social **Pairs/Flocks** | Lifespan **Up to 20 years** | Status **Secure (p)** |

DATE SEEN	WHERE	NOTES
....	....	....
....	....	....
....	....	....
....	....	....
....	....	....

| Order **Charadriiformes** | Family **Scolopacidae** | Species *Limnodromus scolopaceus* |

Long-billed Dowitcher

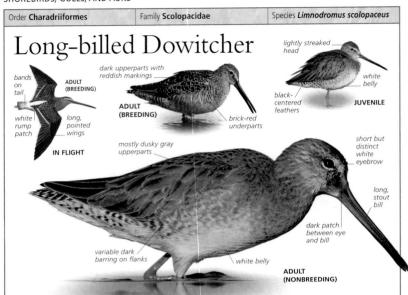

IN FLIGHT
bands on tail
white rump patch
long, pointed wings

ADULT (BREEDING)
dark upperparts with reddish markings
brick-red underparts

JUVENILE
lightly streaked head
white belly
black-centered feathers

ADULT (NONBREEDING)
mostly dusky gray upperparts
short but distinct white eyebrow
long, stout bill
dark patch between eye and bill
variable dark barring on flanks
white belly

It was not until 1950 that, after museum and field studies, scientists recognized two separate species of dowitcher in North America. The Long-billed Dowitcher is usually slightly larger, longer-legged, and heavier in the chest and neck than the Short-billed Dowitcher. The breeding ranges of the two species are separate, but their migration and en route stop-over areas overlap. The Long-billed Dowitcher is usually found in freshwater wetlands, and in the fall most of its population occurs west of the Mississippi River.

VOICE Flight and alarm call sharp, whistled *keek*, given singly or in series when agitated; song buzzy *pipipipipipi-chi-drrr*.

NESTING Deep sedge or grass-lined depression in sedge or grass; 4 eggs; 1 brood; May–June.

FEEDING Probes wet ground with "sewing-machine" motion for spiders, snails, worms, insects, and seeds.

FLIGHT: swift, direct flier with fast, powerful wing beats.

TOUCHY FEELY
Sensitive touch-receptors at the tip of the bird's bill enable it to feel in the mud for food.

OCCURRENCE
Breeds in wet, grassy meadows or coastal sedge tundra near freshwater pools. Migrates to Mexico and Central America, south to Panama, when found in freshwater habitats, including ponds, flooded fields, lake shores, also sheltered lagoons, salt marsh pools, and tidal mudflats.

SIMILAR SPECIES

WILSON'S SNIPE see p.162
pale, central crown stripe
shorter legs

SHORT-BILLED DOWITCHER see p.163
slightly smaller overall
orangish underparts

| Length **9½–10in (24–26cm)** | Wingspan **18–20½in (46–52cm)** | Weight **3–4oz (85–125g)** |
| Social **Pairs/Flocks** | Lifespan **Unknown** | Status **Secure** |

DATE SEEN	WHERE	NOTES

| Order **Charadriiformes** | Family **Scolopacidae** | Species *Limosa haemastica* |

Hudsonian Godwit

white wing stripe

ADULT (NONBREEDING)

brownish gray upperparts

pale eyebrow

long, orange-based bill

white rump

off-white underparts

IN FLIGHT

pale, buffy feather fringes

JUVENILE

black-and-white upperparts

brownish streaked head and neck

unpatterned brownish wing feathers

black tail

rich chestnut underparts with black barring

white-feathered chestnut breast

FLIGHT: swift and straight, with fast and powerful wing beats.

MALE (BREEDING)

FEMALE (BREEDING)

This large, graceful sandpiper, with a long and slightly upturned bill, undertakes a remarkable annual migration from its tundra breeding grounds in Alaska and Canada all the way to extreme southern South America, a distance probably close to 10,000 miles (16,000km) in one direction, with very few stopovers. The number of breeding birds is unknown, but counts in Tierra del Fuego indicate totals of perhaps 30,000 to 40,000 birds, all found in two areas of tidal mudflats. Between the far North and the far South, North American stops are few, and only in the spring, along a central route mid-continent. Hudsonian Godwits spend six months wintering, two months breeding, and four flying between the two locations.

VOICE Flight call emphatic *peed-wid*; also high *peet* or *kwee*; display song *to-wida to-wida to-wida*, or *to-wit, to-wit, to-wit*.

NESTING Saucer-shaped depression on dry hummock or tussocks under cover; 4 eggs; 1 brood; May–July.

FEEDING Probes in mud for insects, insect grubs, worms, crustaceans and mollusks; also eats plant tubers in fall.

LONG-HAUL BIRD
Hudsonian Godwits only make a few stops on their long flights to and from South America.

SIMILAR SPECIES

BAR-TAILED GODWIT see p.472
more streaks

shorter legs

longer bill

OCCURRENCE
Breeds in the high Arctic, in sedge meadows and bogs in scattered tundra; scarce along the Atlantic Coast in fall near coastal freshwater reservoirs; but locally common in flooded rice fields, pastures, and reservoirs in spring. Winters in extreme southern Chile and Argentina.

| Length **14–16in (35–41cm)** | Wingspan **27–31in (68–78cm)** | Weight **7–12oz (200–350g)** |
| Social **Flocks** | Lifespan **Up to 29 years** | Status **Declining** |

DATE SEEN	WHERE	NOTES

Order **Charadriiformes**	Family **Scolopacidae**	Species *Limosa fedoa*

Marbled Godwit

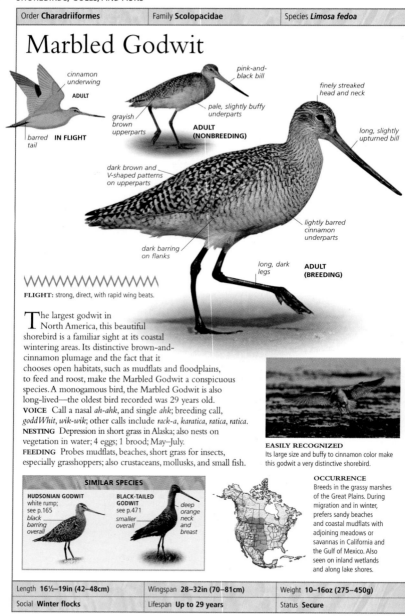

cinnamon underwing

ADULT

barred **IN FLIGHT** tail

pink-and-black bill

grayish brown upperparts

pale, slightly buffy underparts

ADULT (NONBREEDING)

finely streaked head and neck

long, slightly upturned bill

dark brown and V-shaped patterns on upperparts

lightly barred cinnamon underparts

dark barring on flanks

long, dark legs

ADULT (BREEDING)

FLIGHT: strong, direct, with rapid wing beats.

The largest godwit in North America, this beautiful shorebird is a familiar sight at its coastal wintering areas. Its distinctive brown-and-cinnamon plumage and the fact that it chooses open habitats, such as mudflats and floodplains, to feed and roost, make the Marbled Godwit a conspicuous species. A monogamous bird, the Marbled Godwit is also long-lived—the oldest bird recorded was 29 years old.

VOICE Call a nasal *ah-ahk*, and single *ahk*; breeding call, *goddWhit*, *wik-wik*; other calls include *rack-a*, *karatica*, *ratica*, *ratica*.

NESTING Depression in short grass in Alaska; also nests on vegetation in water; 4 eggs; 1 brood; May–July.

FEEDING Probes mudflats, beaches, short grass for insects, especially grasshoppers; also crustaceans, mollusks, and small fish.

EASILY RECOGNIZED
Its large size and buffy to cinnamon color make this godwit a very distinctive shorebird.

SIMILAR SPECIES

HUDSONIAN GODWIT white rump; see p.165 black barring overall

BLACK-TAILED GODWIT see p.471 smaller overall

deep orange neck and breast

OCCURRENCE
Breeds in the grassy marshes of the Great Plains. During migration and in winter, prefers sandy beaches and coastal mudflats with adjoining meadows or savannas in California and the Gulf of Mexico. Also seen on inland wetlands and along lake shores.

Length **16½–19in (42–48cm)**	Wingspan **28–32in (70–81cm)**	Weight **10–16oz (275–450g)**
Social **Winter flocks**	Lifespan **Up to 29 years**	Status **Secure**

DATE SEEN	WHERE	NOTES

Order **Charadriiformes**	Family **Scolopacidae**	Species **Numenius phaeopus**

Whimbrel

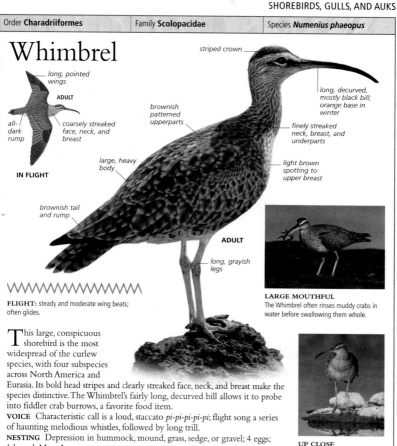

striped crown

long, pointed wings

ADULT

all-dark rump

coarsely streaked face, neck, and breast

IN FLIGHT

brownish patterned upperparts

long, decurved, mostly black bill; orange base in winter

finely streaked neck, breast, and underparts

light brown spotting to upper breast

large, heavy body

brownish tail and rump

ADULT

long, grayish legs

FLIGHT: steady and moderate wing beats; often glides.

LARGE MOUTHFUL
The Whimbrel often rinses muddy crabs in water before swallowing them whole.

This large, conspicuous shorebird is the most widespread of the curlew species, with four subspecies across North America and Eurasia. Its bold head stripes and clearly streaked face, neck, and breast make the species distinctive. The Whimbrel's fairly long, decurved bill allows it to probe into fiddler crab burrows, a favorite food item.

VOICE Characteristic call is a loud, staccato *pi-pi-pi-pi-pi*; flight song a series of haunting melodious whistles, followed by long trill.

NESTING Depression in hummock, mound, grass, sedge, or gravel; 4 eggs; 1 brood; May–August.

FEEDING Probes for crabs, in addition to worms, mollusks, and fish; also eats insects and berries.

UP CLOSE
A close look at the Whimbrel shows this bird's beautiful, fine patterning.

SIMILAR SPECIES

BRISTLE-THIGHED CURLEW

longer, slightly curved bill

pale rump

more spotted

LONG-BILLED CURLEW, see p.450

larger overall

long, decurved bill

OCCURRENCE
Several populations breed in northern, sub-Arctic, and low-Arctic regions of North America; during migration and in winter, found mostly in coastal marshes, tidal creeks, flats, and mangroves; also at inland Salton Sea, California. Winters along rocky coasts in South America.

Length **15½–16½in (39–42cm)**	Wingspan **30–35in (76–89cm)**	Weight **11–18oz (300–500g)**
Social **Flocks**	Lifespan **Up to 19 years**	Status **Secure**

DATE SEEN	WHERE	NOTES
....	....	....
....	....	....
....	....	....
....	....	....

Order **Charadriiformes**	Family **Scolopacidae**	Species *Bartramia longicauda*

Upland Sandpiper

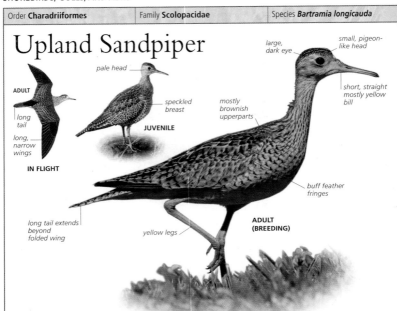

large, dark eye

small, pigeon-like head

pale head

short, straight mostly yellow bill

ADULT

long tail

speckled breast

mostly brownish upperparts

long, narrow wings

JUVENILE

IN FLIGHT

buff feather fringes

long tail extends beyond folded wing

yellow legs

ADULT (BREEDING)

Unlike other sandpipers, this graceful bird spends most of its life away from water in grassy habitats. The Upland Sandpiper's coloration helps it camouflage itself in the grasslands, especially while nesting on the ground. It is well known for landing on fence posts and raising its wings while giving its tremulous, whistling call. The bird is currently listed as endangered in many of its breeding states due to the disappearance of its grassland habitat.

VOICE Flight call a low *qui-pi-pi-pi*; song consists of gurgling notes followed by long, descending "wolf whistle" *whooooleeeeee*, *wheeelooooo-ooooo*.

NESTING Simple depression in ground among grass clumps; 4 eggs; 1 brood; May.

FEEDING Feeds with head-bobbing motion on adult and larval insects, spiders, worms, centipedes; occasionally seeds.

FLIGHT: strong and swift; rapid, fluttering flight in breeding display.

DRY GROUND WADER
A true grassland species, the Upland Sandpiper is rarely found away from this habitat.

SIMILAR SPECIES

WHIMBREL see p.167

long, curved bill

dull bluish gray legs

LONG-BILLED CURLEW ♂ see p.450

very long, curved bill

much larger overall

OCCURRENCE
Breeds in native tallgrass or mixed-grass prairies. Airports make up large portion of its breeding habitat in the northeast US. During migration and in winter it prefers shortgrass habitats such as grazed pastures, turf farms, cultivated fields.

Length **11–12½in (28–32cm)**	Wingspan **25–27in (64–68cm)**	Weight **4–7oz (150–200g)**
Social **Migrant flocks**	Lifespan **Unknown**	Status **Declining**

DATE SEEN	WHERE	NOTES

| Order **Charadriiformes** | Family **Scolopacidae** | Species *Tringa melanoleuca* |

Greater Yellowlegs

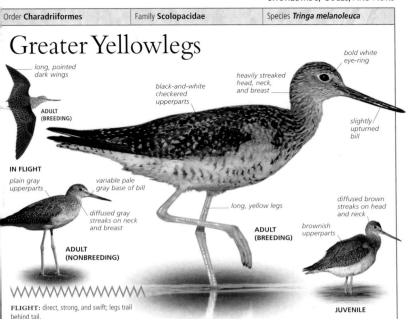

long, pointed
dark wings

**ADULT
(BREEDING)**

IN FLIGHT

bold white
eye-ring

heavily streaked
head, neck,
and breast

black-and-white
checkered
upperparts

slightly
upturned
bill

plain gray
upperparts

variable pale
gray base of bill

diffused gray
streaks on neck
and breast

long, yellow legs

diffused brown
streaks on head
and neck

brownish
upperparts

**ADULT
(NONBREEDING)**

**ADULT
(BREEDING)**

JUVENILE

FLIGHT: direct, strong, and swift; legs trail
behind tail.

This fairly large shorebird often runs frantically in many
directions while pursuing small prey. It is one of the first
northbound spring shorebird migrants, and one of the first to
return south in late June or early July. Its plumage, a mixture
of brown, black, and white checkered upperparts, and streaked
underparts, is more streaked during the breeding season.
VOICE Call a loud, penetrating *tew-tew-tew*; agitated birds make
repetitive *keu* notes; song a continuous *too-whee.*
NESTING Simple scrape in moss or peat, usually close to water;
4 eggs; 1 brood; May–June.
FEEDING Picks water surface and mud for small aquatic and
terrestrial crustaceans and worms; also eats small fish, frogs,
seeds, and berries.

EFFECTIVE METHOD
The Greater Yellowlegs often catches its prey
by sweeping its bill sideways through water.

SIMILAR SPECIES

LESSER YELLOWLEGS
see p.170

less
angular
body
contours

thinner,
more
pointed
bill

WILLET
see p.173
lacks checkered
upperparts

heavier,
thicker bill

OCCURRENCE
Breeds in openings in northerly
forests with bogs and wet
meadows, a habitat called
muskegs. In migration and
winter, uses a wide variety
of shallow water habitats,
including freshwater and
saltwater marshes, reservoirs,
and tidal mudflats.

| Length **11½–13in (29–33cm)** | Wingspan **28–29in (70–74cm)** | Weight **4–8oz (125–225g)** |
| Social **Solitary/Flocks** | Lifespan **Unknown** | Status **Secure** |

DATE SEEN	WHERE	NOTES

| Order **Charadriiformes** | Family **Scolopacidae** | Species *Tringa flavipes* |

Lesser Yellowlegs

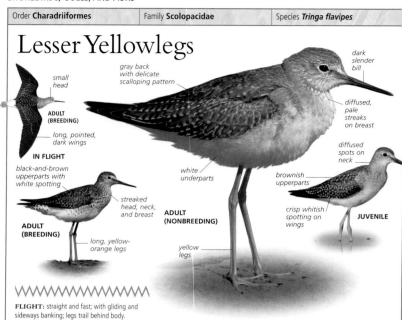

ADULT (BREEDING)
small head

long, pointed, dark wings

IN FLIGHT

gray back with delicate scalloping pattern

dark slender bill

diffused, pale streaks on breast

diffused spots on neck

black-and-brown upperparts with white spotting

white underparts

ADULT (BREEDING)

streaked head, neck, and breast

brownish upperparts

crisp whitish spotting on wings

JUVENILE

ADULT (NONBREEDING)

long, yellow-orange legs

yellow legs

FLIGHT: straight and fast; with gliding and sideways banking; legs trail behind body.

With its smaller head, thinner bill, and smoother body shape, the Lesser Yellowlegs has a more elegant profile than the Greater Yellowlegs. It prefers smaller, freshwater, or brackish pools to open saltwater habitats, and it walks quickly and methodically while feeding. Although this species is a solitary feeder, it is often seen in small to large loose flocks in migration and winter.

VOICE Low, whistled *tu*, or *tu-tu* call; series of *tu* or *cuw* notes when agitated; display song a *pill-e-wee, pill-e-wee, pill-e-wee.*
NESTING Depression in ground or moss, lined with grass and leaves; 4 eggs; 1 brood; May–June.
FEEDING Eats a wide variety of aquatic and terrestrial insects, mollusks, and crustaceans, especially flies and beetles; also seeds.

READY TO FLY
This Lesser Yellowlegs raises its wings before takeoff.

SIMILAR SPECIES

GREATER YELLOWLEGS
see p.169

larger and heavier

longer, thicker bill

SOLITARY SANDPIPER
see p.171

shorter, greenish yellow legs

more defined breast streaks

OCCURRENCE
Breeds in northerly forest with clearings, and where forest meets tundra. In migration and in winter, uses wide variety of shallow wetlands, including flooded pastures and agricultural fields, swamps, lake and river shores, tidal creeks, and brackish mudflats. Winters from Mexico to Argentina.

| Length **9–10in (23–25cm)** | Wingspan **23–25in (58–64cm)** | Weight **2–3⅜oz (55–95g)** |
| Social **Flocks** | Lifespan **Unknown** | Status **Secure** |

DATE SEEN	WHERE	NOTES

| Order **Charadriiformes** | Family **Scolopacidae** | Species ***Tringa solitaria*** |

Solitary Sandpiper

long, pointed wings

ADULT (BREEDING)

dark flight feathers

IN FLIGHT

brown-and-white checkered upperparts

brownish streaked crown and head

JUVENILE

dark-and-white checkered upperparts

ADULT (BREEDING)

conspicuous white eye-ring

roundish forehead

straight dark, tapered bill

finely streaked breast

greenish olive legs

FLIGHT: graceful and strong, with deep, stiff wing beats.

Alexander Wilson described this species in 1813, naming it, quite appropriately, "Solitary." This sandpiper seldom associates with other shorebirds as it moves nervously along margins of wetlands. When feeding, the Solitary Sandpiper constantly bobs its head like the Spotted Sandpiper. When disturbed, the Solitary Sandpiper often flies directly upward, and when landing, it keeps its wings upright briefly, flashing the white underneath, before carefully folding them to its body.

VOICE Flight and alarm call a high-pitched *weet-weet-weet* or *pit*; display song a *pit-pit-pit-pit; kik-kik-kik.*

NESTING Abandoned nests in trees (a unique behavior for a North American shorebird); 4 eggs; 1 brood; May–June.

FEEDING Eats insects, small crustaceans, snails, and small frogs.

LONE RANGER
This sandpiper is indeed solitary and is found in quiet, sheltered habitats and along river shores.

SIMILAR SPECIES

LESSER YELLOWLEGS ♂
see p.170
slimmer body
yellow-orange legs

SPOTTED SANDPIPER
see p.172
bulkier body
shorter bill
shorter legs

OCCURRENCE
Breeds primarily in bogs in northern forests; in winter and during migration, occurs in sheltered pools or muddy areas near forests. Winters from Mexico down to South America, sometimes in tiny pools at high altitude in the Andes; also riverbanks, streams, rain pools, and ditches.

Length **7½–9in (19–23cm)**	Wingspan **22–23in (56–59cm)**	Weight **1¹⁄₁₆–2¼oz (30–65g)**
Social **Solitary/Small flocks**	Lifespan **Unknown**	Status **Secure**

DATE SEEN	WHERE	NOTES

| Order **Charadriiformes** | Family **Scolopacidae** | Species *Actitis macularia* |

Spotted Sandpiper

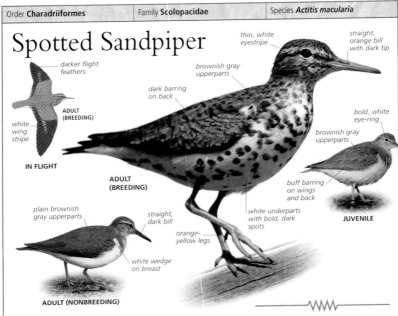

darker flight feathers

ADULT (BREEDING)

white wing stripe

IN FLIGHT

thin, white eyestripe

straight, orange bill with dark tip

brownish gray upperparts

dark barring on back

ADULT (BREEDING)

bold, white eye-ring

brownish gray upperparts

buff barring on wings and back

white underparts with bold, dark spots

JUVENILE

plain brownish gray upperparts

straight, dark bill

orange-yellow legs

white wedge on breast

ADULT (NONBREEDING)

One of only two species of the genus *Actitis*, from the Latin meaning "a coastal inhabitant," this small, short-legged sandpiper is the most widespread shorebird in North America. It is characterized by its quick walking pace, its habit of constantly teetering and bobbing its tail, and its unique style of flying low over water with stiff wing beats. These birds have an unusual mating behavior, in which the females take on an aggressive role, defending territories and mating with three or more males per season.
VOICE Call a clear, ringing note *tee-tee-tee-tee*; flight song a monotonous *cree-cree-cree*.
NESTING Nest cup shaded by or scrape built under herbaceous vegetation; 3 eggs; 1–3 broods; May–June.
FEEDING Eats many items, including adult and larval insects, mollusks, small crabs, and worms.

FLIGHT: mostly shallow, rapidly, stiffly fluttering wing beats, usually low above water.

BEHAVIORAL QUIRKS
This sandpiper "teeters," raising and lowering its tail while walking along the water's edge.

OCCURRENCE
Breeds across North America in a wide variety of grassy, brushy, forested habitats near water, but not high Arctic tundra. During migration and in winter found in habitats near freshwater, including lake shores, rivers, streams, beaches, sewage ponds, ditches, seawalls, sometimes estuaries.

SIMILAR SPECIES

SOLITARY SANDPIPER ♀
see p.171

more slender body

longer legs

streaked breast

COMMON SANDPIPER

longer tail

more grayish green legs

| Length **7¼–8in (18.5–20cm)** | Wingspan **15–16in (38–41cm)** | Weight **1⁹⁄₁₆–1¾oz (45–50g)** |
| Social **Small flocks** | Lifespan **Up to 12 years** | Status **Secure** |

DATE SEEN	WHERE	NOTES

Order **Charadriiformes**	Family **Scolopacidae**	Species ***Catoptrophorus semipalmatus***

Willet

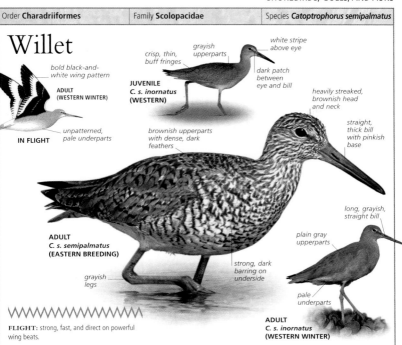

bold black-and-white wing pattern

ADULT (WESTERN WINTER)

IN FLIGHT — unpatterned, pale underparts

grayish upperparts

crisp, thin, buff fringes

JUVENILE *C. s. inornatus* (WESTERN)

white stripe above eye

dark patch between eye and bill

heavily streaked, brownish head and neck

straight, thick bill with pinkish base

brownish upperparts with dense, dark feathers

ADULT *C. s. semipalmatus* (EASTERN BREEDING)

grayish legs

strong, dark barring on underside

long, grayish, straight bill

plain gray upperparts

pale underparts

ADULT *C. s. inornatus* (WESTERN WINTER)

FLIGHT: strong, fast, and direct on powerful wing beats.

The two distinct subspecies of the Willet, Eastern (*C. s. semipalmatus*) and Western (*C. s. inornatus*), differ in breeding habit, plumage coloration, vocalizations, and migratory habits. The Eastern Willet leaves North America from September to March; whereas the Western Willet winters along southern North American shorelines south to South America.

VOICE Flight call a loud *kyah-yah*; alarm call a sharp, repeated *kleep*; song an urgent, rapid *pill-will-willet*.

NESTING Depression in vegetated dunes, wetlands, prairies, or salt marshes; 4 eggs; 1 brood; April–June.

FEEDING Picks, probes, or swishes for crustaceans such as fiddler and mole crabs, aquatic insects, marine worms, small mollusks, and fish.

EXPOSED PERCH
Willets display on exposed perches at breeding grounds.

OCCURRENCE
Eastern subspecies breeds in coastal saltwater habitats: salt marshes, barrier islands, beaches, mangroves; winters in similar habitats. Western subspecies breeds near sparsely vegetated prairie wetlands or adjacent semi-arid grasslands; winters in coastal regions.

SIMILAR SPECIES

GREATER YELLOWLEGS see p.169

longer neck

yellowish orange legs

WANDERING TATTLER ✿1ST✿

stockier body

yellowish legs

Length **12½–16½in (32–42cm)**	Wingspan **21½–28½in (54–72cm)**	Weight **7–12oz (200–350g)**
Social **Flocks**	Lifespan **Up to 10 years**	Status **Secure**

DATE SEEN	WHERE	NOTES

| Order **Charadriiformes** | Family **Scolopacidae** | Species *Arenaria interpres* |

Ruddy Turnstone

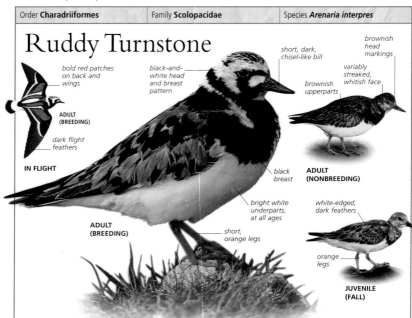

bold red patches on back and wings

ADULT (BREEDING)

dark flight feathers

IN FLIGHT

black-and-white head and breast pattern

short, dark, chisel-like bill

brownish head markings

variably streaked, whitish face

brownish upperparts

ADULT (NONBREEDING)

black breast

bright white underparts, at all ages

white-edged, dark feathers

orange legs

JUVENILE (FALL)

ADULT (BREEDING)

short, orange legs

This tame, medium-sized, and stocky sandpiper with a chisel-shaped bill is a common visitor along the shorelines of North and South America. On its high-Arctic breeding grounds, it is bold and aggressive and is able to drive off predators as large as the Glaucous Gull and Parasitic Jaeger. The Ruddy Turnstone was given its name because of its reddish back color and because of its habit of flipping and overturning items like mollusk shells and pebbles, or digging in the sand and looking for small crustaceans and other marine invertebrates. Two subspecies live in Arctic North America: *A. i. interpres* in northeastern Canada and *A. i. morinellas* elsewhere in Canada and Alaska.

VOICE Rapid chatter on breeding ground: *TTT-wooo TTT-woooRITititititititit*; flight call a low, rapid *kut-a-kut.*

NESTING Simple scrape lined with lichens and grasses in dry, open areas; 4 eggs; 1 brood; June.

FEEDING Forages along shoreline for crustaceans, insects, including beetles, spiders; also eats plants.

FLIGHT: swift and strong flight, with quick wing beats.

WINTER GATHERINGS
Ruddy Turnstones often congregate in large winter flocks on rocky shorelines.

SIMILAR SPECIES

BLACK TURNSTONE

darker overall

no rust color in plumage

duller legs

OCCURRENCE
Breeds in high Arctic: wide-open, barren, and grassy habitats and rocky coasts, usually near water. In winter, on sandy or gravel beaches and rocky shorelines, from northern California to South America, and from northern Massachusetts south along Atlantic and Gulf Coasts.

| Length **8–10½in (20–27cm)** | Wingspan **20–22½in (51–57cm)** | Weight **3½–7oz (100–200g)** |
| Social **Flocks** | Lifespan **Up to 7 years** | Status **Secure** |

DATE SEEN	WHERE	NOTES

Order **Charadriiformes**	Family **Scolopacidae**	Species *Calidris canutus*

Red Knot

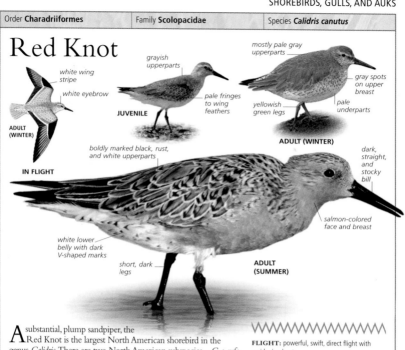

grayish upperparts

mostly pale gray upperparts

white wing stripe

white eyebrow

JUVENILE

pale fringes to wing feathers

gray spots on upper breast

yellowish green legs

pale underparts

ADULT (WINTER)

ADULT (WINTER)

IN FLIGHT

boldly marked black, rust, and white upperparts

dark, straight, and stocky bill

salmon-colored face and breast

white lower belly with dark V-shaped marks

short, dark legs

ADULT (SUMMER)

A substantial, plump sandpiper, the Red Knot is the largest North American shorebird in the genus *Calidris*. There are two North American subspecies—*C. c. rufa* and *C. c. roselaari*. Noted for its extraordinary long-distance migration, *C. c. rufa* flies about 9,300 miles (15,000km) between its high-Arctic breeding grounds and wintering area in South America, especially in Tierra del Fuego, at the tip of South America. Recent declines have occurred in this population, attributed to over-harvesting of horseshoe crab eggs—its critical food source. With the population of *C. c. rufa* having declined from over 100,000 birds in the mid-1980s to below 15,000 today, the Red Knot is now listed as endangered in New Jersey, and faces possible extinction.

VOICE Flight call a soft *kuEEt* or *kuup*; display song *eerie por-meeee por-meeee*, followed by *por-por por-por*.

NESTING Simple scrape in grassy or barren tundra, often lined; 4 eggs; 1 brood; June.

FEEDING Probes mud or sand for insects, plant material, small mollusks, crustaceans, especially small snails, worms, and other invertebrates.

FLIGHT: powerful, swift, direct flight with rapid wing beats.

STAGING AREAS
Red Knots form dense flocks during migration and on their wintering grounds.

SIMILAR SPECIES

BLACK-BELLIED PLOVER
see p.155
large, dark eye

longer, dark legs

OCCURRENCE
Breeds in flat, barren tundra in high-Arctic islands and peninsulas. Mostly coastal during migration and winter, preferring sandbars, beaches, and tidal flats, where it congregates in huge flocks.

Length **9–10in (23–25cm)**	Wingspan **23–24in (58–61cm)**	Weight **3¾–8oz (95–225g)**
Social **Large flocks**	Lifespan **Unknown**	Status **Declining**

DATE SEEN	WHERE	NOTES

Order **Charadriiformes**	Family **Scolopacidae**	Species **Calidris alba**

Sanderling

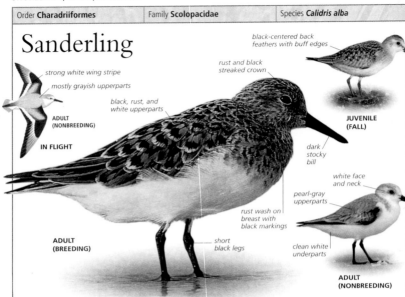

strong white wing stripe

mostly grayish upperparts

ADULT (NONBREEDING)

IN FLIGHT

black, rust, and white upperparts

rust and black streaked crown

black-centered back feathers with buff edges

JUVENILE (FALL)

dark stocky bill

white face and neck

pearl-gray upperparts

rust wash on breast with black markings

ADULT (BREEDING)

short black legs

clean white underparts

ADULT (NONBREEDING)

The Sanderling is probably the best-known shorebird in the world. It breeds in some of the most remote, high-Arctic habitats, from Greenland to Siberia, but occupies just about every temperate and tropical shoreline in the Americas when not breeding. Indeed, its wintering range spans both American coasts, from Canada to Argentina. Feeding in flocks, it is a common sight in winter on sandy beaches. In many places, though, the bird is declining rapidly, with pollution of the sea and shore, and the disturbance caused by people using beaches for various recreational purposes, the main causes.

VOICE Flight call squeaky *pweet*, threat call *sew-sew-sew*; display song harsh, buzzy notes and chattering *cher-cher-cher*.

NESTING Small, shallow depression on dry, stony ground; 4 eggs; 1–3 broods; June–July.

FEEDING Probes along the surf-line in sand for insects, small crustaceans, small mollusks, and worms.

FLIGHT: rapid, free-form; birds in flocks twisting and turning as if they were one.

CHASING THE WAVES
The sanderling scampers after retreating waves to pick up any small creatures stranded by the sea.

SIMILAR SPECIES

SEMIPALMATED SANDPIPER ✿ see p.177

less contrasting upperparts

WESTERN SANDPIPER see p.178

prominent eyebrow

paler throat and breast

tapering bill

OCCURRENCE
Breeds in barren high-Arctic coastal tundra of northernmost Canada, including the islands, north to Ellesmere Island. During winter months and on migration, found along all North American coastlines, but especially sandy beaches; inland migrants found along lake and river edges.

Length **7½–8in (19–20cm)**	Wingspan **16–18in (41–46cm)**	Weight **1⁷⁄₁₆–3½oz (40–100g)**
Social **Small flocks**	Lifespan **Up to 10 years**	Status **Declining**

DATE SEEN	WHERE	NOTES

| Order **Charadriiformes** | Family **Scolopacidae** | Species *Calidris pusilla* |

Semipalmated Sandpiper

SUMMER

IN FLIGHT

white eyebrow

crisp, pale fringed feathers

short bill with blunt tip

pale grayish black legs

dark-centered back feathers with buff fringes

slightly paler grayish nape

streaked black and rust crown

pale wing stripe along flight feathers

JUVENILE

short, dark bill

wing tips extend to tail tip

ADULT (SUMMER)

lightly streaked breast

This is the most abundant of the so-called "peep" *Calidris* sandpipers, especially in the eastern US. Flocks of up to 300,000 birds gather on migration staging areas. As a species, though, it can be hard to identify, due to plumage variation between juveniles and breeding adults, and a bill that varies markedly in size and shape from west to east. Semipalmated sandpipers from northeasterly breeding grounds may fly nonstop to their South American wintering grounds in the fall.

VOICE Flight call *chrrk* or higher, sharper *chit*; display song monotonous, droning trill, often repeated for minutes at a time.

NESTING Shallow, lined scrape in short grass habitat; 4 eggs; 1 brood; May–June.

FEEDING Probes mud for aquatic and terrestrial invertebrates such as mollusks, worms, and spiders.

FLIGHT: fast and direct on narrow, pointed, wings; flies in large flocks in winter.

SLEEPING TOGETHER
Semipalmated Sandpipers form large feeding or resting flocks on migration and in winter.

OCCURRENCE
Breeds in Arctic and sub-Arctic tundra habitats near water; in Alaska, on outer coastal plain. Migrants occur in shallow fresh- or saltwater and open muddy areas with little vegetation, such as intertidal flats or lake shores. Winters in Central and South America, south to Brazil and Peru.

SIMILAR SPECIES		
SANDERLING see p.176 more contrasting upperparts	**WESTERN SANDPIPER** ✷ see p.178	puffier head
		LEAST SANDPIPER ✷ see p.179
darker breast	usually longer legs	usually more pointed bill
	yellowish legs	smaller overall

Length **5¼–6in (13.5–15cm)**	Wingspan **13½–15in (34–38cm)**	Weight **½–1⅜oz (14–40g)**
Social **Large flocks**	Lifespan **Up to 12 years**	Status **Secure**

DATE SEEN	WHERE	NOTES

Order **Charadriiformes**	Family **Scolopacidae**	Species *Calidris mauri*

Western Sandpiper

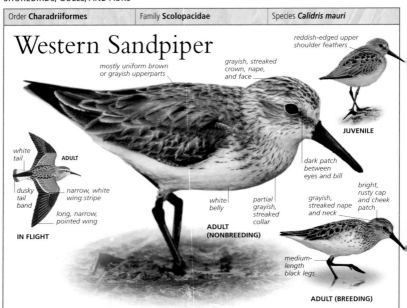

reddish-edged upper shoulder feathers

mostly uniform brown or grayish upperparts

grayish, streaked crown, nape, and face

JUVENILE

white tail

ADULT

dusky tail band

narrow, white wing stripe

long, narrow, pointed wing

IN FLIGHT

dark patch between eyes and bill

white belly

partial grayish, streaked collar

ADULT (NONBREEDING)

grayish, streaked nape and neck

bright, rusty cap and cheek patch

medium-length black legs

ADULT (BREEDING)

Despite its restricted breeding range in western Alaska, the Western Sandpiper is one of the most common shorebirds in the Western Hemisphere. During its spring migration spectacularly large flocks are seen at several Pacific coast locations. At the Copper River Delta in Alaska, for instance, over four million Western Sandpipers stop on their way to their tundra breeding grounds to fatten up and refuel for the last hop northward. Many of these migrate over relatively short distances to winter along US coastlines. In spite of its name, the Western Sandpiper is common in the East along the Atlantic coast.

VOICE Flight call loud *chir-eep*; flushed birds make *sirp* call, or *chir-ir-ip*; song *tweer, tweer, tweer*, followed by descending trill.

NESTING Shallow depression on drained Arctic and sub-Arctic tundra; 4 eggs; 1 brood; May–June.

FEEDING Probes mud for insect larvae, crustaceans, and worms.

FLIGHT: direct, rapid flight on narrow, pointed wings; in large flocks.

FORAGING FOR FOOD
The Western Sandpiper feels for hidden prey with the touch-sensitive tip of its bill.

OCCURRENCE
Breeds in wet sedge, grassy habitats with well-drained microhabitats; in migration and in winter, prefers shallow freshwater or saltwater habitats with open muddy or sandy are and little vegetation, su s intertidal mudflats and lake shores. Winters along both coasts.

SIMILAR SPECIES

SEMIPALMATED SANDPIPER ☼
see p.177

smaller, more rounded head

slightly shorter legs

smaller, more blunt-tipped bill

DUNLIN ❄
see p.184

longer, downcurved bill

dusky head and neck

Length **5½–6½in (14–16cm)**	Wingspan **14–15in (35–38cm)**	Weight **¹¹⁄₁₆–1¼oz (19–35g)**
Social **Flocks**	Lifespan **Up to 9 years**	Status **Secure**

DATE SEEN	WHERE	NOTES

Order **Charadriiformes**	Family **Scolopacidae**	Species *Calidris minutilla*

Least Sandpiper

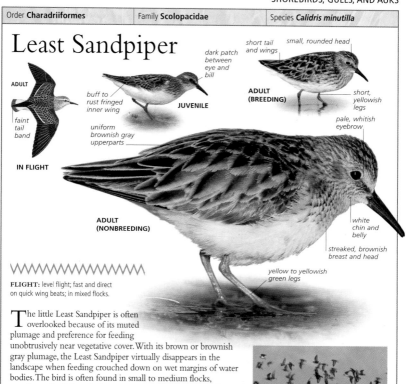

ADULT

IN FLIGHT

faint tail band

buff to rust fringed inner wing

uniform brownish gray upperparts

dark patch between eye and bill

JUVENILE

short tail and wings

small, rounded head

ADULT (BREEDING)

short, yellowish legs

pale, whitish eyebrow

white chin and belly

streaked, brownish breast and head

yellow to yellowish green legs

ADULT (NONBREEDING)

FLIGHT: level flight; fast and direct on quick wing beats; in mixed flocks.

The little Least Sandpiper is often overlooked because of its muted plumage and preference for feeding unobtrusively near vegetative cover. With its brown or brownish gray plumage, the Least Sandpiper virtually disappears in the landscape when feeding crouched down on wet margins of water bodies. The bird is often found in small to medium flocks, members of which typically are nervous when foraging, and frequently burst into flight, only to alight a short way off.
VOICE Its flight call, *kreeeep*, rises in pitch, often repeated 2-syllable *kree-eep*; display call trilled *b-reeee, b-reeee, b-reeee*.
NESTING Depression in open, sub-Arctic habitat near water; 4 eggs; 1 brood; May–June.
FEEDING Forages for variety of small terrestrial and aquatic prey, especially sand fleas, mollusks, and flies.

FLOCK IN FLIGHT
The narrow pointed wings of the Least Sandpiper allow it to fly fast and level.

SIMILAR SPECIES	
SEMIPALMATED SANDPIPER ☼ see p.177 — grayer overall, whiter throat, larger overall	**PECTORAL SANDPIPER** see p.182 — larger overall, heavier bill

OCCURRENCE
Breeds in wet low-Arctic areas from Alaska and the Yukon to Québec and Newfoundland. During migration and in winter, uses muddy areas such as lake shores, riverbanks, flooded fields, and tidal flats. Winters from southern North America south to Peru and Brazil.

Length **4¾in (12cm)**	Wingspan **13–14in (33–35cm)**	Weight **5/16–1oz (9–27g)**
Social **Flocks**	Lifespan **Up to 16 years**	Status **Secure**

DATE SEEN	WHERE	NOTES

| Order **Charadriiformes** | Family **Scolopacidae** | Species *Calidris fuscicollis* |

White-rumped Sandpiper

easily visible white rump

long, tapered wings

ADULT

IN FLIGHT

dark feathers with rust edges

IMMATURE (1ST SUMMER)

dark bill with curved tip

heavily streaked breast

grayish brown upperparts

rust-colored cap and cheek

streaked head

fine streaks on breast

crisp, pale fringed feathers

JUVENILE

The White-rumped Sandpiper undertakes one of the longest migrations of any bird in the Western Hemisphere. From its high-Arctic breeding grounds in Alaska and Canada, it migrates in several long jumps to extreme southern South America—about 9,000–12,000 miles (14,500–19,300km), twice a year. Almost the entire population migrates through the central US in spring, with several stopovers, which are critical to the success of its journey. While associating with other shorebird species during migration and winter, it can be overlooked in the crowd. Its insect-like call and white rump aid identification.

VOICE Call a very high-pitched, insect-like *tzeet*; flight song an insect-like, high-pitched, rattling buzz, interspersed with grunts.

NESTING Shallow depression in usually wet but well-vegetated tundra; 4 eggs; 1 brood; June.

FEEDING Picks and probes for insects, spiders, earthworms, and marine worms; also some plant matter.

FLIGHT: fast, strong, and direct flight with deep wing beats.

WING POWER
Long narrow wings enable this species to migrate to and from the Arctic and Tierra del Fuego.

SIMILAR SPECIES

| **SEMIPALMATED SANDPIPER** see p.177 | *slightly rufous crown* | **BAIRD'S SANDPIPER** see p.181 |

no white rump

more distinct streaks on breast

OCCURRENCE
Breeds in wet but well-vegetated tundra, usually near ponds, lakes, or streams. In migration and winter, grassy areas: flooded fields, grassy lake margins, rivers, ponds, grassy margins of tidal mudflats, and roadside ditches. On wintering grounds, often associates with Baird's Sandpiper.

| Length **6–6¾in (15–17cm)** | Wingspan **16–18in (41–46cm)** | Weight **⅞–1¾oz (25–50g)** |
| Social **Flocks** | Lifespan **Unknown** | Status **Secure** |

DATE SEEN	WHERE		NOTES

Order **Charadriiformes**	Family **Scolopacidae**	Species *Calidris bairdii*

Baird's Sandpiper

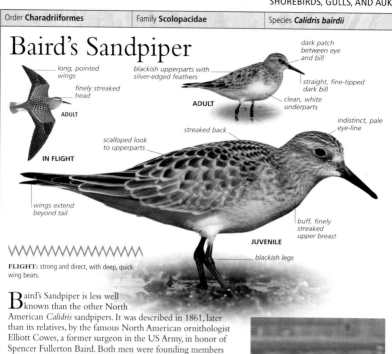

long, pointed wings

finely streaked head

ADULT

IN FLIGHT

wings extend beyond tail

blackish upperparts with silver-edged feathers

dark patch between eye and bill

ADULT

straight, fine-tipped dark bill

clean, white underparts

indistinct, pale eye-line

streaked back

scalloped look to upperparts

buff, finely streaked upper breast

JUVENILE

blackish legs

FLIGHT: strong and direct, with deep, quick wing beats.

Baird's Sandpiper is less well known than the other North American *Calidris* sandpipers. It was described in 1861, later than its relatives, by the famous North American ornithologist Elliott Cowes, a former surgeon in the US Army, in honor of Spencer Fullerton Baird. Both men were founding members of the AOU (the American Ornithologists' Union). From its high Arctic, tundra habitat, Baird's Sandpiper moves across North America and the western US, into South America, and all the way to Tierra del Fuego, a remarkable biannual journey of 6,000–9,000 miles (9,700–14,500km).

VOICE Flight call a low, dry *preep*; song on Arctic breeding ground: *braay, bray, brray*, followed by *hee-aaw, hee-aaw, hee-aaw*.
NESTING Shallow depression in coastal or upland tundra; 4 eggs; 1 brood; June.
FEEDING Picks and probes for insects and larvae; also spiders and pond crustaceans.

FEEDING IN FLOCKS
Flocks of this sandpiper rush about in search of food in shallow water and muddy areas.

SIMILAR SPECIES

WHITE-RUMPED SANDPIPER
see p.180

prominent, white eyebrow

slightly bulkier body

PECTORAL SANDPIPER
larger; see p.182

yellowish legs

streaked breast-band

OCCURRENCE
Breeds in tundra habitats of high Arctic Alaska and Canada. During migration and winter, inland freshwater habitats: lake and river margins, wet pastures, rice fields; also tidal flats at coastal locations. In winter, common in the high Andes of South America, and sometimes all the way to Tierra del Fuego.

Length **5¾–7¼in (14.5–18.5cm)**	Wingspan **16–18½in (41–47cm)**	Weight **1¹⁄₁₆–2oz (30–55g)**
Social **Flocks**	Lifespan **Unknown**	Status **Secure**

DATE SEEN	WHERE	NOTES

| Order **Charadriiformes** | Family **Scolopacidae** | Species *Calidris melanotos* |

Pectoral Sandpiper

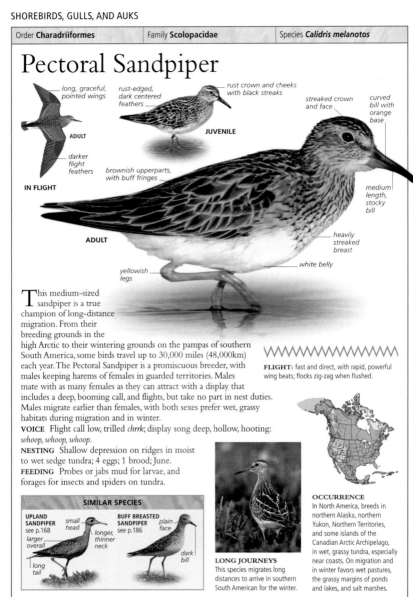

long, graceful, pointed wings

rust-edged, dark centered feathers

rust crown and cheeks with black streaks

streaked crown and face

curved bill with orange base

ADULT

JUVENILE

darker flight feathers

brownish upperparts, with buff fringes

IN FLIGHT

medium length, stocky bill

ADULT

heavily streaked breast

yellowish legs

white belly

This medium-sized sandpiper is a true champion of long-distance migration. From their breeding grounds in the high Arctic to their wintering grounds on the pampas of southern South America, some birds travel up to 30,000 miles (48,000km) each year. The Pectoral Sandpiper is a promiscuous breeder, with males keeping harems of females in guarded territories. Males mate with as many females as they can attract with a display that includes a deep, booming call, and flights, but take no part in nest duties. Males migrate earlier than females, with both sexes prefer wet, grassy habitats during migration and in winter.

FLIGHT: fast and direct, with rapid, powerful wing beats; flocks zig-zag when flushed.

VOICE Flight call low, trilled *chrrk*; display song deep, hollow, hooting: *whoop, whoop, whoop*.

NESTING Shallow depression on ridges in moist to wet sedge tundra; 4 eggs; 1 brood; June.

FEEDING Probes or jabs mud for larvae, and forages for insects and spiders on tundra.

SIMILAR SPECIES

UPLAND SANDPIPER see p.168

small head

larger overall

long tail

longer, thinner neck

BUFF BREASTED SANDPIPER see p.186

plain face

dark bill

LONG JOURNEYS
This species migrates long distances to arrive in southern South American for the winter.

OCCURRENCE
In North America, breeds in northern Alaska, northern Yukon, Northern Territories, and some islands of the Canadian Arctic Archipelago, in wet, grassy tundra, especially near coasts. On migration and in winter favors wet pastures, the grassy margins of ponds and lakes, and salt marshes.

| Length **7½–9in (19–23cm)** | Wingspan **16½–19½in (42–49cm)** | Weight **1¾–4oz (50–125g)** |
| Social **Migrant flocks** | Lifespan **Up to 4½ years** | Status **Secure** |

DATE SEEN	WHERE	NOTES

| Order **Charadriiformes** | Family **Scolopacidae** | Species *Calidris maritima* |

Purple Sandpiper

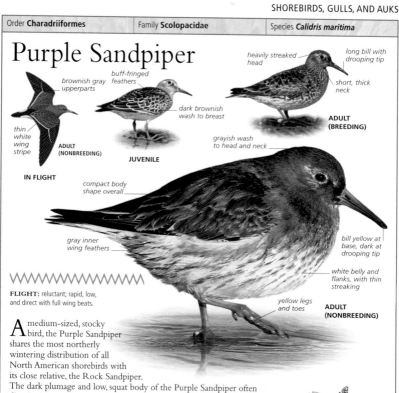

heavily streaked head

long bill with drooping tip

short, thick neck

ADULT (BREEDING)

buff-fringed feathers

brownish gray upperparts

dark brownish wash to breast

grayish wash to head and neck

ADULT (NONBREEDING)

JUVENILE

thin white wing stripe

IN FLIGHT

compact body shape overall

gray inner wing feathers

bill yellow at base, dark at drooping tip

white belly and flanks, with thin streaking

yellow legs and toes

ADULT (NONBREEDING)

WWWWWWWWWW

FLIGHT: reluctant; rapid, low, and direct with full wing beats.

A medium-sized, stocky bird, the Purple Sandpiper shares the most northerly wintering distribution of all North American shorebirds with its close relative, the Rock Sandpiper. The dark plumage and low, squat body of the Purple Sandpiper often disguise its presence on dark tidal rocks, until a crashing wave causes a previously invisible flock to explode into flight.

VOICE Flight call low *kweesh*; when disturbed, *eh-eh-eh*; breeding *kwi-ti-ti-ti-bli-bli-bli* followed by *dooree-dooree-dooree*.

NESTING Simple lined scrape in high-alpine-like or barren low-lying Arctic tundra; 4 eggs; 1 brood; June.

FEEDING Feeds on various invertebrates, including crustaceans, snails, insects, spiders, and worms.

SIMILAR SPECIES		
ROCK SANDPIPER *slightly smaller bill* *darker, plainer upperparts* *less orange color to base of bill*	**DUNLIN** *see p.184* *plain, pale gray-brown upperparts*	*longer black bill*

WINTER EXPOSURE
The Purple Sandpiper winters mainly on exposed rocky shores along the eastern seaboard.

OCCURRENCE
On breeding grounds, found on barren Arctic and alpine tundra habitats in the Canadian Arctic Archipelago. On migration and in winter, predominantly found on rocky, wave-pounded shores on the eastern seaboard.

Length **8–8½in (20–21cm)**	Wingspan **16½–18½in (42–47cm)**	Weight **1¾–3½oz (50–100g)**
Social **Small flocks**	Lifespan **Up to 20 years**	Status **Declining**

DATE SEEN	WHERE	NOTES

Order **Charadriiformes**	Family **Scolopacidae**	Species **Calidris alpina**

Dunlin

black-and-cream stripes on back

JUVENILE

black streaks on buff underside

JUVENILE

dull gray-brown head and back

white sided rump

thin white wing bar

IN FLIGHT

long, tapered, black bill

dull, gray-streaked breast

rich chestnut-and-black back

fine dark streaks on whitish breast

large, squarish, black belly patch

ADULT (BREEDING)

ADULT (NONBREEDING)

FLIGHT: swift and direct flight, with rapid wing beats.

OLD RED BACK
The Dunlin was once known as the Red-backed Sandpiper because of its distinct breeding plumage.

The Dunlin is one of the most abundant and widespread of North America's shorebirds, but of the ten recognized subspecies, only three breed in North America: *C. a. arcticola*, *C. a. pacifica*, and *C. a. hudsonia*. The Dunlin is unmistakable in its striking, red-backed, black-bellied breeding plumage. In winter it sports much drabber colors, but more than makes up for this by gathering in spectacular flocks of many thousands of birds on its favorite coastal mudflats.

VOICE Call accented trill, *drurr-drurr*, that rises slightly, then descends; flight call *jeeezp*; song *wrraah-wrraah*.

NESTING Simple cup lined with grasses, leaves, and lichens in moist to wet tundra; 4 eggs; 1 brood; June–July.

FEEDING Probes for marine, freshwater, terrestrial invertebrates: clams, worms, insect larvae, crustaceans; also plants and small fish.

SIMILAR SPECIES

STILT SANDPIPER ✳
see p.185

longer, thinner neck

yellowish green legs

CURLEW SANDPIPER ✳
see p.450

less streaking on chest

longer legs

OCCURRENCE
Breeds in Arctic and sub-Arctic moist, wet tundra, often near ponds, with drier islands for nest sites. In migration and winter, prefers coastal areas with extensive mudflats and sandy beaches; also feeds in flooded fields and seasonal inland wetlands.

Length **6½–8½in (16–22cm)**	Wingspan **12½–17½in (32–44cm)**	Weight **1⁹⁄₁₆–2¼oz (45–65g)**
Social **Large flocks**	Lifespan **Up to 24 years**	Status **Declining**

DATE SEEN	WHERE	NOTES

Order **Charadriiformes**	Family **Scolopacidae**	Species **Calidris himantopus**

Stilt Sandpiper

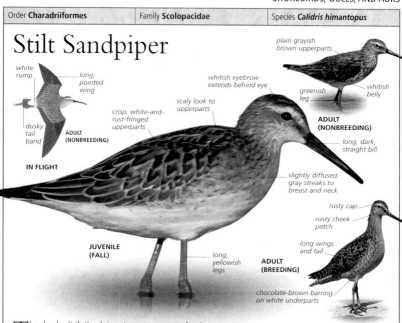

white rump

long, pointed wing

dusky tail band

ADULT (NONBREEDING)

IN FLIGHT

crisp, white-and-rust-fringed upperparts

scaly look to upperparts

whitish eyebrow extends behind eye

plain grayish brown upperparts

greenish leg

whitish belly

ADULT (NONBREEDING)

long, dark, straight bill

slightly diffused gray streaks to breast and neck

JUVENILE (FALL)

long, yellowish legs

rusty cap

rusty cheek patch

long wings and tail

ADULT (BREEDING)

chocolate-brown barring on white underparts

The slender Stilt Sandpiper is uncommon and unique to North America, where it breeds in several small areas of northern tundra. It favors shallow, freshwater habitats, where it feeds in a distinctive style, walking slowly through belly-deep water with its neck outstretched and bill pointed downward. It either picks at the surface, or submerges itself, keeping its tail raised up all the while. During migration it forms dense, rapidly moving flocks that sometimes include other sandpiper species.

VOICE Flight or alarm call low, muffled *chuf*; also *krrit* and sharp *kew-it*; display call *xxree-xxree-xxree-xxree-ee-haw, ee-haw*.

NESTING Shallow depression on raised knolls or ridges in tundra; 4 eggs; 1 brood; June.

FEEDING Eats mostly adult and larval insects; also some snails, mollusks, and seeds.

FLIGHT: fast and direct, with rapid beats of its long wings.

SIMILAR SPECIES	
DUNLIN ✳ see p.184 — shorter neck — shorter, black legs	**CURLEW SANDPIPER** ✳ see p.450 — black legs — curved bill

PALE BELOW
Wading through shallow water, this Stilt Sandpiper displays its whitish underparts.

OCCURRENCE
Breeds in moist to wet coastal tundra on well-drained, raised knolls or ridges in Alaska, Yukon, and northwestern territories and Hudson Bay. During migration and in winter, prefers freshwater habitats, such as flooded fields, marsh pools, reservoirs, and sheltered lagoons to tidal mudflats.

Length **8–9in (20–23cm)**	Wingspan **17–18½in (43–47cm)**	Weight **1¾–2⅛oz (50–60g)**
Social **Pairs/Flocks**	Lifespan **At least 3 years**	Status **Secure**

DATE SEEN	WHERE	NOTES

Order **Charadriiformes**	Family **Scolopacidae**	Species **Tryngites subruficollis**

Buff-breasted Sandpiper

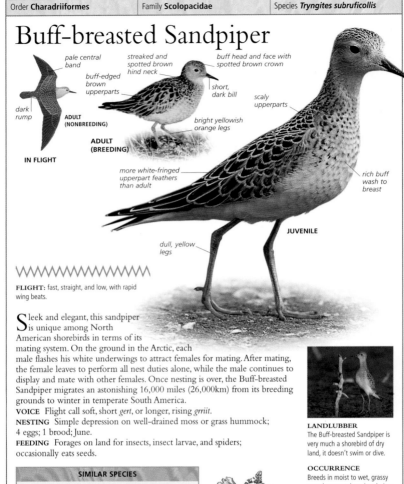

pale central band

buff-edged brown upperparts

dark rump

ADULT (NONBREEDING)

IN FLIGHT

streaked and spotted brown hind neck

buff head and face with spotted brown crown

short, dark bill

scaly upperparts

bright yellowish orange legs

ADULT (BREEDING)

rich buff wash to breast

more white-fringed upperpart feathers than adult

JUVENILE

dull, yellow legs

FLIGHT: fast, straight, and low, with rapid wing beats.

Sleek and elegant, this sandpiper is unique among North American shorebirds in terms of its mating system. On the ground in the Arctic, each male flashes his white underwings to attract females for mating. After mating, the female leaves to perform all nest duties alone, while the male continues to display and mate with other females. Once nesting is over, the Buff-breasted Sandpiper migrates an astonishing 16,000 miles (26,000km) from its breeding grounds to winter in temperate South America.

VOICE Flight call soft, short *gert*, or longer, rising *grriit*.

NESTING Simple depression on well-drained moss or grass hummock; 4 eggs; 1 brood; June.

FEEDING Forages on land for insects, insect larvae, and spiders; occasionally eats seeds.

LANDLUBBER
The Buff-breasted Sandpiper is very much a shorebird of dry land, it doesn't swim or dive.

OCCURRENCE
Breeds in moist to wet, grassy or sedge coastal tundra; during migration, favors short grass areas such as pastures, sod farms, meadows, rice fields, or agricultural areas. Winters in the pampas region of South America in short, wet grass habitats.

SIMILAR SPECIES

UPLAND SANDPIPER
see p.168
larger overall
longer wings and tail

PECTORAL SANDPIPER
see p.182
darker cap with pale eyebrow
longer bill
longer, streaked neck

Length **7¼–8in (18.5–20cm)**	Wingspan **17–18½in (43–47cm)**	Weight **1⁷⁄₁₆–3³⁄₈oz (40–95g)**
Social **Large flocks**	Lifespan **Unknown**	Status **Declining**

DATE SEEN	WHERE	NOTES

Order **Charadriiformes**	Family **Scolopacidae**	Species **Phalaropus tricolor**

Wilson's Phalarope

plain gray-and-black upperparts

paler head markings

MALE

white eyebrow

reddish brown markings on sides of back

plain gray upperparts

largely white face

white cheek

FEMALE (BREEDING)

yellowish legs

white underparts

fairly long, straight bill

grayish brown wings

IN FLIGHT

JUVENILE (MOLTING TO 1ST WINTER)

black stripe from bill to nape

gray and reddish brown back

rust neck and throat

FEMALE (BREEDING)

A truly American phalarope, Wilson's is the largest of the three phalarope species. Unlike its two relatives, it does not breed in the Arctic, but in the shallow wetlands of western North America, and winters mainly in continental habitats of Bolivia and Argentina instead of in the ocean. This species can be found employing the feeding technique of spinning in shallow water to churn up adult and larval insects, or running in various directions on muddy wetland edges with its head held low to the ground while chasing and picking up insects. This bird is quite tolerant of humans on its breeding grounds, but this attitude changes immediately before migration, as it has gained weight and its movement is sluggish.

VOICE Flight call a low, nasal *werpf*; also higher, repetitive *emf, emf, emf,* or *luk, luk, luk.*

NESTING Simple scrape lined with grass; 4 eggs; 1 brood; May–June.

FEEDING Eats brine shrimp, various insects, and insect larvae.

FLIGHT: fast and direct with quick wing beats.

ODD ONE OUT
Unlike its two essentially oceanic relatives, Wilson's Phalarope is also found in freshwater habitats.

SIMILAR SPECIES

LESSER YELLOWLEGS see p.170

darker, spotted back

RED-NECKED PHALAROPE ♀ see p.188

streaked head and neck

black cheek patch

shorter bill

OCCURRENCE
Breeds in shallow, grassy wetlands of interior North America; during migration and winter, occurs in salty lakes and saline ponds as well as inland waterbodies. In winter, tens of thousands can be seen in the middle of Titicaca Lake in Bolivia.

Length **8½–9½in (22–24cm)**	Wingspan **15½–17in (39–43cm)**	Weight **1¼–3oz (35–85g)**
Social **Large flocks**	Lifespan **Up to 10 years**	Status **Secure**

DATE SEEN	WHERE	NOTES

| Order **Charadriiformes** | Family **Scolopacidae** | Species *Phalaropus lobatus* |

Red-necked Phalarope

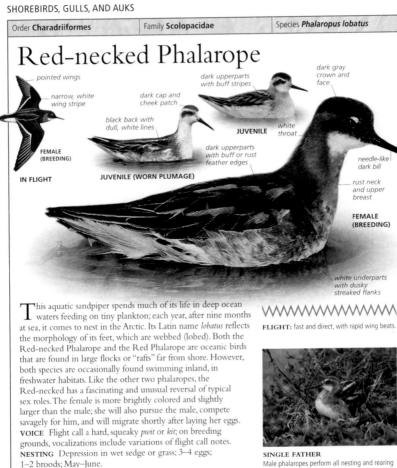

pointed wings

narrow, white wing stripe

FEMALE (BREEDING)

IN FLIGHT

black back with dull, white lines

dark cap and cheek patch

JUVENILE (WORN PLUMAGE)

dark upperparts with buff stripes

JUVENILE

dark upperparts with buff or rust feather edges

dark gray crown and face

white throat

needle-like dark bill

rust neck and upper breast

FEMALE (BREEDING)

white underparts with dusky streaked flanks

This aquatic sandpiper spends much of its life in deep ocean waters feeding on tiny plankton; each year, after nine months at sea, it comes to nest in the Arctic. Its Latin name *lobatus* reflects the morphology of its feet, which are webbed (lobed). Both the Red-necked Phalarope and the Red Phalarope are oceanic birds that are found in large flocks or "rafts" far from shore. However, both species are occasionally found swimming inland, in freshwater habitats. Like the other two phalaropes, the Red-necked has a fascinating and unusual reversal of typical sex roles. The female is more brightly colored and slightly larger than the male; she will also pursue the male, compete savagely for him, and will migrate shortly after laying her eggs.
VOICE Flight call a hard, squeaky *pwit* or *kit*; on breeding grounds, vocalizations include variations of flight call notes.
NESTING Depression in wet sedge or grass; 3–4 eggs; 1–2 broods; May–June.
FEEDING Eats plankton; also insects, brine shrimp, and mollusks.

FLIGHT: fast and direct, with rapid wing beats.

SINGLE FATHER
Male phalaropes perform all nesting and rearing duties after the female lays the eggs.

SIMILAR SPECIES

WILSON'S PHALAROPE ♀
see p.187

paler face

larger overall

RED PHALAROPE ♀ *slightly thicker bill*
see p.189

larger head and thicker neck

OCCURRENCE
Breeds in wet tundra, on raised ridges, or hummocks, but during migration and in winter, occurs far out at sea and away from shores, although sometimes found in freshwater habitats.

| Length **7–7½in (18–19cm)** | Wingspan **12½–16in (32–41cm)** | Weight **1¹⁄₁₆–1⁹⁄₁₆oz (30–45g)** |
| Social **Flocks** | Lifespan **Unknown** | Status **Secure** |

DATE SEEN	WHERE	NOTES

| Order **Charadriiformes** | Family **Scolopacidae** | Species ***Phalaropus fulicarius*** |

Red Phalarope

bold white wing bar

FEMALE (BREEDING)

white rump with black line in center, and white edges

buff feather fringes

scalloped upperparts

dull rust crown with black streaks

broad, pointed wings

IN FLIGHT

brick-red underparts; paler than female

MALE (BREEDING)

black cheek patch and nape

mostly gray upperparts

white neck and head

white underparts

ADULT (NONBREEDING)

bold white cheek patch

black crown

tan-fringed feathers on upperparts

FEMALE (BREEDING)

stout, yellow bill with black tip

deep brick-red neck, throat, and underparts

Wilson's Phalarope more terrestrial; see p.187

The Red Phalarope spends over ten months each year over deep ocean waters. It also migrates across the ocean, which explains why few birds of this species are ever seen inland. Many Red Phalaropes winter in tropical waters, with concentrations in the Humboldt Current off Peru and Chile, and in the Benguela Current off southwestern Africa. During migration over Alaskan waters, flocks of Red Phalaropes feed on crustaceans in the mud plumes that are created by the foraging of gray and bowhead whales on the ocean floor.

VOICE Flight call a sharp *psip* or *pseet*, often in rapid succession; alarm call a drawn-out, 2-syllabled *sweet*.

NESTING Depression on ridge or hummock in coastal sedge; 3–4 eggs; 1 brood; June.

FEEDING Plucks prey from sea; marine crustaceans, fish eggs, larval fish; adult or larval insects.

FLIGHT: direct with rapid wing beats, birds in flocks often synchronize.

DIFFERENT COLOR
In nonbreeding plumage, phalaropes are gray and white.

NO TIES
After breeding, female Red Phalaropes leave the male and play no role in raising young.

SIMILAR SPECIES

WILSON'S PHALAROPE
more terrestrial; see p.187

larger overall

RED-NECKED PHALAROPE
see p.188

no black mask

smaller head

more slender body

OCCURRENCE
Breeds in coastal Arctic tundra; during migration and in winter, occurs in deep ocean waters; small numbers are seen near the shore in coastal California in fall and winter. The Red Phalarope is rare inland.

| Length **8–8½in (20–22cm)** | Wingspan **16–17½in (41–44cm)** | Weight **1¼–2⅝oz (35–75g)** |
| Social **Large flocks** | Lifespan **Unknown** | Status **Secure** |

DATE SEEN	WHERE	NOTES

| Order **Charadriiformes** | Family **Laridae** | Species *Larus delawarensis* |

Ring-billed Gull

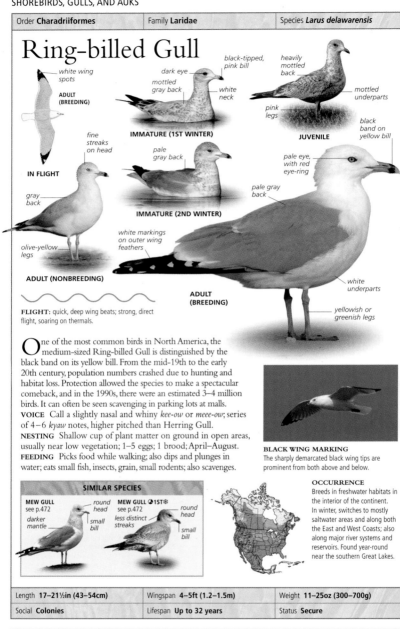

ADULT (BREEDING)

white wing spots

IN FLIGHT

fine streaks on head

gray back

olive-yellow legs

ADULT (NONBREEDING)

black-tipped, pink bill

dark eye

mottled gray back

white neck

IMMATURE (1ST WINTER)

pale gray back

IMMATURE (2ND WINTER)

white markings on outer wing feathers

heavily mottled back

mottled underparts

pink legs

JUVENILE

black band on yellow bill

pale eye, with red eye-ring

pale gray back

white underparts

yellowish or greenish legs

ADULT (BREEDING)

FLIGHT: quick, deep wing beats; strong, direct flight, soaring on thermals.

One of the most common birds in North America, the medium-sized Ring-billed Gull is distinguished by the black band on its yellow bill. From the mid-19th to the early 20th century, population numbers crashed due to hunting and habitat loss. Protection allowed the species to make a spectacular comeback, and in the 1990s, there were an estimated 3–4 million birds. It can often be seen scavenging in parking lots at malls.

VOICE Call a slightly nasal and whiny *kee-ow* or *meee-ow*; series of 4–6 *kyaw* notes, higher pitched than Herring Gull.

NESTING Shallow cup of plant matter on ground in open areas, usually near low vegetation; 1–5 eggs; 1 brood; April–August.

FEEDING Picks food while walking; also dips and plunges in water; eats small fish, insects, grain, small rodents; also scavenges.

BLACK WING MARKING
The sharply demarcated black wing tips are prominent from both above and below.

SIMILAR SPECIES

MEW GULL see p.472

darker mantle

round head

small bill

MEW GULL 1ST✷ see p.472

less distinct streaks

round head

small bill

OCCURRENCE
Breeds in freshwater habitats in the interior of the continent. In winter, switches to mostly saltwater areas and along both the East and West Coasts; also along major river systems and reservoirs. Found year-round near the southern Great Lakes.

| Length **17–21½in (43–54cm)** | Wingspan **4–5ft (1.2–1.5m)** | Weight **11–25oz (300–700g)** |
| Social **Colonies** | Lifespan **Up to 32 years** | Status **Secure** |

DATE SEEN	WHERE	NOTES

Order **Charadriiformes**	Family **Laridae**	Species *Larus marinus*

Great Black-backed Gull

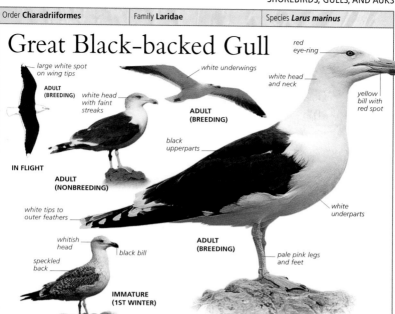

red eye-ring

large white spot on wing tips

ADULT (BREEDING)

white underwings

white head and neck

white head with faint streaks

ADULT (BREEDING)

yellow bill with red spot

black upperparts

IN FLIGHT

ADULT (NONBREEDING)

white tips to outer feathers

white underparts

whitish head

black bill

ADULT (BREEDING)

speckled back

pale pink legs and feet

IMMATURE (1ST WINTER)

The largest gull in North America, the Great Black-backed Gull is known for its bullying dispostion. In breeding colonies, it is especially aggressive in the morning and early evening, and after chicks hatch; adults dive at ground predators and strike them with their wings and feet. Other birds benefit from this forceful behavior, for example eiders nesting in Great Black-backed Gull colonies suffer a low rate of nest predation.

VOICE Low, growling flight call, often repeated, low-pitched *heyaa…heyaa…heyaa…heyaa*, similar to the Herring Gull.

NESTING Shallow bowl on ground, lined with vegetation, feathers, and trash; 2–3 eggs; 1 brood; April–August.

FEEDING Scavenges and hunts fish, marine invertebrates, small mammals, eggs, chicks, adult seabirds, and waterfowl.

FLIGHT: heavy lumbering with deep wing beats.

SOLITARY BIRDS
While all gulls are social animals, the Great Black-backed Gull is the most solitary.

SIMILAR SPECIES

LESSER BLACK-BACKED GULL ✱
see p.195

smaller body

slate-gray back

yellow legs

SLATY-BACKED GULL
see p.472

gray back

bright pink legs

OCCURRENCE
Breeds on natural and artificial islands, barrier beaches, salt marshes, sand dunes; during winter, found along the coast, near shore water, major rivers, landfills, and harbors; in all seasons, often found together with Herring Gulls and Ring-billed Gulls. Also occurs also in Europe.

Length **28–31in (71–79cm)**	Wingspan **5–5¼ft (1.5–1.6m)**	Weight **2¾–4½lb (1.3–2kg)**
Social **Pairs/Colonies**	Lifespan **Up to 27 years**	Status **Secure**

DATE SEEN	WHERE	NOTES

SHOREBIRDS, GULLS, AND AUKS

| Order **Charadriiformes** | Family **Laridae** | Species *Larus hyperboreus* |

Glaucous Gull

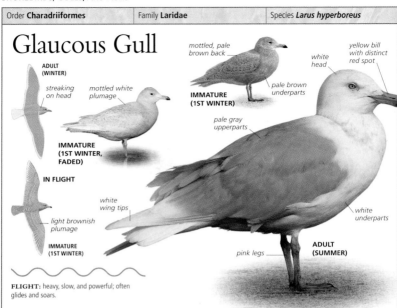

ADULT (WINTER)
streaking on head
mottled white plumage

IMMATURE (1ST WINTER, FADED)

IN FLIGHT
white wing tips
light brownish plumage
IMMATURE (1ST WINTER)

mottled, pale brown back

IMMATURE (1ST WINTER)
pale brown underparts

white head
yellow bill with distinct red spot

pale gray upperparts

white underparts

ADULT (SUMMER)
pink legs
white underparts

FLIGHT: heavy, slow, and powerful; often glides and soars.

The Glaucous Gull is the largest of the "white-winged" gulls. Its large, pale shape is immediately apparent in a group of gulls as it appears like a large white spectre among its smaller, darker cousins. In the southern part of its US winter range, pale immatures are encountered more frequently than adults. In the Arctic, successful pairs of Glaucous Gulls maintain the bonds with their mates for years, often returning to the same nest site year after year.

VOICE Similar to that of the Herring Gull, but slightly harsher and deeper; hoarse, nasal *ku-ku-ku*.
NESTING Shallow cup lined with vegetation on ground, at edge of tundra pools, on cliffs and ledges and islands; 1–3 eggs; 1 brood; May–July.
FEEDING Eats fish, crustaceans, mollusks; also eggs and chicks of waterfowl, small seabirds, and small mammals.

NORTHERN VISITOR
This large gull is an uncommon visitor over most of North America during the winter months.

SIMILAR SPECIES

GLAUCOUS-WINGED GULL
dusky wing tips

ICELAND GULL
see p.193
much smaller bill
much smaller overall

OCCURRENCE
Breeds along the high-Arctic coast, rarely inland; winters along northern Atlantic and Pacific coasts and the Great Lakes; frequently seen at Niagara Falls. Strays, usually immatures, can occur inland anywhere where concentrations of gulls are found, such as trash sites dumps.

| Length **26–30in (65–75cm)** | Wingspan **5–6ft (1.5–1.8m)** | Weight **2¾–6lb (1.2–2.7kg)** |
| Social **Colonies** | Lifespan **Up to 21 years** | Status **Secure** |

DATE SEEN	WHERE	NOTES

Order **Charadriiformes**	Family **Laridae**	Species ***Larus glaucoides***

Iceland Gull

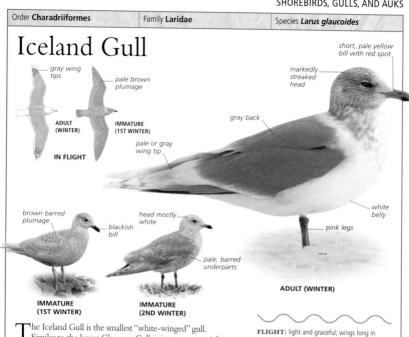

short, pale yellow
bill with red spot

markedly
streaked
head

gray wing
tips

pale brown
plumage

**ADULT
(WINTER)**

**IMMATURE
(1ST WINTER)**

IN FLIGHT

gray back

pale or gray
wing tip

white
belly

pink legs

brown barred
plumage

blackish
bill

head mostly
white

pale, barred
underparts

**IMMATURE
(1ST WINTER)**

**IMMATURE
(2ND WINTER)**

ADULT (WINTER)

The Iceland Gull is the smallest "white-winged" gull.
Similar to the larger Glaucous Gull, it is a common sight
in winter, and immatures are seen more often than adults.
North American breeding birds have gray wing tips, and have
been considered a separate species called the "Kumlien's Gull."
The subspecies *L. g. glaucoides* is distinguishable as it possesses
white wing tips; it breeds in Greenland, and winters in Greenland
and Iceland, but a few birds travel to the western North Atlantic.
VOICE Call a *clew, clew, clew* or *kak-kak-kak*; vocal around
breeding colonies; virtually silent on wintering grounds.
NESTING Loose nest of moss, vegetation, and feathers, usually
on narrow rock ledge; 2–3 eggs; 1 brood; May–August.
FEEDING Grabs small fish from surface while in flight;
also eats crustaceans, mollusks, carrion, and garbage.

FLIGHT: light and graceful; wings long in
proportion to body.

WING TIP COLOR VARIATION
Some adult Iceland Gulls found in North America
have wing tips that are almost pure white.

SIMILAR SPECIES

GLAUCOUS GULL
see p.192
much larger
body

white wing
tips

THAYER'S GULL
see p.450   dark eye

larger
bill

slightly larger
and darker
overall

OCCURRENCE
Uncommon far from sea
coast; usually nests on ledges
on vertical cliffs overlooking
the sea; winters where it finds
regions of open water in frozen
seas and along coast. A few
wander to open water areas
in the interior, such as the
Great Lakes and major rivers;
Niagara Falls.

Length **20½–23½in (52–60cm)**	Wingspan **4½–5ft (1.4–1.5m)**	Weight **21–39oz (600–1,100g)**
Social **Colonies**	Lifespan **Up to 33 years**	Status **Secure**

DATE SEEN	WHERE	NOTES

Order **Charadriiformes**	Family **Laridae**	Species *Larus argentatus*

Herring Gull

white spots near wing tips

ADULT (BREEDING)

light head

barred gray-brown overall

gray wings

IMMATURE (2ND WINTER)

streaked head

ADULT (NONBREEDING)

IN FLIGHT

black outer wing feathers

mottled brown back

IMMATURE (1ST WINTER)

barred brown body

white head and neck

large, yellow bill with red spot

gray back

white underparts

pink legs

ADULT (BREEDING)

streaked head and neck

ADULT (NONBREEDING)

The Herring Gull is the archetypal, large "white-headed" gull to which nearly all other gulls are compared. When people mention "seagulls" they usually refer to the Herring Gull. The term, however, is misleading because the Herring Gull, like most other gulls, does not commonly go far out to sea—it is a bird of near-shore waters, coasts, lakes, rivers, and inland waterways. Now very common, the Herring Gull was nearly wiped out in the late 19th and early 20th century by plumage hunters and egg collectors.
VOICE Typical call a high-pitched, shrill, repeated *heyaa… heyaa…heyaa…heyaa*; vocal throughout the year.
NESTING Shallow bowl on ground lined with feathers, vegetation, detritus; 2–4 eggs; 1 brood; April–August.
FEEDING Eats fish, crustaceans, mollusks, worms; eggs and chicks of other seabirds; scavenges carrion, garbage; steals from other birds.

FLIGHT: steady, regular, slow wing beats; also commonly soars and glides.

MASTER SCAVENGER
A common sight near any water body, the Herring Gull is an expert scavenger of carrion and trash.

OCCURRENCE
Found throughout North America along coasts and inland on lakes, rivers, and reservoirs; also frequents garbage dumps. Breeds in northeastern US and across Canada. Migrates southward across much of the continent to winter in coastal areas and along lakes and major rivers.

SIMILAR SPECIES

RING-BILLED GULL
see p.190
smaller overall

black ring on bill

yellow-green legs

CALIFORNIA GULL
see p.472

black-and-red spot on bill

greenish legs

Length **22–26in (56–66cm)**	Wingspan **4–5ft (1.2–1.5m)**	Weight **28–42oz (800–1,200g)**
Social **Colonies**	Lifespan **At least 35 years**	Status **Secure**

DATE SEEN	WHERE	NOTES

| Order **Charadriiformes** | Family **Laridae** | Species *Larus fuscus* |

Lesser Black-backed Gull

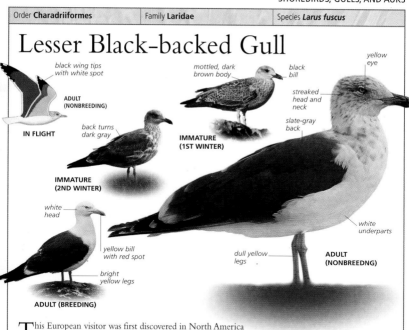

black wing tips with white spot

ADULT (NONBREEDING)

IN FLIGHT

mottled, dark brown body

black bill

IMMATURE (1ST WINTER)

back turns dark gray

IMMATURE (2ND WINTER)

white head

yellow bill with red spot

bright yellow legs

ADULT (BREEDING)

yellow eye

streaked head and neck

slate-gray back

dull yellow legs

white underparts

ADULT (NONBREEDNG)

This European visitor was first discovered in North America on the New Jersey coast on September 9, 1934 and in New York City a few months later. In recent decades, it has become an annual winter visitor. Nearly all the Lesser Black-backed Gulls found in North America are of the Icelandic and western European subspecies *L. f. graellsii*, with a slate–gray back. Another European subspecies, with a much darker back, has rarely been reported in North America, but it is probably only a matter of time before it nests here.

VOICE A *kyow…yow…yow…yow* call, similar to that of Herring Gull; also a deeper and throaty, repeated *gah-gah-gah-gah*.

NESTING Scrape on ground lined with dry lichens, dry grass, and feathers; 3 eggs; 1 brood; April–September.

FEEDING Eats mollusks, crustaceans, and various insects; also scavenges carrion and garbage.

FLIGHT: powerful and direct; regular wing beats; long wings make it appear graceful.

SIMILAR SPECIES

| GREAT BLACK-BACKED GULL see p.191 | SLATY-BACKED GULL see p.472 |

darker back

larger overall

pink legs and feet

larger overall

pink legs

EXCITING FIND
In recent years, gull enthusiasts and birdwatchers have found these birds visiting from Europe.

OCCURRENCE
Regular and increasingly common winter visitor to eastern North America, usually along the coast, but also in the interior; wherever gulls commonly concentrate such as harbors, lakeshores, landfills, and around fishing boats.

| Length **20½–26in (52–67cm)** | Wingspan **4¼–5ft (1.3–1.5m)** | Weight **22–35oz (625–1,000g)** |
| Social **Colonies** | Lifespan **Up to 26 years** | Status **Secure** |

DATE SEEN	WHERE	NOTES

| Order **Charadriiformes** | Family **Laridae** | Species *Larus ridibundus* |

Black-headed Gull

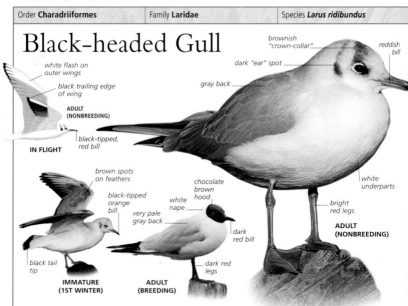

white flash on outer wings

black trailing edge of wing

ADULT (NONBREEDING)

IN FLIGHT

black-tipped, red bill

brownish "crown-collar"

reddish bill

dark "ear" spot

gray back

white underparts

bright red legs

ADULT (NONBREEDING)

brown spots on feathers

black-tipped orange bill

white nape

very pale gray back

black tail tip

IMMATURE (1ST WINTER)

chocolate brown hood

dark red bill

dark red legs

ADULT (BREEDING)

An abundant breeder in Eurasia, the Black-headed Gull colonized North America in the 20th century. It was first seen in the 1920s, not long after nests were discovered in Iceland in 1911. It has become common in Newfoundland after being found nesting there in 1977, and has nested as far south as Cape Cod. However, it has not spread far to the West and remains an infrequent visitor or stray over most of the continent.

VOICE Loud laughing (its French name is Laughing Gull) or a chattering *kek kek keeaar*; very vocal at breeding sites.

NESTING Loose mass of vegetation, on ground or on top of other vegetation; may be a large mound in wet areas; 2–3 eggs; 1 brood; April–August.

FEEDING Picks insects, small crustaceans, and mollusks off water's surface while flying or hovering; eats some vegetation; also forages in plowed farm fields; raids garbage dumps.

FLIGHT: graceful, light, and buoyant; agile.

BEAUTIFUL BREEDING PLUMAGE
Most American birders never see the elegant summer plumage of the Black-headed Gull.

SIMILAR SPECIES

BONAPARTE'S GULL see p.197

smaller and more delicate

black bill

white underwing

LITTLE GULL see p.200

much smaller overall

all gray upperwing

OCCURRENCE
Rare breeder in northeastern North America; singles or a few individuals may be found along the coast, often with Bonaparte's Gulls, at harbors, inlets, bays, rivers, lakes, sewage outlets, or garbage dumps; strays may occur anywhere. One of the most common European gulls.

| Length **13½–14½in (34–37cm)** | Wingspan **3ft 3in–3½ft (1–1.1m)** | Weight **7–14oz (200–400g)** |
| Social **Colonies** | Lifespan **Up to 18 years** | Status **Localized** |

DATE SEEN	WHERE	NOTES

| Order **Charadriiformes** | Family **Laridae** | Species *Larus philadelphia* |

Bonaparte's Gull

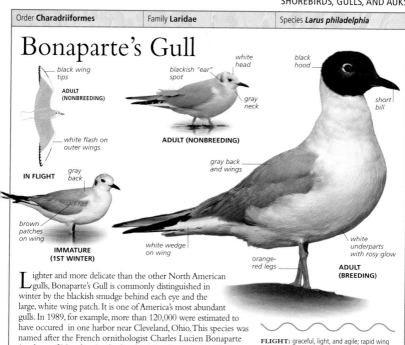

black wing tips

ADULT (NONBREEDING)

white flash on outer wings

IN FLIGHT

gray back

brown patches on wing

IMMATURE (1ST WINTER)

white wedge on wing

blackish "ear" spot

white head

gray neck

ADULT (NONBREEDING)

gray back and wings

black hood

white head

short bill

white underparts with rosy glow

orange-red legs

ADULT (BREEDING)

Lighter and more delicate than the other North American gulls, Bonaparte's Gull is commonly distinguished in winter by the blackish smudge behind each eye and the large, white wing patch. It is one of America's most abundant gulls. In 1989, for example, more than 120,000 were estimated to have occured in one harbor near Cleveland, Ohio. This species was named after the French ornithologist Charles Lucien Bonaparte (nephew of Napoleon), who lived in New Jersey in the 1820s.

VOICE Harsh *keek, keek*; can be vocal in feeding flocks, *kew, kew, kew.*

NESTING Stick nest of twigs, branches, tree bark, lined with mosses or lichens; usually in conifers 5–20ft (1.5–6m) above ground; also in rushes over water; 1–4 eggs; 1 brood; May–July.

FEEDING Catches insects in flight on breeding grounds; picks crustaceans, mollusks, and small fish from water's surface; also plunge-dives.

FLIGHT: graceful, light, and agile; rapid wing beats; can be mistaken for a tern in flight.

TERN-LIKE GULL
Bonaparte's Gulls are very social and, flying in flocks, these pale, delicate birds look like terns.

WHITE UNDERWINGS
In all plumages, Bonaparte's Gulls have white underwings, unlike other similar small gulls.

SIMILAR SPECIES

BLACK-HEADED GULL
see p.196
dark outer wing feathers
red bill
larger overall

LITTLE GULL
see p.200
smaller overall
uniform gray upperwing

OCCURRENCE
During breeding season, found in northern forest zone, in lakes, ponds, or bogs; on migration, may be found anywhere where there is water: ponds, lakes, sewage pools, or rivers. Winters on Great Lakes and along the coast; often found in large numbers at coastal inlets.

| Length **11–12in (28–30cm)** | Wingspan **35in–3ft 3in (90–100cm)** | Weight **6–8oz (175–225g)** |
| Social **Flocks** | Lifespan **Up to 18 years** | Status **Secure** |

DATE SEEN	WHERE		NOTES

| Order **Charadriiformes** | Family **Laridae** | Species *Larus atricilla* |

Laughing Gull

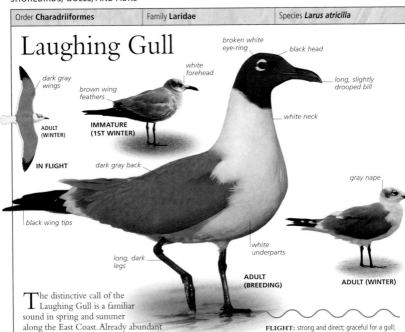

broken white eye-ring

black head

white forehead

long, slightly drooped bill

dark gray wings

brown wing feathers

ADULT (WINTER)

IN FLIGHT

IMMATURE (1ST WINTER)

white neck

dark gray back

gray nape

black wing tips

long, dark legs

white underparts

ADULT (BREEDING)

ADULT (WINTER)

The distinctive call of the Laughing Gull is a familiar sound in spring and summer along the East Coast. Already abundant when the Europeans arrived in North America, it was greatly reduced in the 19th century by egg collectors and the millinery trade. Its numbers increased in the 1920s, following protection, but declined again due to competition with larger gulls from the North. With the closing of landfills however, the Laughing Gull population has recovered.

VOICE Typical call strident laugh, *ha...ha...ha...ha...ha*; very vocal in breeding season; quiet in winter.

NESTING Mass of grass on dry land with heavy vegetation, sand, rocks, and salt marshes; 2–4 eggs, 1 brood; April–July.

FEEDING Picks from surface while walking and swimming; feeds on various invertebrates: insects, earthworms, squid, crabs, crab eggs, and larvae; also eats small fish, garbage, and berries.

FLIGHT: strong and direct; graceful for a gull; agile enough to catch flying insects.

DARK WING TIPS
Unlike many gulls, the Laughing Gull usually shows little or no white in the wing tips.

SIMILAR SPECIES

FRANKLIN'S GULL
see p.199

short, straight bill

white band in wing tips

FRANKLIN'S GULL ◑ ☼
see p.199

short, straight bill

darker head

pink blush on underparts

OCCURRENCE
During breeding season usually found near saltwater. Post-breeders and juveniles wander widely; strays can turn up anywhere. Rare in winter in the Northeast. Small numbers once nested at the Salton Sea but only a visitor there for the last 50 years.

| Length **15½–18in (39–46cm)** | Wingspan **3¼–4ft (1–1.2m)** | Weight **7–13oz (200–375g)** |
| Social **Colonial** | Lifespan **Up to 20 years** | Status **Secure** |

DATE SEEN	WHERE	NOTES

| Order **Charadriiformes** | Family **Laridae** | Species *Larus pipixcan* |

Franklin's Gull

black wing tips set-off by white band

dark gray wings

ADULT (WINTER)

IN FLIGHT

white in outer wing feathers

dark back of head

gray back

short, straight bill

ADULT (WINTER)

dark gray back

partial hood

IMMATURE (1ST SUMMER)

broken white eye crescent

black head

red bill

pink blush underneath

ADULT (SUMMER)

~~~~~~~~~~
FLIGHT: stiff and direct; relatively fast wing beats; agile flier.

Since its discovery, Franklin's Gull has carried a number of names: Prairie Dove, Rosy Dove, and Franklin's Rosy Gull—"Dove" alluding to its dainty appearance and "rosy" to the pink blush of its undersides. Its official name honors British Arctic explorer, John Franklin, on whose first expedition, the bird was discovered in 1823. Unlike other gulls, this species has two complete molts each year. As a result, its plumage usually looks fresh and it rarely has the scruffy look of some other gulls.

VOICE Nasal *weeh-a, weeh-a*; shrill *kuk kuk kuk kuk*; extremely vocal around breeding colonies.

NESTING Floating mass of bulrushes or other plants; material added as nest sinks; 2–4 eggs; 1 brood; April–July.

FEEDING Feeds mainly on earthworms and insects during breeding and some seeds, taken while walking or flying; opportunistic feeder during migration and winter.

PROMINENT EYES
In all plumages, Franklin's Gull has much more prominent white eye-crescents than similar species.

OCCURRENCE
In summer, a bird of the high prairies; always nests over water. On migration often found in agricultural areas; large numbers frequent plowed fields or follows plows. Winters mainly along the Pacific Coast of South America.

SIMILAR SPECIES

LAUGHING GULL see p.198
longer, drooped bill
longer legs

LAUGHING GULL ♂ ❋ see p.198
smaller eye-crescents
longer legs
longer, drooped bill

| Length **12½–14in (32–36cm)** | Wingspan **33in–3ft 1in (85–95cm)** | Weight **8–11oz (225–325g)** |
| Social **Colonial** | Lifespan **At least 10 years** | Status **Secure** |

DATE SEEN	WHERE	NOTES

Order **Charadriiformes**	Family **Laridae**	Species *Larus minutus*

Little Gull

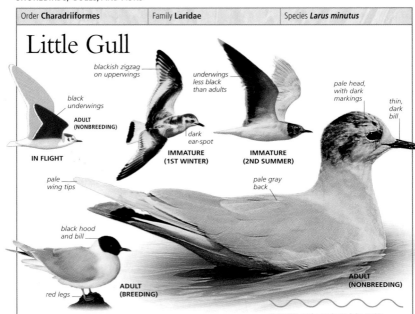

blackish zigzag on upperwings

underwings less black than adults

pale head, with dark markings

thin, dark bill

black underwings

ADULT (NONBREEDING)

dark ear-spot

IMMATURE (1ST WINTER)

IMMATURE (2ND SUMMER)

IN FLIGHT

pale wing tips

pale gray back

black hood and bill

pale gray back

ADULT (NONBREEDING)

black hood and bill

red legs

ADULT (BREEDING)

A Eurasian species distributed from the Baltic to China, the Little Gull is the smallest gull in the world. Whether it is a recent immigrant to North America or has actually been here, unnoticed, in small numbers for many years remains a mystery. It was first recorded in North America in the early 1800s, but a nest was not found until 1962, in Ontario, Canada. Known nesting areas are still few, but winter numbers have been increasing steadily in recent decades.

VOICE Nasal *kek, kek, kek, kek*, reminiscent of a small tern.

NESTING Thick, floating mass of dry cattails, reeds, or other vegetation, in marshes and ponds; 3 eggs; 1 brood; May–August.

FEEDING Seizes prey from water's surface, while swimming or plunge-diving; typical prey includes flying insects, aquatic invertebrates such as shrimps, and small fish.

FLIGHT: quick wing beats; light, nimble, and agile.

SIMPLE ELEGANCE
Its long, pale gray wings with a thin white border make this bird one of the most elegant gulls.

SIMILAR SPECIES

BLACK-HEADED GULL see p.196

BONAPARTE'S GULL see p.197

larger overall

red bill

white flash in wing

white flash in wing

OCCURRENCE
Breeds in extensive freshwater marshes in Hudson Bay and Great Lakes region, but the full extent of its breeding range in North America is unknown; can appear almost anywhere while migrating. Winters primarily along sea coasts, at sewage outfalls; often with groups of Bonaparte's Gulls.

Length **10–12in (25–30cm)**	Wingspan **23½–26in (60–65cm)**	Weight **3½–5oz (100–150g)**
Social **Colonies**	Lifespan **Up to 6 years**	Status **Secure**

DATE SEEN	WHERE	NOTES

Order **Charadriiformes**	Family **Laridae**	Species ***Xema sabini***

Sabine's Gull

white triangle on wing

black outer wing feathers

ADULT　**JUVENILE**

black band on tail

IN FLIGHT

gray hood

red eye-ring

black border

yellow-tipped black bill

gray back

white underparts

black legs

ADULT (BREEDING)

barring on gray-brown back

black bill

JUVENILE

This strikingly patterned gull was discovered in Greenland by the English scientist Edward Sabine during John Ross's search for the Northwest Passage in 1818 (it was described in 1819). The distinctive wing pattern and notched tail make it unmistakable in all plumages—only juvenile kittiwakes are superficially similar. Previously thought to be related to the larger, but similarly patterned, Swallow-tailed Gull of the Galápagos, recent research indicates that Sabine's Gull is more closely related to the Ivory Gull. This species breeds in the Arctic and winters at sea, off the coasts of the Americas (south to Peru) and Africa (south to the Cape region).
VOICE Raucous, harsh *kyeer, kyeer, kyeer*; tern-like.
NESTING Shallow depression in marsh or tundra vegetation usually near water, lined with grass or unlined; 3–4 eggs; 1 brood; May–August.
FEEDING Catches aquatic insects from the water surface while swimming, wading, or flying during breeding season; winter diet mainly includes crustaceans, small fish, and plankton.

FLIGHT: wing beats shallow and stiff; tern-like, buoyant.

STRIKING WING PATTERN
Juvenile Sabine's Gulls have a muted version of the distinctive triangular wing pattern seen in the adults.

SIMILAR SPECIES

BLACK-LEGGED KITTIWAKE ○ see p.202　*partial black collar*

black wing bar

OCCURRENCE
In the summer, breeds near the Arctic coast and on wet tundra in freshwater and brackish habitats, but also occurs near saltwater. Winters far offshore in tropical and subtropical waters; widespread in Pacific and Atlantic oceans on migration.

Length **13–14in (33–36 cm)**	Wingspan **35in–3ft 3in (90–100cm)**	Weight **5–9oz (150–250g)**
Social **Colonies**	Lifespan **At least 8 years**	Status **Secure**

DATE SEEN	WHERE	NOTES

Order **Charadriiformes**	Family **Laridae**	Species *Rissa tridactyla*

Black-legged Kittiwake

IN FLIGHT

pale outer wing feathers

pale gray upperparts

black tip to tail

ADULT

black "M" pattern in wings

black bill

JUVENILE

black wing tip

greenish yellow bill

white head

pale gray back feathers

ADULT

dark neck collar

dark wing bar

black legs and feet

JUVENILE

A kittiwake nesting colony is an impressive sight, with sometimes thousands of birds lined up along steep cliff ledges overlooking the sea. The ledges are often so narrow that the birds' tails stick out over the edge. Kittiwakes have sharper claws than other gulls, probably to give them a better grip on their ledges. In the late 20th century, the Black-legged Kittiwake population expanded greatly in the Canadian maritime provinces, with numbers doubling in the Gulf of St. Lawrence.

VOICE Repeated, nasal *kit-ti-wake, kit-ti-wake* call; vocal near nesting cliffs; usually silent in winter.

NESTING Mound of mud and vegetation on narrow cliff ledge; 1–3 eggs; 1 brood; April–August.

FEEDING Snatches small marine fish and invertebrates from the surface, or dives just below the water's surface; feeds in flocks.

FLIGHT: very stiff-winged; rapid, shallow wing beats; overall more buoyant than most gulls.

LIVING ON THE EDGE
Young and adult kittiwakes pack together tightly on their precariously narrow cliff ledges.

OCCURRENCE
Rarely seen far from the ocean; common in summer around sea cliffs, with ledges suitable for nesting, and nearby offshore waters; winters at sea; most likely to be seen from land during and after storms; strays have appeared throughout the interior.

SIMILAR SPECIES	
RING-BILLED GULL see p.190	**RED-LEGGED KITTIWAKE**

heavier, dark-marked bill

white spots in outer wing feathers

darker shoulder feathers

red legs

gray underwings

Length **15–16in (38–41cm)**	Wingspan **3ft 1in–4ft (0.95m–1.2m)**	Weight **11–18oz (300–500g)**
Social **Colonies**	Lifespan **Up to 26 years**	Status **Secure**

DATE SEEN	WHERE	NOTES

Order **Charadriiformes**	Family **Laridae**	Species *Sterna nilotica*

Gull-billed Tern

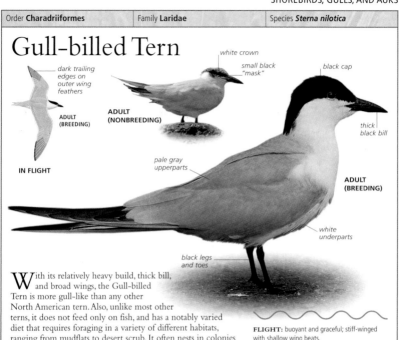

white crown

small black "mask"

black cap

dark trailing edges on outer wing feathers

ADULT (NONBREEDING)

ADULT (BREEDING)

IN FLIGHT

thick black bill

pale gray upperparts

ADULT (BREEDING)

white underparts

black legs and toes

With its relatively heavy build, thick bill, and broad wings, the Gull-billed Tern is more gull-like than any other North American tern. Also, unlike most other terns, it does not feed only on fish, and has a notably varied diet that requires foraging in a variety of different habitats, ranging from mudflats to desert scrub. It often nests in colonies with other terns—particularly Common and Caspian terns— and skimmers, and will occasionally hunt their chicks and steal their prey. During the 19th century, Gull-billed Terns were hunted ruthlessly for their eggs and feathers. Their numbers have at least partially recovered, but increasing human disturbance at nesting sites is a long-term conservation concern.

VOICE Short, two-noted, nasal yapping, *kay-wek, kay-wek.*
NESTING Simple, camouflaged scrape on ground, usually on sand, shell bank, or bare rock; shells and other debris used to build up nest; 2–3 eggs; 1 brood; April–July.
FEEDING Eats insects, lizards, small fish, and chicks. Catches insects in flight; plucks prey from ground or water's surface.

FLIGHT: buoyant and graceful; stiff-winged with shallow wing beats.

LONG WINGS
The Gull-billed Tern has very long, pointed wings with a dusky edge on the outer feathers.

SIMILAR SPECIES

SANDWICH TERN ✿
see p.205

crest

yellow-tipped, thin, black bill

ROSEATE TERN ☙
see p.207

thin bill

long, forked tail

smaller overall

OCCURRENCE
Rarely found away from saltwater. Historically considered a species of salt marshes, but now breeds primarily on sandy beaches and barrier islands; most birds leave the US to winter in Central America, where they favor mudflats or flooded fields.

Length **13–15in (33–38cm)**	Wingspan **3¼–4ft (1–1.2m)**	Weight **5–7oz (150–200g)**
Social **Colonies**	Lifespan **Up to 16 years**	Status **Localized**

DATE SEEN	WHERE	NOTES

Order **Charadriiformes**	Family **Laridae**	Species *Sterna caspia*

Caspian Tern

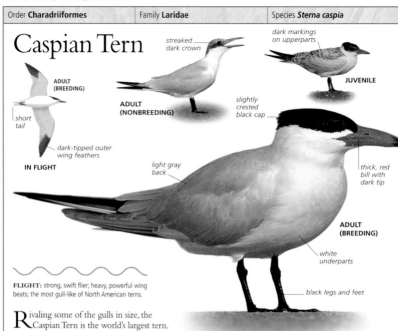

streaked dark crown

dark markings on upperparts

JUVENILE

ADULT (BREEDING)

short tail

dark-tipped outer wing feathers

IN FLIGHT

ADULT (NONBREEDING)

slightly crested black cap

light gray back

thick, red bill with dark tip

ADULT (BREEDING)

white underparts

black legs and feet

FLIGHT: strong, swift flier; heavy, powerful wing beats; the most gull-like of North American terns.

Rivaling some of the gulls in size, the Caspian Tern is the world's largest tern. Unlike other "black-capped" terns, it never has a completely white forehead, even in winter. In nonbreeding plumage, when the cap is very heavily streaked. The Caspian Tern is known for its predatory habits, stealing prey from other seabirds, as well as snatching eggs from, and hunting the chicks of, other gulls and terns. It is aggressive in defending its nesting territory, giving hoarse alarm calls and rhythmically opening and closing its beak in a threatening display to intruders.

VOICE Hoarse, deep *kraaa, kraaa*; also barks at intruders; male's wings vibrate loudly in courtship flight.

NESTING Shallow scrape on ground; 2–3 eggs; 1 brood; May–August.

FEEDING Plunges into water to snatch fish, barnacles, and snails.

AGGRESSIVE BIRDS
The Caspian Tern is one of the most aggressive terns, though actual physical contact is rare.

OCCURRENCE
Found in a variety of aquatic habitats, freshwater and marine; rare offshore; breeds on interior lakes, salt marsh, and on coastal barrier islands; winters on and near the coast. May be seen on marshes and wetlands during migration.

SIMILAR SPECIES

ELEGANT TERN
smaller overall

thin, orange-yellow bill

ROYAL TERN
see p.206

thinner, orange bill

slender build

Length **18½–21½in (47–54cm)**	Wingspan **4¼–5ft (1.3–1.5m)**	Weight **19–27oz (525–775g)**
Social **Colonies/Pairs**	Lifespan **Up to 30 years**	Status **Declining**

DATE SEEN	WHERE	NOTES

| Order **Charadriiformes** | Family **Laridae** | Species ***Sterna sandvicensis*** |

Sandwich Tern

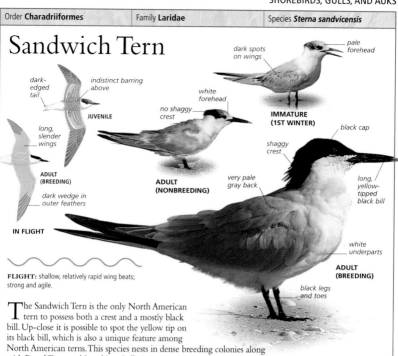

dark spots on wings

pale forehead

dark-edged tail

indistinct barring above

white forehead

no shaggy crest

JUVENILE

IMMATURE (1ST WINTER)

black cap

shaggy crest

long, slender wings

ADULT (BREEDING)

ADULT (NONBREEDING)

very pale gray back

long, yellow-tipped black bill

dark wedge in outer feathers

IN FLIGHT

white underparts

ADULT (BREEDING)

FLIGHT: shallow, relatively rapid wing beats; strong and agile.

black legs and toes

The Sandwich Tern is the only North American tern to possess both a crest and a mostly black bill. Up-close it is possible to spot the yellow tip on its black bill, which is also a unique feature among North American terns. This species nests in dense breeding colonies along with Royal Terns and Laughing Gulls. It is not an aggressive species and, like the Elegant Tern, is thought to benefit from the protection the other, more aggressive species offer it from potential predators. Worldwide, there are three subspecies of Sandwich Tern, but only one of these inhabits North America.

VOICE Loud, harsh two-syllabled *kirr-ick*; vocal when breeding, less elsewhere.
NESTING Shallow scrape on bare ground in open area, often alongside other tern species; debris added during incubation, but sometimes unlined; 1–2 eggs; 1 brood; April–August.
FEEDING Plunge-dives from medium height to catch fish, squid, and crustaceans; also snatches prey from surface and catches insects in flight.

SIMILAR SPECIES

GULL-BILLED TERN
see p.203

more compact body

stout, all black bill

ROSEATE TERN
see p.207

no yellow tip on bill

smaller overall

CLOSE NESTING
Sandwich Terns often nest in extremely dense colonies with nests packed closely together.

OCCURRENCE
An East Coast and Caribbean species, it is rarely far from saltwater; breeds on barrier beaches, barrier islands, and man-made dredge islands. Winters in similar areas; roosts on sandbars. May occur north of normal range after tropical storms and hurricanes.

| Length **13½–17½in (34–45cm)** | Wingspan **3ft 1in–3ft 4in (95–105cm)** | Weight **6–11oz (175–300g)** |
| Social **Colonies** | Lifespan **Up to 22 years** | Status **Secure** |

DATE SEEN	WHERE	NOTES

| Order **Charadriiformes** | Family **Laridae** | Species *Sterna maxima* |

Royal Tern

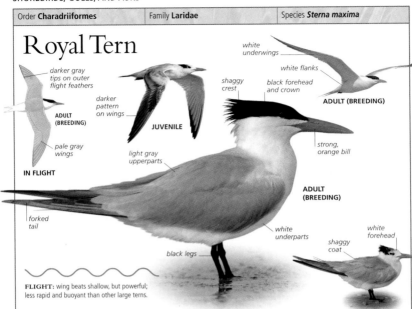

white underwings

white flanks

shaggy crest

black forehead and crown

ADULT (BREEDING)

darker gray tips on outer flight feathers

ADULT (BREEDING)

darker pattern on wings

JUVENILE

light gray upperparts

pale gray wings

IN FLIGHT

strong, orange bill

ADULT (BREEDING)

forked tail

white underparts

black legs

white forehead

shaggy coat

ADULT (NONBREEDING)

FLIGHT: wing beats shallow, but powerful; less rapid and buoyant than other large terns.

Royal Terns have a full black cap for only a very short time at the beginning of the breeding season; for most of the year, they have white foreheads. The color of a Royal Tern's bill is quite variable, ranging from yellowish orange to red. Some possess a reddish bill similar to that of the Caspian Tern, but the latter does not have a pure white forehead and its bill is thicker. Perhaps it was these red-billed Royal Terns that caused the renowned ornithologist, John James Audubon, to confuse the two species.

VOICE Call *keer-reet*, usually during courtship; higher pitched and less raspy than Caspian Tern; more vocal around colonies.
NESTING Shallow scrape on bare ground, usually unlined, rim of guano reinforces nest; 1 egg; 1 brood; April–August.
FEEDING Mostly plunge-dives, but also plucks prey from surface while flying; sometimes skims surface; almost exclusively eats fish and crustaceans, such as crabs and barnacles.

BREEDING HABITS
Royal Terns appear monogamous, but it is unclear whether the pair bond is kept between seasons.

SIMILAR SPECIES

CASPIAN TERN ☼ see p.204

stout red bill

larger overall

ELEGANT TERN

smaller overall

thinner, curved bill

OCCURRENCE
Normally restricted to warm saltwater habitats. Breeds in dense colonies, often on barrier islands; post-breeders wander north of regular breeding range; some are carried north by tropical storms and hurricanes, and may be found in the interior of the US.

| Length **17½–19½in (45–50cm)** | Wingspan **4–4¼ft (1.2–1.3m)** | Weight **12–16oz (350–450g)** |
| Social **Colonies** | Lifespan **Up to 29 years** | Status **Secure** |

DATE SEEN	WHERE	NOTES

| Order **Charadriiformes** | Family **Laridae** | Species ***Sterna dougallii*** |

Roseate Tern

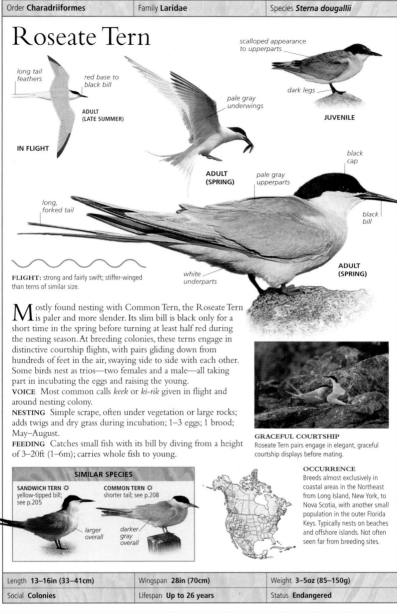

long tail feathers

red base to black bill

ADULT (LATE SUMMER)

IN FLIGHT

scalloped appearance to upperparts

dark legs

JUVENILE

pale gray underwings

ADULT (SPRING)

pale gray upperparts

black cap

long, forked tail

black bill

FLIGHT: strong and fairly swift; stiffer-winged than terns of similar size.

white underparts

ADULT (SPRING)

Mostly found nesting with Common Tern, the Roseate Tern is paler and more slender. Its slim bill is black only for a short time in the spring before turning at least half red during the nesting season. At breeding colonies, these terns engage in distinctive courtship flights, with pairs gliding down from hundreds of feet in the air, swaying side to side with each other. Some birds nest as trios—two females and a male—all taking part in incubating the eggs and raising the young.

VOICE Most common calls *keek* or *ki-rik* given in flight and around nesting colony.

NESTING Simple scrape, often under vegetation or large rocks; adds twigs and dry grass during incubation; 1–3 eggs; 1 brood; May–August.

FEEDING Catches small fish with its bill by diving from a height of 3–20ft (1–6m); carries whole fish to young.

GRACEFUL COURTSHIP
Roseate Tern pairs engage in elegant, graceful courtship displays before mating.

SIMILAR SPECIES

SANDWICH TERN ☼
yellow-tipped bill; see p.205

larger overall

COMMON TERN ☼
shorter tail; see p.208

darker gray overall

OCCURRENCE
Breeds almost exclusively in coastal areas in the Northeast from Long Island, New York, to Nova Scotia, with another small population in the outer Florida Keys. Typically nests on beaches and offshore islands. Not often seen far from breeding sites.

| Length **13–16in (33–41cm)** | Wingspan **28in (70cm)** | Weight **3–5oz (85–150g)** |
| Social **Colonies** | Lifespan **Up to 26 years** | Status **Endangered** |

DATE SEEN	WHERE	NOTES
....	....	....
....	....	....
....	....	....
....	....	....
....	....	....

| Order **Charadriiformes** | Family **Laridae** | Species *Sterna hirundo* |

Common Tern

dark wedge on outer feathers

brown bars on upperparts

whitish forehead

white forehead

bill mostly dark

dark bill with red-orange base

black wing bar

blackish leg

ADULT (BREEDING)

JUVENILE

ADULT (NONBREEDING)

IN FLIGHT

black cap

gray upperparts

forked tail

black-tipped red bill

pale gray-white underparts

red leg

ADULT (BREEDING)

FLIGHT: graceful, steady and strong; wing beats relatively deep.

One of North America's most widespread terns, the Common Tern was nearly wiped out in the late 19th century by hunters seeking its feathers. The 1918 Migratory Bird Treaty helped protect it, and numbers increased, but populations have declined again in recent decades due to human disturbance, habitat loss, and pollution.
VOICE Common call loud *keeee-aarr* descending at end; emits *kek-kek-kek-kek* call when attacking intruders; vocal in colonies; also calls elsewhere.
NESTING Shallow scrape on bare sand, often gravel or similar surface, dry vegetation and debris used during incubation; 2–3 eggs; 1 brood; May–August.
FEEDING Plunges for prey, snatches from water's surface, catches insects in flight; mainly eats fish but also crustaceans, squid, and insects.

SIMILAR SPECIES

ARCTIC TERN ☼
see p.209

shorter red bill

shorter neck

shorter legs

FORSTER'S TERN
see p.210

paler wings

longer tail

FEEDING FLOCK
A flock of Common Terns focus on a school of fish, diving to catch them. Fishermen watch for such flocks to locate fish.

OCCURRENCE
Found almost anywhere with water during migration. Winters in Central and South America. One population breeds along the barrier beaches and coasts northwards from the Carolinas; a second population occurs around lakes and wetland areas in the northern interior.

| Length **12–14in (31–35cm)** | Wingspan **30–31in (75–80cm)** | Weight **3⅜–5oz (95–150g)** |
| Social **Colonies** | Lifespan **Up to 26 years** | Status **Declining** |

DATE SEEN	WHERE	NOTES

Order **Charadriiformes**	Family **Laridae**	Species **Sterna paradisaea**

Arctic Tern

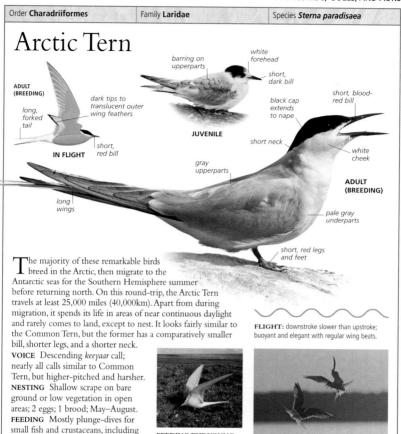

ADULT (BREEDING)

long, forked tail

dark tips to translucent outer wing feathers

short, red bill

IN FLIGHT

barring on upperparts

white forehead

short, dark bill

JUVENILE

short neck

gray upperparts

long wings

black cap extends to nape

short, blood-red bill

white cheek

ADULT (BREEDING)

pale gray underparts

short, red legs and feet

The majority of these remarkable birds breed in the Arctic, then migrate to the Antarctic seas for the Southern Hemisphere summer before returning north. On this round-trip, the Arctic Tern travels at least 25,000 miles (40,000km). Apart from during migration, it spends its life in areas of near continuous daylight and rarely comes to land, except to nest. It looks fairly similar to the Common Tern, but the former has a comparatively smaller bill, shorter legs, and a shorter neck.

VOICE Descending *keeyaar* call; nearly all calls similar to Common Tern, but higher-pitched and harsher.

NESTING Shallow scrape on bare ground or low vegetation in open areas; 2 eggs; 1 brood; May–August.

FEEDING Mostly plunge-dives for small fish and crustaceans, including crabs and shrimps; will also take prey from surface, sometimes catches insects in flight.

FLIGHT: downstroke slower than upstroke; buoyant and elegant with regular wing beats.

FEEDING THE YOUNG
Both parents feed chicks—males bring more food than females, especially right after hatching.

TRANSLUCENT FEATHERS
The translucent outer wing feathers of the Arctic Tern are evident on these two flying birds.

SIMILAR SPECIES

COMMON TERN ☼
see p.208

longer neck

longer legs

longer bill

FORSTER'S TERN
see p.210

longer, orange bill

longer legs

OCCURRENCE
Breeds in far North, mostly in open, unforested areas near water and along the coast; generally migrates far offshore. Spends more time away from land than other northern terns. Winters on edge of pack ice in Antarctica.

Length **11–15½in (28–39cm)**	Wingspan **26–30in (65–75cm)**	Weight **3⅛–4oz (90–125g)**
Social **Colonies**	Lifespan **Up to 34 years**	Status **Vulnerable**

DATE SEEN	WHERE	NOTES

| Order **Charadriiformes** | Family **Laridae** | Species *Sterna forsteri* |

Forster's Tern

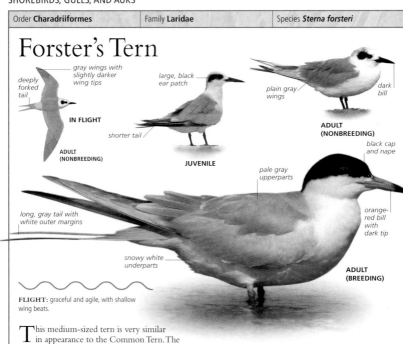

gray wings with slightly darker wing tips

deeply forked tail

IN FLIGHT

large, black ear patch

shorter tail

ADULT (NONBREEDING)

JUVENILE

plain gray wings

dark bill

ADULT (NONBREEDING)

black cap and nape

pale gray upperparts

orange-red bill with dark tip

long, gray tail with white outer margins

snowy white underparts

ADULT (BREEDING)

FLIGHT: graceful and agile, with shallow wing beats.

This medium-sized tern is very similar in appearance to the Common Tern. The features that differentiate it from the Common Tern are its lighter outer wing feathers and longer tail. Early naturalists could not tell the two species apart until 1834 when English botanist Thomas Nuttall made the distinction. He named this tern after Johann Reinhold Forster, a naturalist who accompanied the English explorer Captain Cook on his epic second voyage (1772-75).
VOICE Harsh, descending *kyerr*; more nasal than Common Tern.
NESTING Shallow scrape in mud or sand, but occasionally nests on top of muskrat lodge or on old grebe nest; sometimes constructs raft of floating vegetation; 2–3 eggs; 1 brood; May–August.
FEEDING Catches fish and crustaceans with shallow plunge-diving, often only head submerges; also catches insects in flight.

BLACK EARS
With its black ear patch, Foster's Tern is more distinctive in nonbreeding than breeding plumage.

SIMILAR SPECIES

COMMON TERN
see p.208

ARCTIC TERN
see p.209

shorter red bill

redder bill

shorter neck

shorter tail

shorter legs

OCCURRENCE
Breeds in northeastern Mexico, in freshwater and saltwater marshes with large stretches of open water. Winters on both coasts and across southern US states, unlike the Common Tern, which primarily winters in South America.

| Length **13–14in (33–36cm)** | Wingspan **29–32in (73–82cm)** | Weight **4–7oz (125–190g)** |
| Social **Colonies** | Lifespan **Up to 16 years** | Status **Secure** |

DATE SEEN	WHERE	NOTES

| Order **Charadriiformes** | Family **Laridae** | Species *Sterna antillarum* |

Least Tern

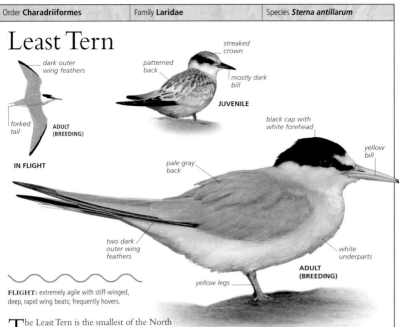

dark outer wing feathers

forked tail

ADULT (BREEDING)

IN FLIGHT

streaked crown

patterned back

mostly dark bill

JUVENILE

black cap with white forehead

yellow bill

pale gray back

two dark outer wing feathers

white underparts

ADULT (BREEDING)

yellow legs

FLIGHT: extremely agile with stiff-winged, deep, rapid wing beats; frequently hovers.

The Least Tern is the smallest of the North American terns and, in summer, its distinctive black cap and white forehead distinguish it from other members of its family. In the 19th century the population of Least Terns declined rapidly as its feathers were prized fashion accessories. Protected by the Migratory Bird Treaty of 1916, its numbers grew again, but it is still threatened by ongoing habitat loss.

VOICE Extremely vocal during breeding; a high-pitched *ki-deek*, *ki-deek*; also a rapid, almost non-stop chatter.

NESTING Shallow scrape on ground lined with dry vegetation, broken shells, and pebbles; 2–3 eggs; 1 brood; April–September.

FEEDING Plunge-dives, often after hovering, for fish and aquatic invertebrates, does not submerge completely; also skims surface for food; catches insects in flight.

COURTSHIP FEEDING
As with many other species of tern, Least Tern males offer fish to females during courtship.

OCCURRENCE
Breeds along both coasts, major rivers, lakes, reservoirs, and in Great Plains wetlands; favors sandy areas such as barrier islands, beaches, sandbars, and nearby waters. Winters from Mexico to South America. Also breeds in the West Indies and Mexico.

SIMILAR SPECIES

COMMON TERN
see p.208

black-tipped red bill

all-black cap

larger overall

FORSTER'S TERN
larger overall; see p.210

black-tipped orange bill

longer tail

| Length **8½–9in (21–23cm)** | Wingspan **19–21in (48–53cm)** | Weight **1¼–2oz (35–55g)** |
| Social **Colonies** | Lifespan **Up to 24 years** | Status **Endangered** |

DATE SEEN	WHERE		NOTES

| Order **Charadriiformes** | Family **Laridae** | Species *Chlidonias niger* |

Black Tern

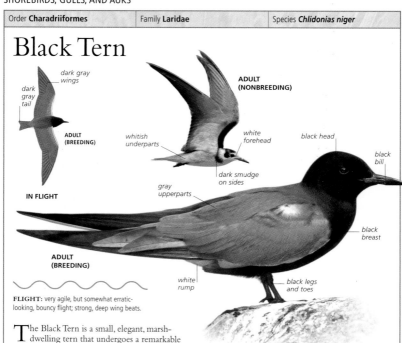

dark gray wings

dark gray tail

ADULT (BREEDING)

ADULT (NONBREEDING)

whitish underparts

white forehead

black head

black bill

dark smudge on sides

gray upperparts

IN FLIGHT

black breast

ADULT (BREEDING)

white rump

black legs and toes

FLIGHT: very agile, but somewhat erratic-looking, bouncy flight; strong, deep wing beats.

The Black Tern is a small, elegant, marsh-dwelling tern that undergoes a remarkable change in appearance from summer to winter—more so than any other regularly occurring North American tern. The Black Tern's breeding plumage can cause the bird to be confused with the closely related White-winged Tern, which is an accidental visitor to North America. The Black Tern's nonbreeding plumage is much paler than its breeding plumage—the head turns white with irregular black streaks, and the neck, breast, and belly become whitish gray.

VOICE Call nasal and harsh *krik, kip,* or *kik*; most vocal during breeding, but calls throughout the year.

NESTING Shallow cup on top of floating mass of vegetation, sometimes on top of muskrat lodges; usually 3 eggs; 1 brood; May–August.

FEEDING Picks prey off water's surface or vegetation; rarely plunge dives; in summer, feeds on mainly insects, caught from the air or ground, also freshwater fish; in winter, eats mainly small sea fish.

FLOATING NEST
A floating nest is a dry place to lay eggs and raise chicks in a watery environment.

SIMILAR SPECIES

SOOTY TERN Ⓖ
see p.451

white spots on back

much larger overall

OCCURRENCE
Freshwater marshes in summer, but nonbreeding plumaged birds—probably young—occasionally seen along the coast. During migration, can be found almost anywhere near water. Winters in the marine coastal waters of Central and South America.

| Length **9–10in (23–26cm)** | Wingspan **25–35in (63–88cm)** | Weight **1¾–2½ oz (50–70g)** |
| Social **Colonies** | Lifespan **Up to 9 years** | Status **Vulnerable** |

DATE SEEN	WHERE	NOTES

| Order **Charadriiformes** | Family **Laridae** | Species *Rynchops niger* |

Black Skimmer

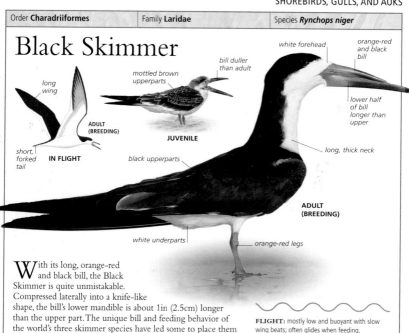

white forehead

orange-red and black bill

bill duller than adult

mottled brown upperparts

long wing

ADULT (BREEDING)

JUVENILE

lower half of bill longer than upper

long, thick neck

short, forked tail **IN FLIGHT**

black upperparts

ADULT (BREEDING)

white underparts

orange-red legs

With its long, orange-red and black bill, the Black Skimmer is quite unmistakable. Compressed laterally into a knife-like shape, the bill's lower mandible is about 1in (2.5cm) longer than the upper part. The unique bill and feeding behavior of the world's three skimmer species have led some to place them in their own family, although they are usually grouped with gulls and terns. When disturbed, Black Skimmer chicks kick up sand with their feet, forming a depression and throwing sand over their backs, which helps to camouflage them.

VOICE Calls given by both sexes, more often at night; distinctive sound like the yapping of a small dog.

NESTING Shallow scrape or depression on sandy beach or dead saltmarsh vegetation, also on gravel rooftops; 1–5 eggs; 1 brood; May–August.

FEEDING Skims surface with the lower part of its bill in water; bill snaps shut when prey is within reach; catches small fish in relatively calm waters.

FLIGHT: mostly low and buoyant with slow wing beats; often glides when feeding.

GREGARIOUS BIRDS
The Black Skimmer is often seen in flocks on sandy beaches and mudflats.

SLICING THE SURFACE
The unique way in which skimmers such as the Black Skimmer feed gave rise to the old common name for these birds—Cutwaters.

OCCURRENCE
Breeds on East Coast from Massachusetts south to Mexico; West Coast only in southern California, including Salton Sea; rarely found far from saltwater. Found on beaches; feeds in bays, estuaries, lagoons, and areas with relatively calm waters. Winters in Central America.

| Length **15½–19½in (40–50cm)** | Wingspan **3½–4¼ft (1.1–1.3m)** | Weight **8–14oz (225–400g)** |
| Social **Colonies** | Lifespan **Up to 20 years** | Status **Vulnerable** |

DATE SEEN	WHERE	NOTES

Order **Charadriiformes**	Family **Stercorariidae**	Species **Stercorarius pomarinus**

Pomarine Jaeger

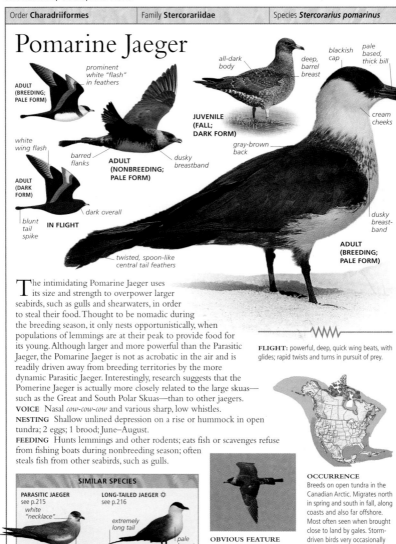

ADULT (BREEDING; PALE FORM)

prominent white "flash" in feathers

all-dark body

deep, barrel breast

blackish cap

pale based, thick bill

white wing flash

JUVENILE (FALL; DARK FORM)

cream cheeks

ADULT (NONBREEDING; PALE FORM)

barred flanks

dusky breastband

gray-brown back

ADULT (DARK FORM)

dark overall

blunt tail spike

IN FLIGHT

dusky breast-band

twisted, spoon-like central tail feathers

ADULT (BREEDING; PALE FORM)

The intimidating Pomarine Jaeger uses its size and strength to overpower larger seabirds, such as gulls and shearwaters, in order to steal their food. Thought to be nomadic during the breeding season, it only nests opportunistically, when populations of lemmings are at their peak to provide food for its young. Although larger and more powerful than the Parasitic Jaeger, the Pomarine Jaeger is not as acrobatic in the air and is readily driven away from breeding territories by the more dynamic Parasitic Jaeger. Interestingly, research suggests that the Pomerine Jaeger is actually more closely related to the large skuas—such as the Great and South Polar Skuas—than to other jaegers.

VOICE Nasal *cow-cow-cow* and various sharp, low whistles.

NESTING Shallow unlined depression on a rise or hummock in open tundra; 2 eggs; 1 brood; June–August.

FEEDING Hunts lemmings and other rodents; eats fish or scavenges refuse from fishing boats during nonbreeding season; often steals fish from other seabirds, such as gulls.

FLIGHT: powerful, deep, quick wing beats, with glides; rapid twists and turns in pursuit of prey.

SIMILAR SPECIES

PARASITIC JAEGER see p.215

white "necklace"

gray breastband

LONG-TAILED JAEGER ☼ see p.216

extremely long tail

pale breast

OBVIOUS FEATURE
The twisted, spoon-like central tail feathers are clearly visible when the Pomarine Jaeger flies.

OCCURRENCE
Breeds on open tundra in the Canadian Arctic. Migrates north in spring and south in fall, along coasts and also far offshore. Most often seen when brought close to land by gales. Storm-driven birds very occasionally found inland. More commonly seen on West Coast than East Coast; winters far out at sea.

Length **17–20in** (43–51cm)	Wingspan **4ft** (1.2m)	Weight **23–26oz** (650–750g)
Social **Solitary**	Lifespan **Unknown**	Status **Secure**

DATE SEEN	WHERE		NOTES

Order **Charadriiformes**	Family **Stercorariidae**	Species ***Stercorarius parasiticus***

Parasitic Jaeger

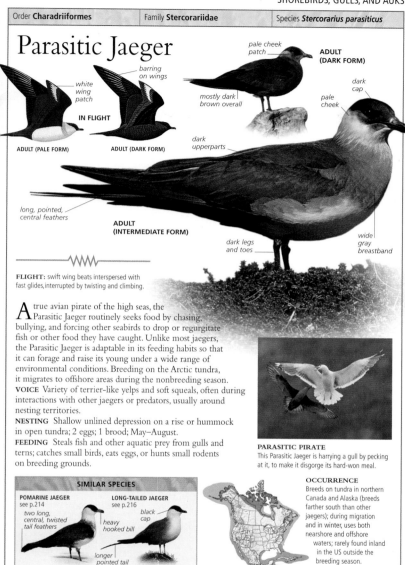

pale cheek patch

ADULT (DARK FORM)

barring on wings

white wing patch

mostly dark brown overall

IN FLIGHT

ADULT (PALE FORM)

ADULT (DARK FORM)

dark upperparts

dark cap

pale cheek

long, pointed, central feathers

ADULT (INTERMEDIATE FORM)

dark legs and toes

wide gray breastband

FLIGHT: swift wing beats interspersed with fast glides, interrupted by twisting and climbing.

A true avian pirate of the high seas, the Parasitic Jaeger routinely seeks food by chasing, bullying, and forcing other seabirds to drop or regurgitate fish or other food they have caught. Unlike most jaegers, the Parasitic Jaeger is adaptable in its feeding habits so that it can forage and raise its young under a wide range of environmental conditions. Breeding on the Arctic tundra, it migrates to offshore areas during the nonbreeding season.

VOICE Variety of terrier-like yelps and soft squeals, often during interactions with other jaegers or predators, usually around nesting territories.

NESTING Shallow unlined depression on a rise or hummock in open tundra; 2 eggs; 1 brood; May–August.

FEEDING Steals fish and other aquatic prey from gulls and terns; catches small birds, eats eggs, or hunts small rodents on breeding grounds.

PARASITIC PIRATE
This Parasitic Jaeger is harrying a gull by pecking at it, to make it disgorge its hard-won meal.

OCCURRENCE
Breeds on tundra in northern Canada and Alaska (breeds farther south than other jaegers); during migration and in winter, uses both nearshore and offshore waters; rarely found inland in the US outside the breeding season.

SIMILAR SPECIES

POMARINE JAEGER
see p.214

two long, central, twisted tail feathers

LONG-TAILED JAEGER
see p.216

black cap

heavy hooked bill

longer pointed tail

Length **16–18½in (41–47cm)**	Wingspan **3ft 3in–3½ft (1–1.1m)**	Weight **13–18oz (375–500g)**
Social **Solitary/Small flocks**	Lifespan **Up to 18 years**	Status **Secure**

DATE SEEN	WHERE	NOTES

| Order **Charadriiformes** | Family **Stercorariidae** | Species *Stercorarius longicaudus* |

Long-tailed Jaeger

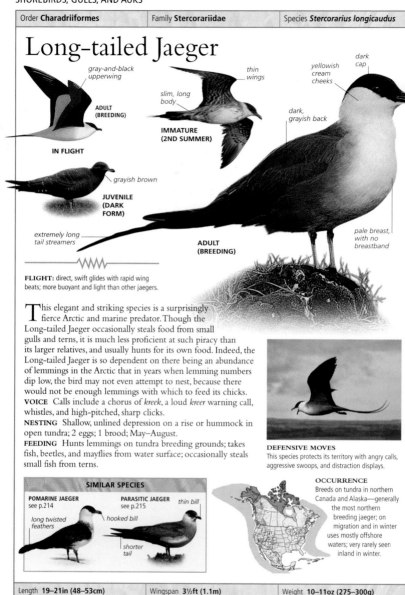

gray-and-black upperwing

ADULT (BREEDING)

IN FLIGHT

thin wings

slim, long body

IMMATURE (2ND SUMMER)

yellowish cream cheeks

dark cap

dark, grayish back

grayish brown

JUVENILE (DARK FORM)

extremely long tail streamers

ADULT (BREEDING)

pale breast, with no breastband

FLIGHT: direct, swift glides with rapid wing beats; more buoyant and light than other jaegers.

This elegant and striking species is a surprisingly fierce Arctic and marine predator. Though the Long-tailed Jaeger occasionally steals food from small gulls and terns, it is much less proficient at such piracy than its larger relatives, and usually hunts for its own food. Indeed, the Long-tailed Jaeger is so dependent on there being an abundance of lemmings in the Arctic that in years when lemming numbers dip low, the bird may not even attempt to nest, because there would not be enough lemmings with which to feed its chicks.
VOICE Calls include a chorus of *kreek*, a loud *kreer* warning call, whistles, and high-pitched, sharp clicks.
NESTING Shallow, unlined depression on a rise or hummock in open tundra; 2 eggs; 1 brood; May–August.
FEEDING Hunts lemmings on tundra breeding grounds; takes fish, beetles, and mayflies from water surface; occasionally steals small fish from terns.

DEFENSIVE MOVES
This species protects its territory with angry calls, aggressive swoops, and distraction displays.

SIMILAR SPECIES

POMARINE JAEGER see p.214

long twisted feathers

PARASITIC JAEGER see p.215

thin bill

hooked bill

shorter tail

OCCURRENCE
Breeds on tundra in northern Canada and Alaska—generally the most northern breeding jaeger; on migration and in winter uses mostly offshore waters; very rarely seen inland in winter.

| Length **19–21in (48–53cm)** | Wingspan **3½ft (1.1m)** | Weight **10–11oz (275–300g)** |
| Social **Solitary/Flocks** | Lifespan **Up to 8 years** | Status **Secure** |

DATE SEEN	WHERE	NOTES

| Order **Charadriiformes** | Family **Alcidae** | Species *Alle alle* |

Dovekie

short, dark tail

dark wings

ADULT (BREEDING)

IN FLIGHT

dark head and upper breast

white triangle on side of breast

ADULT (BREEDING)

white collar at back of head

dark crown

small bill

dark back

white throat

white undertail

ADULT (NONBREEDING)

Also known widely as the Little Auk, the stocky and diminutive black-and-white Dovekie is a bird of the High Arctic. Most Dovekies breed in Greenland in large, noisy, crowded colonies (the largest one containing 15–20 million birds), but some breed in northeastern Canada, and others on a few islands in the Bering Sea off Alaska. On their breeding grounds, both adult and immature Dovekies are hunted ruthlessly by Glaucous Gulls, as well as mammalian predators, such as the Arctic Fox. Vast numbers of Dovekies winter on the Low Arctic waters off the northeastern North American seaboard, in immense flocks. Occasionally, severe onshore gales cause entire flocks to become stranded along the East Coast of North America.

VOICE Variety of calls at breeding colony, including high-pitched trilling that rises and falls; silent at sea.

NESTING Pebble nest in crack or crevice in boulder field or rocky outcrop; 1 egg; 1 brood; April–August.

FEEDING Mostly picks tiny crustaceans from just below the sea's surface.

FLIGHT: rapid, whirring wing beats; flies in flocks low over the water's surface.

SOCIABLE LITTLE AUK
After initial squabbles over nest sites, Dovekies in breeding colonies become highly sociable.

SIMILAR SPECIES

BLACK GUILLEMOT ☾
see p.221

black-and-white barring on wing

whitish head

longer bill

OCCURRENCE
Breeds on islands inside the Arctic Circle; in Greenland, mostly, but also in northeastern Canada and the Bering Sea. Many birds remain just south of the Arctic pack ice throughout the winter; others fly south to winter off the northeastern seaboard of North America.

| Length **8½in (21cm)** | Wingspan **15in (38cm)** | Weight **6oz (175g)** |
| Social **Colonies** | Lifespan **Unknown** | Status **Secure** |

DATE SEEN	WHERE		NOTES

| Order **Charadriiformes** | Family **Alcidae** | Species *Uria lomvia* |

Thick-billed Murre

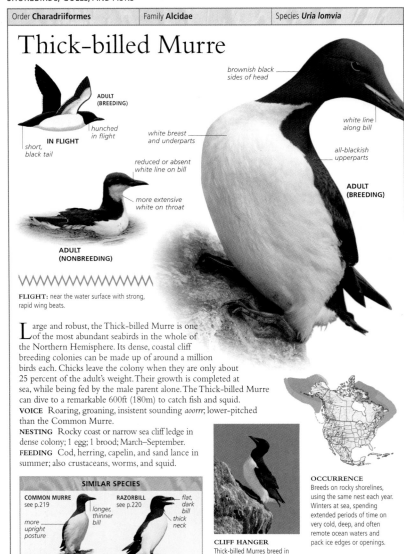

ADULT (BREEDING)

IN FLIGHT

short, black tail

hunched in flight

brownish black sides of head

white line along bill

white breast and underparts

all-blackish upperparts

ADULT (BREEDING)

reduced or absent white line on bill

more extensive white on throat

ADULT (NONBREEDING)

FLIGHT: near the water surface with strong, rapid wing beats.

Large and robust, the Thick-billed Murre is one of the most abundant seabirds in the whole of the Northern Hemisphere. Its dense, coastal cliff breeding colonies can be made up of around a million birds each. Chicks leave the colony when they are only about 25 percent of the adult's weight. Their growth is completed at sea, while being fed by the male parent alone. The Thick-billed Murre can dive to a remarkable 600ft (180m) to catch fish and squid.

VOICE Roaring, groaning, insistent sounding *aoorrr*; lower-pitched than the Common Murre.

NESTING Rocky coast or narrow sea cliff ledge in dense colony; 1 egg; 1 brood; March–September.

FEEDING Cod, herring, capelin, and sand lance in summer; also crustaceans, worms, and squid.

SIMILAR SPECIES

COMMON MURRE see p.219

more upright posture

longer, thinner bill

RAZORBILL see p.220

flat, dark bill

thick neck

CLIFF HANGER
Thick-billed Murres breed in dense colonies on steep cliffs, often in very remote areas.

OCCURRENCE
Breeds on rocky shorelines, using the same nest each year. Winters at sea, spending extended periods of time on very cold, deep, and often remote ocean waters and pack ice edges or openings.

| Length **18in (46cm)** | Wingspan **28in (70cm)** | Weight **34oz (975g)** |
| Social **Colonies** | Lifespan **At least 25 years** | Status **Secure** |

DATE SEEN	WHERE	NOTES

| Order **Charadriiformes** | Family **Alcidae** | Species *Uria aalge* |

Common Murre

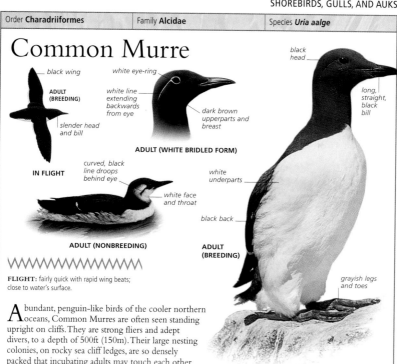

black head

black wing

ADULT (BREEDING)

white eye-ring

white line extending backwards from eye

dark brown upperparts and breast

slender head and bill

long, straight, black bill

ADULT (WHITE BRIDLED FORM)

IN FLIGHT

curved, black line droops behind eye

white underparts

white face and throat

black back

ADULT (NONBREEDING)

ADULT (BREEDING)

grayish legs and toes

FLIGHT: fairly quick with rapid wing beats; close to water's surface.

Abundant, penguin-like birds of the cooler northern oceans, Common Murres are often seen standing upright on cliffs. They are strong fliers and adept divers, to a depth of 500ft (150m). Their large nesting colonies, on rocky sea cliff ledges, are so densely packed that incubating adults may touch each other on both sides. Common Murre eggs are pointed at one end—when pushed, they roll around in a circle, reducing the risk of rolling off the nesting ledge. It has been suggested that unique egg markings may help adults recognize their own eggs.
VOICE Low-pitched, descending call given from cliffs or water, reminiscent of trumpeting elephant.
NESTING Directly on bare rock near shore, on wide cliff ledge, or large crevice; 1 egg; 1 brood; May–July.
FEEDING Pursues small schooling fish, such as herring, sand lance, and haddock; also crustaceans, marine worms, and squid.

BREEDING COLONY
Crowded together, Common Murres are not territorial but will defend a personal space.

SIMILAR SPECIES

THICK-BILLED MURRE see p.218

thick, pale line between eye and bill

RAZORBILL ☼ see p.220

bill with white bar near tip

OCCURRENCE
Breeds close to rocky shorelines, nesting on coastal cliff ledges or flat rocks on top of sea stacks on both East and West coasts. Found farther offshore during nonbreeding season, spending extended periods on the open ocean and in large bays. Winters at sea.

| Length **17½in (44cm)** | Wingspan **26in (65cm)** | Weight **35oz (1,000g)** |
| Social **Colonies** | Lifespan **At least 40 years** | Status **Localized** |

DATE SEEN	WHERE	NOTES

| Order **Charadriiformes** | Family **Alcidae** | Species *Alca torda* |

Razorbill

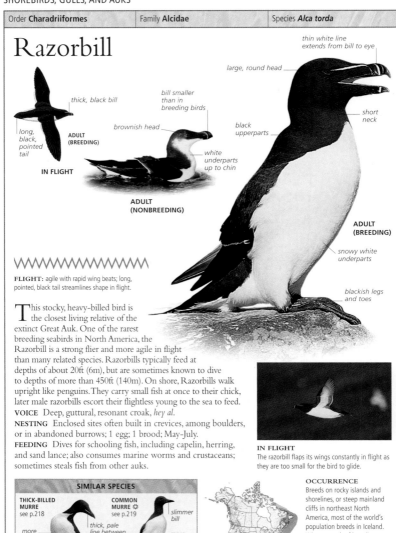

thin white line extends from bill to eye

large, round head

IN FLIGHT

thick, black bill

long, black, pointed tail

ADULT (BREEDING)

bill smaller than in breeding birds

brownish head

white underparts up to chin

ADULT (NONBREEDING)

black upperparts

short neck

ADULT (BREEDING)

snowy white underparts

blackish legs and toes

FLIGHT: agile with rapid wing beats; long, pointed, black tail streamlines shape in flight.

This stocky, heavy-billed bird is the closest living relative of the extinct Great Auk. One of the rarest breeding seabirds in North America, the Razorbill is a strong flier and more agile in flight than many related species. Razorbills typically feed at depths of about 20ft (6m), but are sometimes known to dive to depths of more than 450ft (140m). On shore, Razorbills walk upright like penguins. They carry small fish at once to their chick, later male razorbills escort their flightless young to the sea to feed.

VOICE Deep, guttural, resonant croak, *hey al.*
NESTING Enclosed sites often built in crevices, among boulders, or in abandoned burrows; 1 egg; 1 brood; May–July.
FEEDING Dives for schooling fish, including capelin, herring, and sand lance; also consumes marine worms and crustaceans; sometimes steals fish from other auks.

IN FLIGHT
The razorbill flaps its wings constantly in flight as they are too small for the bird to glide.

SIMILAR SPECIES

THICK-BILLED MURRE see p.218

more slender body

thick, pale line between eye and bill

COMMON MURRE ☼ see p.219

slimmer bill

more slender body

OCCURRENCE
Breeds on rocky islands and shorelines, or steep mainland cliffs in northeast North America, most of the world's population breeds in Iceland. Winters south of breeding range on ice-free coastal waters reaching New Jersey and Virginia. Forages in cool, shallower water, near shore.

| Length **17in (43cm)** | Wingspan **26in (65cm)** | Weight **26oz (725g)** |
| Social **Colonies** | Lifespan **At least 30 years** | Status **Localized** |

DATE SEEN	WHERE	NOTES

Order **Charadriiformes**	Family **Alcidae**	Species *Cepphus grylle*

Black Guillemot

ADULT (BREEDING)

broad, rounded wings

oval, snowy white upperwing patch

IN FLIGHT

gray bars in white wing patch

gray cap

gray neck

JUVENILE

large white patch

thin, straight bill

dark belly

scarlet legs and toes

ADULT (BREEDING)

round, black body

Black Guillemots, also known as "sea pigeons," are medium-sized auks with distinctive black plumage and white wing patches. Their striking scarlet legs and mouth lining help attract a mate during the breeding season. Like the other two species of the *Cepphus* genus, Black Guillemots prefer shallow, inshore waters to the open ocean. They winter near the shore, sometimes moving into the mouths of rivers.

VOICE Very high-pitched whistles and squeaks given on land and water near nesting habitat that resonate like an echo.

NESTING Shallow scrape in soil or pebbles within cave or crevice, site may be reused; 1–2 eggs; 1 brood; May–August.

FEEDING Dives under water near shore to hunt small, bottom-dwelling fish, such as rock eels, sand lance, and sculpin; propels down to depths of 59ft (18m) using partly opened wings, webbed feet as a rudder; feeds close to nesting islands.

FLIGHT: flies low over the water with very rapid wing beats.

FOOD FOR CHICKS
The birds carry food for the chicks in their bills and often pause near the nest before dashing home.

SIMILAR SPECIES

DOVEKIE ❊
smaller; see p.217

dark back

white patch behind eye

PIGEON GUILLEMOT ✿
dusky underwings in flight

black bar on white wing patch

OCCURRENCE
Primarily an Atlantic species. Breeds in crevices on remote rocky islands and cliffs that provide protection from predators. At sea prefers shallow waters, close to rocky coasts. At end of breeding season, adults and young move closer to shore to avoid pack ice.

Length **13in (33cm)**	Wingspan **21in (53cm)**	Weight **15oz (425g)**
Social **Colonies**	Lifespan **At least 20 years**	Status **Localized**

DATE SEEN	WHERE	NOTES

Order **Charadriiformes**	Family **Alcidae**	Species *Fratercula arctica*

Atlantic Puffin

dusky gray face

dull bill

black back, collar, and underwings

blue-gray, orange, and red stripes on bill

ADULT (BREEDING)

short tail

IN FLIGHT

orange legs and toes

ADULT (BREEDING)

gray face

red eye-ring

thick black line

ADULT (NONBREEDING)

stocky, rounded body

large, colorful, triangular bill

white breast

ADULT (BREEDING)

With its black-and-white "tuxedo," ungainly upright posture, and enormous, colorful bill, the Atlantic Puffin is often known as the "clown of the sea." Certainly it looks comical, whether strutting about or simply bobbing on the sea. It is seen in summer, when large breeding colonies gather on remote, rocky islands. To feed itself and its young, it can dive down to 200ft (60m) with partly folded wings, essentially "flying" underwater in pursuit of small schooling fish.

VOICE Rising and falling buzzy growl, resembling a chainsaw.
NESTING Underground burrow or deep rock crevice lined with grass and feathers; 1 egg; 1 brood; June–August.
FEEDING Dives deep for capelin, herring, hake, sand lance, and other small fish, which it swallows underwater, or stores crossways in its bill to take back to its chicks.

FLIGHT: swift and direct, with rapid wing beats; often circles breeding islands.

CATCH AND CARRY
When returning to breeding colonies to feed chicks, most birds carry more than one fish in their bill.

SIMILAR SPECIES

LONG-TAILED DUCK ♂ ❄
see p.65

long tail

white eye-ring

stubby bill

dark flanks

HORNED PUFFIN

fleshy "horn" above eye

yellow base to bill

OCCURRENCE
This northern North Atlantic seabird (found on both sides of the ocean) breeds in colonies on small, rocky, offshore islands, where it excavates nesting burrows or nests under boulders. Between breeding seasons, it heads for the high seas and remains far offshore, favoring cold, open waters.

Length **12½in (32cm)**	Wingspan **21in (53cm)**	Weight **12oz (350g)**
Social **Colonies**	Lifespan **At least 30 years**	Status **Localized**

DATE SEEN	WHERE	NOTES

PIGEONS & DOVES

THE LARGER SPECIES WITHIN the family Columbidae are known as pigeons, and the smaller ones as doves, although there is no actual scientific basis for this distinction. They are all fairly heavy, plump birds with relatively small heads and short necks. They have slender bills with the nostrils positioned in a fleshy mound at the base. Among other things, members of this family have strong wing muscles, making them powerful and agile

TINY DOVE
Slightly larger than a sparrow, the Common Ground-Dove has well-marked black wing-spots.

fliers. When alarmed, they burst into flight, with their wings emitting a distinctive clapping or swishing sound. Pigeons and doves secrete a nutritious "crop-milk" to feed their young. Despite human activity having severely affected members of this family in the past (the leading cause of the Passenger Pigeon's extinction in the 19th century is thought to be overhunting), the introduced Rock Pigeon has adapted and proliferated worldwide, as has the recently introduced Eurasian Collared-Dove, albeit on a smaller scale. The introduced Spotted Dove has not shown a similar tendency for explosive expansion, however, and remains limited to southern California and the islands of Hawaii. Among the species native to North America, only the elegant Mourning Dove is as widespread as the various species of introduced birds.

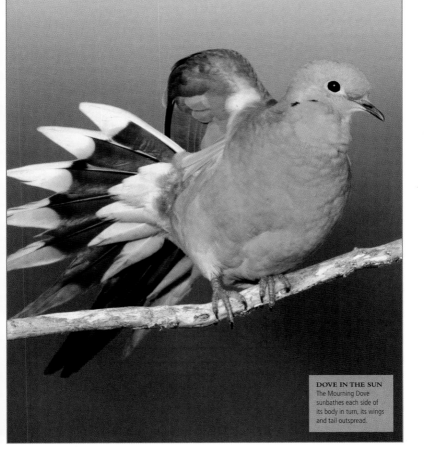

DOVE IN THE SUN
The Mourning Dove sunbathes each side of its body in turn, its wings and tail outspread.

| Order **Columbiformes** | Family **Columbidae** | Species *Columba livia* |

Rock Pigeon

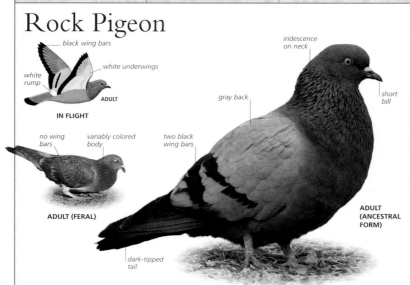

IN FLIGHT

black wing bars

white underwings

white rump

ADULT

iridescence on neck

gray back

short bill

no wing bars

variably colored body

two black wing bars

ADULT (FERAL)

ADULT (ANCESTRAL FORM)

dark-tipped tail

The Rock Pigeon was introduced to the Atlantic coast of North America by 17th century colonists. Now feral, this species is found all over the continent, especially around farms, cities, and towns. This medium-sized pigeon comes in a wide variety of plumage colors and patterns, including bluish gray, checkered, rusty red, and nearly all-white. Its wings usually have two dark bars on them—unique among North American pigeons. The variability of the Rock Pigeon influenced Charles Darwin as he developed his theory of natural selection.
VOICE Soft, gurgling *coo*, *roo-c'too-coo*, for courtship and threat.
NESTING Twig nest on flat, sheltered surface, such as caves, rocky outcrops, and buildings; 2 eggs; several broods; year-round.
FEEDING Eats seeds, fruit, and rarely insects; human foods such as popcorn, bread, peanuts; various farm crops in rural areas.

FLIGHT: strong, direct; can reach speeds up to around 60mph (95kph).

CITY PIGEONS
Most Rock Pigeons in North America descend from domesticated forms and exhibit many colors.

SIMILAR SPECIES

WHITE-CROWNED PIGEON
mangroves; see p.452

white crown

dark gray overall

BAND-TAILED PIGEON
western

yellow bill with dark tip

white band on nape

OCCURRENCE
Across southern Canada and North America; nests in human structures of all sorts; resident. Original habitat in the Old World was (and still is) sea cliffs and inland canyons; found wild in some places, such as dry regions of North Africa, but feral in much of the world.

| Length **11–14in (28–36cm)** | Wingspan **20–26in (51–67cm)** | Weight **9–14oz (250–400g)** |
| Social **Solitary/Flocks** | Lifespan **Up to 6 years** | Status **Secure** |

DATE SEEN	WHERE	NOTES

| Order **Columbiformes** | Family **Columbidae** | Species ***Streptopelia decaocto*** |

Eurasian Collared-Dove

dark outer wing feathers

gray wing feathers

ADULT

IN FLIGHT

dark bill

black collar on hind neck

pale gray body

ADULT

square tail

gray undertail wing feathers

A stocky bird, the Eurasian Collared-Dove is easily recognized by the black collar on the back of its neck and its square tail. First released at New Providence, Bahamas, in the mid-1970s, this species is spreading rapidly across the continental mainland, thanks to multiple local releases, the planting of trees in urban and suburban habitats, the popularity of bird feeders making food readily available, and the bird's extraordinarily high reproductive rate. This species soon becomes very confiding and tolerant of humans, regularly nesting and feeding in urban areas. One consequence of this is that it often falls prey to domestic cats, but this has little effect on the expanding population. Based on sightings from locations all over North America—and on the evidence from Europe, throughout which it has spread since only the 1940s—it is highly likely that the Eurasian Collared-Dove will soon become a common species in North America.

VOICE Repeated four-note *coo-hoo-HOO-cook* that is quick and low-pitched; also harsh, nasal *krreeew* in flight.

NESTING Platform of twigs, stems, and grasses in trees or on buildings; 2 eggs; multiple broods; March–November.

FEEDING Eats seed and grain, plant stems and leaves, berries, and some invertebrates; feeds on the ground for seed, but also visits elevated feeders.

FLIGHT: strong, stiff flight reminiscent of hawks; occasional swoops and dives.

COLLARED COLONIZER
The Eurasian Collared-Dove has spread throughout Europe in just a few decades, and now looks set to do the same in North America.

SIMILAR SPECIES

MOURNING DOVE
see p.226

black dot on face

black spots on wings

pointed tail

OCCURRENCE
Can be seen almost anywhere in North America south of the northern forest zone, but occurs mainly in suburban and urban areas (though not large cities) with seeds and grain for food and deciduous trees for nesting and roosting. May roost in man-made structures such as barns.

| Length **11½–12in (29–30cm)** | Wingspan **14in (35cm)** | Weight **5–6oz (150–175g)** |
| Social **Large flocks** | Lifespan **Up to 13 years** | Status **Localized** |

DATE SEEN	WHERE	NOTES

| Order **Columbiformes** | Family **Columbidae** | Species *Zenaida macroura* |

Mourning Dove

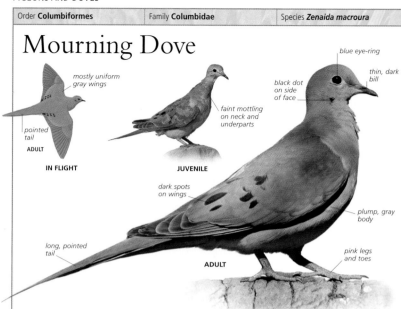

blue eye-ring

thin, dark bill

black dot on side of face

mostly uniform gray wings

faint mottling on neck and underparts

pointed tail

ADULT

IN FLIGHT

JUVENILE

dark spots on wings

plump, gray body

long, pointed tail

pink legs and toes

ADULT

One of the most familiar, abundant, and widespread of North American birds, the Mourning Dove is a long-tailed, plump, medium-sized dove with a small head. It has a grayish tan body with a pale, rosy breast and black spots on folded wings. While coveted by hunters—as many as 70 million are shot annually—the Mourning Dove is also well known to those who live on farms and in suburbia. The species is divided into four subspecies, two of which occur in North America—the larger grayish brown *Z. m. carolinensis*, east of the Mississippi River, and the smaller, paler *Z. m. marginella* in the west.

VOICE Mellow, owl-like call: *hoO-Oo-oo, hoo-hoo-hoo.*

NESTING Flat, flimsy twig platform, mostly in trees, sometimes on the ground; 2 eggs; 2 broods; February–October.

FEEDING Forages mainly for seeds on the ground; obtains food quickly and digests it later at roost.

FLIGHT: swift, direct flight, with fairly quick wing beats; twists and turns sometimes.

SIMILAR SPECIES

EURASIAN COLLARED-DOVE
see p.225

WHITE-WINGED DOVE ♂
see p.227

black collar on hind-neck

square tail

white in wings

square tail

FAMILIAR SIGHT
The Mourning Dove is North America's most widespread member of this family.

OCCURRENCE
Breeds in a wide variety of habitats but shuns extensive forests; human-altered vegetation favored for feeding, including farmland and suburbia. Winters in small to medium sheltered woodland while feeding in grain fields; winters in southern Mexico and Central America.

| Length **9–13½in (23–34cm)** | Wingspan **14½–17½in (37–45cm)** | Weight **3–6oz (85–175g)** |
| Social **Pairs/Winter flocks** | Lifespan **Up to 19 years** | Status **Secure** |

DATE SEEN	WHERE	NOTES

| Order **Columbiformes** | Family **Columbidae** | Species *Zenaida asiatica* |

White-winged Dove

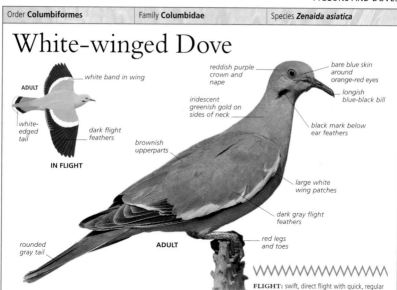

ADULT

white band in wing

white-edged tail

dark flight feathers

IN FLIGHT

brownish upperparts

reddish purple crown and nape

bare blue skin around orange-red eyes

longish blue-black bill

iridescent greenish gold on sides of neck

black mark below ear feathers

large white wing patches

dark gray flight feathers

red legs and toes

rounded gray tail

ADULT

FLIGHT: swift, direct flight with quick, regular wing beats; maximum height about 200ft (60m).

As one of the larger gray-colored dove species in North America, the White-winged Dove is best identified in flight by the conspicuous white bands on its wings. When perched, the bright blue skin around its orange eyes and its longish, square tail with a white tip can be seen. This species has been expanding its population northwards in recent decades, though not as quickly as the Eurasian Collared-Dove. Increased farmland habitat and ornamental trees, both favorite roosting places, are the most likely cause. In common with many other doves, the nest is a somewhat flimsy structure, and eggs or nestlings frequently fall to their end if the nest is disturbed, or when there are high winds.

VOICE Distinctive, drawn-out cooing: *who-cooks-for-you*; also makes five-note variation from the nest: *la-coo-kla-coo-kla*.

NESTING Frail platform of twigs, moss, and grasses, on a sturdy branch in dense-canopied trees; 2 eggs; 2 broods; March–September.

FEEDING Forages for seeds, wild nuts, and fruit on the ground and in elevated locations; prefers corn, sorghum, wheat, and sunflower.

DESERT DWELLER
The White-winged Dove is much more at home in semi-arid and desert areas than the Mourning Dove.

SIMILAR SPECIES

MOURNING DOVE see p.226 — smaller, rounder head

no white wing patch

longer tail

OCCURRENCE
Breeds and winters in dense, thorny woodlands dominated by mesquite and Texas Ebony; deserts with cactus, palo verde, and other scrub plants; riverine woodlands, orchards, and residential areas. Formerly only abundant in the US in the Rio Grande Valley, it has now expanded north to Oklahoma.

| Length **11½in (29cm)** | Wingspan **19in (48cm)** | Weight **5oz (150g)** |
| Social **Solitary/Flocks** | Lifespan **Up to 21 years** | Status **Localized** |

DATE SEEN	WHERE	NOTES

Order **Columbiformes**	Family **Columbidae**	Species ***Columbina inca***

Inca Dove

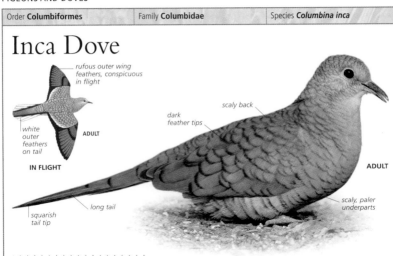

rufous outer wing feathers, conspicuous in flight

white outer feathers on tail

ADULT

IN FLIGHT

scaly back

dark feather tips

ADULT

scaly, paler underparts

long tail

squarish tail tip

FLIGHT: fast, direct flights of short duration, with a noisy takeoff.

This small, brownish gray dove has expanded its range from Central America and Mexico into the southern US in the last 100 years or so, and now breeds in all of the southwestern states from California east to the Mississippi River. Resembling a baby Mourning Dove because of its slender shape and long tail, the Inca Dove can be distinguished by its "scaly" pattern. Although it is a secretive species, hiding in low, dense vegetation, it is tame and frequently occurs in human settlements. When encountered, the Inca Dove often flushes almost from underfoot, flashing the reddish coloration of its wings.

VOICE Repeated 2-note chant, *pol-pah*, which can sound like the words "no hope;" sometimes low, trilling *coo*.

NESTING Compact platform of twigs and leaves in a variety of trees and shrubs; 2 eggs; several broods; March–November.

FEEDING Pecks at grains, seeds, and weeds on the ground, among vegetation; also fruit.

WING-UP DISPLAY
The wing-up posture is used by territorial male Inca Doves in aggressive displays.

A "TALL" TAIL
An Inca Dove's tail makes up a third of the bird's total length.

OCCURRENCE
Breeds and winters all year in areas of human habitation: cities, towns, farms containing shrubs and small trees for nesting. Forages on lawns and barnyards and occasionally near rivers and streams but appears to favor drier areas in the south of its range.

SIMILAR SPECIES

RUDDY GROUND-DOVE
see p.472

smaller overall

shorter tail

Length **7–9in (18–23cm)**	Wingspan **11in (28cm)**	Weight **1¹⁄₁₆–2oz (30–60g)**
Social **Solitary/Large flocks**	Lifespan **Up to 7 years**	Status **Localized**

DATE SEEN	WHERE	NOTES

| Order **Columbiformes** | Family **Columbidae** | Species *Columbina passerina* |

Common Ground-Dove

rufous outer wing feathers

MALE

short tail

IN FLIGHT

pinkish or red base to bill

scaly, gray breast

FEMALE

black spots on wings

scaly looking head

scaly breast with pink tinge

square tail

MALE

The Common Ground-Dove, the smallest of all North American doves, is only slightly larger than a sparrow. Both of these qualities are reflected in its scientific name—*Columbina*—meaning "little dove," and *passerina* being the Latin for sparrow. It is also different from other doves in that it retains its pair-bond throughout the year and tends not to form flocks. Birds in a pair usually remain within a few yards of each other. Besides its diminutive size, the Common Ground-Dove is recognizable by prominent black spots on its wings, scaly underparts (seen while perched), the reddish appearance of its wings, and its square, blackish tail while in flight. It is found coast to coast along the most southerly regions of the continent, but vagrants can appear almost anywhere.

VOICE Simple, repeated, ascending double-note *wah-up* given every 2–3 seconds.

NESTING Depression on ground lined with grasses and palm fibers, or frail nest in trees; 2 eggs; several broods; April–August.

FEEDING Pecks on the ground at grass and weed seeds, grains, small berries, insects, and snails; also takes seeds from feeders; prefers drier, scrubby ground.

FLIGHT: direct, quick, sometimes jerky flight with stiff, rapid wing beats; usually short duration.

EASILY OVERLOOKED
Ground-Doves blend in with the ground and can be overlooked as they quietly feed.

SIMILAR SPECIES

RUDDY GROUND-DOVE
see p.472

plain gray head

dark bill

OCCURRENCE
Mostly prefers dry, sandy areas with short, open vegetation, although it can be found in a variety of habitats, such as open pine woodlands, woodland edges, citrus groves, mesquite and riverine thickets, farm fields, suburban areas, and cultivated land, including orchards.

| Length **6–7in (15–18cm)** | Wingspan **11in (28cm)** | Weight **1¹⁄₁₆–1⁷⁄₁₆oz (30–40g)** |
| Social **Pairs** | Lifespan **Up to 7 years** | Status **Localized** |

DATE SEEN	WHERE	NOTES

PARAKEETS & PARROTS

ALTHOUGH THEY VARY in size, shape, plumage, and behavior, all psittacids—parakeets and parrots—have certain features in common: a large, powerful, sharply hooked bill; a large, stocky head, with no noticeable neck; and short legs with what are called zygodactyl feet, in which two toes point forward and two back. Most species are brightly colored and have red, orange, or yellow patches on the wings or tail. Some birds are entirely white, black, yellow, red, or blue, but most are various shades of green. Psittacids live primarily in forests, where their green plumage enables the birds to disappear from view against a background of thick foliage. Even brightly colored parrots and parakeets are surprisingly well camouflaged in trees. Some species frequently forage on the ground, and many readily visit birdfeeders in suburban and urban areas. Psittacids are mainly vegetarian, feeding on a variety of fruits, nuts, flowers, and grains. They are very social and vocal, with loud calls that help to keep members of a flock together. In addition to feeding and roosting together, many species nest close together; a few even nest colonially. Except for the Monk Parakeet, which builds an elaborate stick nest, parrots and parakeets are secondary cavity nesters, breeding in rock crevices, existing tree cavities, and birdhouses.

SECONDHAND HOME
The Red-crowned Parrot will readily nest in an existing tree cavity, such as an abandoned woodpecker hole.

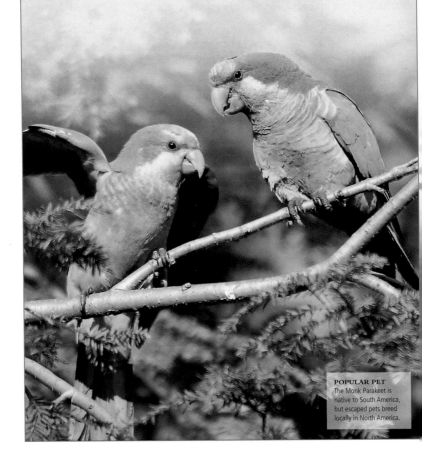

POPULAR PET
The Monk Parakeet is native to South America, but escaped pets breed locally in North America.

| Order **Psittaciformes** | Family **Psittacidae** | Species *Myiopsitta monachus* |

Monk Parakeet

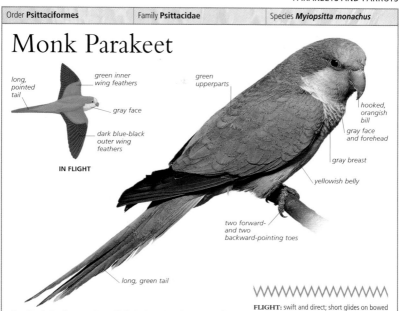

long, pointed tail

green inner wing feathers

gray face

dark blue-black outer wing feathers

IN FLIGHT

green upperparts

hooked, orangish bill

gray face and forehead

gray breast

yellowish belly

two forward- and two backward-pointing toes

long, green tail

Monk Parakeets, native to Bolivia, Argentina, Paraguay, and Brazil, have been introduced to a number of places in the United States. They are the most abundant and widespread species of introduced parrot in North America, locally breeding in huge colonies. Their large communal nests of sticks are unique among parrots and parakeets. These nests are used both for breeding and for roosting. If food is abundant, Monk Parakeets are perfectly capable of surviving cold winters in places such as Chicago or New York City, although supplementary food from feeders is welcome.
VOICE Wide variety of calls, mostly loud and grating squawks, can mimic human voice and other sounds.
NESTING Large, bulky stick nests placed in trees, palms, or on man-made structures; 5–8 eggs; 2 broods; March–July.
FEEDING Eats seeds, buds, flowers, fruits, nuts; occasionally eats insects; visits birdfeeders.

FLIGHT: swift and direct; short glides on bowed wings; often changes direction, usually in flocks.

PLANT FEEDER
Monk Parakeets feed on a wide variety of plant material, including bottlebrush flowers.

SIMILAR SPECIES

GREEN PARAKEET
see p.453
green breast and face

green upperparts and flight feathers

ACROBATIC FLIGHT
Flocks of vividly colored Monk Parakeets twist and turn in flight, and are notoriously vocal.

OCCURRENCE
In North America mainly restricted to urban or suburban habitats, where nests can be built in palms, deciduous trees, telephone poles, or electrical substations. Common in southern Florida; found in several other areas, north to New York City, Chicago, and Portland, Oregon.

| Length **11½in (29cm)** | Wingspan **21in (53cm)** | Weight **3½oz (100g)** |
| Social **Flocks/Colonies** | Lifespan **Up to 6 years** | Status **Localized** |

DATE SEEN	WHERE		NOTES
....	....		....
....	....		....
....	....		....
....	....		....
....	....		....

CUCKOOS & RELATIVES

Cuckoos are notorious for laying eggs in other birds' nests, but of the three species in North America, one never does this, and two seldom do so. Their close relatives on the continent are the Greater Roadrunner, and two species of anis.

CUCKOOS

Generally shy and reclusive, the Black-billed Cuckoo, Yellow-billed Cuckoo, and Mangrove Cuckoo all favor dense, forested habitats. All three species usually build a nest and raise their own offspring. The Black-billed Cuckoo and the Yellow-billed Cuckoo occasionally lay their eggs in other birds' nests, including each other's, and even the nests of their own species. In flight, cuckoos are often mistaken for small birds of prey. They sometimes pounce on lizards, frogs, and other small animals—even small birds—but mostly they glean insects from the foliage of trees. Much remains to be learned about these birds.

WEATHER BIRD
Folklore has it that the Yellow-billed Cuckoo, or "Raincrow," calls mostly on cloudy days.

GREATER ROADRUNNER

The Greater Roadrunner is a ground-based member of the Cuckoo family and an inhabitant of the arid Southwest. It is capable of running at over 15mph (25kph), and is one of the few species of birds that actively hunts rattlesnakes, doing so in pairs. The Greater Roadrunner has been seen pulling small birds out of mist nets set by scientists for research purposes. It does not fly often, and rarely above a few yards.

STRONG STOMACH
The Black-billed Cuckoo can safely eat caterpillars that are poisonous to other birds.

ANIS

In North America both the Groove-billed Ani and the Smooth-billed Ani are at the northern edge of their known range, being much more widespread in open country in tropical and subtropical regions farther south. Anis are typically weak, short-distance fliers, but, like the Greater Roadrunner, they are sturdy on their feet and often run and hop after their insect prey. They breed communally, several pairs of birds laying their eggs in one nest, then all help to raise the young.

PERCHED TO KILL
After catching a lizard, the Greater Roadrunner bashes it repeatedly against a rock before gulping it down.

| Order **Cuculiformes** | Family **Cuculidae** | Species *Coccyzus erythropthalmus* |

Black-billed Cuckoo

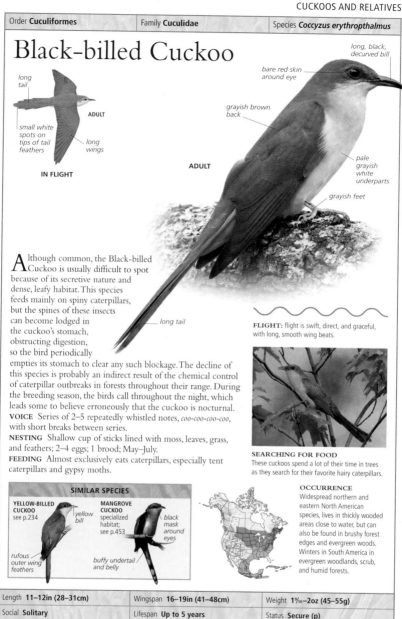

long tail

ADULT

small white spots on tips of tail feathers

long wings

IN FLIGHT

long, black, decurved bill

bare red skin around eye

grayish brown back

ADULT

pale grayish white underparts

grayish feet

long tail

Although common, the Black-billed Cuckoo is usually difficult to spot because of its secretive nature and dense, leafy habitat. This species feeds mainly on spiny caterpillars, but the spines of these insects can become lodged in the cuckoo's stomach, obstructing digestion, so the bird periodically empties its stomach to clear any such blockage. The decline of this species is probably an indirect result of the chemical control of caterpillar outbreaks in forests throughout their range. During the breeding season, the birds call throughout the night, which leads some to believe erroneously that the cuckoo is nocturnal.

VOICE Series of 2–5 repeatedly whistled notes, *coo-coo-coo-coo*, with short breaks between series.

NESTING Shallow cup of sticks lined with moss, leaves, grass, and feathers; 2–4 eggs; 1 brood; May–July.

FEEDING Almost exclusively eats caterpillars, especially tent caterpillars and gypsy moths.

FLIGHT: flight is swift, direct, and graceful, with long, smooth wing beats.

SEARCHING FOR FOOD
These cuckoos spend a lot of their time in trees as they search for their favorite hairy caterpillars.

SIMILAR SPECIES

YELLOW-BILLED CUCKOO see p.234

yellow bill

rufous outer wing feathers

MANGROVE CUCKOO specialized habitat; see p.453

black mask around eyes

buffy undertail and belly

OCCURRENCE
Widespread northern and eastern North American species, lives in thickly wooded areas close to water, but can also be found in brushy forest edges and evergreen woods. Winters in South America in evergreen woodlands, scrub, and humid forests.

| Length **11–12in (28–31cm)** | Wingspan **16–19in (41–48cm)** | Weight **1⁹⁄₁₆–2oz (45–55g)** |
| Social **Solitary** | Lifespan **Up to 5 years** | Status **Secure (p)** |

DATE SEEN	WHERE	NOTES

Order **Cuculiformes**	Family **Cuculidae**	Species **Coccyzus americanus**

Yellow-billed Cuckoo

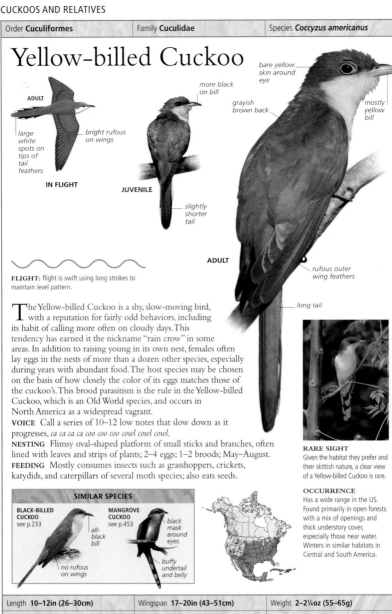

ADULT

IN FLIGHT

large white spots on tips of tail feathers

bright rufous on wings

JUVENILE

more black on bill

slightly shorter tail

ADULT

bare yellow skin around eye

grayish brown back

mostly yellow bill

rufous outer wing feathers

long tail

FLIGHT: flight is swift using long strokes to maintain level pattern.

The Yellow-billed Cuckoo is a shy, slow-moving bird, with a reputation for fairly odd behaviors, including its habit of calling more often on cloudy days. This tendency has earned it the nickname "rain crow" in some areas. In addition to raising young in its own nest, females often lay eggs in the nests of more than a dozen other species, especially during years with abundant food. The host species may be chosen on the basis of how closely the color of its eggs matches those of the cuckoo's. This brood parasitism is the rule in the Yellow-billed Cuckoo, which is an Old World species, and occurs in North America as a widespread vagrant.

VOICE Call a series of 10–12 low notes that slow down as it progresses, *ca ca ca ca coo coo coo cowl cowl cowl*.

NESTING Flimsy oval-shaped platform of small sticks and branches, often lined with leaves and strips of plants; 2–4 eggs; 1–2 broods; May–August.

FEEDING Mostly consumes insects such as grasshoppers, crickets, katydids, and caterpillars of several moth species; also eats seeds.

RARE SIGHT
Given the habitat they prefer and their skittish nature, a clear view of a Yellow-billed Cuckoo is rare.

OCCURRENCE
Has a wide range in the US. Found primarily in open forests with a mix of openings and thick understory cover, especially those near water. Winters in similar habitats in Central and South America.

SIMILAR SPECIES		
BLACK-BILLED CUCKOO see p.233	**MANGROVE CUCKOO** see p.453	

all-black bill

no rufous on wings

black mask around eyes

buffy undertail and belly

Length **10–12in (26–30cm)**	Wingspan **17–20in (43–51cm)**	Weight **2–2¼oz (55–65g)**
Social **Small winter flocks**	Lifespan **Up to 4 years**	Status **Secure (p)**

DATE SEEN	WHERE	NOTES

| Order **Cuculiformes** | Family **Cuculidae** | Species *Geococcyx californianus* |

Greater Roadrunner

long, thick, powerful bill

large crest

ADULT

light brown body

ADULT

large, whitish crescent on wings

heavily streaked upperparts

IN FLIGHT

dark brown, glossy green, and black streaks

heavily streaked head, neck, and chest

long, dark tail with white-edged tip

unstreaked, lower belly

FLIGHT: weak flutter to high perches; open wing glide from elevated perch; prefers to run.

Unlike the other species of North American cuckoo, the Greater Roadrunner is a ground bird, but it can fly, despite preferring to run. Its speed enables it to overcome and chase prey on foot, especially lizards and small birds. Its generalized feeding habits allow this bird to take advantage of whatever food resources it comes across. This may be one of the main reasons roadrunners are expanding their range.

VOICE Cooing *coo-coo-coo-cooo-cooooo* series of 4–5 descending notes.

NESTING Shallow, loosely organized cup of twigs and branches, lined with grass, animal hair, and feathers; 3–5 eggs; 2 broods; April–September.

FEEDING Eats a wide variety of insects, small reptiles such as lizards, birds, and mammals; also eggs and carrion.

DRINKING
Roadrunners obtain much of their moisture from the food they eat, but will take full advantage of water whenever it's available.

LOFTY ABODE
This species nests off the ground, and can occasionally be seen occupying elevated perches.

SIMILAR SPECIES

PLAIN CHACHALACA
see p.444

darker, solid color

RING-NECKED PHEASANT ♀
see p.33

lighter brown overall

unstreaked upperparts

larger overall

no crest

plump body

OCCURRENCE
Widespread across southeastern US, from California to Louisiana, and north to Utah, Colorado, Kansas, and Arkansas; lives at low elevations in open brushy areas mixed with thorn scrub such as mesquite; also pinyon-juniper shrubbery, and deserts and chaparral. Resident.

| Length **21in (53cm)** | Wingspan **23in (58cm)** | Weight **11oz (300g)** |
| Social **Solitary/Pairs** | Lifespan **Up to 6 years** | Status **Secure** |

DATE SEEN	WHERE	NOTES

OWLS

OWLS HAVE FASCINATED humans throughout history, partly because of their nocturnal habits and eerie cries. They are placed in the order Strigiformes, and two families are represented in North America: the Barn Owl is classified in Tytonidae, other North American owl species are in the Strigidae. Most owls are active primarily at night and have developed adaptations for living in low-light environments. Their large eyes are sensitive enough to see in the dark, and face forward to maximize binocular vision. Since the eyes are fixed in their sockets, a flexible

neck helps owls turn their heads almost 180° toward a direction of interest. Ears are offset on each side of the head to help identify the source of a sound; "ear tufts" on some species are for visual effect and unrelated to hearing. Many owls have serrations on the forward edges of their flight feathers to cushion airflow, so their

BIG HORNS
The "ear" tufts of the Great Horned Owl are taller than those of other "tufted" owls.

flight is silent while stalking prey. All North American owls are predatory to some degree and they inhabit most areas of the continent. The Burrowing Owl is unique in that it hunts during the day and nests underground.

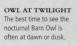

OWL AT TWILIGHT
The best time to see the nocturnal Barn Owl is often at dawn or dusk.

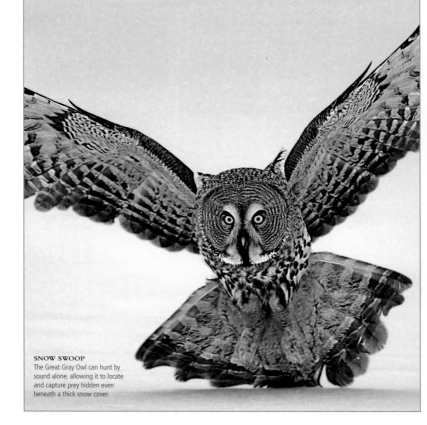

SNOW SWOOP
The Great Gray Owl can hunt by sound alone, allowing it to locate and capture prey hidden even beneath a thick snow cover.

| Order **Strigiformes** | Family **Tytonidae** | Species *Tyto alba* |

Barn Owl

barring on wings and tail

head lacks "ear" tufts

rounded, heart-shaped facial disk

relatively small eyes

long wings

ADULT

ADULT

IN FLIGHT

pale buff upperparts

white underparts

dark eyes

gray and black spots

ruff surrounds facial disk

feathered legs

ADULT

FLIGHT: irregular bursts of flapping, interspersed with short glides, banking, doubling back, fluttering.

Aptly named, the Barn Owl inhabits old sheds, sheltered rafters, and empty buildings in rural fields. With its affinity for human settlement, and 32 subspecies, this owl has an extensive range covering every continent except Antarctica. Although widespread, the Barn Owl is secretive. Primarily nocturnal, it can fly undetected until its screeching call pierces the air. The Barn Owl is endangered in several Midwestern states as a result of modern farming practices, which have decimated prey populations and reduced the number of barns for nesting.

VOICE Typical call loud, raspy, screeching shriek, *shkreee,* often given in flight; also clicking sounds associated with courtship.

NESTING Unlined cavity in tree, cave, building, hay bale, or nest box; 5–7 eggs; 1–2 broods; March–September.

FEEDING Hunts on the wing for small rodents such as mice; research reveals it can detect the slightest rustle made by prey even in total darkness.

NOCTURNAL HUNTER
The Barn Owl hunts at night for small rodents, but may be seen before sunset feeding its young.

OCCURRENCE
In North America breeds from northwestern and northeastern US south to Mexico. Resident in all except very north of range. Prefers open habitats, such as desert, grassland, and fields, wherever prey and suitable nest sites are available. Generally not found in mountainous or heavily forested areas.

SIMILAR SPECIES

SNOWY OWL see p.239

black markings on female and juvenile

SHORT-EARED OWL see p.248

dark patches on outer wing

dark barring on underparts

| Length **12½–15½in (32–40cm)** | Wingspan **3ft 3in (100cm)** | Weight **14–25oz (400–700g)** |
| Social **Solitary** | Lifespan **Up to 8 years** | Status **Declining** |

DATE SEEN	WHERE		NOTES

Order **Strigiformes**	Family **Strigidae**	Species **Otus asio**

Eastern Screech-Owl

"ear" tufts

dark gray bars on short, rounded wings

ADULT

yellow eyes

white spots on inner wing feathers

streaked underparts

short tail **IN FLIGHT**

ADULT (GRAY FORM)

feathered legs

FLIGHT: direct, purposeful flight; straight with steady wing beats, typically below tree cover.

This widespread little owl has adapted to suburban areas, and its distinctive call is a familiar sound across the eastern US at almost any time of the year. An entirely nocturnal species, it may be found roosting (and hidden) during the day in a birdhouse or tree cavity. With gray and red color forms, this species shows more plumage variation than the Western Screech-Owl. The relatively high mortality rate of Eastern Screech-Owls, especially juveniles, is caused in part by predation by Great Horned Owls and collisions with motor vehicles.

VOICE Most familiar call a descending whinny and often used in movie soundtracks; also an even trill; occasional barks and screeches; female higher-pitched than male.

NESTING No nest; lays eggs in cavity in tree, woodpecker hole, rotted snag, nest box; 2–6 eggs; 1 brood; March–August.

FEEDING Captures prey with toes; eats insects, earthworms, rodents, songbirds, crayfish, small fish, tadpoles, snakes, and lizards.

STANDING OUT
The striking red color form of the Eastern Screech-Owl is less common than the gray.

SIMILAR SPECIES

BOREAL OWL see p.245

brown back

no ear tufts

NORTHERN SAW-WHET OWL see p.246

white spots

long brown streaks

OCCURRENCE
In the US and southern Canada, breeds in a variety of lowland wooded areas east of the Rockies. Also breeds south to northeastern Mexico. Can be found in suburban and urban parks and gardens; avoids mountain forests above 1,000ft (300m).

Length **6½–10in (16–25cm)**	Wingspan **19–24in (48–61cm)**	Weight **5–7oz (150–200g)**
Social **Solitary**	Lifespan **Up to 13 years**	Status **Secure**

DATE SEEN	WHERE	NOTES

Order **Strigiformes**	Family **Strigidae**	Species **Nyctea scandiaca**

Snowy Owl

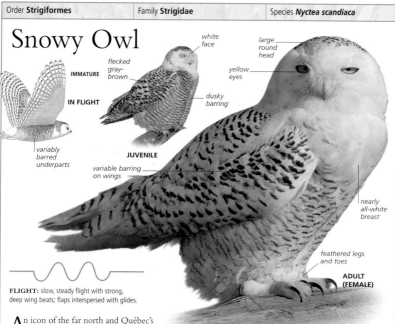

white face

flecked gray-brown

large round head

IMMATURE

yellow eyes

IN FLIGHT

dusky barring

variably barred underparts

JUVENILE

variable barring on wings

nearly all-white breast

feathered legs and toes

ADULT (FEMALE)

FLIGHT: slow, steady flight with strong, deep wing beats; flaps interspersed with glides.

An icon of the far north and Québec's Provincial Bird, the Snowy Owl has gained celebrity status for its occasional winter forays into northern US states. This is a bird of the open tundra, where it hunts from headlands or hummocks and nests on the ground. In such a harsh environment, the Snowy Owl largely depends on lemmings for prey. It is fiercely territorial, and will valiantly defend its young in the nest even against larger animals, such as the Arctic Fox.

VOICE Deep hoots, doubled or given in a short series, usually by male; also rattles, whistles, and hisses.

NESTING Scrape in ground vegetation or dirt, with no lining; 3–12 eggs; 1 brood; May–September.

FEEDING Mostly hunts lemmings, but takes whatever other small mammals, birds, and occasionally fish it can find.

SNOWY MALE
Some adult males show no barring at all and have pure white plumage.

SIMILAR SPECIES

BARN OWL
see p.237

black eyes

golden brown

SHORT-EARED OWL
see p.248

mottled brown markings

larger overall

OCCURRENCE
Breeds in the tundra of Eurasia and northern North America, north to Ellesmere Island; North American birds winter south to the Great Plains. In some years, many North American birds winter south of their normal range, including in dunes, marshes, and airfields, as far south as Idaho and New Jersey.

Length **20–27in (51–68cm)**	Wingspan **4¼–5¼ft (1.3–1.6m)**	Weight **3½–6½lb (1.6–2.9kg)**
Social **Solitary**	Lifespan **Up to 9 years**	Status **Vulnerable**

DATE SEEN	WHERE	NOTES

Order **Strigiformes**	Family **Strigidae**	Species **Bubo virginianus**

Great Horned Owl

large "ears"

yellow eye

rusty facial disk

ADULT

long, broad wing

dark arc on wing

IN FLIGHT

white throat and chin

barred underparts

mottled, barred, brownish and gray upperparts

ADULT

ADULT

heavy barring of underparts

barring on undertail

FLIGHT: fairly slow with heavy wing beats alternating with short glides; swoops when hunting.

The Great Horned Owl is perhaps the archetypal owl. Large and adaptable, it is resident from Alaska to Tierra del Fuego. With such a big range, geographical variation occurs; at least 13 subspecies have been described. The southernmost populations—*B. v. magellanicus*, from Peru to Patagonia—are often considered a distinct species. The Great Horned Owl's deep hoots are easily recognized, and can often be heard in movie soundtracks. The bird is the top predator in its food chain, often killing and eating other owls, and even skunks. An early breeder, it starts hooting in the middle of winter, and often lays its eggs in January.

VOICE Series of hoots *whoo-hoo-oo-o*; also screams, barks, and hisses; female higher-pitched.

NESTING Old stick nest, in tree, exposed cavity, cliff, human structure, or on the ground; 1–5 eggs; 1 brood; January–April.

FEEDING Hunts mammals, reptiles, amphibians, birds, and insects; mostly nocturnal.

SIMILAR SPECIES

RED-TAILED HAWK diurnal; see p.135	smaller head	**GREAT GRAY OWL** see p.242	no tufts large, round head

long, red tail

RECYCLING
The Great Horned Owl breeds in old stick nests constructed by other large birds, like crows.

OCCURRENCE
In North America, found in nearly every type of habitat except Arctic tundra. Prefers fragmented landscapes: desert, swamp, prairie, woodland, and urban areas. Rare only in the Appalachian Mountains in the East and in the Sonoran and Mohave Deserts in the West.

Length **18–25in (46–63cm)**	Wingspan **3–5ft (0.9–1.6m)**	Weight **1⅞–5½lb (0.9–2.5kg)**
Social **Solitary**	Lifespan **Up to 28 years**	Status **Secure**

DATE SEEN	WHERE	NOTES

| Order **Strigiformes** | Family **Strigidae** | Species *Strix varia* |

Barred Owl

rounded wings

ADULT

IN FLIGHT

large round head

dark eyes

conspicuously yellowish bill

brown upperparts

heavy white spotting

ADULT

barred tail

barring on breast

streaking on belly

ADULT

FLIGHT: glides silently among trees, interspersed with flaps; rarely hovers.

The Barred Owl is more adaptable and aggressive than its close relative the Spotted Owl. Recent range expansions have brought the two species into closer contact, which has resulted in the Barred Owl displacing the Spotted Owl, as well as occasional interbreeding. The Barred Owl is mostly nocturnal, but may also call or hunt during the day.

VOICE Series of hoots in rhythm: *who-cooks-for-you, who-cooks-for-you-all*; also pair duetting (at different pitches), cawing, cackling, and guttural sounds.

NESTING No nest; lays eggs in broken-off branches, cavities, old stick nests; 1–5 eggs; 1 brood; January–September.

FEEDING Perches quietly and waits to spot prey below, then pounces; eats small mammals, birds, amphibians, reptiles, insects, and spiders.

WOODED HABITATS
The Barred Owl is very much at home in dense woodlands, including conifer forests.

OCCURRENCE
Widespread, though not evenly so, in North America from British Columbia across to the Maritimes and much of the eastern US. Found in a variety of wooded habitats—from cypress swamps in the south to conifer rain forest in the Northwest—and in mixed hardwoods.

SIMILAR SPECIES

GREAT HORNED OWL see p.240

"ear" tufts

yellow eyes

larger overall

horizontal barring on underparts

longer tail

SPOTTED OWL

pale oval bars

| Length **17–19½in (43–50cm)** | Wingspan **3½ft (1.1m)** | Weight **17–37oz (475–1,050g)** |
| Social **Solitary** | Lifespan **Up to 18 years** | Status **Secure** |

DATE SEEN	WHERE	NOTES

| Order **Strigiformes** | Family **Strigidae** | Species *Strix nebulosa* |

Great Gray Owl

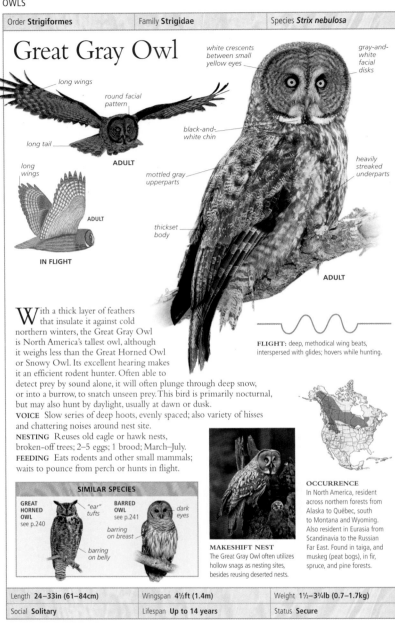

white crescents between small yellow eyes

gray-and-white facial disks

long wings

round facial pattern

black-and-white chin

long tail

ADULT

heavily streaked underparts

long wings

mottled gray upperparts

ADULT

thickset body

ADULT

IN FLIGHT

FLIGHT: deep, methodical wing beats, interspersed with glides; hovers while hunting.

With a thick layer of feathers that insulate it against cold northern winters, the Great Gray Owl is North America's tallest owl, although it weighs less than the Great Horned Owl or Snowy Owl. Its excellent hearing makes it an efficient rodent hunter. Often able to detect prey by sound alone, it will often plunge through deep snow, or into a burrow, to snatch unseen prey. This bird is primarily nocturnal, but may also hunt by daylight, usually at dawn or dusk.

VOICE Slow series of deep hoots, evenly spaced; also variety of hisses and chattering noises around nest site.

NESTING Reuses old eagle or hawk nests, broken-off trees; 2–5 eggs; 1 brood; March–July.

FEEDING Eats rodents and other small mammals; waits to pounce from perch or hunts in flight.

SIMILAR SPECIES

GREAT HORNED OWL see p.240

"ear" tufts

barring on belly

BARRED OWL see p.241

dark eyes

barring on breast

MAKESHIFT NEST
The Great Gray Owl often utilizes hollow snags as nesting sites, besides reusing deserted nests.

OCCURRENCE
In North America, resident across northern forests from Alaska to Québec, south to Montana and Wyoming. Also resident in Eurasia from Scandinavia to the Russian Far East. Found in taiga, and muskeg (peat bogs), in fir, spruce, and pine forests.

| Length **24–33in (61–84cm)** | Wingspan **4½ft (1.4m)** | Weight **1½–3¾lb (0.7–1.7kg)** |
| Social **Solitary** | Lifespan **Up to 14 years** | Status **Secure** |

DATE SEEN	WHERE	NOTES

| Order **Strigiformes** | Family **Strigidae** | Species **Surnia ulula** |

Northern Hawk Owl

fine spotting on forehead and crown

yellowish eyes

black line around white face

brownish black upperparts

heavy white marking

whitish facial disks

ADULT — long wings

patterned face

long tail — IN FLIGHT

ADULT

heavy barring below

ADULT

regularly barred underparts

ADULT

Whether swooping low through a bog or perching at the tip of a branch, the Northern Hawk Owl is as falcon-like as it is owl-like, being streamlined, a powerful flier, and an active daytime hunter. It is patchily distributed across the northern North American forests, far from most human settlements, so is seldom seen—and is not well studied—on its breeding grounds. In winter, the bird is somewhat nomadic and is occasionally seen south of its breeding range for a few days or weeks in southern Canada and the northern US.

VOICE Ascending, whistled, drawn-out trill; also chirps, screeches, and yelps.
NESTING Cavities, hollows, broken-off branches, old stick nests, nest boxes; 3–13 eggs; 1 brood; April–August.
FEEDING Swoops like a falcon, from an elevated perch, to pounce on prey; preys mainly on rodents in summer, and on grouse, ptarmigan, and other birds in summer.

FLIGHT: powerful, deep wing beats; glides; highly maneuverable, occasionally soars.

SIMILAR SPECIES

MERLIN see p.119 — small head — smaller overall — buffy orange underneath

GREAT HORNED OWL see p.240 — "ear" tufts — chunky shape — much larger overall

KEEN-EYED OWL
This owl hunts mainly by sight, swooping down on prey spotted from a high perch.

OCCURRENCE
Breeds across the forests of northern Canada, from Alaska to Québec and Newfoundland, in sparse woodland or mixed conifer forest with swamps, bogs, burnt areas, or storm damage. In winter occasionally moves south to southern Canada, Great Lakes region and New England.

| Length **14–17½in (36–44cm)** | Wingspan **31in (80cm)** | Weight **11–12oz (300–350g)** |
| Social **Family groups** | Lifespan **Up to 10 years** | Status **Secure** |

DATE SEEN	WHERE		NOTES

Order **Strigiformes**	Family **Strigidae**	Species **Athene cunicularia**

Burrowing Owl

yellow eyes

short, rounded wings

white streaking on forehead and crown

white contrasting with dark brown band below

ADULT

chest spotted with white

brown upperparts with white spotting

IN FLIGHT

brown ear feathers

white spots

short tail

ADULT

short tail

brown streaks on lower belly

ADULT

FLIGHT: buoyant, often undulating; close to ground; sometimes hovers while hunting.

short tail

long, feathered legs

The Burrowing Owl is unique among North American owls in nesting underground. Usually it uses the abandoned burrows of prairie dogs, ground squirrels, armadillos, badgers, and other mammals. Where such burrows are scarce, however—in built-up areas of Florida, notably—it excavates its own burrow, digging out the soil with its bill and scraping it away with its feet. Usually it nests in loose colonies, too. Active by day or night, the Burrowing Owl hunts prey on foot or on the wing. Populations of the bird in southern areas of North America tend to stay there year-round, but those farther north move south to Mexico for the winter.

VOICE *Coo-cooo*, or *ha-haaa*, with accent on second syllable; also clucks, chatters, warbles, and screams.

NESTING Cavity lined with grass, feathers, sometimes animal dung, at end of burrow; 8–10 eggs; 1 brood; March–August.

FEEDING Walks, hops, runs, hovers, or flies from perch to capture mainly insects, and occasionally small mammals, birds, reptiles, and amphibians.

ON THE ALERT
A Burrowing Owl keeps watch from the entrance of its burrow, which can be 10ft (3m) long.

SIMILAR SPECIES
SHORT-EARED OWL see p.248
larger overall
streaked below

OCCURRENCE
Breeds in Florida, the western US, and southwestern Canada, in a wide range of open, well-drained habitats not prone to flooding, including pastures, plains, deserts, grasslands, and steppes, but also developed area, up to about 6,500ft (2,000m). Partial migrant.

Length **7½–10in (19–25cm)**	Wingspan **21½in (55cm)**	Weight **5oz (150g)**
Social **Loose colonies**	Lifespan **Up to 9 years**	Status **Declining**

DATE SEEN	WHERE	NOTES

| Order **Strigiformes** | Family **Strigidae** | Species ***Aegolius funereus*** |

Boreal Owl

ADULT

rounded wings

IN FLIGHT

finely spotted crown

usually flat-topped head, with fine white spots

yellow eyes

pale bill

black border around face

white and brown streaked underparts

ADULT

short tail

ADULT

WWWWWWWWWW

FLIGHT: quick, strong wing beats; adept at maneuvering; glides down to attack prey.

Unusually for owls, the female Boreal Owl is bigger than the male. Males will mate with two or three females in years when voles and other small rodents are abundant. The Boreal Owl roosts on an inconspicuous perch by day and hunts at night, detecting its prey by sound. In the US it is elusive and rarely seen, as it breeds at high elevations in isolated western mountain ranges. White spotting on the crown, a grayish bill, and a black facial disk distinguish the Boreal Owl from the Northern Saw-whet Owl.

VOICE Prolonged series of whistles, usually increasing in volume and intensity toward the end; also screeches and hisses; can be heard from afar.

NESTING Natural and woodpecker-built tree cavities, also nest boxes; 3–6 eggs; 1 brood; March–July.

FEEDING Mainly eats small mammals, occasionally birds and insects; pounces from elevated perch; sometimes stores prey.

DAYTIME ROOSTING
The Boreal Owl roosts in dense vegetation by day, even when the branches are laden with snow.

| | SIMILAR SPECIES | |

NORTHERN PYGMY-OWL

black streaks on belly

longer tail

NORTHERN SAW-WHET OWL
see p.246

lacks dark frame to facial disk

dark bill

OCCURRENCE
Breeds in northern forests from Alaska to Newfoundland and Québec, south into the Rockies to Colorado and New Mexico. Largely sedentary, but irregular movements take place south of the breeding range, southward to New England and New York. In the Old World it is called Tengmalm's Owl.

| Length **8½–11in (21–28cm)** | Wingspan **21½–24in (54–62cm)** | Weight **3⅛–8oz (90–225g)** |
| Social **Solitary** | Lifespan **Up to 11 years** | Status **Secure** |

DATE SEEN	WHERE	NOTES

| Order **Strigiformes** | Family **Strigidae** | Species *Aegolius acadicus* |

Northern Saw-whet Owl

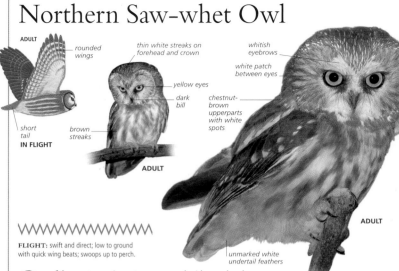

ADULT

rounded wings

thin white streaks on forehead and crown

whitish eyebrows

white patch between eyes

yellow eyes

dark bill

chestnut-brown upperparts with white spots

short tail
IN FLIGHT

brown streaks

ADULT

ADULT

FLIGHT: swift and direct; low to ground with quick wing beats; swoops up to perch.

unmarked white undertail feathers

One of the most secretive yet common and widespread owls in North America, the Northern Saw-whet Owl is much more often heard than seen. Strictly nocturnal, it is concealed as it sleeps by day in thick vegetation, usually in conifers. Although the same site may be used for months if it remains undisturbed, it is never an easy bird to locate and, like most owls, it is elusive, even though it sometimes roosts in large garden trees. When it is discovered, the Northern Saw-whet Owl "freezes," and relies on its camouflage rather than flying off. At night it watches intently from a perch, before swooping down to snatch its prey.

VOICE Series of rapid whistled notes, on constant pitch; can continue for minutes on end; also whines and squeaks.

NESTING Unlined cavity in tree, usually old woodpecker hole or nest box; 4–7 eggs; 1 brood; March–July.

FEEDING Hunts from elevated perch; eats small mammals, including mice and voles; also eats insects and small birds.

RARE SIGHT
Despite being abundant in its range, this shy species is rarely seen.

SIMILAR SPECIES

ELF OWL
see p.454

gray back

smaller overall

BOREAL OWL
see p.245

darker face

spotted crown

black facial border

OCCURRENCE
Breeds from Alaska and British Columbia to Maritimes; in the West, south to Mexico; in the East, south to Appalachians; coniferous and mixed deciduous forests, swampy forests, wooded wetlands, bogs. Winters in southern to central states, in open woodlands, pine plantations, and shrubby areas.

| Length **7–8½in (18–21cm)** | Wingspan **16½–19in (42–48cm)** | Weight **3½oz (100g)** |
| Social **Solitary** | Lifespan **Up to 10 years** | Status **Secure** |

DATE SEEN	WHERE	NOTES

Order **Strigiformes**	Family **Strigidae**	Species *Asio otus*

Long-eared Owl

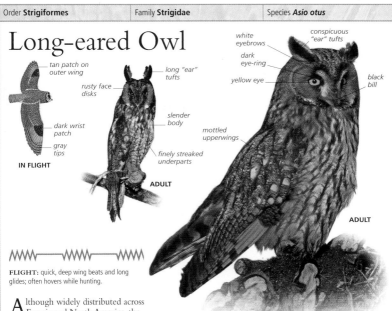

tan patch on outer wing

rusty face disks

dark wrist patch

gray tips

IN FLIGHT

long "ear" tufts

slender body

finely streaked underparts

ADULT

white eyebrows

dark eye-ring

yellow eye

conspicuous "ear" tufts

black bill

mottled upperwings

ADULT

FLIGHT: quick, deep wing beats and long glides; often hovers while hunting.

Although widely distributed across Eurasia and North America, the Long-eared Owl is seldom seen, being secretive and nocturnal. By day it roosts high up and out of sight in thick cover. Only at nightfall does it fly out to hunt on the wing over open areas, patrolling for small mammals. Its wing feathers, like those of many other owls, have sound-suppressing structures that allow it to fly almost silently.

VOICE Evenly spaced *hooo* notes, continuously repeated, about 3 seconds apart, typically 10–50 per series, sometimes more; barks when alarmed.

NESTING Old stick nests of ravens, crows, magpies, and hawks; 2–7 eggs; 1 brood; March–July.

FEEDING Preys mainly on mice and other small rodents, occasionally small birds.

OWL ON THE WING
In flight this bird's "ear" tufts are flattened back and not visible, but the face and underwing markings are clearly revealed.

SIMILAR SPECIES

GREAT HORNED OWL see p.240

tufts farther apart

much larger overall

horizontal barring on underparts

SHORT-EARED OWL see p.248

patterned buffy above

pale below

larger overall

OCCURRENCE
Breeds in old nests, especially in dense stands of cottonwood, willow, juniper, and conifers near open areas suitable for hunting. Occasionally uses old nests in tree holes, cliffs, or on ground in dense vegetation; in winter, up to 100 birds in roosts. Northern birds move south for winter; some western birds resident.

Length **14–15½in (35–40cm)**	Wingspan **34–39in (86–98cm)**	Weight **8–15oz (225–425g)**
Social **Solitary/Winter flocks**	Lifespan **Up to 27 years**	Status **Secure**

DATE SEEN	WHERE		NOTES

Order **Strigiformes**	Family **Strigidae**	Species **Asio flammeus**

Short-eared Owl

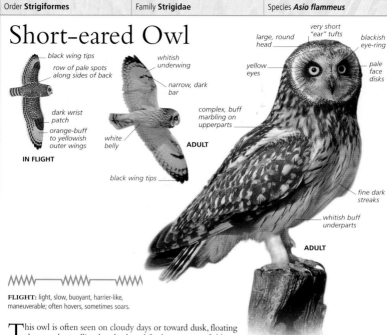

black wing tips

row of pale spots along sides of back

dark wrist patch

orange-buff to yellowish outer wings

IN FLIGHT

whitish underwing

narrow, dark bar

white belly

black wing tips

ADULT

very short "ear" tufts

large, round head

blackish eye-ring

yellow eyes

pale face disks

complex, buff marbling on upperparts

fine dark streaks

whitish buff underparts

ADULT

FLIGHT: light, slow, buoyant, harrier-like, maneuverable; often hovers, sometimes soars.

This owl is often seen on cloudy days or toward dusk, floating above and patrolling low, back and forth, over open fields, looking and listening for prey, sometimes with Northern Harriers. Although territorial in the breeding season, it may winter in communal roosts of up to 200 birds, occasionally alongside Long-eared Owls. About 10 subspecies are widely distributed across five continents and numerous islands, including the Greater Antilles, Galápagos, the Falklands, and Hawaii. Unlike other North American owls, the Short-eared Owl builds its own nest.
VOICE Usually silent; male courtship call a rapid *hoo hoo hoo*, often given during display flights; about 16 notes in 3 seconds; also barking, *chee-oww*.
NESTING Scrape lined with grass and feathers on ground; 4–7 eggs; 1–2 broods; March–June.
FEEDING Eats small mammals and some birds.

SIMILAR SPECIES

NORTHERN HARRIER
see p.128

gray upperparts

whitish underparts

long tail

LONG-EARED OWL
see p.247

"ear" tufts

rusty face disks

LOOKOUT POST
Perched on a branch, a Short-eared Owl keeps a wary eye on any intruder on its territory.

OCCURRENCE
Breeds in open areas, including prairie, grasslands, tundra, fields, and marshes across northern North America, from Alaska, the Yukon, and British Columbia to Québec, and Newfoundland, south to the western and central prairies, and east to New England. Partial migrant.

Length **13½–16in (34–41cm)**	Wingspan **2¾–3½ft (0.9–1.1m)**	Weight **11–13oz (325–375g)**
Social **Solitary/Winter flocks**	Lifespan **Up to 13 years**	Status **Vulnerable**

DATE SEEN	WHERE	NOTES

NIGHTJARS & NIGHTHAWKS

ALTHOUGH WIDESPREAD and common throughout North America, species of the family Caprimulgidae are heard more often than they are seen. The exceptions to this rule are the two species of Common Nighthawks that regularly forage for insects at dawn and dusk. Nighthawks are medium-sized birds that use their long wings and wide tails to make rapid and graceful turns to capture their insect prey in the air. They feed predominantly on large flying insects such as moths. Their wide, gaping mouths are surrounded by bristles that aid foraging efforts, and they have very small legs and toes. Both nightjars and nighthawks are similar in coloration and pattern, with a mottled mixture of various browns, grays, and blacks that provides impeccable camouflage when they hide during daylight hours. This ability to hide in plain sight is useful during the nesting season, when all nightjars lay their patterned eggs directly on the ground, without any nest material. The nature of the camouflage pattern of their feathers makes it difficult to distinguish between species when they rest in trees or on the ground. The most reliable means of telling species apart is their voice. If seen, the placement and nature of white markings, combined with the style of flight, are the best means of identification. Most members of the family migrate and move southward as insects become dormant in the North. Nightjars are also known as "Goatsuckers" because in ancient Greece it was believed that they sucked blood from goats.

PART OF THE LITTER
Not many bird species match the leaf litter of the forest floor as well as nightjars, as this Chuck-will's-widow shows.

SITTING PRETTY
Unusually for birds, members of the nightjar family, such as this Common Nighthawk, often perch lengthwise on branches.

ELEGANT HUNTER
This Lesser Nighthawk male soars through the air, hunting for insects, which it catches on the wing.

Order **Caprimulgiformes**	Family **Caprimulgidae**	Species ***Chordeiles minor***

Common Nighthawk

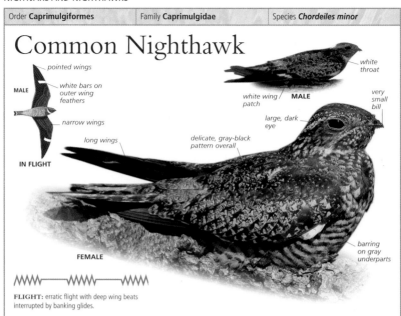

MALE
- pointed wings
- white bars on outer wing feathers
- narrow wings

long wings

IN FLIGHT

white wing patch   **MALE**

white throat

very small bill

large, dark eye

delicate, gray-black pattern overall

barring on gray underparts

FEMALE

FLIGHT: erratic flight with deep wing beats interrupted by banking glides.

Common Nighthawks are easy to spot as they swoop over parking lots, city streets, and athletics fields during the warm summer months. They are more active at dawn and dusk than at night, pursuing insect prey up to 250ft (80m) in the air. The species once took the name Booming Nighthawk, a reference to the remarkable flight display of the male birds, during which they dive rapidly towards the ground, causing their feathers to vibrate and produce a characteristic "booming" sound.

VOICE Nasal *peeent*; also soft clucking noises from both sexes.
NESTING Nests on ground on rocks, wood, leaves, or sand, also on gravel-covered rooftops in urban areas; 2 eggs; 1 brood; May–July.
FEEDING Catches airborne insects, especially moths, mayflies, and beetles, also ants; predominantly active at dusk and dawn.

A RARE SIGHT
Common Nighthawks are seen in flight more often than other caprimulgids, but it is a rare treat to see one resting on a perch.

SIMILAR SPECIES

LESSER NIGHTHAWK more buffy barring on underside of wings; see p.454

COMMON PAURAQUE longer, rounded tail with white patches; see p.455

browner plumage

larger overall

OCCURRENCE
Wide variety of open habitats such as cleared forests, fields, grassland, beaches, and sand dunes; also common in urban areas, including cities. The most common and widespread North American nighthawk, this species also occurs in Central and South America.

Length **9–10in (23–26cm)**	Wingspan **22–24in (56–61cm)**	Weight **2⅞oz (80g)**
Social **Solitary/Flocks**	Lifespan **Up to 9 years**	Status **Declining**

DATE SEEN	WHERE	NOTES

Order **Caprimulgiformes**	Family **Caprimulgidae**	Species ***Caprimulgus carolinensis***

Chuck-will's-widow

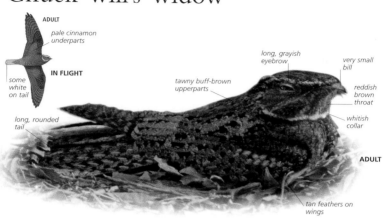

ADULT

pale cinnamon underparts

IN FLIGHT

some white on tail

long, rounded tail

tawny buff-brown upperparts

long, grayish eyebrow

very small bill

reddish brown throat

whitish collar

ADULT

tan feathers on wings

The larger of the two species of North American nightjar, the Chuck-will's-widow is also one of the least known. This species is very tolerant of human development and nests in suburban and urban areas. Unlike other nightjars it often feeds by hawking—flying continuously and capturing its prey in the air. It is also known to forage on the ground under streetlights and has occasionally been observed chasing down and swallowing bats and small birds, such as warblers, whole. Chuck-will's-widow is crepuscular, meaning that it hunts mostly at dawn and dusk. It is also active whenever there is a full moon, possibly because levels of light are similar to its preferred foraging times.

VOICE Whistled *chuck-will's-wid-ow*; begins softly, then increases in volume with emphasis on the two middle syllables.

NESTING Eggs laid directly on ground litter, including evergreen needles and fallen leaves; 2 eggs; 1 brood; May–June.

FEEDING Primarily catches flying insects, especially moths and beetles; usually hunts at dusk and dawn.

FLIGHT: alternation of slow flapping flight with erratic glides.

DAYTIME SLEEPER
Well-camouflaged on the forest floor, this species of nightjar sleeps during the day.

SIMILAR SPECIES	
COMMON POORWILL see p.455 grayer overall	**WHIP-POOR-WILL** see p.252 darker with more gray than brown more white on tail

OCCURRENCE
Breeds in forests composed of a mixture of deciduous and evergreen trees, and in open fields. A truly North American species, it is found mainly in the eastern US. Winters in Mexico and in northern Central America.

Length **11–12½in (28–32cm)**	Wingspan **25–28in (63–70cm)**	Weight **3½oz (100g)**
Social **Solitary**	Lifespan **Up to 14 years**	Status **Secure**

DATE SEEN	WHERE	NOTES

| Order **Caprimulgiformes** | Family **Caprimulgidae** | Species ***Caprimulgus vociferus*** |

Whip-poor-will

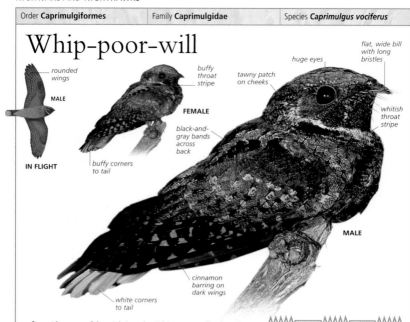

rounded wings

MALE

IN FLIGHT

buffy corners to tail

buffy throat stripe

FEMALE

black-and-gray bands across back

tawny patch on cheeks

huge eyes

flat, wide bill with long bristles

whitish throat stripe

MALE

cinnamon barring on dark wings

white corners to tail

As with many of the nightjars, the Whip-poor-will is heard more often than seen. Its camouflage makes it extremely difficult to spot on the forest floor and it usually flies away only when an intruder is very close—sometimes only a few feet. This species apparently has an unusual breeding pattern—while the male feeds the first brood until fledging, the female lays eggs for a second brood. The two eggs from each brood may hatch simultaneously during full moon, when there is most light at night, allowing the parents more time to forage for their young.
VOICE Loud, 3-syllable whistle *WHIP-perrr-WIIL*.
NESTING Lays eggs on leaf litter on forest floor, often near overhead plant cover; 2 eggs; 2 broods; April–July.
FEEDING Flies upward quickly from perch to capture passing moths and other insects, such as mosquitoes.

FLIGHT: slow, erratic flight, with alternating bouts of flapping and gliding.

WAITING IN AMBUSH
This species waits in ambush for its prey from a perch on the forest floor, or on a rock.

SIMILAR SPECIES		
COMMON POORWILL see p.455	**CHUCK-WILL'S-WIDOW** see p.251	
smaller, grayer overall	cinnamon-brown chin	
	larger overall	
square tail		

OCCURRENCE
Mixed mature forests with open understory, especially oak and pine forests on dry upland sites. Breeds north to southern and south-central Canada and south to El Salvador. Eastern and southwestern populations are widely separated.

| Length **9–10in (23–26cm)** | Wingspan **17–20in (43–51cm)** | Weight **1⁹⁄₁₆–2¼oz (45–65g)** |
| Social **Solitary** | Lifespan **Up to 15 years** | Status **Secure** |

DATE SEEN	WHERE	NOTES

SWIFTS

SWIFTS SPEND VIRTUALLY ALL their daylight hours as well as many night hours plying the skies. The most aerial birds in North America—if not the world—swifts eat, drink, court, mate, and even sleep on the wing. Swifts are some of the fastest and most acrobatic flyers of the bird world. Several species have been clocked at over 100mph (160kph). They feed on insects caught in aerial pursuits. The family name, based on the Greek *apous*, which means "without feet," originates from the ancient belief that swifts had no feet and lived their entire lives in the air.

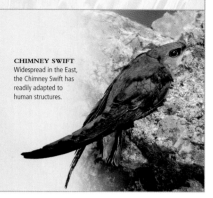

CHIMNEY SWIFT
Widespread in the East, the Chimney Swift has readily adapted to human structures.

HUMMINGBIRDS

FOUND ONLY IN THE Americas, hummingbirds are sometimes referred to as the crown jewels of the bird world. The first sight of a glittering hummingbird can be a life-changing experience. The amount of iridescence in their plumage varies from almost none to what seems like every feather. Most North American male hummingbirds have a colorful throat patch called a gorget, but females tend to lack this gorgeous attribute. Because iridescent colors are structural and not pigment-based, a gorget can often appear blackish until seen at the correct angle toward the light. Hummingbirds are the only birds that can fly backward, an adaptation that allows them to move easily between flowers. Flying sideways, up, down, and hovering are also within hummingbirds' abilities, and all are achieved by their unique figure-eight, rapid wing strokes and reduced wing bone structure. Their long, thin bills allow them access to nectar in tubular flowers. The only common hummingbird in the East is the Ruby-throated Hummingbird.

AGGRESSIVE MALES
This male Ruby-throated Hummingbird defends his territory from a perch.

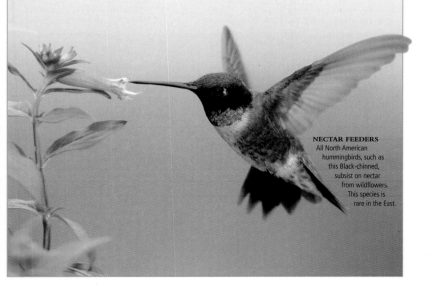

NECTAR FEEDERS
All North American hummingbirds, such as this Black-chinned, subsist on nectar from wildflowers. This species is rare in the East.

Order **Apodiformes**	Family **Apodidae**	Species ***Chaetura pelagica***

Chimney Swift

large eyes

short bill

long, sickle-shaped wings

dark brown upperparts

pale brown throat

ADULT

throat slightly paler than body

short, square tail

IN FLIGHT

very long, black wings

stiff spined tail

Nicknamed "spine-tailed," the Chimney Swift is a familiar summer sight and sound, racing through the skies east of the Rockies, its rolling twitters often heard. These birds do almost everything on the wing—feeding, drinking, and even bathing. Chimney Swifts have adapted to nest in human structures, including chimneys, although they once nested in tree holes. It remains a common bird, although local populations have declined; and it has expanded its range west and south.
VOICE High, rapid chips and twittering; notes from individuals in a flock run together into a rapid, descending chatter.
NESTING Shallow cup of twigs and saliva attached to inside of chimney or other artificial structure, rarely hollow tree; 4–5 eggs; 1 brood; April–August.
FEEDING Pursues a large variety of small aerial insects.

FLIGHT: fast, acrobatic, and erratic; very rapid, vibrating wing beats; soars with tail fanned.

HIGH FLYER
Swifts feed at heights on sunny days, and only feed near the ground when it is cold and cloudy.

SIMILAR SPECIES		

BLACK SWIFT

larger overall

broader wings

VAUX'S SWIFT

paler rump

shorter wings and tail

paler throat

OCCURRENCE
Widespread in eastern North America, over many habitats: urban and suburban areas, small towns; in sparsely populated areas nests in hollow trees and caves; regular in summer in southern California, present late March to early November. Winters in Amazonian South America.

Length **5in (13cm)**	Wingspan **14in (36cm)**	Weight ⅝–1¹⁄₁₆oz (17–30g)
Social **Flocks**	Lifespan **Up to 15 years**	Status **Secure**

DATE SEEN	WHERE	NOTES

| Order **Apodiformes** | Family **Trochilidae** | Species *Archilochus colubris* |

Ruby-throated Hummingbird

MALE

IN FLIGHT (MALE)

dark, forked tail

bronzy-green upperparts

pale-tipped crown feathers

greenish speckling on throat

IMMATURE MALE

green crown

black face

straight, black bill

orange-red throat

white chest

greenish sides and flanks

glittering green upperparts

white chin and throat

FEMALE

white underparts with buff wash on sides and flanks

rounded tail

grayish white underparts

MALE

The only hummingbird to breed east of the Mississippi River, the Ruby-throated Hummingbird is a welcome addition to gardens throughout its range. It is easily identified in most of its range, though more difficult to distinguish in areas where other species are found, particularly during migration. Males perform a deep diving display for females. Before migration, these birds add about ¹⁄₁₆oz (2g) of fat to their weight to provide enough fuel for their nonstop 800-mile (1,300km) flight across the Gulf of Mexico.
VOICE Call a soft, thick *chic*, sometimes doubled; twittered notes in interactions; chase call a fast, slightly buzzy *tsi-tsi-tsi-tsi-tsi-tsi-tsi-tsi*; soft, rattling song very rarely heard.
NESTING Tiny cup of plant down, with bud scales and lichen on the exterior, bound with spider's silk, usually in deciduous trees; 2 eggs; 1–2 broods; April–September.
FEEDING Drinks nectar from many species of flowers; feeds on small insects and spiders, caught aerially or gleaned from foliage.

FLIGHT: swift, forward flight with very fast wing beats; hovers at flowers and darts after insects.

CATCHING THE LIGHT
Although the throat patch often appears all black, the right lighting sets it afire with color.

SIMILAR SPECIES

BLACK-CHINNED HUMMINGBIRD ♀
see p.455

broader outer feathers

longer bill

ANNA'S HUMMINGBIRD ♀
harder, sharper call notes

thicker neck

grayer underparts

OCCURRENCE
Favors a variety of woodlands and gardens; earliest migrants appear in the South as early as late February; most leave by November; regular in winter in southern Florida; small numbers winter elsewhere on the Gulf Coast; rare in the West. The bulk of the population migrates to Central America for the winter.

Length **3½in (9cm)**	Wingspan **4¼in (11cm)**	Weight **¹⁄₁₆–⁷⁄₃₂oz (2–6g)**
Social **Solitary**	Lifespan **Up to 9 years**	Status **Secure**

DATE SEEN	WHERE	NOTES

Order **Apodiformes**	Family **Trochilidae**	Species *Selasphorus rufus*

Rufous Hummingbird

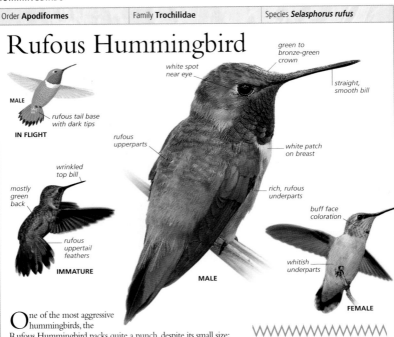

MALE

IN FLIGHT

rufous tail base
with dark tips

white spot
near eye

green to
bronze-green
crown

straight,
smooth bill

rufous
upperparts

white patch
on breast

wrinkled
top bill

mostly
green
back

rufous
uppertail
feathers

IMMATURE

rich, rufous
underparts

buff face
coloration

whitish
underparts

MALE

FEMALE

One of the most aggressive hummingbirds, the Rufous Hummingbird packs quite a punch, despite its small size; it often chases other hummingbirds away from nectar sources. This bird also breeds farther north than any other North American species of hummingbird and undertakes a lengthy migration. Males are recognizable by their overall fiery orange-rufous color, but females and immature birds are difficult to distinguish from Allen's Hummingbirds.

VOICE Call a hard *chuk*, sometimes in steady series or doubled; also short, buzzy warning call, *tssrr*; chase call a fast, raspy twitter, *tzzerr tichupy tichupy*.

NESTING Tiny cup of plant down, lichen, and other plant matter on exterior, bound with spider's silk, in shrubs or trees; 2 eggs; 1–2 broods; April–July.

FEEDING Drinks nectar from flowers and sap from trees; catches small insects and other arthropods in the air or gleans them off foliage.

FLIGHT: fast flight with extremely rapid wing beats; hovers at flowers; darts after insects.

SIMILAR SPECIES

BROAD-TAILED HUMMINGBIRD ♀
higher-pitched call

dull pinkish
flanks

broad
tail

ALLEN'S HUMMINGBIRD ♂

entirely
green
back

FIERY MALE
With temperaments matching their bold, flame-like color, males aggressively defend territories.

OCCURRENCE
This Western species has become a regular fall visitor in the East. Breeds in old-growth forest clearings, bushy country, and urban gardens; early migrants appear in March; most leave by August; it has become a regular winter inhabitant along the Gulf Coast and southern California.

Length **3½in (9cm)**	Wingspan **5in (13cm)**	Weight ³⁄₃₂–⁷⁄₃₂oz **(3–6g)**
Social **Solitary**	Lifespan **Up to 12 years**	Status **Secure**

DATE SEEN	WHERE	NOTES

KINGFISHERS

K INGFISHERS ARE PRIMARILY a tropical family (Alcedinidae) that apparently originated in the Australasian region. Three species are found in the US and Canada, but only one, the Belted Kingfisher, is widespread. Like most species of kingfishers, these birds are large-headed and large-billed but have comparatively short legs and toes. Although North American kingfishers lack the array of bright blues, greens, and reds associated with their tropical and European counterparts, they are striking birds, distinguished by chestnut-colored chest bands and white underparts. While they also eat frogs and crayfish, North American species are primarily fish-eaters. After catching a fish, they routinely stun their prey by beating it against a perch before turning the fish around so that it can be eaten head first. Smaller species such as the Green Kingfisher are shy and not often seen.

FISH DINNER
A female Belted Kingfisher uses its large bill to catch and hold slippery prey.

Order **Coraciiformes**	Family **Alcedinidae**	Species **Megaceryle alcyon**

Belted Kingfisher

MALE

large head

single blue breastband

barred tail

IN FLIGHT

bluish gray head with shaggy crest

white collar

bluish slate upperparts

white belly

MALE

prominent crest

long, thick, powerful bill

chestnut band across breast

chestnut flanks

FEMALE

double crest

white collar

single dark breastband

IMMATURE MALE

FLIGHT: strongly flaps its wings and then glides after two or three beats; frequently hovers.

Its stocky body, double-pointed crest, large head, and contrasting white collar distinguish the Belted Kingfisher from other species in its range. This kingfisher's loud and far-carrying rattles are heard more often than the bird is seen. Interestingly, it is one of the few birds in North America in which the female is more colorful than the male. The Belted Kingfisher can be found in a large variety of aquatic habitats, both coastal and inland, vigorously defending its territory, all year round.
VOICE Harsh mechanical rattle given in flight or from a perch; sometimes emits screams or trill-like warble during breeding.
NESTING Unlined chamber in subterranean burrow 3–6ft (1–2m) deep, excavated in earthen bank usually over water, but sometimes in ditches, sand, or gravel pits; 6–7 eggs; 1 brood; March–July.
FEEDING Plunge-dives from branches or wires to catch a wide variety of fish near the surface, including sticklebacks and trout; also takes crustaceans, such as crayfish.

SIMILAR SPECIES
RINGED KINGFISHER ♂ see p.456   larger overall   chestnut belly

CATCH OF THE DAY
The female's chestnut belly band and flanks are clearly visible here as she perches with her catch.

OCCURRENCE
Breeds and winters around clear, open waters of streams, rivers, lakes, estuaries, and protected marine shorelines, where perches are available and prey is visible. Avoids water with emergent vegetation. Northern populations migrate south to Mexico, Central America, and the West Indies.

Length **11–14in (28–35cm)**	Wingspan **19–23in (48–58cm)**	Weight **5–6oz (150–175g)**
Social **Solitary**	Lifespan **Unknown**	Status **Secure**

DATE SEEN	WHERE	NOTES

WOODPECKERS

THE THREE GROUPS of closely related species that constitute the family Picidae are found throughout North America. They are a physically striking group adapted to living on tree trunks.

WOODPECKERS
The typical North American woodpecker species share a distinct set of physical characteristics and behaviors. They use pecking and drumming to construct nests and communicate. This is made possible by a very thick skull, adapted to withstand the shock of continually pecking wood. Woodpeckers nest in cavities in dead trees, and are vulnerable to the loss of their specialized habitats due to forest clearing.

SAPSUCKERS
Sapsuckers feed on tree sap as a primary source of nourishment for both adults and their young. They have tongues tipped with stiff hairs to allow sap to stick to them. The holes sapsuckers create in order to extract the sap from trees also attract insects, which make up the main protein source in the sapsucker diet. Because sapsuckers damage living trees, some orchard growers consider them to be pests.

BALANCING ACT
The Yellow-bellied Sapsucker rests its stiff tail against a tree to maintain its balance.

FLICKERS
Flickers are relatively large members of the family Picidae and spend more time feeding on the ground than other woodpeckers, consuming ants and other insects. They often forage in open areas around human habitation. Flickers are notable for their colorful underwing feathers and their distinctive white rumps.

RED ALERT
With its crimson head, the Red-headed Woodpecker is an instantly recognizable North American bird.

COMMON FLICKER
The Northern Flicker can be found across the entire North American continent. This is the Red-shafted form of Northern Flicker, which is only found in the West.

| Order **Piciformes** | Family **Picidae** | Species *Melanerpes erythrocephalus* |

Red-headed Woodpecker

white rump

red head

ADULT

IN FLIGHT

wing feathers white with black barring

brownish head

JUVENILE

bright red head

bluish gray bill

upperparts black with bluish sheen

narrow black "necklace"

ADULT

white secondary wing feathers

The Red-headed Woodpecker is the only member of this family that has a completely red head, and is therefore easy to identify. Unlike most other woodpecker species, it forages for food—both insects and nuts—and stores it for eating at a later time. It is one of the most skilled flycatchers in the woodpecker family. Its numbers have declined, largely because of the destruction of its habitat, especially the removal of dead trees in urban and rural areas, and clearing and cutting of trees for firewood in rural areas. The Red-headed Woodpecker is a truly North American bird, not extending south of the Rio Grande.

VOICE Primary call an extremely harsh and loud *churr*, also produces breeding call and alarm; no song; active drummer.

NESTING Excavates cavity in dead wood; 3–5 eggs; 1–2 broods; May–August.

FEEDING Forages in flight, on ground, and in trees; feeds on a variety of insects, spiders, nuts seeds, berries, and fruit, and, in rare cases, small mammals such as mice.

WORK IN PROGRESS
The Red-headed Woodpecker excavates its breeding cavities in tree trunks and stumps.

FLIGHT: strong flapping; undulation not as marked as in other woodpecker species.

OCCURRENCE
Breeds in a variety of habitats, especially open deciduous woodlands, including riverine areas, orchards, municipal parks, agricultural areas, forest edges, and forests affected by fire. Uses the same habitats during the winter and in the breeding season.

| Length 8½–9½in (22–24cm) | Wingspan **16–18in (41–46cm)** | Weight **2–3oz (55–85g)** |
| Social **Solitary** | Lifespan **At least 10 years** | Status **Declining** |

DATE SEEN	WHERE		NOTES

Order **Piciformes**	Family **Picidae**	Species *Melanerpes carolinus*

Red-bellied Woodpecker

white patches at base of outer wing

gray crown   red crown

MALE

pale grayish tan face

pale grayish tan underparts

red nape

IN FLIGHT

red nape

FEMALE

regular black-and-white barring

FLIGHT: undulating flight, as with other woodpecker species.

MALE

This attractive, abundant woodpecker is found throughout the eastern half of the US, and has expanded its range both northward and westward in the last decade or two. Despite its common name, it does not actually possess a red belly. The male is distinguished by its red forehead, crown, and nape, while the female only has a red nape; both have pale-colored underparts and evenly barred upperparts. Male Red-bellied Woodpeckers excavate several holes in trees, one of which the female chooses for nesting. They also use previously available cavities, but often lose them to aggressive European Starlings. Unlike many woodpecker species, although the Red-bellied eats insects, it does not excavate trees to find them.

VOICE Rather soft, clearly rolling, slightly quivering *krrurrr* call.
NESTING Cavity nester; 4–5 eggs; 1–3 broods; May–August.
FEEDING Eats insects, fruit, seeds, acorns, and other nuts; in winter, eats mainly vegetable matter.

SIMILAR SPECIES

GILA WOODPECKER   red crown

brown head

rump bars

GOLDEN-FRONTED WOODPECKER ♂
see p.456   red crown

orange-yellow nape

white rump

SUBURBAN SPECIES
These birds can be seen and heard on tree trunks in suburban and urban woods.

OCCURRENCE
Resident in the eastern and southeastern US, where it breeds in a wide range of habitats; found in forests, swamps, suburban wooded areas, open woodlands, and parks. Winter habitats resemble the breeding areas.

Length **9–10½in (23–27cm)**	Wingspan **16in (41cm)**	Weight **2½oz (70g)**
Social **Solitary/Pairs**	Lifespan **Up to 12 years**	Status **Secure**

DATE SEEN	WHERE	NOTES

| Order **Piciformes** | Family **Picidae** | Species *Sphyrapicus varius* |

Yellow-bellied Sapsucker

MALE

MALE

white patch on inner wing

white rump

IN FLIGHT

dark brown forehead

red forehead

black-and-white patterned face

red throat

pale yellow to breast and belly

no red on throat

white throat

black-and-white barring on back

JUVENILE   **FEMALE**   **MALE**

The Yellow-bellied Sapsucker, with its red, black, and white coloring and soft yellow wash on its underparts, is a striking bird. Like its relatives, the Red-breasted Sapsucker and the Red-naped Sapsucker, it drills holes in trees to drink sap. It was not until 1983 that the sapsuckers were allocated to four separate species. This is one of only two North American woodpeckers that are completely migratory, with females moving farther south than males. The other is the Red-naped Sapsucker, in the West.

VOICE Primary call a mewing *wheer-wheer-wheer*.

NESTING Cavities in dead trees; 5–6 eggs; 1 brood; May–June.

FEEDING Drinks sap; eats ants and other small insects; feeds on the inner bark of trees, also a variety of fruit.

FLIGHT: typical woodpecker, undulating flight pattern with intermittent flapping and gliding.

STRIKING SPECIES
The Yellow-bellied Sapsucker's white rump and black-and-white forked tail are clearly evident here.

SIMILAR SPECIES

WILLAMSON'S SAPSUCKER ♀

brown head

more extensive barring on back

RED-NAPED SAPSUCKER

red patch on forehead

two rows of white bars on back

OCCURRENCE
Breeds in eastern Alaska, Canada, and south to the Appalachians. Prefers either deciduous forests or mixed deciduous-coniferous forests; preferably young forests. In winter, it is found in open wooded areas in southeastern states, Caribbean islands, and Central America.

| Length **8–9in (20–23cm)** | Wingspan **16–18in (41–46cm)** | Weight **1¾ oz (50g)** |
| Social **Solitary/Pairs** | Lifespan **Up to 7 years** | Status **Secure** |

DATE SEEN	WHERE	NOTES

| Order **Piciformes** | Family **Picidae** | Species **Picoides pubescens** |

Downy Woodpecker

barred wings

white back

MALE

IN FLIGHT

black wings with white spots

MALE

red nape patch

short, pointed black bill

white underparts

MALE

black shoulders

black crown patch

FEMALE

white back

spotted outermost tail feathers

FLIGHT: glides and short bursts of wing beats, giving an undulating flight pattern.

The smallest North American woodpecker, the Downy Woodpecker is seen all year round from coast to coast in Canada, north to Alaska, and southward, in the US, from California to the Eastern Seaboard. It is distinguishable from the similar Hairy Woodpecker by its shorter bill and much smaller size. After breeding, Downy Woodpeckers remain in the same area, but wander around in search of food in a variety of habitats, including suburbs, gardens; also reedbeds, a winter habitat that no other North American woodpecker uses.

VOICE Two main calls—a high-pitched *pik*, and an even higher-pitched whinny; also rattles and chirps.

NESTING Excavates cavity in dead wood; 4–5 eggs; 1 brood; May–July.

FEEDING Forages for insects and spiders from the surfaces and bark crevices of live and dead trees, but also eats fruits, seeds, and other vegetable matter, depending on the season.

SIMILAR SPECIES

HAIRY WOODPECKER ♂
see p.264

long bill

red crown patch

HAIRY WOODPECKER ♀
see p.264

long bill

no red crown patch

SUET LOVERS
Downy Woodpeckers will feed on suet provided in feeders during the winter.

OCCURRENCE
Breeds in a wide variety of habitats, including deciduous and mixed deciduous-coniferous woodlands, parks, wooded suburban areas, and areas near rivers. Although it uses nature's bounty of dead trees, it will also breed in man-made objects such as fenceposts. Resident, but local movements occur.

| Length **6–7in (15–18cm)** | Wingspan **10–12in (25–30cm)** | Weight **1¹⁄₁₆oz (30g)** |
| Social **Solitary/Flocks** | Lifespan **Up to 11 years** | Status **Secure** |

DATE SEEN	WHERE		NOTES

| Order **Piciformes** | Family **Picidae** | Species *Picoides villosus* |

Hairy Woodpecker

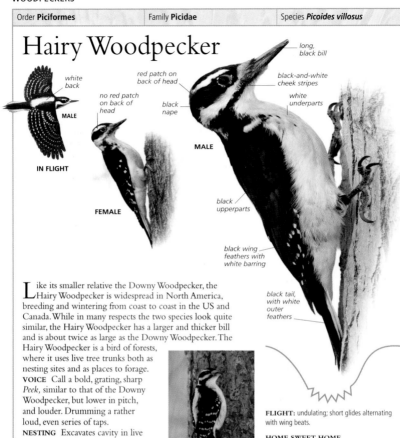

white back

MALE

IN FLIGHT

long, black bill

red patch on back of head

no red patch on head

black nape

black-and-white cheek stripes

white underparts

MALE

FEMALE

black upperparts

black wing feathers with white barring

black tail, with white outer feathers

Like its smaller relative the Downy Woodpecker, the Hairy Woodpecker is widespread in North America, breeding and wintering from coast to coast in the US and Canada. While in many respects the two species look quite similar, the Hairy Woodpecker has a larger and thicker bill and is about twice as large as the Downy Woodpecker. The Hairy Woodpecker is a bird of forests, where it uses live tree trunks both as nesting sites and as places to forage.

VOICE Call a bold, grating, sharp *Peek,* similar to that of the Downy Woodpecker, but lower in pitch, and louder. Drumming a rather loud, even series of taps.

NESTING Excavates cavity in live trees; 4 eggs; 1 brood; May–July.

FEEDING Eats mainly insects and their larvae; also nuts and seeds.

FLIGHT: undulating; short glides alternating with wing beats.

HOME SWEET HOME
The Hairy Woodpecker is generally found in forests and prefers mature woodland areas, using both deciduous and coniferous trees.

SIMILAR SPECIES

DOWNY WOODPECKER ♂
see p.263

shorter bill

black markings on outer wing feathers

DOWNY WOODPECKER ♀
see p.263

shorter bill

black markings on outer wing feathers

OCCURRENCE
Breeds primarily in forests, both deciduous and coniferous, but also in more open woodlands, swamps, suburban parks, and wooded areas. Resident in North America all year-round, though in the far north of its range it may move south for the winter.

| Length **9–9½in (23–24cm)** | Wingspan **15–16in (38–41cm)** | Weight **2½oz (70g)** |
| Social **Solitary/Winter flocks** | Lifespan **At least 16 years** | Status **Secure** |

DATE SEEN	WHERE	NOTES

| Order **Piciformes** | Family **Picidae** | Species *Picoides borealis* |

Red-cockaded Woodpecker

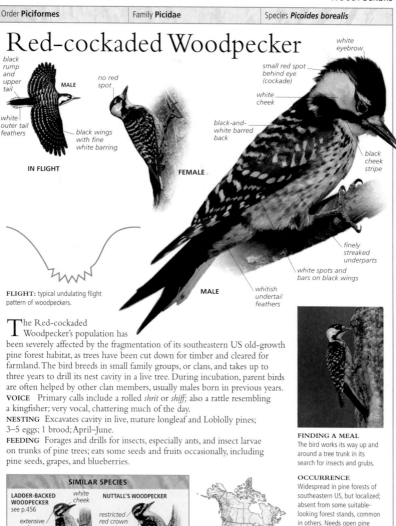

black rump and upper tail

MALE

no red spot

white outer tail feathers

black wings with fine white barring

IN FLIGHT

FEMALE

white eyebrow

small red spot behind eye (cockade)

white cheek

black-and-white barred back

black cheek stripe

finely streaked underparts

white spots and bars on black wings

whitish undertail feathers

MALE

FLIGHT: typical undulating flight pattern of woodpeckers.

The Red-cockaded Woodpecker's population has been severely affected by the fragmentation of its southeastern US old-growth pine forest habitat, as trees have been cut down for timber and cleared for farmland. The bird breeds in small family groups, or clans, and takes up to three years to drill its nest cavity in a live tree. During incubation, parent birds are often helped by other clan members, usually males born in previous years.

VOICE Primary calls include a rolled *shrit* or *shiff*; also a rattle resembling a kingfisher; very vocal, chattering much of the day.

NESTING Excavates cavity in live, mature longleaf and Loblolly pines; 3–5 eggs; 1 brood; April–June.

FEEDING Forages and drills for insects, especially ants, and insect larvae on trunks of pine trees; eats some seeds and fruits occasionally, including pine seeds, grapes, and blueberries.

FINDING A MEAL
The bird works its way up and around a tree trunk in its search for insects and grubs.

OCCURRENCE
Widespread in pine forests of southeastern US, but localized; absent from some suitable-looking forest stands, common in others. Needs open pine forests maintained without much understory by regular forest fires. Resident.

SIMILAR SPECIES

LADDER-BACKED WOODPECKER see p.456
white cheek
extensive red crown
black stripe behind eye

NUTTALL'S WOODPECKER
restricted red crown
black stripe behind eye

| Length **7½–8⅜in (19–22cm)** | Wingspan **14–15in (36–38cm)** | Weight **1⁷⁄₁₆–1⁹⁄₁₆oz (40–45g)** |
| Social **Family groups** | Lifespan **12 years** | Status **Endangered** |

DATE SEEN	WHERE	NOTES

Order **Piciformes**	Family **Picidae**	Species *Picoides tridactylus dorsalis*

American Three-toed Woodpecker

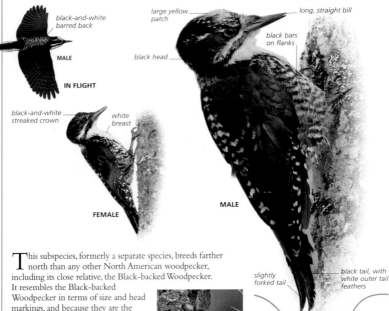

black-and-white barred back

MALE

IN FLIGHT

large yellow patch

black head

long, straight bill

black bars on flanks

black-and-white streaked crown

white breast

FEMALE

MALE

This subspecies, formerly a separate species, breeds farther north than any other North American woodpecker, including its close relative, the Black-backed Woodpecker. It resembles the Black-backed Woodpecker in terms of size and head markings, and because they are the only two North American woodpeckers with three toes on each foot. The population of this woodpecker is decreasing as a result of habitat loss. This species and its relative require matures forests with old or dead trees.

VOICE Call notes *queep*, *quip*, or *pik*; generally quiet, likened to the Yellow-bellied Sapsucker.

NESTING Excavates cavity mainly in dead or dying wood, sometimes in live wood; 4 eggs; 1 brood; May–July.

FEEDING Flakes off bark and eats insects underneath, mainly the larvae of Bark Beetles.

slightly forked tail

black tail, with white outer tail feathers

FLIGHT: undulating flight with rapid wing beats typical of other woodpeckers.

COLOR VARIATION
The streaks on this species' back are highly variable; some populations have nearly all-white backs.

SIMILAR SPECIES

BLACK-BACKED WOODPECKER shorter call; see p.267

solid black back

OCCURRENCE
Breeds in mature northern coniferous forests across Canada and through the Rockies. Since it is largely nonmigratory, this is also the winter habitat for most populations, although it is found in more open areas in winter.

Length **8–9in (20–23cm)**	Wingspan **15in (38cm)**	Weight **2¼–2½ oz (65–70g)**
Social **Solitary/Pairs**	Lifespan **Unknown**	Status **Vulnerable**

DATE SEEN	WHERE	NOTES

| Order **Piciformes** | Family **Picidae** | Species *Picoides arcticus* |

Black-backed Woodpecker

white spots on
outer wings

long, black bill

yellow cap on
black head

black back

white stripe
on head

white
underparts

MALE

IN FLIGHT

black cap

black back
and wings

MALE

FEMALE

Formerly called the Black-backed Three-toed Woodpecker, this species has a black back and heavily barred flanks. Despite being widespread across the northern US, southern Canada, and southern Alaska, this bird is difficult to find. The Black-backed Woodpecker often occurs in areas of burned forest, eating wood-boring beetles that occur after outbreaks of fire. This diet is very specialized, and the species is greatly affected by forestry programs, which prevent the spread of fire. Although it overlaps geographically with the American Three-toed Woodpecker, the two are rarely found together in the same locality.

VOICE Main call a single *pik*.

NESTING Cavity excavated in tree; 3–4 eggs; 1 brood; May–July.

FEEDING Eats beetles, especially larvae of wood-boring beetles, by flaking off bark.

FLIGHT: typical undulating flight of woodpeckers.

FREQUENT MOVING
This bird excavates a new nest cavity each year, rarely returning in subsequent years.

SIMILAR SPECIES

AMERICAN THREE-
TOED WOODPECKER
see p.266

black-and-
white barred
upperparts

OCCURRENCE
Inhabitant of northern and mountain coniferous forests that require fire for renewal. Breeding occurs soon after sites are burned as new colonies are attracted to the habitat. In Michigan's Upper Peninsula, the bird uses trees similar to those in its northern habitat.

Length **9–9½in (23–24cm)**	Wingspan **15–16in (38–41cm)**	Weight **2½oz (70g)**
Social **Pairs**	Lifespan **Unknown**	Status **Secure**

DATE SEEN	WHERE	NOTES

| Order **Piciformes** | Family **Picidae** | Species **Colaptes auratus** |

Northern Flicker

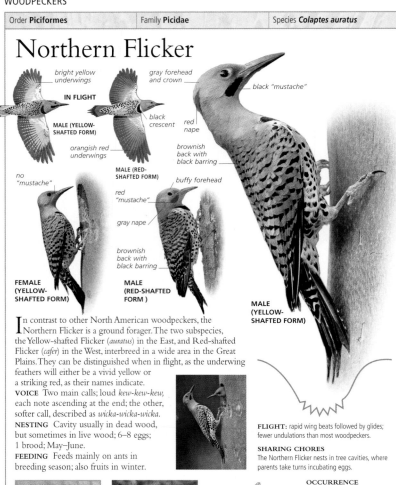

bright yellow underwings

IN FLIGHT

gray forehead and crown

black "mustache"

MALE (YELLOW-SHAFTED FORM)

black crescent

red nape

orangish red underwings

brownish back with black barring

MALE (RED-SHAFTED FORM)

buffy forehead

no "mustache"

red "mustache"

FEMALE (YELLOW-SHAFTED FORM)

gray nape

brownish back with black barring

MALE (RED-SHAFTED FORM)

MALE (YELLOW-SHAFTED FORM)

In contrast to other North American woodpeckers, the Northern Flicker is a ground forager. The two subspecies, the Yellow-shafted Flicker (*auratus*) in the East, and Red-shafted Flicker (*cafer*) in the West, interbreed in a wide area in the Great Plains. They can be distinguished when in flight, as the underwing feathers will either be a vivid yellow or a striking red, as their names indicate.

VOICE Two main calls; loud *kew-kew-kew*, each note ascending at the end; the other, softer call, described as *wicka-wicka-wicka*.

NESTING Cavity usually in dead wood, but sometimes in live wood; 6–8 eggs; 1 brood; May–June.

FEEDING Feeds mainly on ants in breeding season; also fruits in winter.

FLIGHT: rapid wing beats followed by glides; fewer undulations than most woodpeckers.

SHARING CHORES
The Northern Flicker nests in tree cavities, where parents take turns incubating eggs.

SIMILAR SPECIES

GILDED FLICKER

cinnamon crown

paler brown back

FEET ON THE GROUND
Unlike other woodpeckers, flickers can be found foraging for ants on the ground.

OCCURRENCE
A common species found in woodland in every part of the US, the southern half of Canada, and north into Alaska. During breeding season, prefers open woodlands and forest edge; also suburbs. Little is known about this bird's winter habitat.

| Length **12–13in (31–33cm)** | Wingspan **19–21in (48–53cm)** | Weight **4oz (125g)** |
| Social **Solitary** | Lifespan **9 years** | Status **Secure** |

DATE SEEN	WHERE	NOTES

Order **Piciformes**   Family **Picidae**   Species *Dryocopus pileatus*

Pileated Woodpecker

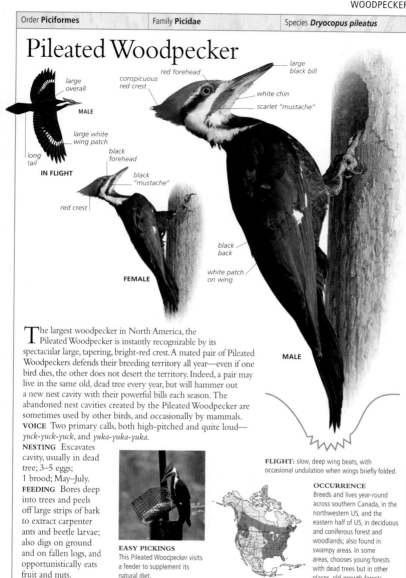

MALE

large overall

large white wing patch

long tail

IN FLIGHT

conspicuous red crest

red forehead

large black bill

white chin

scarlet "mustache"

black forehead

black "mustache"

red crest

FEMALE

black back

white patch on wing

MALE

MALE

The largest woodpecker in North America, the Pileated Woodpecker is instantly recognizable by its spectacular large, tapering, bright-red crest. A mated pair of Pileated Woodpeckers defends their breeding territory all year—even if one bird dies, the other does not desert the territory. Indeed, a pair may live in the same old, dead tree every year, but will hammer out a new nest cavity with their powerful bills each season. The abandoned nest cavities created by the Pileated Woodpecker are sometimes used by other birds, and occasionally by mammals.
VOICE Two primary calls, both high-pitched and quite loud—*yuck-yuck-yuck*, and *yuka-yuka-yuka*.
NESTING Excavates cavity, usually in dead tree; 3–5 eggs; 1 brood; May–July.
FEEDING Bores deep into trees and peels off large strips of bark to extract carpenter ants and beetle larvae; also digs on ground and on fallen logs, and opportunistically eats fruit and nuts.

FLIGHT: slow, deep wing beats, with occasional undulation when wings briefly folded.

EASY PICKINGS
This Pileated Woodpecker visits a feeder to supplement its natural diet.

OCCURRENCE
Breeds and lives year-round across southern Canada, in the northwestern US, and the eastern half of US, in deciduous and coniferous forest and woodlands; also found in swampy areas. In some areas, chooses young forests with dead trees but in other places, old-growth forests.

Length **16–18in (41–46cm)**	Wingspan **26–30in (66–76cm)**	Weight **10oz (275g)**
Social **Pairs**	Lifespan **Up to 9 years**	Status **Secure**

DATE SEEN	WHERE		NOTES

FLYCATCHERS

BIRDS POPULARLY known as "flycatchers" occur in many parts of the world, but several different families of songbirds have this name. With the exception of some Old World species that stray into Alaska, the North American flycatchers are members of a single family—the Tyrant Flycatchers (Tyrannidae). With about 400 species, this is the largest bird family in the New World. These birds are uniform in appearance, with only a hint of the diversity in the family that is found in Central and South America. Most are drab-colored, olive-green or gray birds, sometimes with yellow underparts. The Vermilion Flycatcher is a striking exception, as is the gray and salmon-pink Scissor-tailed Flycatcher, which also has elongated outer tail

ERECT STANCE
A large headed look and erect posture are typical of this Eastern Phoebe.

feathers. Members of the genus *Empidonax* include some of the most difficult birds to identify in North America; they are best distinguished by their songs. Typical flycatcher feeding behavior is to sit on a branch or exposed perch, then sally to catch flying insects. Tyrannid flycatchers are found across North America, except in Arctic regions. Many live in wooded habitats, though others prefer woodland edges and deserts. Nearly all flycatchers are long-distance migrants and spend the northern winter in Central and South America.

TYRANT BEHAVIOR
Such aggressive display by Couch's Kingbird reflects its English and generic names. Couch's Kingbird is rare in the East.

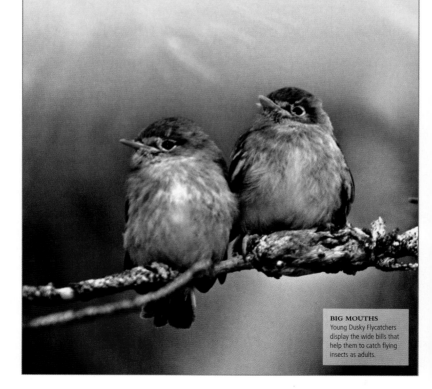

BIG MOUTHS
Young Dusky Flycatchers display the wide bills that help them to catch flying insects as adults.

| Order **Passeriformes** | Family **Tyrannidae** | Species *Sayornis phoebe* |

Eastern Phoebe

ADULT

rounded wings with two faint wing bars

IN FLIGHT

white throat

round, dark-capped head

dark eye

ADULT (FALL)

yellowish tint on lower belly

olive tint to sides and breast

long, dark tail

ADULT (BREEDING)

The Eastern Phoebe is an early spring migrant that tends to nest under bridges, culverts, and on buildings, in addition to rocky outcroppings. Not shy, it is also familiar because of its *fee-bee* vocalization and constant tail wagging. By tying a thread on the leg of several Eastern Phoebes, ornithologist John James Audubon established that individuals return from the south to a previously used nest site. Although difficult to tell apart, males tend to be slightly larger and darker than females.

VOICE Common call a clear, weak *chip*; song an emphatic *fee-bee* or *fee-b-be-bee*.

NESTING Open cup of mud, moss, and leaves, almost exclusively on man-made structures; 3–5 eggs; 2 broods; April–July.

FEEDING Feeds mainly on flying insects; also consumes small fruits from fall through winter.

FLIGHT: direct, with steady wing beats; hovers occasionally; approaches nest with a low swoop.

PALE EDGES
Perched on a twig, a male shows off the pale margins of his wing feathers.

LIGHTER FEMALE
They are difficult to distinguish, but the female is slightly lighter overall than the male.

OCCURRENCE
Found in open woodland and along deciduous or mixed forest edges, in gardens and parks, near water. Breeds across Canada from the Northwest Territories south of the tundra belt and in the eastern half of the US. Winters in the southeast US and Mexico.

SIMILAR SPECIES

EASTERN WOOD-PEWEE
lacks tail-wag; see p.273
distinct wing bars

WILLOW FLYCATCHER
flicks tail upwards; see p.276
more distinct wing bars

often has eye-ring

smaller overall

| Length **5½–7in (14–17cm)** | Wingspan **10½in (27cm)** | Weight **¹¹⁄₁₆oz (20g)** |
| Social **Solitary** | Lifespan **Up to 9 years** | Status **Secure** |

DATE SEEN	WHERE	NOTES

| Order **Passeriformes** | Family **Tyrannidae** | Species *Contopus cooperi* |

Olive-sided Flycatcher

short tail

ADULT (SUMMER)

pointed wings

IN FLIGHT

large, dark head

lower base of bill often dull orange

brownish gray back

dull white throat

brownish olive flanks

white belly

ADULT (SUMMER)

FLIGHT: fast and direct, with deep, rapid wing beats; turns sharply to chase prey.

The Olive-sided Flycatcher is identified by its distinctive song, large size, and contrasting belly and flank colors, which make its underside appear like a vest with the buttons undone. Both members of a breeding pair are known to aggressively defend their territory. This flycatcher undertakes a long journey from northern parts of North America to winter in Panama and the Andes.

VOICE Call an evenly spaced *pip-pip-pip*; song a loud 3-note whistle: *quick-THREE-BEERS* or *whip-WEE-DEER*.

NESTING Open cup of twigs, rootlets, lichens; 2–5 eggs; 1 brood; May–August.

FEEDING Sits and waits for prey to fly past its perch before swooping after it; eats flying insects, such as bees, wasps, and flying ants.

BUILDING THE NEST
The female Olive-sided Flycatcher usually constructs the nest on her own.

EXPOSED PERCH
This species can often be found singing from an exposed twig emerging from the canopy.

OCCURRENCE
Breeds in mountainous, northern coniferous forests at edges or openings around ponds, bogs, meadows where standing dead trees occur. Also found in post-fire forests with abundant stumps. Winters in forest edges with tall trees and stumps.

SIMILAR SPECIES

EASTERN PHOEBE
see p.271

lacks "vest"

WESTERN WOOD-PEWEE
see p.472

lack "vest"

longer tail

| Length **7–8in (18–20cm)** | Wingspan **13in (33cm)** | Weight **1¹⁄₁₆–1¼oz (30–35g)** |
| Social **Solitary** | Lifespan **Up to 7 years** | Status **Declining** |

DATE SEEN	WHERE		NOTES

Order **Passeriformes**	Family **Tyrannidae**	Species **Contopus virens**

Eastern Wood-pewee

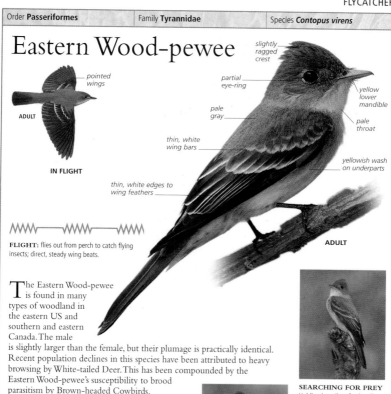

slightly ragged crest

pointed wings

ADULT

partial eye-ring

pale gray

thin, white wing bars

IN FLIGHT

thin, white edges to wing feathers

yellow lower mandible

pale throat

yellowish wash on underparts

ADULT

FLIGHT: flies out from perch to catch flying insects; direct, steady wing beats.

The Eastern Wood-pewee is found in many types of woodland in the eastern US and southern and eastern Canada. The male is slightly larger than the female, but their plumage is practically identical. Recent population declines in this species have been attributed to heavy browsing by White-tailed Deer. This has been compounded by the Eastern Wood-pewee's susceptibility to brood parasitism by Brown-headed Cowbirds.

VOICE Call terse *chip*; song slurred *pee-ah-wee*, plaintive *wee-ooo*, or *wee-ur*, and slurred *ah di dee*.

NESTING Shallow cup of grass, lichens on horizontal limb; 2–4 eggs; 1 brood; May–September.

FEEDING Consumes mainly flying insects, such as flies, beetles, and bees; occasionally forages for insects on foliage on the ground.

SEARCHING FOR PREY
Holding its tail perfectly still, this Wood-pewee is perched upright, scanning for prey.

COLORATION
The Eastern Wood-pewee has yellowish underparts and a yellow lower mandible.

OCCURRENCE
Widely distributed in eastern US and adjacent Canadian provinces. Breeds in deciduous and coniferous forests, often near clearings or edges; uses waterside areas in Midwest, less so in the East. Late-arriving migrant. Winters in shrubby, second-growth forests of South America.

SIMILAR SPECIES

WESTERN WOOD-PEWEE
range barely overlaps;
see p.472

dark gray back

WILLOW FLYCATCHER
tendency to wag tail;
see p.276

smaller size

stronger eye-ring

lighter breast and head

Length **6in (15cm)**	Wingspan **9–10in (23–26cm)**	Weight **⅜–¹¹⁄₁₆oz (10–19g)**
Social **Solitary**	Lifespan **Up to 7 years**	Status **Secure**

DATE SEEN	WHERE	NOTES

| Order **Passeriformes** | Family **Tyrannidae** | Species *Empidonax flaviventris* |

Yellow-bellied Flycatcher

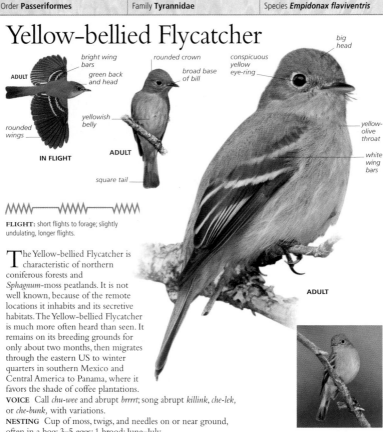

big head

ADULT

bright wing bars

green back and head

rounded crown

broad base of bill

conspicuous yellow eye-ring

yellowish belly

rounded wings

IN FLIGHT

ADULT

square tail

yellow-olive throat

white wing bars

ADULT

FLIGHT: short flights to forage; slightly undulating, longer flights.

The Yellow-bellied Flycatcher is characteristic of northern coniferous forests and *Sphagnum*-moss peatlands. It is not well known, because of the remote locations it inhabits and its secretive habitats. The Yellow-bellied Flycatcher is much more often heard than seen. It remains on its breeding grounds for only about two months, then migrates through the eastern US to winter quarters in southern Mexico and Central America to Panama, where it favors the shade of coffee plantations.

VOICE Call *chu-wee* and abrupt *brrrrt*; song abrupt *killink, che-lek,* or *che-bunk,* with variations.

NESTING Cup of moss, twigs, and needles on or near ground, often in a bog; 3–5 eggs; 1 brood; June–July.

FEEDING Catches insects in the air or gleans mosquitoes, midges, and flies from foliage; sometimes eats berries and seeds.

YELLOW BELLY
A frontal view clearly shows this species' field mark.

OCCURRENCE
Breeds from Alaska to Québec, Newfoundland, and the northeast US (New England) in boreal forests and bogs dominated by spruce trees. Winters in Mexico and Central America to Panama, in lowland forests, second-growth, and riverine habitats.

SIMILAR SPECIES

ACADIAN FLYCATCHER see p. 275

larger overall

longer, wider tail

larger bill

lacks olive on breast

LEAST FLYCATCHER distinctive call; see p.278

darker lower mandible

distinct, pale throat patch

| Length **5½in (14cm)** | Wingspan **8in (20cm)** | Weight **⁹⁄₃₂–½oz (8–15g)** |
| Social **Solitary** | Lifespan **At least 4 years** | Status **Secure** |

DATE SEEN	WHERE	NOTES

| Order **Passeriformes** | Family **Tyrannidae** | Species ***Empidonax virescens*** |

Acadian Flycatcher

slight crest

narrow, eye-ring

ADULT

prominent wing bars

IN FLIGHT

greenish nape and back

broad bill with yellowish lower mandible

two wing bars

white-edged flight feathers

pale belly

yellowish wash on lower belly

ADULT

I ts often-drooped wings and minimal wing and tail flicking give the Acadian Flycatcher an outwardly calm appearance compared to other flycatchers. It bathes by diving into water, then preens on a perch. It suffers more parasitism from Brown-headed Cowbirds in small woodlots than in large forests. Where Cowbirds lay their eggs in the flycatcher's nest, they displace the flycatcher's young.

broad tail

FLIGHT: direct, fast with quick wing beats; short flights to and from perches; hovers while foraging.

VOICE Contact call soft *peet*, one of many calls; territorial song *tee-chup*, *peet-sah* or *flee-sick*, loud and "explosive" sounding.

NESTING Shallow, open cup in tree fork or shrub near water; 3 eggs; 2 broods; May–August.

FEEDING Takes insects from undersides of leaves, also catches them in the air and occasionally on the ground; eats berries.

SIMILAR SPECIES

WILLOW FLYCATCHER flicks tail; see p.276

lacks distinct eye-ring

LEAST FLYCATCHER smaller overall; see p.278

smaller bill

more gray overall

TOP PERFORMER This flycatcher is seen typically perched on a treetop from where it sings forcefully.

OCCURRENCE Breeds in eastern US in mature deciduous forests associated with water; prefers large undisturbed tracts. Winters in Nicaragua, Costa Rica, and Panama, and in South America along the Andes from Venezuela and Colombia to Ecuador, in tropical forests and woodlands with evergreen trees.

| Length **6in (15cm)** | Wingspan **9in (23cm)** | Weight **⅜–½oz (11–14g)** |
| Social **Solitary** | Lifespan **Up to 10 years** | Status **Secure** |

DATE SEEN	WHERE	NOTES

| Order **Passeriformes** | Family **Tyrannidae** | Species *Empidonax traillii* |

Willow Flycatcher

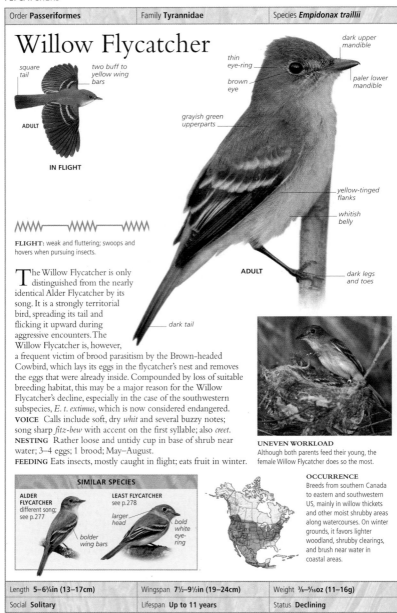

ADULT

IN FLIGHT

square tail

two buff to yellow wing bars

grayish green upperparts

thin eye-ring

brown eye

dark upper mandible

paler lower mandible

yellow-tinged flanks

whitish belly

ADULT

dark legs and toes

dark tail

FLIGHT: weak and fluttering; swoops and hovers when pursuing insects.

The Willow Flycatcher is only distinguished from the nearly identical Alder Flycatcher by its song. It is a strongly territorial bird, spreading its tail and flicking it upward during aggressive encounters. The Willow Flycatcher is, however, a frequent victim of brood parasitism by the Brown-headed Cowbird, which lays its eggs in the flycatcher's nest and removes the eggs that were already inside. Compounded by loss of suitable breeding habitat, this may be a major reason for the Willow Flycatcher's decline, especially in the case of the southwestern subspecies, *E. t. extimus*, which is now considered endangered.
VOICE Calls include soft, dry *whit* and several buzzy notes; song sharp *fitz-bew* with accent on the first syllable; also *creet*.
NESTING Rather loose and untidy cup in base of shrub near water; 3–4 eggs; 1 brood; May–August.
FEEDING Eats insects, mostly caught in flight; eats fruit in winter.

UNEVEN WORKLOAD
Although both parents feed their young, the female Willow Flycatcher does so the most.

SIMILAR SPECIES

ALDER FLYCATCHER different song; see p.277

bolder wing bars

LEAST FLYCATCHER see p.278

larger head

bold white eye-ring

OCCURRENCE
Breeds from southern Canada to eastern and southwestern US, mainly in willow thickets and other moist shrubby areas along watercourses. On winter grounds, it favors lighter woodland, shrubby clearings, and brush near water in coastal areas.

| Length **5–6¾in (13–17cm)** | Wingspan **7½–9½in (19–24cm)** | Weight **⅜–⁹⁄₁₆oz (11–16g)** |
| Social **Solitary** | Lifespan **Up to 11 years** | Status **Declining** |

DATE SEEN	WHERE	NOTES

| Order **Passeriformes** | Family **Tyrannidae** | Species **Empidonax alnorum** |

Alder Flycatcher

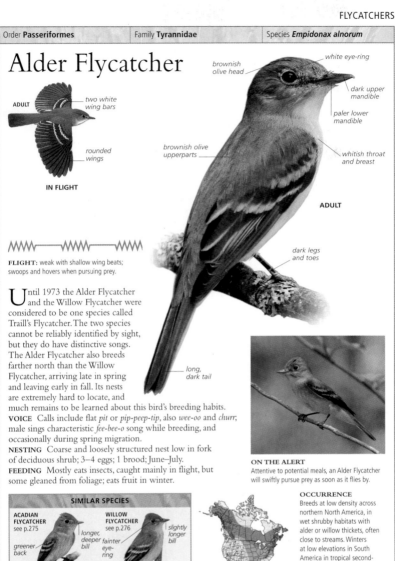

brownish olive head

white eye-ring

dark upper mandible

paler lower mandible

ADULT

two white wing bars

rounded wings

IN FLIGHT

brownish olive upperparts

whitish throat and breast

ADULT

dark legs and toes

FLIGHT: weak with shallow wing beats; swoops and hovers when pursuing prey.

Until 1973 the Alder Flycatcher and the Willow Flycatcher were considered to be one species called Traill's Flycatcher. The two species cannot be reliably identified by sight, but they do have distinctive songs. The Alder Flycatcher also breeds farther north than the Willow Flycatcher, arriving late in spring and leaving early in fall. Its nests are extremely hard to locate, and much remains to be learned about this bird's breeding habits.

long, dark tail

VOICE Calls include flat *pit* or *pip-peep-tip*, also *wee-oo* and *churr*; male sings characteristic *fee-bee-o* song while breeding, and occasionally during spring migration.

NESTING Coarse and loosely structured nest low in fork of deciduous shrub; 3–4 eggs; 1 brood; June–July.

FEEDING Mostly eats insects, caught mainly in flight, but some gleaned from foliage; eats fruit in winter.

ON THE ALERT
Attentive to potential meals, an Alder Flycatcher will swiftly pursue prey as soon as it flies by.

SIMILAR SPECIES

ACADIAN FLYCATCHER see p.275

greener back

longer, deeper bill

WILLOW FLYCATCHER see p.276

fainter eye-ring

slightly longer bill

OCCURRENCE
Breeds at low density across northern North America, in wet shrubby habitats with alder or willow thickets, often close to streams. Winters at low elevations in South America in tropical second-growth forest and forest edges.

| Length **5¾in (14.5cm)** | Wingspan **8½in (22cm)** | Weight **½oz (14g)** |
| Social **Solitary** | Lifespan **At least 3 years** | Status **Secure** |

DATE SEEN	WHERE	NOTES

Order **Passeriformes**	Family **Tyrannidae**	Species **Empidonax minimus**

Least Flycatcher

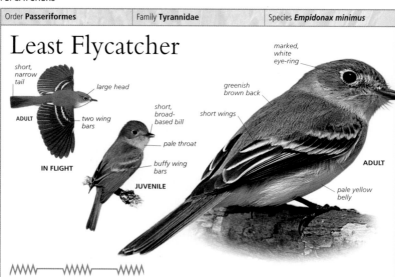

short, narrow tail

large head

ADULT

two wing bars

IN FLIGHT

short, broad-based bill

pale throat

buffy wing bars

JUVENILE

marked, white eye-ring

greenish brown back

short wings

ADULT

pale yellow belly

FLIGHT: direct, short forays with rapid wing beats to catch prey; sometimes hovers briefly.

The smallest eastern member of the *Empidonax* genus is a solitary bird and is very aggressive towards intruders encroaching upon its breeding territory, including other species of flycatcher. This combative behavior reduces the likelihood of acting as unwitting host parents to eggs laid by the Brown-headed Cowbird. The Least Flycatcher is very active, and frequently flicks its wings and tail upward. Common in the eastern US in mixed and deciduous woodland, especially at the edges, it spends a short time—up to only two months—on its northern breeding grounds before migrating south. Adults molt in winter, while young molt before and during fall migration.

VOICE Call soft, short *whit*; song frequent, persistent, characteristic *tchebeck*, sings during spring migration and breeding season.

NESTING Compact cup of tightly woven bark strips and plant fibers in fork of deciduous tree; 3–5 eggs; 1 brood; May–July.

FEEDING Feeds principally on insects, such as flies, midges, beetles, ants, butterflies, and larvae; occasionally eats berries and seeds.

YELLOW TINGE
The subtle yellow tinge to its underparts and white undertail feathers are evident here.

OCCURRENCE
Breeds in coniferous and mixed deciduous forests across North America, east of Rockies to East Coast; occasionally in conifer groves or wooded wetlands, often near openings or edges. Winters in Central America in varied habitat from second-growth evergreen woodland to arid scrub.

SIMILAR SPECIES

WILLOW FLYCATCHER see p.276

larger body

longer bill

ALDER FLYCATCHER see p.277

larger overall

wider tail

Length **5¼in (13.5cm)**	Wingspan **7¾in (19.5cm)**	Weight **⁹⁄₃₂–⁷⁄₁₆oz (8–13g)**
Social **Solitary**	Lifespan **Up to 6 years**	Status **Secure**

DATE SEEN	WHERE	NOTES

| Order **Passeriformes** | Family **Tyrannidae** | Species *Tyrannus verticalis* |

Western Kingbird

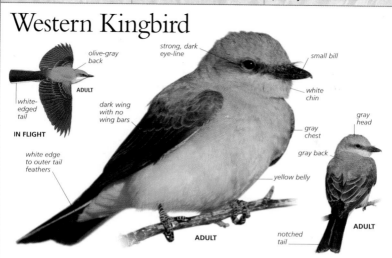

olive-gray back

strong, dark eye-line

small bill

ADULT

white-edged tail

dark wing with no wing bars

white chin

IN FLIGHT

gray head

gray chest

gray back

white edge to outer tail feathers

yellow belly

ADULT

ADULT

notched tail

A conspicuous summer breeder in the US, the Western Kingbird occurs in open habitats in much of western North America. The white outer edges on its outer tail feathers distinguish it from other kingbirds. Its population has expanded eastward over the last 100 years. A large, loosely defined territory is defended against other kingbirds when breeding begins in spring; a smaller core area is defended as the season progresses.

VOICE Calls include *whit*, *pwee-t*, and chatter; song, regularly repeated sharp *kip* notes and high-pitched notes.

NESTING Open, bulky cup of grass, rootlets, and twigs in tree, shrub, utility pole; 2–7 eggs; 1 brood; April–July.

FEEDING Feeds on a wide variety of insects; also berries and fruit.

FLIGHT: agile, fast, direct, flapping flight; flies to catch insects; hovers to pick bugs on vegetation.

FENCE POST
A favorite place for the Western Kingbird to perch, and look around, is on fenceposts.

QUENCHING THIRST
A juvenile Western Kingbird drinks at the edge of a shallow pools of water.

SIMILAR SPECIES

TROPICAL KINGBIRD see p.458

heavier bill

CASSIN'S KINGBIRD

paler wings

olive-yellow chest

gray tip to tail

OCCURRENCE
Widespread in southern Canada and the western US, in open habitats such as grasslands, savannah, desert shrub, pastures, and cropland, near elevated perches; particularly near water. Winters in similar habitats and in tropical forest and shrubbery from Mexico to Costa Rica.

| Length **8–9in (20–23cm)** | Wingspan **15–16in (38–41cm)** | Weight **1¼–1⁹⁄₁₆oz (35–45g)** |
| Social **Solitary** | Lifespan **Up to 6 years** | Status **Secure** |

DATE SEEN	WHERE	NOTES

| Order **Passeriformes** | Family **Tyrannidae** | Species **Tyrannus forficatus** |

Scissor-tailed Flycatcher

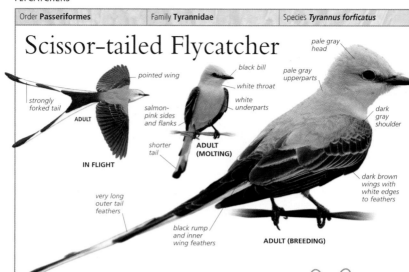

pale gray head

pointed wing

black bill

pale gray upperparts

white throat

strongly forked tail

white underparts

ADULT

salmon-pink sides and flanks

dark gray shoulder

shorter tail

ADULT (MOLTING)

IN FLIGHT

very long outer tail feathers

dark brown wings with white edges to feathers

black rump and inner wing feathers

ADULT (BREEDING)

The Scissor-tailed Flycatcher is a beautiful sight when observed flying or when perched on a wire or fence in the south–central US. Its aerial courtship display, with its long tail streaming behind it, is rather spectacular. The Scissor-tailed Flycatcher's nest incorporates many human products, such as string, cloth, paper, and wrapping material. High winds or thunderstorms may be responsible for many nest failures in some years. This flycatcher forms impressive pre-migratory roosts in large trees during late summer. Flocks usually consist of more than 100 individuals, but groups of over 1,000 birds have been recorded.

VOICE Males vocalize in breeding territories and communal roosts; song variable number of *pups* followed by *perleep* or *peroo*.

NESTING Open cup of plant stems or strings, in small isolated tree or large shrub; 3–6 eggs; 1 brood; March–August.

FEEDING Catches insects in midair, also from trees or from ground; eats fruits and berries in winter.

FLIGHT: rapid wing beats, flies with folded tail, hovers with spread tail; abrupt, midair turns.

MALE IN FLIGHT
The male bird's tail seems to float behind him in flight and vivid pink can be seen under the wings.

SIMILAR SPECIES

WESTERN KINGBIRD
see p.279

wider body

shorter tail

LOVES TO PERCH
Fenceposts, wires, and barbed-wire fences are all excellent perches for these birds.

OCCURRENCE
Breeds in southern states and northeast Mexico; savanna, open grasslands, agricultural fields, pastures, golf courses, and wherever occasional trees and shrubs give perches or nest sites. Winters in similar habitats and at edges of tropical forests in southern Mexico and Central America south to Costa Rica.

| Length **9–15in (23–38cm)** | Wingspan **15in (38cm)** | Weight **1¼–2oz (35–55g)** |
| Social **Flocks** | Lifespan **Unknown** | Status **Secure** |

DATE SEEN	WHERE	NOTES

Order **Passeriformes**	Family **Tyrannidae**	Species **Tyrannus tyrannus**

Eastern Kingbird

ADULT

white-tipped tail

white throat

IN FLIGHT

pale edges to wing feathers

white belly

white undertail feathers

dark crown and cheeks, almost black

dark eyes

faint gray "necklace"

white throat and underparts

relatively short, thick bill

slate-gray back

ADULT

black legs and toes

ADULT

black tail with white tip

The Eastern Kingbird is a tame and widely distributed bird. It is a highly territorial species and is known for its aggressive behavior toward potential predators, particularly crows and hawks, which it pursues relentlessly. It is able to identify and remove the eggs of the Brown-headed Cowbird when they are laid in its nest. The Eastern Kingbird is generally monogamous and pairs will return to the same territory in subsequent years. This species winters in tropical South America, where it forages for fruit in the treetops of evergreen forests.

VOICE Principal call is loud, metallic *chatter-zeer*; song rapid, electric *kdik-kdik-kdik-pika-pika-pika-kzeeeer*.

NESTING Open cup of twigs, roots, stems in hawthorn, elm, stump, fence, or post; 2–5 eggs; 1 brood; May–August.

FEEDING Catches flying insects from elevated perch or gleans insects from foliage; eats berries and fruit, except in spring.

FLIGHT: strong, direct, and very agile with vigorous, rapid wing beats; hovers and sails.

WHITE-TIPPED
The white-tipped tails of these two Eastern Kingbirds are conspicuous as they sit on a budding twig.

SIMILAR SPECIES		
THICK-BILLED KINGBIRD	dark mask	**GRAY KINGBIRD** see p.458
	thicker bill	larger bill
	yellowish belly	gray crown and back
	no white on tail	

OCCURRENCE
Breeds across much of North America in a variety of open habitats, including urban areas, parks, golf courses, fields with scattered shrubs, beaver ponds, and along forest edges. Long distance migrant; winters in South America, south to Argentina.

Length **7–9in (18–23cm)**	Wingspan **13–15in (33–38cm)**	Weight **1¹⁄₁₆–2oz (30–55g)**
Social **Solitary/Pairs**	Lifespan **Up to 7 years**	Status **Secure**

DATE SEEN	WHERE	NOTES
....	....	....
....	....	....
....	....	....
....	....	....
....	....	....

| Order **Passeriformes** | Family **Tyrannidae** | Species *Myiarchus crinitus* |

Great Crested Flycatcher

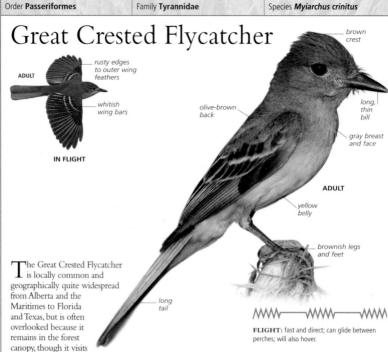

brown crest

ADULT

rusty edges to outer wing feathers

whitish wing bars

IN FLIGHT

olive-brown back

long, thin bill

gray breast and face

ADULT

yellow belly

brownish legs and feet

long tail

The Great Crested Flycatcher is locally common and geographically quite widespread from Alberta and the Maritimes to Florida and Texas, but is often overlooked because it remains in the forest canopy, though it visits the ground for food and nest material. Its presence is usually given away by its loud, sharp, double-syllabled notes. It lines its nest with shed snakeskins like other *Myiarchus* flycatchers.

FLIGHT: fast and direct; can glide between perches; will also hover.

VOICE Principal call a loud, abrupt *purr-it* given by both sexes; male song repeated *whee-eep*, occasionally *wheeyer*.

NESTING In deep cavity, usually woodpecker hole, lined with leaves, bark, trash, and snakeskins; 4–6 eggs; 1 brood; May–July.

FEEDING Picks flying insects, moths, and caterpillars mainly from leaves and brances in the canopy; also small berries and fruits.

SIMILAR SPECIES

ASH-THROATED FLYCATCHER see p.459

silvery white throat

paler yellow belly

BROWN-CRESTED FLYCATCHER see p.459

heavier bill

more rufous wings

paler yellow belly

TRICOLORED SPECIES
Viewed from the front, the eastern Great Crested Flycatcher is tricolored.

OCCURRENCE
Widespread in eastern North America, from Alberta to the Maritimes in Canada, and, in the US, south to Texas and Florida. Migrates to Mexico, Central America, and northern South America. Breeds in deciduous and mixed woodlands with clearings.

| Length **7–8in (18–20cm)** | Wingspan **13in (33cm)** | Weight **⅞–1⁷⁄₁₆oz (25–40g)** |
| Social **Solitary** | Lifespan **Up to 13 years** | Status **Secure** |

DATE SEEN	WHERE	NOTES

SHRIKES & VIREOS

SHRIKES
Two of the thirty species of shrikes (Laniidae) occur in Canada and the United States. The Loggerhead Shrike is truly North American, but the other North American species, the Northern (or Gray) Shrike, is also widespread in Europe and western Asia. Shrikes have a strongly hooked bill, almost like a bird of prey. In fact, shrikes capture not only insects, but also birds, rodents, and lizards, which they impale on a thorn in a shrub (a larder). Shrikes pounce down on their prey from high perches in trees or on fenceposts, catching it on or near the ground. Many shrike species are declining.

VIREOS
Vireos are a family of songbirds restricted to the New World, with about 15 species occurring in the United States and Canada. Their classification has long been problematic— traditionally they were associated with warblers, but recent molecular

KEEN SONGSTER
The White-eyed Vireo sings almost continuously, even on the hottest of summer days.

studies suggest that they are actually related to crow-like birds. Vireo plumage is drab, often predominantly greenish or grayish above and whitish below, augmented by eye-rings, ("spectacles,") eyestripes, and wing bars. Most vireos have a preference for broadleaved habitats, where they move about deliberately, hopping and climbing as they slowly forage for their prey. They are mainly insect-eaters. Most species are mid- to long-distance migrants, retreating to warmer climes in winter, when insects are dormant. Vireos are most often detected by the male's loud and clear territorial song, which is repetitive and persistent.

SEPARATE SPECIES
The Blue-headed Vireo is one of three species, formerly known as just one species, the Solitary Vireo.

JAYS & CROWS

ALTHOUGH JAYS AND crows belong to a highly diverse family, the Corvidae, most members share some important characteristics. They are remarkably social, some species even breeding cooperatively, but at the same time they can be quiet and stealthy. Always opportunistic, corvids use strong bills and toes to obtain a varied, omnivorous diet. Ornithologists have

shown that ravens, magpies, and crows are among the most intelligent birds. They exhibit self-awareness when looking into mirrors, can make tools, and successfully tackle difficult counting and problem-solving. As a rule, most corvid plumage comes in shades of blue, black, and white. The plumage of adult corvids does not vary by season. Corvidae are part of an ancient bird lineage (Corvoidea) that originated in Australasia. Crows and jays were among the birds most affected by the spread of West Nile virus in the early 2000s, but most populations seem to have recovered quickly.

WHITE AND BLUE
Everybody knows at least one bird, and it is likely to be the Blue Jay.

Order **Passeriformes**	Family **Laniidae**	Species *Lanius ludovicianus*

Loggerhead Shrike

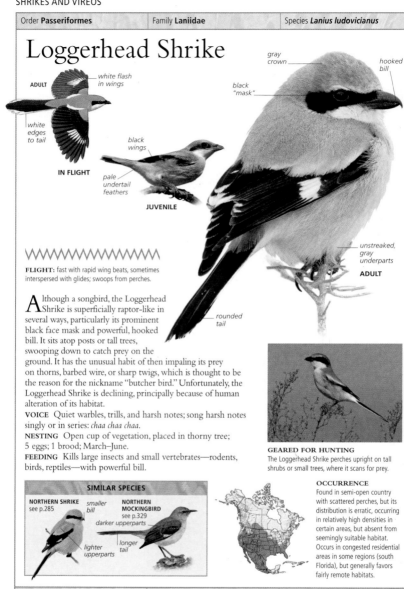

ADULT

white flash in wings

gray crown

hooked bill

black "mask"

white edges to tail

black wings

pale undertail feathers

IN FLIGHT

JUVENILE

unstreaked, gray underparts

ADULT

FLIGHT: fast with rapid wing beats, sometimes interspersed with glides; swoops from perches.

rounded tail

Although a songbird, the Loggerhead Shrike is superficially raptor-like in several ways, particularly its prominent black face mask and powerful, hooked bill. It sits atop posts or tall trees, swooping down to catch prey on the ground. It has the unusual habit of then impaling its prey on thorns, barbed wire, or sharp twigs, which is thought to be the reason for the nickname "butcher bird." Unfortunately, the Loggerhead Shrike is declining, principally because of human alteration of its habitat.

VOICE Quiet warbles, trills, and harsh notes; song harsh notes singly or in series: *chaa chaa chaa.*

NESTING Open cup of vegetation, placed in thorny tree; 5 eggs; 1 brood; March–June.

FEEDING Kills large insects and small vertebrates—rodents, birds, reptiles—with powerful bill.

GEARED FOR HUNTING
The Loggerhead Shrike perches upright on tall shrubs or small trees, where it scans for prey.

SIMILAR SPECIES

NORTHERN SHRIKE see p.285

smaller bill

NORTHERN MOCKINGBIRD see p.329

darker upperparts

longer tail

lighter upperparts

OCCURRENCE
Found in semi-open country with scattered perches, but its distribution is erratic, occurring in relatively high densities in certain areas, but absent from seemingly suitable habitat. Occurs in congested residential areas in some regions (south Florida), but generally favors fairly remote habitats.

Length **9in (23cm)**	Wingspan **12in (31cm)**	Weight **1¼–2⅛oz (35–60g)**
Social **Solitary**	Lifespan **Unknown**	Status **Declining**

DATE SEEN	WHERE	NOTES

Order **Passeriformes**	Family **Laniidae**	Species *Lanius excubitor*

Northern Shrike

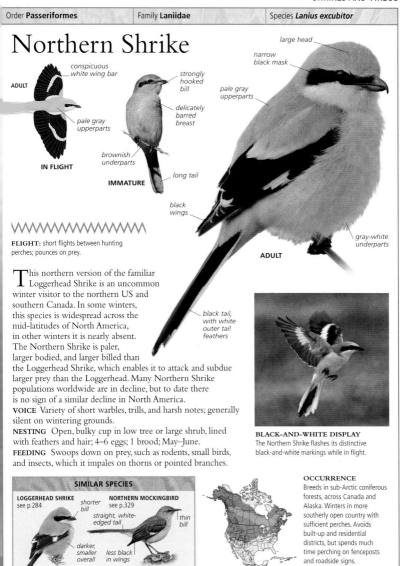

ADULT

conspicuous white wing bar

pale gray upperparts

IN FLIGHT

strongly hooked bill

delicately barred breast

brownish underparts

long tail

IMMATURE

large head

narrow black mask

pale gray upperparts

black wings

gray-white underparts

ADULT

black tail, with white outer tail feathers

FLIGHT: short flights between hunting perches; pounces on prey.

This northern version of the familiar Loggerhead Shrike is an uncommon winter visitor to the northern US and southern Canada. In some winters, this species is widespread across the mid-latitudes of North America, in other winters it is nearly absent. The Northern Shrike is paler, larger bodied, and larger billed than the Loggerhead Shrike, which enables it to attack and subdue larger prey than the Loggerhead. Many Northern Shrike populations worldwide are in decline, but to date there is no sign of a similar decline in North America.

VOICE Variety of short warbles, trills, and harsh notes; generally silent on wintering grounds.

NESTING Open, bulky cup in low tree or large shrub, lined with feathers and hair; 4–6 eggs; 1 brood; May–June.

FEEDING Swoops down on prey, such as rodents, small birds, and insects, which it impales on thorns or pointed branches.

BLACK-AND-WHITE DISPLAY
The Northern Shrike flashes its distinctive black-and-white markings while in flight.

SIMILAR SPECIES

LOGGERHEAD SHRIKE
see p.284

shorter bill

darker, smaller overall

NORTHERN MOCKINGBIRD
see p.329

straight, white-edged tail

less black in wings

thin bill

OCCURRENCE
Breeds in sub-Arctic coniferous forests, across Canada and Alaska. Winters in more southerly open country with sufficient perches. Avoids built-up and residential districts, but spends much time perching on fenceposts and roadside signs.

Length **10in (25cm)**	Wingspan **14in (35cm)**	Weight **1¾–2⅝oz (50–75g)**
Social **Solitary**	Lifespan **Unknown**	Status **Vulnerable**

DATE SEEN	WHERE	NOTES
....	....	....
....	....	....
....	....	....
....	....	....
....	....	....

| Order **Passeriformes** | Family **Vireonidae** | Species *Vireo griseus* |

White-eyed Vireo

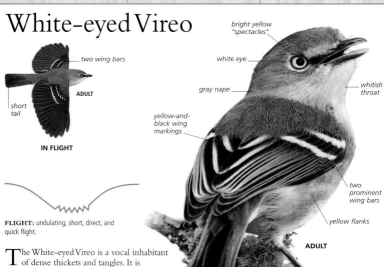

bright yellow "spectacles"

white eye

two wing bars

gray nape

ADULT

yellow-and-black wing markings

whitish throat

short tail

IN FLIGHT

two prominent wing bars

yellow flanks

FLIGHT: undulating, short, direct, and quick flight.

ADULT

The White-eyed Vireo is a vocal inhabitant of dense thickets and tangles. It is generally heard more often than it is seen, singing persistently into the heat of the day and late into the year, long after most birds have become silent. A small-bodied but large-headed vireo, it looks and behaves like a plump warbler as it forages actively in shrubbery. It is heavily parasitized by the Brown-headed Cowbird, and as many as half of the White-eyed Vireo's offspring do not survive.

VOICE Call a raspy, angry scold; male's song a highly variable and complex repertoire of over a dozen distinct songs.

NESTING Deep cup in dense vegetation, outer layer composed of coarse material, lined with finer fibers, often near water, suspended from twigs by the rim; 3–5 eggs; 2 broods; March–July.

FEEDING Hops from branch to branch pursuing bees, flies, beetles, and bugs, plucking them from leaves or sallying out to snatch them in the air; feeds primarily on fruit in winter.

WHITE EYE, WHITE WING BARS
The White-eyed Vireo's distinctive markings ensure that it is highly conspicuous.

SIMILAR SPECIES

BELL'S VIREO
see p.287

yellow flanks

BLUE-HEADED VIREO
see p.289

white eye-ring

bright greenish flanks

OCCURRENCE
A common breeder in dense brush and scrub across the eastern US, from Texas to the Great Lakes region and southern New England. Retreats to southern states of the US, the Atlantic slope of Mexico, Cuba, and the Bahamas in winter.

| Length **5in (13cm)** | Wingspan **7½in (19cm)** | Weight **⅜oz (10g)** |
| Social **Solitary** | Lifespan **Up to 7 years** | Status **Secure** |

DATE SEEN	WHERE	NOTES

| Order **Passeriformes** | Family **Vireonidae** | Species *Vireo bellii* |

Bell's Vireo

single bright
wing bar

gray head

greenish back
and rump

ADULT

IN FLIGHT

long tail

faint
"spectacles"

thin, dark
eye-line

short bill

ADULT

yellowish
lower sides

bright bluish
legs

This pale, grayish, and nondescript vireo is hard to see as it moves through dense brushy vegetation searching for food. Its most distinctive feature is a long tail which it flicks as it moves. In the arid western parts of its range, in northern Mexico and Arizona, Bell's Vireo is usually found close to rivers or streams. The Eastern subspecies (*V. b. belli*) is distinctly brighter in plumage than the three western subspecies, one of which, the Least Bell's Vireo (*V. b. pusillus*) of southern California, is endangered.

VOICE Call high, raspy, and nasal; males highly vocal and sing all day long during the breeding season; song quite fast for a vireo.

NESTING Deep, rounded cup constructed of coarse materials, lined with fine grasses and hair, and bound with spider webs, in dense shrubbery woven to twigs by the rim; 3–5 eggs; 2 broods; April–May.

FEEDING Actively gleans its insect and spider prey from leaves and twigs, hopping from branch to branch in brushy vegetation.

FLIGHT: slightly undulating flight with rapid wing beats followed by short glides.

TAIL FLICKING
Unlike other vireos, Bell's Vireo is known for flicking its long tail as it sings.

SIMILAR SPECIES		
WARBLING VIREO see p.290	white eyebrow	**PHILADELPHIA VIREO** see p.291
	greenish upperparts	
no wing bar		

OCCURRENCE
Fairly common breeder in the bushy habitats of the central US, and the riverine thickets of the southwestern US, southward into northern Mexico. Winters along the Pacific slopes of Mexico.

Length **4¾in (12cm)**	Wingspan **7in (18cm)**	Weight **5/16 oz (9g)**
Social **Solitary**	Lifespan **Up to 8 years**	Status **Vulnerable**

DATE SEEN	WHERE	NOTES

| Order **Passeriformes** | Family **Vireonidae** | Species *Vireo flavifrons* |

Yellow-throated Vireo

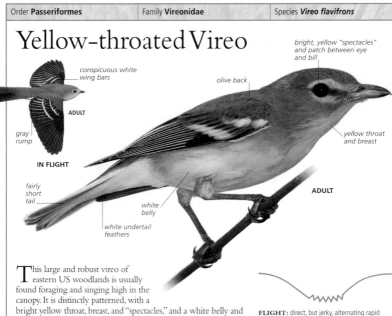

bright, yellow "spectacles" and patch between eye and bill

conspicuous white wing bars

olive back

ADULT

gray rump

IN FLIGHT

yellow throat and breast

fairly short tail

white belly

white undertail feathers

ADULT

This large and robust vireo of eastern US woodlands is usually found foraging and singing high in the canopy. It is distinctly patterned, with a bright yellow throat, breast, and "spectacles," and a white belly and flanks. The fragmentation of forests, spraying of insecticides, and cowbird parasitism have led to regional declines in Yellow-throated Vireo populations, but the bird's range, as a whole, has actually expanded.

VOICE Scolding, hoarse, rapid calls; male song a slow, repetitive, two- or three-note phrase, separated by long pauses.

NESTING Rounded cup of plant and animal fibers bound with spider webs, usually located towards the top of a large tree and hung by the rim; 3–5 eggs; 1 brood; April–July.

FEEDING Forages high in trees, picking spiders and insects from the branches; also eats fruit when available.

FLIGHT: direct, but jerky, alternating rapid wing beats with brief pauses.

CANOPY SINGER
The Yellow-throated Vireo sings from the very tops of tall trees.

HIGH FORAGER
This bird finds much of its food in the peeling bark of mature trees.

OCCURRENCE
Breeds in extensive, mature deciduous, and mixed woodlands in the eastern half of the US, and extreme southern Canada. Winters mainly from southern Mexico to northern South America, primarily in wooded areas.

SIMILAR SPECIES

PINE WARBLER ♂
see p.374

streaked flanks

greenish yellow rump

YELLOW-BREASTED CHAT ♂
see p.391

white "spectacles"

long tail

no wing bars

| Length **5½in (14cm)** | Wingspan **9½in (24cm)** | Weight **⅝oz (18g)** |
| Social **Solitary/Pairs** | Lifespan **Up to 6 years** | Status **Secure** |

DATE SEEN	WHERE	NOTES

| Order **Passeriformes** | Family **Vireonidae** | Species *Vireo solitarius* |

Blue-headed Vireo

gray head

conspicuous white "spectacles"

looks "big-headed"

contrasting white throat

two wing bars

greenish back

ADULT

IN FLIGHT

ADULT

white belly

bright greenish flanks

relatively short tail

Closely related to the Cassin's Vireo and Plumbeous Vireo, the fairly common Blue-headed Vireo is the brightest and most colorful of the three. Its blue-gray, helmeted head, adorned with striking white "spectacles" around its dark eyes also helps to distinguish it from other vireos in its range. This stocky and slow moving bird is heard more often than it is seen in its forest breeding habitat. However, during migration it can be more conspicuous and, is the first vireo to return in spring.
VOICE Call a harsh, scolding chatter; male's song a series of rich, sweet, high phrases of two to six notes slurred together.
NESTING Shallow, rounded cup loosely constructed of animal and plant fibers, lined with finer material and suspended from twigs by the rim; 3–5 eggs; 2 broods; May–July.
FEEDING Gleans insects from branches and leaves, usually high in shrubs and trees; often makes short sallies after prey.

FLIGHT: slow, heavy, undulating flight with a series of deep wing beats followed by short pauses.

SPECTACLED VIREO
Its rather thick head with conspicuous "spectacles" and gray color are distinctive field marks.

SIMILAR SPECIES

BLACK-CAPPED VIREO ♂
see p.459

smaller overall

CASSIN'S VIREO

thin bill

duller overall

OCCURRENCE
Breeds in large tracts of undisturbed coniferous and mixed forests with a rich understory, largely across eastern North America. It winters in woodlands across the southeastern US from Virginia to Texas, as well as in Mexico and northern Central America to Costa Rica.

| Length **5½in (14in)** | Wingspan **9½in (24cm)** | Weight **⁹⁄₁₆oz (16g)** |
| Social **Solitary/Pairs** | Lifespan **Up to 7 years** | Status **Secure** |

DATE SEEN	WHERE	NOTES

Order **Passeriformes**	Family **Vireonidae**	Species *Vireo gilvus*

Warbling Vireo

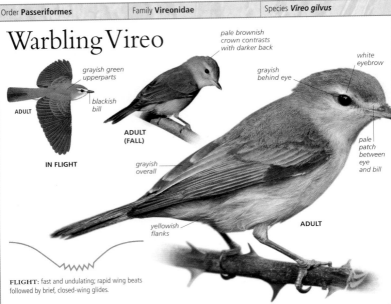

pale brownish crown contrasts with darker back

grayish green upperparts

blackish bill

ADULT

ADULT (FALL)

IN FLIGHT

grayish overall

white eyebrow

grayish behind eye

pale patch between eye and bill

yellowish flanks

ADULT

FLIGHT: fast and undulating; rapid wing beats followed by brief, closed-wing glides.

Widely distributed across North America, this rather drab vireo is better known for its cheerful warbling song than for its plumage, and coincidentally, its thin bill and longish tail give this rather active vireo a somewhat warbler-like appearance. The eastern subspecies (*V. g. gilvus*), which is heavier and has a larger bill, and the western subspecies (*V. g. swainsonii*) are quite different and may in fact be separate species. Out of all the vireos, the Warbling Vireo is most likely to breed in human developments, such as city parks, suburbs, and orchards.

VOICE Harsh, raspy scold call; male's persistent song a high, rapid, and highly variable warble.

NESTING Rough cup placed high in a deciduous tree, hung from the rim between forked twigs; 3–5 eggs; 2 broods; March–July.

FEEDING Gleans a variety of insects, including grasshoppers, aphids, and beetles from leaves; eats fruit in winter.

PLAIN-LOOKING SONGSTER
The Warbling Vireo makes up for its plain appearance by its colorful voice, full of rounded notes and melodious warbles.

SIMILAR SPECIES

BELL'S VIREO
see p.287

faint wing bar

longer tail

PHILADELPHIA VIREO
see p.291

no wing bar

dark line extends to bill

shorter bill

yellow on breast and throat

OCCURRENCE
Extensive distribution across most of temperate North America, from Alaska, around the northern limit of the northerly zone, and through western, central, and eastern North America. Breeds in deciduous and mixed forests, particularly near water. Winters in southern Mexico and Central America.

Length **5½in (14cm)**	Wingspan **8½in (21cm)**	Weight **7/16oz (12g)**
Social **Solitary/Pairs**	Lifespan **Up to 13 years**	Status **Secure**

DATE SEEN	WHERE	NOTES

Order **Passeriformes**	Family **Vireonidae**	Species *Vireo philadelphicus*

Philadelphia Vireo

white eyebrow

dark line through eye

gray cap

greenish upperparts

slightly hooked, black bill

ADULT

yellow throat

yellowish underparts

IN FLIGHT

ADULT

FLIGHT: fast, bouncy, undulating flight with strong wing beats.

Despite being widespread, the Philadelphia Vireo remains rather poorly studied. It shares its breeding habitat with the similar looking, but larger and more numerous, Red-eyed Vireo, and, interestingly, it modifies its behavior to avoid competition. It is the most northerly breeding vireo, with its southernmost breeding range barely reaching the US. Its scientific and English names derive from the fact that the bird was first discovered near Philadelphia in the mid-19th century.

VOICE Song a series of two and four note phrases, remarkably similar to the song of the Red-eyed Vireo.

NESTING Rounded cup of plant fibers bound by spider webs, hanging between forked twigs that narrows at the rim; 3–5 eggs; 1–2 broods; June–August.

FEEDING Gleans caterpillars, bees, flies, and bugs from leaves; usually forages high in trees, moving with short hops and flights.

DISTINGUISHED APPEARANCE
The Philadelphia Vireo's gentle expression and pudgy appearance help separate it from its neighbor, the Red-eyed Vireo.

SIMILAR SPECIES

BELL'S VIREO
see p.287

faint wing bar

longer tail

WARBLING VIREO
see p.290

plainer face

less yellow below

OCCURRENCE
Breeds in deciduous woodlands, mixed woodlands, and woodland edges, in a wide belt across Canada, reaching the Great Lakes and northern New England. The Philadelphia Vireo winters from Mexico to Panama and northern Colombia.

Length **5¼in (13.5cm)**	Wingspan **8in (20cm)**	Weight **7/16oz (12g)**
Social **Solitary/Pairs**	Lifespan **Up to 8 years**	Status **Secure**

DATE SEEN	WHERE	NOTES

| Order **Passeriformes** | Family **Vireonidae** | Species *Vireo olivaceus* |

Red-eyed Vireo

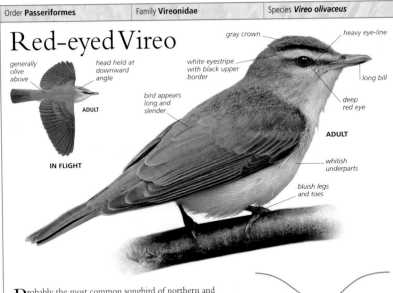

gray crown

heavy eye-line

generally olive above

head held at downward angle

white eyestripe with black upper border

long bill

ADULT

bird appears long and slender

deep red eye

ADULT

IN FLIGHT

whitish underparts

bluish legs and toes

Probably the most common songbird of northern and eastern North America, the Red-eyed Vireo is perhaps the quintessential North American vireo, although it is heard far more often than it is seen. It sings persistently and monotonously all day long and late into the season, long after other species have stopped singing. It generally stays high in the canopy of the deciduous and mixed woodlands where it breeds. The entire population migrates to central South America in winter. To reach their Amazonian winter habitats, Red-eyed Vireos migrate in fall (August–October) through Central America, Caribbean Islands, and northern South America to Ecuador, Peru, and Brazil.

VOICE Nasal mewing call; male song consists of slurred three-note phrases.

NESTING Open cup nest hanging on horizontal fork of tree branch; built with plant fibers bound with spider's web; exterior is sometimes decorated with lichen; 3–5 eggs; 1 brood; May–July.

FEEDING Gleans insects from leaves, hopping methodically in the canopy and sub-canopy of deciduous trees; during fall and winter, primarily feeds on fruit.

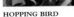

FLIGHT: fast, strong, and undulating with the body angled upwards.

HOPPING BIRD
The Red-eyed Vireo's primary form of locomotion is hopping; at ground level and in trees.

OCCURRENCE
Breeds across North America from the Yukon and British Columbia east to the Canadian maritimes, southward from Washington to south central Texas, and west to Canada in central and northern states. Inhabits the canopy of deciduous forests and pine hardwood forests.

SIMILAR SPECIES

BLACK-WHISKERED VIREO
see p.460

faint black "mustache"

duller green upperparts

BROWN EYES
Immature Red-eyed Vireos have brown eyes, but those of the adult birds are red.

| Length **6in (15cm)** | Wingspan **10in (25cm)** | Weight **⅝oz (17g)** |
| Social **Solitary/Pairs** | Lifespan **Up to 10 years** | Status **Secure** |

DATE SEEN	WHERE	NOTES

Order **Passeriformes**	Family **Corvidae**	Species *Perisoreus canadensis*

Gray Jay

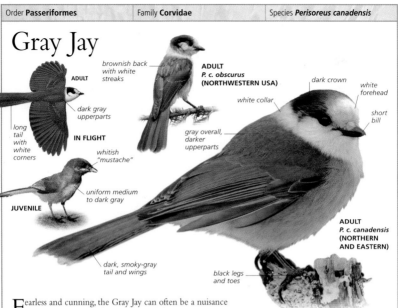

ADULT

brownish back
with white
streaks

**ADULT
P. c. obscurus
(NORTHWESTERN USA)**

dark crown

white
forehead

white collar

short
bill

dark gray
upperparts

gray overall,
darker
upperparts

long
tail
with
white
corners

IN FLIGHT

whitish
"mustache"

uniform medium
to dark gray

JUVENILE

**ADULT
P. c. canadensis
(NORTHERN
AND EASTERN)**

dark, smoky-gray
tail and wings

black legs
and toes

Fearless and cunning, the Gray Jay can often be a nuisance to campers because of its inquisitive behavior. It is particularly adept at stealing food and shiny metal objects, which has earned it the colloquial name of "Camp Robber." One of the interesting aspects of its behavior is the way it stores food for later use, by sticking it to trees with its viscous saliva. This is thought to be one of the reasons that enable it to survive the long northern winters. Gray Jays can often gather in noisy groups of three to six birds in order to investigate intruders encroaching upon their territory.

VOICE Mostly silent, but also produces variety of odd clucks and screeches; sometimes Blue Jay-like *jay!* and eerie whistles, including bisyllabic *whee-oo* or *ew*.

NESTING Bulky platform of sticks with cocoons on south side of coniferous tree; 2–5 eggs; 1 brood; February–May.

FEEDING Forages for insects and berries; also raids birds' nests.

FLIGHT: hollow-sounding wing beats followed by slow, seemingly awkward, rocking glides.

BUILT FOR COLD
The Gray Jay's short extremities and dense, fluffy plumage are perfect for long, harsh winters.

SIMILAR SPECIES

CLARK'S NUTCRACKER

white
wing
patch

longer
bill

longer
tail

NORTHERN MOCKINGBIRD
see p.329

no dark
crown

white
wing
patch

OCCURRENCE
Northern forests, especially lichen-festooned areas with firs and spruce. Found in coniferous forests across northern North America from Alaska to Newfoundland, the Maritimes, and northern New York and New England; south to western mountains; an isolated population in the Black Hills.

Length **10–11½in (25–29cm)**	Wingspan **18in (46cm)**	Weight **2⅛–2⅞ oz (60–80g)**
Social **Family groups**	Lifespan **Up to 10 years**	Status **Secure**

DATE SEEN	WHERE	NOTES

| Order **Passeriformes** | Family **Corvidae** | Species *Cyanocitta cristata* |

Blue Jay

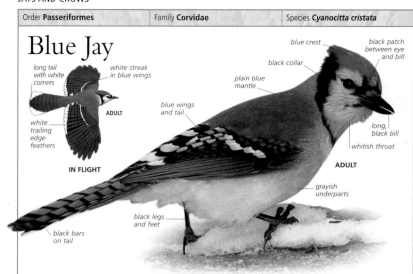

long tail with white corners

white streak in blue wings

ADULT

white trailing edge feathers

IN FLIGHT

blue wings and tail

blue crest

black patch between eye and bill

black collar

plain blue mantle

long, black bill

whitish throat

ADULT

grayish underparts

black legs and feet

black bars on tail

The Blue Jay is one of the best known birds in North America; it is loud, flashy, and common in rural and suburban backyards across the eastern US and southern Canada. Beautiful as it is, this bird has a darker side. It often raids the nests of smaller birds for eggs and nestlings. Although usually thought of as a nonmigratory species, some Blue Jays undergo impressive migrations, with loose flocks sometimes numbering in the hundreds visible overhead in spring and fall.

VOICE Harsh, screaming *jay! jay!*; other common call an odd ethereal, chortling *queedle-ee-dee;* soft clucks when feeding.

NESTING Cup of strong twigs at variable height in trees or shrubs; 3–6 eggs; 1 brood; March–July.

FEEDING Eats insects, acorns, small vertebrates, such as lizards, rodents, bird eggs, birds, tree frogs; fruits and seeds.

FLIGHT: bursts of flapping followed by long glides on flat wings.

UNIQUE FEATURES
The Blue Jay is unique among American jays in having white patches on its wings and tail.

VERSATILE BIRD
Blue Jays are true omnivores, eating almost anything they can find. They are also excellent imitators of other bird calls.

SIMILAR SPECIES

STELLER'S JAY

black head and breast

blue belly

FLORIDA SCRUB-JAY
see p.461

lacks crest

sand-colored shoulder feathers

OCCURRENCE
Native to eastern deciduous, coniferous, and mixed woodlands, but also at home in suburban vegetation; often found in backyards. The Blue Jay is fond of oak trees and their acorns. Blue Jays from northeast Canada and northeast US migrate in the fall to more southern locations.

| Length **9½–12in (24–30cm)** | Wingspan **16in (41cm)** | Weight **2¼–3½oz (65–100g)** |
| Social **Small flocks** | Lifespan **Up to 7 years** | Status **Secure** |

DATE SEEN	WHERE	NOTES

| Order **Passeriformes** | Family **Corvidae** | Species *Pica hudsonia* |

Black-billed Magpie

- large, white patches on outer wings
- white shoulders
- black back and head
- thick, black bill
- black breast

ADULT

IN FLIGHT

- blue-green iridescence to wings and tail

ADULT

- white belly

- long black tail

L oud, flashy, and conspicuous, the Black-billed Magpie is abundant in the northwestern quarter of the continent, from Alaska to interior US. It has adapted to suburbia, confidently strutting across front lawns locally. Until recently, it was considered the same species as the Eurasian Magpie (*P. pica*), and even though they look nearly identical, scientific evidence points instead to a close relationship with the other North American magpie, the Yellow-billed Magpie. Its long tail enables it to make rapid changes in direction in flight. The male uses his tail to display while courting a female. Why the Black-billed Magpie does not occur widely in eastern North America is a biological mystery.

VOICE Common call a questioning, nasal *ehnk*; also raspy *shenk*, *shenk*, *shenk*, usually in series.

NESTING Large, domed, often made of thorny sticks; 5–8 eggs; 1 brood; March–June.

FEEDING Omnivorous; forages on ground, mainly for insects, worms, seeds and carrion; even picks ticks from mammals.

FLIGHT: direct, with slow, steady, and often shallow wing beats; occasional shallow glides.

IRIDESCENT SHEEN
In bright sunlight, beautiful iridescent blues, greens, golds, and purples appear on the wings and tail.

SIMILAR SPECIES

YELLOW-BILLED MAGPIE
- yellow bill
- yellow patch around eye

OCCURRENCE
Found in open habitats, foothills, and plains of the western US and Canada; nests in streamside vegetation; persecution has made it wary and restricted to wilderness in some areas, but in others it has adapted to suburbs of towns and cities.

| Length **17–19½in (43–50cm)** | Wingspan **25in (63cm)** | Weight **6–7oz (175–200g)** |
| Social **Small flocks** | Lifespan **Up to 15 years** | Status **Secure** |

DATE SEEN	WHERE	NOTES

| Order **Passeriformes** | Family **Corvidae** | Species **Corvus brachyrhynchos** |

American Crow

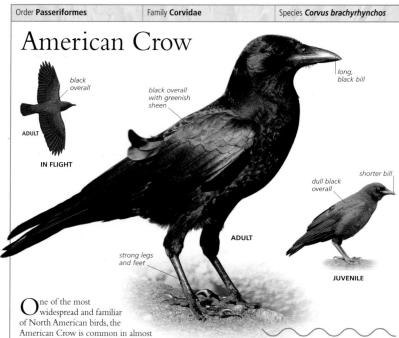

black
overall

ADULT

IN FLIGHT

black overall
with greenish
sheen

long,
black bill

shorter bill

dull black
overall

ADULT

JUVENILE

strong legs
and feet

One of the most widespread and familiar of North American birds, the American Crow is common in almost all habitats—from wilderness to urban centers. Like most birds with large ranges, there is substantial geographical variation in this species. Birds are black across the whole continent, but size and bill shape vary from region to region. Birds from western Canada and western USA (*C. b. hesperis*), are on average smaller and have a lower-pitched voice; birds from southern Florida (*C. b. pascuus*) are more solitary and more wary.
VOICE Call a loud, familiar *caw!*; juveniles' call higher-pitched.
NESTING Stick base with finer inner cup; 3–7 eggs; 1 brood; April–June.
FEEDING Feeds omnivorously on fruit, carrion, garbage, insects, spiders; raids nests.

FLIGHT: direct and level with slow, steady flapping; does not soar.

LOOKING AROUND
Extremely inquisitive, American Crows are always on the lookout for food or something of interest.

SIMILAR SPECIES

FISH CROW
higher, more nasal
call; see p.297
slightly
smaller
overall

smaller
head

CHIHUAHUAN
RAVEN
see p.461

larger
bill

larger
overall

wedge-
shaped tail

OCCURRENCE
Often seen converging at dusk toward favored roosting areas; most numerous in relatively open areas with large and widely spaced trees; has become abundant in some cities; a partial migrant, some populations are more migratory than others.

| Length **15½–19½in (39–49cm)** | Wingspan **3ft (1m)** | Weight **15–22oz (425–625g)** |
| Social **Social** | Lifespan **Up to 15 years** | Status **Secure** |

DATE SEEN	WHERE	NOTES

Order **Passeriformes**	Family **Corvidae**	Species *Corvus ossifragus*

Fish Crow

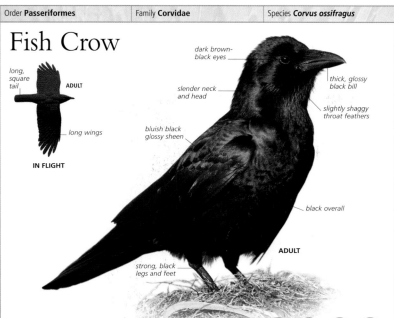

long, square tail

ADULT

long wings

IN FLIGHT

dark brown-black eyes

slender neck and head

bluish black glossy sheen

thick, glossy black bill

slightly shaggy throat feathers

black overall

ADULT

strong, black legs and feet

The Fish Crow is, in many respects, the East Coast version of the Northwestern Crow. Like the Northwestern Crow, it is a highly social species, and not only forages in flocks but also breeds in small colonies. The Fish Crow is common along the eastern seaboard of the US, where it occurs alongside the nearly identical, but slightly larger, American Crow. The Fish Crow is also distinguishable as it has a higher-pitched and more nasal call. Its Latin species name *ossifragus* translates as "bone-breaker."
VOICE Call a paired *ehn uhn* with the second note lower.
NESTING Bulky stick platform with finer inner bowl in fork of tree, often high up; 3–5 eggs; 1 brood; April–August.
FEEDING Takes arthropods such as crabs and insects, small live fish and reptiles, nestling birds, bird and turtle eggs, fruit, carrion, and garbage; notorious for raiding nests in heron rookeries.

FLIGHT: rowing motion with quick, snappy wing beats; soars occasionally.

OMNIVORE
Fish Crows are numerous along coastlines and riverbanks where they eat virtually anything edible.

SIMILAR SPECIES

AMERICAN CROW
lower-pitched, huskier voice;
see p.296

shorter head

larger body

shorter tail

COMMON RAVEN
see p.298

massive bill

wedge-shaped tail

shaggier throat feathers

OCCURRENCE
Found in lowland coastal and riverbank habitats such as beaches, estuaries, and marshes; also found inland and near human structures such as parking lots in suburban malls. Northern populations appear to be migratory.

Length **14–16in (36–41cm)**	Wingspan **36in (91cm)**	Weight **8–11oz (225–325g)**
Social **Flocks**	Lifespan **Up to 15 years**	Status **Secure**

DATE SEEN	WHERE	NOTES
....	....	....
....	....	....
....	....	....
....	....	....
....	....	....

| Order **Passeriformes** | Family **Corvidae** | Species **Corvus corax** |

Common Raven

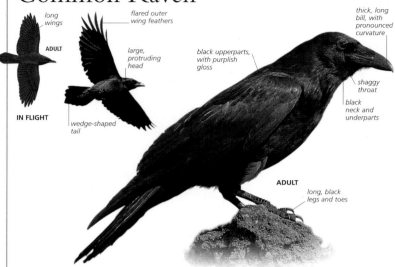

long wings

ADULT

flared outer wing feathers

large, protruding head

black upperparts, with purplish gloss

thick, long bill, with pronounced curvature

shaggy throat

black neck and underparts

IN FLIGHT

wedge-shaped tail

ADULT

long, black legs and toes

The Common Raven, twice the size of the American Crow, is a bird of Viking legend, literature, and scientific wonder, and the Yukon Official Bird. Its Latin name, *Corvus corax*, means "crow of crows." Ravens are perhaps the most brilliant of all birds: they learn quickly, adapt to new circumstances with remarkable mental agility, and communicate with each other through an array of vocal and motional behaviors. They are master problem solvers and deceivers, tricking each other with ingenious methods.

VOICE Varied and numerous vocalizations, including hoarse, rolling *krnuuk*, twangy peals, guttural clicks, and resonant *bonks*.

NESTING Platform of sticks with fine inner material on trees, cliffs, or man-made structure; 4–5 eggs; 1 brood; March–June.

FEEDING Feeds omnivorously on carrion, small crustaceans, fish, rodents, fruit, grain, and garbage; also raids nests.

FLIGHT: slow, steady, powerful, and direct; can also be quite acrobatic; commonly soars.

SHARING INFORMATION
Ravens in flocks can communicate information about food sources.

SIMILAR SPECIES

AMERICAN CROW
lacks shaggy throat feathers;
see p.296

smaller bill

much smaller overall

lacks wedge-shaped tail

CHIHUAHUAN RAVEN
see p.461

slightly smaller overall

OCCURRENCE
Found in almost every kind of habitat, including tundra, mountains, northern forest, woodlands, prairies, arid regions, coasts, and around human settlements; has recently recolonized areas at southern edge of range, from which it was once expelled by humans.

| Length **23½–27in (60–69cm)** | Wingspan **4½ft (1.4m)** | Weight **2½–3¼lb (1–1.5kg)** |
| Social **Solitary/Pairs/Small flocks** | Lifespan **Up to 15 years** | Status **Secure** |

DATE SEEN	WHERE	NOTES

WAXWINGS

WAXWINGS HAVE A crest, a black mask, silky smooth rosy-brown plumage, secondary wing feathers with waxy red tips, and bright yellow tail bands. Of the three species of waxwings, one (the Cedar Waxwing) breeds only in North America. Waxwings are fond of fruit, including mistletoe berries, of which they help to spread the seeds. Waxwings are nomadic, and emigrate following years of food abundance, nesting in areas quite distant from their regular breeding ranges. Bohemian Waxwings are especially notorious wanderers, and in "irruption" years many thousands can be seen far away from their normal Alaskan and north Canadian breeding areas.

CEDAR WAXWING
The Cedar Waxwing breeds across North America, from coast to coast.

CHICKADEES & TITMICE

CHICKADEES

Chickadees are among the best-known and most widespread birds in North America. Tolerant of people, they are frequent visitors to backyards and birdfeeders. The name "chickadee" is derived from the calls of several species. These energetic birds form flocks in winter. Some species, like the Black-capped Chickadee, can lower their body temperature in extreme cold.

TITMICE

Distinguished from chickadees by their crests and lack of black throats (except the Bridled Titmouse from the Southwest), titmice usually have more restricted North American distributions than chickadees.

TAME BIRDS
Black-capped Chickadees have distinctive black-and-white markings and are often very tame.

SWALLOWS, LARKS, & KINGLETS

SWALLOWS

Ornithologists usually call the short-tailed species in this group "martins," and the longer-tailed species "swallows." This nomenclature also has a geographic component. For example, one species is called Bank Swallow in America, but Sand Martin in the United Kingdom. As a family, swallows are cosmopolitan. North American species are migratory, and winter in Central and South America. Barn Swallows have been observed migrating over the Atacama Desert, and as far south as the Diego Ramírez Islands, not far from the Antarctic Peninsula.

LARKS

The only widespread North American species of lark, the Horned Lark, also occurs in the Old World, where it is named the Shore Lark. Larks are brownish birds, usually streaked, and live in open habitats, where they live on the ground. Display flights take the birds high up in the air, and are accompanied with musical songs.

KINGLETS

The five species of kinglets belong to one genus, *Regulus*. They are small, greenish birds, and males have a conspicuous crest of a different color. Two species are widespread in North American coniferous forests. Energetic and hardy, kinglets lay large clutches, eat insects and can survive harsh winters. The Ruby-crowned Kinglet has a very loud and ringing song for a bird weighing only $\frac{3}{16}$ to $\frac{3}{8}$ of an ounce (5–10 grams).

SURFACE SKIMMER
This Tree Swallow flies low over fresh water to catch insects .

| Order **Passeriformes** | Family **Bombycillidae** | Species ***Bombycilla garrulus*** |

Bohemian Waxwing

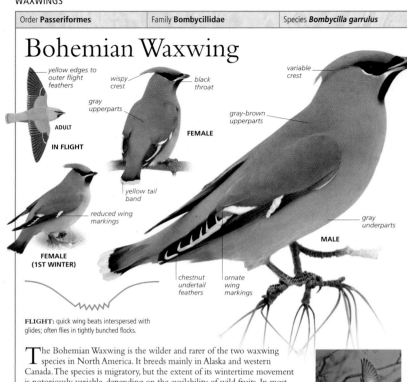

yellow edges to outer flight feathers

wispy crest

gray upperparts

black throat

variable crest

ADULT

IN FLIGHT

FEMALE

gray-brown upperparts

yellow tail band

reduced wing markings

FEMALE (1ST WINTER)

chestnut undertail feathers

ornate wing markings

gray underparts

MALE

FLIGHT: quick wing beats interspersed with glides; often flies in tightly bunched flocks.

The Bohemian Waxwing is the wilder and rarer of the two waxwing species in North America. It breeds mainly in Alaska and western Canada. The species is migratory, but the extent of its wintertime movement is notoriously variable, depending on the availability of wild fruits. In most winters, relatively few Bohemian Waxwings visit the lower 48 states, but in special "irruption" years, tens of thousands may reach as far south as Colorado.
VOICE Call a dull trill, but effect of hundreds of birds calling at the same time is remarkable and sounds like a high-pitched chorus; flocks vocalize constantly.
NESTING Dishevelled cup of sticks and grasses, placed in tree; 4–6 eggs; number of broods unknown; June–July.
FEEDING Catches insects on the wing in summer; flocks devour berries of native and exotic trees and shrubs throughout the year.

STRIKING TAIL
The Bohemian Waxwing's yellow tail band and chestnut undertail are evident here.

OCCURRENCE
Breeds in sub-Arctic coniferous forest, favoring disturbed areas such as beaver ponds and logging sites. Flocks gather at forest edges, hedges, and residential areas in winter. Hundreds or thousands of birds appear in an area, then disappear once food is depleted.

SIMILAR SPECIES		
CEDAR WAXWING see p.301	**CEDAR WAXWING** ☾ see p.301	
plainer wing markings	warmer tones overall	
	unmarked wings	smaller overall

Length **8½in (21cm)**	Wingspan **14½in (37cm)**	Weight **1⁹⁄₁₆–2½oz (45–70g)**
Social **Flocks**	Lifespan **Up to 12 years**	Status **Localized**

DATE SEEN	WHERE	NOTES
....	....	....
....	....	....
....	....	....
....	....	....
....	....	....

| Order **Passeriformes** | Family **Bombycillidae** | Species ***Bombycilla cedrorum*** |

Cedar Waxwing

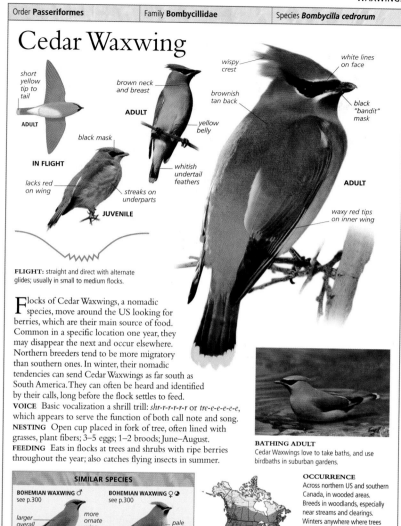

short yellow tip to tail

ADULT

IN FLIGHT

brown neck and breast

ADULT

black mask

lacks red on wing

streaks on underparts

JUVENILE

wispy crest

brownish tan back

yellow belly

whitish undertail feathers

white lines on face

black "bandit" mask

ADULT

waxy red tips on inner wing

ADULT

FLIGHT: straight and direct with alternate glides; usually in small to medium flocks.

Flocks of Cedar Waxwings, a nomadic species, move around the US looking for berries, which are their main source of food. Common in a specific location one year, they may disappear the next and occur elsewhere. Northern breeders tend to be more migratory than southern ones. In winter, their nomadic tendencies can send Cedar Waxwings as far south as South America. They can often be heard and identified by their calls, long before the flock settles to feed.

VOICE Basic vocalization a shrill trill: *shr-r-r-r-r-r* or *tre-e-e-e-e-e*, which appears to serve the function of both call note and song.

NESTING Open cup placed in fork of tree, often lined with grasses, plant fibers; 3–5 eggs; 1–2 broods; June–August.

FEEDING Eats in flocks at trees and shrubs with ripe berries throughout the year; also catches flying insects in summer.

BATHING ADULT
Cedar Waxwings love to take baths, and use birdbaths in suburban gardens.

SIMILAR SPECIES

BOHEMIAN WAXWING ♂
see p.300

larger overall

BOHEMIAN WAXWING ♀ ☾
see p.300

more ornate wing pattern

rufous undertail

pale gray breast

OCCURRENCE
Across northern US and southern Canada, in wooded areas. Breeds in woodlands, especially near streams and clearings. Winters anywhere where trees and shrubs have ripe fruits, especially in Mexico and South America. Spends a lot of time in treetops, but sometimes comes down to shrub level.

| Length **7½in (19cm)** | Wingspan **12in (30cm)** | Weight **1¹⁄₁₆–1¼oz (30–35g)** |
| Social **Flocks** | Lifespan **Up to 7 years** | Status **Secure** |

DATE SEEN	WHERE	NOTES
....	....	....
....	....	....
....	....	....
....	....	....

| Order **Passeriformes** | Family **Paridae** | Species *Parus carolinensis* |

Carolina Chickadee

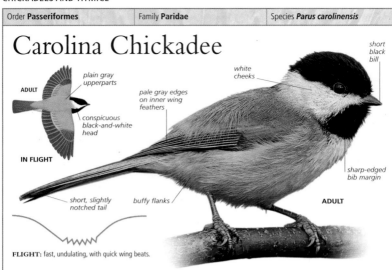

ADULT

plain gray
upperparts

conspicuous
black-and-white
head

IN FLIGHT

pale gray edges
on inner wing
feathers

white
cheeks

short
black
bill

sharp-edged
bib margin

ADULT

short, slightly
notched tail

buffy flanks

FLIGHT: fast, undulating, with quick wing beats.

The Carolina Chickadee is the only chickadee found in the southeastern US, and was first described and named by John James Audubon in 1834, when he was in South Carolina. Its northern range limit locally overlaps the Black-capped Chickadee's southern limit in a narrow band from Kansas to New Jersey, where the two species interbreed regularly, creating hybrids with mixed plumage that are hard to identify. The Carolina Chickadee hides food in caches under branches or even within curled dead leaves, returning for it within a few days. It has a strong preference for sunflower seeds, and can be seen at birdfeeders along with the Black-capped Chickadee, where the Carolina's characteristic call is the easiest way to distinguish the two species.

VOICE Fast *dee-dee-dee* call; song clear, whistled, 4-note sequence *wee-bee wee-bay*, second note lower in pitch.

NESTING Cavity lined with moss, fur, hair, plant down in soft, rotting tree; 5–8 eggs; 1–2 broods; April–May.

FEEDING Forages for insects and spiders; visits birdfeeders in winter.

DULL EXTREME
In worn plumage, and in its southwestern range, this bird has grayish white flanks.

BRIGHT EXTREME
In fresh plumage, some Carolina Chickadees have brighter, buffy flanks.

OCCURRENCE
Year-round dweller in deciduous, mixed and conifer woodlands, urban parks, and suburbs. In the Appalachians, prefers lower elevations than Black-capped. Range is expanding northward, especially in Ohio and Pennsylvania, where it is gradually replacing Black-capped as the resident species.

SIMILAR SPECIES

BLACK-CAPPED CHICKADEE see p.303	**MEXICAN CHICKADEE**
brighter overall	larger black bib
longer tail	larger overall
	dark gray underparts

Length **4¾in (12cm)**	Wingspan **7½in (19cm)**	Weight **⅜oz (11g)**
Social **Mixed flocks**	Lifespan **Up to 10 years**	Status **Secure**

DATE SEEN	WHERE	NOTES

| Order **Passeriformes** | Family **Paridae** | Species *Parus atricapillus* |

Black-capped Chickadee

white on wings and tail

black-and-white head

ADULT

grayish brown upperparts

white edges on wing feathers

IN FLIGHT

bright white cheeks

short black bill

black cap and bib

white edges on outer tail feathers

faded buff flanks

ADULT

The Black-capped Chickadee, the State Bird of Maine and Massachusetts, is the most widespread chickadee in North America, equally at home in the cold far north and in warm Appalachian valleys. To cope with the harsh winters in the northern parts of its range, this species can decrease its body temperature, entering a controlled hypothermia to conserve energy. There is variation in appearance depending upon geographical location, northern birds being slightly larger and possessing brighter white wing edgings than southern birds. Although it is largely nonmigratory, in winter chickadee flocks occasionally travel south of their traditional range.

VOICE Raspy *tsick-a-dee-dee-dee* call; song loud, clear whistle *bee-bee* or *bee-bee-be*, first note higher in pitch.

NESTING Cavity in rotting tree stump, lined with hair, fur, feathers, plant fibers; 6–8 eggs; 1 brood; April–June.

FEEDING Forages for insects and their eggs, and spiders in trees and bushes; mainly seeds in winter; may take seeds from an outstretched hand.

FLIGHT: swift and undulating, with fast wing beats.

ROUGH-EDGED BIB
The Black-capped Chickadee has a less well-defined lower bib margin than the Carolina Chickadee.

SIMILAR SPECIES

CAROLINA CHICKADEE
see p.302
lacks white wing edges

no white tail edges

MEXICAN CHICKADEE

large bib extends to upper breast

OCCURRENCE
Variety of wooded habitats, from vast forests in the far north to small woodlands in urban parks and suburbs. In years of poor seed crops in northern parts of the range, large numbers migrate southward as far as the Carolina Chickadee's range.

| Length **5¼in (13.5cm)** | Wingspan **8½in (22cm)** | Weight **⅜oz (11g)** |
| Social **Mixed flocks** | Lifespan **Up to 12 years** | Status **Secure** |

DATE SEEN	WHERE	NOTES

| Order **Passeriformes** | Family **Paridae** | Species *Parus hudsonicus* |

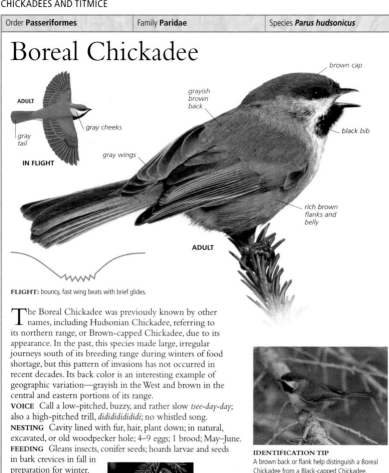

Boreal Chickadee

brown cap

ADULT

grayish brown back

gray cheeks

gray tail

black bib

IN FLIGHT

gray wings

rich brown flanks and belly

ADULT

FLIGHT: bouncy, fast wing beats with brief glides.

The Boreal Chickadee was previously known by other names, including Hudsonian Chickadee, referring to its northern range, or Brown-capped Chickadee, due to its appearance. In the past, this species made large, irregular journeys south of its breeding range during winters of food shortage, but this pattern of invasions has not occurred in recent decades. Its back color is an interesting example of geographic variation—grayish in the West and brown in the central and eastern portions of its range.

VOICE Call a low-pitched, buzzy, and rather slow *tsee-day-day*; also a high-pitched trill, *didididididi*; no whistled song.

NESTING Cavity lined with fur, hair, plant down; in natural, excavated, or old woodpecker hole; 4–9 eggs; 1 brood; May–June.

FEEDING Gleans insects, conifer seeds; hoards larvae and seeds in bark crevices in fall in preparation for winter.

IDENTIFICATION TIP
A brown back or flank help distinguish a Boreal Chickadee from a Black-capped Chickadee.

SIMILAR SPECIES

CHESTNUT-BACKED CHICKADEE *narrow, white cheeks*

chestnut sides

ACROBATIC FORAGER
This acrobatic feeder is able to cling on to conifer needles as it searches for insects and spiders.

OCCURRENCE
Found across the vast northern spruce-fir forests from Alaska to Newfoundland, and from the treeline at the tundra south to the northeastern and northwestern states. The southern edge of the range appears to be retracting, for unknown reasons.

| Length **5½in (14cm)** | Wingspan **8½in (21cm)** | Weight **⅜oz (10g)** |
| Social **Flocks** | Lifespan **Up to 5 years** | Status **Secure** |

DATE SEEN	WHERE	NOTES

Order **Passeriformes**	Family **Paridae**	Species ***Parus bicolor***

Tufted Titmouse

tufted dark gray head

ADULT

crest may be flattened

conspicuous black eye in whitish face

black fore-head

gray wings

orange flanks

IN FLIGHT

gray tail

ADULT

gray-black legs and feet

gray underparts

FLIGHT: swift and undulating, with irregular wing beats; usually across short distances.

A familiar and friendly sight, the Tufted Titmouse is widespread in eastern North America. Its lack of fear of people has enabled the Tufted Titmouse to adapt to human surroundings. In the last century its range has expanded significantly northward to southern Canada, probably due to the increased numbers of birdfeeders, which allow the Tufted Titmouse to survive cold northern winters. Its loud and cheerful song is a sure sign of spring!

VOICE Call a loud, harsh *pshurr, pshurr, pshurr,* song a ringing, far-carrying *peto peto peto,* sometimes shortened to *peer peer peer.*
NESTING Tree cavities, old woodpecker holes, and nest boxes, lined with damp leaves, moss, grass, hair; 5–6 eggs; 1 brood; March–May.
FEEDING Forages actively in trees and shrubs for insects, spiders, and their eggs; in winter, corn kernels, seeds, and small fruits, can split an acorn by hammering it with its bill.

COLOR VARIATION
The orange on an adult's flanks varies from bright in freshly molted feathers to dull in worn plumage.

SIMILAR SPECIES

BLACK-CRESTED TITMOUSE see p.462

high, black crest

pale forehead

BLUE-GRAY GNATCATCHER see p.323

lacks crest

smaller, slimmer body

OCCURRENCE
Lives year-round in areas of large and small deciduous and coniferous woodlands in the eastern half of the US. It has flourished in parks and gardens and can often be found using nest boxes in suburban backyards.

Length **6½in (16cm)**	Wingspan **10in (25cm)**	Weight **¹¹⁄₁₆oz (20g)**
Social **Mixed flocks**	Lifespan **Up to 13 years**	Status **Secure**

DATE SEEN	WHERE	NOTES

| Order **Passeriformes** | Family **Hirundinidae** | Species *Riparia riparia* |

Bank Swallow

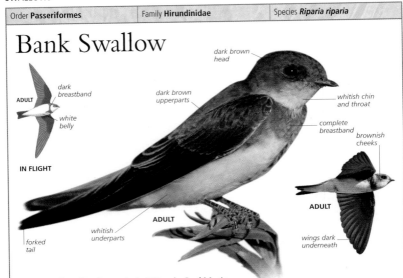

dark brown head

ADULT

dark breastband

dark brown upperparts

whitish chin and throat

white belly

complete breastband

brownish cheeks

IN FLIGHT

whitish underparts

ADULT

ADULT

forked tail

wings dark underneath

The Bank Swallow, known in the UK as the Sand Martin, is the slimmest and smallest of North American swallows. As its scientific name *riparia* (meaning "riverbanks") and common names suggest, the Bank Swallow nests in the banks and bluffs of rivers, streams, and lakes. It also favors sand and gravel quarries in the East. It is widely distributed across North America, breeding from south of the tundra–taiga line south to the central US. Nesting colonies can range from as few as 10 pairs to as many as 2,000, which are quite busy and noisy when all the birds are calling or coming in simultaneously to feed the young.
VOICE Call a soft *brrrrr* or *breee* often issued in pairs; song a harsh twittering or continuous chatter.
NESTING Both sexes excavate burrows in sandy banks containing a flat platform of grass, feathers, and twigs; 2–6 eggs; 1 brood; April–August.
FEEDING Catches insects, such as flies, moths, dragonflies, and bees in flight, but occasionally skims aquatic insects or their larvae off the water or terrestrial insects from the ground.

FLIGHT: fast, frantic, butterfly-like flight with glides, twists, and turns; shallow, rapid wing beats.

WAITING FOR MOM OR DAD
Hungry youngsters still expect to be fed, even when they're ready to fledge.

SIMILAR SPECIES

TREE SWALLOW larger; gray-brown upperparts with greenish tinge; see p.307

incomplete breastband

NORTHERN ROUGH-WINGED SWALLOW larger overall; see p.309

uniformly colored upperparts

OCCURRENCE
Widespread in North America. Breeds in lowland habitats associated with rivers, streams, lakes, reservoirs, and coasts, as well as in sand and gravel quarries. Often prefers man-made sites; winters in grasslands, open farm habitat, and freshwater areas in South America, south to Chile and Argentina.

| Length **4¾–5½in (12–14cm)** | Wingspan **10–11in (25–28cm)** | Weight **⅜–¹¹⁄₁₆oz (10–19g)** |
| Social **Colonies** | Lifespan **Up to 9 years** | Status **Secure** |

DATE SEEN	WHERE	NOTES

| Order **Passeriformes** | Family **Hirundinidae** | Species *Tachycineta bicolor* |

Tree Swallow

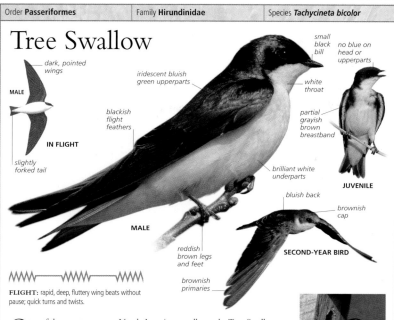

small black bill

no blue on head or upperparts

dark, pointed wings

iridescent bluish green upperparts

MALE

white throat

blackish flight feathers

IN FLIGHT

partial grayish brown breastband

slightly forked tail

brilliant white underparts

JUVENILE

bluish back

brownish cap

MALE

reddish brown legs and feet

SECOND-YEAR BIRD

brownish primaries

FLIGHT: rapid, deep, fluttery wing beats without pause; quick turns and twists.

One of the most common North American swallows, the Tree Swallow is found from coast to coast in the northern two-thirds of the continent, all the way north to Alaska. As its Latin name *bicolor* suggests, it is a two-toned bird, with iridescent bluish green upperparts and white underparts. Juveniles can be confused with the smaller Bank Swallow, which has a more complete breastband. The Tree Swallow lives in a variety of habitats, but its hole-nesting habit makes it dependent on crevices in old trees, abandoned woodpecker cavities, and on artificial "housing" such as nest boxes. The size of the population fluctuates according to the availability of nesting sites.

VOICE Ranges from variable high, chirping notes to chatters and soft trills; also complex high and clear 2-note whistle phrases.

NESTING Layer of fine plant matter in abandoned woodpecker hole or nest box, lined with feathers; 4–6 eggs; 1 brood; May–July.

FEEDING Swoops after flying insects from dawn to dusk; also takes bayberries.

KEEPING LOOKOUT
This species uses nest boxes, which the males occupy and defend as soon as they arrive.

OCCURRENCE
Typically breeds close to water in open habitat such as fields, marshes, lakes, and swamps, especially those with standing dead wood for cavity-nesting. Winters in roosts of hundreds of thousands of birds in marshes, in the southern US, and from Mexico to Panama; also Cuba.

SIMILAR SPECIES

BANK SWALLOW
paler brown rump; see p.306

VIOLET-GREEN SWALLOW
white flank patch;

white eye patch

distinct dusky breastband

violet-green upperparts

| Length **5–6in (13–15cm)** | Wingspan **12–14in (30–35cm)** | Weight ⅝–⅞oz (17–25g) |
| Social **Large flocks** | Lifespan **Up to 11 years** | Status **Secure** |

DATE SEEN	WHERE	NOTES

| Order **Passeriformes** | Family **Hirundinidae** | Species **Progne subis** |

Purple Martin

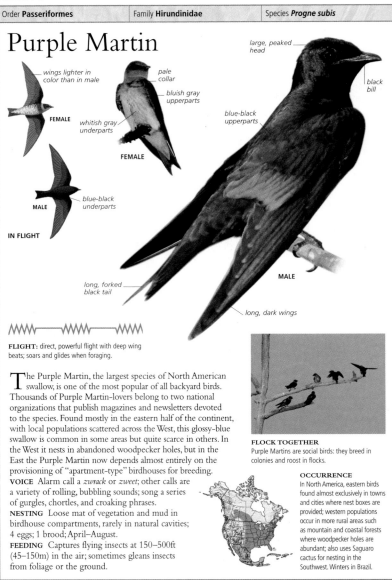

large, peaked head

black bill

wings lighter in color than in male

FEMALE

pale collar

bluish gray upperparts

blue-black upperparts

whitish gray underparts

FEMALE

blue-black underparts

MALE

IN FLIGHT

long, forked black tail

MALE

long, dark wings

FLIGHT: direct, powerful flight with deep wing beats; soars and glides when foraging.

The Purple Martin, the largest species of North American swallow, is one of the most popular of all backyard birds. Thousands of Purple Martin-lovers belong to two national organizations that publish magazines and newsletters devoted to the species. Found mostly in the eastern half of the continent, with local populations scattered across the West, this glossy-blue swallow is common in some areas but quite scarce in others. In the West it nests in abandoned woodpecker holes, but in the East the Purple Martin now depends almost entirely on the provisioning of "apartment-type" birdhouses for breeding.

VOICE Alarm call a *zwrack* or *zweet*; other calls are a variety of rolling, bubbling sounds; song a series of gurgles, chortles, and croaking phrases.

NESTING Loose mat of vegetation and mud in birdhouse compartments, rarely in natural cavities; 4 eggs; 1 brood; April–August.

FEEDING Captures flying insects at 150–500ft (45–150m) in the air; sometimes gleans insects from foliage or the ground.

FLOCK TOGETHER
Purple Martins are social birds: they breed in colonies and roost in flocks.

OCCURRENCE
In North America, eastern birds found almost exclusively in towns and cities where nest boxes are provided; western populations occur in more rural areas such as mountain and coastal forests where woodpecker holes are abundant; also uses Saguaro cactus for nesting in the Southwest. Winters in Brazil.

| Length **7–8in (18–20cm)** | Wingspan **15–16in (38–41cm)** | Weight **1⁷⁄₁₆–2⅛oz (40–60g)** |
| Social **Large flocks/Colonies** | Lifespan **Up to 13 years** | Status **Secure** |

DATE SEEN	WHERE	NOTES

| Order **Passeriformes** | Family **Hirundinidae** | Species *Stelgidopteryx serripennis* |

Northern Rough-winged Swallow

IN FLIGHT
dark brown overall
square tail
ADULT
dark face

JUVENILE
black eye
tan-buffy wing bars
pale underparts

light crescent from cheek to crown
brown head
pale brown breast
pale, grayish brown belly
ADULT

long, brown wings

Given the name *serripennis*, "saw-like," by Audubon in 1888, and characterized by the serrations on its outer wing feathers, this species is otherwise somewhat drab in color and aspect. The Northern Rough-winged Swallow has a broad distribution in North America, across southern Canada and throughout the US. Often overlooked by birdwatchers, this brown-backed, dusky-throated swallow can be spotted hunting insects over water. In size and habit, the Northern Rough-winged Swallow shares many similarities with the Bank Swallow, including breeding habits and color, but the latter's notched tail and smaller size help tell them apart.

VOICE Steady repetition of short, rapid *brrrt* notes inflected upward; sometimes a buzzy *jee-jee-jee* or high-pitched *brzzzzzt*.

NESTING Loose cup of twigs and straw in a cavity or burrow in a bank, such as road cuts; 4–7 eggs; 1 brood; May–July.

FEEDING Captures flying insects, including flies, wasps, bees, damselflies, and beetles in the air; more likely to feed over water and at lower altitudes than other swallows.

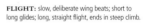

FLIGHT: slow, deliberate wing beats; short to long glides; long, straight flight, ends in steep climb.

BROWN BIRD
This swallow is brownish above and grayish below, with a brown smudge on the sides of its neck.

SIMILAR SPECIES

BANK SWALLOW
see p.306
smaller overall
whitish belly and throat
long, notched tail

TREE SWALLOW ⊙
see p.307
brownish breastband
white throat
grayish breastband
white belly

OCCURRENCE
In North America widespread from coast to coast. Nests at a wide variety of altitudes, prefers exposed banks of clay, sand, or gravel such as gorges, shale banks, and gravel pits. Forages along watercourses where aerial insects are plentiful. Breeds south to Costa Rica. Winters in Central America.

| Length **4¾–6in (12–15cm)** | Wingspan **11–12in (28–30cm)** | Weight **⅜–⅝oz (10–18g)** |
| Social **Solitary** | Lifespan **Unknown** | Status **Secure** |

DATE SEEN	WHERE	NOTES
....	....	....
....	....	....
....	....	....
....	....	....
....	....	....

Order **Passeriformes**	Family **Hirundinidae**	Species *Hirundo rustica*

Barn Swallow

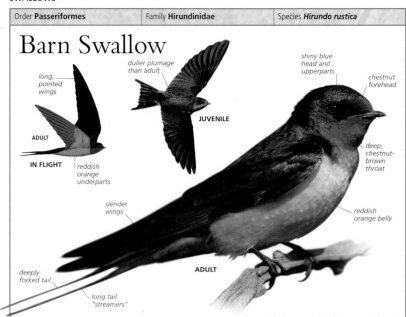

long, pointed wings

ADULT

IN FLIGHT

reddish orange underparts

duller plumage than adult

JUVENILE

shiny blue head and upperparts

chestnut forehead

deep, chestnut-brown throat

reddish orange belly

slender wings

deeply forked tail

long tail "streamers"

ADULT

FLIGHT: bursts of straight flight; close to the ground; weaves left and right, with sharp turns.

The most widely distributed and abundant swallow in the world, the Barn Swallow is found just about everywhere in North America south of the Arctic timberline. Originally a cave-nester before Europeans settlers came to the New World, the Barn Swallow readily adapted to nesting under the eaves of houses, under bridges, and inside buildings such as barns. It is now rare to find this elegant swallow breeding in a natural site. Steely blue upperparts, reddish underparts, and a deeply forked tail identify the Barn Swallow. North American breeders have deep, reddish orange underparts, but birds from Eurasia are white-bellied.

VOICE High-pitched, squeaky *chee-chee* call; song a long series of chatty, pleasant churrs, squeaks, chitterings, and buzzes.

NESTING Deep cup of mud and grass-stems attached to vertical surfaces or on ledges; 4–6 eggs; 1–2 broods; May–September.

FEEDING Snatches flying insects, such as flies, mosquitoes, wasps, and beetles in the air at lower altitudes than other swallows; sometimes eats wild berries and seeds.

WELL PROTECTED
Whether in a barn or other structure, a Barn Swallow nest is totally protected from wind and rain.

SIMILAR SPECIES

TREE SWALLOW ♂
see p.307
lacks forked tail and dark breast-band

white under-parts

OCCURRENCE
Breeds across North America south to central Mexico. Prefers agricultural regions and towns. Winters near sugarcane fields, grain fields, and marshes, south in South America as far as Patagonia. Hundreds of thousands winter in marshes of northern Argentina.

Length **6–7½in (15–19cm)**	Wingspan **11½–13in (29–33cm)**	Weight **⅝–¹¹⁄₁₆oz (17–20g)**
Social **Small colonies/Flocks**	Lifespan **Up to 8 years**	Status **Secure**

DATE SEEN	WHERE		NOTES

| Order **Passeriformes** | Family **Hirundinidae** | Species ***Petrochelidon pyrrhonata*** |

Cliff Swallow

long, roundish wings

brown-tinged, black back

rusty cheek patch

mottled throat

JUVENILE

bluish black back

ADULT

IN FLIGHT

bluish black cap

rusty-brown cheeks

pale hind neck collar

whitish forehead

dark throat

ADULT

pale underparts

slight notch in squared tail

pale reddish rump

The Cliff Swallow is one of North America's most social land birds, sometimes nesting in colonies of over 3,500 pairs, especially in the western US. It is more locally distributed in the East. It can be distinguished from other North American swallows by its square tail and orange rump, but it resembles its close relative, the Cave Swallow, in color, pattern, and in affixing its mud nests to the sides of highway culverts, bridges, and buildings. The considerable increase in such structures has allowed the species to expand its range from the west to breed almost everywhere on the continent south of the tundra.

VOICE Gives *purr* and *churr* calls when alarmed; song a low, squeaky, 6-second twitter given in flight and near nests.

NESTING Domed nests of mud pellets on cave walls, buildings, culverts, bridges, and dams; 3–5 eggs; 1–2 broods; April–August.

FEEDING Catches flying insects (often swarming varieties) while on the wing; sometimes forages on the ground; ingests grit to aid digestion.

FLIGHT: strong, fast wing beats; glides more often but less acrobatically than other swallows.

GATHERING MUD
The Cliff Swallow gathers wet mud from puddles, pond edges, and streamsides to build its nest.

SIMILAR SPECIES

CAVE SWALLOW see p.312 — *brighter orange cheek* — *paler overall*

INDIVIDUAL HOMES
In a Cliff Swallow colony, each nest has a single opening.

OCCURRENCE
Breeds in North America from Alaska to Mexico. Prefers walls, culverts, buildings, cliffs, and undersides of piers on which to affix mud nests. Migrates to South America. Hundreds of thousands winter in marshes of northern Argentina.

| Length **5in (13cm)** | Wingspan **11–12in (28–30cm)** | Weight **¹¹⁄₁₆–1¼oz (20–35g)** |
| Social **Colonies** | Lifespan **Up to 11 years** | Status **Secure** |

DATE SEEN	WHERE	NOTES

| Order **Passeriformes** | Family **Hirundinidae** | Species ***Petrochelidon fulva*** |

Cave Swallow

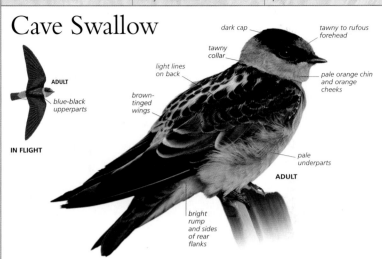

dark cap

tawny to rufous forehead

tawny collar

light lines on back

pale orange chin and orange cheeks

brown-tinged wings

ADULT

blue-black upperparts

IN FLIGHT

pale underparts

ADULT

bright rump and sides of rear flanks

Distinguished from its close relative, the Cliff Swallow, by a pale rather than black throat and rufous rather than white forehead, the buffy-rumped Cave Swallow is limited in its breeding range to parts of New Mexico, Arizona, Texas, and southern Florida. As its name suggests, the Cave Swallow cements its cup nest to the walls of caves, which it often shares with bats; it also builds nests on bridges, water culverts, and buildings. The Cave Swallow was once rare in North America, but in recent years it has expanded both geographically and numerically because it has adapted to nesting on man-made structures. In winter the US Cave Swallow population moves south to Mexico.

VOICE Call a low *wheet*; song a series of bubbly sounds blending into warbling trill, ending in series of double-toned notes.

NESTING Open flat cup with tall, broad rim, made of mud and guano, glued to concrete structure or cave wall; 3–5 eggs; 1–2 broods; April–July.

FEEDING Captures a variety of flying insects while on the wing, including beetles, flies, and bees; sometimes flushes its prey out into the air by flying into vegetation.

FLIGHT: uses rapid wing beats to swoop and dive, but also likes to glide.

MUD BOWL NEST
Cave Swallow nests are cup-like, and not domed like those of the Cliff Swallow.

SIMILAR SPECIES

CLIFF SWALLOW see p.311

light forehead

dark throat

OCCURRENCE
In US, breeds in the arid central West (Arizona, Texas) and southern Florida, wherever nests can be attached to walls of caves, sinkholes, bridges, buildings, and culverts; preferably near open water for feeding on flying insects. Outside US, breeds in Mexico and the Greater Antilles.

| Length **5½in (14cm)** | Wingspan **13in (33cm)** | Weight **⅝–⅞oz (17–25g)** |
| Social **Colonies** | Lifespan **Up to 9 years** | Status **Localized** |

DATE SEEN	WHERE	NOTES

| Order **Passeriformes** | Family **Alaudidae** | Species *Eremophila alpestris* |

Horned Lark

muted facial markings

brown wings

variable brown on upperparts

dark streaks on reddish brown upperparts

tiny "horns"

bold black-and-yellow face

ADULT

IN FLIGHT

ADULT (POSTBREEDING)

whitish underparts

streaked upperparts

black tail with narrow, white edges to outer feathers

short legs

JUVENILE

ADULT (BREEDING)

FLIGHT: undulating, with wings folded in after every few beats.

The Horned Lark is a bird of open country, especially places with extensive bare ground. The species is characteristic of arid, alpine, and Arctic regions; in these areas, it flourishes in the bleakest of habitats imaginable, from sun-scorched, arid lakeshores in the Great Basin, to windswept tundra north of the timberline. In some places, the only breeding bird species are the Horned Lark and the equally resilient Common Raven. In Europe and Asia, this species is known as the Shorelark.

VOICE Flight call a sharp *sweet* or *soo-weet*; song, either in flight or from the ground, pleasant, musical tinkling series, followed by *sweet… swit… sweet… s'sweea'weea'witta'swit.*

NESTING In depression in bare ground, somewhat sheltered by grass or low shrubs, lined with plant matter; 2–5 eggs; 1–3 broods; March–July.

FEEDING Survives exclusively on seeds of grasses and sedges in winter; eats mostly insects in summer.

GROUND FORAGER
With its short legs bent under its body, an adult looks for insects and seeds.

OCCURRENCE
Breeds widely, in any sort of open, even barren habitat with extensive bare ground, especially short-grass prairies and deserts. Winters wherever there are snow-free openings, including along beaches and roads. Winters from southern Canada southward to Florida and Mexico.

SIMILAR SPECIES

SPRAGUE'S PIPIT
see p.343

shorter tail

SKYLARK

shorter wings

streaked crest

streaked overall

VERY VOCAL
The Horned Lark is a highly vocal bird, singing from the air, the ground, or low shrubs.

| Length **7in (18cm)** | Wingspan **12in (30cm)** | Weight **1¹/₁₆oz (30g)** |
| Social **Winter flocks** | Lifespan **Up to 8 years** | Status **Secure** |

DATE SEEN	WHERE	NOTES

Order **Passeriformes**	Family **Regullidae**	Species *Regulus satrapa*

Golden-crowned Kinglet

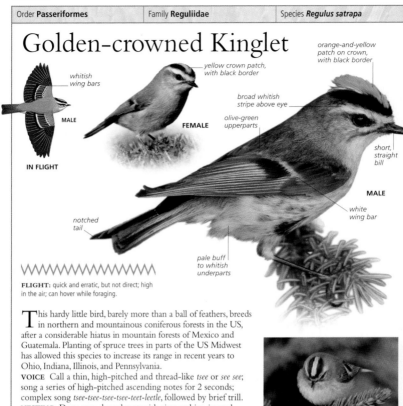

whitish wing bars

MALE

IN FLIGHT

yellow crown patch, with black border

FEMALE

orange-and-yellow patch on crown, with black border

broad whitish stripe above eye

olive-green upperparts

short, straight bill

MALE

white wing bar

notched tail

pale buff to whitish underparts

FLIGHT: quick and erratic, but not direct; high in the air; can hover while foraging.

This hardy little bird, barely more than a ball of feathers, breeds in northern and mountainous coniferous forests in the US, after a considerable hiatus in mountain forests of Mexico and Guatemala. Planting of spruce trees in parts of the US Midwest has allowed this species to increase its range in recent years to Ohio, Indiana, Illinois, and Pennsylvania.

VOICE Call a thin, high-pitched and thread-like *tsee* or *see see*; song a series of high-pitched ascending notes for 2 seconds; complex song *tsee-tsee-tsee-tsee-teet-leetle*, followed by brief trill.

NESTING Deep, cup-shaped nest with rims arching inward, made of moss, lichen, and bark, and lined with finer strips of the same; 8–9 eggs; 1–2 broods; May–August.

FEEDING Gleans flies, beetles, mites, spiders, and their eggs from tips of branches, under bark, tufts of conifer needles; eats seeds, and persimmon fruits.

EXPANDING RANGE
This bird has expanded its range southward following spruce forestation.

SIMILAR SPECIES

RUBY-CROWNED KINGLET
see p.315

white eye-ring

no eye-stripe

olive underparts

HIGHER VOICE
The Golden-crowned has a higher-pitched and less musical song than the Ruby-crowned.

OCCURRENCE
Breeds in remote northern and subalpine spruce or fir forests, mixed coniferous–deciduous forests, single-species stands, and pine plantations; winters in a wide variety of habitats—coniferous and deciduous forests, pine groves, low-lying hardwood forests, swamps, and urban and suburban habitats.

Length 3¼–4¼in (8–11cm)	Wingspan 5½–7in (14–18cm)	Weight ⁵⁄₃₂–⁹⁄₃₂oz (4–8g)
Social **Solitary/Pairs**	Lifespan **Up to 5 years**	Status **Secure**

DATE SEEN	WHERE	NOTES

| Order **Passeriformes** | Family **Regulidae** | Species *Regulus calendula* |

Ruby-crowned Kinglet

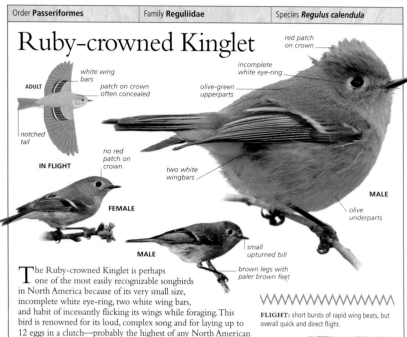

red patch on crown

ADULT

white wing bars

patch on crown often concealed

incomplete white eye-ring

olive-green upperparts

notched tail

IN FLIGHT

no red patch on crown

two white wingbars

FEMALE

MALE

small upturned bill

brown legs with paler brown feet

MALE

olive underparts

The Ruby-crowned Kinglet is perhaps one of the most easily recognizable songbirds in North America because of its very small size, incomplete white eye-ring, two white wing bars, and habit of incessantly flicking its wings while foraging. This bird is renowned for its loud, complex song and for laying up to 12 eggs in a clutch—probably the highest of any North American songbird. Despite local declines resulting from logging and forest fires, the Ruby-crowned Kinglet is common across the continent. It will sometimes be found in mixed-species flocks in winter, together with nuthatches and titmice.
VOICE Call a low, husky *jidit*; song, remarkably loud for such a small bird, begins with 2–3 high, clear notes *tee* or *zee* followed by 5–6 lower *tu* or *turr* notes, and ends with ringing galloping notes *tee-da-leet, tee-da-leet, tee-da-leet*.
NESTING Globular or elongated nest hanging from or on large branch with an enclosed or open cup, made of mosses, feathers, lichens, spider's silk, bark, hair, and fur; 5–12 eggs; 1 brood; May–October.
FEEDING Gleans a wide variety of insects, spiders, and their eggs among the leaves on the outer tips of higher, smaller branches; eats fruit and seeds; often hovers to catch prey.

FLIGHT: short bursts of rapid wing beats, but overall quick and direct flight.

CONCEALED COLOR
This bird's red patch is often concealed unless the bird is agitated or excited.

OCCURRENCE
Within the northern forest zone, breeds near water in Black Spruce and tamarack forests, muskegs, forests with mixed conifers and northern hardwoods; in the mountainous West, spruce-fir, Lodgepole Pine, and Douglas Fir forests. Winters in a broad range of forests, thickets, and borders.

SIMILAR SPECIES

HUTTON'S VIREO
see p.460

larger head

stouter bill

heavier overall

ALWAYS FLICKING
Ruby-crowned Kinglets are easily identified by their habit of constantly flicking their wings.

| Length **3½–4¼in (9–11cm)** | Wingspan **6–7in (15–18cm)** | Weight **³⁄₁₆–³⁄₈oz (5–10g)** |
| Social **Winter flocks** | Lifespan **Up to 5 years** | Status **Secure** |

DATE SEEN	WHERE	NOTES

WRENS & GNATCATCHERS

WITH ONE EXCEPTION, the Eurasian Winter Wren, wrens are all small American songbirds. Most are brown with light and dark streaking. The scientific family name, Troglodytidae, which derives from a Greek word meaning "cave-dweller," seems apt in light of the furtive habits of wrens, which are heard more often than they are seen. Wrens are renowned for their remarkable songs, and, in some species, for their precisely synchronized duets. Of the 13 species of gnatcatchers, small songbirds with subdued plumage and discreet habits, three occur in Canada and the USA.

COCKED TAIL
As they sing, Winter Wrens often hold their tails upward in a near-vertical position.

NUTHATCHES & TREECREEPER

EASILY RECOGNIZED BY their distinctive shape and feeding technique, nuthatches are common North American woodland birds. They are plump-bodied and short-tailed, with blue-gray backs, and often have a contrasting darker crown. These birds use their bills to probe for insects in the crevices of tree trunks and branches. Strong feet and long claws allow them to move along the underside of branches. This contrasts with many other birds, which only move upward on a tree trunk. This characteristic movement is one of the easiest ways to identify nuthatches. Only one species of treecreeper is found in North America. Often overlooked, treecreepers forage by searching methodically in bark crevices.

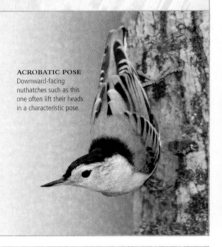

ACROBATIC POSE
Downward-facing nuthatches such as this one often lift their heads in a characteristic pose.

THRASHERS & RELATIVES

THE FAMILY NAME for catbirds, mockingbirds, and thrashers is from the Latin for "to imitate," and no other word better defines the ten species of these birds that are found in North America. The Northern Mockingbird is especially well known for its ability to incorporate the songs of other species into its own song. Members of the Mimidae have long, curved bills and reclusive habits. Some members of this group are able to recognize and remove the eggs of brood parasites such as the Brown-headed Cowbird. The Gray Catbird is recognized by its cat-like *meeow* calls and its overall gray plumage. Only one species of thrasher, the Brown Thrasher, is found in the eastern US.

DISTINCTIVE BILL
This Long-billed Thrasher is characterized by its slender, curved bill, long, thin legs, and long, rounded tail.

| Order **Passeriformes** | Family **Troglodytidae** | Species *Cistothorus platensis* |

Sedge Wren

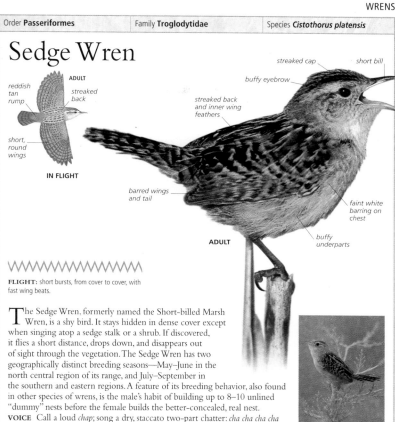

reddish tan rump

ADULT

streaked back

short, round wings

IN FLIGHT

streaked cap

short bill

buffy eyebrow

streaked back and inner wing feathers

barred wings and tail

ADULT

faint white barring on chest

buffy underparts

FLIGHT: short bursts, from cover to cover, with fast wing beats.

The Sedge Wren, formerly named the Short-billed Marsh Wren, is a shy bird. It stays hidden in dense cover except when singing atop a sedge stalk or a shrub. If discovered, it flies a short distance, drops down, and disappears out of sight through the vegetation. The Sedge Wren has two geographically distinct breeding seasons—May–June in the north central region of its range, and July–September in the southern and eastern regions. A feature of its breeding behavior, also found in other species of wrens, is the male's habit of building up to 8–10 unlined "dummy" nests before the female builds the better-concealed, real nest.

VOICE Call a loud *chap*; song a dry, staccato two-part chatter: *cha cha cha cha ch'ch'ch ch'ch'ch'ch'*.

NESTING Globular, woven structure of sedges with side entrance; lined with plant matter, down, and hair; 4–8 eggs; 1–2 broods; May–August.

FEEDING Forages for spiders and insects, such as grasshoppers, flies, mosquitoes, and bugs, close to or on ground in cover of sedges and grass.

LOOK CLOSELY
Close study is necessary to appreciate the Sedge Wren's subtle patterning, which is plainer than the Marsh Wren's.

OCCURRENCE
In North America, breeds in wet meadows and sedge marshes with low water levels. Widely distributed from the Canadian prairies, east to Québec and from northern US, to the south central states, and from there to Chile and Argentina. Winters from Texas to Florida in grassy fields and coastal-plain prairies.

SIMILAR SPECIES

MARSH WREN
see p.318
heavily striped back
plain cap
white eyebrow

HOUSE WREN
see p.322
plain back
faint eyebrow
grayish brown underparts

| Length **4½in (11.5cm)** | Wingspan **5½–6in (14–15.5cm)** | Weight **⁹⁄₁₆oz (9g)** |
| Social **Loose colonies** | Lifespan **Unknown** | Status **Secure** |

DATE SEEN	WHERE	NOTES

Order **Passeriformes**	Family **Troglodytidae**	Species *Cistothorus palustris*

Marsh Wren

ADULT

boldly striped black-and-white back

rusty rump

plain, rusty wing patches

IN FLIGHT

barred tail feathers

heavily streaked, black-and-white back

whitish eyebrow

brown forehead and cap

rusty flanks and uppertail feathers

dull whitish, buff underparts

long bill

ADULT

FLIGHT: straight, with rapid wing beats over short distances, from one reed patch to another.

The Marsh Wren, a common resident of saltwater and freshwater marshes, is known for singing loudly through both day and night. The males perform fluttery, aerial courtship flights while singing, and are polygamous, mating with two or more females. Like the Sedge Wren, the male builds several dummy nests before his mate constructs one herself. The Marsh Wren nests in taller vegetation than the Sedge Wren and over deeper water. Eastern (*C. p. palustris*) and Western (*C. p. paludicola*) Marsh Wrens differ in voice and behavior, and some ornithologists classify them as separate species.
VOICE Calls a low *chek* and a raspy *churr*; song a loud *chuk chuk chuk*, then fast *tih-tih-tih-rih-tih-tih*, an enthusiastic singer.
NESTING Oblong structure with side entrance, woven of reeds and lined with soft materials; 4–5 eggs; 2 broods; March–July.
FEEDING Forages acrobatically for insects, such as mosquitoes, dragonflies, and beetles, within dense clusters of cattails and reeds.

DELICATELY PERCHED
This wren perches on vertical reeds and often holds itself up by spreading its legs across two stalks.

SIMILAR SPECIES

SEDGE WREN
see p.317

streaked cap

HOUSE WREN
see p.322

plain back

barred wings

buffy underparts

grayish brown underparts

OCCURRENCE
Breeds across North America from Canada to the mountains of the western and central northern states. Inhabits freshwater and saltwater marshes with tall vegetation, above water, sometimes more than 3ft (1m) deep. It is irregularly distributed in its range. Winters in grassy marshes and wetlands.

Length **5in (13cm)**	Wingspan **6in (15cm)**	Weight **⅜oz (11g)**
Social **Loose colonies**	Lifespan **Unknown**	Status **Localized**

DATE SEEN	WHERE	NOTES

Order **Passeriformes**	Family **Troglodytidae**	Species ***Thryomanes bewickii***

Bewick's Wren

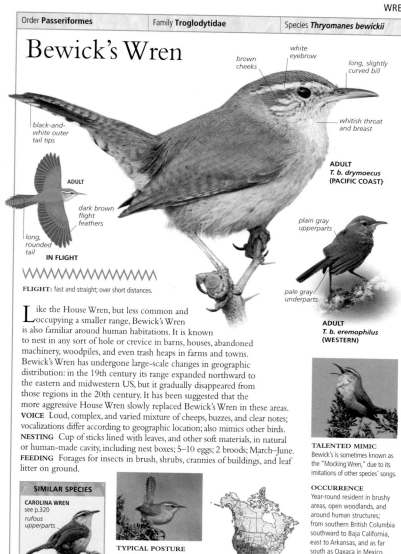

white
eyebrow

brown
cheeks

long, slightly
curved bill

whitish throat
and breast

ADULT
T. b. drymoecus
(PACIFIC COAST)

black-and-
white outer
tail tips

ADULT

dark brown
flight
feathers

long,
rounded
tail

IN FLIGHT

FLIGHT: fast and straight; over short distances.

plain gray
upperparts

pale gray
underparts

ADULT
T. b. eremophilus
(WESTERN)

Like the House Wren, but less common and occupying a smaller range, Bewick's Wren is also familiar around human habitations. It is known to nest in any sort of hole or crevice in barns, houses, abandoned machinery, woodpiles, and even trash heaps in farms and towns. Bewick's Wren has undergone large-scale changes in geographic distribution: in the 19th century its range expanded northward to the eastern and midwestern US, but it gradually disappeared from those regions in the 20th century. It has been suggested that the more aggressive House Wren slowly replaced Bewick's Wren in these areas.
VOICE Loud, complex, and varied mixture of cheeps, buzzes, and clear notes; vocalizations differ according to geographic location; also mimics other birds.
NESTING Cup of sticks lined with leaves, and other soft materials, in natural or human-made cavity, including nest boxes; 5–10 eggs; 2 broods; March–June.
FEEDING Forages for insects in brush, shrubs, crannies of buildings, and leaf litter on ground.

TALENTED MIMIC
Bewick's is sometimes known as the "Mocking Wren," due to its imitations of other species' songs.

OCCURRENCE
Year-round resident in brushy areas, open woodlands, and around human structures; from southern British Columbia southward to Baja California, east to Arkansas, and as far south as Oaxaca in Mexico. May withdraw slightly southward from northernmost portions of range in winter.

SIMILAR SPECIES

CAROLINA WREN
see p.320
rufous
upperparts

buffy
underparts

TYPICAL POSTURE
Bewick's Wren may often be spotted with its distinctive tail cocked vertically.

Length **5in (13cm)**	Wingspan **7in (18cm)**	Weight **⅜oz (11g)**
Social **Solitary/Pairs**	Lifespan **At least 8 years**	Status **Secure**

DATE SEEN	WHERE	NOTES

319

| Order **Passeriformes** | Family **Troglodytidae** | Species ***Thryothorus ludovicianus*** |

Carolina Wren

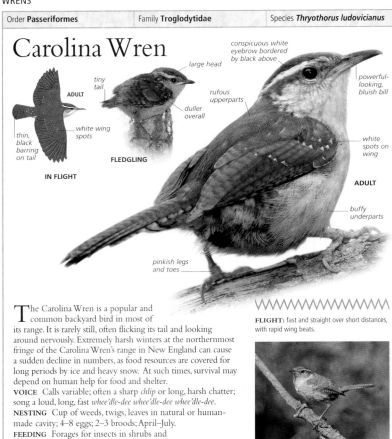

conspicuous white eyebrow bordered by black above

large head

ADULT

tiny tail

thin, black barring on tail

white wing spots

IN FLIGHT

rufous upperparts

duller overall

FLEDGLING

powerful-looking, bluish bill

white spots on wing

ADULT

buffy underparts

pinkish legs and toes

The Carolina Wren is a popular and common backyard bird in most of its range. It is rarely still, often flicking its tail and looking around nervously. Extremely harsh winters at the northernmost fringe of the Carolina Wren's range in New England can cause a sudden decline in numbers, as food resources are covered for long periods by ice and heavy snow. At such times, survival may depend on human help for food and shelter.

VOICE Calls variable; often a sharp *chlip* or long, harsh chatter; song a loud, long, fast *whee'dle-dee whee'dle-dee whee'dle-dee*.

NESTING Cup of weeds, twigs, leaves in natural or human-made cavity; 4–8 eggs; 2–3 broods; April–July.

FEEDING Forages for insects in shrubs and on ground; in winter, favorite foods are peanut butter or suet at a feeder.

FLIGHT: fast and straight over short distances, with rapid wing beats.

DISTINCTIVE BORDER
A unique feature of this wren, not always noticed but visible here, is the black border on the eyebrow.

OCCURRENCE
Breeds in a variety of bushy woodland habitats, such as thickets, parks with shrubby undergrowth, suburban yards with dense, low trees or bushes, and gardens; from northeastern Mexico to the Great Lakes and northeastward to New England. Four subspecies occur from Mexico to Nicaragua.

SIMILAR SPECIES

BEWICK'S WREN see p.319

dull brown or gray upperparts

longer tail

TIRELESS SINGER
Unlike many birds, the male Carolina Wren sings all year long, even on cold winter days.

| Length **5¼in (13.5cm)** | Wingspan **7½in (19cm)** | Weight **¹¹⁄₁₆oz (19g)** |
| Social **Pairs/Family groups** | Lifespan **At least 9 years** | Status **Secure** |

DATE SEEN	WHERE	NOTES

| Order **Passeriformes** | Family **Troglodytidae** | Species ***Troglodytes troglodytes*** |

Winter Wren

distinct, tan eyebrow

stubby tail, usually cocked straight up

dark brown, barred back

small, thin bill

ADULT

short, barred tail

ADULT

flanks strongly barred

barred, rounded wings

IN FLIGHT

The Winter Wren has one of the loudest songs of any North American bird of a similar size: the male's song carries far through its forest haunts. It is widespread, found throughout Eurasia, and from the Aleutians and Alaska eastward to Newfoundland, and as far south as California in the West and the Appalachians in the East, where the subspecies *T. t. pullus* resides. Its winter range is also western (to California) and eastern (to Texas), with a wide hiatus in between. This bird spends its time foraging in tangles of fallen trees and shrubs, appearing mouse-like as it creeps amid the shadows. In Europe, as its family's sole species, it is simply called "the Wren."

VOICE Call a double *chek-chek* or *chimp-chimp*; song a loud, extremely long, complex series of warbles, trills, and single notes.

NESTING Well-hidden in a cavity near ground with dead wood and crevices; nest a messy mound lined with feathers; 4–7 eggs; 1–2 broods; April–July.

FEEDING Forages for insects in low, dense undergrowth, often in wet areas along streams; sometimes thrusts its head into water to capture prey.

FLIGHT: fast and direct, with rapid beats of its short, broad wings.

VOCAL VIRTUOSO
The Winter Wren is a skulker, but in the breeding season singing males show up on lower perches.

SIMILAR SPECIES

HOUSE WREN
see p.322
pale brown back

long tail

plain, unbarred flanks

NERVOUS REACTION
When alarmed, this wren cocks its tail almost vertically, before escaping into a mossy thicket.

OCCURRENCE
Breeds in northern and mountain forests dominated by evergreen trees with a dense understory, fallen trees, and banks of streams. In the Appalachians, breeds in treeless areas with grass near cliffs. Northernmost birds migrate south to winter in woodlands, brush piles, tangles, and secluded spots.

| Length **4in (10cm)** | Wingspan **5½in (14cm)** | Weight **⁵⁄₁₆oz (9g)** |
| Social **Solitary/Family groups** | Lifespan **At least 4 years** | Status **Secure** |

DATE SEEN	WHERE	NOTES

| Order **Passeriformes** | Family **Troglodytidae** | Species *Troglodytes aedon* |

House Wren

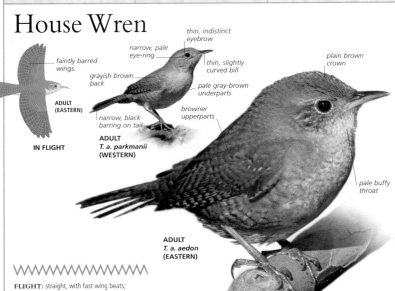

thin, indistinct eyebrow

narrow, pale eye-ring

faintly barred wings

ADULT (EASTERN)

IN FLIGHT

grayish brown back

thin, slightly curved bill

pale gray-brown underparts

plain brown crown

narrow, black barring on tail

ADULT T. a. parkmanii (WESTERN)

browner upperparts

pale buffy throat

ADULT T. a. aedon (EASTERN)

WWWWWWWWWWWW

FLIGHT: straight, with fast wing beats; typically over short distances.

Of all the North American wrens, the House Wren is the plainest, yet one of the most familiar and endearing, especially when making its home in a backyard nest box. However, it can be a fairly aggressive species, driving away nearby nesting birds of its own and other species by destroying nests, puncturing eggs, and even killing young. In the 1920s, distraught bird lovers mounted a campaign calling for the eradication of House Wrens, though the campaign did not last long as most people were in favor of letting nature take its course.

VOICE Call a sharp *chep* or *cherr*; song opens with several short notes, followed by bubbly explosion of spluttering notes.

NESTING Cup lined with soft material on stick platform in natural, manmade cavities, such as nest boxes; 5–8 eggs; 2–3 broods; April–July.

FEEDING Forages for insects and spiders in trees and shrubs, gardens, and yards.

SIMILAR SPECIES

WINTER WREN see p.321 shorter tail

dark brown overall

heavily barred flanks

NESTING MATERIAL This small bird has brought an unusually large twig to its nest inside an old woodpecker hole.

OCCURRENCE Breeds in cities, towns, parks, farms, yards, gardens, and woodland edges. Rarely seen during migration period (late July to early October). Winters south of its breeding range, from southern US to Mexico, in woodlands, shrubby areas, and weedy fields. Nests, or is resident as far south as Tierra del Fuego.

| Length **4½in (11.5cm)** | Wingspan **6in (15cm)** | Weight **⅜oz (11g)** |
| Social **Solitary** | Lifespan **Up to 9 years** | Status **Secure** |

DATE SEEN	WHERE		NOTES

| Order **Passeriformes** | Family **Polioptilidae** | Species *Polioptila caerulea* |

Blue-gray Gnatcatcher

MALE

paler
upperparts

lacks black line

blue-gray
nape

black
line above
eye; absent
in winter

FEMALE

pale gray
overall

white
outer tail
feathers

IN FLIGHT

white
eye-ring

blue-gray
upperparts

white
throat

black central
tail feathers

pale patch
on wing

pale gray
underparts

MALE

FLIGHT: short, straight and fluttering; usually in short bursts from tree-top to tree-top.

If it did not give its continual wheezy call, the Blue-gray Gnatcatcher might often be missed, as it spends much of its time foraging high up in tall trees. In winter it becomes even harder to find as it is generally silent. This species is the most northern of the North American gnatcatchers and is also the only one to migrate. It can exhibit aggressive behavior and is capable of driving off considerably larger birds than itself. The range of the Blue-gray Gnatcatcher appears to be expanding and populations are increasing.

VOICE Call soft, irregular *zhee, zhee*, uttered constantly while foraging; song soft combination of short notes and nasal wheezes.

NESTING Cup of plant fibers, spider webs, mosses; usually high on branch; lined with soft plant material; 4–5 eggs; 1–2 broods; April–June.

FEEDING Forages for small insects and spiders by acrobatically flitting from twig to twig, while twitching long tail.

LISTEN CLOSELY
The rather faint complex song is best heard when the bird is singing from a low perch.

SIMILAR SPECIES

BLACK-TAILED GNATCATCHER
see p.463

black
cap

tail
white
only at
tip

short
tail

TENNESSEE WARBLER
see p.357

greenish
upperparts

no eye-
ring

white
underparts

OCCURRENCE
In eastern North America, breeds in deciduous or pine woodlands; in the West, in scrubby habitats, often near water. Winters in brushy habitats in southern US, Mexico, and Central America. Also breeds in Mexico, Belize, and the Bahamas.

| Length **4¼in (11cm)** | Wingspan **6in (15cm)** | Weight **7⁄32oz (6g)** |
| Social **Solitary/Flocks** | Lifespan **At least 4 years** | Status **Secure** |

DATE SEEN	WHERE	NOTES

| Order **Passeriformes** | Family **Sittidae** | Species *Sitta pusilla* |

Brown-headed Nuthatch

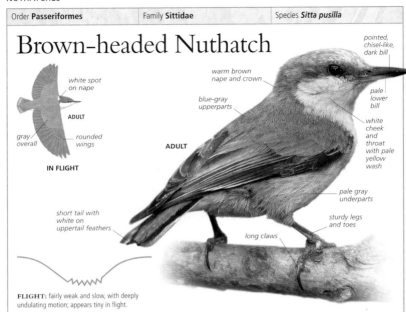

pointed, chisel-like, dark bill

white spot on nape

ADULT

gray overall

rounded wings

IN FLIGHT

warm brown nape and crown

blue-gray upperparts

ADULT

pale lower bill

white cheek and throat with pale yellow wash

pale gray underparts

sturdy legs and toes

long claws

short tail with white on uppertail feathers

FLIGHT: fairly weak and slow, with deeply undulating motion; appears tiny in flight.

This pine-loving species is the southeastern counterpart of the western Pygmy Nuthatch, but separated from it by the Great Plains. In most aspects of their history, these two nuthatch species are very similar and play the same ecological roles in their respective ecosystems. Like the Pygmy, the Brown-headed is a busy bird that travels in noisy packs. In each species, the young are raised by both parents and one or more nonparental relatives, or "helpers."

VOICE Call a short *bek*; foraging flocks *bwee! tutututu*, emphatic first note followed by soft series; chorus of sounds when calling in flocks.

NESTING Excavates cavity in pine tree; nest of plant material lined with fur and feathers; 4–6 eggs; 1–2 broods; March–May.

FEEDING Forages high in pine trees; in summer, gleans beetles, bugs, other insects, and also spiders; in winter, supplements diet with pine seeds.

INTREPID FORAGING
The Brown-headed Nuthatch forages upside down along branches, and head-first down tree trunks.

SIMILAR SPECIES

PYGMY NUTHATCH

grayish crown

pale yellowish wash

PERCHED ADULT
This bird depends upon forest tracts with standing dead wood and snags for nesting.

OCCURRENCE
Breeds in pine forests and oak-pine woods in southeastern US: Delaware, Virginia, and Maryland southward to Florida, westward to Oklahoma and Texas; also in the Bahamas. Prefers old and extensive forest stands with dead trunks for nesting. Resident; small groups wander in fall, but not far from breeding areas.

| Length **4¼in (11cm)** | Wingspan **8in (20cm)** | Weight **⅜oz (10g)** |
| Social **Small flocks** | Lifespan **Up to 2 years** | Status **Declining** |

DATE SEEN	WHERE	NOTES

| Order **Passeriformes** | Family **Sittidae** | Species *Sitta canadensis* |

Red-breasted Nuthatch

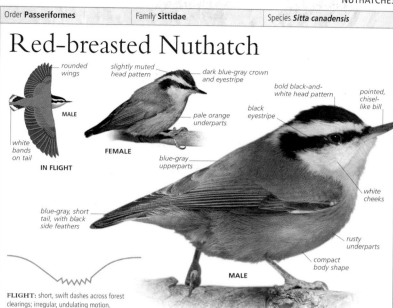

rounded wings

MALE

white bands on tail

IN FLIGHT

slightly muted head pattern

dark blue-gray crown and eyestripe

pale orange underparts

FEMALE

blue-gray upperparts

bold black-and-white head pattern

black eyestripe

pointed, chisel-like bill

white cheeks

blue-gray, short tail, with black side feathers

rusty underparts

compact body shape

MALE

FLIGHT: short, swift dashes across forest clearings; irregular, undulating motion.

This aggressive, inquisitive nuthatch, with its distinctive black eyestripe, breeds in conifer forests across North America. The bird inhabits mountains in the West; in the East, it is found in lowlands and hills. However, sometimes it breeds in conifer groves away from its core range. Each fall, birds move from their main breeding grounds, but the extent of this exodus varies from year to year, depending on population cycles and food availability.
VOICE Call a one-note tooting sound, often repeated, with strong nasal yet musical quality: *aaank, enk, ink,* rather like a horn.
NESTING Excavates cavity in pine tree; nest of grass lined with feathers, with sticky pine resin applied to entrance; 5–7 eggs, 1 brood; May–July.
FEEDING Probes bark for beetle grubs; also eats insect larvae found on conifer needles; seeds in winter.

TASTY GRUB
This nuthatch has just extracted its dinner from the bark of a tree, a favorite foraging habitat.

SIMILAR SPECIES

BROWN-HEADED NUTHATCH
see p.324

brown nape

slightly smaller overall

pale gray

WHITE-BREASTED NUTHATCH
see p.326

larger overall

lacks black eye-stripe

white belly

chestnut undertail

OCCURRENCE
Found year-round in coniferous and mixed hardwood forests. During breeding season, absent from southeastern pine forests, except in the Appalachians. In the west, shares its habitat with Pygmy Nuthatch, but ranges to higher elevations.

| Length **4¼in (11cm)** | Wingspan **8½in (22cm)** | Weight **⅜–⁷⁄₁₆oz (10–13g)** |
| Social **Solitary/Pairs** | Lifespan **Up to 7 years** | Status **Secure** |

DATE SEEN	WHERE	NOTES

| Order **Passeriformes** | Family **Sittidae** | Species **Sitta carolinensis** |

White-breasted Nuthatch

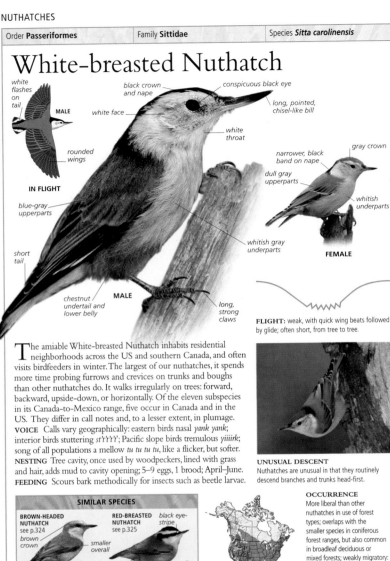

white flashes on tail

MALE

black crown and nape

conspicuous black eye

white face

long, pointed, chisel-like bill

white throat

IN FLIGHT

rounded wings

blue-gray upperparts

short tail

chestnut undertail and lower belly

MALE

long, strong claws

whitish gray underparts

narrower, black band on nape

gray crown

dull gray upperparts

whitish underparts

FEMALE

FLIGHT: weak, with quick wing beats followed by glide; often short, from tree to tree.

The amiable White-breasted Nuthatch inhabits residential neighborhoods across the US and southern Canada, and often visits birdfeeders in winter. The largest of our nuthatches, it spends more time probing furrows and crevices on trunks and boughs than other nuthatches do. It walks irregularly on trees: forward, backward, upside-down, or horizontally. Of the eleven subspecies in its Canada-to-Mexico range, five occur in Canada and in the US. They differ in call notes and, to a lesser extent, in plumage.
VOICE Calls vary geographically: eastern birds nasal *yank yank*; interior birds stuttering *st't't't'*; Pacific slope birds tremulous *yiiiirk*; song of all populations a mellow *tu tu tu tu*, like a flicker, but softer.
NESTING Tree cavity, once used by woodpeckers, lined with grass and hair, adds mud to cavity opening; 5–9 eggs, 1 brood; April–June.
FEEDING Scours bark methodically for insects such as beetle larvae.

UNUSUAL DESCENT
Nuthatches are unusual in that they routinely descend branches and trunks head-first.

OCCURRENCE
More liberal than other nuthatches in use of forest types; overlaps with the smaller species in coniferous forest ranges, but also common in broadleaf deciduous or mixed forests; weakly migratory: little movement in most falls, but moderate departures from breeding grounds in some years.

SIMILAR SPECIES

BROWN-HEADED NUTHATCH see p.324

brown crown

smaller overall

RED-BREASTED NUTHATCH see p.325

black eye-stripe

smaller overall

reddish underparts

| Length **5¾in (14.5cm)** | Wingspan **11in (28cm)** | Weight **¹¹⁄₁₆–⅞oz (19–25g)** |
| Social **Solitary/Pairs** | Lifespan **Up to 9 years** | Status **Secure** |

DATE SEEN	WHERE	NOTES

| Order **Passeriformes** | Family **Certhiidae** | Species **Certhia americana** |

Brown Creeper

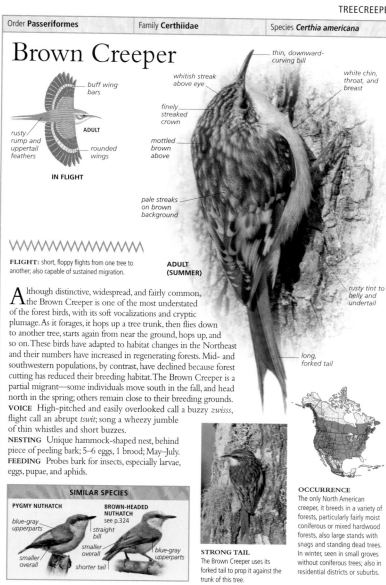

buff wing bars

ADULT

rusty rump and uppertail feathers

rounded wings

IN FLIGHT

thin, downward-curving bill

whitish streak above eye

finely streaked crown

mottled brown above

white chin, throat, and breast

pale streaks on brown background

FLIGHT: short, floppy flights from one tree to another; also capable of sustained migration.

ADULT (SUMMER)

rusty tint to belly and undertail

long, forked tail

Although distinctive, widespread, and fairly common, the Brown Creeper is one of the most understated of the forest birds, with its soft vocalizations and cryptic plumage. As it forages, it hops up a tree trunk, then flies down to another tree, starts again from near the ground, hops up, and so on. These birds have adapted to habitat changes in the Northeast and their numbers have increased in regenerating forests. Mid- and southwestern populations, by contrast, have declined because forest cutting has reduced their breeding habitat. The Brown Creeper is a partial migrant—some individuals move south in the fall, and head north in the spring; others remain close to their breeding grounds.

VOICE High-pitched and easily overlooked call a buzzy *zwiss*, flight call an abrupt *tswit*; song a wheezy jumble of thin whistles and short buzzes.

NESTING Unique hammock-shaped nest, behind piece of peeling bark; 5–6 eggs, 1 brood; May–July.

FEEDING Probes bark for insects, especially larvae, eggs, pupae, and aphids.

SIMILAR SPECIES

PYGMY NUTHATCH

blue-gray upperparts

smaller overall

BROWN-HEADED NUTHATCH
see p.324

straight bill

smaller overall

blue-gray upperparts

shorter tail

STRONG TAIL
The Brown Creeper uses its forked tail to prop it against the trunk of this tree.

OCCURRENCE
The only North American creeper, it breeds in a variety of forests, particularly fairly moist coniferous or mixed hardwood forests, also large stands with snags and standing dead trees. In winter, seen in small groves without coniferous trees; also in residential districts or suburbs.

| Length **5¼in (13.5cm)** | Wingspan **8in (20cm)** | Weight **¼–⅜oz (7–10g)** |
| Social **Solitary** | Lifespan **Up to 4 years** | Status **Secure** |

DATE SEEN	WHERE		NOTES

| Order **Passeriformes** | Family **Mimidae** | Species ***Dumetella carolinensis*** |

Gray Catbird

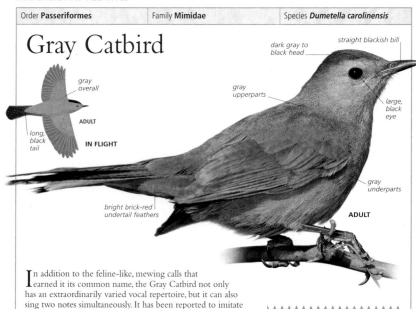

straight blackish bill

dark gray to black head

gray overall

gray upperparts

large, black eye

ADULT

IN FLIGHT

long, black tail

gray underparts

bright brick-red undertail feathers

ADULT

In addition to the feline-like, mewing calls that earned it its common name, the Gray Catbird not only has an extraordinarily varied vocal repertoire, but it can also sing two notes simultaneously. It has been reported to imitate the vocalizations of over 40 bird species, at least one frog species, and several sounds produced by machines and electronic devices. Despite their shy, retiring nature, Gray Catbirds tolerate human presence and will rest in shrubs in suburban and urban lots. Another fascinating skill is the Gray Catbird's ability to recognize and remove eggs of the brood parasite, the Brown-headed Cowbird.

VOICE *Mew* call, like a young kitten; song a long, complex series of unhurried, often grouped notes, sometimes interspersed with whistles and squeaks.

NESTING Large, untidy cup of woven twigs, grass, and hair lined with finer material; 3–4 eggs; 1–2 broods; May–August.

FEEDING Feeds on a wide variety of berries and insects, usually whatever is most abundant in season.

FLIGHT: short flights between habitat patches with constant, medium-speed wing beats.

ANGLED ATTITUDE
Between bouts of feeding, a Gray Catbird often rests with its body and tail at a 50-degree angle.

LARGE BLACK EYES
Peering from the foliage, a Gray Catbird investigates its surroundings.

OCCURRENCE
Breeds in mixed young to mid-aged forests with abundant undergrowth, from British Columbia east to Maritimes and Newfoundland, and in the US diagonally west-east from Washington State to New Mexico, east to the Gulf Coast, north to New England. Northern population migratory.

SIMILAR SPECIES

NORTHERN MOCKINGBIRD
see p.329
white wing patch
longer tail edged in white

CRISSAL THRASHER
longer, curved bill
brown-gray overall
lighter gray

| Length **8–9½in (20–24cm)** | Wingspan **10–12in (25–30cm)** | Weight **1¼–2⅛oz (35–60g)** |
| Social **Solitary/Pairs** | Lifespan **Up to 11 years** | Status **Secure** |

DATE SEEN	WHERE		NOTES

| Order **Passeriformes** | Family **Mimidae** | Species **Mimus polyglottos** |

Northern Mockingbird

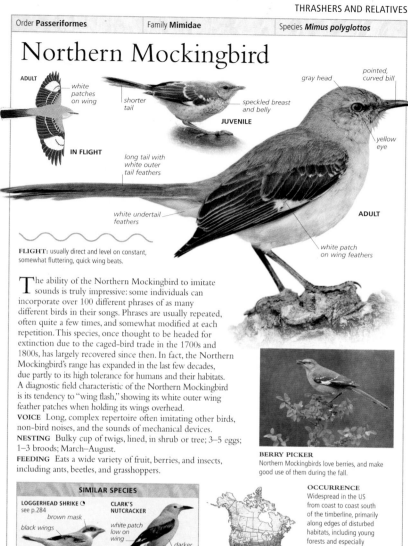

ADULT

white patches on wing

shorter tail

speckled breast and belly

JUVENILE

gray head

pointed, curved bill

IN FLIGHT

yellow eye

long tail with white outer tail feathers

white undertail feathers

ADULT

white patch on wing feathers

FLIGHT: usually direct and level on constant, somewhat fluttering, quick wing beats.

The ability of the Northern Mockingbird to imitate sounds is truly impressive: some individuals can incorporate over 100 different phrases of as many different birds in their songs. Phrases are usually repeated, often quite a few times, and somewhat modified at each repetition. This species, once thought to be headed for extinction due to the caged-bird trade in the 1700s and 1800s, has largely recovered since then. In fact, the Northern Mockingbird's range has expanded in the last few decades, due partly to its high tolerance for humans and their habitats. A diagnostic field characteristic of the Northern Mockingbird is its tendency to "wing flash," showing its white outer wing feather patches when holding its wings overhead.
VOICE Long, complex repertoire often imitating other birds, non-bird noises, and the sounds of mechanical devices.
NESTING Bulky cup of twigs, lined, in shrub or tree; 3–5 eggs; 1–3 broods; March–August.
FEEDING Eats a wide variety of fruit, berries, and insects, including ants, beetles, and grasshoppers.

BERRY PICKER
Northern Mockingbirds love berries, and make good use of them during the fall.

SIMILAR SPECIES

LOGGERHEAD SHRIKE ◐
see p.284

brown mask

black wings

CLARK'S NUTCRACKER

white patch low on wing

darker gray belly

whiter sides to tail

OCCURRENCE
Widespread in the US from coast to coast south of the timberline, primarily along edges of disturbed habitats, including young forests and especially suburban and urban areas with shrubs or hedges.

| Length 8½–10in (22–25cm) | Wingspan **13–15in (33–38cm)** | Weight 1⁹⁄₁₆–2oz (45–55g) |
| Social **Pairs** | Lifespan **Up to 20 years** | Status **Secure** |

DATE SEEN	WHERE	NOTES

| Order **Passeriformes** | Family **Mimidae** | Species *Toxostoma rufum* |

Brown Thrasher

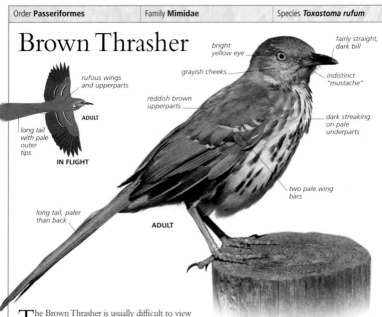

bright yellow eye

grayish cheeks

fairly straight, dark bill

indistinct "mustache"

rufous wings and upperparts

reddish brown upperparts

dark streaking on pale underparts

ADULT

long tail with pale outer tips

IN FLIGHT

two pale wing bars

long tail, paler than back

ADULT

The Brown Thrasher is usually difficult to view clearly because it keeps to dense underbrush. Like most other thrashers, this species prefers running or hopping to flying. When nesting, it can recognize and remove the eggs of brood parasites like the Brown-headed Cowbird. The current population decline is most likely the result of fragmentation of large, wooded habitats into patches, which lack the forest interior habitat this species needs.

VOICE Calls varied, including rasping sounds; song a long series of musical notes, sometimes imitating other species; repeats phrase twice before moving onto the next one.

NESTING Bulky cup of twigs, close to ground, lined with leaves, grass, bark; 3–5 eggs; 1 brood; April–July.

FEEDING Mainly insects (especially beetles) and worms gathered from leaf litter on the forest floor; will peck at cultivated grains, nuts, berries, and fruit.

FLIGHT: slow and heavy with deep wing beats; below treetops, especially in and around ground.

OCCURRENCE
Widespread across central and eastern North America, from Canada to Texas and Florida, in a variety of densely wooded habitats, particularly those with thick undergrowth, but will use woodland edges, hedges, and riverside trees. A partial migrant, it winters in the southern part of its range.

SIMILAR SPECIES

LONG-BILLED THRASHER
see p.464

duller brown back

longer, curved bill

heavily streaked underparts

CURVE-BILLED THRASHER
see p.464

mouse gray-brown upperparts

orange eye

pale brown spots, not streaks

STREAKED BREAST
Displaying its heavily streaked underparts, this Brown Thrasher is perched and ready to sing.

| Length **10–12in (25–30cm)** | Wingspan **11–14in (28–36cm)** | Weight **2⅛–2⅞oz (60–80g)** |
| Social **Solitary/Flocks** | Lifespan **Up to 13 years** | Status **Declining** |

DATE SEEN	WHERE	NOTES

| Order **Passeriformes** | Family **Sturnidae** | Species *Sturnus vulgaris* |

European Starling

short, square tail

pointed, triangular wings

ADULT (BREEDING)

IN FLIGHT

body feathers tipped whitish or buff

wing feathers edged bright orange-buff

large spots on undertail

ADULT (NONBREEDING)

glossy black body with mostly green sheen

black face with hints of shiny, glossy purple

blue-based, sharp, yellow bill; pink-based on female

dark, glossy, blue-black belly

MALE (BREEDING)

long, pinkish brown legs and strong toes

dull brownish head

dark bill

plain brown body

IMMATURE (FALL)

JUVENILE

This distinctive non-native species is perhaps the most successful bird in North America—and probably the most maligned. In the 1890s, 100 European Starlings were released in New York City's Central Park; these were the ancestors of the many millions of birds that now live all across the US. This adaptable and aggressive bird competes with native species for nest sites, and the starling usually wins—even against larger species such as the Northern Flicker.

VOICE Highly varied; gives whooshing *sssssheer*, often in flight; also whistled *wheeeooo*; song an elaborate pulsing series with slurred whistles and clicking notes; imitates other species' vocalizations.

NESTING Natural or artificial cavity of any sort; 4–6 eggs; 1–2 broods; March–July.

FEEDING Omnivorous; picks at anything that might be edible; insects and berries are common food items; also visits birdfeeders and trashcans; often feeds on grubs in lawns.

~~~vvv~~~

FLIGHT: individuals fly in direct, buzzy manner; flocks bunch up tightly in flight.

INSECT EATER
Despite its parents' omnivorous diet, the nestlings are fed almost exclusively on insects and larvae.

SIMILAR SPECIES

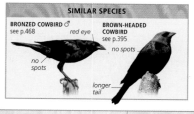

BRONZED COWBIRD ♂ see p.468

red eye

no spots

BROWN-HEADED COWBIRD see p.395

no spots

longer tail

OCCURRENCE
In North America from southern Canada to the US–Mexico border; also Puerto Rico and other Caribbean islands. Common to abundant in cities, towns, and farmlands; also occurs in relatively "wild" settings far from human habitation. Forms flocks at all times, huge in winter.

| Length **8½in (21cm)** | Wingspan **16in (41cm)** | Weight **2⅝– 3⅜oz (75–95g)** |
| Social **Colonies** | Lifespan **Up to 17 years** | Status **Secure** |

DATE SEEN	WHERE	NOTES
....	....	....
....	....	....
....	....	....
....	....	....
....	....	....

THRUSHES

MOST THRUSHES ARE medium-sized brown-or olive-brown-backed birds with varying amounts of spotting underneath. Although undistinguished in color, they more than make up for their drab plumage with beautiful flutelike songs. By contrast, the Varied Thrush, which is the sole member of the genus *Ixoreus*, differs dramatically from other thrushes with its bold black-and-rust pattern, and is one of the most distinctive birds in North America. The brightly colored bluebirds, target of successful conservation efforts, and the duller Townsend's Solitaire both stand out from other thrushes. Thrushes are insectivorous during the breeding season, but have a varied diet at other times, including berries, fruit, snails, and other small invertebrates. Most thrushes are long-distance migrants and spend the northern winter in tropical America.

ORCHARD DWELLER
Bluebirds, for example this Mountain Bluebird, favor orchards far more than other thrushes. This species is rare in the East.

GROUND BIRDS
Though they perch to sing, thrushes, including this Varied Thrush, spend a lot of their time on or near the ground. Varied Thrushes are rare in the East.

PIPITS & DIPPERS

PIPITS
The two species of pipits that breed in North America largely spend the winter south of their breeding range. They are very much birds of open, treeless country—one North American pipit species is montane and arctic, while the other is restricted to the Great Plains.

DIPPERS
Dippers (five species worldwide) are the only song birds that feed underwater. The only North American species of dipper occurs from Alaska in the north, southward through British Colombia to the mountain states of the West, and south to Mexico and Panama. Although they do not breed in the East, dippers dave been recorded in the Great Plains east to Minnesota.

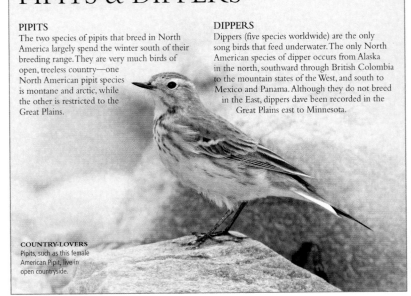

COUNTRY-LOVERS
Pipits, such as this female American Pipit, live in open countryside.

Order **Passeriformes**	Family **Turdidae**	Species *Sialia sialis*

Eastern Bluebird

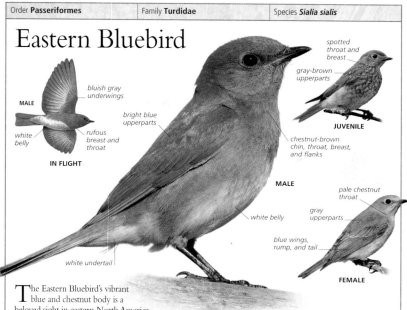

MALE

bluish gray underwings

bright blue upperparts

white belly

rufous breast and throat

IN FLIGHT

white undertail

white belly

MALE

chestnut-brown chin, throat, breast, and flanks

spotted throat and breast

gray-brown upperparts

JUVENILE

pale chestnut throat

gray upperparts

blue wings, rump, and tail

FEMALE

The Eastern Bluebird's vibrant blue and chestnut body is a beloved sight in eastern North America, especially after the remarkable comeback of the species in the past 30 years. It is also New York's State Bird. After much of the bird's habitat was eliminated by agriculture in the mid-1900s, volunteers offered the bluebirds nest boxes as alternatives to their tree cavities, and they took to these like ducks to water. The Eastern Bluebird's mating system involves males seeking (or not minding) multiple partners.

VOICE Main song a melodious series of soft, whistled notes; *churr-wi* or *churr-li*; songs for mating and asserting territoriality.

NESTING Cavity nester, in trees or man-made boxes; nest of grass lined with grass, weeds, and twigs; uses old nests of other species; 3–7 eggs; 2 broods; February–September.

FEEDING Feeds on insects, like grasshoppers, and caterpillars in breeding season; in winter, also takes fruit and plants.

FLIGHT: shallow wing beats; slow and easy.

HOME DELIVERY
A female bluebird delivers food to a nest box.

SIMILAR SPECIES

WESTERN BLUEBIRD ♀

brownish back

grayish throat

MOUNTAIN BLUEBIRD ♀
see p.472

gray-brown head and body

OCCURRENCE
Found in eastern Canada and the eastern US, where it lives in clearings and woodland edges; occupies multiple open habitats in rural, urban, and suburban areas: woodlands, plains, orchards, parks, and spacious lawns. Breeds and winters across the eastern half of the US.

Length **6–8in (15–20cm)**	Wingspan **10–13in (25–33cm)**	Weight **1 1/16 oz (30g)**
Social **Flocks**	Lifespan **8–10 years**	Status **Vulnerable**

DATE SEEN	WHERE	NOTES

| Order **Passeriformes** | Family **Turdidae** | Species *Catharus fuscescens* |

Veery

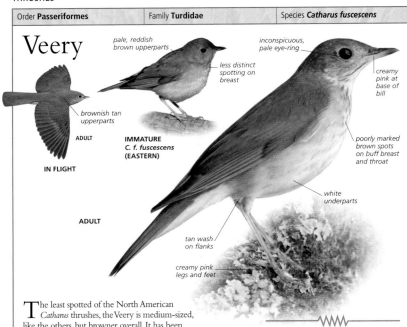

pale, reddish brown upperparts

less distinct spotting on breast

inconspicuous, pale eye-ring

creamy pink at base of bill

brownish tan upperparts

ADULT

IN FLIGHT

IMMATURE
C. f. fuscescens
(EASTERN)

poorly marked brown spots on buff breast and throat

white underparts

ADULT

tan wash on flanks

creamy pink legs and feet

The least spotted of the North American *Catharus* thrushes, the Veery is medium-sized, like the others, but browner overall. It has been described as "dusky," but there is a geographical variation in duskiness; four subspecies have been described to reflect this. The Veery is a long-distance migrant, spending the northern winter months in central Brazil, in a variety of tropical habitats.

VOICE A series of descending *da-vee-ur*, *vee-ur*, *veer*, *veer*, somewhat bi-tonal, sounding like the name Veery; call a rather soft *veer*.

NESTING Cup of dead leaves, bark, weed stems, and moss on or near ground; 4 eggs; 1–2 broods; May–July.

FEEDING Forages on the ground for insects, spiders, snails; eats fruit and berries after breeding.

FLIGHT: rapid and straight, with intermittent hops and glides; makes long hops when on ground.

DAMP DWELLINGS
The Veery breeds in damp habitats such as moist wooded areas or in trees near or in swamps.

OCCURRENCE
In summer, mainly found in damp deciduous forests, but in some places habitat near rivers preferred. In winter, choice of habitat flexible; found in tropical broadleaf evergreen forest, on forest edges, in open woodlands, and in second-growth areas regenerating after fires or clearing.

SIMILAR SPECIES

| **GRAY-CHEEKED THRUSH** see p.335 | gray face | **BICKNELL'S THRUSH** see p.336 | bold brown breast spots | **SWAINSON'S THRUSH** see p.337 | buffy-colored face |
| bold black-brown breast spots | | grayish brown upperparts | | bold brown-black breast spots | |

| Length **7in (18cm)** | Wingspan **11–11½in (28–29cm)** | Weight **1¹⁄₁₆–2oz (28–54g)** |
| Social **Pairs** | Lifespan **Up to 10 years** | Status **Declining** |

DATE SEEN	WHERE	NOTES

| Order **Passeriformes** | Family **Turdidae** | Species *Catharus minimus* |

Gray-cheeked Thrush

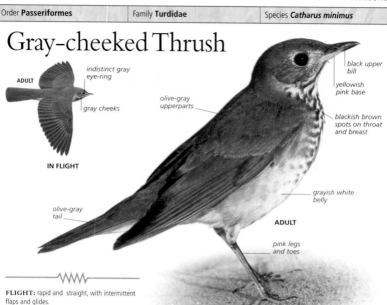

ADULT

indistinct gray
eye-ring

gray cheeks

IN FLIGHT

olive-gray
tail

black upper
bill

yellowish
pink base

olive-gray
upperparts

blackish brown
spots on throat
and breast

grayish white
belly

ADULT

pink legs
and toes

FLIGHT: rapid and straight, with intermittent
flaps and glides.

The Gray-cheeked Thrush is the least known of the four North American *Cathanus* thrushes because it breeds in remote areas of Canada and Alaska. In fact, most of the existing information on this species is a result of research on the Bicknell's Thrush, which was considered to be a subspecies of the Gray-cheeked Thrush until 1993. During migration, the Gray-cheeked Thrush is more likely to be heard in flight at night than seen on the ground by birdwatchers.
VOICE Call a thin *kweer*, sometimes two notes; song flute-like, somewhat nasal, several notes ending on a lower pitch.
NESTING Cup of grass, twigs, moss, dead leaves, and mud, placed near ground in shrubbery; 4 eggs; 1 brood; May–July.
FEEDING Forages insects, including beetles, ants, spiders, earthworms; and also fruit.

FEEDING HABITAT
A Gray-cheeked Thrush hops across the forest floor looking for prey.

SIMILAR SPECIES

BICKNELL'S THRUSH
see p.336

olive-brown
upperparts

brownish
spots

MIGRATION PATTERN
During migration, this bird can be seen near a variety of sites with trees or shrubs.

OCCURRENCE
On breeding grounds occupies densely vegetated areas with small shrubs; preference for spruce forests in northern Canada and Alaska. During migration, favors wooded areas with dense understory. In winter, prefers forested areas and secondary succession woodlands.

| Length **6½–7in (16–18cm)** | Wingspan **11½–13½in (29–34cm)** | Weight **⅞–1¹⁄₁₆ oz (26–30g)** |
| Social **Mixed flocks** | Lifespan **Up to 7 years** | Status **Secure** |

DATE SEEN	WHERE	NOTES

Order **Passeriformes**	Family **Turdidae**	Species *Catharus bicknelli*

Bicknell's Thrush

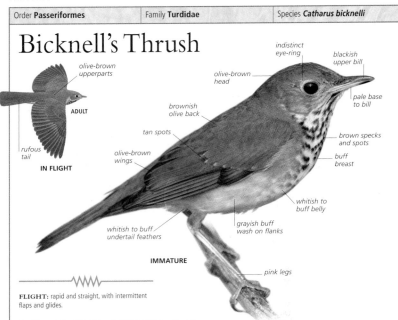

olive-brown upperparts

ADULT

IN FLIGHT

rufous tail

indistinct eye-ring

blackish upper bill

olive-brown head

olive-brown head

pale base to bill

brownish olive back

tan spots

brown specks and spots

olive-brown wings

buff breast

whitish to buff belly

whitish to buff undertail feathers

grayish buff wash on flanks

IMMATURE

pink legs

FLIGHT: rapid and straight, with intermittent flaps and glides.

Named for E.P. Bicknell (1859-1925), a founding member of the American Ornithologists' Union, Bicknell's Thrush was considered a subspecies of the Gray-cheeked Thrush. In 1993, it was shown to be a distinct species with slight differences in color, song, habitat, and migration. In the field, it is best distinguished from the Gray-cheeked Thrush by its song, which is less full and lower in pitch. Bicknell's Thrush breeds only in dwarf conifer forests on mountain tops in the northeastern US and adjacent Canada. Habitat loss threatens this species on its wintering grounds in Cuba, Hispaniola, and Puerto Rico. Males and females mate with multiple partners in a single season; because of this, males may care for young in multiple nests.
VOICE Call *pheeuw*, one or two notes; complicated flute-like song of about four parts, ending with rising pitch; males sing, especially during flight.

NESTING Cup of moss and evergreen twigs, near ground; 3–4 eggs; 1 brood; June–August.
FEEDING Feeds mainly on caterpillars and insects; eats fruit during migration and possibly in winter.

MOUNTAIN-TOP BREEDING
This species breeds in high-elevation woodland areas, especially in conifers.

SIMILAR SPECIES

GRAY-CHEEKED THRUSH
see p.335
olive-gray brown

grayish face

OCCURRENCE
Restricted to dense spruce or fir forest at or near the treeline, at 3,000ft (1,000m), often in disturbed areas undergoing successional changes. During migration, found in a variety of habitats, such as woodlots and beaches. In winter, strong preference for wet mountain Caribbean forests.

Length **6½–7in (16–18cm)**	Wingspan **12in (30cm)**	Weight **⅞–1¹⁄₁₆ oz (26–30g)**
Social **Solitary/Small flocks**	Lifespan **Up to 8 years**	Status **Vulnerable**

DATE SEEN	WHERE	NOTES

| Order **Passeriformes** | Family **Turdidae** | Species *Catharus ustulatus* |

Swainson's Thrush

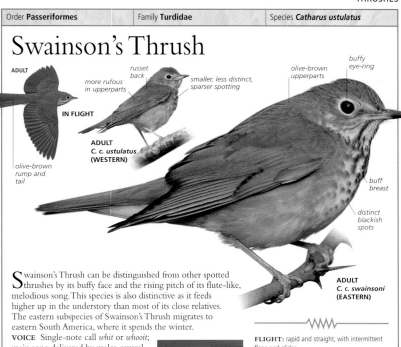

ADULT

IN FLIGHT

olive-brown rump and tail

more rufous in upperparts

russet back

smaller, less distinct, sparser spotting

ADULT
C. c. ustulatus
(WESTERN)

olive-brown upperparts

buffy eye-ring

buff breast

distinct blackish spots

ADULT
C. c. swainsoni
(EASTERN)

Swainson's Thrush can be distinguished from other spotted thrushes by its buffy face and the rising pitch of its flute-like, melodious song. This species is also distinctive as it feeds higher up in the understory than most of its close relatives. The eastern subspecies of Swainson's Thrush migrates to eastern South America, where it spends the winter.

VOICE Single-note call *whit* or *whooit*; main song delivered by males, several phrases, each one spiraling upward; flute-like song is given during breeding and migration.

NESTING Open cup of twigs, moss, dead leaves, bark, and mud, on branches near trunks of small trees or in shrubs; 3–4 eggs; 1–2 broods; April–July.

FEEDING Forages in the air, using fly-catching methods to capture a wide range of insects during breeding season; berries during migration and in winter.

FLIGHT: rapid and straight, with intermittent flaps and glides.

DISTINCTIVE SONG
This bird's song distinguishes it from other thrushes.

TREE DWELLER
Shy and retiring, Swainson's Thrush feeds higher in trees than other *Catharus* thrushes.

SIMILAR SPECIES

VEERY
see p.334

tawny brown back

HERMIT THRUSH
see p.338

lightly spotted breast

rust-colored tail

grayish cheeks

streaks on sides of breast

OCCURRENCE
Breeds mainly in coniferous forests, especially spruce and fir, except in California, where it prefers deciduous riverine woodlands and damp meadows with shrubbery. During spring and fall migrations, dense understory is preferred. Winter habitat is mainly old-growth forest.

| Length **6½–7½in (16–19cm)** | Wingspan **11½–12in (29–31cm)** | Weight **⅞–1⁹⁄₁₆ oz (25–45g)** |
| Social **Pairs/Flocks** | Lifespan **Up to 11 years** | Status **Declining** |

DATE SEEN	WHERE	NOTES

Order **Passeriformes**	Family **Turdidae**	Species *Catharus guttatus*

Hermit Thrush

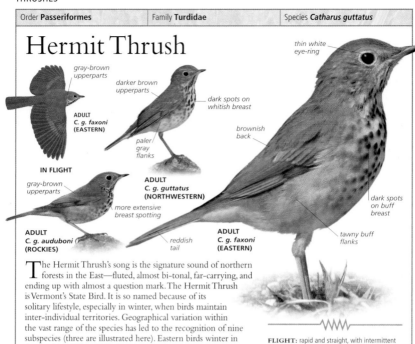

thin white eye-ring

gray-brown upperparts

darker brown upperparts

dark spots on whitish breast

brownish back

ADULT
C. g. faxoni
(EASTERN)

IN FLIGHT

paler gray flanks

ADULT
C. g. guttatus
(NORTHWESTERN)

dark spots on buff breast

gray-brown upperparts

more extensive breast spotting

ADULT
C. g. auduboni
(ROCKIES)

reddish tail

ADULT
C. g. faxoni
(EASTERN)

tawny buff flanks

The Hermit Thrush's song is the signature sound of northern forests in the East—fluted, almost bi-tonal, far-carrying, and ending up with almost a question mark. The Hermit Thrush is Vermont's State Bird. It is so named because of its solitary lifestyle, especially in winter, when birds maintain inter-individual territories. Geographical variation within the vast range of the species has led to the recognition of nine subspecies (three are illustrated here). Eastern birds winter in the southern US and Mexico.

FLIGHT: rapid and straight, with intermittent flaps and glides.

VOICE Calls *tchek*, soft, dry; song flute-like, ethereal, falling, repetitive, and varied; several phrases delivered on a different pitch.
NESTING Cup of grasses, mosses, twigs, leaves, mud, hair, on ground or in low tree branches; 4 eggs; 1–2 broods; May–July.
FEEDING Mainly forages on ground for insects, larvae, earthworms, and snails; in winter, also eats fruit.

URBAN VISITOR
This thrush is frequently seen in wooded areas in urban and suburban parks.

OCCURRENCE
Occurs in coniferous forests and mixed conifer–deciduous woodlands; prefers to nest along the edges of a forest interior, like a bog. During migration, found in many wooded habitats. Found in forest and other open woodlands during winter in Mexico.

SIMILAR SPECIES

VEERY
see p.334

tawny brown back

lightly spotted breast

BICKNELL'S TRUSH
see p.336

olive-brown back

yellow base of bill

SWAINSON'S THRUSH
see p.337

olive-brown upperparts

Length **6–7in (15–18cm)**	Wingspan **10–11in (25–28cm)**	Weight **⅞–1¹⁄₁₆ oz (25–30g)**
Social **Solitary**	Lifespan **Up to 9 years**	Status **Secure**

DATE SEEN	WHERE	NOTES

Order **Passeriformes**	Family **Turdidae**	Species *Hylocichla mustelina*

Wood Thrush

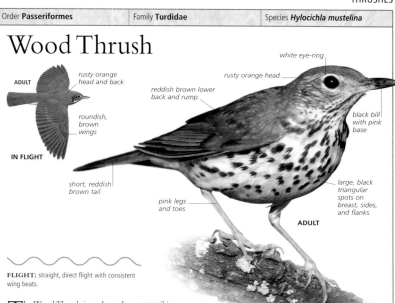

ADULT

rusty orange head and back

roundish, brown wings

IN FLIGHT

short, reddish brown tail

pink legs and toes

reddish brown lower back and rump

white eye-ring

rusty orange head

black bill with pink base

large, black triangular spots on breast, sides, and flanks

ADULT

FLIGHT: straight, direct flight with consistent wing beats.

The Wood Thrush is perhaps the most striking of the small North American thrushes, because of the triangular black spots that cover its underparts, and its rich rufous head and back. In the breeding season, its flute-like song echoes through the Northeastern hardwood forests and suburban wooded areas. Wood Thrush populations have sharply decreased over the past 30 years, as a direct result of forest destruction and fragmentation. Sadly, this decline has been exacerbated by its susceptibility to parasitism by the Brown-headed Cowbird.

VOICE Rapid *pip-pippipip* or *rhuu-rhuu*; a three-part flute-like song—first part indistinct, second part loudest, third part trilled; males have variations of all three parts; mainly before sunrise.

NESTING Cup-shaped nest made with dried grass and weeds in trees or shrubs; 3–4 eggs; 1–2 broods; May–July.

FEEDING Forages in leaf litter, mainly for worms, beetles, moths, caterpillars; eats fruit after breeding season.

STUNNING SOLOIST
The Wood Thrush can often be seen singing its melodious songs from a conspicuous perch.

SIMILAR SPECIES

VEERY
see p.334

smaller overall

longer tail

fainter spotting

HERMIT THRUSH
see p.338

reddish tail

spotting only on throat and upper breast

OCCURRENCE
Hardwood forests in the East, from Texas and Florida northward to Minnesota and the Canadian Maritimes. Breeds in interior and at edges of deciduous and mixed forests; needs dense understory, shrubbery, and moist soil. Winters in Texas, Louisiana, Florida, and south through Central America to Panama; also Cuba.

Length **7½–8½in (19–21cm)**	Wingspan **12–13½in (30–34cm)**	Weight **1⁷⁄₁₆–1¾oz (40–50g)**
Social **Pairs/Flocks**	Lifespan **Up to 9 years**	Status **Declining**

DATE SEEN	WHERE	NOTES

| Order **Passeriformes** | Family **Turdidae** | Species ***Turdus migratorius*** |

American Robin

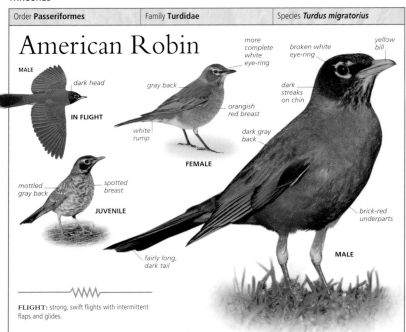

MALE

dark head

IN FLIGHT

more complete white eye-ring

gray back

orangish red breast

white rump

FEMALE

broken white eye-ring

yellow bill

dark streaks on chin

dark gray back

brick-red underparts

MALE

mottled gray back

spotted breast

JUVENILE

fairly long, dark tail

FLIGHT: strong, swift flights with intermittent flaps and glides.

The American Robin, the largest and most abundant of the North American thrushes, is probably also the most familiar bird across the entire continent. Its presence on suburban lawns is a clear sign of spring. Unlike other species, it has adapted and prospered in human-altered habitats. It breeds in the entire US and Canada, winters across the US, and migrates out of most of Canada in fall. The decision to migrate is largely governed by changes in the availability of food. As the breeding season approaches, it is the males that sing first, either late in winter or early spring. The bird's brick-red breast—more vivid in males than in females—is its most distinguishing feature.

VOICE Calls a high pitch *tjip* and a multi-note, throaty *tjuj-tjuk*; primary song a melodious *cheer-up, cheer-up, cheer-wee*, one of the first birds to be heard during the dawn chorus, and one of the last to cease singing in the evening.

NESTING Substantial cup of grass, weeds, twigs, strengthened with mud, in tree or shrub, in fork of tree, or on branch on tree; 4 eggs; 2–3 broods; April–July.

FEEDING Forages in leaf litter, mainly for earthworms and small insects; mostly consumes fruit in the winter season.

SEASONAL DIET
Robins are particularly dependent on the availability of fruit during the winter months.

OCCURRENCE
Breeding habitat a mix of forest, woodland, suburban gardens, lawns, municipal parks, and farms. A partial migrant, these robins tend to be found in woodlands where berry-bearing trees are present. Nonmigrating populations' winter habitat is similar to breeding habitat. Winters in Guatemala.

SIMILAR SPECIES

VARIED THRUSH
see p.472
bluish gray upperparts

orange eyebrow

wide black necklace

| Length **8–11in (20–28cm)** | Wingspan **12–16in (30–41cm)** | Weight **2⅝oz (75g)** |
| Social **Flocks** | Lifespan **Up to 13 years** | Status **Secure** |

DATE SEEN	WHERE		NOTES

| Order **Passeriformes** | Family **Passeridae** | Species ***Passer domesticus*** |

House Sparrow

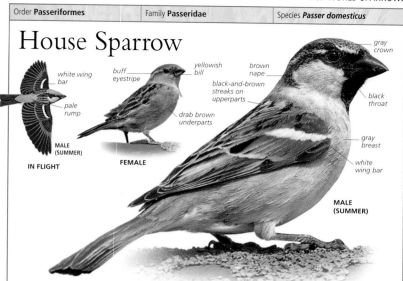

gray crown

white wing bar

pale rump

buff eyestripe

yellowish bill

brown nape

black-and-brown streaks on upperparts

black throat

drab brown underparts

gray breast

white wing bar

MALE (SUMMER)

IN FLIGHT

FEMALE

MALE (SUMMER)

This is the familiar "sparrow" of towns, cities, suburbs, and farms. The House Sparrow is not actually a sparrow as understood in North America, but rather, a member of a Eurasian family called the weaver-finches. It was first introduced in Brooklyn, New York, in 1850. From this modest beginning, and with the help of several other introductions up until the late 1860s, this hardy and aggressive bird eventually spread right through the North American continent. In a little more than 150 years, the House Sparrow has evolved and shows the same sort of geographic variation as some widespread native birds. It is pale in the arid Southwest, and darker in wetter regions.
VOICE Variety of calls, including a *cheery chirp*, a dull *jurv* and a rough *jigga*; song consists of *chirp* notes repeated endlessly.
NESTING Untidy mass of dried vegetable material in either natural or artificial cavities; 3–5 eggs; 2–3 broods; April–August.
FEEDING Mostly seeds; sometimes gleans insects and fruit.

FLIGHT: fast and bouncing, with rapid wing beats; short wings and tail give it a portly profile.

APTLY NAMED
This sparrow is seen near human structures—roofs, outbuildings, loading docks, curbs, and streetlights.

SIMILAR SPECIES

DICKCISSEL ♀
see p.437

pale bill

pale throat

yellowish highlights

DICKCISSEL ♂ ✳
see p.437

black and tan streaks

pale bill

OCCURRENCE
Flourishes in the downtown sections of cities and around human habitations, including agricultural outbuildings in remote areas of the continent. Found also in Mexico, Central and South America, and the West Indies. Also widespread in Eurasia, southeast Asia, North Africa, and Arabia.

| Length **6in (15.5cm)** | Wingspan **9½in (24cm)** | Weight **⅝–1¹⁄₁₆oz (18–30g)** |
| Social **Flocks** | Lifespan **Up to 7 years** | Status **Declining** |

DATE SEEN	WHERE	NOTES

341

PIPITS AND DIPPERS

| Order **Passeriformes** | Family **Motacillidae** | Species *Anthus rubescens* |

American Pipit

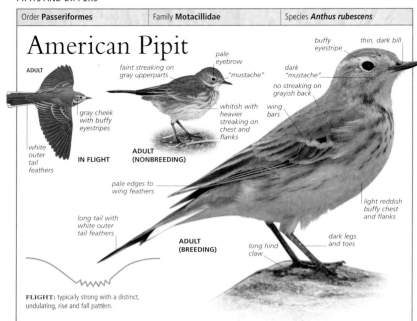

ADULT

faint streaking on
gray upperparts

pale
eyebrow

"mustache"

gray cheek
with buffy
eyestripes

white
outer
tail
feathers

IN FLIGHT

whitish with
heavier
streaking on
chest and
flanks

ADULT
(NONBREEDING)

buffy
eyestripe

thin, dark bill

dark
"mustache"

no streaking on
grayish back

wing
bars

light reddish
buffy chest
and flanks

pale edges to
wing feathers

long tail with
white outer
tail feathers

ADULT
(BREEDING)

long hind
claw

dark legs
and toes

FLIGHT: typically strong with a distinct,
undulating, rise and fall pattern.

The American Pipit is divided into four subspecies, three of
which breed in North America, and the fourth in Siberia.
In nonbreeding plumage, the American Pipit is a drab-looking,
brownish gray bird that forages for insects along waterways and
lake shores, or in cultivated fields with short stems. In the breeding
season, molting transforms it into a beauty—with gray upperparts
and reddish underparts. American Pipits are known for pumping
their tails up and down. When breeding, males display by rising
into the air, then flying down with wings open and singing. Its
migration takes the American Pipit as far south as Guatemala.
VOICE Alarm call a *tzeeep*; song repeated *tzwee-tzooo* from the air.
NESTING Cup in shallow depression on ground, outer frame of
grass, lined with fine grass and hair; 4–6 eggs; 1 brood; June–July.
FEEDING Picks insects; also eats seeds during migration.

WINTER DRAB
Foraging in short vegetation, this bird is almost
the same color as its surroundings.

SIMILAR SPECIES

HORNED LARK ◑
see p.313

less white
on tail
edge

SPRAGUE'S PIPIT
see p.343

heavy streaking
on back

less streaking
on throat
and chest

pale
cheeks
and throat

pale legs

OCCURRENCE
Breeds in Arctic tundra in the
north, and alpine tundra in
the Rockies; also breeds on
treeless mountaintops in
Maine and New Hampshire.
Winters in open coastal areas
and harvested agricultural
fields across the US. Some
North American migrants
fly to Asia for the winter.

| Length **6–8in (15–20cm)** | Wingspan **10–11in (25–28cm)** | Weight **¹¹⁄₁₆oz (20g)** |
| Social **Flocks** | Lifespan **Up to 6 years** | Status **Secure** |

DATE SEEN	WHERE	NOTES

| Order **Passeriformes** | Family **Motacillidae** | Species **Anthus spragueii** |

Sprague's Pipit

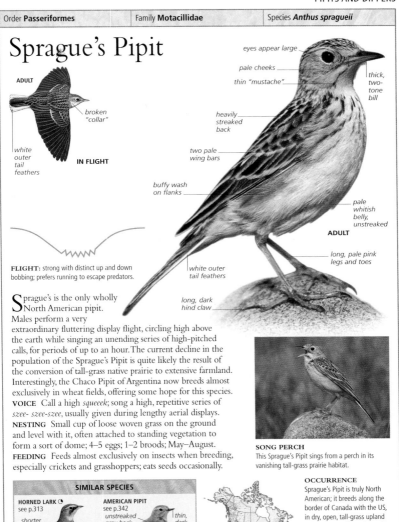

ADULT

IN FLIGHT

broken "collar"

white outer tail feathers

eyes appear large

pale cheeks

thin "mustache"

thick, two-tone bill

heavily streaked back

two pale wing bars

buffy wash on flanks

pale whitish belly, unstreaked

ADULT

long, pale pink legs and toes

FLIGHT: strong with distinct up and down bobbing; prefers running to escape predators.

white outer tail feathers

long, dark hind claw

Sprague's is the only wholly North American pipit. Males perform a very extraordinary fluttering display flight, circling high above the earth while singing an unending series of high-pitched calls, for periods of up to an hour. The current decline in the population of the Sprague's Pipit is quite likely the result of the conversion of tall-grass native prairie to extensive farmland. Interestingly, the Chaco Pipit of Argentina now breeds almost exclusively in wheat fields, offering some hope for this species.

VOICE Call a high *squeeek*; song a high, repetitive series of *szee- szee-szee*, usually given during lengthy aerial displays.

NESTING Small cup of loose woven grass on the ground and level with it, often attached to standing vegetation to form a sort of dome; 4–5 eggs; 1–2 broods; May–August.

FEEDING Feeds almost exclusively on insects when breeding, especially crickets and grasshoppers; eats seeds occasionally.

SONG PERCH
This Sprague's Pipit sings from a perch in its vanishing tall-grass prairie habitat.

OCCURRENCE
Sprague's Pipit is truly North American; it breeds along the border of Canada with the US, in dry, open, tall-grass upland habitat, especially native prairie systems in the northern part of the Great Plains; most birds migrate to Mexico in winter, where habitat is similar to breeding grounds.

SIMILAR SPECIES

HORNED LARK ♂
see p.313
shorter tail, less white

AMERICAN PIPIT
see p.342
unstreaked gray back

less-streaked on throat and chest

dark legs

thin, dark bill

streaked chest, belly and flanks

| Length **4–6in (10–15cm)** | Wingspan **6–8in (15–20cm)** | Weight **$^{11}/_{16}$–$^7/_8$oz (20–25g)** |
| Social **Solitary** | Lifespan **Unknown** | Status **Vulnerable** |

DATE SEEN	WHERE	NOTES

FINCHES

THE NAME "FINCHES" applies to the
Fringillidae, a family of seed-eating songbirds
that includes 16 species in North America.
They vary in size and shape from the small and
fragile-looking redpolls to the robust and chunky
Evening Grosbeak. Finch colors range from
whitish with some pink (redpolls) to gold
(American Goldfinch), bright red (crossbills),
and yellow, white, and black (Evening Grosbeak).
However, irrespective of body shape, size, and
color, all have conical
bills with razor-sharp
edges. Finches do not
crush seeds. Instead,
they cut open the hard
hull, then seize the seed
inside with their tongue
and swallow it. The bills
of conifer-loving
crossbills are crossed at
the tip, a unique
arrangement that
permits them to open
tough-hulled pine
cones. Roughly
50 percent of crossbills
are "left-billed" and
50 percent "right-
billed"—lefties are right-
footed, and vice versa. Most
finches are social. Although
they breed in pairs, after
nesting finches form
flocks, some of
which are huge.
Most finch
populations fluctuate in
size, synchronized with
seed production and
abundance. All finches

NOT REALLY PURPLE
The inaccurately named Purple
Finch actually has a lovely
wine-red color.

are vocal, calling constantly while flying, and
singing in the spring. Calls are usually sharp,
somewhat metallic sounds, although the American
Goldfinch's tinkling calls are sweeter. Songs can be
quite musical, clear-sounding melodies, like that of
the Cassin's Finch. Finches make open cup-shaped
nests of grasses and lichens, in trees or shrubs, and
are remarkably adept at hiding them.

CROSSBILL
Perched on a pine tree branch,
a female Red Crossbill grinds a
seed in her bill to break open
the hull and reach the fat-rich
kernel inside.

GARDEN GLOW
Even pink flower buds
cannot compete with
the yellow of a male
American Goldfinch.

| Order **Passeriformes** | Family **Fringillidae** | Species ***Carduelis pinus*** |

Pine Siskin

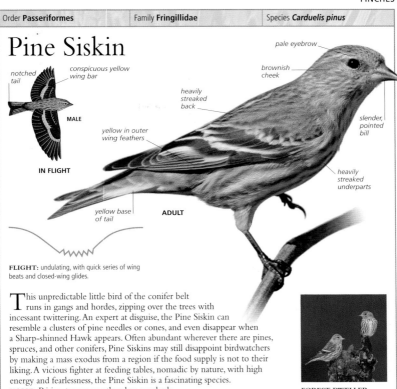

pale eyebrow

brownish cheek

slender, pointed bill

heavily streaked back

heavily streaked underparts

notched tail

conspicuous yellow wing bar

MALE

yellow in outer wing feathers

IN FLIGHT

yellow base of tail

ADULT

FLIGHT: undulating, with quick series of wing beats and closed-wing glides.

This unpredictable little bird of the conifer belt runs in gangs and hordes, zipping over the trees with incessant twittering. An expert at disguise, the Pine Siskin can resemble a clusters of pine needles or cones, and even disappear when a Sharp-shinned Hawk appears. Often abundant wherever there are pines, spruces, and other conifers, Pine Siskins may still disappoint birdwatchers by making a mass exodus from a region if the food supply is not to their liking. A vicious fighter at feeding tables, nomadic by nature, with high energy and fearlessness, the Pine Siskin is a fascinating species.

VOICE Rising *toooeeo*, mostly when perched; also raspy *chit-chit-chit* in flight.

NESTING Shallow cup of grass and lichens near the end of a conifer branch; 3–4 eggs; 1–2 broods; February–August.

FEEDING Eats conifer seeds; gleans insects and spiders; also seen feeding on roadsides, lawns, and weed fields.

FOREST DWELLER
The streaked Pine Siskin inhabits northern and western coniferous forests.

QUARRELSOME
A bird warns off a neighbor at a food source, displaying its yellow wing stripe.

OCCURRENCE
Widespread across North America; occurs in coniferous and mixed coniferous forests, but also seen in parkland and suburbs. In some winters may appear south of regular breeding range to Missouri and Tennessee, also Mexico. Prefers open areas to continuous forest.

SIMILAR SPECIES

COMMON REDPOLL
see p.347

tiny, pale bill

heavier streaking

YELLOW-RUMPED WARBLER ♀
see p.370

yellow rump

yellow patches

| Length 4¼–5½in (11–14cm) | Wingspan 7–9in (18–23cm) | Weight ⁷⁄₁₆–⅝oz (12–18g) |
| Social **Flocks** | Lifespan **Up to 10 years** | Status **Secure** |

DATE SEEN	WHERE	NOTES

| Order **Passeriformes** | Family **Fringillidae** | Species *Carduelis tristis* |

American Goldfinch

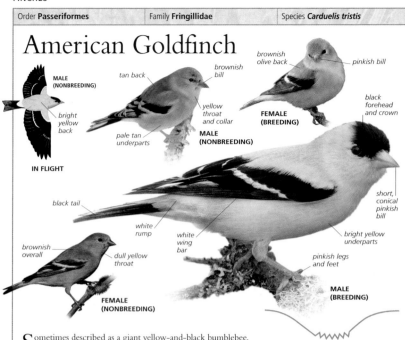

MALE (NONBREEDING)

IN FLIGHT

bright yellow back

tan back

brownish bill

yellow throat and collar

pale tan underparts

MALE (NONBREEDING)

brownish olive back

pinkish bill

FEMALE (BREEDING)

black forehead and crown

short, conical pinkish bill

bright yellow underparts

pinkish legs and feet

MALE (BREEDING)

black tail

white rump

white wing bar

brownish overall

dull yellow throat

FEMALE (NONBREEDING)

Sometimes described as a giant yellow-and-black bumblebee, a male American Goldfinch is a spectacular summer sight. Goldfinches reveal their presence before they are seen by their tinkling, bell-like calls. If there are weeds in seed around, goldfinches will find them and feed energetically on the manna. This all-American species is the State Bird of Washington State.

VOICE Loud, rising, quizzical *pter-yee?* by males; 3–5-note *tit-tse-tew-tew* by both sexes, usually in flight; song complex, warbling, tinkling, and melodious.

NESTING Neat open cup of grass, shaded by leaves, in a tree or tall shrub; 4–5 eggs; 1–2 broods; June–September.

FEEDING Feed mainly on seeds from annuals; also birch and alder; some insects; love sunflower and thistle seed, whether on flower heads or at feeders.

FLIGHT: deeply undulating; wing beats alternating with closed-wing dips.

OCCURRENCE
In low shrubs, deciduous woodlands, farmlands, orchards, suburbs, and gardens across much of North America, from southern Canada to California and Georgia; in winter south to northern Mexico and Florida; winter habitats similar to those used at other times.

SIMILAR SPECIES		
LESSER GOLDFINCH see p.465	**LAWRENCE'S GOLDFINCH**	**WILSON'S WARBLER** see p.389
greenish back, conspicuous wing bars	yellow wing bars, black face, yellow breast	black cap, yellow face

Length **4¼–5in (11–13cm)**	Wingspan **7–9in (18–23cm)**	Weight **⅜–¹¹⁄₁₆oz (11–20g)**
Social **Small flocks**	Lifespan **Up to 11 years**	Status **Secure**

DATE SEEN	WHERE	NOTES

| Order **Passeriformes** | Family **Fringillidae** | Species *Carduelis flammea* |

Common Redpoll

ruby-red cap

small, pointed yellow bill

red cap

MALE

wing bars

IN FLIGHT

MALE (BREEDING)

rosy-red breast

reddish cap

FEMALE

streaked underparts

black streaks on rosy-red breast

MALE (NONBREEDING)

pale wing bars

notched tail

pale wing bar

JUVENILE

Every other year, spruce, birch, and other trees in the northern forest zone fail to produce a good crop of seeds, forcing the Common Redpoll to look for food farther south than usual— as far south as the northern US states. The Common Redpoll is oddly tame around people and is easily attracted to winter feeders. The degree of whiteness in its plumage varies greatly among individuals, related to sex and age. The taxonomy of the Common Redpoll includes four subspecies around the world, and there are suggestions that some may be distinct species.

VOICE Flight call dry *zit-zit-zit-zit* and rattling *chirr*; also high *too-ee* call while perched; song series of rapid trills.

NESTING Cup of small twigs in spruces, larches, willows, alders; 4–6 eggs; 1–2 broods; May–June.

FEEDING Feeds on small seeds from conifers, sedge, birch, willow, alder; also insects and spiders.

FLIGHT: deeply undulating, with dips between bouts of wing beats.

SIMILAR SPECIES		
PINE SISKIN see p.345	**HOARY REDPOLL** see p.465	red cap
yellow on tail	brownish upperparts	
	two wing bars	pale overall · whitish underparts

FRIENDLY FLOCK
Common Redpolls are only weakly territorial, sometimes even nesting close together.

OCCURRENCE
Mainly in extreme northern North America from Alaska to Québec and Labrador, in low forest, sub-Arctic, and shrubby tundra habitats. More southern winter appearances typically occur every other year, rarely south of northern US states, from the Dakotas east to New York and New England.

Length 4¾–5½in (12–14cm)	Wingspan 6½–6¾in (16–17cm)	Weight ⅜–¹¹⁄₁₆oz (11–19g)
Social **Flocks**	Lifespan **Up to 10 years**	Status **Secure**

DATE SEEN	WHERE	NOTES

| Order **Passeriformes** | Family **Fringillidae** | Species **Carpodacus purpureus** |

Purple Finch

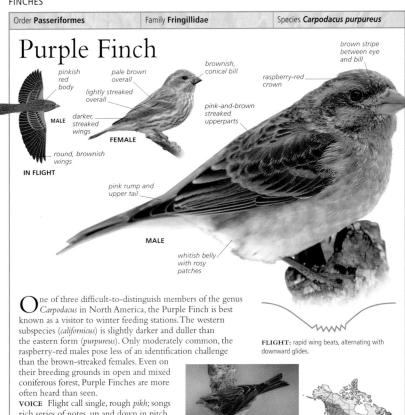

MALE
- pinkish red body
- darker, streaked wings

IN FLIGHT
- round, brownish wings

FEMALE
- pale brown overall
- lightly streaked overall
- brownish, conical bill

MALE
- brown stripe between eye and bill
- raspberry-red crown
- pink-and-brown streaked upperparts
- pink rump and upper tail
- whitish belly with rosy patches

One of three difficult-to-distinguish members of the genus *Carpodacus* in North America, the Purple Finch is best known as a visitor to winter feeding stations. The western subspecies (*californicus*) is slightly darker and duller than the eastern form (*purpureus*). Only moderately common, the raspberry-red males pose less of an identification challenge than the brown-streaked females. Even on their breeding grounds in open and mixed coniferous forest, Purple Finches are more often heard than seen.

VOICE Flight call single, rough *pikh*; songs rich series of notes, up and down in pitch.

NESTING Cup of sticks and grasses on a conifer branch; 4 eggs; 2 broods; May–July.

FEEDING Eats buds, seeds, flowers of deciduous trees; insects and caterpillars in summer; also seeds and berries.

FLIGHT: rapid wing beats, alternating with downward glides.

RASPBERRY TINTED
On a lichen-covered branch this male's delicate coloring is quite striking.

OCCURRENCE
Breeds in northern mixed conifer and hardwood forests in the East, where it is partially migratory, moves as far south as the Gulf Coast. Resident from Baja California north along the Pacific coast and the Cascade Mountains to Yukon Territory.

SIMILAR SPECIES

HOUSE FINCH ♀
western;
see p.349
- thinner streaks

CASSIN'S FINCH ♀
- more marked facial patterning

RED-WINGED BLACKBIRD ♀
see p.396
- larger overall
- heavily streaked
- darker overall

| Length **4¾–6in (12–15cm)** | Wingspan **8½–10in (22–26cm)** | Weight **¹¹⁄₁₆–1¹⁄₁₆oz (20–30g)** |
| Social **Flocks** | Lifespan **Unknown** | Status **Declining** |

DATE SEEN	WHERE	NOTES

| Order **Passeriformes** | Family **Fringillidae** | Species *Carpodacus mexicanus* |

House Finch

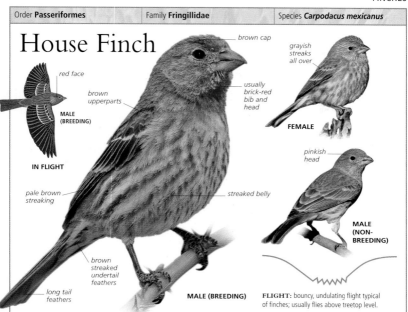

brown cap

grayish streaks all over

red face

brown upperparts

usually brick-red bib and head

MALE (BREEDING)

FEMALE

IN FLIGHT

pinkish head

pale brown streaking

streaked belly

MALE (NON-BREEDING)

brown streaked undertail feathers

long tail feathers

MALE (BREEDING)

FLIGHT: bouncy, undulating flight typical of finches; usually flies above treetop level.

Historically, the House Finch was a western bird, and was first reported in the eastern side of the US on Long Island, New York, in 1941. These birds are said to have originated from the illegal bird trade. The population of the eastern birds started expanding in the 1960s, so much so that by the late 1990s, their population had expanded westward to link up with the original western population. The male House Finch is distinguished from the Purple and Cassin's finches by its brown streaked underparts, while the females have plainer faces and generally blurrier streaking.

VOICE Call note *queet*; varied jumble of notes, often starting with husky notes to whistled and burry notes, and ending with a long *wheeerr*.

NESTING Females build nests from grass stems, thin twigs, and thin weeds in trees and on man-made structures; 1–6 eggs; 2–3 broods; March–August.

FEEDING Eats, almost exclusively, vegetable matter, such as buds, fruits, and seeds; readily comes to feeders.

RED IN THE FACE
The breeding male House Finch can be identified by its stunning brick-red plumage.

OCCURRENCE
Found in urban, suburban, and settled areas; in the East almost exclusively in settled areas, including the centers of large cities; in the West also in wilder areas such as savannas, desert grasslands, and chaparral, particularly near people. Resident, some birds move after breeding.

SIMILAR SPECIES	
PURPLE FINCH see p.348	**CASSIN'S FINCH**

pinkish neck

reddish head

whitish underparts

white underparts

| Length **5–6in (12.5–15cm)** | Wingspan **8–10in (20–25cm)** | Weight **⁹⁄₁₆–1oz (16–27g)** |
| Social **Flocks** | Lifespan **Up to 12 years** | Status **Secure** |

DATE SEEN	WHERE	NOTES

Order **Passeriformes**	Family **Fringillidae**	Species *Pinicola enucleator*

Pine Grosbeak

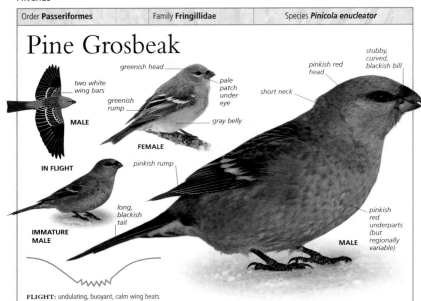

greenish head

pale patch under eye

greenish rump

gray belly

FEMALE

two white wing bars

MALE

IN FLIGHT

pinkish rump

long, blackish tail

IMMATURE MALE

stubby, curved, blackish bill

pinkish red head

short neck

pinkish red underparts (but regionally variable)

MALE

FLIGHT: undulating, buoyant, calm wing beats interrupted by glides.

The largest member of the Fringillidae family in North America, and easily distinguished by the male's unmistakable thick, stubby bill, the Pine Grosbeak is a resident of boreal forests in northeastern Canada and the Adirondacks. The bird is also found across northern Eurasia, where nine subspecies have been identified, four of which are found in North America. Due to extensive color variation of individual plumages, the age and sex of given individuals are not always easily determined.

VOICE Contact calls of eastern birds *tee-tew*, or *tee-tee-tew*; western forms give more complex *tweedle*; warbling song.

NESTING Well-hidden, open cup nest usually in spruce or larch trees; 2–5 eggs, 1 brood; June–July.

FEEDING Eats spruce buds, maple seeds, and mountain ash berries throughout the year; consumes insects in summer.

FRUIT LOVER
This species can often be seen hanging from branches, gorging on ripe fruit.

SIMILAR SPECIES

RED CROSSBILL
see p.351

brownish back

mandibles crossed

WHITE-WINGED CROSSBILL
see p.352

mandibles crossed

white bars on wing

OCCURRENCE
Found in the boreal zone from Alaska to Québec and Newfoundland, in open, northern coniferous forests in summer, usually near fresh water. Winters throughout its breeding range, but may move southward to southern Canada and the northeastern US.

Length **8–10in (20–25cm)**	Wingspan **13in (33cm)**	Weight **2–2½oz (55–70g)**
Social **Flocks**	Lifespan **Up to 10 years**	Status **Secure**

DATE SEEN	WHERE	NOTES

| Order **Passeriformes** | Family **Fringillidae** | Species *Loxia curvirostra* |

Red Crossbill

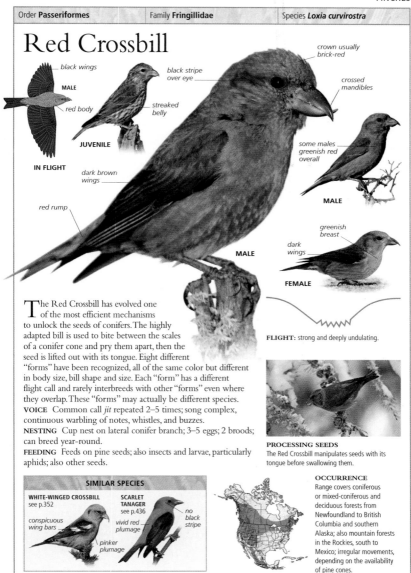

black wings

MALE

red body

IN FLIGHT

JUVENILE

black stripe over eye

streaked belly

dark brown wings

red rump

crown usually brick-red

crossed mandibles

some males greenish red overall

MALE

greenish breast

dark wings

FEMALE

MALE

FLIGHT: strong and deeply undulating.

The Red Crossbill has evolved one of the most efficient mechanisms to unlock the seeds of conifers. The highly adapted bill is used to bite between the scales of a conifer cone and pry them apart, then the seed is lifted out with its tongue. Eight different "forms" have been recognized, all of the same color but different in body size, bill shape and size. Each "form" has a different flight call and rarely interbreeds with other "forms" even where they overlap. These "forms" may actually be different species.

VOICE Common call *jit* repeated 2–5 times; song complex, continuous warbling of notes, whistles, and buzzes.

NESTING Cup nest on lateral conifer branch; 3–5 eggs; 2 broods; can breed year-round.

FEEDING Feeds on pine seeds; also insects and larvae, particularly aphids; also other seeds.

PROCESSING SEEDS
The Red Crossbill manipulates seeds with its tongue before swallowing them.

SIMILAR SPECIES

WHITE-WINGED CROSSBILL see p.352

conspicuous wing bars

pinker plumage

SCARLET TANAGER see p.436

vivid red plumage

no black stripe

OCCURRENCE
Range covers coniferous or mixed-coniferous and deciduous forests from Newfoundland to British Columbia and southern Alaska; also mountain forests in the Rockies, south to Mexico; irregular movements, depending on the availability of pine cones.

| Length **5–6¾in (13–17cm)** | Wingspan **10–10½in (25–27cm)** | Weight **⅞–1¼oz (25–35g)** |
| Social **Flocks** | Lifespan **Up to 10 years** | Status **Secure** |

DATE SEEN	WHERE	NOTES

| Order **Passeriformes** | Family **Fringillidae** | Species *Loxia leucoptera* |

White-winged Crossbill

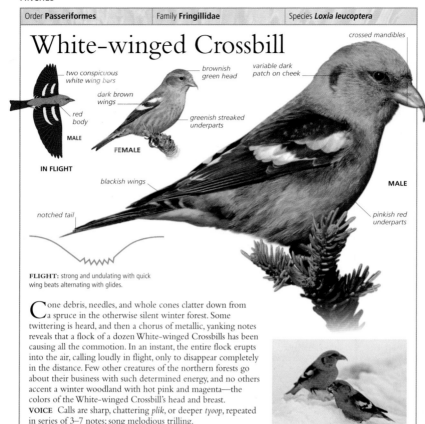

two conspicuous white wing bars

dark brown wings

red body

MALE

IN FLIGHT

brownish green head

crossed mandibles

variable dark patch on cheek

greenish streaked underparts

FEMALE

blackish wings

notched tail

MALE

pinkish red underparts

FLIGHT: strong and undulating with quick wing beats alternating with glides.

Cone debris, needles, and whole cones clatter down from a spruce in the otherwise silent winter forest. Some twittering is heard, and then a chorus of metallic, yanking notes reveals that a flock of a dozen White-winged Crossbills has been causing all the commotion. In an instant, the entire flock erupts into the air, calling loudly in flight, only to disappear completely in the distance. Few other creatures of the northern forests go about their business with such determined energy, and no others accent a winter woodland with hot pink and magenta—the colors of the White-winged Crossbill's head and breast.

VOICE Calls are sharp, chattering *plik*, or deeper *tyoop*, repeated in series of 3–7 notes; song melodious trilling.

NESTING Open cup nest, usually high on end of a spruce branch; eggs 3–5; 2 broods; July, January–February.

FEEDING Eats seeds from small-coned conifers; spruces, firs, larches; feeds on insects when available.

EATING SNOW
The White-winged Crossbill frequently eats snow to provide essential moisture.

SIMILAR SPECIES

PINE GROSBEAK
see p.350

blunt bill

longer tail

RED CROSSBILL
see p.351

no wing bars

redder plumage

OCCURRENCE
Nomadic; most common in the spruce zone of Alaska and Canada but has bred as far south as Colorado in the West; in the East, from Québec and Newfoundland southward to New York City and New England.

| Length **5½–6in (14–15cm)** | Wingspan **10–10½in (26–27cm)** | Weight **¹¹⁄₁₆–1¹⁄₁₆oz (20–30g)** |
| Social **Flocks** | Lifespan **Up to 10 years** | Status **Secure** |

DATE SEEN	WHERE	NOTES

| Order **Passeriformes** | Family **Fringillidae** | Species *Hesperiphona vespertina* |

Evening Grosbeak

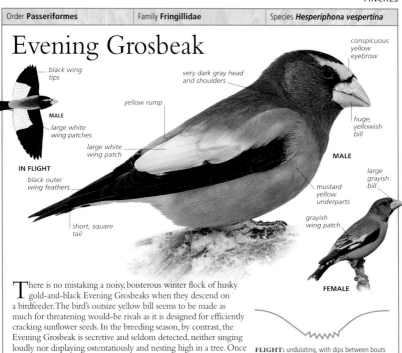

black wing tips

MALE

large white wing patches

IN FLIGHT

black outer wing feathers

short, square tail

very dark gray head and shoulders

yellow rump

large white wing patch

conspicuous yellow eyebrow

huge, yellowish bill

MALE

mustard yellow underparts

large grayish bill

grayish wing patch

FEMALE

There is no mistaking a noisy, boisterous winter flock of husky gold-and-black Evening Grosbeaks when they descend on a birdfeeder. The bird's outsize yellow bill seems to be made as much for threatening would-be rivals as it is designed for efficiently cracking sunflower seeds. In the breeding season, by contrast, the Evening Grosbeak is secretive and seldom detected, neither singing loudly nor displaying ostentatiously and nesting high in a tree. Once a bird of western North America, it has extended its range eastward in the past 200 years, and now breeds as far as Newfoundland. This may be a result of the planting of ornamental box elder, which carries its abundant seeds winter-long, ensuring a ready food supply for the bird.

VOICE Call descending *feeew*; also buzzy notes and beeping chatter.

NESTING Loose, grass-lined twig cup, usually on conifer branch; 3–4 eggs; 1–2 broods; May–July.

FEEDING Eats seeds of pines and other conifers; also maple and box elder seeds; also insects and their larvae, particularly spruce budworms, which are actually Tortricid moths.

FLIGHT: undulating, with dips between bouts of wing beats, may hover briefly.

CAPABLE BILL
This bird's extremely robust bill can deal with all kinds of winter fruits and seeds.

OCCURRENCE
Breeds in mixed conifer and spruce forests from the Rocky Mountain region to eastern Canada, and in western mountain ranges south to Mexico. Winters in coniferous or deciduous woodlands, often in suburban locations; may move south from northern range, depending on food supply.

SIMILAR SPECIES	
PINE GROSBEAK ♀ see p.350 — stubby bill — wing bars — gray underparts	**BALTIMORE ORIOLE** ♀ see p.394 — slender aspect — mottled head — pale orange underparts

| Length **6½–7in (16–18cm)** | Wingspan **12–14in (30–36cm)** | Weight **2–2½oz (55–70g)** |
| Social **Flocks** | Lifespan **Up to 15 years** | Status **Secure** |

DATE SEEN	WHERE	NOTES

WOOD-WARBLERS

THE FAMILY PARULIDAE is restricted to the Americas, and is remarkable for its diversity in plumage, song, feeding, breeding biology, and sexual dimorphism. In general, however, wood-warblers share similar shapes: all are smallish, slender birds with longish, thin bills (unlike thick vireo bills) mostly used for snapping up insects. The odd, chunky, thick-billed Yellow-breasted Chat is an exception. Molecular data suggests what some birders have long thought: that it is not a warbler at all. However, there is not yet any consensus as to what family this bird belongs in.

Ground-dwelling warblers tend to be larger and clad in olives, browns, and yellows, whereas many arboreal species are smaller and sport bright oranges, cool blues, and even ruby reds. The location and presence or absence of wingbars and tail spots is often a good identification aid. Warblers are especially diverse in the East, where over 30 species may be seen in a single morning of spring birding, which may be the highlight of the year for some birdwatchers. Eastern species have three different migration routes to deal with the obstacle of the Gulf of Mexico when going to or coming from their Neotropical wintering grounds. Circum-Gulf migrants fly along the eastern shore of Mexico, Caribbean migrants travel through Florida then island-hop through the West Indies, and trans-Gulf migrants fly directly across the Gulf of Mexico, from the Yucatán Peninsula to the US Gulf Coast. Birds flying this third route are subjected to weather changes that sometimes result in spectacular fallouts at locations such as High Island, Texas.

PLASTIC PLUMAGE
Some male Dendroica warblers (like this Blackburnian) are only brightly colored when breeding.

FEEDING STRATEGIES
Some warblers, such as this Black-and-White, probe the cracks in tree trunks for food.

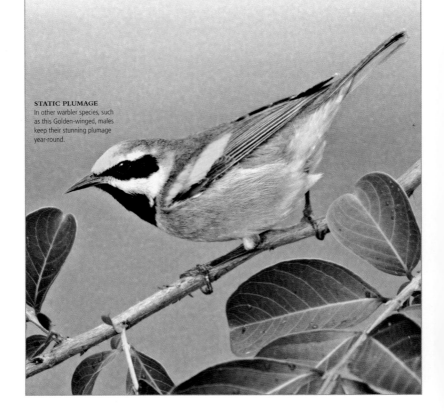

STATIC PLUMAGE
In other warbler species, such as this Golden-winged, males keep their stunning plumage year-round.

| Order **Passeriformes** | Family **Parulidae** | Species ***Vermivora chrysoptera*** |

Golden-winged Warbler

gray back

bright yellow wing panel

MALE

white outer tail feathers

IN FLIGHT

black "mask"

bright yellow crown

gray back suffused with yellow

unstreaked wings

black throat

yellow wing panel

MALE

white undertail

gray "mask"

greenish yellow crown

FEMALE

One of the continent's most beautiful warblers, this species is unfortunately being genetically swamped by the more southerly Blue-winged Warbler. This situation is worsening as more habitat is cleared and climate changes take place. It commonly interbreeds with the Blue-winged, resulting in two more frequently seen hybrid forms: Brewster's Warbler, which resembles the Blue-winged Warbler, and Lawrence's Warbler, which looks like a Blue-winged Warbler with the mask and black throat of a Golden-winged.

VOICE Call a sharp *tsip*; flight call high, slightly buzzy *ziiih*; song buzzy *zee zuu zuu zuu*, first note higher; birds that deviate from this song pattern may be hybrids.

NESTING Shallow bulky cup, on or just above ground; 4–6 eggs; 1 brood; May–July.

FEEDING Hangs upside-down at clusters of curled-up dead leaves; feeds on moth larvae, other winged insects, and spiders.

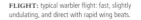

FLIGHT: typical warbler flight: fast, slightly undulating, and direct with rapid wing beats.

SMALL TREES REQUIRED
Golden-winged Warblers breed in shrubby habitats created by clearance and re-growth.

SIMILAR SPECIES

| CAROLINA CHICKADEE see p.302 yellowish wash on underparts | black cap | BLACK-CAPPED CHICKADEE see p.303 | black cap white cheek buffy underparts |

OCCURRENCE
Breeds in the northeastern US and southern Canada in secondary growth habitat with dense patches of deciduous shrubs or tangles, or in marshes with a forest edge; uses any wooded habitat on migration; winters in Central America from Guatemala to northern Colombia; mostly along the Caribbean.

| Length **4¾in (12cm)** | Wingspan **7½in (19cm)** | Weight **⁹⁄₃₂–³⁄₈oz (8–11g)** |
| Social **Migrant/Winter flocks** | Lifespan **Unknown** | Status **Declining** |

DATE SEEN	WHERE	NOTES

| Order **Passeriformes** | Family **Parulidae** | Species **Vermivora pinus** |

Blue-winged Warbler

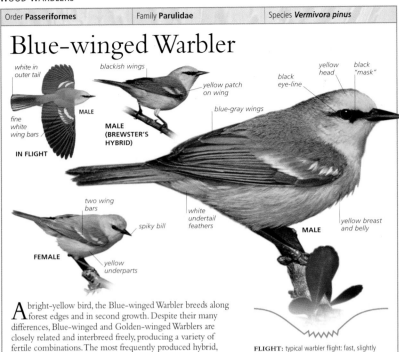

white in outer tail

blackish wings

yellow patch on wing

yellow head

black "mask"

black eye-line

blue-gray wings

MALE

fine white wing bars

IN FLIGHT

MALE (BREWSTER'S HYBRID)

two wing bars

spiky bill

white undertail feathers

MALE

yellow breast and belly

FEMALE

yellow underparts

A bright-yellow bird, the Blue-winged Warbler breeds along forest edges and in second growth. Despite their many differences, Blue-winged and Golden-winged Warblers are closely related and interbreed freely, producing a variety of fertile combinations. The most frequently produced hybrid, Brewster's Warbler, named in 1874, was once believed to be a different species. It is similar to the Golden-winged Warbler (yellowish breast, two yellow wing bars), but has the Blue-winged's facial pattern, minus the black mask and throat.

VOICE Sharp *tsip* call, like *Spizella* sparrows; flight call: a high, slightly buzzy *ziiih*; song is a low, harsh, buzzy *beee-burrrrr*, second note very low in pitch and rattling; deviation from this song pattern may hint at hybrid origin.

NESTING Deep, bulky cup of vegetation, just off the ground in grasses; 4–5 eggs; 1 brood; May–June.

FEEDING Hangs upside-down at clusters of dead leaves; probes for moth larvae and small insects.

FLIGHT: typical warbler flight: fast, slightly undulating, and direct with rapid wing beats.

DECEPTIVE HYBRID The black border to this bird's ear patch indicates a Blue- or Golden-winged ancestry.

OCCURRENCE Breeds in areas of second-growth forest, but is less choosy than the Golden-winged Warbler and can use older and taller stands. Occurs in any wooded habitat during migration. Migrates across the Gulf of Mexico to winter in southeastern Mexico, central Panama, and the West Indies.

SIMILAR SPECIES

YELLOW WARBLER ♀ see p.362

yellow wings

lacks black mask

PROTHONOTARY WARBLER ♀ see p.378

shorter tail

lacks white wing bars

| Length **4¾in (12cm)** | Wingspan **7½in (19cm)** | Weight **9/32–3/8oz (8–11g)** |
| Social **Loose flocks** | Lifespan **Up to 7 years** | Status **Secure** |

DATE SEEN	WHERE	NOTES

Order **Passeriformes**	Family **Parulidae**	Species *Vermivora peregrina*

Tennessee Warbler

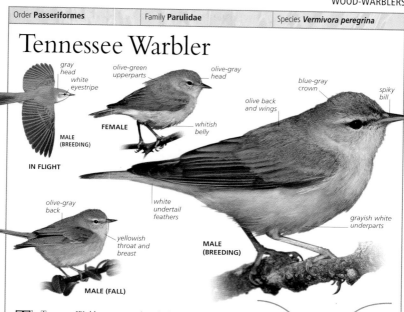

gray head
white eyestripe

MALE (BREEDING)

IN FLIGHT

olive-green upperparts

FEMALE

olive-gray head

whitish belly

blue-gray crown

spiky bill

olive back and wings

grayish white underparts

MALE (BREEDING)

olive-gray back

white undertail feathers

yellowish throat and breast

MALE (FALL)

The Tennessee Warbler was named on the basis of a specimen found in that state on migration, as this species breeds almost entirely in Canada and winters in Central America. These warblers inhabit fairly remote areas and their nests are difficult to find. It is one of a number of species that takes advantage of outbreaks of spruce budworms (actually Tortricid moths); their populations tend to increase in years when budworms themselves increase.

VOICE Call a sharp *tzit*; flight call a thin slightly rolling *seet*; song usually three-part staccato series, *chip-chip-chip*, each series increasing in pitch and usually in tempo.

NESTING Nest woven of fine plant matter, in ground depression, concealed from above by shrubbery; 4–7 eggs; 1 brood; June.

FEEDING Searches outer branches of trees for caterpillars, bees, wasps, beetles, and spiders; also eats fruits in winter and drinks nectar by piercing base of flowers.

FLIGHT: fast, slightly undulating, and direct with rapid wing beats.

UNIQUE UNDERPARTS
The breeding male is the only North American wood-warbler with unmarked grayish white underparts.

SIMILAR SPECIES

PHILADELPHIA VIREO see p.291
white eyebrow
yellowish underparts

ORANGE-CROWNED WARBLER see p.358
shorter wings
greenish yellow rump
muted markings

OCCURRENCE
Breeds in a variety of habitats, especially woodlands with dense understory and thickets of willows and alders. Very common in suburban parks and gardens during migration, particularly in the Midwest. Winters from southern Mexico to northern Ecuador and northern Venezuela; also Cuba.

Length 4¾in (12cm)	Wingspan 7⅜in (19.5cm)	Weight ⁹⁄₃₂–⅝oz (8–17g)
Social **Flocks**	Lifespan **Up to 6 years**	Status **Secure**

DATE SEEN	WHERE	NOTES

Order **Passeriformes**	Family **Parulidae**	Species **Vermivora celata**

Orange-crowned Warbler

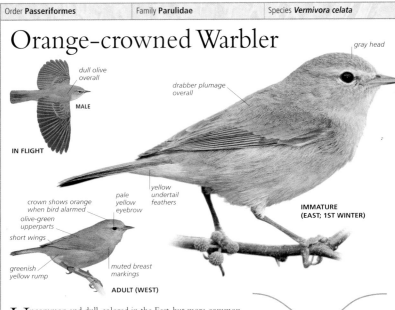

gray head

drabber plumage overall

dull olive overall

MALE

IN FLIGHT

yellow undertail feathers

crown shows orange when bird alarmed

pale yellow eyebrow

olive-green upperparts

short wings

greenish yellow rump

muted breast markings

ADULT (WEST)

IMMATURE (EAST; 1ST WINTER)

Uncommon and dull-colored in the East, but more common and brightly colored in the West, the Orange-crowned Warbler has a large breeding range. The 19th-century American naturalist Thomas Say described this species on the basis of specimens collected in Nebraska. He was struck by the tiny orange cap, but because it was so concealed in the plumage of the crown, he named it *celata*, which is Latin for "hidden." The orange cap is not usually visible in the field.

VOICE Call a clean, sharp *tsik*; flight call a high, short *seet*; song a loose, lazy trill; eastern birds lazier, western birds more emphatic.

NESTING Cup of grasses, fibers, and down, usually on ground under bush; 4–5 eggs; 1 brood; March–July.

FEEDING Gleans mostly arthropods such as beetles, ants, spiders, and their larvae; also eats fruits; collects nectar by piercing base of flower.

FLIGHT: fast, slightly undulating, and direct with rapid wing beats.

FACE MARKINGS
In eastern populations of this warbler, the birds have whitish facial markings during their first winter.

SIMILAR SPECIES

TENNESSEE WARBLER ♀
see p.357

YELLOW WARBLER ♀
see p.362

yellow upperparts

whitish underparts

longer wings

bright yellow breast and belly

OCCURRENCE
Breeds in a variety of habitats across North America from Alaska eastward to Newfoundland, and in the West from British Columbia southward to California, New Mexico, and western Texas. Prefers streamside thickets. Some winter in the West, while others go to Mexico and Guatemala.

Length **5in (13cm)**	Wingspan **7¼in (18.5cm)**	Weight **¼–⅜oz (7–11g)**
Social **Winter flocks**	Lifespan **Up to 6 years**	Status **Secure**

DATE SEEN	WHERE	NOTES

| Order **Passeriformes** | Family **Parulidae** | Species **Vermivora ruficapilla** |

Nashville Warbler

MALE
V. r. ruficapilla
(EASTERN)

olive-green
upperparts

IN FLIGHT

rounded
wings

whitish
eye-ring

little contrast
between gray
and yellow

dull olive
back

olive
wings

dull yellow
underparts

FEMALE
V. r. ruficapilla
(EASTERN)

blue-gray
head

rufous
crown patch

grayish
green back

conspicuous
white eye-ring

yellow
undertail
feathers

olive
wings

MALE
V. r. ridgwayi
(WESTERN)

Although often confused with the ground-walking, chunky Connecticut Warbler, the Nashville Warbler is much smaller, hops about up in trees, and has a yellow throat. Nashville has two subspecies: *V. r. ruficapilla* in the East and *V. r. ridgwayi* in the West. Differences in voice, habitat, behavior, and plumage hint that they may in fact be separate species. *V. r. ridgwayi* can be distinguished by more extensive white on the belly and a grayish green back.

VOICE Call sharp *tik*, sharper in West; flight call high, thin *siit*; eastern song two parts: first part lazy, second faster trill *tee-tsee tee-tsee tee-tsee titititin*; western song slightly lower and fuller with lazier second part, a seldom trilled *tee-tsee tee-tsee tee-tsee weesay weesay way*.

NESTING Cup hidden on ground in dense cover; 3–6 eggs; 1 brood; May–July.

FEEDING Gleans insects and spiders from trees.

FLIGHT: fast, slightly undulating, and direct, with rapid wing beats.

SIMILAR SPECIES

**VIRGINIA'S
WARBLER**

lacks
yellow
belly

**CONNECTICUT
WARBLER** ♂
walks on ground;
see p.385

chunky
pink bill

lacks
olive
wings

shorter
tail

FIELD MARKS
The white eye-ring and belly are evident on this singing male.

OCCURRENCE
Eastern *ruficapilla* breeds in wet habitats from Saskatchewan east to Newfoundland and south to West Virginia; it migrates south to winter in Mexico. Western *ridgwayi* breeds in brushy montane habitats of the Sierras and northern Rockies, and winters in coastal California, and from southern Texas to Guatemala.

| Length **4¾in (12cm)** | Wingspan **7½in (19cm)** | Weight **¼–⁷⁄₁₆oz (7–13g)** |
| Social **Migrant/Winter flocks** | Lifespan **Up to 7 years** | Status **Secure** |

DATE SEEN	WHERE		NOTES

WOOD-WARBLERS

| Order **Passeriformes** | Family **Parulidae** | Species **Parula americana** |

Northern Parula

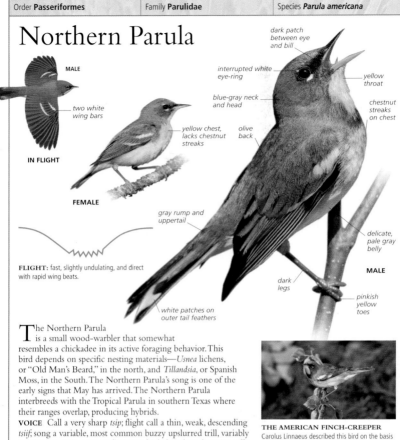

MALE (in flight)

- two white wing bars

IN FLIGHT

- dark patch between eye and bill
- interrupted white eye-ring
- blue-gray neck and head
- yellow throat
- chestnut streaks on chest
- yellow chest, lacks chestnut streaks
- olive back
- gray rump and uppertail
- delicate, pale gray belly
- dark legs
- pinkish yellow toes
- white patches on outer tail feathers

FEMALE

MALE

FLIGHT: fast, slightly undulating, and direct with rapid wing beats.

The Northern Parula is a small wood-warbler that somewhat resembles a chickadee in its active foraging behavior. This bird depends on specific nesting materials—*Usnea* lichens, or "Old Man's Beard," in the north, and *Tillandsia*, or Spanish Moss, in the South. The Northern Parula's song is one of the early signs that May has arrived. The Northern Parula interbreeds with the Tropical Parula in southern Texas where their ranges overlap, producing hybrids.

VOICE Call a very sharp *tsip*; flight call a thin, weak, descending *tsiif*; song a variable, most common buzzy upslurred trill, variably continuous or in steps, ending very high, but then dropping off in an emphatic *zip*.

NESTING Hanging pouch in clump of lichens; 4–5 eggs; 1 brood; May–July (south) or April–August (north).

FEEDING Gleans for caterpillars, flies, moths, beetles, wasps, ants, spiders; also eats berries, nectar, some seeds.

THE AMERICAN FINCH-CREEPER
Carolus Linnaeus described this bird on the basis of a plate in Catesby's *Natural History of Carolina*, called Finch-creeper.

SIMILAR SPECIES

TROPICAL PARULA see p.466 — dark face, more yellow

OCCURRENCE
Nests in almost any kind of wooded area if *Tillandsia* or *Usnea* are available. Migrants (some of which cross the Gulf of Mexico) occur in almost any habitat; winters in varied habitats from southern Texas and Florida across Caribbean and Mexico south to Panama.

| Length **4¼in (11cm)** | Wingspan **7in (18cm)** | Weight **¼–⅜oz (7–10g)** |
| Social **Winter flocks** | Lifespan **Up to 7 years** | Status **Secure** |

DATE SEEN	WHERE	NOTES

| Order **Passeriformes** | Family **Parulidae** | Species *Dendroica pensylvanica* |

Chestnut-sided Warbler

MALE (BREEDING)
two yellow wing bars
IN FLIGHT
white outer tail feathers

yellow cap
black "mustache"
chestnut band along flanks
FEMALE (BREEDING)
white tail spots

yellow-and-black streaks on upperparts
conspicuous white cheeks
yellow crown
white throat
two wing bars
rich chestnut flanks
MALE (BREEDING)

olive crown
bright lime-green above
plain face with white eye-ring
FEMALE (1ST FALL)
plain gray underside

The Chestnut-sided Warbler is one of the few wood-warbler species that has benefited from deforestation, because it depends on deciduous second-growth and forest edges for breeding. Once a rare bird, it is more common now than it was in the early 19th century. These birds vary in appearance, immature females looking quite unlike adult males in breeding. In all plumages, yellowish wing bars and whitish belly are the most distinguishing characteristics. Its pleasant song has long been transcribed as *pleased pleased pleased to MEET'cha*.
VOICE Call a sweet *chip*; flight call a low, burry *brrrt*; song a series of fast, sweet notes, usually ending with emphatic *WEET-chew*.
NESTING Open, easy-to-find cup just off ground in small deciduous tree or shrub; 3–5 eggs; 1 brood; May–August.
FEEDING Eats insects, especially larvae; also berries and seeds.

FLIGHT: fast, slightly undulating, and direct with rapid wing beats.

MALE TERRITORY
This singing, territorial male prefers second-growth thickets as its habitat.

SIMILAR SPECIES

BLACKPOLL WARBLER ♀
see p.363
white wing bars
pale stripe on face
fine streaks on breast

BAY-BREASTED WARBLER ♀
see p.364
olive upperparts
white wing bars
buffy undertail
greenish underside

OCCURRENCE
Breeds in successive stages of regrowth in deciduous forests, from Alberta to the Great Lakes, New England, and the Appalachians; isolated populations in the Midwest. Winters in the West Indies, Mexico, and Central America, south to Venezuela and northern Colombia.

| Length **5in (13cm)** | Wingspan **8in (20cm)** | Weight ⁹⁄₃₂–⁷⁄₁₆oz (8–13g) |
| Social **Winter flocks** | Lifespan **Up to 7 years** | Status **Secure** |

DATE SEEN	WHERE	NOTES

Order **Passeriformes**	Family **Parulidae**	Species *Dendroica petechia*

Yellow Warbler

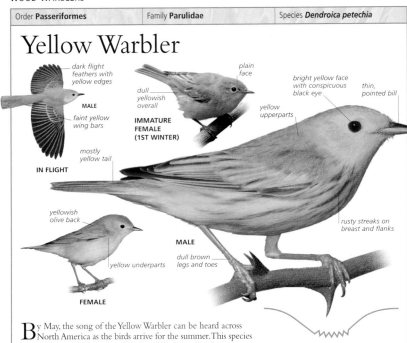

dark flight feathers with yellow edges

MALE

faint yellow wing bars

IN FLIGHT

mostly yellow tail

plain face

dull yellowish overall

IMMATURE FEMALE (1ST WINTER)

bright yellow face with conspicuous black eye

thin, pointed bill

yellow upperparts

rusty streaks on breast and flanks

yellowish olive back

MALE

dull brown legs and toes

yellow underparts

FEMALE

B y May, the song of the Yellow Warbler can be heard across North America as the birds arrive for the summer. This species is extremely variable geographically, with about 40 subspecies, especially on its tropical range (West Indies and Central and South America). The Yellow Warbler is known to build another nest on top of an old one when cowbird eggs appear in it, which can result in up to six different tiers. The Yellow Warbler does not walk, but rather hops from branch to branch.

VOICE Call a variable *chip*, sometimes given in series; flight call buzzy *zeep*; song variable series of fast, sweet notes; western birds often add an emphatic ending.

NESTING Deep cup of plant material, grasses in vertical fork of deciduous tree or shrub; 4–5 eggs; 1 brood; May–July.

FEEDING Eats mostly insects and insect larvae, plus some fruit.

FLIGHT: fast, slightly undulating, and direct, with rapid wing beats.

ONE OF A KIND
This species has more yellow in its plumage than any other North American wood-warbler.

SIMILAR SPECIES

ORANGE-CROWNED WARBLER see p.358

olive-green overall

WILSON'S WARBLER ♀ see p.389

dark crown

longer tail

OCCURRENCE
Widespread in most shrubby and second-growth habitats of North America. Migrates to southern US and southward to Mexico, Central America, and South America. Resident populations live in Florida and the West Indies.

Length **5in (13cm)**	Wingspan **8in (20cm)**	Weight **⁹⁄₃₂–½oz (8–14g)**
Social **Flocks**	Lifespan **Up to 9 years**	Status **Secure**

DATE SEEN	WHERE	NOTES

| Order **Passeriformes** | Family **Parulidae** | Species *Dendroica striata* |

Blackpoll Warbler

white tail spots

MALE

two white wing bars

IN FLIGHT

greenish upperparts with fine black streaks

white cheek

black cap

FEMALE (BREEDING)

faint, fine streaking on underparts

greenish overall

streaking on breast

bold black streaks on gray back

MALE (FALL)

pale feet contrasting with darker legs

white undertail feathers

streaked underparts

orange legs

MALE (BREEDING)

The Blackpoll Warbler is well known for undergoing a remarkable fall migration that takes it over the Atlantic Ocean from the northeastern US to northern Venezuela. Before departing, it almost doubles its body weight with fat to serve as fuel for the nonstop journey. With the return of spring, most of these birds travel the shorter Caribbean route back north.

VOICE Call piercing *chip*; flight call high, buzzy yet sharp *tzzzt*; common song crescendo of fast, extremely high-pitched ticks, ending with a decrescendo *tsst tsst TSST TSST TSST tsst tsst*; less commonly, ticks run into even faster trill.

NESTING Well-hidden cup placed low against conifer trunk; 3–5 eggs; 1–2 broods; May–July.

FEEDING Gleans arthropods, such as worms and beetles, but will take small fruit in fall and winter.

FLIGHT: fast, slightly undulating, and direct, with rapid wing beats.

REACHING THE HIGH NOTES
The song of the male Blackpoll is so high-pitched that it is inaudible to many people.

SIMILAR SPECIES

BAY-BREASTED WARBLER ♀
see p.364

greenish sides to neck

warm wash to flanks

BLACK-AND-WHITE WARBLER ♂
see p.376

black cheek

distinct black-and-white stripes

OCCURRENCE
Breeds in spruce-fir forests across the northern boreal forest zone from Alaska eastward to Newfoundland, southward to coastal coniferous forests in the Maritimes and northern New England. Migrants fly over the Atlantic Ocean to a landfall in the Caribbean and northern South America.

| Length **5½in (14cm)** | Wingspan **9in (23cm)** | Weight **⅜–⅝oz (10–18g)** |
| Social **Flocks** | Lifespan **Up to 8 years** | Status **Secure** |

DATE SEEN	WHERE	NOTES

Order **Passeriformes**	Family **Parulidae**	Species *Dendroica castanea*

Bay-breasted Warbler

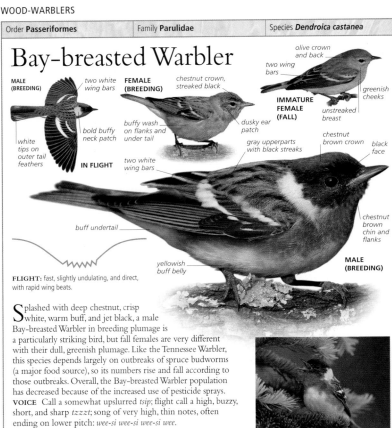

MALE (BREEDING)

two white wing bars

white tips on outer tail feathers

bold buffy neck patch

IN FLIGHT

FEMALE (BREEDING)

chestnut crown, streaked black

buffy wash on flanks and under tail

two white wing bars

dusky ear patch

olive crown and back

two wing bars

greenish cheeks

IMMATURE FEMALE (FALL)

unstreaked breast

gray upperparts with black streaks

chestnut brown crown

black face

chestnut brown chin and flanks

buff undertail

yellowish buff belly

MALE (BREEDING)

FLIGHT: fast, slightly undulating, and direct, with rapid wing beats.

Splashed with deep chestnut, crisp white, warm buff, and jet black, a male Bay-breasted Warbler in breeding plumage is a particularly striking bird, but fall females are very different with their dull, greenish plumage. Like the Tennessee Warbler, this species depends largely on outbreaks of spruce budworms (a major food source), so its numbers rise and fall according to those outbreaks. Overall, the Bay-breasted Warbler population has decreased because of the increased use of pesticide sprays.
VOICE Call a somewhat upslurred *tsip*; flight call a high, buzzy, short, and sharp *tzzzt*; song of very high, thin notes, often ending on lower pitch: *wee-si wee-si wee-si wee*.
NESTING Fragile-looking cup of grass and lichens on horizontal branch at mid-level in forest; 4–5 eggs; 1 brood; May–July.
FEEDING Mostly eats moths, smaller insects, worms, spiders, and caterpillars during migration and on breeding grounds; eats mainly fruit in winter.

SINGING IN THE FOREST
A brilliantly colored breeding male sings its high-pitched song on a spruce branch.

SIMILAR SPECIES

BLACKPOLL WARBLER ♂
see p.363

streaked breast

PINE WARBLER ♀
see p.374

yellow around eye

white sides to tail

OCCURRENCE
Breeds in mature spruce-fir-balsam forest across the forest belt from Yukon to the Maritimes, and south to the Great Lakes area and northern New England. Migrants occur in varied habitat, but especially woodland edges. Winters in wet forest in Central America.

Length 5½in (14cm)	Wingspan 9in (23cm)	Weight ⅜–½oz (11–15g)
Social **Migratory/Winter flocks**	Lifespan **Up to 4 years**	Status **Vulnerable**

DATE SEEN	WHERE	NOTES

| Order **Passeriformes** | Family **Parulidae** | Species *Dendroica fusca* |

Blackburnian Warbler

IN FLIGHT

white edges to outer tail feathers

bold white wing patches

MALE

pale orange line in center of crown

complex black-and-orange face pattern

white streaks on black back

white patch on wing

white belly

MALE

brilliant orange throat

black streaks on breast and belly

more subdued facial pattern

white wing bars

orange throat and breast

black streaks on flanks

FEMALE

This fiery beacon of the treetops is considered one of the most beautiful members of its family; its orange throat is unique among the North American warblers. The Blackburnian Warbler co-exists with many other *Dendroica* warblers in the coniferous and mixed woods of the north and east, but is able to do so by exploiting a slightly different niche for foraging—in this case the treetops. It also seeks the highest trees for nesting.

VOICE Call a slightly husky *chik;* flight-call a high, thin *zzee;* song variable, but always high-pitched; swirling series of lisps, spiraling upward to end in an almost inaudible *trill.*

NESTING Fine cup in conifer on horizontal branch away from trunk, usually high in tree; 4–5 eggs; 1 brood; May–July.

FEEDING Gleans arthropods, such as spiders, worms, and beetles; also fruit.

FLIGHT: fast, slightly undulating, and direct with rapid wing beats.

DISTINGUISHING FEATURES
The female is like a dull adult male, but with two wing bars and no black on the face.

AVIAN FIREFLY
This male in breeding plumage glows when seen against a dark forest background.

OCCURRENCE
Breeds in coniferous and mixed forests from Alberta east through the northern Great Lakes area to Newfoundland and south into the Appalachians of Georgia; migrants found in wooded, shrubby, or forest edge habitats. Winters in wet forests in Costa Rica and Panama, and southward as far as Peru.

SIMILAR SPECIES

BAY-BREASTED WARBLER (FALL) ♀♂
see p.364
greenish back
unstreaked underparts

CERULEAN WARBLER ♀
see p.367
sea-green back
shorter tail
white corners to tail

| Length **5in (13cm)** | Wingspan **8½in (21cm)** | Weight **⁵⁄₁₆–⁷⁄₁₆oz (9–12g)** |
| Social **Winter flocks** | Lifespan **Up to 8 years** | Status **Secure** |

DATE SEEN	WHERE	NOTES

Order **Passeriformes**	Family **Parulidae**	Species *Dendroica magnolia*

Magnolia Warbler

yellow rump

gray crown

MALE (BREEDING)

broken white tail band

IN FLIGHT

greenish back

white undertail feathers

IMMATURE (FALL)

plain face with pale eye-ring

white eyebrow

black face

incomplete eye-ring

large white patch on wing

yellow underparts with black streaks

greenish back with black stripes

black streaking on breast and flanks not as heavy

FEMALE (BREEDING)

MALE (BREEDING)

FLIGHT: fast, slightly undulating, and direct with rapid wing beats.

The bold, flashy, and common Magnolia Warbler is hard to miss as it flits around at eye level, fanning its uniquely marked tail. This species nests in young forests and winters in almost any habitat, so its numbers have not suffered in recent decades, unlike some of its relatives. Although it really has no preference for its namesake plant, the 19th century ornithologist Alexander Wilson discovered a Magnolia Warbler feeding in a magnolia tree during migration, which is how it got its name.

VOICE Call a tinny *jeinf*, not particularly warbler-like; also short, simple whistled series *wee'-sa wee'-sa WEET-a-chew*; short, distinctive, flight call a high, trilled *zeep*.

NESTING Flimsy cup of black rootlets placed low in dense conifer against trunk; 3–5 eggs; 1 brood; June–August.

FEEDING Gleans mostly caterpillars, beetles, and spiders.

SPRUCE WARBLER
The conspicuous male Magnolia Warbler can be found singing its distinctive, loud song, often throughout the day, in a spruce tree.

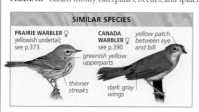

SIMILAR SPECIES

PRAIRIE WARBLER ♀ yellowish undertail; see p.373

thinner streaks

CANADA WARBLER ♀ see p.390

greenish yellow upperparts

yellow patch between eye and bill

dark gray wings

OCCURRENCE
Breeds in dense, young mixed and coniferous forests from Yukon east to Newfoundland and south into Appalachians of Tennessee; migrates across the Gulf and Caribbean; winters in varied habitats in Caribbean and from southeast Mexico to Panama; rare vagrant in the West.

Length **5in (13cm)**	Wingspan **7½in (19cm)**	Weight **7/32–7/16 oz (6–12g)**
Social **Migrant/Winter flocks**	Lifespan **Up to 6 years**	Status **Secure**

DATE SEEN	WHERE	NOTES

Order **Passeriformes**	Family **Parulidae**	Species *Dendroica cerulea*

Cerulean Warbler

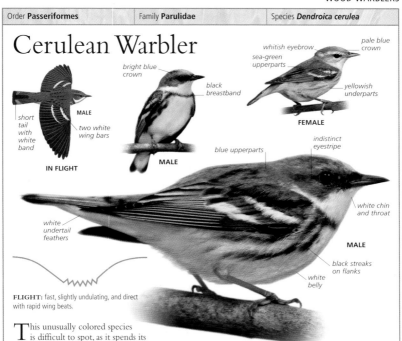

whitish eyebrow

pale blue crown

sea-green upperparts

yellowish underparts

FEMALE

bright blue crown

black breastband

MALE

blue upperparts

indistinct eyestripe

white chin and throat

MALE

black streaks on flanks

white belly

white undertail feathers

short tail with white band

MALE

two white wing bars

IN FLIGHT

FLIGHT: fast, slightly undulating, and direct with rapid wing beats.

This unusually colored species is difficult to spot, as it spends its time foraging high in the canopy of tall deciduous forests. It was once common across the Midwest and the Ohio River Valley, but its habitat is being cleared for agriculture and fragmented by development. In winter, this bird lives high in the canopy of forests in the Andean foothills, but this habitat is threatened by coffee cultivation.

VOICE Call a slurred *chip*; flight call a buzzy *zeet*; three-part, buzzy song consisting of a short series of low paired notes followed by a mid-range trill and upslurred high-pitched *zhree*.

NESTING Compact cup high on fork in deciduous tree, far from trunk; 2–5 eggs; 1 brood; May–July.

FEEDING Gleans insects high in canopy, especially from leaf bases.

UNIQUE COLOR
Female Cerulean Warblers have a unique pale blue color on their crown and back.

SIMILAR SPECIES

BLACKBURNIAN WARBLER ♀
see p.365

pale streaking on back

yellow throat

BLACK-AND-WHITE WARBLER ♀
see p.376

white streaks on upperparts

white eyebrow

black undertail markings

OCCURRENCE
Breeds mostly in mature deciduous forests across the northeastern US; tends to prefer dense woodlands during migration. Winters in evergreen forests along the foothills of the Andes, from Colombia to Peru.

Length **4¾in (12cm)**	Wingspan **7¾in (19.5cm)**	Weight **⁹⁄₃₂–⅜oz (8–10g)**
Social **Migrant/Winter flocks**	Lifespan **Up to 6 years**	Status **Vulnerable**

DATE SEEN	WHERE	NOTES

| Order **Passeriformes** | Family **Parulidae** | Species *Dendroica tigrina* |

Cape May Warbler

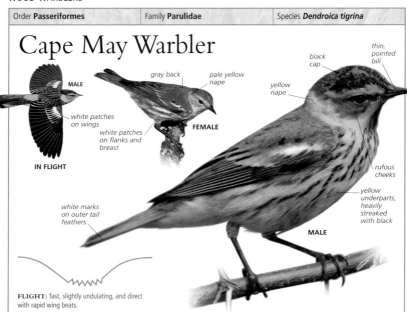

MALE

white patches on wings

gray back

pale yellow nape

FEMALE

white patches on flanks and breast

IN FLIGHT

thin, pointed bill

black cap

yellow nape

yellow nape

rufous cheeks

yellow underparts, heavily streaked with black

MALE

white marks on outer tail feathers

FLIGHT: fast, slightly undulating, and direct with rapid wing beats.

The Cape May Warbler is a spruce budworm (a moth actually, not a worm) specialist, and its populations increase during outbreaks of this pest. Cape May Warblers chase other birds aggressively from flowering trees, where they use their semitubular tongue to suck the nectar from blossoms. In its summer spruce forest habitat, the Cape May Warbler plucks insects from clumps of needles. The "Cape May" Warbler was named this way because the first specimen was collected here, but it doesn't breed at Cape May!
VOICE Song a high, even-pitched series of whistles *see see see*.
NESTING Cup placed near trunk, high in spruce or fir near top; 4–9 eggs; 1 brood; June–July.
FEEDING Gleans arthropods, especially spruce budworms, and also flies, adult moths, and beetles from mid-high levels in canopy; also fruit and nectar during the nonbreeding season.

SPRING FLASH
Magnificently colored, a male shows its chestnut cheek, yellow necklace, and yellow rump.

SIMILAR SPECIES

YELLOW-RUMPED WARBLER (MYRTLE) ♀
see p.370

yellow rump

thicker, heavier bill

yellow flank patches

PALM WARBLER (WESTERN) 🦜
see p.375

browner overall

yellow undertail feathers

OCCURRENCE
Breeds from the Yukon and British Columbia to the Great Lakes, the Maritimes, and New England in mature spruce–fir forests. Migrants occur in a variety of habitats. Winters especially in gardens in Central America, as far south as Honduras.

| Length **5in (13cm)** | Wingspan **8in (20cm)** | Weight **⁵⁄₁₆–⁷⁄₁₆oz (9–13g)** |
| Social **Migrant flocks** | Lifespan **Up to 4 years** | Status **Secure** |

DATE SEEN	WHERE	NOTES

Order **Passeriformes**	Family **Parulidae**	Species *Dendroica caerulescens*

Black-throated Blue Warbler

MALE
dark blue overall
black face
white wing patches
white patches on outer tail feathers
IN FLIGHT

olive upperparts
pale eyebrow
white patch
incomplete eye-ring, only below eye
FEMALE

dark blue upperparts
dark blue crown
black "mask" and throat
white breast ("kerchief")
black flanks
white belly
MALE

FLIGHT: fast, slightly undulating, and direct with rapid wing beats; typical warbler flight.

Male and female Black-throated Blue Warblers look so different that early ornithologists thought they belonged to different species. Many of the females have a blue wash to their wings and tail, and almost all have a subdued version of the male's white "kerchief," so identification is not difficult. This beautiful eastern North American species migrates northward in spring, along the eastern flank of the Appalachians, but a small number of birds fly, along an imaginary line, northwestward to the Great Lakes. This "line" is so clearly defined that this bird is common in Chicago but extremely rare in St. Louis.

VOICE Call a husky junco-like *tchunk*; flight call a distinctive, drawn-out, metallic *ssiiink,* reminiscent of some Northern Cardinal calls; song a relatively low-pitched series of upslurred buzzes *zu zu zo zhray zhree,* or slower *zhray zhray zhreee.*

NESTING Bulky cup of plant material a meter off ground in dense forest; 3–5 eggs; 1–2 broods; May–August.

FEEDING Gleans arthropods, mainly caterpillars, from mid-low level in forest; takes small fruit and nectar.

BLACK, WHITE, AND BLUE
Males are gorgeous year-round, especially when viewed against contrastingly colored fall foliage.

SIMILAR SPECIES

YELLOW-RUMPED WARBLER (MYRTLE) ♀
see p.370

yellow rump
two wing bars

OCCURRENCE
Breeds in relatively undisturbed deciduous and mixed hardwood forests from southern Ontario and northern Minnesota to Nova Scotia and into the Appalachians of Georgia. Fall migration through wooded habitats; a Caribbean migrant. Winters in Central and South America.

Length **5in (13cm)**	Wingspan **7½in (19cm)**	Weight **⁹⁄₃₂–⁷⁄₁₆oz (8–12g)**
Social **Migrant flocks**	Lifespan **Up to 10 years**	Status **Secure**

DATE SEEN	WHERE	NOTES

| Order **Passeriformes** | Family **Parulidae** | Species *Dendroica coronata* |

Yellow-rumped Warbler

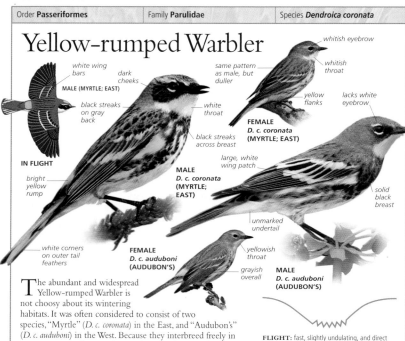

whitish eyebrow

MALE (MYRTLE; EAST)

white wing bars

dark cheeks

same pattern as male, but duller

whitish throat

yellow flanks

lacks white eyebrow

FEMALE
D. c. coronata
(MYRTLE; EAST)

black streaks on gray back

white throat

black streaks across breast

IN FLIGHT

bright yellow rump

MALE
D. c. coronata
(MYRTLE; EAST)

large, white wing patch

solid black breast

white corners on outer tail feathers

FEMALE
D. c. auduboni
(AUDUBON'S)

unmarked undertail

yellowish throat

grayish overall

MALE
D. c. auduboni
(AUDUBON'S)

The abundant and widespread Yellow-rumped Warbler is not choosy about its wintering habitats. It was often considered to consist of two species, "Myrtle" (*D. c. coronata*) in the East, and "Audubon's" (*D. c. auduboni*) in the West. Because they interbreed freely in a narrow zone of contact in British Columbia and Alberta, the American Ornithologists Union merged them. The two forms differ in plumage and voice, and their hybrid zone appears stable.
VOICE Myrtle's call a flat, husky *tchik*; Audubon's a higher-pitched, relatively musical, rising *jip*; flight call of both a clear, upslurred *sviiit*; song loose, warbled trill with an inflected ending; Myrtle's song higher and faster, Audubon's lower and slower.
NESTING Bulky cup of plant matter in conifer; 4–5 eggs; 1 brood; March–August.
FEEDING Feeds mostly on flies, beetles, wasps, and spiders during breeding; takes fruit and berries at other times of the year, often sallies to catch prey.

FLIGHT: fast, slightly undulating, and direct with rapid wing beats.

WIDESPREAD WARBLER
Yellow-rumped Warblers are widespread and are likely to be spotted often.

SIMILAR SPECIES

MAGNOLIA WARBLER ♂ see p.366	CAPE MAY WARBLER ♀ see p.368

dark eye-line

yellow throat and breast

more white in tail

thin, curved bill

OCCURRENCE
Both eastern and western populations are widespread across the continent from Alaska eastward to Québec and Labrador, and westward in the mountains south to Arizona, New Mexico, and Northern Mexico. Prefers coniferous and mixed hardwood coniferous forests.

Length **5in (13cm)**	Wingspan **9in (23cm)**	Weight ⅜–⅝oz **(10–17g)**
Social **Flocks**	Lifespan **Up to 7 years**	Status **Secure**

DATE SEEN	WHERE	NOTES

| Order **Passeriformes** | Family **Parulidae** | Species **Dendroica virens** |

Black-throated Green Warbler

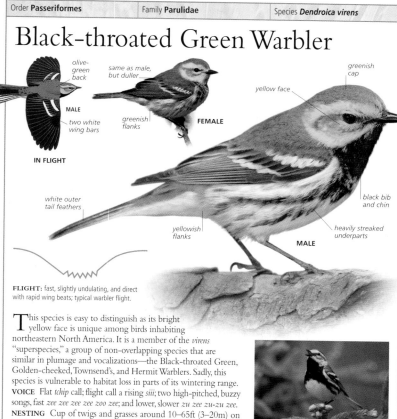

olive-green back

same as male, but duller

greenish cap

yellow face

MALE

two white wing bars

greenish flanks

FEMALE

IN FLIGHT

white outer tail feathers

yellowish flanks

black bib and chin

heavily streaked underparts

MALE

FLIGHT: fast, slightly undulating, and direct with rapid wing beats; typical warbler flight.

This species is easy to distinguish as its bright yellow face is unique among birds inhabiting northeastern North America. It is a member of the *virens* "superspecies," a group of non-overlapping species that are similar in plumage and vocalizations—the Black-throated Green, Golden-cheeked, Townsend's, and Hermit Warblers. Sadly, this species is vulnerable to habitat loss in parts of its wintering range.
VOICE Flat *tchip* call; flight call a rising *siii*; two high-pitched, buzzy songs, fast *zee zee zee zee zoo zee*; and lower, slower *zu zee zu-zu zee*.
NESTING Cup of twigs and grasses around 10–65ft (3–20m) on horizontal branch near trunk in the North, away from trunk in the South; 3–5 eggs; 1 brood; May–July.
FEEDING Gleans arthropods, especially caterpillars; also takes small fruit, including poison ivy berries, in nonbreeding season.

YELLOW-AND-BLACK GEM
From a high perch in a spruce tree, a male advertises his territory with persistent singing.

SIMILAR SPECIES

GOLDEN-CHEEKED WARBLER ♂
see p.466

black crown

thin, black eye-line

GOLDEN-CHEEKED WARBLER ♀
see p.466

darker crown

darker upper breast

OCCURRENCE
Breeds in many forest types, especially a mix of conifers and hardwood, from British Columbia east to Newfoundland and the southeastern US along the Appalachians. Migrants and wintering birds use a variety of habitats. Winters from southern Texas into Venezuela; small numbers in Caribbean.

| Length **5in (13cm)** | Wingspan **8in (20cm)** | Weight **9/32–3/8oz (8–11g)** |
| Social **Migrant/Winter flocks** | Lifespan **Up to 6 years** | Status **Secure** |

DATE SEEN	WHERE		NOTES

Order **Passeriformes**	Family **Parulidae**	Species **Dendroica dominica**

Yellow-throated Warbler

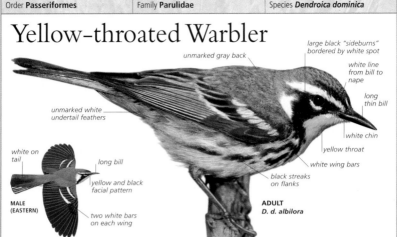

large black "sideburns" bordered by white spot

white line from bill to nape

unmarked gray back

long thin bill

white chin

unmarked white undertail feathers

yellow throat

white wing bars

white on tail

long bill

yellow and black facial pattern

black streaks on flanks

MALE (EASTERN)

two white bars on each wing

IN FLIGHT

ADULT
D. d. albilora

This is one of the earliest warblers to return from its southerly wintering grounds to its breeding grounds in the forests of the eastern US in the spring; in fact, some birds arrive by late March. The Yellow-throated Warbler is perhaps best known for its habit of creeping along branches, much like its cousin, the Black-and-white Warbler. Four subspecies have been described; the subspecies, *D. d. albilora*, has a penchant for sycamore trees. The species occasionally interbreeds with the Northern Parula, creating the so-called "Sutton's Warbler."

VOICE Flight call high, thin *siit*; song long, descending cascade of clear whistles, often with jumbled or slightly emphatic ending *Tseu'-ee tseu'-ee tseu'-oh tseu'-oh tseu'-uh tseu'-uh teedle-ee-EEdle*.

NESTING Cup of fine grasses on branch tip, usually in tree canopy; 3–5 eggs; 1–2 broods; April–July.

FEEDING Gleans spiders, insects, and insect larvae, especially caterpillars, from foliage and bark.

FLIGHT: fast, slightly undulating, and direct, with rapid wing beats.

SOUTHERNER
The Yellow-throated Warbler is a species of southern woodlands, such as cypress swamps.

SIMILAR SPECIES

GRACE'S WARBLER

yellow around eye

BLACK-AND-WHITE WARBLER
see p.376

shorter bill

black and white markings

black streaks

OCCURRENCE
Breeds in the eastern half of North America, but not in southern Florida, in woods with cypress, sycamore, or live oak; wintering birds may prefer tall palms and parklike settings. Range has extended northwards in recent years. Southern US population is non-migratory.

Length **5in (13cm)**	Wingspan **8in (20cm)**	Weight **⁹⁄₃₂–³⁄₈oz (8–11g)**
Social **Winter flocks**	Lifespan **Up to 5 years**	Status **Secure**

DATE SEEN	WHERE	NOTES

| Order **Passeriformes** | Family **Parulidae** | Species *Dendroica discolor* |

Prairie Warbler

MALE

pale yellowish wing bars

no rufous spots on back

paler markings on face

roundish wings

FEMALE

streaks on breast not as bold as male

white sides to tail

IN FLIGHT

rufous spots on back

straight, black bill

yellow face with black markings

black streaks on yellow underparts

white outertail feathers

MALE

FLIGHT: fast, slightly undulating, and direct, with rapid wing beats.

Contrary to its common name, the Prairie Warbler does not live on the "prairie." Its distinctive song is a quintessential sound of scrubby areas across the eastern US. Although its populations increased in the 19th century as a result of the widespread cutting of forests, the later maturation of this habitat, along with human development, is having a negative impact on local populations.

VOICE Call a thick *tsik* or *tchip*, flight call a high, thin *sssip*; song variable in tempo, but always series of husky, buzzy notes that increase in pitch: *zzu zzu zzu zzo zzo zzo zzee zzee.*

NESTING Cup of plant material in fork of sapling or low trees, often within human reach; 3–5 eggs; 1 brood; May–July.

FEEDING Eats various insects, such as flies and crickets; also berries.

HIGH AND LOUD
Males sing from preferred elevated perches, producing their characteristic buzzy song that increases in pitch and tempo.

SIMILAR SPECIES

MAGNOLIA WARBLER ♀
see p.366

white eye-ring

less prominent streaking

PINE WARBLER ♂
see p.374

thin, dark line through eye

white wing bars

larger overall

OCCURRENCE
Breeds in shrubby, open-canopied, second-growth habitats, and mangroves; migrant and wintering birds prefer similar-looking brushy habitats. Florida birds are partially resident. Winters in the Bahamas, Greater and Lesser Antilles, and along the coast from southern Mexico to El Salvador.

Length 4¾in (12cm)	Wingspan 9in (23cm)	Weight ⁷⁄₃₂–⁵⁄₁₆oz (6–9g)
Social **Solitary/Winter flocks**	Lifespan **Up to 10 years**	Status **Declining**

DATE SEEN	WHERE	NOTES

| Order **Passeriformes** | Family **Parulidae** | Species **Dendroica pinus** |

Pine Warbler

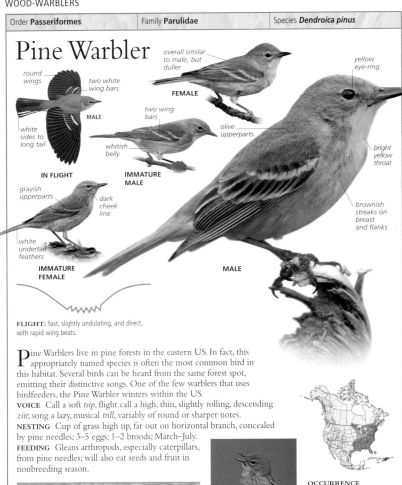

round wings

two white wing bars

MALE

white sides to long tail

IN FLIGHT

overall similar to male, but duller

FEMALE

yellow eye-ring

two wing bars

whitish belly

IMMATURE MALE

olive upperparts

bright yellow throat

grayish upperparts

dark cheek line

white undertail feathers

IMMATURE FEMALE

brownish streaks on breast and flanks

MALE

FLIGHT: fast, slightly undulating, and direct, with rapid wing beats.

Pine Warblers live in pine forests in the eastern US. In fact, this appropriately named species is often the most common bird in this habitat. Several birds can be heard from the same forest spot, emitting their distinctive songs. One of the few warblers that uses birdfeeders, the Pine Warbler winters within the US.

VOICE Call a soft *tsip*, flight call a high, thin, slightly rolling, descending *ziit*; song a lazy, musical *trill*, variably of round or sharper notes.

NESTING Cup of grass high up, far out on horizontal branch, concealed by pine needles; 3–5 eggs; 1–2 broods; March–July.

FEEDING Gleans arthropods, especially caterpillars, from pine needles; will also eat seeds and fruit in nonbreeding season.

SIMILAR SPECIES

BLACKPOLL WARBLER ♀ see p.363

larger overall

streaks on flanks

BAY-BREASTED WARBLER ♀ see p.364

greenish cheeks

buff underparts

WELL NAMED
In many areas, Pine Warblers are the most common breeding birds in mature pine woods.

OCCURRENCE
Pine and mixed forests from southern Canada and the eastern US, south to eastern Texas and Florida. Nests in deciduous forests if individual trees or small stands of pine are present. Resident in southern half of its US range. Also breeds and winters in the Bahamas and Hispaniola.

| Length **5in (13cm)** | Wingspan **9in (23cm)** | Weight **⁵⁄₁₆–½oz (9–15g)** |
| Social **Migrant/Winter flocks** | Lifespan **Up to 7 years** | Status **Secure** |

DATE SEEN	WHERE	NOTES

| Order **Passeriformes** | Family **Parulidae** | Species *Dendroica palmarum* |

Palm Warbler

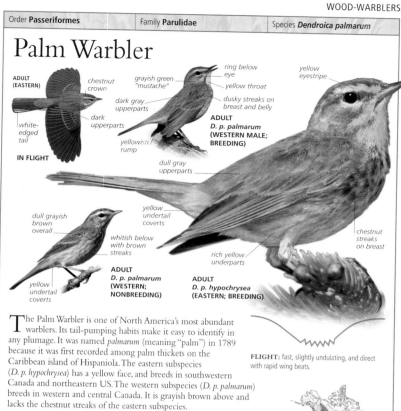

ADULT (EASTERN)
chestnut crown
dark upperparts
white-edged tail
IN FLIGHT

grayish green "mustache"
ring below eye
yellow throat
dark gray upperparts
dusky streaks on breast and belly
yellowish rump
ADULT D. p. palmarum (WESTERN MALE; BREEDING)

yellow eyestripe

dull gray upperparts

dull grayish brown overall
yellow undertail coverts
whitish below with brown streaks
yellow undertail coverts
ADULT D. p. palmarum (WESTERN; NONBREEDING)

rich yellow underparts
ADULT D. p. hypochrysea (EASTERN; BREEDING)

chestnut streaks on breast

The Palm Warbler is one of North America's most abundant warblers. Its tail-pumping habits make it easy to identify in any plumage. It was named *palmarum* (meaning "palm") in 1789 because it was first recorded among palm thickets on the Caribbean island of Hispaniola. The eastern subspecies (*D. p. hypochrysea*) has a yellow face, and breeds in southwestern Canada and northeastern US. The western subspecies (*D. p. palmarum*) breeds in western and central Canada. It is grayish brown above and lacks the chestnut streaks of the eastern subspecies.
VOICE Call a husky *chik* or *tsip*; flight call a light *ziint*; slow, loose, buzzy trill: *zwi zwi zwi zwi zwi zwi zwi zwi*.
NESTING Cup of grasses on or near ground in open area of conifers at forest edge of a bog; 4–5 eggs; 1 brood; May–July.
FEEDING Eats insects, sometimes caught in flight; also takes seeds and berries.

FLIGHT: fast, slightly undulating, and direct with rapid wing beats.

OCCURRENCE
In North America, breeds in spruce bogs within the northern forest zone, across Canada from the Yukon to the Maritimes and Labrador, and in the US from Minnesota to Maine. Often migrates through central portions of eastern US; winters in southeastern US, Florida, and Central America.

FAR FROM THE PALMS
This male Palm Warbler is far north of the coastal palms where its kin spend the winter.

SIMILAR SPECIES

CAPE MAY WARBLER ♀
see p.368
olive gray back
thin patch of yellow on throat and neck

YELLOW-RUMPED WARBLER (MYRTLE) ♀
see p.370
streaking on back
white throat

| Length **5½in (14cm)** | Wingspan **8in (20cm)** | Weight **¼–⁷⁄₁₆oz (7–13g)** |
| Social **Flocks** | Lifespan **Up to 6 years** | Status **Secure** |

DATE SEEN	WHERE		NOTES

Order **Passeriformes**	Family **Parulidae**	Species *Mniotilta varia*

Black-and-white Warbler

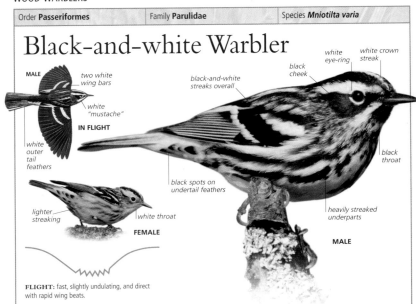

MALE
two white wing bars
white "mustache"
IN FLIGHT
white outer tail feathers

black-and-white streaks overall

white eye-ring
white crown streak
black cheek

black throat

black spots on undertail feathers

heavily streaked underparts

MALE

lighter streaking
white throat
FEMALE

FLIGHT: fast, slightly undulating, and direct with rapid wing beats.

The Black-and-white Warbler is best known for its creeper-like habit of feeding in vertical and upside-down positions as it pries into bark crevices, where its relatively long, curved bill allows it to reach tiny nooks and crannies. These habits, combined with streaked plumage, make this bird one of the most distinctive warblers in North America. It is a long-distance migrant, with some birds wintering in parts of northern South America.
VOICE Sharp *stik* call; flight call a very high, thin *ssiit*, often doubled; song a thin, high-pitched, wheezy series *wheesy wheesy wheesy wheesy wheesy.*
NESTING Cup on ground against stump, fallen logs, or roots; 4–6 eggs; 1 brood; April–August.
FEEDING Creeps along branches and trunks, probing into bark for insects and insect larvae.

SQUEAKY WHEEL
The high-pitched, wheezy song of this warbler is said to be reminiscent of a squeaky wheel.

UPSIDE-DOWN
Black-and-white Warblers often creep head-first along trunks and branches of trees.

OCCURRENCE
Breeds in deciduous and mixed mature and second-growth woodlands; migrants occur on a greater variety of habitats; winters in a wide range of wooded habitats in southern US, Mexico and into Central and South America. Rare along West Coast in winter.

SIMILAR SPECIES

BLACKPOLL WARBLER ♂
see p.363
black cap
white cheek patch

BLACK-THROATED GRAY WARBLER ♂
see p.472
yellow patch
bright orange legs

Length **5in (13cm)**	Wingspan **8in (20cm)**	Weight **⁹⁄₁₆–½oz (9–14g)**
Social **Migrant/Winter flocks**	Lifespan **Up to 11 years**	Status **Secure**

DATE SEEN	WHERE	NOTES

| Order **Passeriformes** | Family **Parulidae** | Species ***Setophaga ruticilla*** |

American Redstart

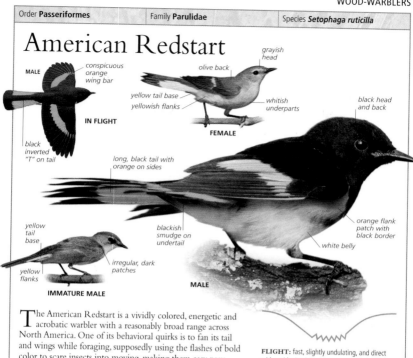

MALE

conspicuous orange wing bar

IN FLIGHT

black inverted "T" on tail

grayish head

olive back

yellow tail base
yellowish flanks

whitish underparts

FEMALE

black head and back

long, black tail with orange on sides

yellow tail base

yellow flanks

blackish smudge on undertail

irregular, dark patches

IMMATURE MALE

MALE

orange flank patch with black border

white belly

The American Redstart is a vividly colored, energetic and acrobatic warbler with a reasonably broad range across North America. One of its behavioral quirks is to fan its tail and wings while foraging, supposedly using the flashes of bold color to scare insects into moving, making them easy prey. It possesses well-developed rictal bristles, hair-like feathers extending from the corners of the mouth, which help it to detect insects.
VOICE Harsh *tsiip* call; flight call a high, thin *sweep*; song a confusingly variable, high, thin, yet penetrating series of notes; one version burry, emphatic, and downslurred *see-a see-a see-a see-a ZEE-urrrr*.
NESTING Cup of grasses and rootlets, lined with feathers; placed low in deciduous tree; 2–5 eggs; 1–2 broods; May–July.
FEEDING Gleans insects and spiders from leaves at mid-levels in trees; also catches moths, flies in flight; will also eat fruit.

FLIGHT: fast, slightly undulating, and direct with rapid wing beats.

COMMON SONG
This bird's short, ringing song is a common sound in the moist deciduous woods of the East and North.

MALE CAREGIVER
As with most warblers, male Redstarts help raise the young, though they may be polygamous.

OCCURRENCE
Breeds in moist deciduous and mixed woodlands across North America; migrants and wintering birds use a wide range of habitats. Winters from Baja California and south Florida through Middle America and the Caribbean to northern South America.

| Length **5in (13cm)** | Wingspan **8in (20cm)** | Weight **7/32–3/8oz (6–11g)** |
| Social **Flocks** | Lifespan **Up to 10 years** | Status **Secure** |

DATE SEEN	WHERE		NOTES

Order **Passeriformes**	Family **Parulidae**	Species ***Protonotaria citrea***

Prothonotary Warbler

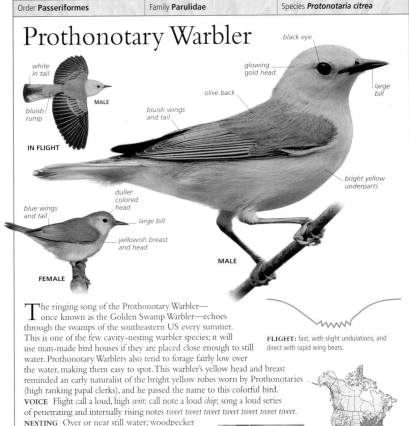

white in tail

MALE

bluish rump

IN FLIGHT

black eye

glowing gold head

large bill

olive back

bluish wings and tail

bright yellow underparts

duller colored head

blue wings and tail

large bill

yellowish breast and head

MALE

FEMALE

The ringing song of the Prothonotary Warbler— once known as the Golden Swamp Warbler—echoes through the swamps of the southeastern US every summer. This is one of the few cavity-nesting warbler species; it will use man-made bird houses if they are placed close enough to still water. Prothonotary Warblers also tend to forage fairly low over the water, making them easy to spot. This warbler's yellow head and breast reminded an early naturalist of the bright yellow robes worn by Prothonotaries (high ranking papal clerks), and he passed the name to this colorful bird.

VOICE Flight call a loud, high *sviit*; call note a loud *chip*; song a loud series of penetrating and internally rising notes *tsveet tsveet tsveet tsveet tsveet tsveet tsveet*.

NESTING Over or near still water; woodpecker holes often used; 3–8 eggs; 1–2 broods; April–July.

FEEDING Mostly eats insects and small mollusks; also seeds, fruit, and nectar.

FLIGHT: fast, with slight undulations, and direct with rapid wing beats.

GOLDEN SONGBIRD
Visible in the darkness of a southern swamp, a Prothonotary Warbler sings its ringing song.

OCCURRENCE
Breeds in wooded areas over or near still water, especially in cypress swamps and bottomlands across the southeastern US. Winters in mangroves and dry forests in southern Mexico.

SIMILAR SPECIES

BLUE-WINGED WARBLER
see p.356

white wing bars

YELLOW WARBLER ♀
see p.362

smaller bill

black eye-line

Length **5½in (14cm)**	Wingspan **9in (23cm)**	Weight **½–⅝oz (14–18g)**
Social **Winter flocks**	Lifespan **Up to 8 years**	Status **Endangered**

DATE SEEN	WHERE	NOTES

| Order **Passeriformes** | Family **Parulidae** | Species *Helmitheros vermivorum* |

Worm-eating Warbler

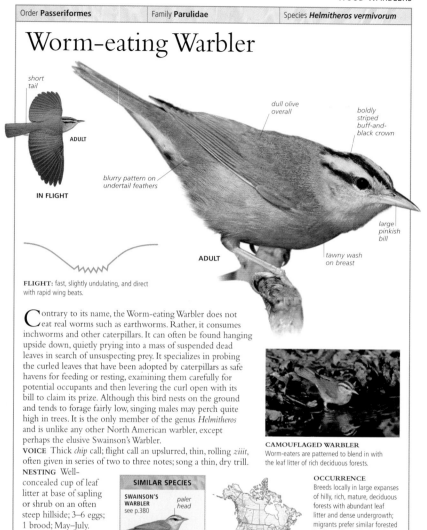

short tail

ADULT

IN FLIGHT

dull olive overall

boldly striped buff-and-black crown

blurry pattern on undertail feathers

ADULT

large pinkish bill

tawny wash on breast

FLIGHT: fast, slightly undulating, and direct with rapid wing beats.

Contrary to its name, the Worm-eating Warbler does not eat real worms such as earthworms. Rather, it consumes inchworms and other caterpillars. It can often be found hanging upside down, quietly prying into a mass of suspended dead leaves in search of unsuspecting prey. It specializes in probing the curled leaves that have been adopted by caterpillars as safe havens for feeding or resting, examining them carefully for potential occupants and then levering the curl open with its bill to claim its prize. Although this bird nests on the ground and tends to forage fairly low, singing males may perch quite high in trees. It is the only member of the genus *Helmitheros* and is unlike any other North American warbler, except perhaps the elusive Swainson's Warbler.

VOICE Thick *chip* call; flight call an upslurred, thin, rolling *ziiit*, often given in series of two to three notes; song a thin, dry trill.

NESTING Well-concealed cup of leaf litter at base of sapling or shrub on an often steep hillside; 3–6 eggs; 1 brood; May–July.

FEEDING Forages in low shrubs, mainly for caterpillars, but also insects and spiders.

CAMOUFLAGED WARBLER
Worm-eaters are patterned to blend in with the leaf litter of rich deciduous forests.

SIMILAR SPECIES

SWAINSON'S WARBLER
see p.380

paler head

paler underparts

see p.380

OCCURRENCE
Breeds locally in large expanses of hilly, rich, mature, deciduous forests with abundant leaf litter and dense undergrowth; migrants prefer similar forested habitats. Winters in Central America and the Caribbean, in varied forested habitats, but prefers dense undergrowth.

| Length **5in (13cm)** | Wingspan **8½in (21cm)** | Weight **7/16–5/8oz (12–17g)** |
| Social **Solitary/Flocks** | Lifespan **Up to 7 years** | Status **Secure** |

DATE SEEN	WHERE	NOTES

| Order **Passeriformes** | Family **Parulidae** | Species *Limnothlypis swainsonii* |

Swainson's Warbler

short tail

ADULT

IN FLIGHT

plain brown upperparts

rusty-brown crown

pale eyebrow

long bill

dusky wash on underparts

ADULT

FLIGHT: fast, slightly undulating, and direct with rapid wing beats.

Few people ever get to see Swainson's Warbler—not even those enthusiasts who regularly go looking for it. The species' remarkable song makes it relatively easy to track, but its reclusive nature, drab plumage, and liking for dense thickets make it one of the most difficult birds in North America to actually spot. The species is also quite unusual in that it has two seemingly identical populations that breed in distinct habitats—one in dense, giant canebreaks in swampy lowlands, and the other in Appalachian rhododendron or mountain laurel thickets.
VOICE Flight call high *siiii*, often doubled; song loud series of downslurred whistles ending emphatically and purposefully *su see-a see-oh WEE-chuh WEE-oh*.
NESTING Bulky mass of vegetation placed low in dense understory thicket; 2–5 eggs; 1 brood; May–July.
FEEDING Forages slowly and methodically on the forest floor for insects, insect larvae, and spiders.

PROUD SURVEYOR
A male Swainson's Warbler surveys his breeding territory from the vantage of a perch.

SIMILAR SPECIES

WORM-EATING WARBLER
see p.379

black head stripe

buff underparts

black eyebrow

LOUISIANA WATERTHRUSH
see p.383

dark gray crown

bold streaks below

OCCURRENCE
Breeds in floodplains, often in areas of dense undergrowth, and in mountain forests with suitable undergrowth; during migration and in winter found in forests with dense understory and abundant leaf litter. Winters in Central America and the West Indies.

| Length **5½in (14cm)** | Wingspan **9in (23cm)** | Weight **⁷⁄₁₆–¹¹⁄₁₆oz (12–20g)** |
| Social **Solitary/Winter flocks** | Lifespan **Up to 7 years** | Status **Declining** |

DATE SEEN	WHERE	NOTES

| Order **Passeriformes** | Family **Parulidae** | Species *Seiurus aurocapillus* |

Ovenbird

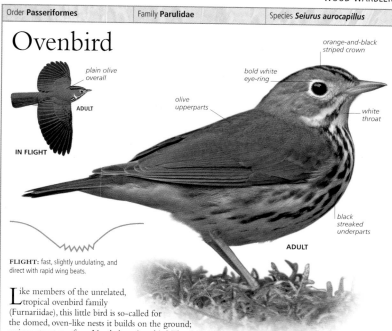

plain olive overall

ADULT

IN FLIGHT

orange-and-black striped crown

bold white eye-ring

olive upperparts

white throat

black streaked underparts

ADULT

FLIGHT: fast, slightly undulating, and direct with rapid wing beats.

Like members of the unrelated, tropical ovenbird family (Furnariidae), this little bird is so-called for the domed, oven-like nests it builds on the ground; unique structures for a North American bird. The Ovenbird is also noted for its singing. Males flit about boisterously, often at night, incorporating portions of their main song into a jumble of spluttering notes. In the forest, one male singing loudly to declare his territory can set off a whole chain of responses from his neighbors, until the whole forest rings.

VOICE Call variably pitched, sharp *chik* in series; flight call high, rising *siiii*; song loud, ringing crescendo of paired notes *chur-tee' chur-tee' chur-tee' chur-tee' chur-TEE chur-TEE chur-TEE.*

NESTING Domed structure of leaves and grass on ground with side entrance; 3–6 eggs; 1 brood; May–July.

FEEDING Forages mainly on the forest floor for insects and other invertebrates.

STRUTTING ITS STUFF
The Ovenbird is noted for the way it struts across the forest floor, a little like a tiny chicken.

SIMILAR SPECIES

NORTHERN WATERTHRUSH much slimmer; see p.382
dark brown upperparts
no eye-ring

LOUISIANA WATERTHRUSH see p.383
dark brown upperparts
white eyebrow

OCCURRENCE
Breeds in closed-canopy mixed and deciduous forests with suitable amount of fallen plant material for nest building and foraging; migrants and wintering birds use similar habitats. Winters in Florida, Central America, and the West Indies.

| Length **6in (15cm)** | Wingspan **9½in (24cm)** | Weight **⁹⁄₁₆–⁷⁄₈oz (16–25g)** |
| Social **Solitary/Flocks** | Lifespan **Up to 7 years** | Status **Declining** |

DATE SEEN	WHERE	NOTES

| Order **Passeriformes** | Family **Parulidae** | Species *Seiurus noveboracensis* |

Northern Waterthrush

pale eyebrow
narrows behind eye

dull brown
upperparts

short tail

small,
short
bill

ADULT

pale
eyebrow

fine, dense
breast
streaking

streaking
on white or
yellowish
flanks

IN FLIGHT

ADULT

dull, fleshy-colored
legs and toes

FLIGHT: fast, slightly undulating, and direct
with rapid wing beats.

The tail-bobbing Northern Waterthrush is often
heard giving a *spink!* call as it swiftly flees from
observers. Although this species may be mistaken for the closely
related Louisiana Waterthrush, there are clues that are helpful in
its identification. While the Northern Waterthrush prefers still
water, its relative greatly prefers running water; in addition, its
song is quite unlike that of the Louisiana Waterthrush.
VOICE Call a sharp, rising, ringing *spink!*; flight call a rising,
buzzy *ziiiit*; song a loud series of rich, accelerating, staccato notes,
usually decreasing in pitch *teet, teet, toh-toh toh-toh tyew-tyew!*.
NESTING Hair-lined, mossy cup placed on or near ground,
hidden in roots of fallen or standing tree or in riverbank;
4–5 eggs; 1 brood; May–August.
FEEDING Mostly eats insects such as ants, mosquitoes, moths,
and beetles, both larvae and adult, plus slugs, and snails; when
migrating, also eats small crustaceans, and even tiny fish.

YELLOW FORM
Many Northern Waterthrushes have yellow
underparts, like this one, while others have white.

SIMILAR SPECIES

OVENBIRD
much rounder;
fatter; see p.381
olive
upperparts

bold
eye-ring

**LOUISIANA
WATERTHRUSH**
see p.383

eyebrow
widens behind
eye

thicker,
longer
bill

orange
wash to
flanks

OCCURRENCE
Breeds right across northern
North America in dark,
still-water swamps and bogs;
also in the still edges of rivers
and lakes; migrant birds use
wet habitats; winters in
shrubby marshes, mangroves,
and occasionally in crops, such
as rice fields and citrus groves.
Rare in Baja California in winter.

| Length **6in (15cm)** | Wingspan **9½in (24cm)** | Weight **½–⅞oz (14–23g)** |
| Social **Solitary** | Lifespan **Up to 9 years** | Status **Secure** |

DATE SEEN	WHERE	NOTES

| Order **Passeriformes** | Family **Parulidae** | Species *Seiurus motacilla* |

Louisiana Waterthrush

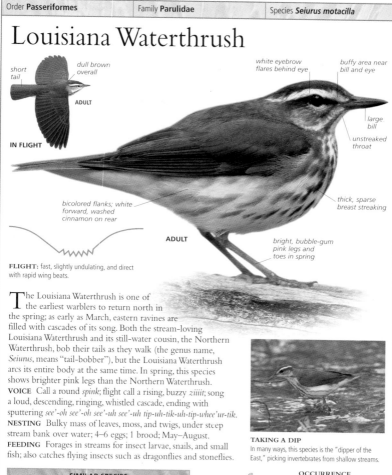

short tail

dull brown overall

ADULT

IN FLIGHT

white eyebrow flares behind eye

buffy area near bill and eye

large bill

unstreaked throat

bicolored flanks; white forward, washed cinnamon on rear

ADULT

thick, sparse breast streaking

bright, bubble-gum pink legs and toes in spring

FLIGHT: fast, slightly undulating, and direct with rapid wing beats.

The Louisiana Waterthrush is one of the earliest warblers to return north in the spring; as early as March, eastern ravines are filled with cascades of its song. Both the stream-loving Louisiana Waterthrush and its still-water cousin, the Northern Waterthrush, bob their tails as they walk (the genus name, *Seiurus*, means "tail-bobber"), but the Louisiana Waterthrush arcs its entire body at the same time. In spring, this species shows brighter pink legs than the Northern Waterthrush.
VOICE Call a round *spink*; flight call a rising, buzzy *ziiiit*; song a loud, descending, ringing, whistled cascade, ending with sputtering *see'-oh see'-oh see'-uh see'-uh tip-uh-tik-uh-tip-whee'ur-tik*.
NESTING Bulky mass of leaves, moss, and twigs, under steep stream bank over water; 4–6 eggs; 1 brood; May–August.
FEEDING Forages in streams for insect larvae, snails, and small fish; also catches flying insects such as dragonflies and stoneflies.

TAKING A DIP
In many ways, this species is the "dipper of the East," picking invertebrates from shallow streams.

SIMILAR SPECIES

OVENBIRD much rounder; fatter; see p.381 olive upperparts

bold eye-ring

NORTHERN WATERTHRUSH see p.382

thinner, shorter bill

fine breast streaks

OCCURRENCE
Breeds along fast-moving streams in deciduous forests in the eastern US; migrants stop over anywhere near running water, including gardens; winters along wooded streams and rivers in mountains and hills in the Caribbean, Mexico, Central America, and northern South America.

| Length **6in (15cm)** | Wingspan **10in (25cm)** | Weight ⅝–⅞oz (18–25g) |
| Social **Solitary** | Lifespan **Up to 8 years** | Status **Secure** |

DATE SEEN	WHERE	NOTES

| Order **Passeriformes** | Family **Parulidae** | Species *Oporornis formosus* |

Kentucky Warbler

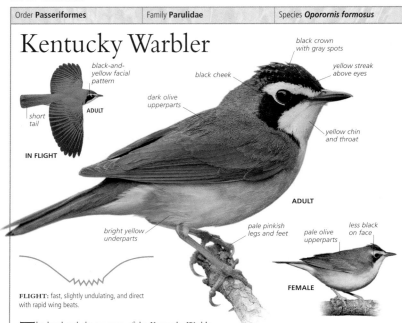

black crown
with gray spots

yellow streak
above eyes

black cheek

black-and-
yellow facial
pattern

dark olive
upperparts

yellow chin
and throat

short
tail

ADULT

IN FLIGHT

ADULT

bright yellow
underparts

pale pinkish
legs and feet

pale olive
upperparts

less black
on face

FEMALE

FLIGHT: fast, slightly undulating, and direct
with rapid wing beats.

The loud and cheery song of the Kentucky Warbler is one of the characteristic sounds of dense, moist eastern US forests. Unlike the Connecticut Warbler, it is appropriately named, because it actually breeds in its namesake state, Kentucky. This species is a rather secretive inhabitant of dense US hardwood forests, where it forages close to or on the ground, looking for insects that live on the forest floor.
VOICE Call a low, hollow *chup*, flight call a buzzy *dziiip*; song a loud rolling series of paired notes *chur-ee' chur-ee' chur-ee' chur-ee' chur-ee'*, with little variation.
NESTING Concealed bulky cup of leaves and grass on or just above ground in shrub; 4–5 eggs; 1–2 broods; May–August.
FEEDING Gleans beetles, spiders, and other arthropods, mainly in low vegetation.

LUCKY SHOT
This bird is mostly seen in the underbrush of moist forests, not out in the open like this migrant.

SIMILAR SPECIES

COMMON YELLOWTHROAT ♂
smaller; see p.387

longer
tail

black-
and-gray
face

HOODED WARBLER ♀
see p.388

greenish
crown

plain,
yellow
face

longer
tail

OCCURRENCE
Breeds in eastern US moist, deciduous forests with dense deciduous understory. Migrants prefer dense woodlands and thickets. Winters from Mexico to Panama and northern South America, in dense, wet lowland thickets and forests.

| Length **5in (13cm)** | Wingspan **8½in (21cm)** | Weight **⁷⁄₁₆–¹¹⁄₁₆oz (12–19g)** |
| Social **Solitary/Flocks** | Lifespan **Up to 7 years** | Status **Secure (p)** |

DATE SEEN	WHERE	NOTES

Order **Passeriformes**	Family **Parulidae**	Species *Oporornis agilis*

Connecticut Warbler

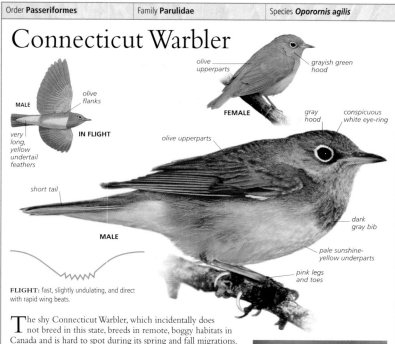

FEMALE
- olive upperparts
- grayish green hood
- gray hood
- conspicuous white eye-ring

MALE IN FLIGHT
- olive flanks
- very long, yellow undertail feathers

MALE
- olive upperparts
- short tail
- dark gray bib
- pale sunshine-yellow underparts
- pink legs and toes

FLIGHT: fast, slightly undulating, and direct with rapid wing beats.

The shy Connecticut Warbler, which incidentally does not breed in this state, breeds in remote, boggy habitats in Canada and is hard to spot during its spring and fall migrations. It arrives in the US in late May and leaves its breeding grounds in August. It is the only warbler that walks along the ground in a bouncy manner, with its tail bobbing up and down.

VOICE Seldom-heard call a nasal *champ*, flight call a buzzy *ziiiit*; song a loud "whippy," accelerating series, often ending with upward inflection *tweet, chuh WHIP-uh chee-uh-WHIP-uh chee-uh-WAY*.

NESTING Concealed cup of grass or leaves, lined with fine plant matter and hair; placed near or on ground in damp moss or grass clump; 3–5 eggs; 1 brood; June–July.

FEEDING Gleans a variety of adult insects, insect larvae, and spiders from under leaves; also eats small fruits.

EXCEPTIONAL UNDERTAIL
The yellow undertail feathers nearly reach the tip of the Connecticut Warbler's tail.

SIMILAR SPECIES

NASHVILLE WARBLER ♀
see p.359
- pale gray back

MOURNING WARBLER ♂
see p.386
- darker breast patch
- yellowish throat

OCCURRENCE
Breeds across Canada from British Columbia to Québec and in the US in Minnesota and the Great Lakes region, in bogs and pine forests. Winters in forest habitats of Amazonian Peru and Brazil.

Length **6in (15cm)**	Wingspan **9in (23cm)**	Weight **⁷⁄₁₆–¹¹⁄₁₆oz (13–20g)**
Social **Solitary**	Lifespan **Up to 4 years**	Status **Secure (p)**

DATE SEEN	WHERE	NOTES

| Order **Passeriformes** | Family **Parulidae** | Species *Oporornis philadelphia* |

Mourning Warbler

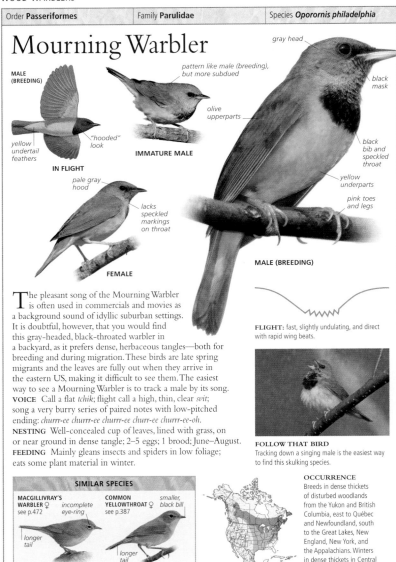

MALE (BREEDING)

pattern like male (breeding), but more subdued

olive upperparts

gray head

black mask

IN FLIGHT

yellow undertail feathers

"hooded" look

IMMATURE MALE

black bib and speckled throat

yellow underparts

pink toes and legs

pale gray hood

lacks speckled markings on throat

FEMALE

MALE (BREEDING)

The pleasant song of the Mourning Warbler is often used in commercials and movies as a background sound of idyllic suburban settings. It is doubtful, however, that you would find this gray-headed, black-throated warbler in a backyard, as it prefers dense, herbaceous tangles—both for breeding and during migration. These birds are late spring migrants and the leaves are fully out when they arrive in the eastern US, making it difficult to see them. The easiest way to see a Mourning Warbler is to track a male by its song.

VOICE Call a flat *tchik*; flight call a high, thin, clear *svit*; song a very burry series of paired notes with low-pitched ending: *churrr-ee churrr-ee churrr-ee churr-ee churrr-ee-oh.*

NESTING Well-concealed cup of leaves, lined with grass, on or near ground in dense tangle; 2–5 eggs; 1 brood; June–August.

FEEDING Mainly gleans insects and spiders in low foliage; eats some plant material in winter.

FLIGHT: fast, slightly undulating, and direct with rapid wing beats.

FOLLOW THAT BIRD
Tracking down a singing male is the easiest way to find this skulking species.

SIMILAR SPECIES

MACGILLIVRAY'S WARBLER ♀ see p.472

incomplete eye-ring

longer tail

COMMON YELLOWTHROAT ♀ see p.387

smaller, black bill

longer tail

OCCURRENCE
Breeds in dense thickets of disturbed woodlands from the Yukon and British Columbia, east to Québec and Newfoundland, south to the Great Lakes, New England, New York, and the Appalachians. Winters in dense thickets in Central and South America.

| Length **5in (13cm)** | Wingspan **7.5in (19cm)** | Weight **⅜–⁷⁄₁₆oz (10–13g)** |
| Social **Solitary** | Lifespan **Up to 8 years** | Status **Secure** |

DATE SEEN	WHERE	NOTES

| Order **Passeriformes** | Family **Parulidae** | Species *Geothlypis trichas* |

Common Yellowthroat

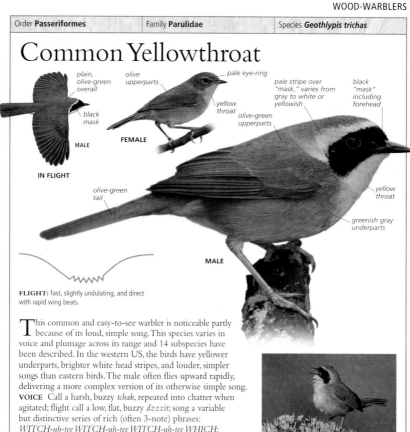

plain, olive-green overall

black mask

olive upperparts

pale eye-ring

yellow throat

olive-green upperparts

FEMALE

MALE

IN FLIGHT

pale stripe over "mask," varies from gray to white or yellowish

black "mask" including forehead

yellow throat

greenish gray underparts

olive-green tail

MALE

FLIGHT: fast, slightly undulating, and direct with rapid wing beats.

This common and easy-to-see warbler is noticeable partly because of its loud, simple song. This species varies in voice and plumage across its range and 14 subspecies have been described. In the western US, the birds have yellower underparts, brighter white head stripes, and louder, simpler songs than eastern birds. The male often flies upward rapidly, delivering a more complex version of its otherwise simple song.

VOICE Call a harsh, buzzy *tchak*, repeated into chatter when agitated; flight call a low, flat, buzzy *dzzzit*; song a variable but distinctive series of rich (often 3-note) phrases: *WITCH-uh-tee WITCH-uh-tee WITCH-uh-tee WHICH*; more complex flight song.

NESTING Concealed, bulky cup of grasses just above ground or water; 3–5 eggs; 1 brood; May–August.

FEEDING Eats insects and spiders in low vegetation; also seeds.

UNFORGETTABLE CALL
The song of the male Common Yellowthroat is an extremely helpful aid in its identification.

SIMILAR SPECIES

KENTUCKY WARBLER ♂ much larger; see p.384

yellow eyebrow

shorter tail

bright yellow belly

MOURNING WARBLER ♀ see p.386

gray head

pink-based bill

bright yellow on belly

OCCURRENCE
Found south of the tundra, from Alaska and the Yukon to Québec and Newfoundland, and south to California, Texas, and to southeastern US. Inhabits dense herbaceous understory, from marshes and grasslands to pine forest and hedgerows. Winters from Mexico to Panama and the Antilles.

| Length **5in (13cm)** | Wingspan **6¾in (17cm)** | Weight **29oz (825g)** |
| Social **Migrant/Winter flocks** | Lifespan **Up to 11 years** | Status **Secure** |

DATE SEEN	WHERE	NOTES

| Order **Passeriformes** | Family **Parulidae** | Species **Wilsonia citrina** |

Hooded Warbler

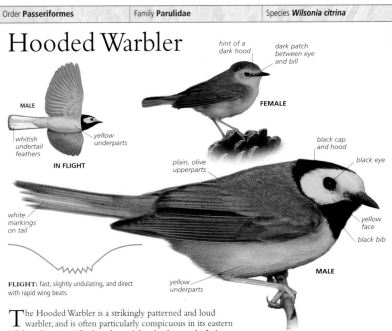

hint of a dark hood

dark patch between eye and bill

MALE

whitish undertail feathers

yellow underparts

FEMALE

IN FLIGHT

plain, olive upperparts

black cap and hood

black eye

white markings on tail

yellow face

black bib

MALE

FLIGHT: fast, slightly undulating, and direct with rapid wing beats.

yellow underparts

The Hooded Warbler is a strikingly patterned and loud warbler, and is often particularly conspicuous in its eastern US breeding range. Both males and females frequently flash the white markings hidden on the inner webs of their tails. The extent of the black hood varies in female Hooded Warblers; it ranges from none in first fall birds to almost as extensive as males in some adult females. Genetic (DNA) and vocal information point to a close relationship with *Dendroica* warblers.

VOICE Call a metallic *tsink*; flight call a high, thin *sweep*; song a rich, whistled series, ending loudly and emphatically: *tu-wee' tu-wee' tu-wee-TEE-tee-yu.*

NESTING Bulky cup of leaves lined with hair, in shrub near eye level; 3–5 eggs; 1–2 broods; May–July.

FEEDING Eats many different kinds of insects found low in vegetation.

STRIKING MASK
The black and yellow face of the Hooded Warbler makes the male an unmistakable bird.

SIMILAR SPECIES

WILSON'S WARBLER ♂
see p.389

smaller overall

WILSON'S WARBLER ♀
see p.389

smaller overall

no black bib

no dark patch

OCCURRENCE
Breeds in moist deciduous forests with dense understory in eastern US; has bred in some moist mountain canyons. Migrants like similar habitat. Winters in moist woodlands with good understory, especially lowland rain forest, from eastern Mexico to Panama and the West Indies.

| Length **5¼in (13.5cm)** | Wingspan **7in (17.5cm)** | Weight **5/16oz–7/16oz (9–12g)** |
| Social **Migrant/Winter flocks** | Lifespan **Up to 8 years** | Status **Secure (p)** |

DATE SEEN	WHERE	NOTES

Order **Passeriformes**	Family **Parulidae**	Species ***Wilsonia pusilla***

Wilson's Warbler

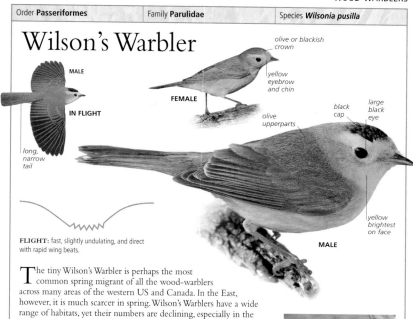

olive or blackish crown

MALE

FEMALE

yellow eyebrow and chin

IN FLIGHT

olive upperparts

black cap

large black eye

long, narrow tail

yellow brightest on face

MALE

FLIGHT: fast, slightly undulating, and direct with rapid wing beats.

The tiny Wilson's Warbler is perhaps the most common spring migrant of all the wood-warblers across many areas of the western US and Canada. In the East, however, it is much scarcer in spring. Wilson's Warblers have a wide range of habitats, yet their numbers are declining, especially in the West, as its riverine breeding habitats are gradually being destroyed by development. This species and the entire genus are named after the renowned early 19th-century ornithologist, Alexander Wilson.

VOICE Call a rich *chimp* or *champ;* flight call a sharp, liquid *tsik;* song a variable, chattering trill, often increases in speed *che che che che chi-chi-chi-chit*.

NESTING Cup of leaves and grass placed on or near ground in mosses or grass, higher along Pacific coast; 4–6 eggs; 1 brood; April–June.

FEEDING Captures insects in foliage, leaf litter, or during flight; also takes berries and honeydew.

BRIGHT WESTERN BIRD
In its western range, male Wilson's Warblers have a glowing yellow-orange face; eastern birds are duller.

EASY IDENTIFICATION
The black cap and yellow face of the otherwise olive-colored Wilson's Warbler are good field marks.

OCCURRENCE
Breeds in wet shrubby thickets with no canopy, often along streams and lakes; Pacific slope birds use more varied habitats, including moist forests. Widespread in forests south of tundra, from Newfoundland, the Great Lakes, and northern New England; British Columbia to California and New Mexico.

SIMILAR SPECIES

YELLOW WARBLER ♀ see p.362

yellow edges to wing feathers

shorter tail

yellow overall

HOODED WARBLER ♀ see p.388

larger body

larger bill

Length **4¾in (12cm)**	Wingspan **7in (17.5cm)**	Weight **⁷⁄₃₂–⁵⁄₁₆oz (6–9g)**
Social **Flocks**	Lifespan **Up to 6 years**	Status **Declining**

DATE SEEN	WHERE	NOTES

| Order **Passeriformes** | Family **Parulidae** | Species ***Wilsonia canadensis*** |

Canada Warbler

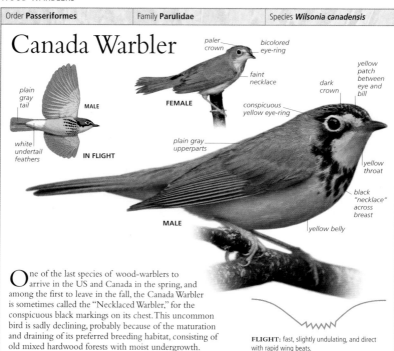

MALE

paler crown

bicolored eye-ring

faint necklace

FEMALE

plain gray tail

IN FLIGHT

white undertail feathers

yellow patch between eye and bill

dark crown

conspicuous yellow eye-ring

plain gray upperparts

yellow throat

black "necklace" across breast

yellow belly

MALE

One of the last species of wood-warblers to arrive in the US and Canada in the spring, and among the first to leave in the fall, the Canada Warbler is sometimes called the "Necklaced Warbler," for the conspicuous black markings on its chest. This uncommon bird is sadly declining, probably because of the maturation and draining of its preferred breeding habitat, consisting of old mixed hardwood forests with moist undergrowth.

VOICE Call a thick *tchip;* flight call a variable, clear *plip;* song a haphazard jumble of sweet notes, often beginning with or interspersed with *tchip,* followed by a pause.
NESTING Concealed cup of leaves, in moss or grass, on or near ground; 4–5 eggs; 1 brood; May–June.
FEEDING Gleans at mid-levels for many species of insects; also flycatches and forages on ground.

FLIGHT: fast, slightly undulating, and direct with rapid wing beats.

TAKING FLIGHT
This species often waits for prey to fly by, before launching into flight to pursue it.

FAMILIAR MEAL
Flying insects, including crane flies, make up the bulk of the Canada Warbler's diet.

SIMILAR SPECIES	
MAGNOLIA WARBLER ♀ see p.366 — white eyebrow — streaked flanks	**KIRTLAND'S WARBLER** ♂ see p.466 — streaked mantle and flanks

OCCURRENCE
Breeds in moist deciduous, mixed, and coniferous forests with well-developed understory, especially swampy woods; migrants use well-vegetated habitats; winters in dense, wet thickets and a variety of tropical woodlands in South America.

| Length **5in (13cm)** | Wingspan **8in (20cm)** | Weight **9⁄32–1⁄2oz (8–15g)** |
| Social **Flocks** | Lifespan **Up to 8 years** | Status **Declining** |

DATE SEEN	WHERE	NOTES

| Order **Passeriformes** | Family **Parulidae** | Species *Icteria virens* |

Yellow-breasted Chat

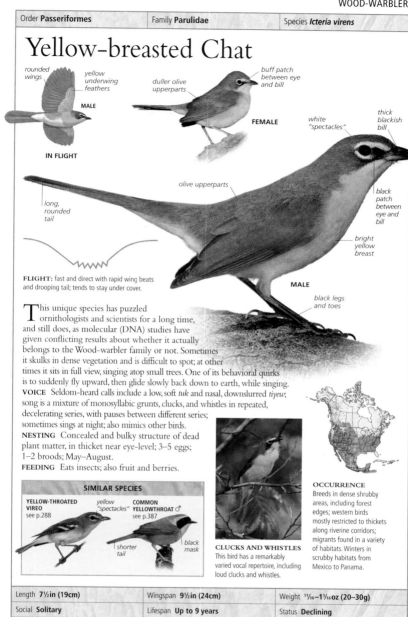

rounded wings

yellow underwing feathers

MALE

IN FLIGHT

duller olive upperparts

buff patch between eye and bill

FEMALE

white "spectacles"

thick blackish bill

olive upperparts

black patch between eye and bill

long, rounded tail

bright yellow breast

FLIGHT: fast and direct with rapid wing beats and drooping tail; tends to stay under cover.

MALE

black legs and toes

This unique species has puzzled ornithologists and scientists for a long time, and still does, as molecular (DNA) studies have given conflicting results about whether it actually belongs to the Wood-warbler family or not. Sometimes it skulks in dense vegetation and is difficult to spot; at other times it sits in full view, singing atop small trees. One of its behavioral quirks is to suddenly fly upward, then glide slowly back down to earth, while singing.

VOICE Seldom-heard calls include a low, soft *tuk* and nasal, downslurred *tiyeu*; song is a mixture of monosyllabic grunts, clucks, and whistles in repeated, decelerating series, with pauses between different series; sometimes sings at night; also mimics other birds.

NESTING Concealed and bulky structure of dead plant matter, in thicket near eye-level; 3–5 eggs; 1–2 broods; May–August.

FEEDING Eats insects; also fruit and berries.

SIMILAR SPECIES

YELLOW-THROATED VIREO see p.288

yellow "spectacles"

COMMON YELLOWTHROAT ♂ see p.387

shorter tail

black mask

CLUCKS AND WHISTLES This bird has a remarkably varied vocal repertoire, including loud clucks and whistles.

OCCURRENCE Breeds in dense shrubby areas, including forest edges; western birds mostly restricted to thickets along riverine corridors; migrants found in a variety of habitats. Winters in scrubby habitats from Mexico to Panama.

| Length **7½ in (19cm)** | Wingspan **9½ in (24cm)** | Weight **¹¹⁄₁₆–1¹⁄₁₆ oz (20–30g)** |
| Social **Solitary** | Lifespan **Up to 9 years** | Status **Declining** |

DATE SEEN	WHERE	NOTES

ORIOLES & BLACKBIRDS

THE ICTERIDS EXEMPLIFY the wonderful diversity that exists among birds. Most members are common and widespread, occurring from coast to coast. They are present in nearly every habitat in North America, from the arid Southwest and Florida to the boreal forest zone in the north but do not live in the tundra. The species reveal a tremendous variety in color, nesting, and social behavior—from solitary orioles to vast colonies of blackbirds. One group of icterids, the cowbirds, are obligatory brood parasites, and make no nest, but lay their eggs in the nests of other species, mostly small songbirds.

ORIOLES

Orioles are generally recognized by their contrasting black and orange plumage, although some species tend more toward yellow or chestnut shades. They are common tropical to subtropical seasonal migrants to North America, and their intricate hanging nests are an impressive combination of engineering and weaving. Most oriole species have a loud and melodious song and show tolerance of humans, a combination that makes them popular throughout their range. The Orchard Oriole and the Baltimore Oriole are widespread in the East, but the other North American species live either in the West, the Southwest, or in southern Texas. The Eastern North American orioles spend the winter in tropical America.

COWBIRDS

These strictly parasitic birds have been known to lay eggs in the nests of nearly 300 different bird species in North and South America. The males of all three North American species are readily identified by their thick bills and dark, iridescent plumage. The females and immatures, however, are drab, brownish, or blackish birds. The eastern species, the Brown-headed Cowbird, has dramatically increased in recent years.

SUBTLE BRILLIANCE
Although its plumage is dark, the Common Grackle displays a beautiful iridescence.

BLACKBIRDS & GRACKLES

This group of birds is largely covered with dark feathers, and has a streamlined appearance due to long, pointed bills and tails. Not as brilliantly colored as some of the other icterids, these are among the most numerous birds on the continent. After the breeding season they gather in huge flocks and form an impressive sight.

BIG VOICE
A Meadowlark's melodious voice is a defining feature in many rural landscapes.

MEADOWLARKS

Meadowlarks occur in both North and South America. The North American species have yellow breasts; the South American species have bright red ones. Only one species breeds in the East. It can be distinguished from its western counterpart by its song.

NECTAR LOVER
The magnificently colored Baltimore Oriole inserts its bill into the base of a flower, taking the nectar, but playing no part in pollination.

| Order **Passeriformes** | Family **Icteridae** | Species *Icterus spurius* |

Orchard Oriole

black back

MALE

IN FLIGHT

deep orange shoulders

dark, rusty orange rump

white-edged flight feathers

MALE

black tail

slightly curved, blue-gray, black-tipped bill

olive upperparts, very similar to female

black face, chin, and throat

IMMATURE MALE (1ST SPRING)

dark, rusty orange belly

olive upperparts

two white wing bars

yellowish underparts

FEMALE

A small bird, the Orchard Oriole resembles a large warbler in size, color, and the way it flits among leaves while foraging for insects. It flutters its tail, unlike other orioles. It spends less time on the breeding grounds than other migrant orioles, often arriving there as late as mid-May and leaving as early as late-July. The Orchard Oriole tolerates humans and can be found breeding in suburban parks and gardens. In recent years, its numbers have increased in the eastern part of its range.
VOICE Fast, not very melodious, series of high warbling notes mixed with occasional shorter notes ending in slurred *shheere*.
NESTING Woven nest of grass suspended in fork between branches; 4–5 eggs; 1 brood; April–July.
FEEDING Mainly eats insects during breeding season, but will also feed on seeds, fruit, and occasionally, nectar; in winter, mostly fruit and nectar, and some insects.

FLIGHT: quite bouncy flight due to shallow, quick wing beats; interrupted by glides.

RUSTY ORANGE SPLASH
The male Orchard Oriole has distinctive black upperparts and dark, rusty-orange underparts.

SIMILAR SPECIES

SCOTT'S ORIOLE
see p.467

yellow shoulder

bright yellow underparts

BALTIMORE ORIOLE
see p.394

black breast

orange underparts

larger overall

OCCURRENCE
Breeds in the eastern US, in open forest and woodland edges with a mixture of evergreen and deciduous trees, especially along river bottoms and in shelter belts surrounding agricultural land. Winters in Mexico, Central America, and South America.

| Length **7–8in (18–20cm)** | Wingspan **9in (23cm)** | Weight **11/16oz (20g)** |
| Social **Pairs** | Lifespan **Up to 9 years** | Status **Secure** |

DATE SEEN	WHERE	NOTES

Order **Passeriformes**	Family **Icteridae**	Species *Icterus galbula*

Baltimore Oriole

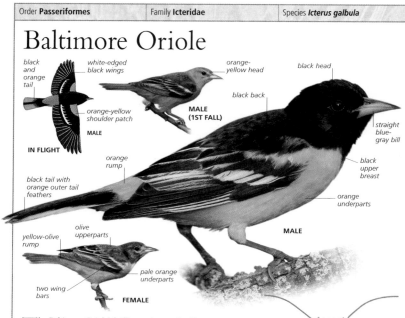

black and orange tail

white-edged black wings

orange-yellow shoulder patch

MALE

IN FLIGHT

orange-yellow head

black back

MALE (1ST FALL)

black head

straight blue-gray bill

black upper breast

orange rump

orange underparts

black tail with orange outer tail feathers

MALE

olive upperparts

yellow-olive rump

two wing bars

pale orange underparts

FEMALE

The Baltimore Oriole's brilliant colors are familiar to many persons in the East because this bird is tolerant of human presence. This species originally favored the American Elm for nesting, but Dutch Elm disease decimated these trees. The oriole has since adapted to using sycamores, cottonwoods, and other tall trees for its nesting sites. Its ability to use suburban gardens and parks has helped expand its range to areas densely occupied by humans. The Baltimore Oriole is Maryland's State Bird, somewhat ironically.
VOICE Loud, clear, melodious song comprising one or two, or several short notes in series, often of varying lengths.
NESTING Round-bottomed basket usually woven of grass, hung toward the end of branches; 4–5 eggs; 1 brood; May–July.
FEEDING Hops or flits among leaves and branches picking insects and spiders; fond of caterpillars; also eats fruits and sips nectar.

FLIGHT: strong with rapid wing beats; full downstrokes during flight provide great power.

PERFECT FOR FORAGING
The Baltimore Oriole forages alone in dense foliage of trees and bushes or on the ground.

SIMILAR SPECIES

ORCHARD ORIOLE
see p.393

darker overall

BULLOCK'S ORIOLE
see p.467

incomplete black hood

chestnut-colored belly

black eyeline

orange cheeks

huge white patch

OCCURRENCE
Forest edges and tall, open mixed hardwoods, especially close to rivers; regularly uses forested parks, suburban and urban areas with abundant tall trees. Small numbers winter in southeastern US and Florida, but most birds move to Mexico, Colombia, and Venezuela.

Length **8–10in (20–26cm)**	Wingspan **10–12in (26–30cm)**	Weight **1¹⁄₁₆–1¼oz (30–35g)**
Social **Solitary/Pairs**	Lifespan **Up to 11 years**	Status **Secure**

DATE SEEN	WHERE	NOTES

| Order **Passeriformes** | Family **Icteridae** | Species *Molothrus ater* |

Brown-headed Cowbird

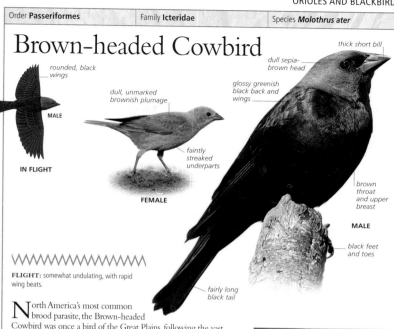

rounded, black wings

MALE

IN FLIGHT

dull, unmarked brownish plumage

faintly streaked underparts

FEMALE

thick short bill

dull sepia-brown head

glossy greenish black back and wings

brown throat and upper breast

MALE

black feet and toes

fairly long black tail

FLIGHT: somewhat undulating, with rapid wing beats.

Ｎorth America's most common brood parasite, the Brown-headed Cowbird was once a bird of the Great Plains, following the vast herds of bison to feed on insects kicked up by their hooves. Now, most likely as a result of forest clearance and suburban development, it is found continent-wide and north to the Yukon and Canada. It has become a serious threat to the breeding success of North American songbirds. It lays its eggs in the nests of more than 220 different species, and its young are raised to fledglings by more than 140 species, including the highly endangered Kirtland's Warbler.
VOICE High-pitched, squeaky whistles and bubbling notes, *dub-dub-come-tzeee*; also various clucks and *cheks*.
NESTING No nest, lays eggs in nests of other species; a female may lay an astounding 25–55 (or more) eggs per season; April–August.
FEEDING Primarily eats grass seeds and cereal grains, but also insects when available, especially grasshoppers and beetles.

AT A FEEDER
A female Brown-headed Cowbird enjoys a snack of seeds at a suburban feeder.

SIMILAR SPECIES

BRONZED COWBIRD ♂
see p.468
red eye
glossy blue-black wings and tail
longer, thicker bill

SHINY COWBIRD ♂
see p.468
glossy purplish-black
thinner, more pointed bill

OCCURRENCE
Favors habitats modified by human activity, such as open wooded patches, low grass fields, orchards, agricultural pastures with livestock, and suburban residential areas. Widespread across North America in both Canada and the US. Eastern birds spend the winter locally, and south to central Mexico.

| Length **6–8in (15–20cm)** | Wingspan **11–13in (28–33cm)** | Weight **1⁷⁄₁₆–1³⁄₄oz (40–50g)** |
| Social **Large flocks** | Lifespan **Up to 16 years** | Status **Secure** |

DATE SEEN	WHERE	NOTES

Order **Passeriformes**	Family **Icteridae**	Species *Agelaius phoeniceus*

Red-winged Blackbird

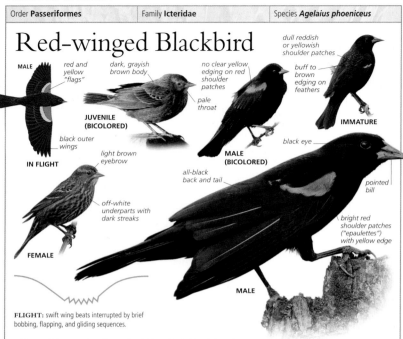

MALE

red and yellow "flags"

dark, grayish brown body

no clear yellow edging on red shoulder patches

dull reddish or yellowish shoulder patches

buff to brown edging on feathers

JUVENILE (BICOLORED)

pale throat

IMMATURE

black outer wings

IN FLIGHT

light brown eyebrow

MALE (BICOLORED)

black eye

all-black back and tail

pointed bill

off-white underparts with dark streaks

bright red shoulder patches ("epaulettes") with yellow edge

FEMALE

MALE

FLIGHT: swift wing beats interrupted by brief bobbing, flapping, and gliding sequences.

One of the most abundant native bird species in North America, the Red-winged Blackbird is also one of the most conspicuous in wetland habitats. The sight and sound of males singing from the tops of cattails is a sure sign that spring is near. This adaptable species migrates and roosts in flocks that may number in the millions. There are 22 subspecies, one of the most distinctive being the "Bicolored" Blackbird (*A. p. gubernator*) from Mexico.

VOICE Various brusk *chek, chit,* or *chet* calls; male song a *kronk-a-rhee* with a characteristic nasal, rolling and metallic "undulating" ending.

NESTING Cup of grasses and mud woven into dense standing reeds or cattails; 3–4 eggs; 1–2 broods; March–June.

FEEDING Forages for seeds and grains; largely insects when breeding.

DENSE FLOCKS
The huge flocks of Red-winged Blackbirds seen in the fall and during migration are an amazing sight.

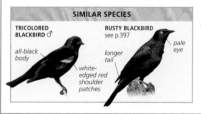

SIMILAR SPECIES		
TRICOLORED BLACKBIRD♂	**RUSTY BLACKBIRD** see p.397	
all-black body	longer tail	pale eye
white-edged red shoulder patches		

OCCURRENCE
Widespread across Canada and the US from Alaska to the Maritimes, and south to Mexico, Central America, and the Bahamas. Lives in wetlands, especially freshwater marshes with cattails, and also saltwater; wet meadows with tall grass and open woodlands with reeds. Migrates south in winter.

Length **7–10in (18–25cm)**	Wingspan **11–14in (28–35cm)**	Weight **1⁹⁄₁₆–2¹⁄₂oz (45–70g)**
Social **Flocks**	Lifespan **At least 14 years**	Status **Secure**

DATE SEEN	WHERE	NOTES

Order **Passeriformes**	Family **Icteridae**	Species ***Euphagus carolinus***

Rusty Blackbird

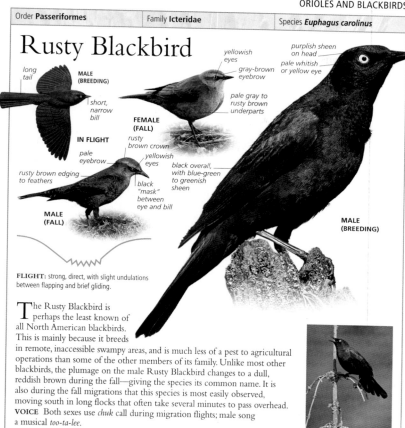

long tail

MALE (BREEDING)

short, narrow bill

IN FLIGHT

pale eyebrow

rusty brown edging to feathers

MALE (FALL)

rusty brown crown

yellowish eyes

black "mask" between eye and bill

yellowish eyes

gray-brown eyebrow

pale gray to rusty brown underparts

FEMALE (FALL)

black overall, with blue-green to greenish sheen

purplish sheen on head

pale whitish or yellow eye

MALE (BREEDING)

FLIGHT: strong, direct, with slight undulations between flapping and brief gliding.

The Rusty Blackbird is perhaps the least known of all North American blackbirds. This is mainly because it breeds in remote, inaccessible swampy areas, and is much less of a pest to agricultural operations than some of the other members of its family. Unlike most other blackbirds, the plumage on the male Rusty Blackbird changes to a dull, reddish brown during the fall—giving the species its common name. It is also during the fall migrations that this species is most easily observed, moving south in long flocks that often take several minutes to pass overhead.
VOICE Both sexes use *chuk* call during migration flights; male song a musical *too-ta-lee*.
NESTING Small bowl of branches and sticks, lined with wet plants and dry grass, usually near water; 3–5 eggs; 1 brood; May–July.
FEEDING Eats seasonally available insects, spiders, grains, seeds of trees, and fleshy fruits or berries.

WIDE OPEN
Seldom seen, the male's courtship display includes gaping and tail-spreading.

OCCURRENCE
Breeds in moist to wet forests up to the timberline in the far north from Alaska to NE Canada; but barely in the continental US (farther north than any other species of North American blackbird); winters in eastern US, in several kinds of swampy forests.

SIMILAR SPECIES

BREWER'S BLACKBIRD see p.398
purplish sheen on head
longer tail

COMMON GRACKLE see p.399
bill thicker at base
large tail

bluish sheen on head
glossy bronze body

Length **8–10in (20–25cm)**	Wingspan **12–15in (30–38cm)**	Weight **1⁹⁄₁₆–2⁷⁄₈oz (45–80g)**
Social **Pairs/Winter flocks**	Lifespan **At least 9 years**	Status **Secure**

DATE SEEN	WHERE		NOTES

Order **Passeriformes**	Family **Icteridae**	Species *Euphagus cyanocephalus*

Brewer's Blackbird

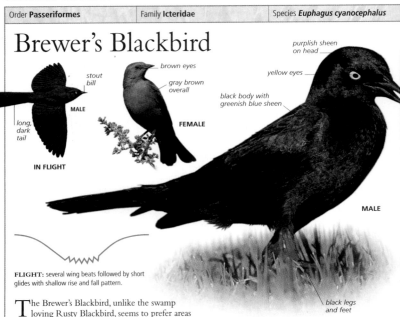

purplish sheen on head

yellow eyes

black body with greenish blue sheen

brown eyes

gray brown overall

FEMALE

stout bill

MALE

long, dark tail

IN FLIGHT

MALE

black legs and feet

FLIGHT: several wing beats followed by short glides with shallow rise and fall pattern.

The Brewer's Blackbird, unlike the swamp loving Rusty Blackbird, seems to prefer areas disturbed by humans to natural ones throughout much of its range. It is likely that the relatively recent eastward range expansion of Brewer's Blackbird has been aided by changes in land practices. Interestingly, when the Brewer's Blackbird range overlaps with that of the Common Grackle, it wins out in rural areas, but loses out in urban areas. This species can be found feasting on waste grains left behind after the harvest.
VOICE Buzzy *tshrrep* song ascending in tone.
NESTING Bulky cup of dry grass, stem and twig framework lined with soft grasses and animal hair; 3–6 eggs; 1–2 broods; April–July.
FEEDING Forages on the ground for many species of insects during breeding season, also snails; seeds, grain, and occasional fruit in fall and winter.

BROWN-EYED BIRD
Brown eyes distinguish the female Brewer's from the yellow-eyed, female Rusty Blackbird.

SIMILAR SPECIES

RUSTY BLACKBIRD see p.397

shorter tail

bill thinner at base

COMMON GRACKLE see p.399

glossy bronze body

long, wedge-shaped tail

OCCURRENCE
Breeds and winters in open areas, readily adapting to, and preferring, disturbed areas and human developments such as parks, gardens, clear-felled forests, and fallow fields edged with dense trees or shrubs.

Length **10–12in (25–30cm)**	Wingspan **13–16in (33–41cm)**	Weight **1¾–2½oz (50–70g)**
Social **Flocks/Colonies**	Lifespan **Up to 13 years**	Status **Secure**

DATE SEEN	WHERE	NOTES

Order **Passeriformes**	Family **Icteridae**	Species *Quiscalus quiscula*

Common Grackle

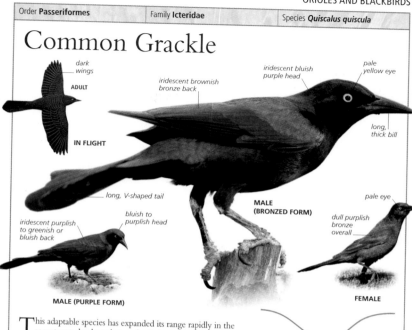

dark wings

ADULT

IN FLIGHT

iridescent brownish bronze back

iridescent bluish purple head

pale yellow eye

long, thick bill

MALE (BRONZED FORM)

long, V-shaped tail

bluish to purplish head

iridescent purplish to greenish or bluish back

MALE (PURPLE FORM)

pale eye

dull purplish bronze overall

FEMALE

This adaptable species has expanded its range rapidly in the recent past, thanks to human land clearing practices. The Common Grackle is so well suited to urban and suburban habitats that it successfully excludes other species from them. During migration and winter, Common Grackles form immense flocks, some of which may be made up of more than one million individuals. This tendency, combined with its preference for cultivated areas, has made this species an agricultural pest in some regions.

VOICE Call a low, harsh *chek*; loud song series of odd squeaks and whistles.

NESTING Small bowl in trees, with a frame of sticks filled with mud and grasses; 4–6 eggs; 1–2 broods; April–July.

FEEDING Eats beetles, flies, spiders, and worms, as well as small vertebrates; also seeds and grain, especially in nonbreeding season; an omnivore.

FLIGHT: straight, level, and direct without the up and down undulation of blackbird species.

SIMILAR SPECIES

GREAT-TAILED GRACKLE larger; see p.400

BOAT-TAILED GRACKLE see p.401

purplish gloss to feathers

very long, deeply wedged tail

longer tail

bluish gloss on black feathers

HIGHLY ADAPTABLE This grackle is comfortable near human developments, resulting in the expansion of its range.

OCCURRENCE
The Common Grackle lives in a wide variety of open woodlands, suburban woodlots, city parks, gardens, and hedgerows. It is absent west of the Great Plains. Wintering range extends south to the Gulf Coast.

Length **11–13½in (28–34cm)**	Wingspan **15–18in (38–46cm)**	Weight **3⅛–4oz (90–125g)**
Social **Flocks**	Lifespan **Up to 20 years**	Status **Secure**

DATE SEEN	WHERE	NOTES

| Order **Passeriformes** | Family **Icteridae** | Species *Quiscalus mexicanus* |

Great-tailed Grackle

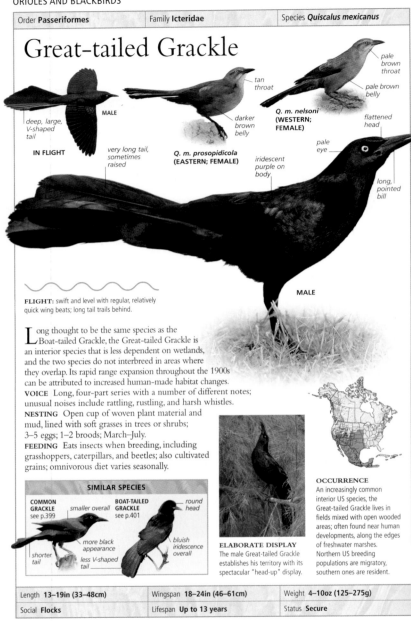

MALE

IN FLIGHT

deep, large, V-shaped tail

very long tail, sometimes raised

Q. m. prosopidicola (EASTERN; FEMALE)

tan throat

darker brown belly

pale brown throat

pale brown belly

Q. m. nelsoni (WESTERN; FEMALE)

flattened head

iridescent purple on body

pale eye

long, pointed bill

MALE

FLIGHT: swift and level with regular, relatively quick wing beats; long tail trails behind.

Long thought to be the same species as the Boat-tailed Grackle, the Great-tailed Grackle is an interior species that is less dependent on wetlands, and the two species do not interbreed in areas where they overlap. Its rapid range expansion throughout the 1900s can be attributed to increased human-made habitat changes.

VOICE Long, four-part series with a number of different notes; unusual noises include rattling, rustling, and harsh whistles.

NESTING Open cup of woven plant material and mud, lined with soft grasses in trees or shrubs; 3–5 eggs; 1–2 broods; March–July.

FEEDING Eats insects when breeding, including grasshoppers, caterpillars, and beetles; also cultivated grains; omnivorous diet varies seasonally.

SIMILAR SPECIES

COMMON GRACKLE see p.399

smaller overall

more black appearance

shorter tail

BOAT-TAILED GRACKLE see p.401

round head

bluish iridescence overall

less V-shaped tail

ELABORATE DISPLAY
The male Great-tailed Grackle establishes his territory with its spectacular "head-up" display.

OCCURRENCE
An increasingly common interior US species, the Great-tailed Grackle lives in fields mixed with open wooded areas; often found near human developments, along the edges of freshwater marshes. Northern US breeding populations are migratory, southern ones are resident.

| Length **13–19in (33–48cm)** | Wingspan **18–24in (46–61cm)** | Weight **4–10oz (125–275g)** |
| Social **Flocks** | Lifespan **Up to 13 years** | Status **Secure** |

DATE SEEN	WHERE	NOTES

Order **Passeriformes**	Family **Icteridae**	Species *Quiscalus major*

Boat-tailed Grackle

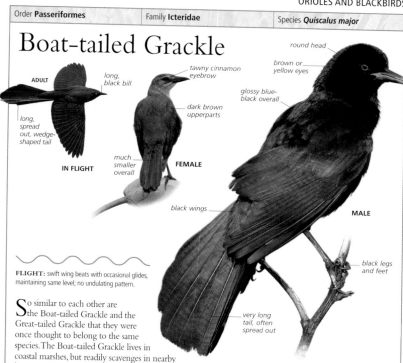

ADULT

long, black bill

tawny cinnamon eyebrow

dark brown upperparts

long, spread out, wedge-shaped tail

much smaller overall

FEMALE

IN FLIGHT

black wings

round head

brown or yellow eyes

glossy blue-black overall

MALE

black legs and feet

very long tail, often spread out

FLIGHT: swift wing beats with occasional glides, maintaining same level; no undulating pattern.

So similar to each other are the Boat-tailed Grackle and the Great-tailed Grackle that they were once thought to belong to the same species. The Boat-tailed Grackle lives in coastal marshes, but readily scavenges in nearby human settlements. In spring, females form large nesting colonies. These attract many males, but only the most dominant males succeed in mating. Their preferred breeding habitat is salt marshes.
VOICE Long, loud, three-part series of high pitched notes, *chreeet chreeet*, followed by low growl, and finally by *shreet shreet*.
NESTING Rough cups of grass and mud, woven into standing marsh vegetation like cattails or branches of shubs or trees; 2–5 eggs; 1–2 broods; March–June.
FEEDING Highly varied diet includes insects, crayfish, clams, seeds, fruit, fish, frogs, lizards, nestling birds; also human refuse.

PLAIN BROWN
Unlike the glossy blue-black males, females are brown, with darker wings and tail.

SIMILAR SPECIES

COMMON GRACKLE see p.399

paler eye

GREAT-TAILED GRACKLE see p.400

shorter tail

smaller overall

longer tail

larger overall

OCCURRENCE
Breeds along the Gulf and Atlantic coasts of the US, and in Florida along interior waterways; resident in tidal areas of coastal marshes and their neighboring upland components; also urban and suburban, human-altered habitats. Roosts colonially in same areas in winter.

Length **13–18in (33–46cm)**	Wingspan **16–24in (41–61cm)**	Weight **3½–8½oz (100–240g)**
Social **Loose colonies/Winter flocks**	Lifespan **Up to 12 years**	Status **Localized**

| Order **Passeriformes** | Family **Icteridae** | Species *Sturnella magna* |

Eastern Meadowlark

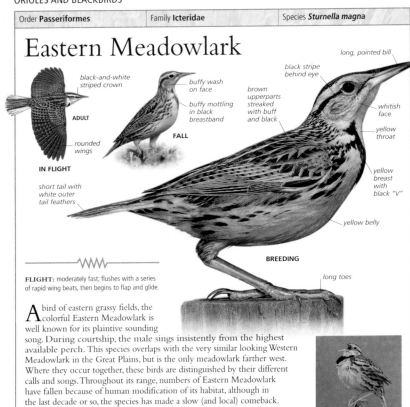

long, pointed bill

black stripe behind eye

black-and-white striped crown

ADULT

rounded wings

IN FLIGHT

buffy wash on face

buffy mottling in black breastband

FALL

brown upperparts streaked with buff and black

whitish face

yellow throat

yellow breast with black "V"

short tail with white outer tail feathers

yellow belly

BREEDING

long toes

FLIGHT: moderately fast; flushes with a series of rapid wing beats, then begins to flap and glide.

A bird of eastern grassy fields, the colorful Eastern Meadowlark is well known for its plaintive sounding song. During courtship, the male sings insistently from the highest available perch. This species overlaps with the very similar looking Western Meadowlark in the Great Plains, but is the only meadowlark farther west. Where they occur together, these birds are distinguished by their different calls and songs. Throughout its range, numbers of Eastern Meadowlark have fallen because of human modification of its habitat, although in the last decade or so, the species has made a slow (and local) comeback.

VOICE Call a sharp *dzzeer*; song a series of clear, descending whistles consisting of 3–8 notes, *tseeeoou tseeeeou*.

NESTING Loosely woven, usually domed, cup of grasses and other plants, located on the ground in tall grass fields; 3–8 eggs; 1 brood; March–May.

FEEDING Forages on ground, mainly for insects, especially grasshoppers, but also caterpillars and grubs; seeds and grain in winter.

FAVORITE PERCH
Eastern Meadowlarks are partial to fenceposts as a favorite perch for singing.

OCCURRENCE
Breeds in native tallgrass openings, pastures, and overgrown roadsides. Widespread in eastern North America, from Québec to New Mexico and Arizona; also in Mexico and Cuba, and locally in northern South America. Partial migrant in the US, resident in Mexico and South America.

SIMILAR SPECIES

AMERICAN PIPIT
see p.342

more slender, shorter bill

no yellow on chest

WESTERN MEADOWLARK
see p.403

slightly paler

more yellow at corner of bill

| Length **7–10in (18–25cm)** | Wingspan **13–15in (33–38cm)** | Weight **2⅛–4oz (60–125g)** |
| Social **Pairs/Winter flocks** | Lifespan **Up to 9 years** | Status **Declining** |

DATE SEEN	WHERE	NOTES

| Order **Passeriformes** | Family **Icteridae** | Species *Sturnella neglecta* |

Western Meadowlark

short wings

ADULT

yellow throat

white outer tail feathers

IN FLIGHT

yellow patch between bill and eye

long, pointed bill

blackish brown stripe behind eye

chunky body

black "V" on yellow chest

black spots and streaks on sides and flanks

yellow underparts

ADULT (BREEDING)

duller pattern than breeding bird

ADULT (NONBREEDING)

short, wide tail

long toes

FLIGHT: several rapid wing beats followed by a short glide.

Although the range of the Western Meadowlark overlaps widely with that of its Eastern counterpart, hybrids between the two species are very rare and usually sterile. The large numbers of Western Meadowlarks in the western Great Plains, the Great Basin, and the Central Valley of California, combined with the male's tendency to sing conspicuously from the tops of shrubs, when fenceposts are not available, make this species attractive to birdwatchers. Where the two meadowlarks overlap they are best identified by their song.

VOICE Series of complex, bubbling, whistled notes descending in pitch.
NESTING Domed grass cup, well hidden in tall grasses; 3–7 eggs; 1 brood; March–August.
FEEDING Feeds mostly on insects, including beetles, grubs, and grasshoppers; also grains and grass seeds.

SIMILAR SPECIES

AMERICAN PIPIT
see p.342

shorter bill

lacks yellow chest and black necklace

EASTERN MEADOWLARK
see p.402

less yellow at corner of beak

slightly darker overall

A SHRUB WILL DO
With few fenceposts in the Western Meadowlark's habitat, it perches on a shrub to sing.

OCCURRENCE
Common in western North America, across much of southern Canada and the western US, south to Mexico. Breeds primarily in open grassy plains, but also uses agricultural fields with overgrown edges and hayfields. Partial migrant in US, winters south to Mexico.

| Length **7–10in (18–26cm)** | Wingspan **13–15in (33–38cm)** | Weight **2⅞–4oz (80–125g)** |
| Social **Pairs/Winter flocks** | Lifespan **Up to 10 years** | Status **Secure** |

DATE SEEN	WHERE	NOTES

| Order **Passeriformes** | Family **Icteridae** | Species *Xanthocephalus xanthocephalus* |

Yellow-headed Blackbird

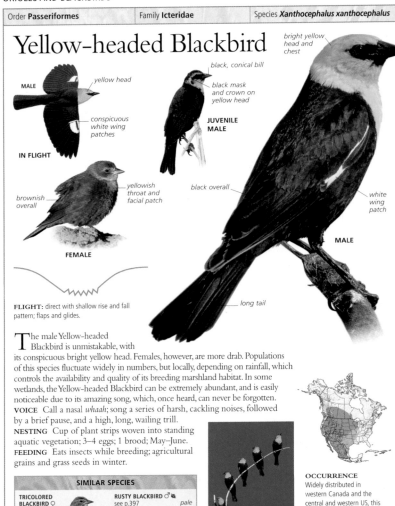

bright yellow head and chest

MALE

yellow head

IN FLIGHT

conspicuous white wing patches

black, conical bill

black mask and crown on yellow head

JUVENILE MALE

black overall

white wing patch

MALE

brownish overall

yellowish throat and facial patch

FEMALE

long tail

FLIGHT: direct with shallow rise and fall pattern; flaps and glides.

The male Yellow-headed Blackbird is unmistakable, with its conspicuous bright yellow head. Females, however, are more drab. Populations of this species fluctuate widely in numbers, but locally, depending on rainfall, which controls the availability and quality of its breeding marshland habitat. In some wetlands, the Yellow-headed Blackbird can be extremely abundant, and is easily noticeable due to its amazing song, which, once heard, can never be forgotten.

VOICE Call a nasal *whaah*; song a series of harsh, cackling noises, followed by a brief pause, and a high, long, wailing trill.

NESTING Cup of plant strips woven into standing aquatic vegetation; 3–4 eggs; 1 brood; May–June.

FEEDING Eats insects while breeding; agricultural grains and grass seeds in winter.

SIMILAR SPECIES

TRICOLORED BLACKBIRD ♀

lacks yellow throat

RUSTY BLACKBIRD ♂ ♀
see p.397

pale eye

lacks yellow throat

larger

YELLOW GARLAND
Five evenly spaced yellow-headed males watch over their wetland habitat from a twig.

OCCURRENCE
Widely distributed in western Canada and the central and western US, this species breeds in marshes with cattail and bullrush vegetation, and also, locally, in wetlands within wooded areas. Winters in Mexico; resident in Baja California.

| Length **8½–10½in (21–27cm)** | Wingspan **15in (38cm)** | Weight **2⅛–3½oz (60–100g)** |
| Social **Flocks/Colonies** | Lifespan **Up to 9 years** | Status **Localized** |

DATE SEEN	WHERE	NOTES

| Order **Passeriformes** | Family **Icteridae** | Species *Dolichonyx oryzivorus* |

Bobolink

black wings

buff-colored hindneck

MALE (BREEDING)

IN FLIGHT

sparrow-like markings

pointed tail feathers

blackish brown crown

gold-buff overall

pinkish bill

central crown stripe

FEMALE (BREEDING)

buffy throat

ADULT (FALL)

white shoulder feathers

white rump

black face and crown

black underparts

MALE (BREEDING)

black tail with pointed feathers

FLIGHT: typically direct flight; series of rapid wing beats; glides of varying length.

The Bobolink is a common summer resident of open fallow fields through much of the northern US and southern Canada. In spring, the males perform a conspicuous circling or "helicoptering" display, which includes singing, to establish territory and to attract females. Bobolink populations have declined on its breeding grounds and in wintering areas because of habitat loss and changing agricultural practices.

VOICE Calls like the end of its name *link*; song a long, complex babbling series of musical notes varying in length and pitch.

NESTING Woven cup of grass close to or on the ground, well hidden in tall grass; 3–7 eggs; 1 brood; May–July.

FEEDING Feeds mostly on insects, spiders, grubs in breeding season, but seasonally variable; also cereal grains and grass seeds.

TAKING A BREAK
This male has fled the sun of the open fields to seek shelter in the shade of a tree.

SIMILAR SPECIES

RED-WINGED BLACKBIRD see p.396
red shoulder patches

lacks buff-colored hindneck

larger overall

LARK BUNTING see p.411
lacks buff-colored hindneck

larger

white wing patches

OCCURRENCE
Breeds in open fields with a mixture of tall grasses and other herbaceous vegetation, especially old hayfields. In Canada from British Columbia to the East Coast; in the US from Idaho to New England. Migrates through the southern US and the Caribbean; winters in northern South America.

| Length **6–8in (15–20cm)** | Wingspan **10–12in (25–30cm)** | Weight **1¹⁄₁₆–2oz (30–55g)** |
| Social **Winter flocks** | Lifespan **Up to 10 years** | Status **Declining** |

DATE SEEN	WHERE	NOTES

LONGSPURS & AMERICAN SPARROWS

THE EMBERIZIDAE IS A FAMILY of finch-like birds that includes longspurs, buntings, and American sparrows. These birds occur everywhere in the world except for Australia and Antarctica. Emberizid finches are a diverse group, with over 300 species worldwide, including about 50 in North America. Although the scientific names of these birds are straightforward, their common names are not, and it is easy to become confused. Early settlers in North America thought these birds resembled European sparrows, and most North American emberizids are named "sparrows," despite having no close relationship with the European species *Passer domesticus*, which was deliberately introduced to the US.

Distinguishing between different North American sparrows can be a daunting job. Many are small, brownish birds, with streaking in their plumage. They usually remain hidden in dense vegetation, and are not easy to see. Clues such as voice, habitat, behavior, and body shape are essential in their identification.

BEST VIEW
Singing males like this Chestnut-collared Longspur are easily seen in summer.

Emberizids tend to forage for seeds on or near the ground, using their stout, conical bills to crush the seeds. Some North American sparrow species are year-round residents, but most are either migrants or partial migrants, and some have both resident and migrant populations. Fox Sparrows and Song Sparrows provide superb examples of species in the making, with numerous subspecies and overlapping ranges: because of geographical and ecological diversification, we are able to observe evolution in action.

TYPICAL SPARROW
A White-crowned Sparrow shows the typical stout emberizid beak.

TANAGERS

THE TANAGERS COMPRISE a large, diverse family of over 200 songbird species, found only in the Americas. Some tropical species are dull-colored, and feed on insects from the forest floor, while others are rainbow-colored fruit-eaters that congregate in the canopy of fruit-bearing trees. North American tanagers belong to the genus *Piranga*, a Tupi-Guarani name from South America. Males are brightly colored in reds or yellows, but females are dull greenish yellow. The Eastern species migrate to South America.

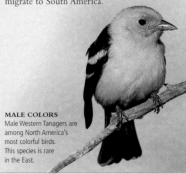

MALE COLORS
Male Western Tanagers are among North America's most colorful birds. This species is rare in the East.

CARDINALS

THE FAMILY CARDINALIDAE includes the well-known Northern Cardinal, but also the Dickcissel, several grosbeaks, and "buntings." These buntings have the same common name as some emberizid finches, but are unrelated to them. All cardinalids are vocal, and some are spectacularly colored, especially the electric-blue Indigo Bunting and the multicolored Painted Bunting. The Pyrrhuloxia, with a parrot-like bill, is a close relative of the Northern Cardinal.

STRONG BILLS
Male Pyrrhuloxias have impressive bills for cutting open seed hulls and nuts, and opening large fruits. Pyrrhuloxias are rare in the East.

Order **Passeriformes**	Family **Emberizidae**	Species *Calcarius lapponicus*

Lapland Longspur

thin white edge to tail

MALE (BREEDING)

black face

rich buffy hood

IN FLIGHT

streaked crown

white eye-line

thick yellowish bill

bright rufous nape

black streak on throat

FEMALE (BREEDING)

rusty wing panel

ADULT (NONBREEDING)

thick streaking on flanks

black flanks

white underparts

MALE (BREEDING)

FLIGHT: deeply undulating, with birds often calling in troughs as they flap.

The genus name, *Calcarius*, refers to the long hind claw of this bird, hence "longspur" in American usage. The Lapland Longspur is one of the most numerous breeding birds in the Arctic tundra, from Labrador west to Alaska, and across northern Eurasia. In winter, they form huge flocks in open habitats of southern Canada and the US. They are found on gravel roads and barren countryside immediately after heavy snowfalls. DNA data suggest that the longspurs and *Plectrophenax* buntings may not belong to the family Emberizidae, but where remains an open question.
VOICE Flight call a dry rattle, *tyew*, unlike other longspurs; song a series of thin tinklings and whistles, melodious often in flight.
NESTING Cup of grass and sedges placed in depression on ground next to a clump of vegetation; 4–6 eggs; 1 brood; May–July.
FEEDING Eats insects during breeding season; seeds in winter.

CONSPICUOUS SPECIES
This longspur is one of the most conspicuous breeding birds of the Arctic tundra.

OCCURRENCE
Breeds in tundra right across the high Arctic of North America and Eurasia. Winters in open grasslands and barren fields, and on beaches across the northern and central US and south-central and northeastern Canada.

SIMILAR SPECIES

SMITH'S LONGSPUR ♀
see p.408
white bars on wing
thin bill

CHESTNUT-COLLARED LONGSPUR ♀ ❋
see p.409
dark cheek patch
more white in tail

Length **6½in (16cm)**	Wingspan **10½–11½in (27–29cm)**	Weight **⅞–1¹⁄₁₆oz (25–30g)**
Social **Large flocks**	Lifespan **Up to 5 years**	Status **Secure**

DATE SEEN	WHERE	NOTES

Order **Passeriformes**	Family **Emberizidae**	Species *Calcarius pictus*

Smith's Longspur

MALE (BREEDING)

white outer tail feathers

white cheek patch

relatively long wings

IN FLIGHT

rich, buffy overall

wings extend past tail

FEMALE

fine breast streaks

white shoulder

black-and-white "helmet"

small bill

orange collar

rich pumpkin-colored underparts

MALE (BREEDING)

white undertail feathers

With their pumpkin colored breast and black-and-white "helmet," breeding males Smith's Longspurs contrast strongly with their drab winter plumage. Females are pale versions of the males. On both its remote breeding grounds in the Arctic, and its restricted shortgrass range in winter, this bird hides on the ground at all times, making it hard to spot. Smith's Longspurs migrate through the Great Plains to reach their wintering grounds, but on the return journey they swing east, making their migration path elliptical. This species breeds communally and does not hold territories: males mate with several females who, in turn, mate with other males.
VOICE Flight call a mechanical, dry, sharp rattle; also a nasal *nief* when squabbling; song a series of thin, sweet whistles.
NESTING Concealed cup of sedges, lined with feathers, placed in hummock on ground; 3–5 eggs; 1 brood; June–July.
FEEDING Eats mainly seeds and insects; migrants may rely heavily upon introduced foxtail grass.

FLIGHT: deeply undulating, with birds often calling in troughs as they flap.

LINEBACK LONGSPUR
On his breeding or spring staging grounds, the male sports a striking black-and-white "helmet."

SIMILAR SPECIES

LAPLAND LONGSPUR ♀ ❄
see p.407

thicker bill

broad, reddish edges to wings

CHESTNUT-COLLARED LONGSPUR ♀ ❄
see p.409

lacks rich buff color and streaks

more white in tail

OCCURRENCE
Breeds along the tundra-taiga timberline from northern Alaska southeastwards to northern Ontario; also mountainous southeastern Alaska and southwestern Yukon. Migrants are found in shortgrass prairies. Winters in open areas with shortgrass in Kansas, Oklahoma, Texas, and Arkansas.

Length **6–6½in (15–16cm)**	Wingspan **10–11½in (25–29cm)**	Weight **⅞–1¹⁄₁₆oz (25–30g)**
Social **Large flocks**	Lifespan **Up to 5 years**	Status **Secure**

DATE SEEN	WHERE	NOTES

| Order **Passeriformes** | Family **Emberizidae** | Species *Calcarius ornatus* |

Chestnut-collared Longspur

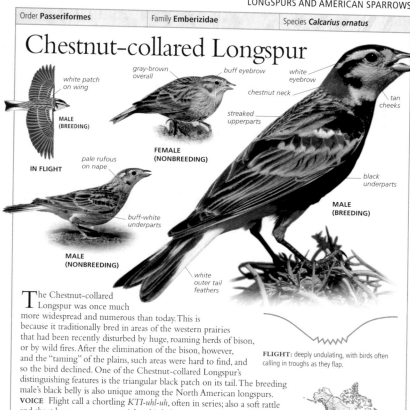

white patch
on wing

**MALE
(BREEDING)**

IN FLIGHT

gray-brown
overall

buff eyebrow

**FEMALE
(NONBREEDING)**

pale rufous
on nape

buff-white
underparts

**MALE
(NONBREEDING)**

white eyebrow

chestnut neck

tan
cheeks

streaked
upperparts

black
underparts

**MALE
(BREEDING)**

white
outer tail
feathers

The Chestnut-collared
Longspur was once much
more widespread and numerous than today. This is
because it traditionally bred in areas of the western prairies
that had been recently disturbed by huge, roaming herds of bison,
or by wild fires. After the elimination of the bison, however,
and the "taming" of the plains, such areas were hard to find, and
so the bird declined. One of the Chestnut-collared Longspur's
distinguishing features is the triangular black patch on its tail. The breeding
male's black belly is also unique among the North American longspurs.
VOICE Flight call a chortling *KTI-uhl-uh*, often in series; also a soft rattle
and short buzz; song a sweet, rich, whistled series, in
fluttering, circular flights over the prairies.
NESTING Grassy cup on ground, in grass clump or
next to rock; 3–5 eggs; 1–2 broods; May–August.
FEEDING Eats seeds year-round; also feeds on
insects when breeding.

FLIGHT: deeply undulating, with birds often
calling in troughs as they flap.

SIMILAR SPECIES

MCCOWN'S LONGSPUR ♀
see p.472

shorter, mostly
white tail

rich, buff
coloration

SMITH'S LONGSPUR ♀ ♣
see p.408

larger, thicker bill

less white
in tail

NOW AND THEN
The male bird usually sings
from the air, but occasionally
from a prominent perch.

OCCURRENCE
Breeds in shortgrass prairie
from Alberta east to Minnesota,
south to northeastern Colorado
and northwestern Nebraska;
on migration, grasslands and
cultivated fields. Winters in
grasslands and other barren
areas in the southern Great
Plains west to southeastern
Arizona and south to Mexico.

| Length **5½–6in (14–15cm)** | Wingspan **10–10½in (25–27cm)** | Weight **⅜–¹¹⁄₁₆oz (11–20g)** |
| Social **Large flocks** | Lifespan **Up to 4 years** | Status **Declining** |

DATE SEEN	WHERE	NOTES
....	....	....
....	....	....
....	....	....
....	....	....
....	....	....

Order **Passeriformes**	Family **Emberizidae**	Species *Plectrophenax nivalis*

Snow Bunting

less white in wings

white outer tail feathers

MALE (NONBREEDING)

black back

yellow bill

IN FLIGHT large white patches on black wings

MALE (BREEDING)

FEMALE (NONBREEDING)

white head and underparts

black bill

FEMALE (BREEDING)

pale rufous crown

white underparts

dark brown eyes

rusty-orange cheek patch

black peeks through buffy feather edgings

rusty-orange breast patch

gray body

white eye-ring

MALE (NONBREEDING)

white underparts

JUVENILE

The bold white wing patches of the Snow Bunting make it immediately recognizable in a whirling winter flock of dark-winged longspurs and larks. In winter, heavy snowfall forces flocks onto roadsides, where they can be seen more easily. To secure and defend the best territories, some males arrive as early as April in their barren high-Arctic breeding grounds; these buntings breed farther north than any other songbirds. The Snow Bunting is very similar in appearance to the rare McKay's Bunting, localized to western Alaska. Although McKay's Bunting generally has less black on the back, in the wings, and on the tail, the two species cannot always be conclusively identified. This is especially true as they sometimes interbreed, producing hybrids.
VOICE Flight a call musical, liquid rattle, also *tyew* notes and short buzz; song a pleasant series of squeaky and whistled notes.
NESTING Bulky cup of grass and moss, lined with feathers, and placed in sheltered rock crevice; 3–6 eggs; 1 brood; June–August.
FEEDING Eats seeds (sedge in Arctic), flies and other insects, and buds on migration.

FLIGHT: deeply undulating; flocks "roll" along as birds at back overtake those in front.

ROCKY GROUND
About the only perches in the Snow Bunting's barren breeding grounds are large boulders.

SIMILAR SPECIES

McKAY'S BUNTING

mostly white tail, back, and wings

OCCURRENCE
Breeds in rocky areas, usually near sparsely vegetated tundra, right across the Arctic in both North America and Eurasia. North American birds winter in open country and along shores across the southern Canada and the northern US, and in southern and western coastal areas of Alaska.

Length **6½–7in (16–18cm)**	Wingspan **12½–14in (32–35cm)**	Weight **1¼–2oz (35–55g)**
Social **Large flocks**	Lifespan **Unknown**	Status **Secure**

DATE SEEN	WHERE	NOTES

| Order **Passeriformes** | Family **Emberizidae** | Species *Calamospiza melanocorys* |

Lark Bunting

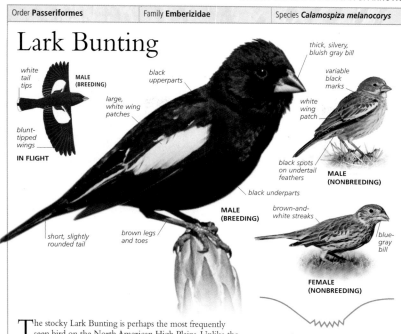

white tail tips

MALE (BREEDING)

black upperparts

thick, silvery, bluish gray bill

variable black marks

large, white wing patches

white wing patch

blunt-tipped wings

IN FLIGHT

black spots on undertail feathers

MALE (NONBREEDING)

black underparts

MALE (BREEDING)

brown-and-white streaks

blue-gray bill

short, slightly rounded tail

brown legs and toes

FEMALE (NONBREEDING)

The stocky Lark Bunting is perhaps the most frequently seen bird on the North American High Plains. Unlike the Chestnut-collared Longspur, which lives alongside it, it has coped with the changes wrought on its habitat by humans, and occurs in extraordinarily high density throughout its range. Nomadic flocks of thousands of birds scour the high deserts, open grasslands, and sage brushlands for seeds. Breeding-plumage males are unmistakable: black with large white wing patches. Females and immature birds are duller, with more subdued wing patches.
VOICE Call a low, soft, whistled *hwoik*; song partly melodious, partly "scratchy," with repetitions of phrases, then whistles.
NESTING Open cup of grass, lined with fine plant material, in depression in ground; 4–5 eggs; 1 brood; May–August.
FEEDING Mainly seeds in winter, a variety of insects in summer.

FLIGHT: low and undulating, short glides alternating with stiff wing beats.

CAUGHT BY ANY MEANS
Lark Buntings hawk, glean, and forage insect prey throughout the breeding season.

SIMILAR SPECIES

PURPLE FINCH ♀
see p.348

no white in notched tail

VESPER SPARROW
see p.431

no white wing patches

pink bill

longer, squarer tail

OCCURRENCE
Breeds in grasslands and sage flats on High Plains from Alberta south to the Texas panhandle. Winters in similar habitats—and also in deserts, cultivated plains, and open shrubsteppes—across interior southwestern US and northern Mexico. Migrants use similar open-country habitats.

| Length **7in (18cm)** | Wingspan **10½–11in (27–28cm)** | Weight **1¹⁄₁₆–1¾oz (30–50g)** |
| Social **Large flocks** | Lifespan **Unknown** | Status **Secure** |

DATE SEEN	WHERE	NOTES

Order **Passeriformes**	Family **Emberizidae**	Species **Passerella iliaca**

Fox Sparrow

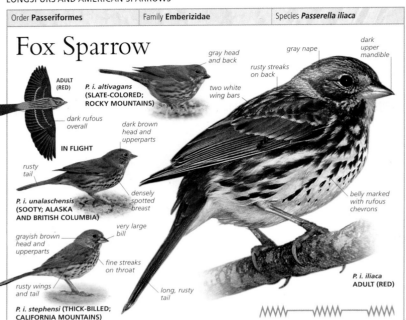

ADULT (RED)

P. i. altivagans (SLATE-COLORED; ROCKY MOUNTAINS)

gray head and back

rusty streaks on back

two white wing bars

gray nape

dark upper mandible

rusty streaks on back

dark rufous overall

IN FLIGHT

dark brown head and upperparts

rusty tail

P. i. unalaschensis (SOOTY; ALASKA AND BRITISH COLUMBIA)

densely spotted breast

belly marked with rufous chevrons

grayish brown head and upperparts

very large bill

fine streaks on throat

rusty wings and tail

long, rusty tail

P. i. stephensi (THICK-BILLED; CALIFORNIA MOUNTAINS)

P. i. iliaca **ADULT (RED)**

FLIGHT: alternates wing beats and glides; straight and fluttery, from cover to cover.

FOXY RED
The Fox Sparrow gets its name from the rusty coloration of the eastern "Red" birds.

Larger, more robust, and more colorful than its close relatives, the Fox Sparrow is a beautiful species. When it appears in backyards, its presence can be detected by its foraging habits; it crouches low in leaf litter, and hops back and forth, noisily, to disturb leaves, under which it finds seeds or insects. It varies considerably over its huge range. Eastern birds are the distinctive "reds." Thick-billed birds are found in the Sierras, sooty ones in the Pacific Northwest, and slate-colored ones in the Rockies.
VOICE Call is sharp, dry *tshak* or *tshuk;* flight call a high-pitched *tzeep!;* song is complex and musical with trills and whistles.
NESTING Dense cup of grasses or moss lined with fine material; usually placed low in shrub; 2–5 eggs; 1 brood; April–July.
FEEDING Forages for insects, seeds, and fruit.

OCCURRENCE
Encompasses the entire boreal forest zone, from Alaska in the West to Québec, Labrador, and Newfoundland in the East. In the East, it occurs in boreal forests. Winters in the Pacific West, south to Baja California; also from Texas to Massachusetts.

SIMILAR SPECIES

HERMIT THRUSH
see p.338
unstreaked flanks

SONG SPARROW
see p.413
different bill shape
thinner bill
longer tail
breast streaking less marked

Length **6–7½in (15–19cm)**	Wingspan **10½–11½in (27–29cm)**	Weight **⅞–1⁹⁄₁₆oz (25–45g)**
Social **Solitary/Small flocks**	Lifespan **Up to 9 years**	Status **Secure**

DATE SEEN	WHERE	NOTES

Order **Passeriformes**	Family **Emberizidae**	Species *Meliospiza melodia*

Song Sparrow

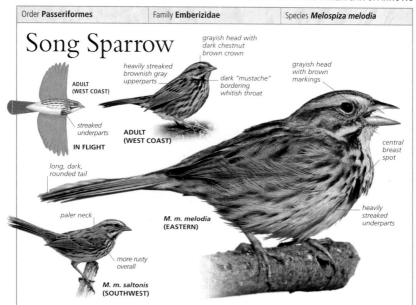

grayish head with dark chestnut brown crown

heavily streaked brownish gray upperparts

dark "mustache" bordering whitish throat

ADULT (WEST COAST)

ADULT (WEST COAST)

grayish head with brown markings

streaked underparts

IN FLIGHT

long, dark, rounded tail

central breast spot

paler neck

M. m. melodia (EASTERN)

heavily streaked underparts

more rusty overall

M. m. saltonis (SOUTHWEST)

The familiar song of this species can be heard in backyards across the continent, including in winter, although it varies both individually and geographically. In the southeastern US, where it does not breed, migrant birds start singing in early spring before departing for northern areas. The Song Sparrow may be the North American champion of geographical variation—about 40 subspecies have been described. These vary from the large, dark birds of the Aleutian Islands (*M. m. maxima*) to the smaller, paler birds of southern Arizona (*M. m. saltonis*). Eastern birds, such as *M. m. melodia*, fall between the two in size.

VOICE A dry *tchip* call; flight call a clear *siiiti*; song a jumble of variable whistles and trills, *deeep deeep deep-deep chrrrr tiiiiiiiiiiii tyeeur* most common.

NESTING Bulky cup on or near ground, in brush or marsh vegetation; 3–5 eggs; 1–3 broods; March–August.

FEEDING In summer, feeds mainly on insects; in winter, eats mainly seeds, but also fruit.

FLIGHT: low and direct, staying within cover whenever possible.

SIMILAR SPECIES

LINCOLN'S SPARROW see p.414

thinner black streaks

less rounded tail

SAVANNAH SPARROW see p.420

yellow eye-stripe

shorter, square tail

BREAST SPOT
The Song Sparrow often sings from exposed perches, showing off its characteristic breast spot.

OCCURRENCE
Widespread in a range of habitats (although not in dense forests) across Canada and the US, from the Atlantic to the Pacific Coasts and north to Alaska. Some populations move south of their breeding range in winter.

Length **5–7½in (13–19cm)**	Wingspan **8½–12in (21–31cm)**	Weight **⁷⁄₁₆–1¾oz (13–50g)**
Social **Solitary/Flocks**	Lifespan **Up to 9 years**	Status **Secure**

DATE SEEN	WHERE	NOTES

| Order **Passeriformes** | Family **Emberizidae** | Species *Melospiza lincolnii* |

Lincoln's Sparrow

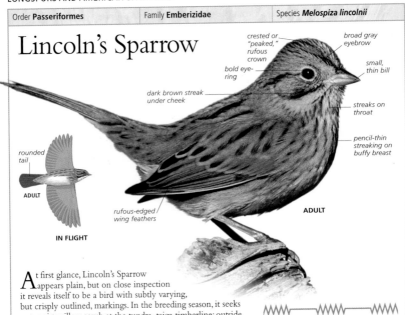

crested or "peaked," rufous crown

broad gray eyebrow

bold eye-ring

small, thin bill

dark brown streak under cheek

streaks on throat

pencil-thin streaking on buffy breast

rounded tail

ADULT

ADULT

rufous-edged wing feathers

IN FLIGHT

At first glance, Lincoln's Sparrow appears plain, but on close inspection it reveals itself to be a bird with subtly varying, but crisply outlined, markings. In the breeding season, it seeks out moist willow scrub at the tundra–taiga timberline; outside the breeding season, Lincoln's Sparrow occurs in scrubby habitats right across North America. It will occasionally visit backyard feeders in winter, but it is generally secretive and stays within fairly dense cover. Lincoln's Sparrow's rich, musical song is unmistakable, and it varies remarkably little from region to region. Audubon named this species in 1834 in honor of his collector Thomas Lincoln.

VOICE Call a variable, loud *tchip*, flight call a rolling *ziiiit*; song series of rich, musical trills, *ju-ju-ju dodododo didididid whrrrrr.*

NESTING Grass cup, lined with fine grass, and hidden in depression in ground under overhanging sedges or grasses; 3–5 eggs; 1 brood; June–August.

FEEDING Mainly seeds in winter; in summer, mostly insects, such as beetles, mosquitoes, and moths.

FLIGHT: low and direct, staying within cover whenever possible.

RAISE THE ALARM
When disturbed, Lincoln's Sparrow often raises its central crown feathers, which form a crest.

SIMILAR SPECIES

SONG SPARROW see p.413
larger overall

more coarse streaking

SAVANNAH SPARROW see p.420

yellow stripe above eye

short, square, notched tail

OCCURRENCE
Breeds in muskeg and wet thickets across northern North America, also south into the western ranges of California and Arizona. Migrants and wintering birds use a variety of scrubby habitats. Winters in southern US (and farther south), and on Pacific Coast north to British Columbia.

| Length 5¼–6in (13.5–15cm) | Wingspan 7½–8½in (19–22cm) | Weight ½–⅞oz (15–25g) |
| Social **Solitary/Small flocks** | Lifespan **Up to 7 years** | Status **Secure** |

DATE SEEN	WHERE	NOTES

| Order **Passeriformes** | Family **Emberizidae** | Species *Melospiza georgiana* |

Swamp Sparrow

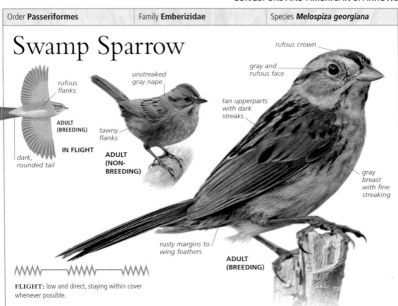

rufous crown

gray and rufous face

unstreaked gray nape

rufous flanks

ADULT (BREEDING)

tawny flanks

IN FLIGHT

dark, rounded tail

tan upperparts with dark streaks

ADULT (NON-BREEDING)

gray breast with fine streaking

rusty margins to wing feathers

ADULT (BREEDING)

FLIGHT: low and direct, staying within cover whenever possible.

The Swamp Sparrow is a common breeder in wet habitats across eastern North America and Canada west to the southern Yukon and eastern British Columbia. It is abundant in its preferred habitat of tall reed and cattail marshes. A somewhat skittish bird, the Swamp Sparrow is often seen darting rapidly into cover, but usually repays the patient observer with a reappearance, giving its characteristic *chimp* call. Though often confused with both the Song Sparrow and Lincoln's Sparrow, the Swamp Sparrow never shows more than a very faint, blurry streaking on its gray breast, and sports conspicuous rusty-edged wing feathers. Its song is also quite different.

VOICE Call a slightly nasal, forceful *chimp*, flight call a high, buzzy *ziiiiii*; song a slow, monotonous, loose trill of chirps.

NESTING Bulky cup of dry plants placed 1–4ft (30–120cm) above water in marsh vegetation; 3–5 eggs; 1–2 broods; May–July.

FEEDING Mostly insects in the breeding season, especially grasshoppers; seeds in winter; occasionally fruit.

HIGH PERCH
This male Swamp Sparrow is checking his territory from atop a seeding cattail flower.

OCCURRENCE
Breeds in marshes, cedar bogs, damp meadows, and wet hayfields, from the Yukon east to Newfoundland and south to Nebraska and the Delmarva Peninsula; winters in marshes in eastern US and south through Mexico; rare but regular along Pacific coast.

SIMILAR SPECIES		
SONG SPARROW see p.413	**LINCOLN'S SPARROW** see p.414	
brown tail		
brown wings	streaked breast	
	less red overall	fine breast streaks

| Length **5–6in (12.5–15cm)** | Wingspan **7–7½in (18–19cm)** | Weight **½–⅞oz (15–25g)** |
| Social **Solitary/Small flocks** | Lifespan **Up to 6 years** | Status **Secure** |

DATE SEEN	WHERE	NOTES

| Order **Passeriformes** | Family **Emberizidae** | Species *Zonotrichia querula* |

Harris's Sparrow

ADULT (NONBREEDING)
indistinct facial markings
IN FLIGHT

two wing bars
ADULT (NONBREEDING)
pinkish bill

gray rump and undertail feathers

gray cheeks
black cheek patch

black crown
pinkish or yellow bill

black chin and throat

tan cheek
white chin
concentration of streaks on chest
JUVENILE

ADULT (BREEDING)

An unmistakable black-faced, pink-billed bird, Harris's Sparrow is the only breeding bird endemic to Canada. It can be seen in the US during migration or in winter on the Great Plains. This species is occasionally found in large flocks of White-throated and White-crowned Sparrows. Harris's Sparrow is the largest sparrow in North America, approaching the Northern Cardinal in size. Its scientific name, *querula*, comes from the plaintive quality of its whistled song. The First Harris's Sparrow nest was found in 1907 in the Northwest Territories.
VOICE Call a sharp *weeek*; song a melancholy series of 2–4 whistles on the same pitch.
NESTING Bulky cup placed on ground among vegetation or near ground in brush; 3–5 eggs; 1 brood; June–August.
FEEDING Eats seeds, insects, buds, and even young conifer needles in summer.

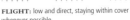

FLIGHT: low and direct, staying within cover whenever possible.

NORTHERN ACROBAT
This nonbreeding Harris's Sparrow grips two different weeds, one in each foot.

SIMILAR SPECIES

HOUSE SPARROW
see p.341
much smaller

WHITE-THROATED SPARROW ♀
see p.418
lacks bright pink bill
no black necklace
smaller and shorter-tailed

OCCURRENCE
Breeds in scrub-tundra along the Canadian taiga–tundra timberline from northern Northwest Territories to northern Ontario. Winters in US Great Plains from South Dakota and Iowa south to northern Texas. Nonbreeders found in thickets, hedges. Casual in the East, and rare in the West.

| Length 6¾–7½in (17–19cm) | Wingspan 10½–11in (27–28cm) | Weight 1¹⁄₁₆–1⁷⁄₁₆oz (30–40g) |
| Social **Flocks** | Lifespan **Up to 12 years** | Status **Secure** |

DATE SEEN	WHERE	NOTES

| Order **Passeriformes** | Family **Emberizidae** | Species *Zonotrichia leucophrys* |

White-crowned Sparrow

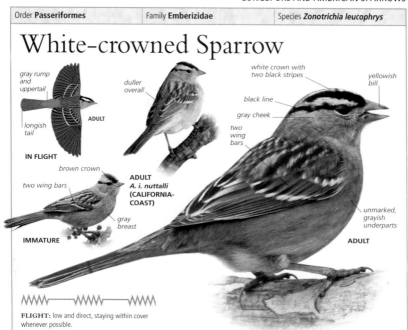

gray rump and uppertail

duller overall

white crown with two black stripes

yellowish bill

black line

gray cheek

two wing bars

longish tail

ADULT

IN FLIGHT

brown crown

ADULT
A. i. nuttalli
(CALIFORNIA-COAST)

two wing bars

gray breast

IMMATURE

unmarked, grayish underparts

ADULT

FLIGHT: low and direct, staying within cover whenever possible.

The White-crowned Sparrow breeds far north in eastern Canada in open boreal forests ranging westward to Alaska. Geographic variation in this species is well-marked, and recognized by five subspecies. Eastern birds belong to *Z. l leucophrys*. Four western subspecies have been described. Eastern birds migrate south to wintering grounds in a number of states, southward of a line from southern Minnesota to New York to the Gulf Coast (but not Florida).

VOICE Call a sharp *tink*; flight call a thin *seep*; song a buzzy whistle.
NESTING Bulky cup of grass placed on or near the ground in bushes; 4–6 eggs; 1–3 broods; March–August.
FEEDING Forages for seeds, insects, fruit, buds, and grass.

LOOKING RESTED
Perched on a shrub, this sparrow's white eyestreak is highly visible.

SIMILAR SPECIES

WHITE-THROATED SPARROW see p.418

yellow patch

gray bill

chunkier overall

more reddish

GOLDEN-CROWNED SPARROW ♀

yellowish forecrown

plain face

gray bill

OCCURRENCE
Widespread across the boreal forest and the taiga-tundra border, from Alaska eastward to Québec and Labrador, and southward from British Columbia to coastal California and the intermontane west. In the North, breeds in willow thickets, wet forest; in the west, habitats are more varied.

| Length 6½–7in (16–18cm) | Wingspan 9½–10in (24–26cm) | Weight 1¹⁄₁₆–1¼oz (20–35g) |
| Social **Flocks** | Lifespan **Up to 13 years** | Status **Secure** |

DATE SEEN	WHERE	NOTES

| Order **Passeriformes** | Family **Emberizidae** | Species ***Zonotrichia albicollis*** |

White-throated Sparrow

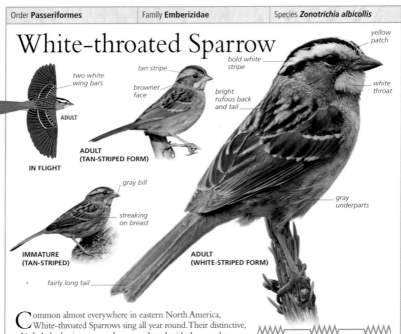

yellow patch

bold white stripe

tan stripe

two white wing bars

ADULT
IN FLIGHT

browner face

bright rufous back and tail

ADULT
(TAN-STRIPED FORM)

white throat

gray bill

streaking on breast

IMMATURE
(TAN-STRIPED)

gray underparts

fairly long tail

ADULT
(WHITE-STRIPED FORM)

C ommon almost everywhere in eastern North America, White-throated Sparrows sing all year round. Their distinctive, whistled, rhythmic song can be remembered with the popular mnemonics *Oh sweet Canada Canada Canada*, or the less accurate *Old Sam Peabody*. This species has two different color forms, one with a white stripe above its eye, and the other with a tan stripe. In the nonbreeding season, large flocks roam the leaf litter of woodlands in search of food. Often the only indication of their presence is the occasional moving leaf or thin, lisping flight call.

VOICE Call loud, sharp *jink*; flight call lisping *tssssst!*; song clear whistle comprising 1–2 higher notes, then three triplets.

NESTING Cup placed on or near ground in dense shrubbery; 2–6 eggs; 1 brood; May–August.

FEEDING Mainly forages on the ground for seeds, fruit, insects, buds, and various grasses.

FLIGHT: low and direct, staying within cover whenever possible.

DIFFERENT COLOR FORMS
The presence of white or tan stripes on White-throated Sparrows is not related to their sex.

SIMILAR SPECIES

WHITE-CROWNED SPARROW
slimmer overall;
see p.417

no yellow patch

orange or pink bill

GOLDEN-CROWNED SPARROW ♀

yellowish forecrown

plain, grayish breast

OCCURRENCE
Breeds in forests from eastern Yukon to Newfoundland, south to the Great Lakes region and northern Appalachians. Nonbreeders prefer wooded thickets and hedges. Winters across the eastern US and extreme south of the Southwest. Rare but regular along the Pacific Coast.

| Length **6½–7½in (16–17.5cm)** | Wingspan **9–10in (23–26cm)** | Weight **¹¹⁄₁₆–1¼oz (20–35g)** |
| Social **Flocks** | Lifespan **Up to 10 years** | Status **Secure** |

DATE SEEN	WHERE	NOTES

| Order **Passeriformes** | Family **Emberizidae** | Species *Junco hyemalis* |

Dark-eyed Junco

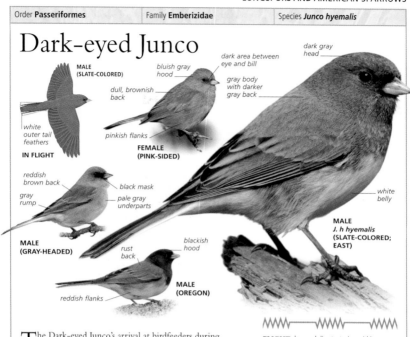

MALE (SLATE-COLORED)

bluish gray hood

dark area between eye and bill

dark gray head

gray body with darker gray back

dull, brownish back

white outer tail feathers

IN FLIGHT

pinkish flanks

FEMALE (PINK-SIDED)

reddish brown back

gray rump

black mask

pale gray underparts

MALE (GRAY-HEADED)

rust back

blackish hood

MALE (OREGON)

reddish flanks

white belly

MALE *J. h hyemalis* (SLATE-COLORED; EAST)

FLIGHT: low and direct, staying within cover whenever possible.

The Dark-eyed Junco's arrival at birdfeeders during winter snowstorms has earned it the colloquial name of "snowbird." The name "Dark-eyed Junco" is used to describe a group of birds that vary geographically in such a strikingly diverse way that 16 subspecies have been described. "Slate-colored" populations are widespread across Canada and the northeastern US. "White-winged" birds nest in the Black Hills. "Pink-sided" ones breed in Idaho, Montana, and Wyoming, and "Oregon" birds breed in the West, from Alaska to British Columbia and the mountains of the western US in the Sierras south to Mexico. Birds from the Appalachians are ascribed to the subspecies *J.h carolinensis*.

VOICE Loud, smacking *tick* and soft *dyew* calls; flight call a rapid, twittering, and buzzy *zzeet*; song a simple, liquid, 1-pitch trill.

NESTING Cup placed on ground hidden under vegetation or next to rocks; 3–5 eggs; 1–2 broods; May–August.

FEEDING Eats insects and seeds; also berries.

BRIGHTER MALE
Like other juncos, this male is brighter than females.

SIMILAR SPECIES

YELLOW-EYED JUNCO

red back

yellow eyes

buff wash to belly

OCCURRENCE
Breeds in coniferous and mixed forests across Canada, the northeastern and northwestern US, south in the east Appalachians to Georgia, and in the west, in mountains from Alaska and British Columbia to New Mexico and northern Baja California. Winters from southern Canada to northern Mexico, but not in Florida.

Length **6–6¾in (15–17cm)**	Wingspan **8–10in (20–26cm)**	Weight **⅝–1¹⁄₁₆oz (18–30g)**
Social **Flocks**	Lifespan **Up to 11 years**	Status **Secure**

DATE SEEN	WHERE	NOTES

419

| Order **Passeriformes** | Family **Emberizidae** | Species ***Passerculus sandwichensis*** |

Savannah Sparrow

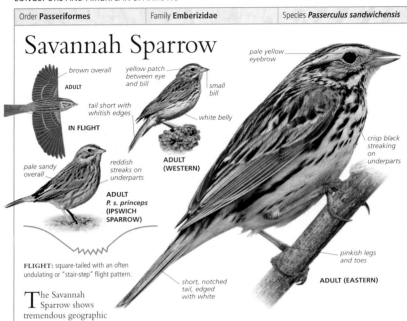

pale yellow eyebrow

ADULT — *brown overall*

IN FLIGHT — *tail short with whitish edges*

yellow patch between eye and bill

small bill

ADULT (WESTERN) — *white belly*

pale sandy overall

reddish streaks on underparts

ADULT P. s. princeps (IPSWICH SPARROW)

FLIGHT: square-tailed with an often undulating or "stair-step" flight pattern.

crisp black streaking on underparts

short, notched tail, edged with white

pinkish legs and toes

ADULT (EASTERN)

The Savannah Sparrow shows tremendous geographic variation—21 subspecies—across its vast range, but it is always brown, with dark streaks above and white with dark streaks below. The pale "Ipswich Sparrow" (*P. s. princeps*), originally described as a species, breeds on the very isolated Sable Island, Nova Scotia, and winters along the East Coast. Eastern Savannah Sparrows breed in eastern Canada and the northwestern US, and winter in the southern half of the US, Mexico, and the West Indies.

VOICE Call a sharp, but full *stip*; flight call a thin, weak, down-slurred *tseew*; song a *sit sit sit sit suh-EEEEE say*, from perch or in display flight with legs dangling.

NESTING Concealed cup of grass placed in depression on ground, protected by overhanging grass or sedges; 2–6 eggs; 1–2 broods; June–August.

FEEDING Forages on the ground, mostly for insects; in summer also eats seeds; in winter berries and fruit when available; also small snails and crustaceans.

SAVANNAH SPARROW
This bird's yellow eyebrow matches the colour of its surroundings.

OCCURRENCE
Breeds in meadows, grasslands, pastures, bushy tundra, and some cultivated land across northern North America. Also along Pacific Coast and in Mexican interior. Nonbreeders use varied open habitats. Eastern birds winter across southern US to Honduras, also Cuba, the Bahamas, and the Cayman Islands.

SIMILAR SPECIES

SONG SPARROW see p.413 — *larger overall* — *longer, rounded tail*

VESPER SPARROW see p.431 — *rusty shoulder* — *dark tail*

| Length **5½–6in (14–15cm)** | Wingspan **6¾in (17cm)** | Weight **½–1¹⁄₁₆oz (15–30g)** |
| Social **Solitary/Loose flocks** | Lifespan **Unknown** | Status **Secure** |

DATE SEEN	WHERE	NOTES

Order **Passeriformes**	Family **Emberizidae**	Species **Ammodramus maritimus**

Seaside Sparrow

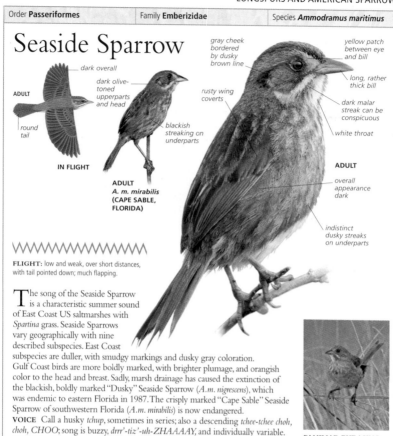

ADULT dark overall

IN FLIGHT

round tail

ADULT A. m. mirabilis (CAPE SABLE, FLORIDA)

dark olive-toned upperparts and head

blackish streaking on underparts

gray cheek bordered by dusky brown line

rusty wing coverts

yellow patch between eye and bill

long, rather thick bill

dark malar streak can be conspicuous

white throat

ADULT

overall appearance dark

indistinct dusky streaks on underparts

FLIGHT: low and weak, over short distances, with tail pointed down; much flapping.

The song of the Seaside Sparrow is a characteristic summer sound of East Coast US saltmarshes with *Spartina* grass. Seaside Sparrows vary geographically with nine described subspecies. East Coast subspecies are duller, with smudgy markings and dusky gray coloration. Gulf Coast birds are more boldly marked, with brighter plumage, and orangish color to the head and breast. Sadly, marsh drainage has caused the extinction of the blackish, boldly marked "Dusky" Seaside Sparrow (*A.m. nigrescens*), which was endemic to eastern Florida in 1987. The crisply marked "Cape Sable" Seaside Sparrow of southwestern Florida (*A.m. mirabilis*) is now endangered.

VOICE Call a husky *tchup*, sometimes in series; also a descending *tchee-tchee choh, choh, CHOO*; song is buzzy, *drrr'-tiz'-uh-ZHAAAAY*, and individually variable.

NESTING Cup of grasses, occasionally domed, placed near ground; 2–5 eggs; 1–3 broods; May–August.

FEEDING Eats seeds of grasses, and sedge; also insects in the breeding season.

FAMILIAR PHRASING
This sparrow's song resembles that of a distant Red-winged Blackbird, but often varies.

OCCURRENCE
Breeds in coastal salt and brackish marshes from the Rio Grande in southeastern Texas northeastward and southward to New Hampshire. Absent from many parts of Florida. Mostly resident, but retreats from areas north of Massachusetts in the winter.

SIMILAR SPECIES	
SAVANNAH SPARROW see p.420 — paler, square tail	**SALTMARSH SHARP-TAILED SPARROW** see p.423 — much smaller bill, shorter, spikier tail, small, pale bill

Length 5¼–6in (13.5–15cm)	Wingspan 7–8in (17.5–20cm)	Weight ¹¹⁄₁₆–⅞oz (20–25g)
Social **Solitary**	Lifespan **Up to 8 years**	Status **Vulnerable**

DATE SEEN	WHERE	NOTES

| Order **Passeriformes** | Family **Emberizidae** | Species *Ammodramus nelsoni* |

Nelson's Sharp-tailed Sparrow

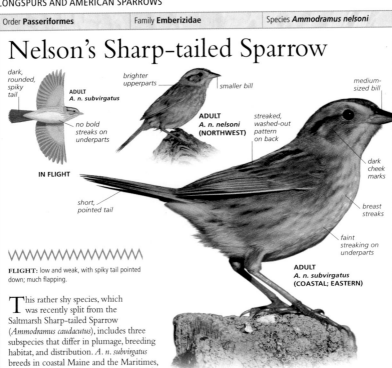

dark, rounded, spiky tail

ADULT
A. n. subvirgatus

no bold streaks on underparts

IN FLIGHT

brighter upperparts

ADULT
A. n. nelsoni
(NORTHWEST)

smaller bill

streaked, washed-out pattern on back

medium-sized bill

dark cheek marks

breast streaks

faint streaking on underparts

ADULT
A. n. subvirgatus
(COASTAL; EASTERN)

short, pointed tail

FLIGHT: low and weak, with spiky tail pointed down; much flapping.

This rather shy species, which was recently split from the Saltmarsh Sharp-tailed Sparrow (*Ammodramus caudacutus*), includes three subspecies that differ in plumage, breeding habitat, and distribution. *A. n. subvirgatus* breeds in coastal Maine and the Maritimes, and along the St. Lawrence River. It is duller colored than *A. n. nelsoni*, with a longer bill and flatter head. The intermediate-looking *A. n. alterus* breeds along the southern and western coasts of Hudson Bay. *A. n. nelsoni* is the most brightly colored, and is found from the southern Northwest Territories south to northwest Wisconsin.

VOICE Sharp *tik* call; song a husky *t-SHHHHEE-uhrr*.

NESTING Cup of grass placed on or just above ground; 4–5 eggs; 1 brood; May–July.

FEEDING Forages on the ground mainly for insects, spiders, and seeds.

SIMILAR SPECIES	
SALTMARSH SHARP-TAILED SPARROW see p.423	**LE CONTE'S SPARROW** see p.424
longer bill	white crown stripe
darker streaks	white stripes on back
	darker streaking

IDENTIFYING MARKS
The orange-and-gray facial pattern and streaks on the breast are distinctive.

OCCURRENCE
Breeds in a variety of marsh habitats across central Canada and the Maritimes and extreme north-central North America; nonbreeders in marshes and wet, weedy fields. *A. n. nelsoni* and *A. n. alterus* winter on coast from Texas northeastward to New Jersey; *A. n. subvirgatus* from eastern Florida to New Jersey.

Length **4¾in (12cm)**	Wingspan **7in (17.5cm)**	Weight **⁷⁄₁₆–¹¹⁄₁₆oz (13–20g)**
Social **Solitary/Flocks**	Lifespan **Unknown**	Status **Secure**

DATE SEEN	WHERE	NOTES

| Order **Passeriformes** | Family **Emberizidae** | Species **Ammodramus caudacutus** |

Saltmarsh Sharp-tailed Sparrow

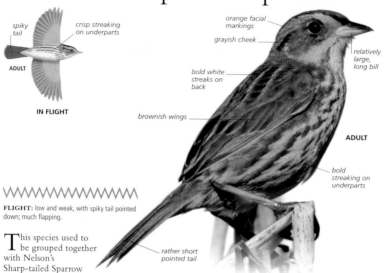

spiky tail

crisp streaking on underparts

ADULT

IN FLIGHT

orange facial markings

grayish cheek

relatively large, long bill

bold white streaks on back

brownish wings

ADULT

bold streaking on underparts

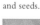

FLIGHT: low and weak, with spiky tail pointed down; much flapping.

rather short pointed tail

This species used to be grouped together with Nelson's Sharp-tailed Sparrow in a single species—the Sharp-tailed Sparrow. Birdwatchers refer to them as "Saltmarsh Sparrows" and "Nelson's Sparrows." The Saltmarsh Sparrow has more defined facial markings, darker streaks on its breast, and a longer bill; it is found only along the East Coast of the US, whereas Nelson's Sparrow is quite widespread inland.

VOICE Call a sharp *tik*; complex flight song given just above the grass; song a series of muted, thin, airy notes, often without pausing.

NESTING Cup, occasionally domed, placed on or near ground; 3–5 eggs; 1 brood; May–August.

FEEDING Forages on ground for insects, spiders, and seeds.

STREAKED BREAST
Its distinct breast streaks distinguish the Saltmarsh Sparrow from Nelson's Sparrow.

OCCURRENCE
Breeds in salt marshes, especially those with salt-meadow cordgrass, from Virginia northward to southern Maine. Nonbreeders use similar-looking habitats. Winters from Florida north to New Jersey, New York, and southern Massachusetts. Does not breed in Canada.

SIMILAR SPECIES

SEASIDE SPARROW
see p.421

longer, less spiky tail

larger, darker bill

NELSON'S SHARP-TAILED SPARROW
see p.422

fainter streaks on underparts

| Length **5in (13cm)** | Wingspan **7–7½in (17.5–19cm)** | Weight **⅝–¹¹⁄₁₆oz (17–20g)** |
| Social **Solitary/Loose flocks** | Lifespan **Up to 10 years** | Status **Declining** |

DATE SEEN	WHERE		NOTES

Order **Passeriformes**	Family **Emberizidae**	Species **Ammodramus leconteii**

Le Conte's Sparrow

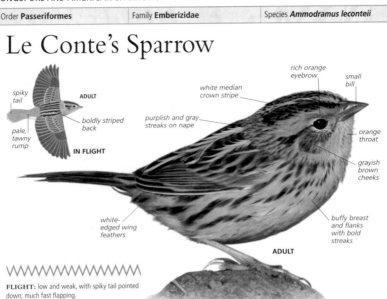

spiky tail

ADULT

boldly striped back

pale, tawny rump

IN FLIGHT

rich orange eyebrow

small bill

white median crown stripe

purplish and gray streaks on nape

orange throat

grayish brown cheeks

white-edged wing feathers

buffy breast and flanks with bold streaks

ADULT

FLIGHT: low and weak, with spiky tail pointed down; much fast flapping.

Intricately patterned in browns and buffs, Le Conte's Sparrow is usually very difficult to see. Not only is it tiny—one of the smallest of all North American sparrows—but in its grassland and marsh habitats of interior North America, it darts for cover, hiding under grasses instead of flushing when disturbed. The flight call and song of this elusive little bird are remarkably insect-like. Many people who hear it believe that the unseen caller is a grasshopper. Its nest is even harder to find, making this bird a real challenge to study as well as observe.

VOICE Call long, down-slurred *zheeep*; flight call similar to grasshopper; song insect-like, buzzy *tik'-uht-tizz-ZHEEEEEE-k*.

NESTING Concealed little cup placed on or near ground; 3–5 eggs; 1 brood; June–August.

FEEDING Forages on the ground and in grasses for insects, insect larvae, spiders, and seeds.

HIDEAWAY BIRD
Le Conte's Sparrow is usually found skulking in medium-to-tall grass.

OCCURRENCE
Breeds in marshes, wet meadows, and bogs from the southwestern Yukon east to Lake Superior and western Québec. Migrants and wintering birds are found in tall grass and marshes from southwestern Kansas to southern Indiana, and from central Texas to the Carolinas.

SIMILAR SPECIES

NELSON'S SHARP-TAILED SPARROW see p.422

gray nape

less streaked

GRASSHOPPER SPARROW see p.426

larger bill

duller overall

Length 4½–5in (11.5–13cm)	Wingspan 6½–7in (16–18cm)	Weight ⁷⁄₁₆–⁹⁄₁₆oz (12–16g)
Social **Solitary/Loose flocks**	Lifespan **Unknown**	Status **Secure**

DATE SEEN	WHERE	NOTES

Order **Passeriformes**	Family **Emberizidae**	Species **Ammodramus henslowii**

Henslow's Sparrow

round, spiky tail

dark reddish overall

ADULT

IN FLIGHT

yellowish green (or olive) head with black stripes

heavy blackish streaking

rufous-edged wing feathers

heavy bill

black streaks on buffy breast

ADULT

pointed tail feathers

The combination of a proportionally large, flat head with a greenish olive cast and heavily streaked back are characteristic marks of Henslow's Sparrow. Audubon named this species in 1829 to honor John Henslow, a distinguished British botanist. A bird of the tallgrass prairies and wet meadows, it has suffered from the drainage, cultivation, and urbanization of its breeding habitats. However, Henslow's Sparrows have recently occupied abandoned strip mines in northwest Missouri and Iowa for breeding.

VOICE Call a sharp *tsik*, flight call a long, high, shrill *tseeeeee*; song a hiccupping sputter with second note higher *tsih-LIK!*

NESTING Cup of grass placed on or near ground; 2–5 eggs; 1–2 broods; May–August.

FEEDING Eats seeds; forages for insects, insect larvae, and spiders in the summer.

FLIGHT: low and weak, with spiky tail pointed down; much flapping.

SIMILAR SPECIES

GRASSHOPPER SPARROW Western; see p.426

gray-brown streaking

no streaks

GRASSHOPPER SPARROW Eastern; see p.426

darker crown

less rounded tail

OUT LOUD
The male puts considerable effort into his short, but surprisingly far-carrying song.

OCCURRENCE
This eastern North American sparrow breeds in tallgrass prairie and wet grasslands from Oklahoma north eastward to New York, and southeast to North Carolina. Winters in weedy, brushy fields, grassy pine woods, and undergrowth along Gulf Coastal Plain from Texas to North Carolina, and northern Florida.

Length **4¾–5in (12–13cm)**	Wingspan **6½in (16cm)**	Weight **⅜–½oz (11–15g)**
Social **Solitary/Loose flocks**	Lifespan **Unknown**	Status **Declining**

DATE SEEN	WHERE	NOTES

| Order **Passeriformes** | Family **Emberizidae** | Species *Ammodramus savannarum* |

Grasshopper Sparrow

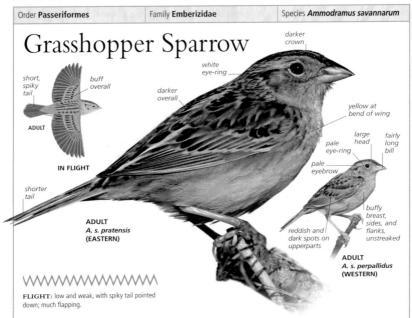

darker crown

white eye-ring

darker overall

short, spiky tail

buff overall

ADULT

IN FLIGHT

yellow at bend of wing

large head

pale eye-ring

fairly long bill

pale eyebrow

shorter tail

ADULT
A. s. pratensis
(EASTERN)

reddish and dark spots on upperparts

buffy breast, sides, and flanks, unstreaked

ADULT
A. s. perpallidus
(WESTERN)

FLIGHT: low and weak, with spiky tail pointed down; much flapping.

A Grasshopper Sparrow singing briefly atop a weed is usually the first glimpse people get of a member of the secretive genus *Ammodramus*. Although its large head and spiky tail are characteristic of species in its genus, it is the only *Ammodramus* sparrow to have a plain breast and two completely different songs. While it does eat grasshoppers, its common name derives from its grasshopper-like song. The Grasshopper Sparrow varies geographically, with about 12 subspecies.

VOICE Sharp *tik* call; flight call a long, high *tseeee*; song an insect-like trill *tik'-tok-TREEEE*, or series of quick buzzes.

NESTING Cup of grass placed in clump of grass; 3–6 eggs; 1–2 broods; April–August.

FEEDING Forages on ground for seeds and insects.

YELLOW STRIPE
The pale crown stripe is quite visible here as the bird faces the photographer.

SIMILAR SPECIES

LE CONTE'S SPARROW
see p.424

brighter overall

gray cheek patch

orange eyebrow

BAIRD'S SPARROW
see p.472

ocher crown

dark, lateral throat stripe

OCCURRENCE
Breeds in short grassland, pastures, and even mown areas across much of the US and in southern Canada. Locally distributed in the Southwest, also patchily through central US. Winters in similar habitats from southern US to Colombia; also in the West Indies.

| Length **5in (13cm)** | Wingspan **8in (20cm)** | Weight **½–¹¹⁄₁₆oz (15–20g)** |
| Social **Solitary/Flocks** | Lifespan **Up to 7 years** | Status **Declining** |

DATE SEEN	WHERE	NOTES

| Order **Passeriformes** | Family **Emberizidae** | Species ***Spizella arborea*** |

American Tree Sparrow

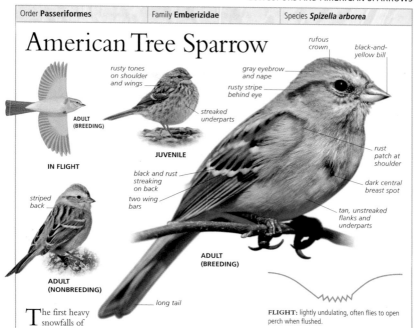

rufous crown

black-and-yellow bill

rusty tones on shoulder and wings

gray eyebrow and nape

rusty stripe behind eye

streaked underparts

ADULT (BREEDING)

JUVENILE

IN FLIGHT

rust patch at shoulder

black and rust streaking on back

two wing bars

dark central breast spot

tan, unstreaked flanks and underparts

striped back

ADULT (NONBREEDING)

long tail

ADULT (BREEDING)

FLIGHT: lightly undulating, often flies to open perch when flushed.

The first heavy snowfalls of winter often bring flocks of American Tree Sparrows to birdfeeders in the Northeast. This bird is commonly mistaken for the smaller Chipping Sparrow, but the two species look different in winter. The American Tree Sparrow's central breast spot, bicolored bill, and relatively large size are unique among *Spizella* sparrows. American Tree Sparrows are social birds and some winter flocks can number in the hundreds. Poorly named, this species actually breeds in boggy habitats of the far North.
VOICE Call a bell-like *teedle-ee*; flight call a thin, slightly descending *tsiiiu*; song *seee seee di-di-di di-di-di dyew dyew*.
NESTING Neat cup on ground concealed within thicket; 4–6 eggs; 1 brood; June–July.
FEEDING Feeds on seeds, berries, and a variety of insects.

WINTER HABITATS
In winter this species frequents barren habitats, like old fields and roadsides, as well as feeders.

SIMILAR SPECIES

CHIPPING SPARROW
see p.428

lacks rusty eye-line

FIELD SPARROW
see p.429

bold white eye-ring

no central, black breast spot

all-pale bill

smaller overall

OCCURRENCE
Breeds in scrubby thickets of birch and willows in the area between taiga and tundra across Alaska and northern Canada. Nonbreeders choose open, grassy, brushy habitats. Winters across southern Canada and the northern US. Casual to Pacific coast and southern US.

| Length 6¼in (16cm) | Wingspan 9½in (24cm) | Weight ⁷⁄₁₆–⁷⁄₈oz (13–25g) |
| Social **Flocks** | Lifespan **Up to 11 years** | Status **Secure** |

DATE SEEN	WHERE	NOTES

427

| Order **Passeriformes** | Family **Emberizidae** | Species *Spizella passerina* |

Chipping Sparrow

pale underparts

ADULT

IN FLIGHT

rusty cast to crown

pinkish bill

ADULT (WINTER)

heavily streaked, especially on breast

JUVENILE

long tail

bright rufous crown

blackish bill

white eyebrow

black eye line

ADULT (BREEDING)

gray underparts

The Chipping Sparrow is a common and trusting bird, which breeds in backyards across most of North America. While they are easily identifiable in the summer, "Chippers" molt into a drab, nonbreeding plumage during the fall, at which point they are easily confused with the Clay-colored and Brewer's Sparrows they flock with. Most winter reports of this species in the north are actually of the larger American Tree Sparrow. In winter, Chipping Sparrows lack their bright, rusty crown and are restricted to southern states.

VOICE Call a sharp *tsip*; flight call a sharp, thin *tsiiit*; song an insect-like trill of *chip* notes, variable in duration and intensity.

NESTING Neat cup usually placed well off the ground in tree or shrub; 3–5 eggs; 1–2 broods; April–August.

FEEDING Eat seeds of grasses and annuals, plus some fruits; when breeding, also eat insects and other invertebrates.

FLIGHT: lightly undulating, often to open perch when flushed.

BACKYARD BIRD
Chipping Sparrows are common in gardens and backyards all across the continent.

SIMILAR SPECIES

CLAY-COLORED SPARROW see p.430

heavy streaks

BREWER'S SPARROW

partial "necklace"

streaked crown

pale underparts

OCCURRENCE
Found in a wide variety of habitats: open forest, woodlands, grassy park-like areas, seashores, and backyards. Breeds in North America south of the Arctic timberline southward to Mexico, and in Central America as far south as Nicaragua. Winters from southern states to Nicaragua.

| Length **5½in (14cm)** | Wingspan **8½in (21cm)** | Weight **⅜–½oz (10–15g)** |
| Social **Large flocks** | Lifespan **Up to 9 years** | Status **Secure** |

DATE SEEN	WHERE	NOTES

| Order **Passeriformes** | Family **Emberizidae** | Species *Spizella pusilla* |

Field Sparrow

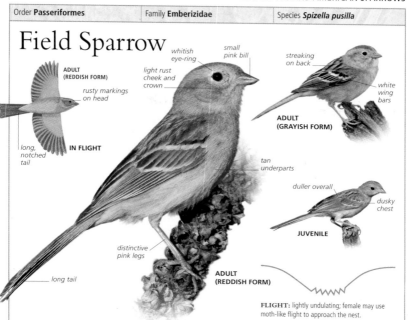

whitish eye-ring

small pink bill

light rust cheek and crown

ADULT (REDDISH FORM)

rusty markings on head

long, notched tail

IN FLIGHT

streaking on back

white wing bars

ADULT (GRAYISH FORM)

tan underparts

duller overall

dusky chest

JUVENILE

distinctive pink legs

long tail

ADULT (REDDISH FORM)

FLIGHT: lightly undulating; female may use moth-like flight to approach the nest.

The distinctive accelerating trill song of the Field Sparrow is a characteristic sound of shrubby fields and scrubby areas in the eastern US. The bird's bright-pink bill, plain "baby face," and whitish eye-ring make this sparrow one of the easiest to identify. The Field Sparrow has a brighter plumage in the eastern part of its range than farther west, a pattern also seen in other sparrows, like the Vesper Sparrow. Although quite dissimilar at first glance, the Black-chinned Sparrow may in fact be the Field Sparrow's closest relative, sharing its pink bill, relatively unpatterned plumage, and song.
VOICE Call a sharp *tsik*; flight call a strongly descending *tsiiiu*; song a series of sweet, down-slurred whistles accelerating to a rapid trill.
NESTING Grass cup placed on or just above ground in grass or bush; 3–5 eggs; 1–3 broods; March–August.
FEEDING Eats seeds; also insects, insect larvae, and spiders in the summer.

FAMILIAR SONG
Male Field Sparrows sing their familiar song, an accelerated trill during the summer.

OCCURRENCE
Breeds in overgrown fields, woodland edges, roadsides, and other shrubby, overgrown areas; occasionally in orchards and parks in the eastern US, west to North Dakota, east to New England. Winters in similar habitats in the southern US. Casual in Atlantic Canada and on the Pacific Coast.

SIMILAR SPECIES		

WHITE-CROWNED SPARROW ♀
see p.417
larger body

pale crown stripe

AMERICAN TREE SPARROW
see p.427

lacks bold, white eye-ring

central, black breast spot

| Length **5½in (14cm)** | Wingspan **8in (20cm)** | Weight **⅜–½oz (11–15g)** |
| Social **Solitary/Flocks** | Lifespan **Up to 6 years** | Status **Declining** |

DATE SEEN	WHERE	NOTES

Order **Passeriformes**	Family **Emberizidae**	Species *Spizella pallida*

Clay-colored Sparrow

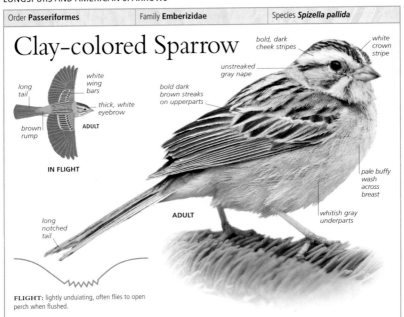

bold, dark cheek stripes

white crown stripe

unstreaked gray nape

white wing bars

long tail

thick, white eyebrow

bold dark brown streaks on upperparts

brown rump

ADULT

IN FLIGHT

long notched tail

ADULT

pale buffy wash across breast

whitish gray underparts

FLIGHT: lightly undulating, often flies to open perch when flushed.

The small Clay-colored Sparrow is best known for its mechanical, buzzy song. This bird spends much of its foraging time away from its breeding habitat; consequently, males' territories are very small, allowing for dense breeding populations. Clay-colored Sparrows have shifted their breeding range eastward and northward over the last century, most likely because of changes in land practices. During the nonbreeding season, they form large flocks in open country, associating with other *Spizella* sparrows, especially Chippings and Brewer's.
VOICE Call a sharp *tsip*; flight a call short, rising *sip*; song a series of 2–7 mechanical buzzes on one pitch.
NESTING Cup of grass placed just off the ground in shrub or small tree; 3–5 eggs; 1–2 broods; May–August.
FEEDING Forages on or near the ground for seeds and insects.

CHRISTMAS PRESENT
The Clay-colored Sparrow is fond of low conifers for breeding, so Christmas tree farms form a perfect habitat.

SIMILAR SPECIES

CHIPPING SPARROW ✳
see p.428

grayish rump

dark stripe through eye

grayer breast

BREWER'S SPARROW

streaked nape

lacks bold, crown stripe

OCCURRENCE
Breeds in open habitats: prairies, shrubland, forest edges, and Christmas tree farms along the US/Canadian border and northward to the southern Northwest Territory. Winters in a large variety of brushy and weedy areas from south Texas to Mexico. Migration takes it to the Great Plains.

Length **5½in (14cm)**	Wingspan **7½in (19cm)**	Weight **⅜–½oz (10–15g)**
Social **Large flocks**	Lifespan **Up to 5 years**	Status **Secure**

DATE SEEN	WHERE	NOTES

| Order **Passeriformes** | Family **Emberizidae** | Species **Pooecetes gramineus** |

Vesper Sparrow

dark bordered ear patches

white eye-ring

rusty shoulders

ADULT

pale brown upperparts

streaked breast

IN FLIGHT

conspicuous white edges

uniformly streaked upperparts

ADULT

ADULT

boldly white-edged long, dark, square tail

white outer tail feathers

ADULT

The Vesper Sparrow got its common name because its song was considered by some ornithologists to sound sweeter in the evening, when "vespers" are sung in the Catholic churches. When Henry David Thoreau wrote of this species, he called it the "Bay-winged Bunting," a name given by Audubon, because of its (sometimes concealed) rusty shoulder patches. The Vesper Sparrow needs areas with bare ground to breed, so it is one of the few species that can successfully nest in areas of intensive agriculture; the bird's numbers seem to be declining in spite of this.

VOICE Full *tchup* call, flight call thin *tseent*; song consists of 2 whistles of same pitch, followed by 2 higher-pitched ones, then trills, ends lazily.

NESTING Cup placed on patch of bare ground, against grass, bush, or rock; 3–5 eggs; 1 brood; April–August.

FEEDING Eats insects and seeds.

FLIGHT: strong, often perches when flushed; often moves on ground.

SIMILAR SPECIES

SAVANNAH SPARROW (EAST) see p.420

smaller bill

SAVANNAH SPARROW (IPSWICH) see p.420

lacks white eye-ring

orange feet

GIFTED SONGSTER
The sweet song of the Vesper Sparrow is a characteristic sound of northern open areas.

OCCURRENCE
In the East, breeds in sparse grassland, cultivated fields, and recently burned areas. It is widely distributed across southern Canada and the northern US. Winters in sparsely vegetated, open habitats from southern US to southwestern Mexico. Found in patches of bare earth in all seasons.

| Length **6¼in (16cm)** | Wingspan **10in (25cm)** | Weight **¹¹⁄₁₆–1¹⁄₁₆oz (20–30g)** |
| Social **Flocks** | Lifespan **Up to 7 years** | Status **Declining** |

DATE SEEN	WHERE	NOTES

| Order **Passeriformes** | Family **Emberizidae** | Species **Chondestes grammacus** |

Lark Sparrow

rounded tail with white corners

ADULT

IN FLIGHT

thick gray bill

pale patch at base of outer wing feathers

central breast spot

JUVENILE

unique bold facial pattern

brown upperparts

long tail

pale plain rump

central breast spot

ADULT

FLIGHT: strong flight, in straight lines; often perches when flushed.

The bold harlequin facial pattern, single central breast spot, and long, rounded black tail with white outer corners make the Lark Sparrow one of the most easily identifiable of North American sparrows. Lark Sparrows have declined precipitously in the East, where they are mostly associated with western-like sandy soils. It is likely, that this species' presence in the East has been possible because of forest clearing. In the West, by contrast, Lark Sparrows are common, and often found singing from the top of a fencepost or small tree, and perched on barbed wire fences.

VOICE Thin, up-slurred *tseep* call, flight call sharp *tink*; song series of trills, whistles, and rattles on varying pitches.

NESTING Cup usually placed on ground at base of plant, or off-ground in tree or bush; 3–5 eggs; 1–2 broods; April–August.

FEEDING Eats seeds and insects.

ON THE FENCE
The Lark Sparrow is a common roadside bird, often found perching on barbed wire fences.

OCCURRENCE
Localized breeder in the East, associated with well-drained soils. Breeds east to Ohio. In the West, breeds in a variety of habitats such as sagebrush flats of the Great Basin, and grasslands from British Columbia and Saskatchewan to Baja California and central Mexico. Winters in southern US and Mexico.

| Length **6–6¾in (15–17cm)** | Wingspan **11in (28cm)** | Weight **¹¹⁄₁₆–1¹⁄₁₆oz (20–30g)** |
| Social **Large flocks** | Lifespan **Up to 8 years** | Status **Secure** |

DATE SEEN	WHERE	NOTES

Order **Passeriformes**	Family **Emberizidae**	Species *Aimophila aestivalis*

Bachman's Sparrow

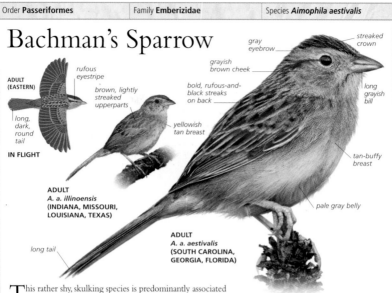

gray eyebrow

streaked crown

grayish brown cheek

ADULT (EASTERN)

rufous eyestripe

brown, lightly streaked upperparts

bold, rufous-and-black streaks on back

long grayish bill

yellowish tan breast

long, dark, round tail

IN FLIGHT

tan-buffy breast

**ADULT
A. a. illinoensis
(INDIANA, MISSOURI,
LOUISIANA, TEXAS)**

pale gray belly

long tail

**ADULT
A. a. aestivalis
(SOUTH CAROLINA,
GEORGIA, FLORIDA)**

This rather shy, skulking species is predominantly associated with pine woods in the South, and can be identified by its melodious song. It was first described in 1833 by John James Audubon in honor of his friend, John Bachman, a social reformer and naturalist. This sparrow invaded the open, shrubby habitats along the Ohio River Valley as far north as Chicago in the early 20th century, only to abandon the area by the 1970s. The reddish subspecies from the south-central US was even named *A. a. illinoensis,* which is now ironic, as it has been extirpated from Illinois. Bachman's Sparrow populations have been declining for some time, primarily as a result of habitat loss.
VOICE Call a thin *tseep*; song a melodious, high, thin whistle followed by a loose, musical trill.
NESTING Cup of grasses, sometimes domed, placed on ground, often in thicket; 2–5 eggs; 1–3 broods; May–September.
FEEDING Forages on the ground for insects, such as weevils and beetles; also eats various seeds.

FLIGHT: direct, low, and fairly weak; usually over short distances.

PINE SPARROW
This species was once known by this name, which refers to its preferred habitat.

OCCURRENCE
Found in open, grassy old-growth and pine woods with dense undergrowth of palmettos, and orchards from eastern Texas and southwestern Missouri to southeastern Kentucky, and south around the Appalachians to southeastern Virginia. Northernmost populations winter in the Southeast and Florida.

SIMILAR SPECIES	
SWAMP SPARROW see p.415	**BOTTERI'S SPARROW** much grayer in Texas; see p.469

gray nape

dark throat stripe

long, dark tail

grayish underparts

Length **6in (15cm)**	Wingspan **7¼in (18.5cm)**	Weight ⅝–¹¹⁄₁₆oz (18–20g)
Social **Solitary**	Lifespan **Unknown**	Status **Vulnerable**

DATE SEEN	WHERE	NOTES

Order **Passeriformes**	Family **Emberizidae**	Species **Pipilo erythrophthalmus**

Eastern Towhee

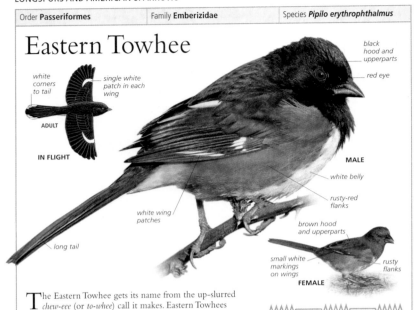

black hood and upperparts

red eye

white corners to tail

single white patch in each wing

ADULT

IN FLIGHT

MALE

white belly

rusty-red flanks

white wing patches

long tail

brown hood and upperparts

small white markings on wings

rusty flanks

FEMALE

FLIGHT: low and direct with much gliding, usually within cover.

The Eastern Towhee gets its name from the up-slurred *chew-eee* (or *to-whee*) call it makes. Eastern Towhees are famous for their vocalizations and have one of the best-known mnemonics for their song: "drink your tea." The Eastern Towhee was once lumped with the western Spotted Towhee under the name "Rufous-sided Towhee," because they interbreed in the Great Plains. Eastern Towhees from the southeast of Florida have increasingly paler eyes; Florida birds have white eyes. Like all towhees, the Eastern Towhee feeds noisily by jumping backwards with both feet at once to move leaves and reveal the insects and seeds that may be hidden underneath.

VOICE Call a nasal, up-slurred *chew-eee*; flight call *zeeeooooweeet*; song sounds like *dwee, dyooo di-i-i-i-i-i-i-i-i-i-i*.

NESTING Large cup in depression on ground under cover, also low in thicket; 3–5 eggs; 1–2 broods; May–August.

FEEDING Eats seeds, fruits, insects, and buds.

TERRESTRIAL LIFE
Eastern Towhees stay near the ground, and are usually found not more than a few feet above it.

SIMILAR SPECIES

SPOTTED TOWHEE ♂
see p.472

SPOTTED TOWHEE ♀
see p.472

two white wing bars

white spots on shoulder

two white wing bars

OCCURRENCE
Found in dense thickets, woodlands, shrubbery, forest edges, and disturbed forests from southeastern Saskatchewan, eastern Nebraska, western Louisiana, east to southern Québec, southern Maine, and southern Florida. Retreats from areas north of Chicago to winter in eastern Texas.

Length **7½–8in (19–20cm)**	Wingspan **10½in (27cm)**	Weight **1¹⁄₁₆–1¾oz (30–50g)**
Social **Solitary/Small flocks**	Lifespan **Up to 12 years**	Status **Secure**

DATE SEEN	WHERE	NOTES

Order **Passeriformes**	Family **Thraupidae**	Species *Piranga rubra*

Summer Tanager

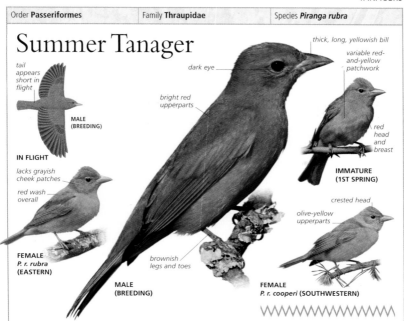

tail appears short in flight

MALE (BREEDING)

IN FLIGHT

dark eye

bright red upperparts

thick, long, yellowish bill

variable red-and-yellow patchwork

red head and breast

IMMATURE (1ST SPRING)

lacks grayish cheek patches

red wash overall

FEMALE
P. r. rubra
(EASTERN)

brownish legs and toes

MALE (BREEDING)

crested head

olive-yellow upperparts

FEMALE
P. r. cooperi (SOUTHWESTERN)

FLIGHT: strong and direct with quick wing beats; occasionally glides.

The stunning male Summer Tanager is the only North American bird that is entirely bright red. Immature males in their first spring plumage are almost equally as striking, with their patchwork of bright yellow-and-red plumage. The two subspecies of Summer Tanager are quite similar—*P. r. rubra* breeds in the East while *P. r. cooperi* breeds in the West. The latter is, on an average, paler, larger, and longer-billed.

VOICE Call an explosive *PIT-tuck!* or *PIT-a TUK*; flight call a muffled, airy *vreee*; song similar to American Robin, but more muffled and with longer pauses.

NESTING Loosely built cup of grasses usually placed high up in tree; 3–4 eggs; 1 brood; May–August.

FEEDING Eats bees, wasps, and other insects; also consumes fruit.

MAD FOR MULBERRIES
All *Piranga* tanagers are frugivores in season, and mulberries are one of their favorites.

SIMILAR SPECIES

HEPATIC TANAGER ♀

yellowish upperparts

reddish brown wings

SCARLET TANAGER ♀
see p.436

greenish overall

smaller, grayish bill

darker, wings and tail

OCCURRENCE
P. r. rubra breeds in deciduous and mixed woodlands from New Jersey and Nebraska south to Texas; *P. r. cooperi* in cottonwood-willow habitats near streams and rivers from California and Utah to Texas and Mexico. Both winter from southern Texas and Mexico to Bolivia and Brazil, and the West Indies.

Length **8in (20cm)**	Wingspan **12in (31cm)**	Weight **⁷⁄₈–1⁷⁄₁₆oz (25–40g)**
Social **Solitary**	Lifespan **Unknown**	Status **Secure**

DATE SEEN	WHERE	NOTES

Order **Passeriformes**	Family **Thraupidae**	Species *Piranga olivacea*

Scarlet Tanager

black wings

red body

vibrant scarlet head and body

MALE (BREEDING)
IN FLIGHT

tail appears short in flight

dark brown eyes

yellow patches in red plumage

grayish yellow bill

MALE (MOLTING)

greenish rump and upper tail

overall greenish upperparts

FEMALE

black wings

black tail

dark gray feet and legs

yellow-green body, head, and rump

MALE (NONBREEDING)

MALE (BREEDING)

I n breeding plumage, the male Scarlet Tanager is one of the brightest and most easily identified North American birds. Its secretive nature and preference for the canopies of well-shaded oak woodlands, however, make it difficult to spot. Males are most easily located by their distinctive and easily recognizable song. Male Scarlet Tanagers vary in appearance—some are orange, not scarlet, and others have a faint reddish wing bar.

VOICE Call a hoarse, drawn out *CHIK-breeer*, often shortened to *CHIK*; flight call an upslurred, whistled *pwee*; song a burry, slurred *querit-queer-query-querit-queer*.

NESTING Loosely woven cup of grass, lined with fine material, high up in tree; 3–5 eggs; 1 brood; May–July.

FEEDING Gleans insects, larvae, fruit, buds, and berries.

FLIGHT: strong and direct; rapid wing beats.

STUNNING MALE
Taking a bath away from the treetops, a male Scarlet Tanager can be seen in all its glory.

SIMILAR SPECIES		
VERMILION FLYCATCHER ♂ see p.457 — brown wings and tail	**SUMMER TANAGER** ♀ see p.435 — olive-yellow upperparts, thinner bill	larger bill, yellowish underparts

OCCURRENCE
Breeds in mature deciduous and mixed forests (especially with large oaks) from southern Manitoba and eastern Oklahoma east to the Maritime Provinces and the Carolinas. Trans-Gulf migrant. Winters in a variety of habitats along the eastern slope of the Andes from eastern Panama to Bolivia.

Length **7in (18cm)**	Wingspan **11½in (29cm)**	Weight **¹¹⁄₁₆–1¼oz (20–35g)**
Social **Solitary/Small flocks**	Lifespan **At least 10 years**	Status **Secure**

DATE SEEN	WHERE	NOTES

| Order **Passeriformes** | Family **Cardinalidae** | Species *Spiza americana* |

Dickcissel

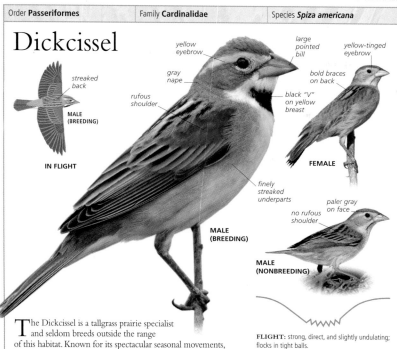

streaked back

MALE (BREEDING)

IN FLIGHT

yellow eyebrow

gray nape

rufous shoulder

large pointed bill

yellow-tinged eyebrow

bold braces on back

black "V" on yellow breast

FEMALE

finely streaked underparts

no rufous shoulder

paler gray on face

MALE (BREEDING)

MALE (NONBREEDING)

The Dickcissel is a tallgrass prairie specialist and seldom breeds outside the range of this habitat. Known for its spectacular seasonal movements, the Dickcissel winters in Venezuela, with flocks in the tens of thousands ravaging rice fields and damaging seed crops, making it a notorious pest. Immature birds, without yellow and rusty plumage, are very similar to female House Sparrows—vagrant and wintering Dickcissels in North America are often mistaken for sparrows.

VOICE Call a flat *chik*; flight call a distinctive, low, electric buzz *frrrrrrrt*; song a short series of sharp, insect-like stutters followed by few longer chirps or trill *dick-dick-dick-SISS-SISS-suhl*.

NESTING Bulky cup placed near ground in dense vegetation; 3–6 eggs; 1–2 broods; May–August.

FEEDING Forages on ground for insects, spiders, and seeds.

FLIGHT: strong, direct, and slightly undulating; flocks in tight balls.

UNIQUE SONG
The Dickcissel's onomatopoetic song is the characteristic sound of a healthy tallgrass prairie.

SIMILAR SPECIES

HOUSE SPARROW ♀
see p.341

shorter bill

shorter tail

no streaking on underparts

EASTERN MEADOWLARK
see p.402

longer bill

bright yellow underparts

OCCURRENCE
Breeds in tallgrass prairie, grasslands, hayfields, unmown roadsides, and untilled cropfields across the eastern and central US. Barely reaches southernmost Canada and northeastern Mexico. Winters in huge flocks in Venezuela, in open areas with tall grass-like vegetation, including rice fields.

| Length **6½in (16cm)** | Wingspan **9½in (24cm)** | Weight **⅞–1¼oz (25–35g)** |
| Social **Large flocks** | Lifespan **Up to 5 years** | Status **Declining** |

DATE SEEN	WHERE	NOTES

| Order **Passeriformes** | Family **Cardinalidae** | Species *Pheucticus ludovicianus* |

Rose-breasted Grosbeak

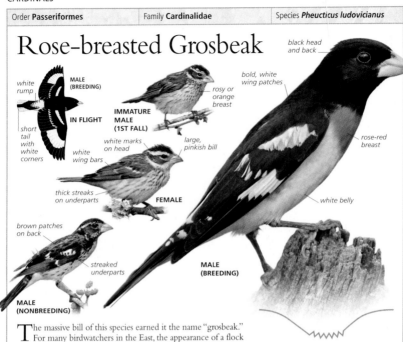

black head and back

white rump

MALE (BREEDING)

bold, white wing patches

IN FLIGHT

rosy or orange breast

IMMATURE MALE (1ST FALL)

short tail with white corners

white wing bars

white marks on head

large, pinkish bill

rose-red breast

thick streaks on underparts

FEMALE

white belly

brown patches on back

streaked underparts

MALE (BREEDING)

MALE (NONBREEDING)

The massive bill of this species earned it the name "grosbeak." For many birdwatchers in the East, the appearance of a flock of dazzling male Rose-breasted Grosbeaks in early May signals the peak of spring songbird migration. Adult males in their tuxedo attire, with rose-red ties, are unmistakable, but females and immature males are more somber. In the fall, immature male Rose-breasted Grosbeaks often have orange breasts, and are commonly mistaken for female Black-headed Grosbeaks. The difference is in the pink wing lining usually visible on perched birds, pink bill, and streaking across the center of the breast.

VOICE Call a high, sharp, explosive *sink* or *eeuk*, flight call an airy *vreee*; song a liquid, flute-like warble, rather slow in delivery, almost relaxed.

NESTING Loose, open cup or platform, usually in deciduous saplings, mid to high level; 2–5 eggs; 1–2 broods; May–July.

FEEDING Eats arthropods, fruit, seeds, and buds.

FLIGHT: undulating but powerful flight with bursts of wing beats.

OCCURRENCE
Breeds in deciduous and mixed woods, parks, and orchards across the northeastern quarter of the US, and across Canada westward from Newfoundland through Ontario to southeast Yukon. Winters from Mexico and the Caribbean, south to Guyana and Peru. Rare in the West.

SIMILAR SPECIES

PURPLE FINCH ♀
see p.348

much smaller

smaller, dark bill

thick, lateral throat stripe

BLACK-HEADED GROSBEAK ♀
see p.472

tawny breast

pencil-thin streaks on underparts

STUNNING MALE
A striking male Rose-breasted Grosbeak in springtime is quite unmistakable on a tree.

| Length **8in (20cm)** | Wingspan **12½in (32cm)** | Weight **1¼–2oz (35–55g)** |
| Social **Solitary/Small flocks** | Lifespan **Up to 13 years** | Status **Secure** |

DATE SEEN	WHERE	NOTES

Order **Passeriformes**	Family **Cardinalidae**	Species *Cardinalis cardinalis*

Northern Cardinal

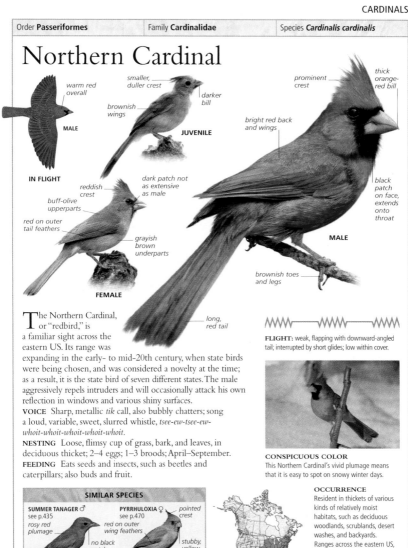

MALE — warm red overall

IN FLIGHT

JUVENILE — smaller, duller crest; brownish wings; darker bill

prominent crest

thick orange-red bill

bright red back and wings

black patch on face, extends onto throat

MALE

FEMALE — reddish crest; buff-olive upperparts; red on outer tail feathers; dark patch not as extensive as male; grayish brown underparts

long, red tail

brownish toes and legs

The Northern Cardinal, or "redbird," is a familiar sight across the eastern US. Its range was expanding in the early- to mid-20th century, when state birds were being chosen, and was considered a novelty at the time; as a result, it is the state bird of seven different states. The male aggressively repels intruders and will occasionally attack his own reflection in windows and various shiny surfaces.

VOICE Sharp, metallic *tik* call, also bubbly chatters; song a loud, variable, sweet, slurred whistle, *tsee-ew-tsee-ew-whoit-whoit-whoit-whoit-whoit.*

NESTING Loose, flimsy cup of grass, bark, and leaves, in deciduous thicket; 2–4 eggs; 1–3 broods; April–September.

FEEDING Eats seeds and insects, such as beetles and caterpillars; also buds and fruit.

FLIGHT: weak, flapping with downward-angled tail; interrupted by short glides; low within cover.

CONSPICUOUS COLOR
This Northern Cardinal's vivid plumage means that it is easy to spot on snowy winter days.

SIMILAR SPECIES

SUMMER TANAGER ♂
see p.435
rosy red plumage
no black patch

PYRRHULOXIA ♀
see p.470
red on outer wing feathers
pointed crest
stubby, yellow bill

OCCURRENCE
Resident in thickets of various kinds of relatively moist habitats, such as deciduous woodlands, scrublands, desert washes, and backyards. Ranges across the eastern US, southernmost Canada, the extreme Southwest, and south into Mexico, northern Guatemala, and northern Belize.

Length **8½in (22cm)**	Wingspan **12in (30cm)**	Weight **1⁷⁄₁₆–1¾oz (40–50g)**
Social **Solitary**	Lifespan **Up to 16 years**	Status **Secure**

DATE SEEN	WHERE	NOTES

439

| Order **Passeriformes** | Family **Cardinalidae** | Species *Passerina caerulea* |

Blue Grosbeak

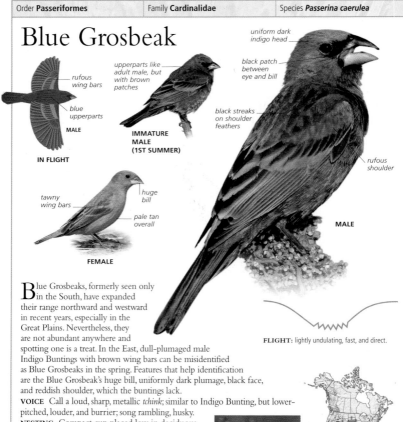

uniform dark indigo head

black patch between eye and bill

black streaks on shoulder feathers

rufous shoulder

MALE

rufous wing bars

blue upperparts

MALE

IN FLIGHT

upperparts like adult male, but with brown patches

IMMATURE MALE (1ST SUMMER)

tawny wing bars

huge bill

pale tan overall

FEMALE

FLIGHT: lightly undulating, fast, and direct.

Blue Grosbeaks, formerly seen only in the South, have expanded their range northward and westward in recent years, especially in the Great Plains. Nevertheless, they are not abundant anywhere and spotting one is a treat. In the East, dull-plumaged male Indigo Buntings with brown wing bars can be misidentified as Blue Grosbeaks in the spring. Features that help identification are the Blue Grosbeak's huge bill, uniformly dark plumage, black face, and reddish shoulder, which the buntings lack.

VOICE Call a loud, sharp, metallic *tchink*; similar to Indigo Bunting, but lower-pitched, louder, and burrier; song rambling, husky.

NESTING Compact cup placed low in deciduous tangle; 3–5 eggs; 1–2 broods; April–July.

FEEDING Eats seeds in winter, insects such as beetles, caterpillars, and grasshoppers in summer, and fruit.

SIMILAR SPECIES	
INDIGO BUNTING ♂ **1ST** ☘ see p.441	**LAZULI BUNTING** ♀ see p.472
pale blue markings overall	pale brown upperparts / much smaller bill

TRUE INDIGO
The Blue Grosbeak is actually indigo in color, with rufous shoulders and wing bars.

OCCURRENCE
Breeds in dense undergrowth of disturbed habitats: old fields, hedgerows, and desert scrub across the southern US from California to New Jersey, and southward to northwestern Costa Rica; breeders are trans-Gulf migrants; winters from Mexico to Panama and West Indies.

| Length **6¾in (17cm)** | Wingspan **11in (28cm)** | Weight **⅞–1¹⁄₁₆oz (25–30g)** |
| Social **Large flocks** | Lifespan **Up to 6 years** | Status **Secure** |

DATE SEEN	WHERE	NOTES

| Order **Passeriformes** | Family **Cardinalidae** | Species ***Passerina cyanea*** |

Indigo Bunting

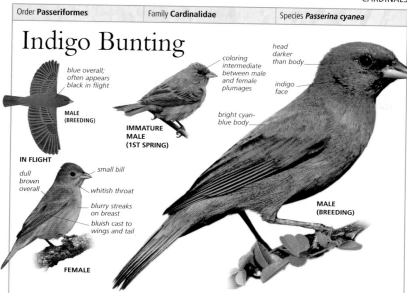

blue overall; often appears black in flight

MALE (BREEDING)

IN FLIGHT

coloring intermediate between male and female plumages

IMMATURE MALE (1ST SPRING)

head darker than body

indigo face

bright cyan-blue body

dull brown overall

small bill

whitish throat

blurry streaks on breast

bluish cast to wings and tail

FEMALE

MALE (BREEDING)

Few other North American birds are more brilliantly colored than the Indigo Bunting. However, it is not particularly well named, because the bird is really not indigo but rather a vibrant, almost cyan-blue. The male's head color is indigo with a rich violet tone on the face. Indigo Buntings are specialists of disturbed habitats, originally depending on tree-falls within forests and the grassland-forest edge. Human activity, especially the clearing of forests, has considerably increased suitable breeding habitats. As a result, Indigo Buntings are much more common and widespread than they were a hundred years ago. This adaptable species has even learned to nest in cornfields.

FLIGHT: lightly undulating, fast, and direct; gliding and fluttering in territorial encounters.

VOICE Call a sharp, dry, rattling *pik*!; flight a call long buzz; song series of simple, high-pitched, paired whistles, often described as "*fire!-fire!*, *where?-where?*, *there!-there!*, *put-it-out!*, *put-it-out!*"

NESTING Open cup above ground in dense tangle or shrub; 3–4 eggs; 1–3 broods; May–September.

FEEDING Eats seeds, insects, fruits, and buds.

SIMILAR SPECIES

BLUE GROSBEAK ♂
see p.440

deep indigo-violet overall

much larger bill

rich reddish rust shoulder

VARIED BUNTING ♀
see p.470

unstreaked underparts

SOUND OF SUMMER
This is one of the most common and cheerful songbirds found in eastern North America.

OCCURRENCE
Breeds in moist disturbed habitats—weedy fields, forest edges, and areas of heavy cultivation across the eastern US, southeastern Canada, and also locally in the Southwest. Winters from Mexico and the Caribbean south to Panama, and in small numbers along the Gulf Coast and in Florida.

| Length **5½in (14cm)** | Wingspan **8in (20cm)** | Weight **⁷⁄₁₆ –¹¹⁄₁₆oz (12–19g)** |
| Social **Large flocks** | Lifespan **Up to 11 years** | Status **Secure** |

DATE SEEN	WHERE	NOTES

| Order **Passeriformes** | Family **Cardinalidae** | Species ***Passerina ciris*** |

Painted Bunting

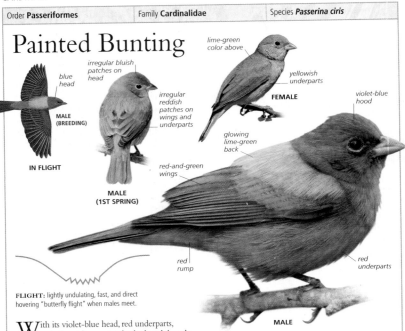

lime-green color above

blue head

MALE (BREEDING)

IN FLIGHT

irregular bluish patches on head

irregular reddish patches on wings and underparts

red-and-green wings

MALE (1ST SPRING)

yellowish underparts

FEMALE

glowing lime-green back

violet-blue hood

red rump

red underparts

MALE

FLIGHT: lightly undulating, fast, and direct hovering "butterfly flight" when males meet.

With its violet-blue head, red underparts, and vibrant lime-green back, the adult male Painted Bunting is the most brightly colored North American bunting. Although duller, the female is distinctive as one of the few truly green songbirds of the region. Young males take on a variety of appearances and can resemble an adult male, a female, or something in between. There are two populations, differing in molt pattern. The more western birds molt after leaving the breeding grounds, whereas the more eastern molt before they depart south for the winter.

VOICE Call a soft, ringing, upward slurred *pwip!;* flight call slurred, softer, and flatter than Indigo Bunting; song a sweet, rambling, relatively clear warble.

NESTING Deep cup in dense tangle or shrub, just above ground; 3–4 eggs; 1–3 broods; May–August.

FEEDING Eats seeds, fruit, and insects.

SIMILAR SPECIES

INDIGO BUNTING ♀
see p.441

lacks green upperparts

bluish wash to tail

VARIED BUNTING ♀
see p.470

streaked breast

tan overall

lacks green / upperparts

stubbier bill

tan overall

"NONPAREIL"
In Louisiana, the French word for "unparalleled" is fittingly used to describe this gorgeous species.

OCCURRENCE
Breeds in thickets and disturbed areas, across the south central US and northern Mexico, and along the East Coast from Florida to North Carolina. Nonbreeders use similar habitats. Western birds (New Mexico, Texas) winter from tropical Mexico to western Panama; eastern birds winter in southern Florida and Cuba.

| Length **5½in (14cm)** | Wingspan **8½in (22cm)** | Weight **⁷⁄₁₆–¹¹⁄₁₆oz (12–21g)** |
| Social **Solitary/Flocks** | Lifespan **Up to 12 years** | Status **Secure** |

DATE SEEN	WHERE	NOTES

Family **Cracidae**	Species ***Ortalis vetula***

Plain Chachalaca

A large, dull-brown to olive-green bird, the Plain Chachalaca deftly moves through trees and shrubs when foraging, running along branches and hopping from tree to tree. Males develop a distinct reddish to pink, naked-skin facial patch and throat during the breeding season.
OCCURRENCE Occurs only along the lower Rio Grande River valley of Texas, in shrubby and wooded areas, and edges of brushy thickets along river bottoms.
VOICE Boisterous, three-syllable *cha-ca-lak*; especially loud when pairs or groups call in chorus.

ADULT

long, fanned-out, white-tipped tail

Length **20–23in (51–58cm)**	Wingspan **24–27in (61–68cm)**

Family **Odontophoridae**	Species ***Callipepla squamata***

Scaled Quail

Named for the scale-like appearance of its chest, neck, and belly feathers, this quail is also called the "Blue Quail," because of its bluish sheen in some lights, or "Cottontop," because of the fluffy white tip to its crest. Its populations periodically go through "boom and bust" cycles that may be tied to rainfall and its impact on their food supply, but are also influenced by grazing practices.
OCCURRENCE Common in arid rangeland and semi desert of western Texas, New Mexico, and eastern Arizona, preferring less dense vegetation than other quails.
VOICE Flushed or separated covey (flock) uses 2-syllable *CHE-kar* call to reunite.

short tail

MALE

Length **10–12in (25–30cm)**	Wingspan **13–15in (33–38cm)**

Family **Anatidae**	Species ***Dendrocygna autumnalis***

Black-bellied Whistling-Duck

With its distinctive red bill and long, pink legs, this Whistling-Duck is spectacular and unmistakable. Unlike most other waterfowl, it has long legs and an upright posture when standing. Whistling-ducks used to be known as "tree-ducks" because they perch on trees when they roost and nest.
OCCURRENCE Prefers shallow, freshwater wetlands; rice fields are a common foraging habitat; also occurs along shorelines and mud bars. Casual west to southeastern California and occasionally east as far as Florida.
VOICE Soft wheezy series of 5–6 notes *pit pit weee do dew*; flight calls include a *chit-chit-chit*.

black belly

ADULT

long pink legs

Length **18½–20in (47–51cm)**	Wingspan **34–36in (86–91cm)**

Family **Anatidae**	Species ***Cygnus buccinator***

Trumpeter Swan

North America's quintessential swan and heaviest waterfowl, the magnificent Trumpeter Swan has made a remarkable comeback after numbers were severely reduced by hunting; by the mid-1930s, fewer than a hundred birds were known to exist. Active reintroduction efforts were made in the upper Midwest and Ontario to re-establish the species to its former breeding range. Its typical far-reaching call is usually the best way to identify it.
OCCURRENCE Alaskan and northern Canadian breeders go south to winter; others remain year round at local places such as Yellowstone National Park. Found on freshwater lakes and marshes with plenty of vegetation. Occurs in estuaries in winter.
VOICE Call nasal, resonant *oh-OH* reminiscent of a French horn, is usually the best way to identify it.

all-white plumage

ADULT

Length **4¼–5ft (1.3–1.5m)**	Wingspan **6½ft (2m)**

Family **Anatidae**	Species **Nomonyx dominicus**

Masked Duck

A small, widespread, Neotropical species, the Masked Duck is rarely seen because of its secretive behavior. Masked Ducks stay hidden in dense vegetation. Like grebes, it sinks below the surface to avoid detection, and drags its tail under the water. In flight, its white wing patch is characteristic. Females have two dark bars across their face, and a mottled brown body. They are related to the Ruddy Duck, both of which are called stiff-tailed ducks.

OCCURRENCE Resident of southern Texas, with scattered records elsewhere. Found in heavily vegetated freshwater marshes and ponds. Resident from Mexico to Argentina, and in the Caribbean.

VOICE Male gives a throaty *coo-coo-coo*, or *kir-roo-kirroo-kiroo* call during courtship; female a short, repeated hiss.

blue bill with black tip

MALE *deep chestnut with black mottling*

Length **13–15in (33–38cm)**	Wingspan **17in (43cm)**

Family **Procellariidae**	Species **Pterodroma hasitata**

Black-capped Petrel

Until recently, the Black-capped Petrel was almost unknown in North America because of its off-shore feeding grounds. After breeding in the West Indies, they move northwestward to feed in the warm Gulf Stream during the summer, where they are seen fairly commonly during deep-water birdwatching trips. Their flight is characteristic of *Pterodroma* species: they rocket up above the ocean and then drop back down while moving forward swiftly, using lift from the air currents above the water.

OCCURRENCE When not breeding, forage at sea over the deep, warm water of the Gulf Stream off the southeastern US.

VOICE Silent at sea but vocal on breeding grounds.

white forehead

long, pointed wings

ADULT

Length **13in (33cm)**	Wingspan **35in (88cm)**

Family **Procellariidae**	Species **Puffinus lherminieri**

Audubon's Shearwater

Audubon's Shearwater, also known as the Tropical Shearwater, is smaller and more slender than all the other regularly occurring shearwaters in North American waters. It has especially short wings that, when combined with its small size, make its flight similar to that of members of the family Alcidae (auks, murres, and puffins).

OCCURRENCE Breeds on Caribbean islands; widespread in tropical waters; spends warmer months feeding in the Gulf of Mexico and along the east coast of the US.

VOICE Occasional thin, high-pitched call; twittering and mewing calls at colonies, but silent at sea.

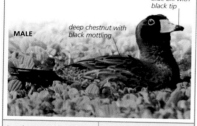

dark undertail feathers

white underparts

ADULT

Length **12in (31cm)**	Wingspan **27in (69cm)**

Family **Hydrobatidae**	Species **Oceanodroma castro**

Band-rumped Storm-Petrel

This uncommon summer visitor forages 25–35 miles (40–56km) in warm offshore waters of the Gulf Stream and the Gulf of Mexico. Its origin is unclear, but it probably comes from colonies in the eastern Atlantic. They appear brawny, long-winged, and square-tailed with the white at the base of their tail extending along the flanks to the belly.

OCCURRENCE A warm-water petrel of the Gulf Stream and Gulf of Mexico. Breeds on islands in the tropical and subtropical Pacific (*O. c. bangsi*) and Atlantic Oceans (*O. c. castro*). Most birds seen in North America probably breed in the eastern Atlantic Ocean.

VOICE Silent at sea; squeaking and purring sounds at nest.

white extends to sides

feet do not extend beyond tail in flight

ADULT

Length **7½–8½in (19–21cm)**	Wingspan **17–18½ in (43–47cm)**

| Family **Podicipedidae** | Species **Tachybaptus dominicus** |

Least Grebe

This tiny, tropical and subtropical species is the most easily overlooked of the North American grebes. This is primarily because it breeds only in fresh or brackish water in southern Texas. It is a good diver, capable of remaining submerged for over 25 seconds. While adults are not seen on land, swimming chicks can clamber ashore when they are threatened.

OCCURRENCE Temporary or permanent bodies of fresh and brackish water, such as mangrove swamps, marsh openings, small ponds, ditches, lakes, and slow-moving rivers, often with very little or no emergent vegetation.

VOICE Metallic, sputtering trill, accelerating at the start, then slowing down then accelerating again; alarm call a single *beep.*

yellowish orange eye

ADULT (SUMMER)

| Length **9–10½in (23–27cm)** | Wingspan **19–21in (48–53cm)** |

| Family **Podicepedidae** | Species **Aechmophorus occidentalis** |

Western Grebe

A strictly North American species, the Western Grebe shares much of its breeding habitat and elaborate mating rituals with Clark's Grebe. Until 1985, they were considered to be different color forms of a single species. Females are smaller than males and have smaller, thinner, slightly upturned bills. This species dives more frequently than Clark's, and remains submerged for about 30 seconds.

OCCURRENCE Western North America, breeds in freshwater lakes and marshes with open water and emergent vegetation; also man-made marshes and artificial habitats. Winters along the Pacific Coast.

VOICE At least nine different calls, each with a specific information content, such as alarm, begging, and mating calls; advertising call a harsh, rolling 2-noted *krrrikk-krrreek.*

black behind eye

ADULT

| Length **21½–30in (55–75cm)** | Wingspan **30–39in (76–100cm)** |

| Family **Podicipedidae** | Species **Aechmophorus clarkii** |

Clark's Grebe

Clark's and Western grebes are closely related and very difficult to distinguish from each other. They rarely fly except when migrating at night. As their legs and toes are set far back making their movement awkward, they seldom come on land. However, they have been reported to run upright rapidly. Their flight muscles are quite reduced when they arrive on their breeding grounds.

OCCURRENCE Breeds in freshwater lakes and marshes bordered by emergent vegetation; has been nesting in man-made Lake Havasu marshes since 1960s. Winters along the Pacific Coast.

VOICE Variety of calls, including a harsh, grating, 2-syllable, single, rising *kree-eekt* advertising call.

ADULT

white around eye

| Length **21½–30in (55–75cm)** | Wingspan **32in (82cm)** |

| Family **Sulidae** | Species **Sula leucogaster** |

Brown Booby

The Brown Booby, which is actually bicolor, sooty brown and white, overlaps with the Masked and Red-footed Boobies and often nests in mixed colonies with them. Unlike juvenile Brown Boobies, the juvenile Masked Booby has a whitish ring around the neck and a pale rump.

OCCURRENCE Breeds on tropical islands of the Atlantic, Pacific, and Indian Oceans, and on Caribbean islands. Rare along Atlantic and Pacific coasts. Occurs closer to shore than Masked Booby.

VOICE Silent, but can make loud or subdued quacking, honking, or braying noises, especially when nesting.

wings black and white underneath

long, yellowish bill

ADULT

| Length **30in (76cm)** | Wingspan **4½ft (1.4m)** |

| Family **Phalacrocoracidae** | Species *Phalacrocorax brasilianus* |

Neotropic Cormorant

The slender Neotropic Cormorant ranges widely in the Western Hemisphere. In the US, it breeds and winters along the Gulf Coast and in the lower Rio Grande Valley. Unlike other cormorant species, it tolerates human activities. In the 1960s, their numbers declined as a result of coastal development and pesticide use, but they have recovered in recent years. The nest is a platform of sticks lined with leaves, grass, and seaweed, cemented with guano.
OCCURRENCE Breeds in coastal marshes, swamps, and inland reservoirs from southeastern Texas and western Louisiana to Tierra del Fuego in South America; found in a wide variety of wetlands in fresh, brackish, or saltwater. Winters close inshore in protected bays, inlets, estuaries, and lagoons.
VOICE Series of low, pig-like grunts; croaks in alarm.

dull orange base to bill

ADULT

| Length **24in (61cm)** | Wingspan **3¼ft (1m)** |

| Family **Falconidae** | Species *Caracara cheriway* |

Crested Caracara

In North America, the large, hawk-like Crested Caracara is only found locally in Texas, southern Arizona, and central Florida. The Crested Caracara is monogamous and territorial. Known locally as the "Mexican Buzzard," the Crested Caracara is a member of the family Falconidae (falcons) not Accipitridae (hawks).
OCCURRENCE Common in Central and South America. Breeds and winters in open areas ranging from desert to grassland with scattered tall trees; around agricultural land; dumps and slaughterhouses.
VOICE Adults disturbed at nest emit cackles, hollow rattles, and high-pitched screams; nestlings utter high-pitched screams and raspy *swee-swee* calls.

dark bars on white breast and nape

ADULT

| Length **19–23in (48–58cm)** | Wingspan **4ft (1.2m)** |

| Family **Accipitridae** | Species *Rostrhamus sociabilis* |

Snail Kite

Formerly known as the Everglade Kite, this bird is found only in peninsular Florida, where it was discovered in 1844. They are nomadic, following the apple snail and breeding in colonies when the snails are abundant. The males may breed with several females in one season, but sequentially, rather than all at one time.
OCCURRENCE In Florida, found locally, year-round, in inland freshwater marshes and along shallow lakes. Outside North America widespread in water habitats, including roadside ditches near towns.
VOICE Grating cackle given by both sexes: *ka-ka-ka-ka-ka-ka* or a harsh *krrrr*, variations of nasal, sheep-like bleating *k-a-a-a-a-a-a-a*, while being harassed or when begging for food.

long pointed bill

bright orange feet

MALE

| Length **14–16in (36–41cm)** | Wingspan **3½ft (1.1m)** |

| Family **Accipitridae** | Species *Chondrohierax uncinatus* |

Hook-billed Kite

This kite occurs in tropical America from Mexico all the way south to Argentina, but in the US is found only in the Rio Grande Valley of southeastern Texas, where fewer than 60 pairs have nested since the late 1960s. The Hooked-billed Kite is long-tailed, and broad at its wing tips. It is mostly seen flying in the morning and is rarely spotted later in the day.

wings broad at tip

OCCURRENCE Breeds and winters only in the Rio Grande Valley of extreme southern Texas; breeds in riverine scrub and woodlands.
VOICE Rapid rattle; *kekekekekekekeke* highest in the middle.

FEMALE

barred underparts

| Length **18in (46cm)** | Wingspan **36in (92cm)** |

Family **Accipitridae**	Species ***Parabuteo unicinctus***

Harris's Hawk

Named by the renowned ornithologist John James Audubon in honor of his friend and patron, Edward Harris, Harris's Hawks nest in social units, unlike other American birds of prey. These groups engage in cooperative hunting: members take turns leading the chase to wear down their prey and share in the kill. This bird is popular with falconers.

OCCURRENCE Forages and breeds year-round in semi-open desert scrub, savanna, grassland, and wetland containing scattered large trees and cacti. Occasionally appears in suburban areas. Essentially a Central and South American species with a restricted range north of the Rio Grande.

VOICE Main territorial alarm call a prolonged, harsh growl lasting about 3 seconds; also chirps, croaks, and screams.

rufous "shoulders"

ADULT

black tail with white tip

Length **18–23in (46–59cm)**	Wingspan **3½–4ft (1.1–1.2m)**

Family **Accipitridae**	Species ***Asturina nitida***

Gray Hawk

The elegant Gray Hawk is found from Mexico south to Argentina, but in North America is only seen in southwestern Texas and southeastern Arizona. The Gray Hawk's breeding system can include trios, one female and two males, all of whom cooperate with chick rearing. About 100 pairs exist in the US, but their numbers are stable and possibly even increasing. Cottonwood and mesquite woodlands are key to their survival.

OCCURRENCE Breeds in riverine woodlands of mesquite and cottonwoods, especially along streams in the Gila River (Arizona) and Rio Grande (Texas) drainages. Little information exists about its winter habitats.

VOICE High-pitched whistled alarm, *creee*, rising and descending.

yellow legs and feet

ADULT

Length **16–17in (41–43cm)**	Wingspan **35in (89cm)**

Family **Accipitridae**	Species ***Buteo brachyurus***

Short-tailed Hawk

In North America this species is found only in peninsular Florida, where it numbers only about 500 individuals. Like some other hawks, it has light and dark forms, the latter the more common one. This hawk is not easy to spot, as it seldom perches in the open and soars quite high. Its habitat is dwindling, and population studies are needed to learn more about its status and its future.

OCCURRENCE Found in woodlands, flooded upland habitats, savanna, prairies, and open country. Nests in cypress or bay swamps with closed canopy; winters where mangrove forest meets tidal sawgrass marsh, in wet prairies, also in suburban areas with forest tracts.

VOICE High-pitched cat-like *keeea* call; also a variety of *keee* calls.

dark brown head and white chin

ADULT (LIGHT FORM)

Length **15½–17½in (39–44cm)**	Wingspan **33–39in (83–100cm)**

Family **Accipitridae**	Species ***Buteo albicaudatus***

White-tailed Hawk

The White-tailed Hawk's distribution in the US is limited to southeastern Texas. An easily identifiable hawk, it is gray above, has a striking white breast, reddish shoulder patches, and black-banded white tail. Unlike other hawks, the adult's outer flight feathers extend noticeably beyond the tail when perched. It is a versatile forager, capturing prey by soaring, hovering, or by still-hunting from a perch. It likes to hunt at the edges of river basins.

OCCURRENCE Found in Texas in savannah, prairie, grasslands, lightly grazed pastures, open woodlands, and woody understory with yucca, mesquite, and thorny shrubs. Widespread in South America.

VOICE Series of scream-like calls *raa kad-ik kad-ik kad-ik kad-ik*.

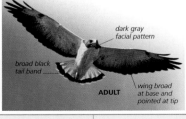

dark gray facial pattern

broad black tail band

ADULT

wing broad at base and pointed at tip

Length **18–23in (46–58cm)**	Wingspan **4¼ft (1.3m)**

Family **Accipitridae** | Species ***Buteo albonotatus***

Zone-tailed Hawk

Widely distributed in Mexico, Central, and South America, the Zone-tailed Hawk's range barely reaches the Southwest. In Arizona, it shares the same riparian woodlands as the Common Black-hawk, but their behavior is quite different. Zone-tailed Hawks join kettles of high-flying Turkey Vultures, which they resemble to the point of mimicry. Using the vultures as a sort of decoy, the hawks spot live prey, then dive to catch it.

OCCURRENCE Nests in lowland riverine woodlands in Arizona, in pine and mixed woodlands at higher elevations in Texas and New Mexico. A migrant in the US, but largely resident from Central America south to Paraguay.

VOICE Harsh scream, 1-syllable *kreeee*, or 2-syllable *kreeee-arr*.

barred flight feathers

long wings

ADULT

Length **17½–22in (45–56cm)** | Wingspan **4–4½ft (1.2–1.4m)**

Family **Accipitridae** | Species ***Buteo regalis***

Ferruginous Hawk

An inhabitant of open country, the Ferruginous Hawk is the largest North American hawk. It is a versatile nester, building its nest on cliffs, nearly level ground, trees, or man-made structures. Its numbers are threatened by its preference for prairie dog habitat, which is declining because of human encroachment, shooting, and pesticide use.

OCCURRENCE Breeds in low-elevation grasslands interrupted by cliffs or isolated trees in western North America; winters in the southwestern US and Mexico.

VOICE Screaming *Kree-aa* or *kaah, kaah* during courtship; quieter, lower-pitched, longer alarm call.

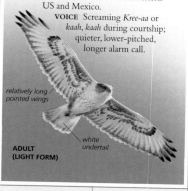

relatively long pointed wings

white undertail

ADULT (LIGHT FORM)

Length **22–27in (56–69cm)** | Wingspan **4¼–4½ft (1.3–1.4m)**

Family **Gruidae** | Species ***Grus americana***

Whooping Crane

The majestic Whooping Crane is one of the most compelling success stories of the US Endangered Species Act. The species has rebounded from just a few dozen birds in the mid-20th century to hundreds of individuals in the early 21st. However, it still remains in a critical state because it reproduces slowly in a restricted range. More intervention measures are required to help this fragile species continue its recovery.

OCCURRENCE Breeds in marshy country with scattered ponds and prairies in a restricted region of Canada; winters in coastal estuaries in Texas; uses marshland and agricultural fields during migration.

VOICE Piercing and trumpeting, *kerloo*! and *kerleeyeur*; bugling calls during courtship dances.

larger than Sandhill Crane

ADULT

Length **4–4½ft (1.2–1.4m)** | Wingspan **7¼ft (2.2m)**

Family **Charadriidae** | Species ***Charadrius montanus***

Mountain Plover

Unlike many other North American shorebirds, this rather plain-looking plover is rarely found near water. Unusually wary, the Mountain Plover often faces away from danger and squats motionless on the ground, "disappearing" into the landscape and earning it the nickname of "Prairie Ghost." It is declining, and endangered because of habitat loss from overgrazing and pesticides.

OCCURRENCE Patchily distributed in west–central North America. Breeds in dry, flat, short grass prairies, semi-desert areas with sparse vegetation; winters south to Mexico.

VOICE Generally silent; flight call grating *kirrp*; wintering birds in flight give short *kip* call; courtship song rolling, drawled, whistled *wee-wee*.

tan-colored overall

ADULT (BREEDING)

Length **8½–9½ in (21–24cm)** | Wingspan **21½–23½in (54–60cm)**

Family **Scolopacidae**	Species **Numenius americanus**

Long-billed Curlew

This large curlew has the southernmost breeding and northernmost wintering ranges of the four North American species of curlew. It is also one of nine bird species that are endemic to the grasslands of the Great Plains. It is remarkably tame on its wintering grounds.

OCCURRENCE Breeds in prairies, short grass and mixed-grass habitats of the Great Basin and Great Plains. Some stragglers occur in Florida, most birds winter in California, Texas, and Mexico.

VOICE Flight call a 2-note *cur-LUoo*, often accompanied by rapid *qui-pi-pi-pi-pi*; flight song haunting whistles, trills *werr-EEEer*.

head less patterned than adult

bill slightly shorter than in adult

barred wing feathers

JUVENILE

Length **20–26in (51–65cm)**	Wingspan **30–39in (75–100cm)**

Family **Scolopacidae**	Species **Calidris ferruginea**

Curlew Sandpiper

The Curlew Sandpiper, a medium-sized Eurasian sandpiper, breeds in northern Siberia. It can be confused with the Dunlin and Stilt Sandpiper in nonbreeding plumage. It is slimmer than the Dunlin, with longer wings, neck, legs, and bill, and differs from the Stilt Sandpiper by its shorter legs and faint white eyebrow.

OCCURRENCE Rare, but regular migrant along the Atlantic Coast; accidental elsewhere. Found in a variety of habitats, including beaches, coastal mudflats, impoundments, and lake margins.

VOICE Flight call a characteristic, musical, trilled, or rolled *chrreep*, dropping in the middle.

JUVENILE

long, decurved bill

black legs

Length **7¼–7½in (18–19cm)**	Wingspan **16¾–18½in (42–46cm)**

Family **Laridae**	Species **Larus thayeri**

Thayer's Gull

The status of Thayer's Gull as a species is puzzling. It was described in 1915, then was considered to be a subspecies of the Herring Gull, but in the 1970s was treated as a full species because of differences between the two. Many authorities now consider the Thayer's Gull to be a subspecies of the Iceland Gull. It is difficult to identify when seen together with the Herring and Iceland Gulls.

OCCURRENCE Nests on cliff ledges of fjords in the High Canadian Arctic. Winter movements are unclear; occurs mainly along the Pacific Coast, but also across the interior and along the East Coast.

VOICE Mewing squeals, like *kee-your*; calls more on breeding grounds than on wintering grounds.

reddish purple eye-ring

ADULT (SUMMER)

Length **22½–25in (57–64cm)**	Wingspan **4¼–5ft (1.3–1.5m)**

Family **Laridae**	Species **Rhodostethia rosea**

Ross's Gull

Named for the great British Polar explorer, James Clark Ross, this species is unmistakable in adult breeding plumage. Dove-gray upperparts, pale-pink underparts, red legs, small black bill, and black collar, make it an elegant and beautiful-looking bird. In winter it lacks the distinctive black neck ring and the delicate pink blush on the underside may be more muted.

OCCURRENCE Siberian breeder found along the north coast of Alaska in fall; breeds along Hudson Bay in Canada; winter strays found across Canada and in northeastern and northwestern US.

VOICE Rarely heard in winter; a tern-like *kik-kik-kik* on the breeding grounds.

black "necklace"

ADULT (BREEDING)

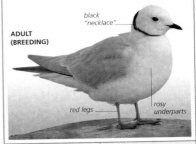

red legs

rosy underparts

Length **11½–12in (29–31cm)**	Wingspan **35–39in (90–100cm)**

Family **Laridae**	Species *Sterna anaethetus*

Bridled Tern

Compared with other terns, the Bridled Tern has darker, browner upperparts, and in strong subtropical light its underparts appear shaded, giving the bird an overall dark look. When perched, breast and shoulders stand out pure white. Note the long white line, or bridle, tapering above each eye, and the black legs and bill, with no hint of red. It first bred in the Florida Keys in 1987, and has nested there occasionally since then. It spends most of its life at sea.

OCCURRENCE Nests in the West Indies and Bahamas, irregularly in Florida. Regular, but mostly far offshore in the Gulf of Mexico.

VOICE Rising, whistled *wheeep* call; also barking *wup, wup*; vocal at colonies.

white supercilium

forked tail

ADULT (BREEDING)

Length **12–12½in (30–32cm)**	Wingspan **30–32in (77–81cm)**

Family **Laridae**	Species *Sterna fuscatus*

Sooty Tern

Except when nesting, the Sooty Tern spends most of its life flying over the tropical and subtropical oceans of the world. After fledging, the young do not return to land for six to eight years. The Sooty Tern's plumage is not particularly waterproof so the bird rarely settles on the water. It sometimes perches on floating debris or even on sea turtles.

OCCURRENCE A large colony breeds at the Dry Tortugas, off the Florida Keys. Small numbers breed along the coast of Texas and near the mouth of the Mississippi River. In summer, found in the Gulf Stream north to Virginia.

VOICE Distinctive nasal call: *wide-a-wake*, *wide-a-wake* has given it the vernacular name of "Wideawake Tern." Vocal throughout year, particularly when breeding.

black upperparts

ADULT (BREEDING)

Length **14–17½in (36–45cm)**	Wingspan **32–37in (82–94cm)**

Family **Laridae**	Species *Anous stolidus*

Brown Noddy

The Brown Noddy resembles a typical tern species but with the colors reversed, its pale gray forehead and crown contrasting with its dark body. Noddies nest on rocks and islands in tropical waters around the world. Its only breeding ground in North America is a few miles off the Florida Keys. It is very tame and shows little fear of humans, hence its scientific name, *Anous stolidus*, which is Latin for "foolish" and "slow-witted."

OCCURRENCE Only nesting site in the US is at Dry Tortugas, off the Florida Keys; during summer occurs offshore in Gulf of Mexico, as far north as the Outer Banks, North Carolina.

VOICE Variety of crow-like *caw* or *kark* calls given around nesting colonies; otherwise silent.

very dark brown upperparts

ADULT

Length **15½–17½in (40–45cm)**	Wingspan **30–33in (77–85cm)**

Family **Laridae**	Species *Anous minutus*

Black Noddy

This species is the rarest and has the most restricted occurrence of any tern that regularly occurs in North America. Since 1962 small numbers of nonbreeding Black Noddies have been seen nearly annually in the Brown Noddy colony of the Dry Tortugas, off the Florida Keys. The Black Noddy is slightly smaller than the Brown Noddy, and has a thinner bill, black upperparts and a white forehead.

OCCURRENCE Subtropical and tropical seas; pelagic away from breeding colonies; regular at Dry Tortugas, but does not breed; accidental along Texas coast.

VOICE High-pitched *caw* or *kark* calls when breeding; otherwise silent.

white forehead

ADULT

black upperparts

Length **14–15½in (35–40cm)**	Wingspan **26–28in (65–72cm)**

| Family **Stercorariidae** | Species *Stercorarius skua* |

Great Skua

The Great Skua can be distinguished from the South Polar Skua by its heavier streaking and usually more reddish tones to its brown body. Known in Scotland as the "bonxie," a name with Nordic origins, the Great Skua is closely related to several species of southern skuas including the Falkland Skua. The Great Skua is aggressive, and is often seen harassing other birds, like Herring Gulls, to make them disgorge their food.

OCCURRENCE Rare visitor, mostly in fall through spring, to pelagic waters off the Atlantic Coast of North America.

VOICE Rough, cackling *rah-rah-rah* at colonies. Usually silent at sea.

strong, hooked bill

dark nape

mottled gray to warm brown plumage

ADULT

| Length **19½–23in (50–58cm)** | Wingspan **4–4½ft (1.2–1.4m)** |

| Family **Stercorariidae** | Species *Stercorarius maccormicki* |

South Polar Skua

Probably a regular visitor to US waters, the South Polar Skua is a large, aggressive relative of the jaegers. It pursues other seabirds to make them disgorge their food, or battles for scraps behind fishing boats. It is a severe threat to penguins on its breeding grounds, roaming around their colonies and waiting to take an egg or snatch a chick. The South Polar Skua takes several years to mature, and stays at sea for long periods until it reaches adulthood.

OCCURRENCE Spends southern winters offshore in the North Atlantic and Pacific; breeds in the South Shetland Islands and along the coast and islands of the Antarctic Peninsula.

VOICE Deep gull-like burbling; generally silent at sea.

ADULT

hooked bill

generally unstreaked parts

| Length **21in (53cm)** | Wingspan **4¼ft (1.3m)** |

| Family **Columbidae** | Species *Columba flavirostris* |

Red-billed Pigeon

The only North American area where this Mexican and Central American pigeon occurs is riverine woodlands of southern Texas. Wine-red below, bluish gray above, with yellow eyes and a red eye-ring, it is unmistakable. It is similar in size and posture to a Rock Pigeon but it has a longer tail and a more slender body. In comparison to a Band-tailed Pigeon, it appears heavier.

OCCURRENCE Prefers to perch in tall trees above brushy understory in wooded bottomlands of Texas's Rio Grande Valley.

VOICE Long, high-pitched, hoarse *coooo* followed by 2–5 *up, cup-a-coos.*

bill red at base

ADULT

| Length **14½in (37cm)** | Wingspan **24in (62cm)** |

| Family **Columbidae** | Species *Columba leucocephala* |

White-crowned Pigeon

Similar in size and shape to the Rock Pigeon, the White-crowned Pigeon has a distinctive white crown, slate-gray back, and slightly longer tail. In addition, it is only found in the Florida Keys and the southern tip of mainland Florida. It occasionally feeds around hotels and in suburban backyards. This strict frugivore is uncommon in the United States.

OCCURRENCE Nests in both red and black mangrove islands. Winters in seasonal deciduous forests of the Florida Keys and Everglades National Park. May travel some distance each day to visit feeding sites.

VOICE Loud, deep *coo-curra-coo*, repeated 5–8 times; also low, purring growl.

white crown

ADULT

| Length **13–14in (33–35cm)** | Wingspan **23in (59cm)** |

Family **Columbidae**	Species *Leptotila verreauxi*

White-tipped Dove

The North American range of the White-tipped Dove is restricted to southern Texas, but it is actually a widespread species, occurring from Mexico through Central and South America to Argentina. A rather shy bird, the White-tipped Dove keeps out of sight, foraging on the floor of mesquite and other woodlands, but its distinctive, two- or three-syllable mournful whistle is often heard.

OCCURRENCE Occurs in the US only in southeastern Texas, where it breeds and winters in dense woodlands of mesquite, Texas Ebony, and Cedar Elm near rivers and oxbow lakes.

VOICE Long, quavering *wh'whoo'oo*, which sounds like someone blowing into an empty bottle.

ADULT

short tail

Length **10–12in (25–30cm)**	Wingspan **18in (46cm)**

Family **Psittacidae**	Species *Aratinga holochlora*

Green Parakeet

A native of Mexico, Central America, and northern South America, this parakeet appeared in southern Texas in the 1980s. Since then, numbers have greatly increased, and are thought to have reached 2,000. Some birds have scattered yellow, orange, or red feathers on the head and breast.

OCCURRENCE Breeds and winters in urban and suburban areas in Texas and Florida; prefers exotic trees and shrubs. In Mexico and Central America, occurs in evergreen and deciduous forests up to 6,500 ft (2,000m).

VOICE High-pitched screeches; also shrill chattering when in flocks.

all green plumage

Length **13in (33cm)**	Wingspan **21in (53cm)**

Family **Psittacidae**	Species *Amazona viridigenalis*

Red-crowned Parrot

Red-crowned Parrots are becoming increasingly rare in their native range in northeastern Mexico because of habitat destruction and their capture for the pet trade. Ironically, the naturalized population in California may now exceed in size that of the native Mexican one. These parrots forage and roost in flocks and often breed in loose nesting colonies.

OCCURRENCE Nonmigratory species, locally common in southern California and uncommon in southern Florida, southern Texas, and Puerto Rico. Lives in deciduous tropical rainforests in its native range.

VOICE Variety of loud squawks or shrieks; can mimic human speech and other sounds.

blue hind crown

red patch on wings

ADULT

Length **12in (30cm)**	Wingspan **25in (63cm)**

Family **Cuculidae**	Species *Cocczyus minor*

Mangrove Cuckoo

The Mangrove Cuckoo's solitary and secretive behavior, as well as its preference for dense, nearly inaccessible mangrove habitats, make it difficult to study. This, combined with the continued human development of mangroves in Florida make the future of this cuckoo uncertain in the US. Widespread in the Caribbean, and from Mexico to Colombia.

OCCURRENCE Found in Florida, in coastal areas from Tampa Bay southward and in the Florida Keys, in mangrove swamps, and also locally in other woodland habitats.

VOICE Series of up to 2 dozen harsh, frog-like notes, *aarhm aarhm aarrhmmm*; also fast *coo coo coo*.

black mask

large, white spots on underside of tail

ADULT

Length **11–12½in (28–32cm)**	Wingspan **16in (41cm)**

Family **Cuculidae**	Species *Crotophaga ani*

Smooth-billed Ani

The Smooth-billed Ani colonized southern Florida in the early 1930s, then steadily declined in the 1980s. It is a communal breeder. Several females lay eggs in the same nest. Their large bills distinguish Smooth-billed Anis from other all-black birds like grackles or crows. They feed on or near the ground on insects, small vertebrates, and fruit.

OCCURRENCE Prefers shrubby areas, agricultural lands, and hedges in southern Florida. Common in the West Indies, Central, and South America.

VOICE Main call is a whiny, ascending *yaahnee*.

upper mandible lacks grooves

ADULT

Length **14½in (37cm)**	Wingspan **18½in (46cm)**

Family **Cuculidae**	Species *Crotophaga sulcirostris*

Groove-billed Ani

Anis, members of the cuckoo family, have black plumage, long tails, and high, narrow, blackish bills. They always appear dishevelled—as if their feathers were about to fall off. Two of their toes point forward and two backward. These social birds have an unusual communal nesting behavior for cuckoos: several females lay eggs in the same nest, and both males and females share incubation duties.

OCCURRENCE Breeds from southern Texas and Mexico to Central and South America.

VOICE Call a liquid *Tee-ho*, accented on first syllable, given in flight and when perched, chorus like when many birds call together.

high blackish bill

long tail

Length **13½in (34cm)**	Wingspan **17in (43cm)**

Family **Strigidae**	Species *Micrathene whitneyi*

Elf Owl

The diminutive Elf Owl is perhaps the most common bird of prey in the upland deserts of the southwestern US. Being strictly nocturnal it is more often heard than seen. Once heard, its distinctive voice is easy to recognize. Elf Owls defend their nests aggressively, and several birds can get together to mob an intruder.

OCCURRENCE Breeds in southern Nevada, Arizona, California, New Mexico, and Texas; also thorn scrub, woodlands along rivers, and suburban areas.

VOICE Call is a loud chatter of 5–6 notes; also trills and barks.

no "ear" tufts

thin white eyebrow

ADULT

Length **4¾–5½in (12–14cm)**	Wingspan **15in (38cm)**

Family **Caprimulgidae**	Species *Chordeiles acutipennis*

Lesser Nighthawk

Well camouflaged when it rests on the ground during daytime, the Lesser Nighthawk is an aerial forager that is most active at dusk and dawn. It swoops low over water, bush, and desert in pursuit of insect prey, which it tracks with agile and abrupt changes in direction. This species was formerly known as the Trilling Nighthawk because of its distinctive call, which distinguishes it from the similar-looking, but different-sounding Common Nighthawk (*peent* calls).

OCCURRENCE Breeds in desert, open scrub, and along watercourses. Occurs from the southern US to Central and South America.

VOICE Low, trilled whistle which lasts up to 12 seconds and resembles the calls of some species of toads.

white band across wing tips

MALE

Length **8–9in (20–23cm)**	Wingspan **21–23in (53–58cm)**

Family **Caprimulgidae**	Species ***Nyctidromus albicollis***

Common Pauraque

The resident Common Pauraque reaches the nothernmost part of its range in southern Texas. It is possible to get quite close to pauraques during the day, as they rely on their camouflage for protection. Common Pauraques feed at night. They perch in open locations and ambush passing insects with sudden bursts of flight.
OCCURRENCE Found in open scrub, sparsely wooded areas, and hedgerows; feeds over open fields, forest clearings, and roads. Breeds from southern Texas to Central and South America.
VOICE Strange, slurred, or buzzed *p'wheeerr* whistle; also various harsh-sounding calls.

dark spots on back

ADULT

Length **10–11in (25–28cm)**	Wingspan **21–23in (53–58cm)**

Family **Caprimulgidae**	Species ***Phalaenoptilus nuttallii***

Common Poorwill

The smallest North American nightjar, the Common Poorwill has shorter wings than its relatives, a stubbier tail, but a comparatively larger head. It can go into a state of torpor, somewhat similar to mammalian hibernation and hummingbird torpor, remaining in this state for several days, perhaps even weeks, during cold weather or when food is unavailable. The male has whitish corners to its tail, while the female is buffy.
OCCURRENCE Breeds in arid habitats from the western US southward to Mexico. Winters in northern Mexico.
VOICE Call low, whistled, *purr-WHEEOO* or *pooor-WEELLUP*.

delicately mottled brownish gray to pale gray plumage

ADULT

Length **7½–8½in (19–21cm)**	Wingspan **15½–19in (40–48cm)**

Family **Trochilidae**	Species ***Amazilia yucatanensis***

Buff-bellied Hummingbird

A resident of the southeastern coast of Texas, the Buff-bellied Hummingbird can be identified by its large size, iridescent emerald body, and tawny belly. It is locally common in gardens, where it is dominant over other species of hummingbirds. Planted flowers and feeders have helped this species expand its range. It now winters from its breeding range eastward to gardens along the Gulf Coast to Florida.
OCCURRENCE In the US, found in a variety of lowland habitats with brushy vegetation, including gardens, mesquite woodland edges; partial migrant.
VOICE Call hard, sharp *tik*, often doubled or rolled into series; chase call buzzier and in fast series; no well-defined song, usually mix of slurred chip notes.

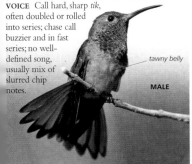

tawny belly

MALE

ength **4in (10cm)**	Wingspan **5½in (14cm)**

Family **Trochilidae**	Species ***Archilochus alexandri***

Black-chinned Hummingbird

The Black-chinned Hummingbird is widespread in the western US, where it occurs in a variety of habitats. It readily accepts sugar water at birdfeeders. During courtship, the males perform a distinctive dive display comprising several broad arcs in addition to a short, back-and-forth shuttle flight. The latter is accompanied by a droning sound produced by the bird's wings.
OCCURRENCE Widespread in scrub and woodlands close to rivers and streams, irrigated urban areas, and semi-arid scrub; also found in drier habitats; forages away from breeding habitats where nectar sources are found. Winters along the Pacific Coast of Mexico
VOICE Call a soft, thick *chic*; fast, buzzy *tsi-tsi-tsi-tsi-tsi-tsi-tsi-tsi* is used to chase off other birds; song soft, warbling, very rarely heard.

MALE

blackish gorget

Length **3½in (9cm)**	Wingspan **4¾in (12cm)**

Family **Alcedinidae**	Species *Chloroceryle americana*

Green Kingfisher

The smallest of the three species of North American kingfishers, the Green Kingfisher can also be distinguished by its proportionately longer bill and conspicuous white collar. Females lack the rufous breast of the male, and instead, have a necklace of white spots. Like other kingfishers, the Green Kingfisher dives from perches over water to catch aquatic prey.

OCCURRENCE Breeds and winters near wooded shorelines of lakes, ponds, and streams. Found in South Texas, Arizona, and from Mexico all the way to southern South America.

VOICE Staccato "ticking" call; also a harsh, buzzy scold; quieter than other two North American kingfishers.

white collar

bronze-green upperparts

long, black bill

MALE

Length **8½in (22cm)**	Wingspan **11in (28cm)**

Family **Alcedinidae**	Species *Megaceryle torquata*

Ringed Kingfisher

The largest of the three North American kingfishers, the Ringed Kingfisher is also easily identified by its color. It perches on trees and branches over water. Because of its shy nature this bird is difficult to spot despite its bright colors. It flies off at the least intrusion, but its loud rattle calls signal where it was. Like other kingfishers it nests in a burrow, which it digs in a muddy or sandy riverbank.

OCCURRENCE Found from the Rio Grande Valley in southern Texas to southern South America. Resident throughout range.

VOICE Loud rattle; also loud, double-syllabled *ktok-ktok* in flight.

white chest band between blue breast and chestnut belly

FEMALE

Length **16in (41cm)**	Wingspan **25in (63cm)**

Family **Picidae**	Species *Melanerpes aurifrons*

Golden-fronted Woodpecker

Although the bright orange color of the nape is more visible than the yellow forehead, this is what gives this woodpecker its name. Males also have a red crown patch; females do not. This species occasionally interbreeds with the closely related Red-bellied Woodpecker.

OCCURRENCE Southern Oklahoma and Texas, Mexico and Central America, south to Nicaragua.

VOICE Call a noisy, "rolled" *churr*, closely resembling the calls of other woodpeckers, especially the Red-bellied Woodpecker, but harsher; drumming rather short.

yellow forehead

MALE

Length **10–12in (25–30cm)**	Wingspan **17in (43cm)**

Family **Picidae**	Species *Picoides scalaris*

Ladder-backed Woodpecker

A bird of the Southwest, the Ladder-backed Woodpecker has conspicuous black-and-white barring on the back and black-and-white facial pattern. Like many other North American woodpeckers, males have a red crown. This resident species uses cacti and trees both for breeding and to forage for insects.

OCCURRENCE Breeds in semi-desert scrub, wooded canyons, and pine-oak woodlands from California eastward to Texas, and from Mexico to Nicaragua.

VOICE Two main calls: a short, sharp *peek!*, and a whinny-like rattle with many notes that descend in pitch at the end.

conspicuous black-and-white facial pattern

MALE

Length **7¼in (18.5cm)**	Wingspan **11–12in (28–30cm**

| Family **Tyrannidae** | Species *Camptostoma imberbe* |

Northern Beardless-Tyrannulet

This tiny flycatcher is usually first detected by its whistled calls. Once seen, it has a distinctive tail-flipping motion, crested look, and vireo-like foraging behavior. Unlike other flycatchers, it lacks bristles at the base of its bill, hence the name "beardless." "Tyrannulet" refers to its diminutive size.
OCCURRENCE Riparian woodlands with mesquite in southeastern Arizona and the lower Rio Grande Valley in Texas. Resident from Mexico to Costa Rica.
VOICE Calls are clear, piping, whistled *peeeuuu* or *peeut di-i-i-i*; song is a descending series of whistles *pee-pee-pee-pee*.

short, stubby bill, pale at base

grayish back

ADULT

| Length **4½–5½in (11.5–14cm)** | Wingspan **7in (18cm)** |

| Family **Tyrannidae** | Species *Sayornis nigricans* |

Black Phoebe

North America's only black-and-white Flycatcher, this species is resident from California to Texas. South of the US, the bird's range extends to Argentina. It commonly forages close to water. Black Phoebes wag their tails like other phoebes, and their calls are also phoebe-like whistles.
OCCURRENCE Breeds and winters in areas close to water such as coastal cliffs, river banks, streams, lakes, and ponds. Also fountains and cattle troughs.
VOICE A whistled *phee-bee*; also a simple *tsip* call; *tweedle-deedle-eek* during courting or when chasing rivals; song a *tee-hee, tee-hoo* or *sisee, sitsew*.

ADULT

black legs and feet

| Length **6in (15.5cm)** | Wingspan **11in (28cm)** |

| Family **Tyrannidae** | Species *Sayornis saya* |

Say's Phoebe

Say's Phoebe breeds farther north than any other flycatcher in North America, reaching the Yukon and Alaska. It is a common sight on ranches and farms from early spring to late fall. Its contrasting dark cap is conspicuous even at a distance as it perches on bushes, boulders, or power lines, wagging its tail.
OCCURRENCE Breeds in dry, open, or semi-open country, such as agricultural areas, desert canyons, and sagebrush; breeds south of the US in Mexico.
VOICE Call a *pee-ee* or *pee-ur*; also a whistled *churr-eep* that may be integrated with a chatter; primary song *pit-see-eur* and *pit-eet*.

ADULT

rufous undertail and lower belly

| ength **7in (17.5cm)** | Wingspan **13in (33cm)** |

| Family **Tyrannidae** | Species *Pyrocephalus rubinus* |

Vermilion Flycatcher

The most colorful North American flycatcher, this species is a resident through most of its vast range, which includes Mexico, Central America, and South America south to Argentina. Only the male is a vibrant red; the female is rather drab by comparison. Breeding territories are defended during spectacular flight displays accompanied with stuttering vocalizations; intruders are chased and if one fails to depart, a fight may ensue.
OCCURRENCE Breeds in riparian woodlands with cottonwoods, willows, and sycamores.
VOICE Contact call *peeent*; male song an excited *p-p-pik-zee*, *pit-a-zee*, or *ching-tink-a-link*.

fiery red head and underparts

MALE

| Length **5–6in (13–15cm)** | Wingspan **10in (25cm)** |

Family **Tyrannidae**	Species *Pitangus sulphuratus*

Great Kiskadee

The Great Kiskadee is named after its loud song, which, together with its black mask, yellow belly, large size, and habit of perching in the open, make it quite a conspicuous bird. In Spanish it is called the Benteveo, which means "I see you well." Aggressive in defense of its roundish nest, the Great Kiskadee attacks birds of prey and snakes.

OCCURRENCE Local in Texas, in riverine woodlands, shady plantations, thorn scrub, and woodland edges. Resident.

VOICE Calls include loud exclamatory *reeee* or *weeer*, *Chik-reee*, and harsh *Reep*, or *ick*; distinctive 3-syllable song *KIK-Chi-wee*, or *Kiss-ka-dee*, is most common during breeding season; highly vocal year-round.

conspicuous yellow belly

JUVENILE

Length **8½–10in (21–26 cm)**	Wingspan **15in (38cm)**

Family **Tyrannidae**	Species *Tyrannus melancholicus*

Tropical Kingbird

Often found in residential areas, the Tropical Kingbird occurs in southeastern Arizona (where it is a migrant) and extreme southern Texas (where it is resident). After the breeding season, young Tropical Kingbirds disperse northward along the West Coast to British Columbia. This species is widespread from Mexico southward to Central and South America.

OCCURRENCE Breeds in open habitats of Arizona and Texas. In its tropical range, occurs in a wide variety of habitats, including pastureland, forest edges, suburban areas, urban parks, and riparian corridors.

VOICE Typical Kingbird-like, loud, high-pitched twittering calls, given all year and throughout the day; song is a longer and more tremulous version of the call.

ADULT
pale grayish olive upperparts
thick bill

Length **7–9in (18–23cm)**	Wingspan **14½in (37cm)**

Family **Tyrannidae**	Species *Tyrannus couchii*

Couch's Kingbird

Spencer Fullerton Baird described this bird in 1860 as *Tyrannus melancholicus couchii*, to honor the famous ornithologist Elliott Coues. It is so similar to the Tropical Kingbird that it was not until the 1980's that W. John Smith realized they were two separate species that can easily be distinguished by their different voices, especially the dawn song.

OCCURRENCE Range restricted to southern Texas and eastern Mexico. Most Texas birds move south to Mexico in winter; occasional in Florida.

VOICE Does not have twittering calls of Tropical flycatcher; instead they are dry *peep* followed by rather jumbled series of notes, increasing in tempo, *tuwit*, *tuwit*, *tuwit*, *tuwitcheer*.

brownish gray wings

ADULT

Length **8–9in (20–23cm)**	Wingspan **15½in (39cm)**

Family **Tyrannidae**	Species *Tyrannus dominicensis*

Gray Kingbird

At first sight the Gray Kingbird appears similar to the widespread and familiar Eastern Kingbird, but careful observation quickly shows its larger size, distinctly longer bill, and paler, less contrasted plumage color (largely grayish above, paler below). Vocalizations are also somewhat different. A species of West Indian, Central and South American distribution, it occurs in the Southeast, especially in Florida.

OCCURRENCE Winters as far south as Colombia; disperses north to New England and west to Texas after nesting. Usually found near water, especially mangroves, but also adapts to suburban areas in the Florida Keys. Often occurs where Mangrove Cuckoos are found.

VOICE A loud *pe-cheeerrr*, rolled and descending in pitch at the end. A strong vocalist.

long black bill

deeply notched tail

ADULT

Length **9in (23cm)**	Wingspan **14in (36cm)**

Family **Tyrannidae**	Species *Myiarchus tyrannulus*

Brown-crested Flycatcher

The Brown-crested Flycatcher is the largest of the three western *Myiarchus* species. It is slender-looking, with a thick black bill, and a ragged, tan or brown crest. In flight, the rufous outer tail feathers are usually conspicuous. Although mostly insectivorous, it will sometimes catch a hummingbird. This late-spring migrant competes aggressively with other birds, such as woodpeckers, for nest holes.

OCCURRENCE Occurs from Nevada to Texas; breeds in riparian woodlands. Migrates south to Mexico and Guatemala. Resident populations from Honduras to South America.

VOICE Call a loud *huit*, often with a question mark at the end. Song a repetition of either *come-here* or *whit-will-do* heard only at dawn.

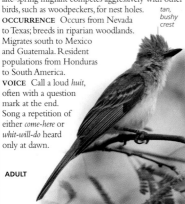

tan, bushy crest

ADULT

Length 8½in (22cm)	Wingspan 13in (33cm)

Family **Tyrannidae**	Species *Myiarchus cinerascens*

Ash-throated Flycatcher

Of the three western species of *Myiarchus* flycatchers found in the US, this is the palest and also the most widespread and ecologically versatile. Desert scrub, mesquite woodland, riparian habitats with cottonwoods, juniper shrublands, and saguaro cactus are all places it chooses for breeding. Ash-throated Flycatchers, which are cavity-nesters, can adapt to man-made structures including pipes, the eaves of houses, and nest boxes.

OCCURRENCE Breeds in a variety of habitats at low to medium elevations. Migrates south to Mexico and Central America. Resident populations from Mexico to Costa Rica.

VOICE Call a rolled whistle, *wheer*, or exclamatory *huit*. Dawn song a repetitious *ha-wheer* or *ka-brick*.

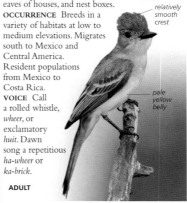

relatively smooth crest

pale yellow belly

ADULT

Length 7–8in (18–20cm)	Wingspan 12–13in (30–33cm)

Family **Vireonidae**	Species *Vireo atricapilla*

Black-capped Vireo

The only vireo to show a sexually dimorphic (different) plumage, the Black-capped Vireo is restricted to the central southern US and Mexico. Despite its broad white "spectacles" and red eye, it is not easy to spot as it forages in dense shrubby vegetation. It sings persistently from near the top of bushes, often long into the day. Habitat changes and Brown-headed Cowbird parasitism have caused declines in the bird's population.

OCCURRENCE Breeds only in the hill country of central southern Texas and adjacent Mexico, casually in Oklahoma. Winters on the foothill country of western Mexico.

VOICE Calls are variable scolds; song an extensive repertoire of trills, whistles, chips, and squeaks, with individual variations.

red eye

broad white "spectacles"

MALE

Length 4½in (11.5cm)	Wingspan 7½in (19cm)

Family **Vireonidae**	Species *Vireo vicinior*

Gray Vireo

A drab, inconspicuous vireo of the hot and arid southwestern US, the Gray Vireo is reminiscent of a miniature shrike in terms of posture and shape. Found mainly in dense, shrubby vegetation such as pinyon and juniper, it is most often detected by its distinctive voice. In its restricted habitat, it can be confused with other small gray birds such as gnatcatchers, titmice, and the Bushtit.

OCCURRENCE Breeds in the hot and arid shrubby scrublands of the southwestern US; short-distance migrant. Winters mostly in Mexico, in similarly arid areas.

VOICE Varied calls, include trills and chatters; song given by male, harsh three- to four-note phrase.

hooked bill

lead-gray body

ADULT

Length 5½in (14cm)	Wingspan 8in (20cm)

Family **Vireonidae**	Species ***Vireo huttoni***

Hutton's Vireo

This unobtrusive bird is geographically variable and has about a dozen subspecies. One of them comprises coastal populations from British Columbia to Baja California; the second subspecies is found from the Southwest to Central America. These two isolated populations, widely separated by desert, may actually represent different species. Very similar in appearance to the Ruby-crowned Kinglet with which it flocks in winter, Hutton's Vireo is distinguishable by its larger size and thicker bill.

OCCURRENCE Year-round resident in mixed evergreen forests; prefers live oak woods. Breeds in mixed oak-pine woodlands along the Pacific coast.

VOICE Varied calls include harsh *mewing* and nasal, raspy *spit*; male's song a repetition of a simple phrase.

white wing bars

pale eye-ring

ADULT

Length **5in (13cm)**	Wingspan **8in (20cm)**

Family **Vireonidae**	Species ***Vireo altiloquus***

Black-whiskered Vireo

This Caribbean breeder is restricted to mangrove and hardwood forests along both coasts of southern Florida. During migration (October–November) it can also be found along the Gulf and Atlantic coasts. Its restricted range and habitat and secretive habits make this vireo difficult to spot. Its song, however, is distinctive, with phrases ending on alternate ascending and descending notes.

OCCURRENCE In the US, found in coastal Florida, along the Atlantic coast south to the Keys, and along the southern Gulf Coast. Winters south to South America; breeds in the West Indies.

VOICE Nasal *mewing* call; male song a series of loud, clear one to four note phrases with distinct pauses between them.

thin "mustache"

ADULT

Length **6½in (16cm)**	Wingspan **10in (26cm)**

Family **Corvidae**	Species ***Cyanocorax yncas***

Green Jay

Known in southern Texas as the "Rio Grande Jay," this brightly colored species is common and conspicuous. It will readily get food at birdfeeders, but away from them it is rather secretive. Its varied vocalizations, however, allow it to be located easily. The Green Jay is a nonmigratory bird.

OCCURRENCE Lives in woodlands and thickets. Occurs southward through Mexico, Central America, and South America to Bolivia.

VOICE Sounds much like the Blue Jay; repeated *chah-chah-chah* calls; also clicks and buzzes, and mewing notes.

long, bluish gray tail

ADULT

Length **10–11½in (25–29cm)**	Wingspan **13½in (34cm)**

Family **Corvidae**	Species ***Cyanocorax morio***

Brown Jay

Both the very large Brown Jay and the colorful Green Jay are hard to miss. Groups of three to six Brown Jays can be heard calling long before they are seen. In the US, they are found very locally along the Rio Grande, in riparian woodlands. Juveniles have bright yellow bare parts, which fade as they become adults.

OCCURRENCE This bird is a resident of dense woodlands from Texas (rare in the Upper Rio Grande Valley) to Panama.

VOICE Makes loud, raucous screams, *keee-uh!* or *kaaah!*, which are often repeated. Begins with percussive popping sound at close range.

yellow bill

dark brown above

1ST YEAR

Length **16½in (42cm)**	Wingspan **26in (66cm)**

Family **Corvidae**	Species *Aphelocoma californica*

Western Scrub-Jay

Easterners visiting the West Coast will immediately notice the Western Scrub-Jay, which is common (to abundant) in open areas, including evergreen oak woodlands, riparian thickets, suburban areas, even city parks. Unlike the familiar Blue Jay, they will notice its lack of crest, whitish underparts, facial mask, gray back, and slender appearance. Like Blue Jays, Western Scrub-Jays are very vocal.
OCCURRENCE Widespread from sea level to mid-elevations in western North America from Washington State to Baja California, and from the Pacific Coast to the hill country of central Texas.
VOICE Most common call a questioning, rising *rehnk?*; other calls include a vaguely robin-like *quill, quill,* and rattles.

A. C. CALIFORNICA (PACIFIC)

rich blue wings and tail

black mask

Length **10–12in (26–31cm)**	Wingspan **15½in (40cm)**

Family **Corvidae**	Species *Aphelocoma coerulescens*

Florida Scrub-Jay

Threatened by increasing habitat loss due to development, the endemic and tame Florida Scrub-Jay has been intensely studied by ornithologists. Young birds stay with their parents after fledging and help them raise their next brood, a social system called cooperative breeding. The Florida, Western, and Island Scrub-Jays used to be considered to comprise one species, the Scrub-Jay.
OCCURRENCE Habitat restricted to chaparral-like evergreen oak scrub, growing on sandy soil and regularly kept open by fire. A highly sedentary bird.
VOICE Harsh and raspy call notes, *krrrahh,* as well as a number of other vocalizations.

whitish forehead

pale back

long, blue tail

ADULT

Length **10–11½in (25–29cm)**	Wingspan **13½in (34cm)**

Family **Corvidae**	Species *Corvus imparatus*

Tamaulipas Crow

Barely larger than the Fish Crow and restricted to southeastern Texas and northeastern Mexico, this bird is easy to identify because it is the only species of crow in this range. The Chihuahuan Raven, which occurs near Brownsville in Texas, is huge by comparison. Tamaulipas Crows have low voices, long wings and tails, and glossy plumage.
OCCURRENCE Lowlands of northeastern Mexico; winters (rarely) near Brownsville, Texas, especially around the dump and the harbor.
VOICE Call a very low, nasal, frog-like croak, sometimes doubled. Also a low-pitched *whaah.*

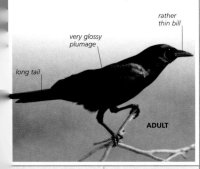

rather thin bill

very glossy plumage

long tail

ADULT

Length **14½in (37cm)**	Wingspan **3ft 3in (1m)**

Family **Corvidae**	Species *Corvus cryptoleucus*

Chihuahuan Raven

Smaller than the Common Raven but bigger than the American Crow, the Chihuahuan Raven was previously called the White-necked Raven. This former name refers to the concealed white feathers of its neck, which are sometimes visible in the bird's windswept environment. A highly gregarious and vocal raven, it is often seen wheeling about in flocks that may contain thousands of individuals.
OCCURRENCE Breeds in the southwestern US and northern Mexico in grasslands, scrublands, and deserts. Northerly populations winter in Mexico.
VOICE High-pitched croak; little variety in vocal repertoire compared to the Common Raven.

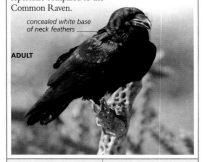

concealed white base of neck feathers

ADULT

Length **17½–20in (44–51cm)**	Wingspan **3½ft (1.1m)**

Family **Paridae**	Species ***Parus bicolor atricristatus***

Black-crested Titmouse

Found only in Texas and Oklahoma in the US, the Black-crested Titmouse is like a Tufted Titmouse with a taller, and black, crest. Black-crested and Tufted Titmice have largely non-overlapping ranges, yet in a small area of Texas they occur together and produce hybrids, a situation that suggests to some ornithologists that they belong to one species. Others disagree. The Black-crested Titmouse is a bird of woodlands, including evergreen oaks.

OCCURRENCE Scrubby oak woodlands; frequents feeders in winter. Sometimes reported as high as 6,000ft (2,000m) in mountain forests of Mexico in the southern part of its range.

VOICE Call a *pew-pew-pew* (or *peter-peter-peter*) like that of the Tufted Titmouse; other calls a rasping, scolding *jhree, jhree, jhree*.

high blackish crest

ADULT

white forehead

Length **6½in (16.5cm)**	Wingspan **10in (25cm)**

Family **Remizidae**	Species ***Auriparus flaviceps***

Verdin

Common in the Southwest from California east to Texas, this yellow-headed, gray-bodied little bird moves constantly from shrub to shrub, inspecting flowers and cobwebs in search of insects. Verdins resemble chickadees and bushtits in behavior and habitat preferences. Interestingly, however, the Verdin is the only American species of a family that is otherwise exclusively Eurasian and African in distribution, the Remizidae (or Penduline Tits): a fascinating evolutionary puzzle!

OCCURRENCE Thorn shrubs, mesquite woodlands, and tamarisk groves in dry creek beds, desert oases, and riverine corridors. Found in northern Mexico besides the southern US.

VOICE Call a bright, simple *beef*, emitted frequently as the bird forages, all day long and throughout the year.

yellow head

ADULT

Length **4½in (11.5cm)**	Wingspan **6½in (16cm)**

Family **Aegithalidae**	Species ***Psaltriparus minimus***

Bushtit

For much of the year, Bushtits roam foothills and valleys of the western US in flocks that usually number just a few birds, but may occasionally include hundreds. It is always on the move, foraging for insects in the foliage of shrubs and small trees. Even during the breeding season, when most other perching birds become territorial, Bushtits retain something of their social nature—raising the young communally, with both siblings and single adults helping in the rearing.

OCCURRENCE Common in open woodlands and shrublands, mainly on hillsides in summer; some birds move down to lower elevations in the fall. Also in cities and gardens.

VOICE Basic call a 2–3-part soft lisp, *ps psss pit*, interspersed with hard *spit* and *spick* notes, like little sparks.

mouse-gray upperparts

tiny bill

MALE

Length **4½in (11.5cm)**	Wingspan **6in (15.5cm)**

Family **Troglodytidae**	Species ***Campylorhynchus brunneicapillus***

Cactus Wren

The largest and most colorful species of North American wren, the Cactus Wren is common and conspicuous in the arid Southwest from California east to Texas. As its name suggests, it prefers areas with cactus, especially perhaps cholla, although it also occurs in other dry habitats. Unlike some other wrens, the Cactus Wren is easy to observe, as it often perches in full view.

OCCURRENCE Lives in deserts and arid hillsides with cacti, yucca, thorn shrubs, and mesquite woodlands; also in suburban areas.

VOICE Call a loud *chack*; song a grating *kchar kchar kchar kchar*, with a cluck-like quality; sings repeatedly from top of cactus or shrub, especially in the morning.

conspicuous white eyebrow

long tail, barred black-and-white

ADULT

Length **8½in (22cm)**	Wingspan **11in (28cm)**

Family **Troglodytidae**	Species *Salpinctes obsoletus*

Rock Wren

The Rock Wren's varied voice, echoing through canyon walls, will usually reveal its owner's presence. Very active, hopping around rock faces, probing crevices for insects, Rock Wrens have the habit of bobbing and swaying when humans approach. A fascinating behavior of Rock Wrens is to "pave" the area in front of their nest entrance with a walkway of pebbles, the purpose of which is unknown.

OCCURRENCE Widespread in the West (and from Mexico to Costa Rica), in arid and rocky country with cliffs and canyons; also quarries and rock piles. Found from lowlands up to mountaintops at 10,000ft (3,000m).

VOICE Call a sharp *ch'keer*; varied series of warbles, trills, chatters, and repeated *chuwee chuwee, teedee teedee.*

pale yellowish or buffy

ADULT

Length **6in (15cm)**	Wingspan **9in (23cm)**

Family **Troglodytidae**	Species *Catherpes mexicanus*

Canyon Wren

Loud, musical, clear, the marvelous whistled song of the Canyon Wren signals this shy bird's presence and often astonishes listeners by its tonal purity. The singer, however, remains usually out of sight, and it takes work to locate it. But the reward is great: Canyon Wrens can walk up, down, or sideways on rock walls, as they search tiny crevices for insect prey.

OCCURRENCE Maintains year-round territory on rocky hillsides, outcroppings, and vertical rock-walled canyons. Sometimes nests in holes in man-made structures.

VOICE Remarkable, musical series of 10–15 loud, ringing whistles, descending in pitch, gradually slowing down, and ending with several buzzes.

ADULT

white throat

Length **5¾in (14.5cm)**	Wingspan **7½in (19cm)**

Family **Polioptilidae**	Species *Polioptila melanura*

Black-tailed Gnatcatcher

Few birds favor the hot, low-elevation deserts of the Southwest. Yet this is the Black-tailed Gnatcatcher's preferred habitat. This tiny bird spends most of its time flitting about in the foliage of shrubs, constantly flicking its long tail from side to side. A monogamous bird, pairs defend their territory aggressively throughout the year.

OCCURRENCE Thorn scrub, acacias, mesquite, saguaro cactus, creosote bush, and dry riverbeds; also bushy groves along waterways. Resident in the southwestern US and northern Mexico.

VOICE Various scolding notes *zhee-zhee-zhee, chih-chih-chih*, and *chee-chee-chee*; song, rarely heard, soft *tse-dee-dee-dee.*

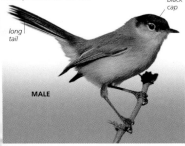

black cap

long tail

MALE

Length **4½in (11.5cm)**	Wingspan **5½in (14cm)**

Family **Mimidae**	Species *Oreoscoptes montanus*

Sage Thrasher

This plain-colored bird is the smallest of the North American thrashers. Like several other species of thrasher, it removes the eggs of the parasitic Brown-headed Cowbird. The English name for this bird, "Sage Thrasher," correctly describes its habitat in the West.

OCCURRENCE Prefers sagebrush habitat in low-elevation, semi-arid valleys of the western US. Winters from southwestern US to Mexico.

VOICE Song varies in duration: low, repeated, very musical notes or phrases that may blend together in a melodious song.

thin "mustache"

dusky, brownish gray upperparts

ADULT

Length **8–9in (20–23cm)**	Wingspan **10–13in (25–33cm)**

Family **Mimidae**	Species *Toxostoma longirostre*

Long-billed Thrasher

In the US, this Mexican species is found only in southern Texas, where the semi-arid thickets and riverine habitats it favors have been largely destroyed by land-clearing. If this habitat loss is offset by an increase in invasive scrubland, and if the thrasher moves into this new habitat, then it will meet the range of the Brown Thrasher, creating an interesting biological problem: will they interbreed?

OCCURRENCE Lives in thick, scrubby vegetation on mountain slopes up to around 3,300ft (1,100m), and in lowlands along the Gulf of Mexico, commonly found in woodland by streams. Sedentary.

VOICE Call a harsh *tchek*; song a loud, harsh series of notes, usually repeated 2–4 times in succession.

ADULT

heavily streaked underparts

Length **10–11in (25–28cm)**	Wingspan **12–13in (30–33cm)**

Family **Mimidae**	Species *Toxostoma curvirostre*

Curve-billed Thrasher

The arid-country loving Curve-billed Thrasher is somewhat unkempt looking, with a thick bill and powerful legs. Less of a mimic than other thrashers, it is nevertheless quite vocal, and its two-note *twit-twit* call is a characteristic sound of the southwestern semi-deserts.

OCCURRENCE In the US, the Curve-billed Thrasher inhabits open, scrubby, arid to semi-arid areas, where it is often found along edges between brush and clearings. Its Mexican range extends south to Veracuz and Oaxaca. It is largely resident throughout its US and Mexican range.

strong bill

VOICE Two-note *qwit-qweet*; song a series of clear, warbled whistles broken into distinct phrases; some mimicry of other species' calls.

ADULT

Length **10–13in (25–33cm)**	Wingspan **12–15in (30–38cm)**

Family **Pycnonotidae**	Species *Pycnonotus jocosus*

Red-whiskered Bulbul

With its black head, large crest and red-and-white cheeks, the Red-whiskered Bulbul is a striking bird. The dark back contrasts with the white underparts and reddish undertail feathers. This shy species is often found in small groups, and is more often heard than seen. The primary breeding population in the US is restricted to the area around and south of Miami.

OCCURRENCE Wooded parks, gardens, and suburbs in Florida. Introduced from tropical and subtropical Asia.

VOICE Call *kinka-choo*; song a choppy, musical whistle.

tall crest

dark back

ADULT

red-and-white cheek

white underparts

Length **6–8in (15–20cm)**	Wingspan **10–12in (25–30cm)**

Family **Muscicapidae**	Species *Oenanthe oenanthe*

Northern Wheatear

Widely distributed in Eurasia, the Northern Wheatear visits North America only during its brief breeding season—the subspecies *O. o. leucorhoa* breeds in the Northeast and *O. o. oenanthe* breeds in the Northwest. Both North American populations winter in sub-Saharan Africa—*oenanthe* flies across Asia, whereas *leucorhoa* crosses the Atlantic Ocean.

OCCURRENCE In North America, breeds in rocky tundra at high latitudes; habitats are more varied in Eurasia.

VOICE Multiple calls, a sharp *tuc* or *tek* common; three types of songs—territorial, conversational, and perched—mixtures of sweet and harsh notes; imitates other species.

tan throat and breast

FEMALE (BREEDING)

Length **5½–6in (14–15cm)**	Wingspan **10¾in (27cm)**

Family **Turdidae**	Species **Turdus grayi**

Clay-colored Robin

The Clay-colored Robin is indeed a clay-colored bird. The upperparts are tawny-brown, darker than the more sandy underparts; the throat is lightly streaked. In good light, the eye looks pale orange. A Mexican and Central American robin, the Clay-colored Robin occurs in Texas, where it is more often heard than seen.

OCCURRENCE Open areas and woodland edges in the lower Rio Grande Valley of southeastern Texas.
VOICE Varied vocalizations including an upward slurring note and 3-syllable *kee-a-wee*; song slow, melodious, with repeated notes.

orange iris

ADULT

light streaks on throat

sandy gray underparts

Length **9–10½in (23–27cm)**	Wingspan **15in (38cm)**

Family **Passeridae**	Species **Passer montanus**

Eurasian Tree Sparrow

Introduced to the US in 1870, this sparrow has not spread widely, unlike the House Sparrow. It occurs locally in parts of Illinois and Missouri, generally in parks, agricultural areas, and woodland edges, and also occasionally near human dwellings. Unlike the House Sparrow, both sexes of the Eurasian Tree Sparrow look alike.

OCCURRENCE In North America, only found locally in Missouri, Iowa, and Illinois. Favors parks, farmyards, and residential neighborhoods.
VOICE Call notes tend to be dry and metallic: *chirp, chep*; song consists of series of dry notes interspersed with few more liquid ones.

rufous-brown cap

white "necklace"

ADULT

Length **6in (15cm)**	Wingspan **9in (23cm)**

Family **Fringillidae**	Species **Carduelis psaltria**

Lesser Goldfinch

A highly vocal bird, the Lesser Goldfinch is common in gardens, suburbs, and farmlands, as well as in its natural habitats of open fields and scrub. The male has a brighter yellow breast and belly than the female, as well as a black cap, which she lacks. Nape and back color varies from black in Texas and Mexico to green along the Pacific coast.

OCCURRENCE Breeds from California to Texas; occurs south to Mexico in winter.
VOICE Call descending *peeyee* and 2-note *tee-eee*, with second note higher; also rapid *dididit*; song warbles and trills.

white wing bar

MALE (PACIFIC COAST)

Length **3½–4¼in (9–11cm)**	Wingspan **6–6¾in (15–17cm)**

Family **Fringillidae**	Species **Carduelis hornemanni**

Hoary Redpoll

Distinctly white, fluffy-looking and with a stubby bill, male Hoary Redpolls are much paler than females. Where the smaller Common Redpoll occurs in the same location as the Hoary Redpoll the two species coexist but do not interbreed. The Hoary Redpoll is a true Arctic bird.

OCCURRENCE Breeds in the High Arctic, including the Canadian Arctic Archipelago; prefers low trees of the open tundra; winters within the boreal forest belt.
VOICE Flight calls dry *zit-zit-zit-zit* and rattling *chirr*; also high *too-ee* call while perched; song series of rapid trills.

small pinkish red patch on forehead

lightly streaked breast

FEMALE

white rump

whitish belly

Length **5–5½in (12.5–14cm)**	Wingspan **8½–9¼in (21–23.5cm)**

Family **Parulidae**	Species ***Parula pitiayumi***

Tropical Parula

The Tropical Parula is widespread in tropical America, but in the US is found only in southern Texas. There, it occasionally interbreeds with the Northern Parula, which is very close to it in appearance. Their offspring are difficult to identify, so that in southern Texas some parula warblers cannot be identified to species.
OCCURRENCE Breeds from the southern edge of the Hill Country to coastal Kleberg County (Texas) southward to central Argentina. Much local movement in the winter months.
VOICE Songs and calls very similar to those of the Northern Parula.

MALE

white wing patch

dark mask

yellow underparts

Length **4½in (11cm)**	Wingspan **6¼in (16cm)**

Family **Parulidae**	Species ***Dendroica chrysoparia***

Golden-cheeked Warbler

Males of this strikingly beautiful warbler species often sing throughout the day, from conspicuous perches in oak-juniper woodlands. The Golden-cheeked Warbler breeds only in a restricted area of Texas, on and near the Edwards Plateau. Habitat loss has made this already scarce species even less common, and it has been listed as an Endangered Species since 1990.
OCCURRENCE Breeds in extensive oak-juniper forests mixed with hardwood trees like maple and ash. Winters in high-elevation pine-oak woodlands.
VOICE Dry *tsk* call; song a variable series of relatively low, buzzy notes, often ending on a high, clear note *zo zu zu zo zu zhray ZHEE*; another version ends at a lower pitch *ZOH zu ZO-ZOH zhray*.

striking yellow-and-black face

MALE

Length **5in (13cm)**	Wingspan **8in (20cm)**

Family **Parulidae**	Species ***Dendroica kirtlandii***

Kirtland's Warbler

Named for a physician from Ohio, Kirtland's Warbler is one of the rarest North American songbirds. The suppression of fires and spread of the parasitic Brown-headed Cowbird decreased this warbler's population to a low of 167 males in 1987, but successful conservation resulted in the population reaching about 5,000 birds in 2007.
OCCURRENCE In northern Michigan, in dense, low, 6- to 20-year-old Jack Pine stands on sandy soil, regrowing after fires.
VOICE A strong *chip*; flight call a high *zit*; song a loud, low-pitched series of staccato *chips*, rising in pitch and intensity and ending with whistled phrase: *tup-CHUP-chup tup-CHEEP-cheep*.

interrupted, white eye-ring

MALE

Length **6in (15cm)**	Wingspan **9in (23cm)**

Family **Icteridae**	Species ***Icterus cucullatus***

Hooded Oriole

Tall palm trees of suburban and urban landscapes, especially in California, have become favored nesting sites for the Hooded Oriole. The increasing number of palm trees and offerings of nectar intended for hummingbirds have led to the expansion of its range in California and the southwestern US. By contrast, its numbers in Texas have been shrinking, in part because of its susceptibility to brood parasitism by Brown-headed and Bronzed Cowbirds.
OCCURRENCE Breeds in open woodlands along water courses, especially those with palm trees, in Mexico, Belize, California, and the southwestern US, and also in southern Texas. Winters in Mexico.
VOICE A harsh *weeek* call; song a weakly whined and rapid series of whistles where notes often run together; imitates other birds.

long, curved bill

MALE (BREEDING)

bright orange

Length **7–8in (18–20cm)**	Wingspan **9–11in (23–28cm)**

Family **Icteridae**	Species *Icterus parisorum*

Scott's Oriole

This Oriole's lemon-yellow plumage is unusual among North American orioles, as most other species are rather orange-colored. Scott's Oriole lives in semi-arid and rocky slopes, a habitat preference that earned it the names of "Desert Oriole" and "Mountain Oriole." Its loud, clear song signals its presence from afar.

OCCURRENCE Breeds at mid-elevations in semi-arid scrub on level ground or along slopes with oak and pinyon. Winters in pine-oak woodlands of Mexico. Individuals can wander widely: the species has even been reported from New York City.

VOICE Call a sharp *chek*; song a musical series of whistles *tew-tew-treew*, loud and ringing.

MALE

black hood and back

black-tipped tail

lemon-yellow underparts

Length **8–9in (20–23cm)**	Wingspan **11–13in (28–33cm)**

Family **Icteridae**	Species *Icterus graduacauda*

Audubon's Oriole

Because it is secretive and lives in dense vegetation, Audubon's Oriole remains little studied, and estimates of its population in the US are few. It was once thought to be declining, because of its restricted habitat (mostly riverine thickets) along the lower Rio Grande Valley in Texas, and because of the negative impact of brood parasitism by the Bronzed Cowbird. However, this oriole has recently adapted to suburban areas and uses birdfeeders, developments that may help its numbers to increase.

OCCURRENCE Woodlands, mesquite thickets, and pine-oak woodlands of southeastern Texas, also parks and gardens; more common in Mexico.

VOICE Low, slow whistle with slurred, broken notes: *heoo-heeooo-heeeww.*

ADULT

yellowish back

Length **9–10in (23–26cm)**	Wingspan **11–13in (28–33cm)**

Family **Icteridae**	Species *Icterus bullockii*

Bullock's Oriole

This oriole is the western counterpart of the Baltimore in both behavior and habitat. The two were considered to belong to a single species, the Northern Oriole (*L. galbula*), because they interbreed where they overlap in the Great Plains, but recent studies suggest that they are actually separate species. The Bullock's is more resistant to brood parasites than other orioles, and either punctures or removes cowbird eggs from its nest.

OCCURRENCE Prefers riverine woodlands with willows and cottonwoods; also mixed hardwood forests, mesquite woodland, and groves of fruit trees.

VOICE Varied string of one- and two-part notes often mumbled or slurred at the end.

black back and wings

MALE

Length **6½–7½in (16–19cm)**	Wingspan **10–12in (25–30cm)**

Family **Icteridae**	Species *Icterus gularis*

Altamira Oriole

The Altamira Oriole, a Central American species, is now common in a restricted area of the Lower Rio Grande Valley. This Texas population has increased since its discovery in 1939. The largest oriole in the US, it can occasionally be seen at birdfeeders. The large size of its hanging nest makes it a target for brood parasites such as cowbirds, but whether the parasites are cared for and fledged successfully remains unknown.

bright orange head

OCCURRENCE Limited to riverine woodlands along the Rio Grande. In Mexico and Central America, occurs in a variety of dry to moist tropical woodlands.

VOICE Call harsh, nasal *drrike*; song loud but musical series of whistles *thoo-thoo-thoo-theeoo.*

ADULT

Length **8–10in (20–25cm)**	Wingspan **13–15in (33–38cm)**

Family **Icteridae**	Species *Molothrus aeneus*

Bronzed Cowbird

The range of the Bronzed Cowbird has been expanding in the US since it was first recorded in the early 1900s. This could be the result of human clearing of its native habitats, which are then replaced with agricultural crops. A brood parasite, it has been recorded as laying eggs in the nests of about 80 bird species, with its young fledging from about 30 of these. Females may work cooperatively to identify and parasitize the nests of other birds.
OCCURRENCE Inhabits open fields, pastures, scattered scrub, and suburban parks. Ranges from Mexico to Panama and northern Colombia, in the US occurs from California to Texas.
VOICE High and metallic with short notes, can be described as *gug-gub-bub-tzee-pss-tzee.*

bright red eye

MALE

Length **8in (20cm)**	Wingspan **13–14in (33–36cm)**

Family **Icteridae**	Species *Molothrus bonariensis*

Shiny Cowbird

The Shiny Cowbird is native to South America, where it ranges south to Chile and Argentina. It has only recently expanded its distribution to Florida, presumably from the West Indies. Over its vast range, the species is known to lay eggs in the nests of about 200 other bird species, 80 of which raise the cowbird's young as their own.
OCCURRENCE Found in open areas with a mixture of woodlands; agricultural fields, and rural and suburban parks, gardens, and backyards.
VOICE Low pitched, rambling series of soft *purr-purr-purr*, interspersed with *tee-tsss-tseeee* running higher to slurred finish.

MALE
(BREEDING)

long tail

Length **7in (18cm)**	Wingspan **10–12in (25–30cm)**

Family **Emberizidae**	Species *Amphispiza bilineata*

Black-throated Sparrow

Because of a certain resemblance in their songs, the Black-throated Sparrow has been called the "Song Sparrow of the desert." This bird is easy to identify as it possesses a bold white "eyebrow" in all plumages. The Black-throated Sparrow is common within its western range, in a variety of arid habitats containing cactus and mesquite.
OCCURRENCE Found in desert scrub of the Great Basin east to Texas, south to Baja California and central Mexico. Breeds locally in eastern Washington state. Casual visitor to the Pacific coast and the East.
VOICE Weak *tink* call; song consists of few short, clear notes, followed by higher trill: *tink tink-tink treeeeee*, also *ti-ti-tink churrrrrrrrrr.*

bold white eyebrow

ADULT

Length **5½in (14cm)**	Wingspan **7¾in (19.5cm)**

Family **Emberizidae**	Species *Aimophila cassinii*

Cassin's Sparrow

Cassin's Sparrow, named for the famous Philadelphia ornithologist John Cassin, is drab-looking, even for an American sparrow. Its modest appearance is made up for by its rather spectacular flight displays, during which it emits a whistled song. This sparrow is found in grasslands interspersed with shrubs, and shows variations in numbers in different years and localities.
OCCURRENCE Grasslands with shrubs, like mesquite and cactus, from western Nebraska to central Mexico; US populations mostly winter in Mexico.
VOICE Calls high seeps and chips, often in series; song *see-eee sii-ii-i-i-i-i-i-i-i zee-zooo' zee-ZWAAAY*, ending on a questioning note.

scalloped upperparts

ADULT

Length **6in (15cm)**	Wingspan **9in (23cm)**

Family **Emberizidae**	Species *Aimophila botterii*

Botteri's Sparrow

Of the nine or ten subspecies of Botteri's Sparrow, a species of the Mexican grasslands, two occur in the US: *A.b. texana* is found in coastal southern Texas, and *A.b. arizonae* in the Southwest. Botteri's Sparrow is usually difficult to spot, as its flees stealthily from disturbance, and quickly hides itself out of sight.

OCCURRENCE Breeds in grasslands of southeastern Arizona and southwestern New Mexico, and in coastal prairies of southern Texas. Winters in Mexico.

VOICE Call a *chip* or double *tsip*; song starts with stuttering, mechanical *chips* and ends in an accelerating trill.

ADULT

dark brown, rusty, and gray streaks on upperparts

Length **18–20in (46–51cm)**	Wingspan **27–38in (68–96cm)**

Family **Emberizidae**	Species *Aimophila ruficeps*

Rufous-crowned Sparrow

The Rufous-crowned Sparrow is a resident of dry canyons and sparsely wooded hillsides across the Southwest, locally up to 5,000ft (1,500m). It tends to run and hide at the first sign of danger. For this reason, it is often first detected by its unique *deeer* call note, which it sometimes gives in a laughter-like series. Visually it is similar to the rarer Rufous-winged Sparrow, but has very different calls, and lives in separate habitats.

OCCURRENCE Breeds in arid scrub and low trees on hillsides and in canyons in California, Colorado, Utah, Arizona, New Mexico, Oklahoma, Texas, and Arkansas; also in Mexico.

VOICE Call a low, nasal *deeer*; song a jumble of chattering notes.

rufous crown

ADULT

Length **6in (15cm)**	Wingspan **7½in (19cm)**

Family **Emberizidae**	Species *Pipilo chlorurus*

Green-tailed Towhee

This is North America's most distinctive towhee, with a rusty crown and green plumage, but it is seldom seen. It tends to stay hidden on the ground in dense cover, both in the breeding season and on its wintering grounds. In winter it sometimes emerges to feed on seeds on deserted, dusty roads, but this bird is more likely to be heard scratching about in the undergrowth than seen.

OCCURRENCE Breeds in a variety of brushy and semi-open habitats of the western US and northern Baja California. Winters along the US–Mexican border southward to central Mexico.

VOICE Call a nasal mewing, rapid chips in excitement; flight call a high *tzhreeee*; song a slurred whistle followed by 1–2 trills.

ADULT

bright, yellow-green tail and wing edgings

Length **7¼in (18.5cm)**	Wingspan **9½in (24cm)**

Family **Emberizidae**	Species *Pipilo fuscus*

Canyon Towhee

Once included with the California Towhee as a single species, the Canyon Towhee is a bird of the arid Southwest, where it occurs in a wide variety of bushy habitats. Its pale, sandy coloration helps it to blend in with the grayish, dusty ground on which it forages. The Canyon Towhee can be distinguished from similarly-colored birds in its range by its stubby, conical bill. Its rusty undertail feathers are not always easy to see.

OCCURRENCE Lives in rocky hillside scrub, desert grasslands, and suburban areas of the southwestern US and central Mexico. Largely resident, but some birds undertake local movements.

VOICE Call a nasal *cheemp*; also various clicking and lisping notes; song a variable slow trill.

ADULT

rusty undertail feathers

Length **8½in (21cm)**	Wingspan **11½in (29cm)**

| Family **Emberizidae** | Species *Sporophila torqueola* |

White-collared Seedeater

As many as 40 species of *Sporophila* seedeaters breed in tropical America, but the White-collared Seedeater is the only species to breed as far north as the US. These tiny birds feed on grass seeds. They remain hidden in vegetation, and it is important to know their calls in order to locate them. While females are drab and tan colored, males have a distinctive black-and-white plumage.

OCCURRENCE Weedy fields and marshy grasslands, from southeastern Texas southward to Panama. In Texas, restricted to the Rio Grande Valley between Laredo and Zapata.

VOICE Calls a nasal *wink!* and *wheer!*; song a sweet, goldfinch-like series of whistles and trills.

brown
upperparts

tan or buffy
underparts

**FEMALE
(BREEDING)**

| Length **4½in (11cm)** | Wingspan **6¼in (16cm)** |

| Family **Emberizidae** | Species *Arremonops rufivirgatus* |

Olive Sparrow

The rather drab, shy Olive Sparrow spends most of its time hopping around in the undergrowth of dense woodlands and thorn scrub. This resident of the Lower Rio Grande Valley can be heard more than it is seen, although some individuals appear at birdfeeders.

OCCURRENCE From southern Texas and northwestern Mexico south locally to northwestern Costa Rica, mostly in thorn scrub.

VOICE Dry *chip* call, also a drawn-out *sreeeeee*; song a series of accelerating chips.

distinctive
head pattern

ADULT

dull olive
upperparts

| Length **6½in (16cm)** | Wingspan **8in (20cm)** |

| Family **Cardinalidae** | Species *Cardinalis sinuatus* |

Pyrrhuloxia

The "Pyro" is the Southwest's equivalent of the Northern Cardinal, and was once known as the "Arizona Cardinal." The ranges of the two species do overlap, and, although the two birds share very similar habits and vocalizations, they tolerate each other's presence.

OCCURRENCE Desert scrub of southwestern US and Mexico. Prefers drier, more upland habitats than the Northern Cardinal, at elevations up to 6,500ft (2000m).

VOICE Call a distinctive, dry, low *chik*, often accelerating into chatter; song generally higher, thinner, and less musical than the Northern Cardinal's.

MALE

long,
conspicuous
crest

red belly

| Length **8½in (22cm)** | Wingspan **12in (30cm)** |

| Family **Cardinalidae** | Species *Passerina versicolor* |

Varied Bunting

The Varied Bunting is the only purple-and-red songbird in North America. When seen in bright light, males are a rich plum color with ruby-red napes and sparkling, sapphire-blue foreheads and rumps. The female, however, is the dullest member of the family Cardinalidae. A Mexican species, the Varied Bunting is localized and hard to find.

OCCURRENCE Breeds in desert scrub in canyons and washes, and in thorn woodlands of the southwestern US. In winter, most migrate to the coastal slopes of Mexico.

VOICE Call a sharp, dry, rattling *pik!*; song a pleasant, rambling, and burry warble.

red nape

MALE

blue
rump

| Length **5½in (14cm)** | Wingspan **7½–8in (19–20cm)** |

VAGRANTS & ACCIDENTALS

T HE LIST THAT FOLLOWS INCLUDES species that occur rarely in eastern North America (defined in this book as Canada and the continental United States *east* of the 100th Meridian). These species can reach North America from Eurasia, Central or South America, Africa, and even Oceania and Antarctica. The US and Canada can receive birds that drift off course, during migration, from eastern Asia across the Pacific Ocean, or from Europe across the Atlantic.

The occurrence of these "vagrant" species is classified by the American Birding Association, depending on their relative frequency, and this terminology is followed in the "status" column for each species. **Rare** species are reported every year in small numbers. **Casual** visitors have been recorded at least a dozen times. **Accidental** species have been recorded no more than five times.

Because of biological, climatological, or other factors, the status of "vagrant" species is constantly changing. The ever greater number of competent birdwatchers also permits the regular, even annual, detection of species that were once considered rare or accidental.

COMMON NAME	SCIENTIFIC NAME	FAMILY NAME	STATUS
Waterfowl			
Pink-footed Goose	*Anser brachyrhynchus*	Anatidae	Accidental from Greenland, Iceland, or Europe to eastern Canada
Lesser White-fronted Goose	*Anser erythropus*	Anatidae	Accidental from Eurasia to Alaska
Muscovy Duck	*Cairina moschata*	Anatidae	Rare from Mexico in southern Texas (also escapees)
Eurasian Wigeon	*Anas penelope*	Anatidae	Rare from Eurasia along East Coast of US
Garganey	*Anas querquedula*	Anatidae	Casual from Eurasia to eastern North America
Cinnamon Teal	*Anas cyanoptera*	Anatidae	Casual from West to eastern US
Tufted Duck	*Aythya fuligula*	Anatidae	Rare from Eurasia to eastern Canada; casual in eastern US
Smew	*Mergellus albellus*	Anatidae	Accidental from Eurasia to eastern US
Loons			
Pacific Loon	*Gavia pacifica*	Gaviidae	Casual from Arctic to East Coast
Yellow-billed Loon	*Gavia adamsii*	Gaviidae	Casual from Arctic to East Coast and Interior US
Petrels			
Fea's Petrel	*Pterodroma feae*	Procellariidae	Rare from eastern Atlantic to East coast; accidental to Nova Scotia
Ibises and Herons			
Jabiru	*Jabiru mycteria*	Ciconiidae	Casual to southern Texas from Central America
Flamingos			
Greater Flamingo	*Phoenicopterus ruber*	Phoenoicpteridae	Rare or casual from West Indies to Florida and Texas
Pelicans and Relatives			
Masked Booby	*Sula dactylatra*	Sulidae	Breeds in Dry Tortugas; rare at sea, Gulf coast, Atlantic coast, Florida to North Carolina
White-tailed Tropicbird	*Phaethon lepturus*	Phaethontidae	Rare visitor from tropical waters off Atlantic coast north to North Carolina
Plovers and Sandpipers			
Pacific Golden Plover	*Pluvialis fulva*	Charadriidae	Casual from Alaska in the Northeast
Common Ringed Plover	*Charadrius hiaticula*	Charadriidae	Casual from high Canadian Arctic to East Coast
Lesser Sand Plover	*Charadrius mongolus*	Charadriidae	Rare visitor from Asia to West Alaska, Pacific coast, and the East
Bar-tailed Godwit	*Limosa lapponica*	Scolopacidae	Casual from Alaska and Eurasia to East Coast
Black-tailed Godwit	*Limosa limosa*	Scolopacidae	Casual from Eurasia along Atlantic Coast
Sharp-tailed Sandpiper	*Calidris acuminata*	Scolopacidae	Casual from eastern Russia to the East
Ruff	*Philomachus pugnax*	Scolopacidae	Rare visitor from Eurasia to East Coast
Wood Sandpiper	*Tringa glareola*	Scolopacidae	Accidental from Eurasia to East Coast
Red-necked Stint	*Calidris ruficollis*	Scolopacidae	Rare visitor from Siberia to both coasts in summer and fall

VAGRANTS & ACCIDENTALS

COMMON NAME	SCIENTIFIC NAME	FAMILY NAME	STATUS
Gulls			
Mew Gull	*Larus canus*	Laridae	Rare visitor from either Alaska or Europe to East coast of Canada and US
California Gull	*Larus californicus*	Laridae	Casual from the West to East Coast
Slaty-backed Gull	*Larus schistisagus*	Laridae	Casual visitor from eastern Eurasia to the East
Ivory Gull	*Pagophila eburnea*	Laridae	Casual visitor from the Arctic to the East Coast; also inland
Pigeons and Doves			
Ruddy Ground-Dove	*Columbina talpacoti*	Columbidae	Casual visitor from Mexico to southern Texas
Owls			
Ferruginous Pygmy-Owl	*Glaucidium brasilianum*	Strigidae	Uncommon breeder from Mexico in southern Texas
Hummingbirds			
Calliope Hummingbird	*Stellula calliope*	Trochilidae	Rare to casual visitor from the West to the East, north to New England
Thrushes and allies			
Varied Thrush	*Ixoreus naevius*	Turdidae	Rare visitor from the West to the East, from Canada to southeastern states
Mountain Bluebird	*Sialia currucoides*	Turdidae	Casual visitor from the West to the eastern states
Townsend's Solitaire	*Myadestes townsendi*	Turdidae	Casual visitor from the West to eastern US
Wood-warblers			
Black-throated Gray Warbler	*Dendroica nigrescens*	Parulidae	Casual visitor from the West to eastern US
Townsend's Warbler	*Dendroica townsendi*	Parulidae	Casual visitor from the Northwest to eastern US
Hermit Warbler	*Dendroica occidentalis*	Parulidae	Casual visitor from the West to eastern US
MacGillivray's Warbler	*Oporornis tolmiei*	Parulidae	Casual visitor from the West to eastern US
Blackbirds and Orioles			
Spot-breasted Oriole	*Icterus pectoralis*	Icteridae	Uncommon in S Florida; introduced from Central America
Flycatchers			
Western Wood-pewee	*Contopus sordidulus*	Tyrannidae	Rare to casual visitor from the West to the East
Tanagers			
Western Tanager	*Piranga ludoviciana*	Thraupidae	Rare to casual visitor from the West to the East
Cardinals and Grosbeaks			
Black-headed Grosbeak	*Pheucticus melanocephalus*	Cardinalidae	Rare visitor from the West to the East
Lazuli Bunting	*Passerina amoena*	Cardinalidae	Casual visitor from the West to the East
American Sparrows			
McCown's Longspur	*Calcarius mccownii*	Emberizidae	Accidental from central Canada and US to East Coast
Baird's Sparrow	*Ammodramus bairdii*	Emberizidae	Accidental from central Canada and US to the East
Spotted Towhee	*Pipilo maculatus*	Emberizidae	Rare to casual visitor from the West to the East
Vireos			
Yellow-green Vireo	*Vireo flavoviridis*	Vireonidae	Casual from Mexico to Gulf coast and central Texas
Woodpeckers			
Lewis's Woodpecker	*Melanerpes lewis*	Picidae	Casual visitor from the West to the East
Nighthawks			
Antillean Nighthawk	*Chordeilis gundlachii*	Caprimulgidae	Rare visitor from Bahamas and West Indies to Florida Keys (breeds) and accidental along mainland coast from Florida to North Carolina

GLOSSARY

Many terms defined here are illustrated in the general introduction (pp.10–21).

adult A fully developed, sexually mature bird. It is in its final plumage, which no longer changes pattern with age and remains the same after yearly molt, although it may change with season. *See also* **immature**, **juvenile**.

aerie The nest of birds of prey, like eagles or peregrine falcons, usually on a cliff, and often used by the same pair of adult birds in successive years.

alarm call A call made by a bird to signal danger. Alarm calls are often short and urgent in tone, and a few species use different calls to signify the precise nature of the threat. *See also* **call**.

allopreening Mutual preening between two birds, the main purpose of which is to reduce the instinctive aggression when birds come into close contact. In the breeding season, allopreening helps to strengthen the pair bond between the male and female.
See also **preening**.

altitudinal migrant *see* vertical migrant
alula A small group of two to six feathers projecting from a bird's "thumb," at the bend of its wing that reduces turbulence when raised.
Audubon, John James (1785–1851) American naturalist and wildlife illustrator, whose best known work was his remarkable collection of prints, *Birds of North America*.

axillary A term describing feathers at the base of the underwing. Axillary feathers often form small patches, with coloration differing from the rest of the underwing.

barred With marks crossing the body, wing, or tail; the opposite of streaked. *See also* **streaks**.
bastard wing *see* alula
beak *see* bill
bill A bird's jaws. A bill is made of bone, with a hornlike outer covering of keratin.

bird of prey Any of the predatory birds in the orders Falconiformes (eagles, hawks, falcons, kites, buzzards, ospreys, and vultures) and Strigiformes (owls). They are characterized by their acute eyesight, powerful legs, strongly hooked bill, and sharp talons. These birds, particularly the Falconiformes, are also known as raptors. *See also* **talon**, **raptor**.

body feather *see* contour feather
booming A sound produced by bitterns and some species of grouse. The booming of male bitterns is a deep, resonant, hollow sound that can carry for several miles. The booming of male grouse is produced by wind from air pouches in the sides of the bird's neck.
brackish Containing a mixture of salt-water and freshwater.

breeding plumage A general term for the plumage worn by adult birds when they display and form breeding pairs. It is usually (but not always) worn in the spring and summer. *See also* nonbreeding plumage.

brood (noun) The young birds produced from a single clutch of eggs and raised together. *See also* **clutch**. **(verb)** In birds, to sit on nestlings to keep them warm. Brooding is usually carried out by the adult female. See also incubate.

brood parasite A bird that lays its eggs in the nest of other birds. Some brood parasites always breed this way, while others do so only occasionally.

brood patch An area of bare skin on the belly of a parent bird, usually the female, that is richly supplied with blood vessels and thus helps keep the eggs warm during incubation. This area loses its feathers in readiness for the breeding season and is fully feathered at other times.
caged-bird A species of bird commonly kept in captivity.

call A sound produced by the vocal apparatus of a bird to communicate a variety of messages to other birds. Calls are often highly characteristic of individual species and can help to locate and identify birds in the field. Most bird calls are shorter and simpler than songs. *See also* **alarm call**, **booming**, **contact call**, **song**.
casque A bony extension on a bird's head.
cere A leathery patch of skin that covers the base of a bird's bill. It occurs only in a few groups, including birds of prey, pigeons, and parrots.
claw In birds, the nail that prolongs their toes.
cloaca An opening toward the rear of a bird's belly. It is present in both sexes and is used in reproduction and excretion.
clutch The group of eggs in a single nest,

usually laid by one female and incubated together.

cock A term sometimes used to describe the adult male in gamebirds and songbirds. *See also* **hen**.
collar The area around a bird's neck, which in some species is a prominent feature of its plumage pattern and can be used for identification.

color form One of two or more clearly defined plumage variations found in the same species. Also known as a color morph or phase, a color form may be restricted to part of a species's range or occur side by side with other color forms over the entire range. Adults of different color forms are able to interbreed, and these mixed pairings can produce young of either form.

comb A fleshy growth of bare skin usually above the eyes.

contact call A call made by a bird to give its location as a means of staying in touch with others of the same species. Contact calls are used by birds in flocks and by breeding pairs. Contact calls are crucial for nocturnal migrants. *See also* **call**.

contour feather A general term for any feather that covers the outer surface of a bird, including its wings and tail. Contour feathers are also known as body feathers, and help streamline the bird.

cooperative breeding A breeding system in which a pair of parent birds are helped in raising their young by several other birds, which are often related to them and may be young birds from previous broods.

courtship display Ritualized, showy behavior used in courtship by the male, and sometimes by the female, involving plumage, sound (vocal and non-vocal), and movements.

covert A small feather covering the base of a bird's flight feather. Together, coverts form a well-defined feather tract on the wing or at the base of the tail. *See also* **feather tract**.

creche A group of young birds of about the same age, produced by different parents but tightly packed together. One or more adults guards the entire creche.

crepuscular Relating to the period just before dawn, when many birds are active, especially during courtship. When used in connection with birds, the term is often used to refer to both dawn and twilight.

crest A group of elongated feathers on top of a bird's head, which may be raised during courtship or to indicate alarm.

crown The area on top of a bird's head. It is often a prominent plumage feature, with a different color from the feathers on the rest of the head.

dabble To feed in shallow water by sieving water and obtain food through comblike filters in the bill; used mostly for ducks (dabbling ducks or dabblers).

decurved A term describing a bird's bill that curves downward from the forehead toward the tip.

dimorphism *see* sexual dimorphism
display *see* courtship display, distraction display, threat display

distraction display A display in which a bird deliberately attempts to attract a predator's attention in order to lure it away from its nest or nestlings.

diurnal Active during the day.
down feather A soft, fluffy feather, lacking the system of barbs of contour or flight feathers, that provides good insulation. Young birds are covered by down feathers until they molt into their first juvenile plumage. Adult birds have a layer of down feathers under their contour feathers. *See also* **contour feather**, **juvenile**.

drake An adult male duck. The adult female is known as the duck.

drift The diversion of migrating birds from their normal migration route by strong winds.

dynamic soaring *see* soaring
ear tuft A distinct tuft of feathers on each side of a bird's forehead, with no connection to the true ears, which can be raised as a visual signal. Many owls have ear tufts.

echolocation A method of sensing nearby objects using pulses of high-frequency sound. Echoes bounce back from obstacles, enabling the sender to build up a "picture" of its surroundings.

eclipse plumage A female-like plumage worn in some birds, especially waterfowl, by adult males for a short period after the breeding

season is over. The eclipse plumage helps camouflage them during their molt, when they are flightless.

elevational migrant *see* vertical migrant
endemic A species (or subspecies) native to a particular geographic area—such as an island, a forest patch, a mountain, or state, or country—and found nowhere else.

escape An individual bird that has escaped from a zoo or other collection to live in the wild. *See also* **exotic**
eye-ring A ring of color, usually narrow and well defined, around the eye of a bird.
eyestripe A stripe of color running as a line through the eye of a bird.
eyrie *see* aerie

exotic A bird found in a region from which it is not native. Some of these are escapees, or were originally, but now live as wild birds.
feather tract A well-defined area on a bird's skin where feathers grow, leaving patches of bare skin inbetween.

fledge In young birds, to leave the nest or acquire the first complete set of flight feathers. Known as fledglings, these birds may still remain dependent on their parents for some time. *See also* **flight feather**.

fledging period The average time taken by the young of a species to fledge, timed from the moment they hatch. Fledging periods in birds range from 11 days in some small songbirds to as long as 280 days in the Wandering Albatross.
fledgling *see* fledge
flight feather A collective term for a bird's wing and tail feathers, used in flight. More specifically, it refers to the largest feathers on the outer part of the wing, the primaries and secondaries.

forewing The front section of a bird's wing, including the primary coverts and secondary coverts. *See also* **hindwing**.
gamebird Generally, any bird that is legally hunted, including some doves and waterfowl. This name is generally used for members of the order Galliformes.

gular sac Also known as a gular pouch, it is a large, fleshy, extendable sac just below the bill of some birds, especially fish-eaters such as pelicans. It forms part of the throat.
habitat The geographical and ecological area where a particular organism usually lives.
hen A term sometimes used to describe the adult female in gamebirds, especially grouse and songbirds. *See also* **cock**.
hindwing The rear section of a bird's spread wing, including the secondary feathers, especially when it has a distinctive color or pattern. *See also* **forewing**.

hybrid The offspring produced when two species, sometimes from different genera, interbreed. Hybrids are usually rare in the wild. Among birds, they are most frequent in gamebirds and waterfowl, especially ducks. Hybrid progeny may or may not be fertile.
immature In birds, an individual that is not yet sexually mature or able to breed. Some birds pass through a series of immature plumages over several years before adopting their first adult plumage and sexual maturity. *See also* **adult**, **juvenile**.

incubate In birds, to sit on eggs to keep them warm, allowing the embryo inside to grow. Incubation is often carried out by the female. *See also* **brood**.

incubation period In birds, the period when a parent incubates its eggs. It may not start until the clutch is completed.

injury feigning *see* distraction display.
inner wing The inner part of the wing, comprising the secondaries and rows of coverts (typically marginal, lesser, median, and greater coverts).

introduced species A species that humans have accidentally or deliberately brought into an area where it does not normally occur.
iridescent plumage Plumage that shows brilliant, luminous colors, which seem to sparkle and change color when seen from different angles.

irruption A sporadic mass movement of animals outside their normal range. Irruptions are usually short-lived and occur in response to food shortage. Also called irruptive migration.
juvenile A term referring to the plumage worn by a young bird at the time it makes its first flight and until it begins its first molt. *See also* **adult**, **immature**.

keratin A tough but lightweight protein. In

birds, keratin is found in the claws, feathers, and outer part of the bill.

kleptoparasite A bird that gets much of its food by stealing it from other birds, usually by following them in flight and forcing them to disgorge their food.

lamellae Delicate, comblike structures on the sides of the bill of some birds used for filtering tiny food particles out of water.

leap-frog migration A pattern of migration in which some populations of a species travel much further than the other populations, by "leap-frogging" over the area where these sedentary (nonmigratory) birds are found. *See also* **migration.**

lek An area, often small, used by males as a communal display arena, where they show off special plumage features accompanied by vocal and non-vocal sounds, to attract females. Females wait along the lek and select the male or males that they will mate with.

lobed feet Feet with loose, fleshy lobes on the toes, adapted for swimming.

lore A small area between a bird's eye and the base of its upper bill.

mandible The upper or lower part of a bird's bill, known as the upper or lower mandible respectively.

mantle The loose term used to define the back of a bird, between its neck and rump.

migrant A species that regularly moves between geographical areas. Most migrants move on an annual basis between a breeding area and a wintering area. *See also* **partial migrant, sedentary.**

migration A journey to a different region, following a well-defined route. *See also* **leap-frog migration, partial migrant, reverse migration, sedentary, vertical migrant.**

mobbing A type of defensive behavior in which a group of birds gang up to harass a predator, such as a bird of prey or an owl, swooping repeatedly to drive it away.

molt In birds, to shed old feathers so that they can be replaced. Molting enables birds to keep their plumage in good condition, change their level of insulation, and change their coloration or markings so that they are ready to breed or display.

monogamous Mating with a single partner, either in a single breeding season or for life. *See also* **polygamous.**

morph *see* **color form**

nape The back of the neck.

nestling A young bird still in the nest.

New World The Americas, from Alaska to Cape Horn, including the Caribbean and offshore islands in the Pacific and Atlantic oceans. *See also* **Old World.**

nictitating membrane A transparent or semiopaque "third eyelid," which moves sideways across the eye. Waterbirds often use the membrane as an aid to vision when swimming underwater.

nocturnal Active at night.

nomadic Being almost constantly on the move. Birds of deserts, grasslands, and the coniferous forests of the far north are commonly nomadic.

nonbreeding plumage The plumage worn by adult birds outside the breeding season. In many species, particularly in temperate regions, it is also known as winter plumage. *See also* **breeding plumage.**

nonmigrant *see* **sedentary**

nonpasserine Any bird that is not a member of the order Passeriformes (or passerines). *See also* **passerine.**

oil gland Also called the preen gland, a gland at the base of a bird's tail that secretes oils that are spread over the feathers for waterproofing them during preening.

Old World Europe, Asia, Africa, and Australasia. *See also* **New World.**

orbital ring A thin, bare, fleshy ring around the eye, sometimes with a distinctive color. *See also* **eye-ring.**

outer wing The outer half of the wing, comprising the primaries, their coverts, and the alula (the "thumb").

partial migrant A species in which some populations migrate while others are sedentary. This situation is common in broadly distributed species that experience a wide range of climatic conditions. *See also* **migration, sedentary.**

passerine A bird belonging to the vast order Passeriformes (the passerines). This group contains more species than all other orders of birds combined. Passerines are also called songbirds or perching birds. *See also* **nonpasserine.**

pelagic Relating to the open ocean. Pelagic birds spend most of their life at sea and only come to land to nest.

phase *see* **color form**

polygamous Mating with two or more partners during the course of a single breeding season. *See also* **monogamous.**

population A group of individual birds of the same species living in a geographically and ecologically circumscribed area.

preening Routine behavior by which birds keep their feathers in good condition. A bird grasps a feather at its base and then "nibbles" upward toward the tip, and repeats the process with different feathers. This helps smooth and clean the plumage. Birds often also smear oil from their preen gland onto their feathers at the same time. *See also* **allopreening.**

primary feather One of the large outer wing feathers, growing from the digits of a bird's "hand." *See also* **secondary feather.**

race *see* **subspecies**

range A term to indicate the geographical distribution of a species or population

raptor A general name for birds belonging to the order Falconiformes, often used interchangeably with bird of prey. *See also* **bird of prey.**

ratite A member of an ancient group of flightless birds that includes the ostrich, cassowaries, emus, rheas, and kiwis. In the past, the group was larger and more diverse.

resident *see* **sedentary**

reverse migration A phenomenon that occurs when birds from a migratory species mistakenly travel in the opposite direction from normal, causing birds to turn up in places far outside their normal range. *See also* **migration.**

roost A place where birds sleep, either at night or by day.

rump The area between a bird's back and the base of its upper tail coverts. In many species, the rump is a different color from the rest of the plumage and can be a useful diagnostic character for identification.

sally A feeding technique (sallying), used especially by tyrant flycatchers, in which a bird makes a short flight from a perch to catch an insect, often in midair, followed by a return to a perch, often the same one.

salt gland A gland located in a depression of the skull, just above the eye of some birds, particularly seabirds. This enables them to extract the fluids they need from saltwater and then expel the excess salts through the nostrils.

scapular Any one of a group of feathers on the "shoulder," forming a more or less oval patch on each side of the back, at the base of the wing.

scrape A simple nest that consists of a shallow depression in the ground, which may be unlined or lined with material such as feathers, bits of grass, or pebbles.

secondary feather One of the row of long, stiff feathers along the rear edge of a bird's wing, between the body and the primary feathers at the wingtip. *See also* **primary feather.**

sedentary Having a settled lifestyle that involves little or no geographic movement. Sedentary birds are also said to be resident or nonmigratory. *See also* **migration.**

semipalmated The condition in which two or more of the toes are partially joined by an incomplete membrane at their base.

sexual dimorphism The occurrence of physical differences between males and females. In birds, the most common differences are in size and plumage.

shorebird Also known as a wader, any member of several families in the order Charadriiformes, including plovers, sandpipers, godwits, snipe, avocets, stilts, oystercatchers, and curlews. Not all species actually wade in water and some live in dry habitats.

soaring In birds, flight without flapping of the wings. A soaring bird stays at the same height or gains height. Updraft soaring is a type of soaring in which a bird benefits from rising currents that form at cliffs or along mountain ridges. Seabirds are expert at dynamic soaring, repeatedly diving into the troughs between waves and then using the rising air deflected off the waves to wheel back up into the air.

song A vocal performance by a bird, usually the adult male, to attract and impress a potential mate, advertise ownership of a territory, or drive away rival birds. Songs are often highly characteristic of individual species and can be a major aid in locating and identifying birds in the field. *See also* **call.**

songbird A general term used to describe a member of the suborder Passeri (or oscines), a subdivision of the largest order of birds, the Passeriformes (passerines).

species A group of similar organisms that are capable of breeding among themselves in the wild and producing fertile offspring that resemble themselves, but that do not interbreed

in the wild with individuals of another similar group, are called a species. *See also* **subspecies, superspecies.**

speculum A colorful patch on the wing of a duck, formed by the secondary feathers. *See also* **secondary feather.**

spur A sharply pointed, clawlike structure at the back of the leg of some birds, like the Wild Turkey.

staging ground A stopover area where migrant birds regularly pause while on migration, to rest and feed.

stoop A near-vertical and often very fast dive made by falcons and some other birds of prey when chasing prey in the air or on the ground.

streaks Marks that run lengthwise on feathers; opposite of bars.

subspecies When species show geographical variation in color, voice, or other characters, these differentiated populations are recognized by ornithologists as subspecies (formerly also called races). *See also* **species.**

superspecies Closely related species that have different geographical ranges. See also species

syrinx A modified section of a bird's trachea (windpipe), equivalent to the voicebox in humans, that enables birds to call and sing.

talon One of the sharp, hooked claws of a bird of prey.

territory An area that is defended by an animal, or a group of animals, against other members of the same species. Territories often include useful resources, such as good breeding sites or feeding areas, which help a male attract a mate.

tertial Any one of a small group of feathers, sometimes long and obvious, at the base of the wing adjacent to the inner secondaries.

thermal A rising bubble or column of warm air over land that soaring birds can use to gain height with little effort. *See also* **soaring.**

threat display A form of defense in which a bird adopts certain postures, sometimes accompanied by loud calls, to drive away a rival or a potential predator.

trachea The breathing tube in animals, also known as the windpipe.

tubenose A general term used to describe members of the order Procellariiformes, including albatrosses, petrels, and shearwaters; their nostrils form two tubes on the upper mandible.

underwing The underside of a bird's wing, usually visible only in flight or when a bird is preening, displaying, or swimming.

upperwing The upper surface of a bird's wing, clearly exposed in flight but often mostly hidden when the bird is perched.

vagrant A bird that has strayed far from its normal range. Usually, vagrants are long-distance migrants that have been blown off course by storms, have overshot their intended destination due to strong winds, or have become disoriented.

vent Also called the crissum, the undertail feathers between the lower belly feathers and tail feathers, which in some species are differently colored from either belly or tail feathers. Can be helpful in identification.

vertical migrant A species that migrates up and down mountains, usually in response to changes in the weather or food supply. *See also* **migration.**

wader *see* **shorebird.**

waterfowl A collective term for members of the family Anatidae, including ducks, geese, and swans.

wattle A bare, fleshy growth that hangs loosely below the bill in some birds. It is often brightly colored, and may play a part in courtship.

wildfowl *see* **waterfowl**

Wilson, Alexander (1766–1813) A contemporary of J.J. Audubon, Wilson's seminal American Ornithology marks the start of scientific ornithology in the US.

wingbar A line or bar of color across the upper surface of a bird's wing. Wingbars can often be seen when a bird is on the ground or perched and its wings are in the closed position, but they are normally much more obvious in flight. Wingbars may be single or in groups of two or more.

wingspan The distance across a bird's outstretched wings and back, from one wingtip to the other.

INDEX

INDEX

ACKNOWLEDGEMENTS

Dorling Kindersley would like to thank the following people for their help in compiling this book: Lucy Baker, Rachel Booth, Kim Bryan, Arti Finn, Peter Frances, Lynn Hassett, Riccie Janus, Megan Jones, Maxine Lea, Ruth O'Rourke, Himanshi Sharma, Catherine Thomas, Yen-Mai Tsang.

Producing such a comprehensive book would be impossible without the research and observations of hundreds of field and museum ornithologists and birdwatchers. The Editor-in-Chief would like to name four who have been especially inspirational and supportive over the years: the late Paul Géroudet, the late Ernst Mayr, Patricia Stryker Joseph, and Helen Hays. In addition, we acknowledge *Birds of North America Online*, edited by Alan Poole, a joint project of the American Ornithologists' Union and Cornell's Laboratory of Ornithology, and *The Howard and Moore Complete Checklist of the Birds of the World*, revised and enlarged 3rd edition, edited by Edward C. Dickinson and published by the Princeton University Press, as invaluable sources of information on the birds of North America.

The publisher would like to thank the following for their kind permission to reproduce their photographs:

Almost without exception, the birds featured in the profiles in this book were photographed in the wild.

(Key: a-above; b-below/bottom; c-centre; f-far; l-left; r-right; t-top)

Alamy Images: AfriPics.com 11cra; Derrick Alderman 18cl; Juniors Bildachiv 13tr; blickwinkel 19cr; Nora Bowers 254t; Bruce Coleman Inc. 14tr, 19br; Gay Bumgarner 18fc; Nancy Camel 19clb; Redmond Durrell 15cb; Elvele Images Ltd. 18-19cb; David Hosking 13fcrb; Don Kates 16cla; William Leaman 334cr; Rick & Nora Bowers 9tc, 360bl, 435fbl, 466tl; Rolf Nussbaumer 16clb; Peter Arnold, Inc. 16cl; Renee Morris 443c; Stock Connection Blue 13cr; tbkmedia.de 16-17c; **Ardea:** Ian Beames 11cr; Peter Steyn 82ca; Jim Zipp 274cr, 274tc, 276fcr, 319tc; **Doug Backlund:** 12-13ca,

26cb, 29cla, 29crb, 40crb, 120cra, 120tc, 122fbl, 129crb, 134bl, 135cra, 140bl, 144tr, 240fbl; **Steve Baldwin** 230b; **The Barn Owl Centre, UK:** 236cla; **Giff Beaton:** 361bl, 363fbl, 364tr, 365fbl, 374bl; **Corbis:** Frank Burek 112; Tim Davis 2-3; Joe McDonald 14cla; David A. Northcott 112; **Mike Danzenbaker:** 77bl, 78bl, 79fbl, 80bl, 80fbl, 81ca, 82bl, 82fbl, 83bl, 83cra, 83fbl, 218cla, 231fbl, 233bl, 234bl, 251bl, 252ca, 252tl, 254bl, 272cb, 369tc, 397cc, 407fbl, 408tc, 409bl, 410bc, 445br, 447br, 453br, 453tr; **Greg & Yvonne Dean / WorldWildlifeImages.com:** 250bl, 455tl; **Dorling Kindersley:** Robin Chittenden 70tr; Chris Gomersall Photography 30crb, 30tr, 48ca, 48crb, 48tr, 51crb, 56bl, 67crb, 79ca, 79tr, 81bl, 102crb, 111crb, 118fbl, 119ca, 119crb, 121fbl, 123cra, 123tc, 129fbl, 172bl, 174crb, 175crb, 183bc, 194cra, 196ca, 203bl, 203fbl, 205bl, 205cra, 207ca, 207crb, 207fbl, 209cb, 218bl, 218fbl, 219bl, 219cla, 219cra, 220bl, 220cra, 221crb, 222crb, 222tc, 224cra, 243fbl, 298bl, 331tc, 341cra, 341tc, 416fbl, 437fbl, 445tl; David Tipling Photo Library 50ca, 57cr, 57cra, 66bl, 70tc, 71bl, 72tc, 74bl, 75bl, 86tc, 87fbl, 88fbl, 123crb, 154cla, 184cla, 191cl, 191cra, 191fbl, 194cl, 195cra, 195fbl, 200cl, 224cla, 313tc; Mark Hamblin 52ca, 57cla, 74ca (1), 113cra, 237cra, 239bl, 239fbl, 244bl, 247bl, 248cra, 464br; Chris Knights 71crb; Mike Lane 30cra, 31bl, 33tc, 45ca, 57tr, 58bl, 62fbl, 65cla, 68fbl, 72tr, 87ca, 111cra, 166bl, 176ca, 177crb, 181fbl, 182tc, 183tr, 196tr, 197fbl, 200fbl, 207bl, 207tc, 208ca, 209fbl, 210fbl, 211fbl, 214bl, 215bl, 216cra, 216crb, 220crb, 221ca, 222ca, 297bl, 298ca, 452tl; Gordon Langsbury 111tc, 156cra, 157fbl, 158fbl, 159fbl, 168tc, 171bl, 172cla, 185tr; Gordon Langsgury 100cra; Tim Loseby 52crb, 189crb, 347cla; George McCarthy 28bl, 31crb, 33tr, 97ca, 98fbl, 100cra, 174cla, 195bc, 214fbl, 215ca, 216bl, 235bl; Natural History Museum, London 10cla, 12cl; Kim Taylor 74tr, 222tr; Roger Tidman 42ca, 42tc, 43fbl, 44ca, 53tr, 61ca, 65bl, 67ca, 70fbl, 72ca, 86fbl, 92ca, 93fbl, 111cla, 165bl, 174tr, 177tc, 179fbl, 183tl, 188bl, 188ca, 189ca, 189tr, 191tc, 203ca, 203crb, 205ca, 205fbl, 208crb, 214cra, 215fbl, 216fbl, 217bl, 217ca, 221fbl, 221tc, 225ca, 226fbl, 331cla, 410cla, 410tc; Ray Tipper 154bl; Steve Young 45tc, 53cr, 57crb, 57tc, 65cra, 65tr, 67tc, 67tr, 68bl, 69bl, 70bl, 71ca, 71tc, 79tc, 83crb, 83tc, 113tc, 184tc, 191crb, 195cla, 196bl, 196ca, 197bl, 198cla, 199bl, 200cra, 200crb, 200tl, 208tc, 228tr, 241tc, 242fbl, 321ca, 322bl, 410cra;

Dudley Edmondson: 23cra, 28fbl, 28tr, 29cra, 29fbl, 31cla, 33bl, 37cra, 37crb, 37tl, 38fbl, 41fbl, 88ca, 88tc, 95cb, 103cla, 105cla, 109cla, 110bl, 110cla, 110tr, 114tc, 118bl, 119bl, 120fbl, 121ca, 122bl, 123bl, 127ca, 127cb, 127cla, 127tc, 129cla, 129cra, 129tc, 130cb, 131crb, 134cla, 134cra, 135crb, 137fbl, 144crb, 148crb, 152ca, 153crb, 160ca, 167fbl, 173crb, 181tc, 190tr, 199crcb, 212crb, 213crb, 238fbl, 242d, 243cb, 245cla, 245cra, 246bl, 250crb, 263bc, 281crb, 294ca, 317crb, 333crb, 378bc, 396crb, 405bl, 411ca, 412cra, 427fbl, 428cra, 449br, 461bl; **Tom Ennis:** 182bl, 186ca; **Hanne & Jens Eriksen:** 111bl, 122crb, 154fbl, 167crb, 191bl, 195bl, 204tc, 217crb, 217tc, 451bl; **Neil Fletcher:** 35cb, 36bc, 36cla, 37cla, 39tc, 43ca, 43cra, 45tr, 46fbl, 48fbl, 49fbl, 52fbl, 52tr, 54fbl, 54tc, 55crb, 55tr, 225crb, 331ca, 341crb; **David Hosking** 78fbl, 445bl; **FLPA:** Goetz Eichhorn/ Foto Natura 75fbl; John Hawkins 17cla; S Jonasson 76cra; Daphne Kinzler 17tr; S & D & K Maslowski 18br; Winfried Wisniewski / Foto Natura 17cr; Tui De Roy / Minden Pictures 17ca; Roger Tidman 76tc; **Joe Fuhrman:** 167ca, 168fbl, 360crb; **Getty Images:** Marc Moritsch 14-15b; Nancy Nehring / Photodisc 112; Brad Sharp 18c; Paul E.Tessier / Photodisc 25tr; **Bob Glover:** 200tc; **Melvin Grey:** 49crb, 50crb, 89bc, 89cra, 91crb, 95fbl, 96ca, 96tr, 97fbl, 98ca, 98cra, 99bl, 99crb, 100crb, 101cla, 101fbl, 103fbl, 104cra, 105bl, 105crb, 119cra, 120cla, 124cla, 124crb, 130crb, 131fbl, 132bl, 133bl, 135cla, 145bl, 145ca, 145crb, 146bl, 146fbl, 147cra, 147fbl, 155tr, 156fbl, 157ca, 157crb, 157tr, 158bl, 159bl, 160cra, 160crb, 160tr, 175bl, 175ca, 176cra, 205tr, 206crb, 206tr, 221bl, 237crb, 296cra, 301tc, 348bc, 396fcla, 396fcra, 452tr; Tom Grey 80cr, 95cra, 116crb, 125tl, 147crb, 190bl, 204crb, 225bl, 226ca, 227bl, 402bl, 403cla, 403cra; **Josef Hlasek:** 188crb; **Barry Hughes:** 219crb; **Arto Juvonen:** 32tc, 78ca, 78crb, 78tc, 113crb, 135bl, 136cra; **Kevin T. Karlson:** 26cla, 27fbl, 27tc, 63bl, 64ca, 64crb, 103tc, 120crb, 133cla, 133tc, 151cla, 163cr, 163cra, 163crb, 163tl, 165ca, 165cra, 166fbl, 186tc, 220ca, 286crb, 297crb, 366fbl, 373tc, 420cla, 431bl, 448bl; **Mike Lane:** Mike Lane 228bl, 229bl; **Barry Mansell:** 34c; **Garth McElroy:** 9clb, 15cl, 44fbl, 47crb, 59fbl, 59tr, 61bl, 62bl, 63tc, 64bl, 64tc, 65ca, 65fbl, 66tc, 67fbl, 68cla, 69crb, 75tc, 86bl, 87bl, 87tc, 88bl, 88cla, 90bl, 90fbl, 91bl, 91fbl, 92bl, 92crb, 93bl, 95bl, 96bl, 97bl, 97tr, 98bl, 99ca, 99fbl, 100bl, 100fbl, 101tc, 102bl, 102ca, 106cra, 106fbl, 106tc, 112crb, 112cr, 112tl, 114bl, 140fbl, 141bl, 142cla, 143cra, 143crb, 144bl, 148fbl, 151cra, 151fbl, 155cra, 156cla, 156crb, 158ca, 159cla, 159crb, 161ca, 161fbl, 162bl, 162cr, 162fbl, 162tc, 163ca, 163fbl, 164bl, 164fbl, 164tr, 165crb, 165tc, 168crb, 169fbl, 169ca, 169cra, 169crb, 169fbl, 170cra, 170fbl, 171crb, 171fbl, 172cra, 173ca, 173cra, 173fbl, 174bl, 176crb, 176tr, 177cb, 179tl, 180bl, 180crb, 180tc, 181cla, 181fbl, 189tc, 196ca, 195ca, 193cla, 193cra, 193crb, 196fbl, 197cra, 198crb, 200bl, 211ca, 211crb, 211tc, 229ca, 232cra, 233crb, 237bl, 241cr, 244crb, 246crb, 247cla, 248bc, 248tc, 255cla, 255tc, 266cb, 266cla, 266cra, 267bl, 271crb, 271tc, 274bl, 275bl, 276bl, 278cla, 278crb, 281ca, 290crb, 292bc, 293cla, 293cra, 293crb, 300bl, 300cla, 300cra, 300tc, 301bl, 301cla, 301fbl, 303crb, 304bl, 304ca, 304crb, 305ca, 306bl, 307ca, 307crb, 309cra, 310bl, 311bl, 311ca, 311crb, 312bl, 313cr, 314crb, 316cr, 316tr, 320crb, 321bl, 323tc, 326cra, 326crb, 327br, 327cra, 328cb, 328crb, 330br, 332b, 333ca, 333cra, 334bl, 334cb, 334tc, 335fbl, 336ca, 336crb, 337bl, 337cb, 337crb, 338bl, 338cb, 338cra, 339bl, 340crb, 340tc, 342cra, 343bl, 344tr, 345crb, 346cra, 346tcc, 347bc, 348cb, 348cra, 348tc, 349fbl, 350bl, 350cra, 350crb, 351cr, 351fbl, 352cra, 352crb, 352fbl, 352tc, 353bc, 353ca, 359bc, 360cra, 361ca, 361crb, 361tc, 363bl, 363cra, 363tc, 364crb, 365cla, 366cla, 366crb, 366tc, 367bl, 367bl, 369crb, 372bl, 373cra, 373fbl, 374bc, 376cb, 376cra, 376fbl, 377fbl, 381ca, 381crb, 382crb, 382fbl, 383crb, 383fbl, 384fbl, 386crb, 387cra, 387crb, 390cb, 390fbl, 391bl, 393fbl, 394crb, 396bl, 396fbl, 397crb, 397tr, 398fbl, 399bc, 400tr, 402fbl, 403fbl, 404fbl, 405crb, 405tc, 411fbl, 411crb, 412fbl, 413bc, 413cra, 413fbl, 414ca, 415bl, 415tc, 416fbl, 418cla, 418crb, 418tc, 419cra, 420bl, 421crb, 422bc, 422tc, 425bl, 426ca, 427cra, 428crb, 428fbl, 429bl, 429crb, 430ca, 430fbl, 431ca, 434bl, 434ca, 434crb, 438cra, 438fbl, 439crb, 441bc, 462tr, 463tr, 467d, 469tr; **Ian Montgomery / Birdway.com.au:** 18tr; **Arthur Morris/ Birds As Art:** 207tr; **Bob Moul:** 87cla, 156crb, 286crb, 339crb, 386bl, 387tc, 399cla, 447tr; **Alan Murphy:** 8tl, 9tr, 23cl, 72bl, 85ca, 103crb, 107tr, 125fbl, 126ca, 126cra, 126crb, 128fbl, 138tr, 141cla, 141crb, 151bl, 151crb, 223ba, 232b, 232cl, 234crb, 235cr, 249tr, 253b, 253crb, 257b, 258bl, 258br, 259b, 262fbl, 270tr, 275cb, 288cb, 288crb, 299cra, 302fbl, 303ca, 354b, 355bl, 356fbl, 358bl, 362cla, 371fbl, 378bl, 389fbl, 392b, 429cra, 429tr, 435bl, 436ca, 436crb, 444tr, 460br, 466tr, 467tr; **Tomi Muukonen:** 45crb, 73cl, 86tr, 128tr, 136cla, 136fbl, 194tl, 196crb, 201bl, 202cla, 202crb, 208fbl, 209ca, 210bl, 407crb, 410crb, 464bl; **naturepl.com:** Vincent Munier 10-11c; Tom Vezo 17br; **NHPA / Photoshot:** Bill Coster 84bc, 150b; Kevin Schafer 76cb; **Wayne Nicholas:** 148bl, 449bl; **Judd Patterson:** 22, 102fbl, 105tc, 106bl, 107bc, 108cb, 108cra, 108tl, 132fbl, 133bc, 133crb, 281bl, 283cra, 458br; **E. J. Peiker:** 56cb, 168bl; **EJ Peiker:** 8ca, 35ca, 35crb, 35fbl, 37bl, 38cra, 42fcra, 42tr, 44bl, 44tc, 46bl, 46cb, 47ca, 50bl, 50fbl, 50tc, 51bl, 53bl, 53cla, 53cra, 53fbl, 54bl, 54ca, 54crb, 54tr, 55ca, 55cb, 55fbl, 55tc, 56crb, 56fbl, 57bl, 57fbl, 58ca, 58crb, 68crb, 69fbl, 69tc, 71fbl, 73br, 75cr, 89crl, 92fbl, 92tc, 93cra, 101cra, 102cra, 110fcla, 112cra, 113bl, 114fbl, 118ca, 118cla, 127fbl, 132cra, 133fbl, 134fbl, 136bl, 146tc, 152crb, 153ca, 153cra, 154cra, 154crb, 157fbl, 159cra, 160bl, 164tc, 167bl, 172crb, 174cr, 185cr, 192crb, 202bl, 202cra, 206tcc, 210tr, 218cb, 226bc, 227crb, 238cla, 238tc, 240cra, 241fbl, 242fbl, 243bl, 247fbl, 255bl, 255crb, 255fbl, 259br, 261fbl, 262cb, 279cb, 280bl, 280cra, 280tc, 282fbl, 286cra, 294cb, 295crb, 300fbl, 301cra, 315c, 315crb, 316br, 322br, 331bl, 345bl, 346tr, 348fbl, 349crb, 349tr, 351bl, 357bl, 358cla, 362crb, 362fbl, 368fbl, 369bl, 370tr, 375bl, 391br, 392tr, 393crb, 395tr, 400bc, 400tc, 402tc, 404bc, 404bb, 406cl, 432ca, 439tc, 438bc, 439bl, 442cla, 444bl, 457tr, 458fbl, 459tr, 461br, 470bl, 470tr; **Jari Peltomäki:** 24bl, 31tc, 32cra, 36ca, 37fbl, 39fbl, 59crb, 65crb, 73bc, 115bc, 123bl, 127bl, 137ca, 137cra, 137crb, 145fbl, 146cla, 146cra, 146crb, 147fbl, 184bl, 185bl, 209crb, 224crb, 237b, 242cb, 285crb, 306cra, 306crb, 344cla, 407cra, 450tr; **Photolibrary:** Tim Zurowski 319fcr; **David Plummer:** 456tl; **Mike Read:** 77crb, 122crb; **Robert Royse:** 26fbl, 27cla, 30bl, 31cra, 39crb, 63ca, 141cra, 141fbl, 142ca, 142crb, 143bl, 167ca, 169cla, 170ca, 175tr, 180ca, 187fbl, 192fbl, 193fbl, 204ca, 204tr, 206fbl, 233cra, 234fbl, 256ca, 265cra, 265tc, 278cra, 296fbl, 297ca, 302ca, 303fbl, 317bl, 318bl, 319cra, 321fbl, 322tc, 332ca, 355fbl, 372fbl, 385crb, 385tr, 386cla, 387bl, 408cra, 408crb, 410tr, 411crb, 419bl, 422bl, 424ca, 424crb, 426bl, 426fbl, 427bl, 429ca, 430crb, 436ca, 441bl, 442bl, 446tr, 450br, 468bl, 468br, 470br; **Chris Schenk:** 65fcla; **Bill Schmoker:** 39bl, 40ca, 42bl, 43tc, 74fbl, 77fbl, 77tr, 80ca, 80crb, 80tr, 81crb, 82crb, 82tc, 88crb, 95ca, 96fbl, 121crb, 135tc, 137bl, 186crb, 254fbl, 284ca, 329fbl; **Brian E. Small:** 1c, 8cr, 8cra, 8crb, 8-9ca, 9cr, 11fcra, 24fbl, 24tc, 24tr, 25bl, 26bl, 27bl, 27cra, 28crb, 29bl, 29tr, 30fbl, 31fbl, 32fbl, 35bl, 36fbl, 39ca, 40fbl, 41bl, 42fbl, 43bl, 45fbl, 46ca, 46tc, 47bl, 49tc, 52bl, 52tc, 55bl, 56ca, 56tc, 58fbl, 58tc, 60bl, 61fbl, 62tc, 63tr, 64fbl, 66ca, 66fbl, 69ca, 74ca, 84tl, 85bl, 90ca, 90cra, 91cla, 91cra, 94cra, 96tc, 101bl, 103bl, 103ca, 104bl, 104cla, 104tc, 105cra, 106cla, 108bl, 109bl, 109cra, 109fbl, 110cra, 110fbl, 111fbl, 114cra, 114crb, 116bl,

116ca, 116tc, 117bl, 117br, 117cra, 117fbl, 117tc, 124fbl, 125bl, 125cra, 126bl, 127cra, 128ca, 129bl, 130cra, 132bc, 139c, 139crb, 140ca, 140crb, 141ca, 142fbl, 143fbl, 144fbl, 145cra, 148c, 148cla, 149ca, 149fbl, 154tc, 155bl, 155fbl, 155tc, 159tc, 166ca, 166tc, 170bl, 170cla, 171ca, 172ca, 175tc, 176fbl, 176fbl, 177bl, 177ca, 178ca, 178cra, 178fbl, 179tr, 180fbl, 187bl, 188tl, 189bl, 190cra, 192bl, 193bl, 194fbl, 198ca, 198ca, 199cra, 199tr, 201ca, 202fbr, 204bl, 204fbl, 206fbl, 206ca, 206cra, 208bl, 209bl, 210ca, 211bl, 212ca, 213ca, 224bl, 224fbl, 226bl, 226tc, 227ca, 231crb, 233fbl, 234ca, 234cra, 235ca, 235fbl, 238cra, 240bl, 240cla, 241ca, 241cra, 242bl, 242cra, 243cla, 243ca, 244cra, 246fbl, 248fbl, 249cf, 250fbl, 251fbl, 252crb, 252fbl, 254crb, 256bc, 256bl, 256fbl, 257tr, 258cra, 258tr, 259cra, 260bc, 260cra, 261bl, 261br, 261cla, 261cra, 262bl, 262cla, 262cra, 263bl, 263fbl, 264cb, 264cla, 264cra, 265bl, 265crb, 265fbl, 267cb, 268ca, 268cb, 268cra, 268fcla, 269cla, 269crb, 271bl, 271cb, 271fbl, 272bl, 272ca, 273bl, 273cb, 273cra, 273fbl, 274fbl, 275cc, 275fbl, 276cra, 276fbl, 277bl, 277ca, 277crb, 277fbl, 278bl, 278fbl, 279fbl, 281cra, 281fbl, 282bl, 282br, 282ca, 283cl, 284bl, 284crb, 285bl, 286bl, 287bl, 287crb, 287fbl, 288bl, 288ca, 288fbl, 289bl, 289ca, 289crb, 289fbl, 290bl, 290cra, 291bl, 291ca, 291crb, 292ca, 292fbl, 292bl, 293fbl, 293tc, 294bl, 294fbl, 301crb, 302cb, 305bl, 305crb, 305fbl, 306ca, 307fbl, 308cra, 309crb, 309fbl, 310ca, 313cb, 313bl, 313tr, 314 bl, 315crb, 315fbl, 317cra, 318crb, 318fbl, 319crb, 319fbl, 320bl, 320cra, 323bl, 323ca, 323fbl, 324bl, 324cra, 324crb, 324fbl, 325bl, 325cra, 325fbl, 325tc, 326bl, 326cla, 326fbl, 327bl, 327fbl, 328ca, 328fbl, 329bl, 329ca, 329crb, 329tc, 330bl, 330fbl, 331fbl, 333bl, 333fbl, 333tr, 334bc, 334fbl, 335bl, 335ca, 336bl, 337cra, 337fbl, 337tc, 338bc, 338cla, 338fbl, 338tc, 339cra, 339fbl, 340bl, 341bl, 341fbl, 342bl, 342tc, 343cra, 343crb, 345ca, 345fbl, 346bc, 346bl, 346cla, 347cra, 347fbl, 349fbl, 350cla, 350fbl, 350tc, 351ca, 351cra, 351tl, 352bl, 353bl, 353fbl, 354tr, 355cla, 355cc, 355crb, 356cb, 356bl, 356cla, 356cra, 357cra, 357fbl, 357tc, 358cb, 359bl, 359fbl, 359tr, 360cla, 362bl, 362cra, 364bl, 364ca, 364tc, 364cb, 365bl, 365tr, 366bl, 366tc, 367crb, 367tc, 367tr, 368bl, 368cra, 368crb, 368tc, 369ca, 370bl, 370cla, 370fbl, 371bl, 371cra, 371crb, 371tc, 372ca, 372crb, 373bl, 373cra, 374ca, 374cla, 374cra, 374tc, 375bc, 375cla, 375fbl, 376bl, 376cla, 377cra, 377tc, 378cla, 378cra, 378bl, 378fbl, 379cra, 379crb, 380bl, 380ca, 380crb, 380fbl, 381bl, 381fbl, 382bl, 382ca, 383bl, 383ca, 384ca, 384cra, 385bl, 385ca, 385fbl, 386bc, 386tr, 387fbl, 388bl, 388ca, 388fbl, 389ca, 389tc, 390tc, 391ca, 391fbl, 393tc, 393ba, 393cra, 393tr, 394cla, 394cra, 394crb, 395bl, 395bl, 395cb, 395ca, 396cra, 397bl, 398bl, 398crb, 399bl, 399ca, 399tr, 399cra, 399fbl, 400bl, 400ca, 400fbl, 401bl, 401cra, 401fbl, 402cra, 402crb, 403bc, 403bl, 404ca, 404cc, 405cla, 405cra, 405fbl, 406tr, 409fbl, 409cra, 409fbl, 411tr, 412bl, 412cl, 413bl, 413tc, 414bl, 414crb, 414fbl, 415cra, 415crb, 415fbl, 416cra, 417cla, 417crb, 417fbl, 417tc, 418cra, 418fbl, 419cl, 419crb, 419fcla, 419tc, 420fbl, 420tc, 421bl, 421fbl, 421tc, 421tr, 422crb, 422fbl, 423bl, 423cra, 423fbl, 424bl, 424fbl, 425bc, 425ca, 425fbl, 426cra, 426fbl, 431cra, 432tc, 433bl, 433cra, 433crb, 433fbl, 434cra, 434fbl, 435ca, 435cla, 435cra, 435crb, 435tr, 436bl, 436fbl, 437bl, 437ca, 437cr, 437crb, 437tr, 438bl, 438cl, 438cla, 438tc, 439cla, 439cra, 439fbl, 439tc, 440bl, 440cla, 440fbl, 440tr, 441cla, 441fbl, 441tc, 441tr, 442bc, 442cra, 442fbl, 442tr, 444br, 444tl, 446tl, 447bl, 448br, 448fbl, 448tr, 449tl, 450bl, 450tl, 451br, 452br, 453bl, 453tl, 454bl, 454br, 454tl, 455bl, 455br, 455tr, 456bl, 456br, 456tr, 457bl, 457br, 457tl, 458bl, 458tr, 459bl, 459br, 460bl, 460tr, 461tr, 462bl, 462br, 463bl, 464bl, 464tr, 465tl, 466br, 467bl, 468tr, 469br, 469tl; **Michelle Lynn St.Sauveur:** 161crb; **Bob Steele:** 8c, 8fcrb, 9ca, 13cb, 25cla, 25fbl, 26ca, 32bl, 36cra, 37tc, 38bl, 38cla, 38crb, 40tc, 40tr, 41crb, 43crb, 44tr, 45fbl, 46crb, 47fbl, 48tc, 49bl, 49crb, 50tr, 51fbl, 58tr, 62crb, 62tr, 66crb, 68tc, 69tr, 75tr, 77cla, 85crb, 85tc, 90crb, 93cla, 93tr, 94bl, 94ca, 96cb, 97crb, 100tc, 104crb, 108fbl, 109tc, 110crb, 112fbl, 114ca, 118crb, 118tr, 119fbl, 124bl, 128ca, 130fbl, 131bl, 132bl, 132tc, 133tc, 134bc, 134ca, 134tr, 135fbl, 136crb, 138br, 138c, 139bl, 143cla, 144ca, 144cr, 147cla, 148cra, 149bl, 149cr, 149crb, 152cra, 152tc, 153cla, 155ca, 156tc, 160cr, 160fbl, 161bl, 162bc, 163cl, 164cra, 164crb, 166crb, 168cca, 170crb, 171tc, 172bl, 173bl, 173tc, 177bc, 178bl, 178cb, 178tr, 179bl, 179ca, 179crb, 181bl, 181crb, 182bc, 182ca, 182fbl, 183bl, 183fbl, 184cra, 184fbl, 185bc, 185ca, 185fbl, 186fbl, 186tl, 187ca, 187crb, 187tl, 187tr, 188fbl, 188tr, 189fbl, 190cla, 190crb, 190fbl, 190tc, 192cla, 192cra, 192tc, 192tr, 194tl, 194crb, 194tc, 197cla, 197tc, 198bl, 199ca, 201cla, 201crb, 203tc, 210crb, 210tc, 212bl, 212tc, 213tc, 214bc, 214cla, 216tc, 218crb, 219bl, 220fbl, 222bl, 228ca, 228cb, 228crb, 229crb, 229tl, 235cb, 236tc, 237fbl, 238bl, 239cra, 239tc, 240cl, 241bl, 244cla, 245bl, 245fbl, 246cra, 246tc, 247crb, 249b, 250ca, 251ca, 252bl, 253tr, 255cra, 256cla, 256cr, 263ca, 263bl, 264bl, 264fbl, 266bl, 267cla, 267cra, 270b, 271cra, 272crb, 272fbl, 273cr, 274crb, 279bl, 279ca, 279cra, 279crb, 280fbl, 283b, 284cra, 284fbl, 285fbl, 286cra, 286fbl, 287ca, 290fbl, 290tc, 291fbl, 292crb, 294crb, 295bl, 295ca, 296bl, 296cra, 296crb, 297fbl, 298bl, 298crb, 298fbl, 299b, 302bl, 302crb, 303bl, 304fbl, 306fbl, 307bl, 307cra, 307tr, 308crb, 308tc, 309bl, 309tc, 310crb, 310tc, 311tc, 313br, 313cla, 314fbl, 314tc, 315bl, 315tcr, 317fbl, 318cra, 319bl, 319ca, 320fbl, 320tc, 322cra, 323cr, 325crb, 330ca, 331fcla, 332cra, 335crb, 340cla, 340cra, 342crb, 342fbl, 343fbl, 344b, 345cb, 346fbl, 347cl, 347tc, 348bl, 349cla, 349cra, 353cra, 354cl, 357cla, 357crb, 358cra, 358fbl, 359cla, 361cla, 361fbl, 362tc, 363cla, 364fbl, 365cb, 365crb, 370c, 370cra, 370crb, 374fbl, 377cra, 377cla, 384bl, 384crb, 385fbl, 388crb, 388tc, 389bl, 389crb, 389tr, 390bl, 390ca, 390crb, 392crb, 394bl, 395cra, 396ca, 396tr, 397bl, 398tr, 398tc, 401crb, 401tc, 404bl, 404cra, 406bl, 407bl, 408bl, 409tr, 411cra, 412cla, 412cr, 413cl, 416cla, 416crb, 416tc, 417bl, 418bl, 420crb, 420tr, 422crb, 426crb, 427cla, 427crb, 427tc, 428bl, 430bl, 431bc, 431fbl, 432bc, 433cla, 440tc, 446bl, 446br, 449tr, 451bl, 451tr, 463br, 464bl, 465bl, 466bl, 467bl, 469bl; **Matthew Studebaker** 356tc; **Andy & Gill Swash:** 77c, 93crb, 94crb, 98cb, 99cra, 109crb, 112bl, 445tl; **Peter Sweber:** 38tc, 49ca, 62ca, 63bl, 104fbl, 105fbl, 110tc; **Markus Varesvuo:** 4-5c, 12-13bl, 23b, 30ca, 32crb, 33cra, 33fbr, 34cra, 36crb, 42crb, 51ca, 51cb, 51tr, 59ca, 59tc, 64fbl, 61cb, 61crb, 61tc, 63crb, 67bl, 68ca, 70ca, 70crb, 74crb, 75ca, 75cb, 84cl, 86ca, 86crb, 87crb, 122cla, 128bl, 128crb, 131cra, 131tr, 136ca, 136tr, 183ca, 184crb, 189cb, 215crb, 215tc, 219tc, 239crb, 247cra, 248bl, 285cra, 300crb, 321crb, 331crb, 347bl, 351crb, 407cla, 407tc, 408bl, 465tr, 465tr; Jim Culbertson 461bl; Robert L. Pitman 79bl; Rick & Nora Bowers 311fbl, 312ca, 312crb; Harold Stiver 81fbl, 445tr; **Cal Vornberger:** 457cr; **Peter S Weber:** 24crb, 25crb, 99tr, 101ca, 106crb, 238crb, 245crb, 250tr, 251crb, 260cla, 262fcla, 263tc, 269bl; **David Welling:** 452bl; **Ian Whetton:** 79crb; **Roger Wilmshurst:** 120bl, 122cra, 126fbl; **Lee Zieger:** 124tr, 230cla, 470d

Jacket images: *Front:* Corbis: Gary Carter. *Back:* **Garth McElroy:** cr, cra (breeding female), crb; **Brian E. Small:** tr; **Bob Steele:** c. *Spine:* **Corbis:** Gary Carter.

All other images © Dorling Kindersley
For further information see: www.dkimages.com